TEACHING AND RESEARCH METHODS FOR ISLAMIC ECONOMICS AND FINANCE

Methods and techniques adopted in teaching, training, learning, research, professional development, or capacity building are generally standardized across most traditional disciplines, particularly within developing countries. This is not the case, however, when it comes to the Islamic disciplines, and, in particular, in relation to the study of Islamic economics and finance, which is influenced by conventional standards and techniques. This is primarily due to the lack of availability of requisite standards and mechanisms designed within the spirit of Maqsid al-Shari'ah.

This book offers a unique resource and a comprehensive overview of the contemporary methods and smart techniques available for teaching, learning, and researching Islamic eco-finance, and it presents solutions to the challenges in implementing them. Further, the book gives deep insight into the most appropriate methodologies that could be employed empirically to explore, model, analyze, and evaluate Islamic finance theories and models, respectively. It also gives recommendations for improving learning, teaching, and research outcomes in Islamic eco-finance. The book also addresses how, in this advanced technological era, smart tools like artificial intelligence, machine learning, big data, Zoom, and the internet of things can be adapted to help equip students, researchers, and scholars with smart skills.

The book will enable those studying Islamic economics and finance to grasp the appropriate tools for research and learning. Additionally, the Islamic economics and finance sector is growing at a significant rate and therefore requires the upskilling and capacity building of its human resources; thus, the book will also be highly beneficial for practitioners involved in the industry.

Mohd Ma'Sum Billah is a Senior Professor of Finance, Insurance, Fintech, and Investment at the Islamic Economics Institute, King Abdulaziz University, Jeddah, Kingdom of Saudi Arabia.

Routledge Studies in Economic Theory, Method and Philosophy

False Feedback in Economics
The Case for Replication
Andrin Spescha

The Economics and Science of Measurement
A Study of Metrology
Albert N. Link

Teaching and Research Methods for Islamic Economics and Finance
Edited by Moh'd Ma'Sum Billah

For more information about this series, please visit: www.routledge.com/Routledge-Studies-in-Economic-Theory-Method-and-Philosophy/book-series/RSEMTP

TEACHING AND RESEARCH METHODS FOR ISLAMIC ECONOMICS AND FINANCE

Edited by Mohd Ma'Sum Billah

Routledge
Taylor & Francis Group
LONDON AND NEW YORK

First published 2022
by Routledge
2 Park Square, Milton Park, Abingdon, Oxon OX14 4RN

and by Routledge
605 Third Avenue, New York, NY 10158

Routledge is an imprint of the Taylor & Francis Group, an informa business

British Library Cataloguing-in-Publication Data
A catalogue record for this book is available from the British Library

Library of Congress Cataloging-in-Publication Data
Names: Mohd. Ma'sum Billah, 1968- editor.
Title: Teaching and research methods for Islamic economics and finance / edited by Mohd Ma'Sum Billah.
Description: Abingdon, Oxon ; New York, NY : Routledge, 2022. |
Series: Routledge studies in economic theory, method and philosophy |
Includes bibliographical references and index.
Identifiers: LCCN 2021042143 (print) | LCCN 2021042144 (ebook) |
ISBN 9781032180816 (hbk) | ISBN 9781032180823 (pbk) |
ISBN 9781003252764 (ebk)
Subjects: LCSH: Finance--Study and teaching--Islamic countries. |
Economics--Study and teaching--Islamic countries. |
Finance--Research--Islamic countries. | Economics--Research--
Islamic countries. | Islamic countries--Economic conditions.
Classification: LCC HG152.5.I74 T43 2022 (print) |
LCC HG152.5.I74 (ebook) | DDC 338.2/3076091767--dc23/eng/20211012
LC record available at https://lccn.loc.gov/2021042143
LC ebook record available at https://lccn.loc.gov/2021042144

ISBN: 978-1-032-18081-6 (hbk)
ISBN: 978-1-032-18082-3 (pbk)
ISBN: 978-1-003-25276-4 (ebk)

DOI: 10.4324/9781003252764

Typeset in Times NR MT Pro
by KnowledgeWorks Global Ltd.

This book is dedicated to the remembrance of my most beloved parents *Allamah Mufti Nur Mohammad (r)* and *Ustazah Akhtarun Nisa(r).*

Also my beloved parents-in-law *Tuan Haji Nawawi Bin Mat Din (r)* and *Puan Hjh Basariah Binti Mat Lia (r)* who have nourished us with their love And wisdom. May *Allah (swt)* shower them with his love and mercy and grant them *Jannat al-Ferdaus.*

I would also like to dedicate this book to my lovely wife, Dr. Khamsiah Binti Nawawi (head, Oshe-hospital UKM) and our heart-touching kids, Dr. Ahmad Mu'izz Billah (HCTM), Ahmad Mu'azz Billah (pursuing his BSc. Honors in Artificial intelligence, UPNM), Ahmad Muniff Billah (pursuing his BSc Honors in aviation management and Piloting, MSU), and Akhtarun Naba' Billah (pursuing her foundation leading to LLB Honors, IIUM), for their continuous supports and sacrifices.

May all be blessed with *Muwaddau Wa Rahmah, Gurratu A'yun* and *Mardhaati Allah (swt)* in this life and the next.

This book is also dedicated to the *Ummah* and the whole of humanity.

CONTENTS

List of figures x
List of tables xii
About the author xiv
Acknowledgement xv
Foreword xvii
Preface xix
List of contributors xxii

Introduction **1**

PART 1
An overview of research and teaching methods for Islamic economics and finance **3**

1 **A critical survey on methodologies and techniques adopted in teaching Islamic economics and finance globally** **5**
IRFAN SYAUQI BEIK, ABDUL AZIZ YAHYA SAOQI AND MUHAMMAD HASBI ZAENAL

2 **Methodological structure in designing academic programs for Islamic economics and finance** **17**
HICHEM HAMZA

3 **SWOT analysis on research methodologies and techniques adopted in Islamic economics and finance** **29**
IRFAN SYAUQI BEIK AND TITA NURSYAMSIAH

4 **Methodologies and smart techniques recommended in analyzing *maqasid al-shari'ah* for Islamic economics and finance** **42**
IRFAN SYAUQI BEIK, RANDI SWANDARU AND PRIYESTA RIZKININGSIH

5 **Mainstream methodologies for analyzing Fiqh in governing Islamic economics and finance** **56**
YOSEPH ATAA ALSAWADY, MOHAMED CHERIF EL AMRI AND MUSTAFA OMAR MOHAMMED

6 **Methods of teaching, learning, and research in Islamic finance: The case of International Islamic University Malaysia (IIUM)** **71**
RUSNI HASSAN, NURDIANAWATI IRWANI ABDULLAH, AKHTARZAITE ABDUL AZIZ AND SAFINAR SALLEH

7 **Impact of the shift from real economy toward the financial economy in deriving new rules (istinbĀt) in mu'amalĀt** **90**
SHEIKH RICKY BAINS AND SHEIKH FAIZAL AHMAD MANJOO

PART 2
Smart teaching methods for Islamic economics and finance **111**

8 **Developing pedagogical methodologies in teaching Islamic economics** **113**
IMRAN H KHAN SUDDAHAZAI AND SHEIKH FAIZAL AHMAD MANJOO

9 **Application of SCL, PBL, and MM in teaching Islamic economics and finance** **137**
IRFAN SYAUQI BEIK AND LAILY DWI ARSYIANTI

10 **Challenges and prospects in adopting ideal methodologies in teaching Islamic finance** **152**
AYMAN MOHAMMAD BAKR, MOHAMED CHERIF EL AMRI, MUSTAFA OMAR MOHAMMED AND ENSARI YÜCEL

11 **Impact of e-learning techniques in conducting the professional shari'ah audit training and employability prospects during the COVID-19 pandemic** **164**
MUHAMMAD IQMAL HISHAM KAMARUDDIN AND MUSTAFA MOHD HANEFAH

12 **Effects of teaching and learning through zoom application** **181**
RAMADHANI MASHAKA SHABANI, MUSTAFA OMAR MOHAMMED, ENSARI YÜCEL AND MOHAMED CHERIF EL AMRI

13 **Rational outlook of teaching and learning Islamic economics and finance through the zoom application** **196**
AHMED AREF

14 Impact analysis of teaching and learning Islamic economics and finance through zoom cloud meeting 209
IRFAN SYAUQI BEIK AND QURROH AYUNIYYAH

PART 3
Smart research methods for Islamic economics and finance 227

15 Methodologies and smart techniques recommended in analyzing qur'anic principles for Islamic economics and finance 229
AHMED AREF

16 Harmonization of mainstream techniques with Maqasid based methodology for Islamic economics and finance research 242
YUSSUF CHARLES YUSSUF, MOHAMED CHERIF EL AMRI AND MUSTAFA OMAR MOHAMMED

17 Standard methodology for research in Islamic economics and finance 255
ASCARYA AND INDRA

18 Recommended methodology for research in Islamic economics and finance 282
ASCARYA AND OMER FARUK TEKDOGAN

19 Acceptable methodology recommended for research in Islamic finance 303
FAUZIA MUBARIK AND SADIA SAEED

20 The best methodology recommended for research in Islamic finance 313
MONSURAT AYOJIMI SALAMI, MUSTAPHA ABUBAKAR AND HARUN TANRIVERMIŞ

21 Challenges in applying standard methodology for research in Islamic economics and finance and the way forward 327
ASCARYA AND ATIKA R. MASRIFAH

22 Challenges faced in adopting standard methodologies for research in Islamic finance and the way out 349
MONSURAT AYOJIMI SALAMI, HARUN TANRIVERMIŞ AND MUSTAPHA ABUBAKAR

Index 363

FIGURES

1.1 The global investment portion of the Islamic economic sector. 6
1.2 Islamic education concepts in Mecca and Medina period. 8
1.3 Education phase transformation in the medieval period of Islam. 9
1.4 Islamic education phase transformation from the colonialism era to the post-colonialism period. 10
1.5 General teaching methodology and technique in learning IEF in various universities in Indonesia. 11
1.6 General teaching methodology and technique in learning IEF in various universities in Malaysia. 13
1.7 Teaching methodology and technique in learning IEF at UK universities. 14
2.1 Institutional development of Islamic economics and finance programs. 20
2.2 Achieving learning outcomes in Islamic economics and finance. 23
4.1 Development of Islamic commercial finance assets, 2012–2019. 43
4.2 Pentagon- and octagon-shaped ethical measurement model. 49
4.3 *Maqasid al-Shari'ah* evaluation framework. 49
4.4 Islamic wealth management based on *Maqasid al-Shari'ah.* 51
4.5 The scope of maqasid theory for assessing human well-being as a higher objective of zakat institutions. 52
7.1 (a) Essential components of analogical reasoning. (b) Ratio legis in *Qiyās* and formulating a new ruling. 99
7.2 Step-by-step guidelines in researching Islamic finance. 106
8.1 The structural framework of the GRIT pedagogical method. 118
10.1 Four quadrants summarizing teaching theories depicting the teacher-centered vs. student- centered approach and high-tech vs. low-tech level. 154
10.2 Four quadrants summarizing curriculum content methods within the student-centered approach depicting horizontally (a) High Industrial Exposure vs. Low Industrial Exposure, and vertically (b) High Knowledge Content vs. Low Knowledge Content. 160

10.3 Tri-perspective holistic approach to address methodological challenges in teaching Islamic finance. 161
11.1 Employment status. 177
11.2 Industry placement. 178
11.3 Job position. 178
11.4 Starting salary. 179
12.1 The growth of online courses (2012–2019). 184
14.1 IPA diagram. 221
17.1 Theory building in Islamic economics and finance. 256
17.2 The spectrum of research. 258
17.3 Procedures of content analysis. 259
17.4 Graph of logistic function. 265
17.5 The comparison graph of logit and probit function. 266
17.6 The volatility of S&P 500 Index. 269
17.7 Selection of the best panel data model. 277
18.1 Causal interrelationships among all variables. 283
18.2 Process of vector autoregression. 286
18.3 Measurement model of latent variables. 287
18.4 Structural model. 288
18.5 Steps of SEM research. 290
18.6 Comparison between AHP and ANP structures. 294
18.7 Steps of ANP research. 295
18.8 Steps of ABM research. 298
19.1 Waqf model. 305
19.2 Neural network. 307
19.3 Global fintech investments (billion dollar). 309
19.4 Fourth Industrial Revolution-driven technologies. 311
20.1 Top-bottom orderliness of best research methodologies in Islamic finance. 323
21.1 A 5-point and a 7-point Likert scale. 329
21.2 Steps of the Delphi method. 331
21.3 Steps of the Delphi-SEM method. 336
21.4 Proposed SEM model of Tamanni *et al.* (2019) before the Delphi method. 337
21.5 Proposed SEM model of Tamanni *et al.* (2019) after the Delphi method. 337
21.6 Steps of Delphi-ANP method. 338
21.7 Proposed ANP model of Sakti *et al.* (2019) based on Delphi results. 338
21.8 The anatomy of econometric modeling. 339
21.9 Interest-profit channels of MPTM under dual financial systems. 340
21.10 Technology acceptance model by Davis (1989). 341
21.11 Modified technology acceptance model. 342
21.12 Overview theory of efficiency. 343

TABLES

1.1 Islamic economics and finance education providers listed in QS Global World Ranking University in 2020 7
1.2 Top education providers of Islamic economics and finance in Indonesia 11
1.3 Top ten education providers of Islamic economics and finance in Malaysia 12
1.4 IEF education providers in the United Kingdom 14
2.1 Matrix of teaching courses identification and balance 25
3.1 The components of SWOT analysis 32
3.2 SWOT matrix 33
3.3 Alternative strategy based on the SWOT matrix 38
4.1 Operational measurement concept of *Maqasid al-Shari'ah* for Islamic banks 47
4.2 Dimensions, element, and measurement for MPEM 48
5.1 Different types of juristic councils 66
6.1 Islamic finance related courses offered by KIRKHS 80
6.2 Courses offered by IIiBF based on Islamic finance domains 81
6.3 Advantages and disadvantages of lectures 83
6.4 Islamic banking and finance research areas in IIUM 86
6.5 Number of Islamic finance courses based on domains 88
7.1 Sources of Islamic law 94
7.2 Qaṭ'ī and Dhannī interpretation and authentication 101
10.1 Gaps in the literature of methodological challenges in teaching Islamic finance 158
10.2 Methodological challenges in teaching Islamic finance 158
11.1 CPSA module outline 170
11.2 Respondents' background information 172
11.3 *Shariah* principles knowledge and skills 173
11.4 *Shariah* governance knowledge and skills 174
11.5 Islamic financial transaction knowledge and skills 174
11.6 *Shariah* risk management knowledge and skills 175
11.7 *Shariah* audit planning and program knowledge and skills 175

11.8 *Shariah* audit fieldwork and communication knowledge and skills 176
14.1 Number of users of five top online meeting platforms in Indonesia, March 2020 210
14.2 Variables 213
14.3 Assessment of performance and importance levels 214
14.4 IPA diagram 215
14.5 Satisfaction index values 217
14.6 Statements 218
14.7 Degree of agreement 218
14.8 Respondents' demographic characteristics 219
14.9 Scores of gap analysis 223
14.10 Score of customer satisfaction index 224
14.11 One-sample statistics 224
17.1 The standard methodology for research in Islamic economics and finance 257
18.1 The best methodology for research in Islamic economics and finance 283
18.2 Comparison of decision-making methods 293
18.3 Pairwise comparison fundamental scale of absolute numbers 295
19.1 The CAMELS system 308
20.1 Comparative features of different research design methodologies 322
21.1 The example of a Likert questionnaire 330
21.2 The example of a Delphi questionnaire 333
21.3 The example of Likert scale results of Delphi-Likert 334
21.4 The example of a Delphi-Likert questionnaire 334
21.5 The example of Delphi results of Delphi-Likert 335
21.6 The development of various DEA methods 346
22.1 Qualitative Islamic finance research involving Islamic scholars 354
22.2 Islamic finance Research and methodologies adopted 356
22.3 Accounting standards complied with in different countries that practice Islamic finance 357
22.4 Basis for different methodologies in Islamic finance research 359

ABOUT THE AUTHOR

Mohd Ma'Sum Billah, PhD, DBA, MBA, MCL, MMB, LLB (hons), is a Senior Professor of finance, insurance, fintech, and investment, Islamic Economics Institute, King Abdulaziz University, Kingdom of Saudi Arabia. He is also currently a member of the Audit Board of ACIG (approved by the Saudi Monetary Authority/Central Bank of Saudi Arabia), Saudi Arabia. Billah has been earlier affiliated with University of South Australia as an Adjunct Professor. Billah has been serving and contributing both to academia as well as corporate industries and international organizations for more than 25 years with management, teaching, research, proving solutions, and sharing strategic and technical know-how toward the advancement of Islamic finance, fintech, business, investment, capital markets, and insurance *(Takaful)* besides *Halal* standard. Billah has published 36 books and chapters in books and more than 200 articles in internationally reputable journals and social media. Most of his books are published by world renowned publishers, namely Thompson Reuters, Sweet & Max Well, Palgrave Mac Millan, Springer, Routledge, Edward Elgar, and others. Most of his books and articles are used as among the lead references (solutions to reality) by universities, industries, professional firms, governments, policy makers, regulators, NGOs, academia, researchers, and students of higher learning in different parts of the contemporary world. He has presented at more than 300 conferences, seminars, executive workshops, and professional development and industrial trainings in different parts of the world. In addition, he has also been affiliated with corporate, academic, and financial industries including central banks, international corporate organizations, governments, and NGOs in his capacity as a member in boards, director, advisor, strategic decision maker, transformer, and reformer with strategic solutions and technical know-how. Among his areas of interest and contributions are: Islamic finance, insurance (*takaful*), crowd-funding, investment, *Zakat, Waqf*, capital market (*Sukuk*), social finance, SDGs, petroleum finance, trade, fintech, e-commerce, crypto-asset, cryptocurrency, industrialization, privatization, national entrepreneurial models, standards, policies strategies, and technical know-how.

ACKNOWLEDGEMENT

There is no strength and power except in Allah (swt), To Him comes the praise, the Savant, the Wise, the Omniscient, the most beautiful names belong to Him. May the blessing of Allah (swt) and peace be upon Muhammad (saw) and all the Prophets (aws) from the first to the last.

I am humbly privileged to acknowledge King Abdulaziz University, Kingdom of Saudi Arabia, and its prestigious wing Islamic Economics Institute for supporting us with every facility in research, academics, human capital, and professional development activities reaching out to the global *Ummah*. It is also a great honor for me to humbly acknowledge His Excellency Professor Dr Abdulrahman Obaid Al-Youbi, the President of King Abdulaziz University, Professor Dr Amin Yousef Mohammad Noaman, the Vice President of King Abdulaziz University; Dr Mohammad A. Naseef, the Dean of the Islamic Economics Institute (IEI), King Abdulaziz University (KAU); Dr Abdullah Qurban Turkistani (former Dean of the IEI, KAU); Dr Faisal Mahmoud Atbani (Vice Dean, IEI, KAU); Dr Hasan Mohammad Makhethi (Vice Dean, IEI-KAU); Dr Maha Alandejani (Vice Dean, IEI, KAU); Dr Adnan M. A. Al-Khiary (Head, Department of Finance, IEI-KAU); Dr Albara Abdullah Abulaban (Head, Department of Economics); Professor Dr Ahmed Mahdi Belouafi (Editor–in-Chief, Journal of King Abdulaziz University-Islamic Economics); and Dr Majed Mohammed Aljohani (Director of the Administration, IEI-KAU) for their continuous support and encouragement toward dynamic professional development, excellent academic contributions, and specialized advanced scientific research activities. Heartiest acknowledgement is also extended to my respected fellow colleagues from the Islamic Economics Institute, King Abdulaziz University, including Professor Dr Abdulrahim Al-Saati, Professor Dr Abderrazak Belabes, Dr Omar Hafiz, Sheikh Dr Ali Ahmed Al-Nadwi, Sheikh Mujib AlRahman Mohammad Amin Al-Bashir, Dr Hichem Salem Hamza, Dr Esmat Almustafa, and my talented colleague Mr Mohammed Alabdulraheem, Lecturer in FinTech and Islamic finance. I would like to express my heartiest thanks with appreciation to scholars, researchers, industrialists, universities, industries, and professional firms whose direct and indirect supports with knowledge, experiences, and resources are heartily recorded.

Mohd Ma'Sum Billah, PhD
Islamic Economics Institute
King Abdulaziz University
Saudi Arabia

FOREWORD

The entire globe has witnessed numerous catastrophes, namely the global attack by the unexpected pandemic novel coronavirus outbreak (COVID-19); the negative hit on the global oil price; political turmoil and racial and ethnic war in many parts of the world, which destabilized in the world's eco-peace and smooth progress of the socio-economic and financial movement. It has recently been predicted that social finance may play a significant role in rescuing the global economic future from the existing catastrophic status quo. In the present century, the world has enjoyed the advancement of science and technology in cyberspace in almost every sector of day-to-day life and culture, whether personal, private, domestic, social, political, economic, global, or cyber. The economic, corporate, financial, and trade sectors have still been dominated by traditional culture in coping with gradual science and technological advancement. It has been observed that, in the recent phenomena, the economic, financial, and non-financial corporate sectors appreciate social financing with multiple smart mechanisms and structures in facilitating contemporary socioeconomic solutions. Despite such a phenomenon optimized by the eco-financial industries, there are obstacles and challenges in the ethical financial movement, which slows the way forward for true achievement. It may be recorded that among those obstacles are lack of regulatory standards, less political support, poor understanding of the impact, misuse and fraud cultures, poor systems, inefficient professionalism and skills, unskilled corporate governance, lack of confidence, poor etiquette, and insufficient support and cooperation from decision makers and policy controllers. However, most of these challenges might be due to invention with new dimension, but with temporary effect, perhaps. Such challenges may not last long in the promising journey or the emerging era of the ethical finance with its smart teaching and research methods in producing skilled professionals in the fields of Islamic eco-finance toward dynamism and impact offerings. Smart teaching and research methods adapted for Islamic eco-finance are not an exception in coping with the global emergence of producing smart professionals serving the Islamic eco-financial industries. Hence, dynamic teaching and research methods may be an added value to the existing solutions to the advancement of Islamic economics and finance, particularly in this catastrophic socioeconomic experience.

The scientific and smart methods of adopting teaching and research in Islamic eco-finance intellectual development may be among the sound solutions to the contemporary eco-turmoil of the globe addressed by professional concern. Economic and financial academia, researchers, students, professionals, authorities, regulators, decision makers, operators, and customers are moving with greater prospects toward appreciating the socio-impact and/or value-based eco-financial system with promising benefits and better services with rational returns and sharing. Such an achievement phenomenon is not only realized among the socioeconomically developing states, but a rising global dimension. The contemporary Islamic financial market is growing faster than its conventional counterpart, with an annual growth rate ranging from 13–23%, with sustainability appreciated by all irrespective of religion, nationality, color, gender, status, or age across the today's economy. Thus, the methods of teaching and research shall not be confined to focusing on literature alone; the methods shall concern adding the empirical analysis by problem-based learning (PBL) and solutions.

Indeed, a world-renowned Islamic finance scholar, Prof. Dr. Mohd Ma'Sum Billah, has produced this unique book, *Teaching and Research Methods for Islamic Economics and Finance*, to meet the emerging demand of the global socioeconomic environment with numerous solutions to smart methods in teaching and research of Islamic eco-finance, with dynamic results toward better serving the industries with socioeconomic impact within the spirit of *Maqasid al-Shari'ah*. The book is thus a value-added holistic empirical solution to teaching and research methods for Islamic eco-finance in the socioeconomic environment by contributing several notable chapters on specialized issues of smart methods of teaching and research in Islamic eco-finance. It is thus, an honor for me to appreciate and acknowledge that this unique book is a solution to core issues of methods of teaching and research of Islamic eco-finance, which is rightfully produced by Prof. Billah of Islamic Economics Institute, King Abdulaziz University, Saudi Arabia, along with the cooperation and intellectual contributions of reputable researchers from different parts of the world as contributors, which will meet the global demand of researchers, academia, professionals, students, industrialists, financial authorities, decision makers, and technical experts. The book may be timely and a useful reference in smart methodologies of teaching and research of Islamic eco-finance toward preparing skilled and smart professionals in the fields of Islamic economics and finance in this era of advanced technology, *enSha Allah (swt)*.

Dr Mohammad A. Naseef
Dean
Islamic Economics Institute
King Abdulaziz University
Kingdom of Saudi Arabia

PREFACE

Teaching and research are among the prime concerns toward a sustainable development of Islamic economics and finance. It is undeniably admitted that the methods and techniques adopted in teaching and research in Islamic economics and finance in different parts of the world today are in most situations neither standardized nor with globally acceptable quality. It has also been observed in recent years that quality in teaching and research get a poor concern rather it has been dominated by quantity and that ought to be a serious threat to the advancement of Islamic economics and finance with significant impact. It is thus important to adopt standard teaching and research methods by coping up with the up-to-date world of teaching and research methods adopted among the top learning institutions in aiming to produce quality professionals who may be able to ensure both academic and the industrial performances with expected results. It has also been closely observed that at the postgraduate level in particular, the subject of research methodology is a compulsory one, yet no standard and or comprehensive refereed book on research methodology specializing in Islamic economics and finance is available. As a result, lecturers, researchers, and students are compelled to refer references, which are even not direct solution to Islamic economics or finance rather on conventional based write-ups. This book, however, is perhaps among the pioneers with a comprehensive solution to different core issues of methodologies, mechanisms, and techniques of teaching, learning, and research in Islamic economics and finance in this contemporary world of reality. Thus, the book *Teaching and Research Methods for Islamic Economics and Finance* contributes some specialized issues with solutions to teaching and research methods for Islamic economics and finance, which consist of three parts with 22 specialized chapters, plus an introduction and index.

Part 1 provides an *Overview of Research and Teaching Methods for Islamic Economics and Finance.* It consists of seven specialized chapters that address different core issues of benchmarking. *Chapter 1* contributes on "A Critical Survey on Methodologies and Techniques Adopted in Teaching Islamic Economics and Finance Globally." *Chapter 2* discovers a solution to "Methodological Structure in Designing Academic Programs for Islamic Economics and Finance." *Chapter 3* provides a paradigm of "SWOT Analysis on Research Methodologies and Techniques Adopted in Islamic Economics and Finance." *Chapter 4* focuses on "Methodologies and Smart Techniques Recommended in Analyzing Maqasid al-Shari'ah for Islamic Economics and Finance." *Chapter 5* contributes to "Mainstream Methodologies for Analyzing *Fiqh* in Governing Islamic Economics and Finance." *Chapter 6* provides a discussion of "Methods of Teaching, Learning and Research in Islamic Finance: The Case of International Islamic University Malaysia (IIUM)." *Chapter Seven* discovers an Impact of the Shift from Real Economy Toward the Financial Economy in Deriving New Rules (Istinbāt) in Mu'amalāt."

Part 2 focuses on the "*Smart Teaching Methods for Islamic Economics and Finance*," which consists of seven specialized chapters. *Chapter 8* advocates for "Developing Pedagogical Methodologies in Teaching Islamic Economics." *Chapter 9* presents the "Application of SCL, PBL, and MM in Teaching Islamic Economics and Finance." *Chapter 10* discusses the "Challenges and Prospects in Adopting Ideal Methodologies in Teaching Islamic Finance." *Chapter 11* in addition, provides "Impact of e-Learning Techniques in Conducting the Professional Shari'ah Audit Training and Employability Prospects during COVID-19." *Chapter 12* analyzes the "Effects of Teaching and Learning through the Zoom Application." *Chapter 13* discusses "Rational Outlook of Teaching and Learning Islamic Economics and Finance through the Zoom Application." *Chapter 14* contributes "Impact Analysis of Teaching and Learning Islamic Economics and Finance through Zoom Cloud Meeting."

Part 3 contributes on "*Smart Research Methods for Islamic Economics and Finance*." The part consists of eight specialized chapters contributing legal and compliance solutions to benchmarking Islamic financial products and services. *Chapter 15* provides a comprehensive analysis on "Methodologies and Smart Techniques Recommended in Analyzing Qur'anic Principles for Islamic Economics and Finance." *Chapter 16* analyzes "Harmonization of Mainstream Techniques with Maqasid-Based Methodology for Islamic Economics and Finance Research." *Chapter 17* contributes on "Standard Methodology for Research in Islamic Economics and Finance." *Chapter 18* provides "Recommended Methodology for Research in Islamic Economics and Finance." *Chapter 19* analyzes an "Acceptable Methodology Recommended for Research in Islamic Finance." *Chapter 20* discovers a "Best Methodology Recommended for Research in Islamic Finance." *Chapter 21* analyzes "Challenges in Applying Standard Methodology for Research in Islamic Economics and Finance and the Way Forward." *Chapter 22* discusses "Challenges Faced in Adopting Standard Methodologies for Research in Islamic Finance and the Way Out."

This title, *Teaching and Research Methods for Islamic Economics and Finance*, is, however, expected to be among the pioneers with organized and comprehensive applied solutions to methodologies and techniques of teaching, learning, and research adopted and recommended for Islamic economics and finance, which may be a useful resource and guide to academia, researchers, financial industries, practitioners, decision makers, programmers, professionals, course leaders, and students for their teaching, training, learning, and research in Islamic economics and finance in this contemporary advanced reality. It is not impossible for the book contains any shortcomings, even though we tried with every humble effort to avoid any inaccuracy. We are thus grateful to all readers should any shortcomings be brought to us for further improvement.

Mohd Ma'Sum Billah, PhD
Islamic Economics Institute
King Abdulaziz University
Saudi Arabia

CONTRIBUTORS

Imran H Khan Suddahazai, PhD is the Head of the Education Program at MIHE and a Visiting Associate Researcher at Lancaster University. After an academic hiatus that entailed senior leadership, management, and coaching roles in diverse industries across the world, he completed his doctoral program in educational leadership from the University of Gloucestershire and MIHE. Imran has now returned to MIHE to develop and further the work of his predecessors and is focused on developing paradigms on educational thought, pedagogy, and reasoning. This embraces attention on the pragmatic dimensions of education from an Islamic worldview, as a propaedeutic science to for the individual to understand the role of God and society. The research also entails the exploration of human self-development models and ideals derived from ancient philosophical schools and technologically driven contemporary perspectives. Imran's particular focus is on examining the relationship between notions of pedagogy/leadership roles and the development of phenomenon related to creativity and intuition. Methodologically, Imran is inclined to adopt frameworks and concepts derived from ethnographic and pragmatic approaches as he endeavors to blend the multifarious aspects of his knowledge and professional experience to deliver a critically reflective perspective on pedagogical methodology via his academic role and research interests.

Hichem Hamza, PhD is currently an Associate Professor of Islamic Economics and Finance at the Islamic Economics Institute – King Abdulaziz University in Jeddah. He holds a master's degree and a PhD in Sciences of Economics from the University of Auvergne – France. He began his academic experience at the Higher School of Commerce in Tunis – Manouba University, where he taught financial markets, Islamic finance, risks of Islamic banking, and economic analysis for undergraduate and postgraduate students. He further taught in many other Tunisian Universities. Since 2016, Dr. Hamza has been with the Institute of Islamic Economics at King Abdulaziz University as a faculty member, participating in many academic projects and designing educational programs for graduate studies, in addition to his research activity in the field of Islamic economics and finance. Among his research interests: Islamic finance and banking, monetary systems, and endowments. Dr. Hamza has published many research papers in refereed journals and has participated in many international seminars and conferences.

Rusni Hassan, PhD is a Professor at the IIUM Institute of Islamic Banking and Finance, IIUM. She graduated with LLB (Honors), LLB (Shariah) (First Class), Master of Comparative Laws (MCL), and PhD in Law. Her area of specialization includes legal, governance, and Shariah aspects of Islamic Banking and Finance. She is an active researcher and expert trainer in IBF. Her publications include books on Islamic banking and finance, chapters in books, and articles published in local and international journals. She is listed as top 10 contributors for research in Islamic finance in the Scopus database. She is on the Shariah Committee for a number of Islamic financial institutions in Malaysia and Maldives. Her works and contributions to Islamic finance have also been recognized internationally. She has been listed among the top women in Islamic finance since 2013. Most recently, she was among the Top 10 Most Influential Women in Islamic Finance 2018, 2019, and 2020 according to Cambridge IFA.

Akhtarzaite Abdul Aziz, PhD is currently an Assistant Professor at the Department of Fiqh and Usul al Fiqh, Kulliyyah of Islamic Revealed Knowledge and Human Sciences, International Islamic University Malaysia (IIUM). She graduated from IIUM in LLB in 1995 and completed her LLB (Shari'ah) in 1996. She also has a master's degree (2000) and PhD (2005) in Fiqh and Usul al Fiqh from the same university. Her research interest is modern issues in Islamic jurisprudence, particularly in Islamic banking, Islamic capital markets, and Takaful as well as the halal management industry. She is currently a member of the Maybank Islamic Bank Shariah Advisory Committee, Chairman of Great Eastern Takaful Shariah Advisory Committee, and a member of the Shariah Advisory of IIUM Endowment.

Safinar Salleh, PhD is an Assistant Professor at Ahmad Ibrahim Kulliyyah of Laws (AIKOL), International Islamic University Malaysia (IIUM). She obtained her Bachelor in Shariah (Hons.) from Al-Azhar University Cairo in 1999. She then pursued her master's in Shariah and became a tutor in the Department of Fiqh and Usul, Academy of Islamic Studies, University of Malaya, where she started developing her expertise in the area of Islamic law of contracts and completed a dissertation on Islamic pawnbroking. Upon completion of her master's in 2005, she took up a lecturer position at AIKOL, IIUM. In July 2013, she obtained her PhD from Glasgow Caledonian University, and her research was on Takaful (Islamic insurance). Currently, Dr. Safinar is a Shariah Committee member for several financial institutions in Malaysia, including Swiss Reinsurance Company Ltd. (Swiss Re Retakaful), Export–Import Bank of Malaysia Berhad (EXIM Bank) and Hong Leong Islamic Bank Berhad (HLISB). She is also a Shariah Committee member of MUA Life Ltd. in Mauritius.

Nurdianawati Irwani Abdullah, PhD is an Associate Professor in law and Shari'ah at the Department of Finance, Kuliyyah of Economics and Management Sciences (KENMS), International Islamic University Malaysia (IIUM). She is also the member of the Shari'ah Advisory Board of AmMetlife Takaful Berhad, Affin Islamic Bank Malaysia, and an AIF-certified assessor and trainer. She holds an LL.B, LL.B (Shari'ah), and Master of Comparative Laws (MCL) from the International Islamic University Malaysia, and a PhD in Islamic banking and finance from Loughborough University–Markfield Institute of Higher Education, United Kingdom. She has conducted training in areas related to legal and Shari'ah issues in Islamic financial products, Shariah governance, regulatory framework of Islamic finance, and takaful. She is directly involved in the legal working committee for the Ministry of Domestic Trade, Cooperatives, and Consumerism together with the Association of Islamic Banks of Malaysia (AIBIM) in respect to legal reforms. Given her involvement and contribution to Islamic finance education, research, and consultancy, she was listed as among the World's 50 Most Influential Women in Islamic Business and Finance in 2017 and 2018 by the Islamic Finance Review Special Report (ISFIRE). In 2019 and 2020, she listed among the Top 50 Most Influential Women in Islamic Finance by the Cambridge International Financial Advisory.

Sheikh Faizal Ahmad Manjoo, PhD has studied a blend of three disciplines – Islamic finance, Sharia, and secular law – that helps him to contribute toward the improvement of the Islamic finance industry. Currently he is the CEO of Minarah Consulting, lawyer, Shariah scholar, and academic. He is both a lawyer and a Muslim scholar (Shariah scholar). He sits on the Shariah supervisory boards of well-known Islamic financial institutions in various jurisdictions, ranging from re-takaful to unit trust and IREITs. He is likewise an active academician at many universities in the United Kingdom and other countries, developing their curricula for Islamic finance and Islamic law. He has also developed about 40 executive training programs in various fields like pedagogy and Islamic finance, which he delivered in France, Dubai, Brunei, South Africa, Morocco, Tunisia, Cameroon, India, and the United Kingdom. He had the privilege of being one of the founding members of the Muslim Mediation and Arbitration Council of South Africa, which is a well-established platform for resolving conflicts between Muslims; and the Johannesburg-based Muslim Lawyers Association. He earned an award for his contribution toward the Islamic finance industry in 2012 and an Emerald Literati Award for his academic reviews in 2018. As a corporate lawyer he often submits legal expert opinion in the high courts in jurisdictions. He structures financial products for companies and is involved in legal documentation. He additionally acts as consultant for law firms and accounting firms on Islamic finance and law.

Sheikh Ricky Bains, MEd works as a teaching fellow at the Markfield Institute of Higher Education, United Kingdom, where he delivers courses on Arabic language and Islamic law. He is also a Lecturer at As-Suffa Institute, a traditional Muslim seminary, where he teaches Arabic and Islamic law as well as leading on curriculum development. Ricky graduated with an LLB (Hons) from the University of Leicester, completed an MEd in Islamic education from Newman University, and is currently studying for an MSc in applied linguistics at Oxford University. He has studied the traditional Islamic sciences in the UK, Egypt, and Saudi Arabia and completed an ʿĀlimiyyah degree program.

Fauzia Mubarik, PhD is an Assistant Professor in the Faculty of Management Sciences, National University of Modern Languages (NUML), Islamabad Campus. She earned her doctor of philosophy in management sciences (finance) in 2017 with honors. Since 2017, she has served as the Finance Cluster In-charge in the Faculty of Management Sciences. She is a member of the National Curriculum Review Committee (NCRC), HEC. Fauzia Mubarik has published numerous research papers in HEC-recognized journals and editorials in the *Frontier Post* newspaper and has had the honor to attend and present research papers at the local conferences. She also has conducted and attended various trainings and workshops in the Faculty Development Programs.

Sadia Saeed, PhD is a Lecturer in the Faculty of Management Sciences, National University of Modern Languages (NUML), Islamabad Campus. She joined NUML in spring 2009. She earned a doctorate of philosophy in management sciences (finance) in 2020. She has published numerous research papers in HEC-recognized journals and has had the honor to attend and present the research papers in national conferences. She has attended various trainings and workshops under the Faculty Development Programs. She also supervises the theses of MBA students.

Harun Tanrıvermiş, PhD is a professor at the Department of Real Estate Development and Management, Faculty of Applied Sciences, Ankara University, Turkey. He received his MSc and PhD degrees from the Department of Agricultural Economics at Ankara University, in the field of land and real estate economics, land, and real estate valuation. He also obtained another MSc degree in environmental management under the MED-CAMPUS Programme. His research interests include real estate and asset valuation, real estate project development and project appraisal, land acquisition and expropriation, facility and property economics and management, and environmental economics. He has been a staff member at Ankara University since 1991 and has worked as a research specialist and consultant in the fields of real estate and asset valuation, project development and appraisal, real estate project financing, facility and property management, corporate and sustainable real estate, land acquisition, expropriation, and impact assessment studies in many public and private sector projects. He has many academic publications, such as articles, books, and proceedings. He has 30 international and 25 national peer-reviewed articles in variety of high-impact factor journals. He published 48 international and 43 national full or abstract proceedings for conferences. He is the author of 39 books and 14 book chapters. He published in total 21 proceedings/articles about sustainable use of land resources, local sustainability indicators, real estate sectors within the scope of sustainable development, sustainable urban transformation, and sustainable real estate development projects and valuation of sustainability. He is the Head of the Department of Real Estate Development and Management and the Dean of the Faculty of Applied Sciences at Ankara University. He has been acting as coordinator of university property development and construction works, and he has also attending research groups on real estate development, project cycle analysis, project appraisal and financing, sustainable real estate, corporate real estate and social responsibility, international standards on valuation, financial reporting, property measurement, and facility management. He has coordinated graduate students' research and theses as well as postdoctoral researchers. He is a member of the Royal Institution of Chartered Surveyors (MRICS) and other national and international occupational institutions.

Monsurat Ayojimi Salami, PhD is an Assistant Professor in the Department of Real Estate Development and Management, Ankara University, Turkey. She received her MSc and PhD from International Islamic University Malaysia (in the field of finance and business administration). She was a postdoctoral research fellow (PDF) at IIUM Institute of Islamic Banking and Finance (IIiBF) between September 2018 and August 2019, and received an Honorable Mention in CIFE from Ethica Institute of Islamic Finance in the United States in October, 2019. She also earned a professional certificate as a certified quantitative risk management (CQRM) on March, 2018 from International Institute of Professional Education and Research (IIPER), Washington, DC. She has successfully trained groups of participants for professional examinations on real options in Malaysia. In addition, she has published several academic articles in journals indexed in Scopus and Web of Science (WoS). She has presented academic papers at national and international conferences, and participated in several econometrics workshops. She has published several chapters in books, and she is an academic article reviewer for journals published by Emerald and Springer.

Mustapha Abubakar, PhD is a Senior Lecturer in the Department of Banking and Finance at Ahmadu Bello University Business School, Zaria-Nigeria. Prior to joining the academic community, he worked as a banking officer at Union Bank of Nigeria for nearly 3 years from 1996 to 1999. He obtained a diploma in accounting, BSc in business administration, MBA, MSc in Business Administration, and PhD from Ahmadu Bello University, Zaria-Nigeria in 1989, 1993, 1995, 2010, and 2017, respectively. He has participated in many academic conferences as a paper presenter in conventional and Islamic finance, banking, and economics areas in Nigeria, Malaysia, Saudi Arabia, and Bangladesh. He has also published a number of papers in academic journals and books in Nigeria and abroad. He is also a member of editorial advisory board of international journals. He has reviewed academic papers for seminars, theses, journal articles, and books in areas of Islamic banking, economics, and finance. This is in addition to supervising the works of undergraduate and postgraduate students. He also served as a member of the advisory committee of experts for Halal Takaful Company in Nigeria.

Muhammad Iqmal Hisham Kamaruddin, PhD is a Lecturer of Islamic Accounting at the Faculty of Economics and Muamalat, Universiti Sains Islam Malaysia (USIM). He obtained his bachelor's degree in accountancy (Hons) and his master's degree in economics and muamalat administration from USIM. He then obtained his doctor of philosophy, specify in Islamic accounting, from Universiti Kebangsaan Malaysia (UKM). He was a recipient of the Royal Education Award for his bachelor's degree and the Accounting Best Student Award 2014 from the Malaysian Institute of Accountants (MIA). He also received the Faculty Book Award (Master by Research) for his master's degree. He has published 15 books and chapters in books, in addition to more than 40 journals and conference papers on national and international levels. He has also presented more than 20 conferences, seminars, executive workshops, and industrial trainings in different parts of the world. In addition, he was also affiliated with corporate, academic, industrial players, and associations as well as regulators in his capacity as a member, advisor, strategic decision-maker, transformer and reformer with strategic solution providers. Among his areas of interest and contributions are Islamic accounting, Islamic finance, Shariah audit and governance, Islamic nonprofit organizations, and halal management.

Mustafa Mohd Hanefah, PhD is a Professor of Accounting, Shariah Auditing and Zakat, Faculty of Economics and Muamalat, Universiti Sains Islam Malaysia (USIM). He was a former Deputy Vice-Chancellor (Research and Innovation), USIM, the Dean of Research and Innovation, and Faculty of Economics and Muamalat. He also was a Visiting Professor at the Economic Research Centre, Nagoya University (2011) and Aoyama

Business School, Aoyama Gakuin University (2016), Japan. Prof. Dato' Dr. Mustafa obtained his bachelor's degree in accounting (Hons.) from Universiti Kebangsaan Malaysia (UKM). Later, he obtained his master's degree in accountancy from the University of Wollongong, Australia, and his PhD in Islamic accounting from Memphis University, USA. He is currently serving as a member of the board of directors of USIM. He has published many papers in international journals and books in the areas of Islamic financial reporting and accounting, Shariah auditing, taxation, zakat, and waqf. He also serves as a member of the editorial boards for a number of international journals.

Irfan Syauqi Beik, PhD is an Associate Professor at the Department of Islamic Economics, IPB University, Indonesia. He currently serves as a commissioner of the Indonesia Waqf Board (BWI), which is an independent state agency responsible for managing the waqf sector in Indonesia. He is responsible for managing strategic research and digital transformation of national waqf system at BWI. Previously, Irfan served as Director of Zakat Distribution and Empowerment and Director of the Center of Strategic Studies (Puskas) at the National Zakat Board of the Republic of Indonesia (BAZNAS). He received his bachelor's degree from IPB University in 2002, his master's degree from International Islamic University Islamabad in 2005, and his PhD from International Islamic University Malaysia in 2010. Furthermore, Irfan also serves as a member of Plenary Board at the National Shariah Board of the Indonesia Council of Ulama (DSN MUI), Vice Chairman VI of the Indonesian Association of Islamic Economists (IAEI), Executive Secretary of the World Zakat Forum, and Member of Executive Council of the International Association for Islamic Economics (IAIE). In addition, Irfan has published books, book chapters, scientific articles in reputable national and international journals, and popular media articles.

Laily Dwi Arsyianti, PhD is an Assistant Professor at IPB University. She currently serves as Deputy Head of the Department of Islamic Economics, Faculty of Economics and Management, IPB University. She graduated from IPB University with a bachelor's degree in economics (Hons), and from International Islamic University of Malaysia with a master of science in finance and a PhD in Islamic banking and finance. Her area of interest includes Islamic wealth management, Islamic social finance, and behavioral finance. She has published papers in various journals, including Scopus-indexed journals and national accredited journals. She also has presented selected papers at various reputable conferences, especially those that are organized by IRTI-IDB and Bank Indonesia.

Muhammad Hasbi Zaenal, PhD is the Director at the BAZNAS Center of Strategic Studies (PUSKAS BAZNAS), the Republic of Indonesia. He is also part-time lecturer in IPB University, Tazkia University College of Islamic Economics, and Syarif Hidayatullah State Islamic University. He obtained a master's degree and PhD from Universiti Kebangsaan Malaysia (2012 and 2018) and a bachelor's degree in Sharia from Al-Azhar University, Egypt in 2009. Currently, he is active in research and publications in the area of Islamic social finance, such as zakat, waqf, and poverty studies.

Qurroh Ayuniyyah, PhD is a Lecturer in the master's program in Islamic economics, Postgraduate School, Bogor Ibn Khaldun University, Indonesia. She received her PhD from International Islamic University Malaysia (IIUM) in 2019 and won the award for "Best Student for PhD In *Kuliyyah* of Economics and Management Sciences." She obtained her bachelor's and master's degrees in economics at IPB University and IIUM, respectively. She was also awarded the "Best Student" prize at each level. She worked as a project manager at Program Bimbingan Usahawan Tijaari (i-Taajir), Centre for Islamic Economics (CIE), IIUM in collaboration with CIMB Islamic Bank Berhad Malaysia from 2018 to 2020. She has been involved in various academic activities and has published several journal articles and book chapters at national and international levels.

Randi Swandaru is a Graduate Academic Assistant at INCEIF, Malaysia. He conducts research and supports faculty members in teaching activities. Formerly, he worked at the Head Division of Zakat Utilization at The National Board of Zakat, the Republic of Indonesia (BAZNAS). He was responsible for utilizing zakat funds for economic empowerment programs with the aims of alleviating poverty. He graduated from the master's program of Islamic finance and management Durham University in 2017 as the best academic performance student. He has received recognition such as the Young Southeast Asian Leaders Initiative (2020), Obama Foundation Leaders Asia Pacific (2019), Future Leaders Connect British Council (2018), and third place in the Indonesia Financial Authority Financial Inclusion Paper Competition.

Priyesta Rizkiningsih is an Economic Empowerment Manager at The National Board of Zakat, the Republic of Indonesia (BAZNAS). She is responsible for zakat distribution at BAZNAS Microfinance and BAZNAS Institute of Mustahik Economic Empowerment. Previously, she was a researcher in BAZNAS Center of Strategic Studies and a research assistant at the Central Bank of Indonesia. She earned her master's degree in Islamic finance and management from Durham University, UK, with a full scholarship from Indonesia Endowment Fund for Education. Her research interests are Islamic social finance as well as governance and social reporting.

Abdul Aziz Yahya Saoqi is the Head of Strategic Research, Partnership and Publication at BAZNAS Center of Strategic Studies and Researcher at World Zakat Forum Research and Development. He also serves as a founder and director of at the Center of Indonesian Poverty Studies (CIPS). He was also a former research fellow at the Department of Islamic Economics and Finance of the Central Bank of Indonesia. He received his bachelor's degree in Islamic economics in 2012 from Tazkia University. He obtained his master's degree in Islamic finance in 2017 from International Islamic University Malaysia with a Sponsor from Maybank Islamic Bank Berhad. As Research Fellow and Head of Strategic Research at BAZNAS, he has been involved as lead researcher in several strategic national zakat and waqf projects, such as Designing Shariah Control and Internal Audit Framework for Zakat Institutions, National Zakat and Waqf Literacy Index, Zakat Shariah Compliance Index, Zakat Transparency Index, Indonesian Zakat Outlook, and World Zakat Performance Indicator. His areas of expertise and interest are Islamic economics and finance, Islamic social finance, Shariah auditing for zakat institutions, good governance for zakat institutions, poverty, and inequality studies.

Tita Nursyamsiah is a Lecturer in the Islamic Economics Department, Faculty of Economics and Management, and Secretary of the Center for Islamic Business and Economic Studies (CI-BEST), IPB University. She received her bachelor's degree at IPB University and her master's degree at International Islamic University Malaysia (IIUM). She has been involved in a lot of government and non-government research programs, including the Financial Services Authority, Indonesia Deposit Insurance Corporation, Center of Strategic Studies (PUSKAS) BAZNAS, National Islamic Finance Committee, and national Islamic philanthropic organizations such as Inisiasi Zakat Indonesia (IZI) and PPPA Daarul Qur'an. Her research areas are mainly in Islamic financial institutions, Islamic social funds, and halal industry. She has published articles in reputable journals and delivered a number of research papers and speeches at conferences. She was awarded as the Best Paper Finalist at the 1st Islamic Economics and Finance Research Forum in 2012 and Best Paper Winner in the 2nd Islamic Economics and Finance Research Forum in 2013.

Ascarya, PhD is a Research Adviser and managing editor of *Journal of Islamic Monetary Economics and Finance* (JIMF), at Bank Indonesia Institute, Bank Indonesia. He also is a senior lecturer at Magister of Economics and Waqf, University of Darussalam Gontor, Indonesia. He serves as editorial team member of several international scientific journals (Scopus indexed) and editorial board member of other international scientific journals. He is also a reviewer of several international (Scopus Indexed) and national scientific journals. He is an expert in the field of Islamic economics, monetary, banking, Islamic microfinance, and Islamic social finance (especially zakat and waqf), as well as a lecturer in several universities. In addition, he is a trainer in the Analytic Network Process (ANP) and Data Envelopment Analysis (DEA) research methods. He holds PhD in Islamic economics and finance from IEF-Trisakti University, Indonesia. He has also received PhD in International Development, MBA in Finance and MSc in Management Information System from University of Pittsburgh, USA. He has produced 28 international journals and books, 70 international papers, 23 national journals, 23 national papers, 41 working papers, three occasional papers, 22 books, four proceedings, 12 periodical publications, and six research notes. He has presented in 73 international conferences and 100 national conferences. He has received four International Best Paper Awards in 2013, 2014, 2015, and 2016. He has also received the BAZNAS Award 2018 as "Tokoh Pendukung Kebangkitan Zakat."

Indra, PhD obtained his bachelor's degree in mathematics from IPB University, a master's degree in economics from IPB University, and a doctorate in economics from the University of Indonesia. Indra has been a Lecturer in economics in the postgraduate program in economics of IPB University since 2015. Indra is also a lecturer at the department of Sharia economics, Tazkia Islamic University College, since 2012. He has expertise in economic modeling, development economics, and welfare economics. Some of his works in this area have been published in international journals indexed by Scopus, such as the *International Journal of Development Studies*, *Asian Economic Journal*, and *International Journal of Social Economics*. On several occasions, Indra has been invited as an instructor in econometric workshops at several universities in Indonesia, as well as at several state institutions such as the Central Bank of Indonesia, Central Bureau of Statistics, the Ministry of Finance, and the Ministry of Industry of the Republic of Indonesia.

Omer Faruk Tekdogan, PhD is the Head of Department at the Ministry of Treasury and Finance – DG Economic Programs and Research. He worked as Senior Specialist at the Prime Ministry Undersecretariat of Treasury. He was a policy analyst at Development Co-Operation Directorate in the Organization for Economic Co-Operation and Development (OECD), where his main research areas were official development finance for infrastructure, investment, private sector development, and regional connectivity. He received his PhD in Islamic Economics and Finance from İstanbul University and he holds a Master's in Economics from North Carolina State University. He is visiting lecturer in Ankara Yildirim Beyazit University Faculty of Political Sciences. His past and present research fields cover Islamic economics and finance, monetary economics, banking, financial economics and agent-based modeling.

Atika R. Masrifah, MSc received her bachelor's degree in Islamic economics and master's degree in Shari'ah economics from Tazkia Islamic

University College. In 2018, she joined the University of Darussalam (UNIDA) Gontor as Secretary of the Islamic Economics Department. She is currently Head of Research and Publication at the International Center for Awqaf Studies (ICAST) UNIDA Gontor. Her research interests include Islamic economics, waqf, zakat, micro- and small-sized enterprises, and Islamic banking and finance. She has published a variety of publications in referenced journals and delivered papers at national and international conferences. Some of her articles have won prizes for best article. Her work has also recently received Best Paper Awards at the 6th Sharia Banking Research Paper Forum in the Young Researchers category. Her work was made possible by obtaining funding in the form of grants from different agencies and organizations at the national level.

Ahmed Aref, CMA has utilized his analytical thinking for strategic decision making in organizations with a broad experience of 23 years as an internal and external financial advisor. During this time in his career, he became aware of an interpersonal communication gap that affected organizations' culture. He learned and understood the reason for this gap by gaining knowledge in executive coaching. In the second part of his life and career, he has addressed this source by assuming a coach-consultant role. As a coach, he guides the leader to decide what they want to do, and as a consultant, he makes sure the leader learned how to do it. His effective methods help the people visualize the beauty within them and use that realization to multiply their contributions toward aligning their spiritual values with business outcomes. Moreover, he has discovered a novel practical roadmap in business through the Values and Leadership podcast by connecting with purposeful business owners and executives from five continents. Those leaders want to pay it forward with their resources, time, talents, and experiences through their day-to-day work and businesses. Now, he finds himself at the intersection of business, economics, and human psychology – what he calls "The Well-Being Experience." His philosophy is that hope and stability are what leaders and their teams want most, and inspiring them is his motivation in work. Inspirational leadership happens with the existence of effective leadership behavior and clear communication.

Mustafa Omar Mohammed, PhD is presently an Associate Professor at the Department of Economics, and the Director of Islamic Economics at the International Islamic University Malaysia (IIUM). He has won several quality academic awards. He has published more than 50 refereed journal articles and presented more than 80 papers. He has supervised more than 50 dissertations. He is also a journal editorial member and reviewer panel to 11 academic entities. Dr. Mustafa has conducted several training workshops on Islamic economics, banking, and finance. He earned his bachelor's and master's degrees in economics at IIUM, and a PhD in finance from USM (2011).

Mohamed Cherif El Amri, PhD is currently working as an Assistant Professor at the Faculty of Business and Management Sciences, Islamic Economics and Finance Department, at Istanbul Sabahattin Zaim University. He completed his bachelor's degree in Islamic Studies from Ibn Tofail University in Morocco. He earned his master's in Islamic jurisprudence and its principles, and his PhD in Islamic banking and finance from International Islamic University Malaysia. He has industrial exposure to and experience in several Islamic financial institutions internationally. He is also a member of various international journal editorial and reviewer panels. He has several research publications and presentations in the field of Islamic economics and finance.

Ayman Mohammad Bakr, MBA is currently a PhD student at the Department of Islamic Economics and Finance at Istanbul Sabahattin Zaim University. He holds two bachelor's degrees, one in electrical electronics engineering from Bilkent University and the other in mathematics from Southern New Hampshire University, from which he earned two outstanding academic achievement awards. Ayman earned his master's degree in business administration with distinction from Strathclyde University. He has several industrial experiences; more than 10 years are in an international financial institution. He wrote several research papers, and his interests are e-waste, circular economy, econometrics of FX rates and trade, waqf, and waqf worldview.

Ensari Yücel, PhD is currently working as an Assistant Professor at the Faculty of Business and Management Sciences, Islamic Economics and Finance Department, at Istanbul Sabahattin Zaim University. He earned his bachelor's degree in business administration from Erciyes University in Turkey (1993). He completed his MSc. in Islamic economics from the International Islamic University, Islamabad, Pakistan (1997). He completed his PhD in international trade and EU law from Istanbul Commerce University in Turkey (2015). He worked in a firm in the information technology (IT) sector for a while, and then he established his own IT Company. He also served as a member and manager in various professional chambers and business organizations. He served as the president of the IT Board of MUSIAD between 2010 and 2011 and the president of the IT Committee of the Istanbul Chamber of Commerce between 2009 and 2013.

Yussuf Charles Yussuf, MSc is currently a PhD candidate at the Department of Islamic Economics and Finance at Istanbul Sabahattin Zaim University. He holds a bachelor's degrees in economics from Zanzibar University, Zanzibar, Tanzania. Yussuf earned his master's degree in economics and finance from Zanzibar University. He also attended short courses in capital market and investment banking in Ahmedabad, India. He has 6 years of experience in the banking industry in Tanzania and worked in two different banks as credit analyst, customer service representative, and banking operation officer. He participated in several international conferences including the 12th International conference in Islamic Economics and Finance and the 33rd SASE Annual conference. His research interests include circular economy, application of econometrics, application of Maqasid al Shariah worldview, economic growth, economic policy and analysis, and Islamic banking and finance.

Yoseph Ataa Alsawady, MA is currently a PhD Candidate in Islamic Economics and Finance at Istanbul Sabahattin Zaim University (IZU). He is also an Awqaf Investment Specialist at the Islamic Development Bank (IsDB) working with the Awqaf Properties Investment Fund (APIF), an impact investment fund dedicated to financing awqaf projects globally. He joined the IsDB in 2017 as part of the Young Professionals Program (YPP). Prior to the IsDB, he worked in construction, engineering, and business development. He holds a Master of Liberal Arts (ALM) degree in International Relations from the Harvard Extension School. He also holds a master's degree in engineering management (MEM) and a bachelor's degree in civil engineering (CE), both from Kansas State University, as well as a minor in Arabic Language and Literature from the American University of Beirut (AUB).

Ramadhani Mashaka Shabani, MSc is currently a master's student at the Faculty of Business and Management Sciences, Islamic Economics and Finance Department, at Istanbul Sabahattin Zaim University. He obtained his bachelor's degree in Customs and Tax Management from the Institute of Tax Administration in Tanzania. He worked as an Assistant Tax Officer for 1 year in the Tanzania Revenue Authority.

INTRODUCTION

The methodology and technique used for teaching, learning, and research in any discipline are generally a prime factor as a driving force to knowledge, skills, capacity building, and contributory impacts toward creating dynamic leadership, skilled nation, and smart human capital in view of transforming a dynamic nation while contributing to the advancement of the world. It had been often observed that the methodology and techniques adapted in teaching, training, learning, research, and professional development or capacity building in any conventional discipline are generally standardized, particularly among the developing countries.

In the contemporary era, on the other hand, the methodology, techniques, and culture adapted in the teaching, learning, research, training, or capacity building in the Islamic discipline are without standardization, and economics and finance are no exception. They have decentralized and diversified mechanisms, cultures, and independent styles. Today, institutions, professionals (i.e., academics, researchers, trainers, and capacity builders), and generally young intellectuals and students particularly in the Islamic economics and finance disciplines have been trying to adapt the standard methodology and techniques in teaching, learning, training, capacity building, and research in Islamic economics and finance, but are still somehow influenced by the mindset from mechanisms appreciated by conventional disciplines. It has also been observed that on some occasions, academics, researchers, capacity builders, trainers, professionals, and students in the Islamic economics and finance disciplines adapt methodologies, techniques, and mechanisms in their teaching, research, learning, professional development, and capacity building by referring to the conventional standards customizing with Islamic sentiments. It is thus submitted that there is no exclusive standard methodology or techniques in teaching, learning, research, capacity building, or professional development in the Islamic economics and finance discipline yet.

In witnessing the above phenomena, it may be concluded that the rapid growth of Islamic eco-finance in ratio (20% pa) is more significant compared with its conventional counterpart globally. But the outcomes of the professional development, research, capacity building and training in the field of Islamic eco-finance are far behind compared with the industrial outcome.

DOI: 10.4324/9781003252764-1

Industries or even the academic and research environments of Islamic eco-finance disciplines are on some occasions influenced by conventional standards and techniques due to unavailability of the required standards and mechanisms designed within the spirit of *Maqasid al-Shari'ah*. If the existing phenomena ought to be allowed to be continued, Islamic eco-financial industrial growth, creating skilled professionals and having significant impact on all levels of Islamic eco-finance industries, may eventually be frustrated.

It is thus time to undertake exclusive research focusing on the standard methodologies, smart techniques, mechanisms, and globally acceptable culture and style within the spirit of *Maqasid al-Shari'ah* in teaching, learning, research, capacity building, professional development, human capital development, and training in Islamic eco-finance in view of creating impact-oriented, skilled professionals, smart academics, researchers, trainers, intellectuals, decision makers, and industrialists to cope with the contemporary world of advanced technology. Thus, this title is an effort to contribute to the aforementioned expectations.

Part 1

AN OVERVIEW OF RESEARCH AND TEACHING METHODS FOR ISLAMIC ECONOMICS AND FINANCE

1

A CRITICAL SURVEY ON METHODOLOGIES AND TECHNIQUES ADOPTED IN TEACHING ISLAMIC ECONOMICS AND FINANCE GLOBALLY

Irfan Syauqi Beik, Abdul Aziz Yahya Saoqi and Muhammad Hasbi Zaenal

Introduction

In the last two decades, the Islamic economic and finance industry has shown very rapid developments indicated by the increasing number of countries involved in developing Islamic economic and financial systems in their respective countries to capture investment opportunities from Muslim investors. The current development of the Islamic economy and finance industry is not only focused on financial institutions development but also in the other sectors, such as halal food, halal travel, modest fashion, pharma and cosmetics, and media and recreation. Investments made by various countries in these sectors have had a considerable impact on the development of each sector. The data shows that the halal food sector is getting enough attention; it can be seen from the data that investment in both the halal food sector and Islamic finance still dominates the total investment in the Islamic economic and financial industry. These sectors reach 52% and 42% of the total investment value in the Islamic economy and finance industry (Figure 1.1) (DinarStandard, 2020).

Apart from total investment, the development of assets or the value of the sharia economic and financial sectors has also developed significantly. Data from the State of the Global Islamic Economic Report shows that the value of assets and spending in each sector has increased. However, as with investment, the development of assets and values in the Islamic finance industry is still dominated by the Islamic finance and halal food sectors of US$2.8 trillion and US$1.17 trillion, respectively, in 2019. The extraordinary development of the Islamic economy and finance industry cannot be separated from the role of human resources (HR). Hence, human resources with special competencies

DOI: 10.4324/9781003252764-3

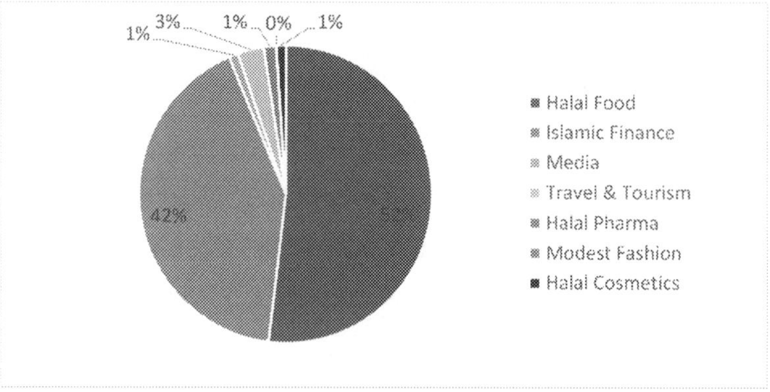

Figure 1.1 The global investment portion of the Islamic economic sector.

Source: DinarStandard (2020), drawn by author.

in economics and Islamic finance are the key to sustainable development in Islamic economics and finance in the future. However, the fulfilment of human resources in the field of Islamic economics and finance is still facing challenges due to the limitation of human resources who have an educational background in Islamic economics and finance. This condition leads the industry to recruit HR from other fields (Amalia, 2014). The education sector has a significant role in providing human resources in accordance with the needs of the rapidly growing economic and financial industry (Nu'man & Ali, 2016). Therefore, the offer of Islamic economics and finance programs is increasingly in demand and opened by various universities. Globally, the number of universities that provide faculties or majors in sharia economics and finance has increased significantly. Even in 2020, at least 21 universities in the world provide Islamic economics and finance programs included in the QS Global World Ranking University list.

Table 1.1 illustrates the list of universities that provide Islamic economics and finance education that is included in the QS Global World Ranking University list. This data shows that Malaysia and Indonesia still dominate in providing Islamic economics and finance programs at various universities. Thus, the two countries are still the main players in the global Islamic economy and finance industry. The adoption of teaching methodologies and techniques at universities providing Islamic economics and finance programs is also one of the keys to the university's success in producing human resources who have competencies following the needs of the Islamic economy and finance industry. Therefore, this study intends to investigate and describe the learning models and techniques in Islamic civilization starting from an early stage of Islam to the modern phase as a critical discussion framework. Moreover, the study aims to explore the current application of methodology and techniques used by various countries in the world in learning Islamic economics and finance. Nevertheless, the study also provides future challenges and opportunities in developing the issue so that the study will deliver valuable input for relevant

Table 1.1 Islamic economics and finance education providers listed in QS Global World Ranking University in 2020

No.	*QS ranking*	*University*	*Country*
1	59	University of Malaya	Malaysia
2	86	Durham University	United Kingdom
3	132	Universiti Putra Malaysia	Malaysia
4	143	King Abdulaziz University	Saudi Arabia
5	165	Al-Farabi Kazakh National University	Kazakhstan
6	187	Universiti Teknologi Malaysia	Malaysia
7	254	Gadjah Mada University	Indonesia
8	254	Universiti Brunei Darussalam	Brunei
9	305	University of Indonesia	Indonesia
10	474	Umm Al-Qura University	Saudi Arabia
11	521–530	Airlangga University	Indonesia
12	531–540	Bogor Agricultural University	Indonesia
13	531–540	Universiti Utara Malaysia	Malaysia
14	551–560	Management and Science University	Malaysia
15	601–650	International Islamic University Malaysia	Malaysia
16	601–650	University of Sharjah	UAE
17	801–1,000	COMSATS University Islamabad	Pakistan
18	801–1,000	Istanbul University	Turkey
19	801–1,000	Kuwait University	Kuwait
20	801–1,000	Prince of Songkla University	Thailand
21	801–1,000	Universitas Padjadjaran	Indonesia

Source: Hidayat and Nasution (2020).

authorities to develop and improve further the quality of education, notably in Islamic economics and finance.

Development of teachings and methodologies in Islamic studies

This chapter elaborates on the historical phase and development of teachings and methodologies in Islamic economics and finance area. The phase was started during the early stages of Islam when building the education system in Mecca and Medina. Subsequently, the discussion continued in the education system during the medieval phase. Moreover, the debate ended when exploring Islamic studies development in the colonialism era and afterwards.

Early phase

Generally, in the early days of the advent of Islam, the education system underwent a transformation in two places, in Mecca and in Medina. In the city of Mecca, the center of Islamic education took place in the house of al-Arqam bin Abi al-Arqam al-Makhzumi, called Darul Arqam, where the house marked the establishment of an Islamic educational institution. Darul Arqam was chosen because the Islamic faith of its owner, al-Arqam, was unknown to the

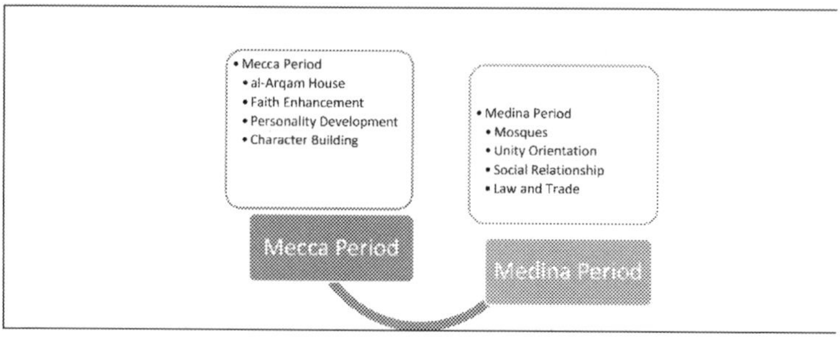

Figure 1.2 Islamic education concepts in Mecca and Medina period.

Source: Hafidhin (2015), Sudan (2017), Rasyidah (2020), drawn by author.

Quraysh, who often prevented the Prophet Muhammad from spreading Islam. The educational method used in the city of Mecca is a simple model in the form of *halaqah*, or a circle with a focus on the theme of education related to behavior development and good character in aspects of strengthening faith, character building, and personality development (Sudan, 2017). These themes become fundamental foundations in the development of Islamic civilization in the future. After the Prophet migrated to the city of Medina, the center of education was located in the Nabawi Mosque. The educational method used is still the same as the method applied in Mecca, such as the memorization method, discussion, question and answer, demonstration, and example (Hafidhin, 2015). However, the education system in Medina had several developments, such as bringing in expert teachers from prisoners of war to teach the Muslim community in Medina to read, write and count. The theme of education was further developed at that time, not only focusing on building faith and personality but also focusing on aspects of practice level in daily life such as unity orientation, social relations, law, and trade (Figure 1.2) (Rasyidah, 2020).

Medieval phase

The end of the period of Al-Khulafa' al-Rashidun, which was full of turmoil and conflict, became the background for changes in the political system of Muslims. The transfer of the center of political power from Medina to Damascus, Syria, has also triggered an increase in the intensity of Islam's contact with Greek cultural heritage. The result of the contact of Muslims with Greek culture in the West and Persian scientific civilization in the eastern hemisphere had a very important influence on Islamic education activities during the Umayyad and Abbasiyah period. Muslims found the Greek scientific heritage in the conquered territories in handwritten manuscripts, and this was very influential in the development of Islamic education at that time (Akhtar & Rawat, 2014). The educational methods that were practiced in the early phases of the history of Islamic education continued to be used, developed, and perfected until the medieval Islamic period. At the peak of Islamic glory,

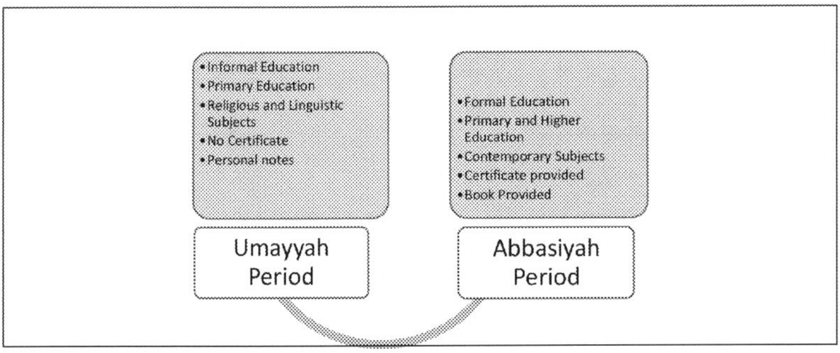

Figure 1.3 Education phase transformation in the medieval period of Islam.

Source: Akhtar and Rawat (2014), Wahyuningsih (2014), Khairuddin (2018).

several methods were most popular at that time, namely the Memorization Method, Lecture Method, *Imla* Method, Reading Method in Front of Teachers, *Munzarah* Method (debate), *Murasalah* Method (correspondence), and *Rihlah 'Ilmiyyah* Method (scientific adventure) (Wahyuningsih, 2014). The entry of the treasures of knowledge into the Islamic educational system has had a tremendous effect on the development of Islamic civilization, with formal institutions established in the Abbasiyah period (Khairuddin, 2018). The advancement of education in the period of Abbasiyah was started by selecting a formal education system from the entry-level to the higher level with the various object of studies not only on religious and linguistic studies but also on contemporary studies such as astronomy, medicine, physics (Figure 1.3) (Akhtar & Rawat, 2014).

Colonialism and post-colonialism period

Since the fall of the Islamic caliphate under the Abbasid dynasty, Western countries have carried out invasions and colonialism in almost all areas that had been controlled by the caliphate for decades. Colonialism has a very significant impact on the development of the education system in Islamic areas. One of the impacts is secularization in education and also the imposition of the Western education system (Tan, 2017). On the other hand, this condition also causes Muslim scholars to reject the entire system and focus on religious education. Therefore, this condition leads to Islamic education closing itself off from contemporary subjects, which causes the decline of Muslims' capability in various scientific fields. After colonialism ended and Islamic territories gained their independence, Islamic countries began to organize educational methods and systems, one of which was the Islamization of knowledge, which was started in late 1976 on the recommendation of the First World Conference on Muslim Education in Mecca in 1976 (1398 H) as an attempt to tackle the Malaise of the Ummah (al-Faruqi, 1982). The Organization of Islamic Cooperation responded positively to the conference results by establishing Islamic universities in the Muslim world, which was

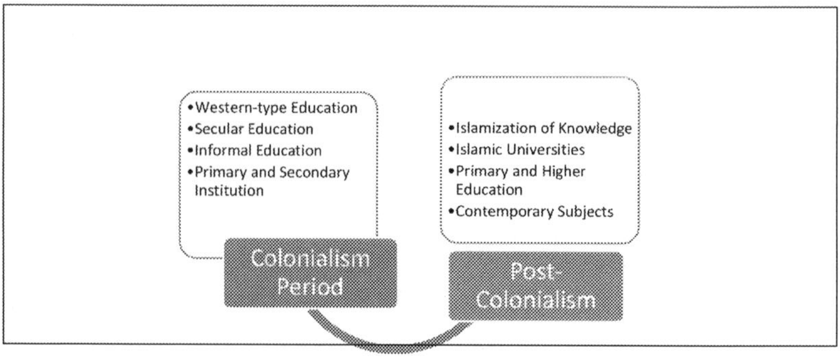

Figure 1.4 Islamic education phase transformation from the colonialism era to the post-colonialism period.

Source: al-Faruqi (1982), Furqani (2012), Tan (2017), drawn by author.

followed up with the establishment of two Islamic universities, namely the International Islamic University in Pakistan in 1980 and the International Islamic University in Malaysia in 1983. The two universities carry a mission of integration of Islamic and conventional knowledge, known as Islamization of knowledge (Figure 1.4) (Furqani, 2012).

Global survey of Islamic economics and finance teaching and methodology

The process of Islamization of knowledge since the 1970s has had a very significant impact on strengthening the education system in Muslim countries up to now. The success of implementing the Islamization of knowledge can be seen in the emergence of knowledge of Islamic economics and finance from various universities in the world, which has contributed to the development and strengthening of the Islamic economic system in various countries. On the other hand, the teaching technique and methodology are also emerged in various universities to support the education system in learning Islamic economics and finance. Hence, this chapter explores the development as well as the techniques and methodology adopted by selected countries, such as Indonesia, Malaysia, and the United Kingdom, in learning Islamic economics and finance.

Indonesia

As the country with the largest Muslim population in the world, Indonesia pays great attention to Islamic economics and finance education. The beginning of the development of Islamic economics and finance education began with the widespread study of Islamic economics and finance, which was then followed by the formalization of Islamic economics and finance education at various universities in Indonesia, starting at the undergraduate level (bachelor's degree) to the graduate level (master's and doctoral degree) (Table 1.2).

Table 1.2 Top education providers of Islamic economics and finance in Indonesia

No	*University*	*QS world ranking*
1	Gadjah Mada University	254
2	Indonesia University	290
3	Airlangga University	465
4	IPB University	511–520
5	Padjadjaran University	801–1000
6	Diponegoro University	1001–1200
7	Brawijaya University	1001–1200

Source: BAN-PT (2021), QS Top Universities (2022).

Indonesia is also known as the country with the most significant number of universities in the world that provide Islamic Economics and Finance (IEF) study programs. According to data obtained from the National Higher Education Accreditation Board (BAN-PT), in 2018, there were 411 Islamic economics and finance study programs provided by various universities, which were dominated by undergraduate study programs (Figure 1.5) (BAN-PT, 2021; KNEKS, 2019).

In terms of applying the technique and methodology in teaching Islamic economics and finance, in general, various universities in Indonesia apply several methodologies or learning approaches, namely class-based learning, project-based learning, and field-based learning. In the class-based learning method, the teaching techniques used are presentations from lecturers, explanations of textbooks and journal reviews, and students are also given the opportunity to make presentations at every meeting of Islamic economics

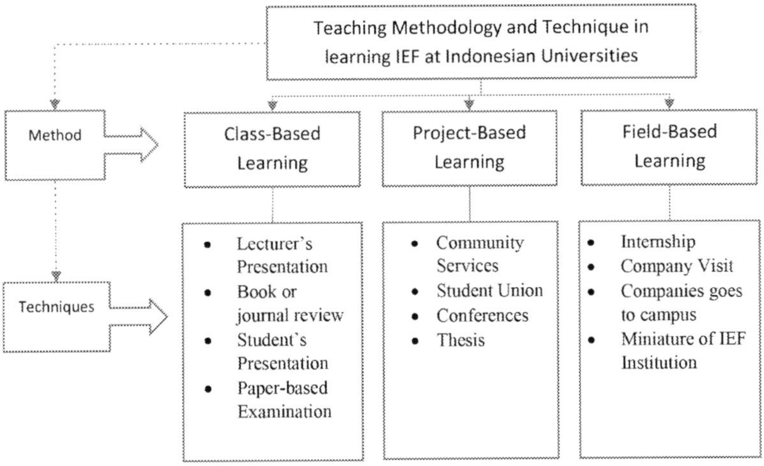

Figure 1.5 General teaching methodology and technique in learning IEF in various universities in Indonesia.

Source: Author's document.

and finance lectures. In addition, the project-based learning method used in Islamic economics and finance learning techniques are community services, activities at student unions, participating in conference activities with relevant topics, and research at the end of the program in the form of a thesis or dissertation. Furthermore, in the field-based learning method, there are several teaching techniques implemented, such as internship programs at Islamic economics and finance institutions, company visits to the Islamic finance industry, and the company goes to campus programs to introduce best practices in the field of Islamic economics and finance. Nevertheless, to get more exposure in IEF institutions, many universities in Indonesia established a miniature of IEF institution to give practical understanding for the students.

Malaysia

Malaysia is known as a very progressive country in Islamic economics and finance education, and this is inseparable from the Malaysian government's efforts to support the establishment of the International Islamic University in 1983, which has a mission to integrate general knowledge with Islamic knowledge, known as the Islamization of knowledge (Furqani, 2012). In the same year, Malaysia has also ratified the Islamic Banking Act, which led to the establishment of Bank Islam Malaysia Berhad (BIMB). Since then, the transformation of the Islamic economics and finance system has greatly progressed in Malaysia. The tremendous development of the IEF system in Malaysia also led the higher education institutions to provide IEF programs. Generally, there are five main IEF programs in Malaysia: *muamalat* (shariah and law in IEF), Islamic economics, Islamic finance, Islamic accounting, and Islamic management. Almost all higher institutions in Malaysia serve as IEF education providers (ICIFE, 2016). Table 1.3 shows the top ten IEF education providers in Malaysia based on QR World University Ranking 2022.

In general, the methodologies and techniques of learning in the field of IEF at various universities in Malaysia are similar to the methodologies and

Table 1.3 Top ten education providers of Islamic economics and finance in Malaysia

No	*University*	*QS world ranking*
1	Universiti Malaya	65
2	University Putra Malaysia	143
3	Universiti Kebangsaan Malaysia	144
4	Universiti Sains Malaysia	147
5	Universiti Teknologi Malaysia	191
6	Taylor's University	332
7	UCSI University	347
8	Universiti Utara Malaysia	511–520
9	International Islamic University Malaysia	651–700
10	Universiti Teknologi MARA	651–700

Source: QS Top Universities (2022).

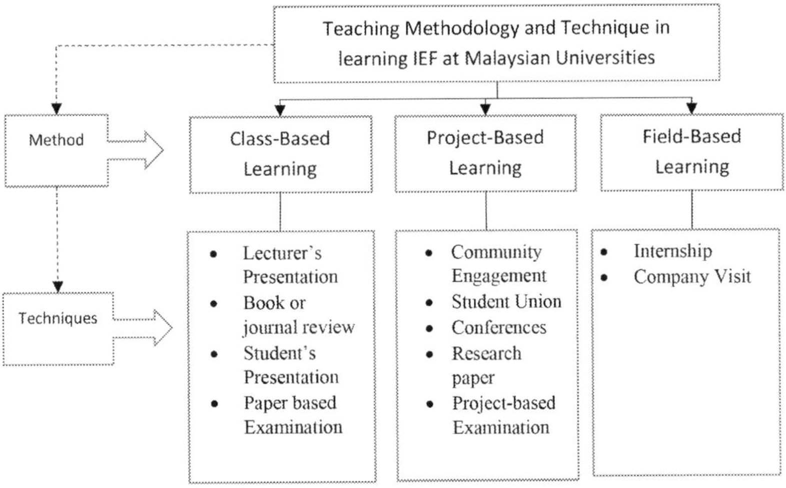

Figure 1.6 General teaching methodology and technique in learning IEF in various universities in Malaysia.

Source: ICIFE (2016), Lathifah (2021).

techniques applied in Indonesia. However, there are some differences in the application of learning techniques. The learning techniques used in the class-based learning method are presentations from lecturers, book or journal reviews, student presentations, and paper-based presentations. In addition, in terms of project-based learning methods for students, many universities in Malaysia use community engagement techniques, student unions, conferences, and applied research activities. And the most exciting things in the education system in Malaysia are project-based examinations. Nevertheless, it has the same technicality in the field-based learning method, namely, an internship program for students and field trips, such as company visits to the Islamic finance industry (Figure 1.6) (Lathifah, 2021).

The United Kingdom

The United Kingdom is one of the countries outside of the Muslim world that gives considerable attention to the Islamic economic and financial system, so this phenomenon is often called by experts a standalone experiment phenomenon (Belouafi & Chachi, 2014). Historically, in the field of Islamic economics and finance education, the Islamic Foundation in the United Kingdom established an Islamic economics and finance research unit to support the UK's Islamic economics and finance ecosystem immediately after the conference in Jeddah in 1976. Then in 1981, the International Association for Islamic Economics was established to strengthen this ecosystem, one of which organized the 4th Conference on Islamic Economics (Belouafi & Chachi, 2014). And in the following years, the United Kingdom experienced a

Table 1.4 IEF education providers in the United Kingdom

No	*University*	*QS world ranking*
1	Durham University	82
2	University of Birmingham	90
3	University of Reading	202
4	Bangor University	601–650
5	University of Salford	801–1000
6	Markfield Institute	-

Source: MES UK (2017), QS Top Universities (2022).

progressive transformation in the field of Islamic economics and finance, and even the UK government had quite ambitious plans to become the Islamic financial hub in Europe. The UK's strong Islamic economic and financial ecosystem is also supported by a robust Islamic economic and financial education system. Table 1.4 presents the list of universities in the United Kingdom that provide Islamic economics and finance programs.

In terms of methodologies and techniques for teaching Islamic economics and finance at UK universities, it is not much different from the system applied in Indonesia and Malaysia. Principally, the method used is still the same as the method applied in Indonesia and Malaysia, only in terms of teaching techniques. The most prominent thing at UK universities is the mastery of textbooks and very strong research applications. Students have a reliable knowledge base to fulfill the demand of the Islamic finance industry at a local level (Figure 1.7) (Al-Anshory, 2021).

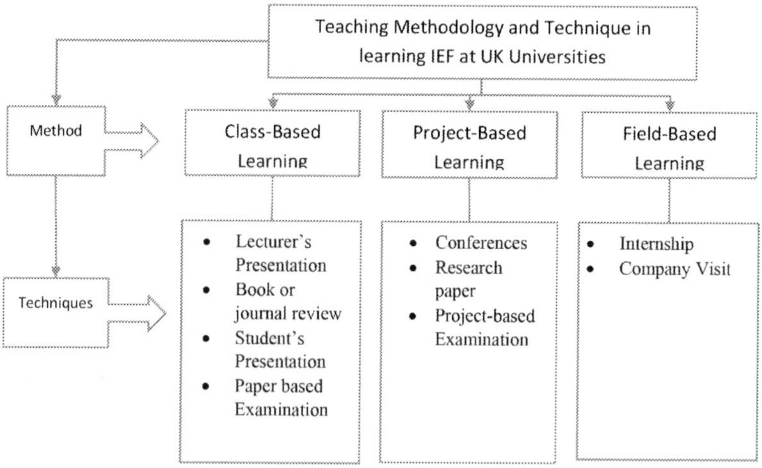

Figure 1.7 Teaching methodology and technique in learning IEF at UK universities.

Source: Al-Anshory (2021).

Conclusion

The growth of Islamic finance and industry has shown a tremendous performance. This is inseparable from the Islamic economics and finance education sector, which has shown a very progressive development in providing competent and quality human resources. The presence of quality human resources is the key to the success of the Islamic economy and finance industry. And indeed, human resources are closely related to the quality of the education system. Historically, the education system in Islam has experienced various challenges starting from the early phase of Islam, the medieval phase, and the colonial and post-colonial phase. All these phases have formed a strong Islamic education system so that the concept of Islamization of knowledge emerges. The implementation of Islamization of knowledge has significant implications for the quality of human resources in Islamic economics and finance to meet the needs of the Islamic economics and finance industry. The excellent quality of human resources is the impact of applying appropriate methodology and techniques for teaching Islamic economics and finance at the higher education level. Indonesia, Malaysia, and the United Kingdom are among the best examples of Islamic economics and finance teaching methods and techniques. This is what drives them to become leading players in the Islamic economics and finance industry so that the study of teaching methods and techniques from the three countries is important to be explored to construct a model for other countries to adopt similar methods and techniques in order to have good quality human resources in accelerating the Islamic economy and finance industry.

References

Akhtar, M. & Rawat, K. J., 2014. A Historiography of the Educational System on the Muslim during the Ummayad's and the Abbasid's Period. *The Dialogue Journal*, IX(4), pp. 356–372.

Al-Anshory, A. C., 2021. *Islamic Economics and Finance Education System in the United Kingdom* [Interview] (4 July 2021).

al-Faruqi, I., 1982. *Islamization of Knowledge: General Principles and Work Plan*. Virginia: International Institute of Islamic Thought.

Amalia, E., 2014. Evaluation of the Model of Education in Islamic Economics and Finance: Empirical Evidences from Indonesia and United Kingdom. *Inferensi Journal*, VIII(2), pp. 373–394.

Belouafi, A. & Chachi, A., 2014. Islamic Finance in the United Kingdom: Factors behind its Development and Growth. *Journal of Islamic Economic Studies*, 22(1), pp. 37–78.

DinarStandard, 2020. *State of the Global Islamic Economy Report*. Dubai: DinarStandard.

Furqani, H., 2012. Islamisasi Ilmu Ekonomi. *SHARE Journal*, 1(2), pp. 83–97.

Hafidhin, H., 2015. Pendidikan Islam pada Masa Rasulullah. *Tarbiya Journal*, I(1), pp. 17–29.

Hidayat, S. E. & Nasution, A., 2020. *IFN News. Universities Offering Islamic Economics and Finance Programs in QS Rankings for 2021*, 1 July, p. 27.

ICIFE, 2016. *Malaysia Islamic Finance Education Report*. Kedah: UUM Press.
Khairuddin, 2018. Pendidikan Pada Masa DInasti Abbasiyah. *Ittihad Education Journal*, II(1), pp. 98–109.
KNEKS, 2019. *Masterplan Ekonomi dan Keuangan Syariah Indonesia 2019–2024*. Jakarta: Komite Nasional Ekonomi dan Keuangan Syariah.
Lathifah, U., 2021. *Islamic Economics and Finance Education in Malaysia* [Interview] (4 July 2021).
Nu'man, R. & Ali, N., 2016. Islamic Economics and Finance Education: Consensus on Reform. *Journal of Islamic Economics, Banking and Finance*, XII(3), pp. 75–97.
Rasyidah, A., 2020. Pendidikan Pada Masa Rasulullah SAW di Makkah dan di Madinah. *Al-Hikmah Journal*, II(1), pp. 32–44.
Sudan, S. A., 2017. The Nature of Islamic Education. *American International Journal of Contemporary Research*, 7(3), pp. 22–27.
Tan, C., 2017. Colonialism, Post-Colonialism, Islam and Islamic Education. In: *Handbook of Islamic Education*. Dordrecht: Springer.
Wahyuningsih, S., 2014. Implementasi Sistem Pendidikan Islam pada Masa Daulah Abbasiyah dan Pada Masa Sekarang. *Education Journal*, II(2), pp. 109–126.

2

METHODOLOGICAL STRUCTURE IN DESIGNING ACADEMIC PROGRAMS FOR ISLAMIC ECONOMICS AND FINANCE

Hichem Hamza

Introduction

The history of teaching Islamic economics and finance began decades ago. During that time, it witnessed institutional developments and educational achievements, the most important of which was the establishment of academic programs, scientific departments, and colleges specializing in Islamic economics and finance. Their establishment represents the knowledge incubator for teaching Islamic economics and finance, as these scientific structures contributed to the process of reviving the economic and financial heritage and its origins, highlighting its richness of knowledge, the alternatives to the conventional system, and solutions to contemporary economic and financial issues. In this regard, the utmost importance of this chapter is highlighted in enriching interest in designing the knowledge and skill content of academic programs in Islamic economics and finance[1] by covering all the theoretical and applied knowledge components of the related courses. In addition, it is important to link the Islamic heritage of knowledge with the contemporary era and give it its rightful place in the content of Islamic economics and finance courses. The content design methodology comes from the core of the curriculum development, and the term and concept of the methodology are mentioned in the Holy Quran in the words of Allah Almighty, "To each of you we prescribed a law and a method."[2] This gives importance to the Islamic method of acquiring knowledge. This appears in the context of what was approved by the Islamic Fiqh Academy in its resolution No. 138 (4/15) of 2004 regarding the Islamization of educational curricula[3] and the support of authenticity and Islamic vision in the formulation of educational subjects and courses.

The academic programs in Islamic economics and finance seek to build knowledge and skill capacities in the field of Islamic economics, Islamic

DOI: 10.4324/9781003252764-4

finance, financial Fiqh, its principles, rules, and purposes. The design of learning outcomes is the main title of academic programs, as the preparation of outcomes requires a background of knowledge of the vocabulary and dimensions of the program and courses, and a reflection of the philosophy of Islam and the fundamentals of Islamic economics and finance in its doctrinal, legal, ethical, and scientific aspects. Upon completion of the selecting and building learning outcomes of the program, they are disassembled in order to prepare a list and content of courses in its compulsory, optional, theoretical, applied, general, and specialized parts. During this process, each faculty member prepares a course description, starting with preparing the course learning outcomes that are serving the program outcomes. After that starts the process of preparing the plan and course content according to a scientific methodology based on identifying the sources and references of the course in addition to mastering the basics of scientific formulation, robustness of style, and what this requires in terms of originality methodology, keeping pace with the development of teaching topics, comparison with other programs, monitoring future trends, comprehensive literary survey, depth of analysis, and accuracy of data.

Institutional development of Islamic economics and finance programs: An experimental study

By institutional development, we mean the establishment of scientific departments in Islamic economics or Islamic finance, as well as the establishment of specialized colleges in this field, and this development is what would effectively contribute to the development of the educational operation. This institutional classification does not underestimate the importance of establishing programs in Islamic economics and finance outside the framework of specialized departments and colleges, as it is noticeable that these programs have been established and spread in many colleges and universities under a conventional umbrella in North Africa, the Middle East, Central Asia, Britain, and France.

Belouafi and Belabes (2012) indicate that the year 1904 witnessed the birth of the first course on economics from an Islamic perspective at the Thaalibiya High School in Algiers. At the beginning of the second half of the last century, specifically during the 1960s, Islamic economics courses were included in the educational curricula at Al-Azhar University in Egypt, King Abdulaziz University in the Kingdom of Saudi Arabia, and Omdurman University in Sudan, where the Islamic Economics Department had been established in 1965 (Mohammad, 2008). This trend accelerated its pace after the Cairo Conference in 1972 and the First Makkah Conference on Islamic Economics, which was organized by King Abdulaziz University in 1976 and called for the inclusion of Islamic economics and finance courses in the curricula of the faculties of economics and business. In this regard, the year 1977 witnessed the establishment of the Institute of Islamic Economics in Jeddah, Kingdom of Saudi Arabia, which was the first research institution in Islamic economics, to which the educational aspect was added in 2013, as the scientific departments in Islamic economics, Islamic finance, and takaful insurance were established in 2017. The outcomes of the First Makkah Conference on Islamic Economics also led to the establishment of the Islamic Economics Division in the Shari'ah Graduate Studies department in 1977 at the College of Shari'ah and Islamic Studies at Umm Al-Qura University in Makkah (formerly King Abdulaziz University branch), and in 1980 the division was transformed into the Islamic Economics Department, which grants scientific degrees in Islamic economics. After that, Umm Al-Qura University established the College of Islamic Economics and Finance in 2012, which has various departments and includes economics, banking, financial markets, finance, and insurance. In Riyadh, the College of Shari'ah affiliated to Imam Mohammad Ibn Saud Islamic University first established a program in Islamic economics, followed by the Department of Islamic Economics in 1979, and then the department turned into a college specializing in economics and administrative sciences. In 2010, the faculty of Shari'ah at the Islamic University of Madinah witnessed the establishment of the Department of Islamic Economics, which offers master's and doctoral programs.

In Egypt, Al-Azhar University established in 1982 the Saleh Centre for Islamic Economics, which is concerned with the dissemination of Islamic economics and commercial thought. In Pakistan, the International Islamic University of Islamabad established in 1983 the International Institute for Islamic Economics, which later established academic programs for all educational levels in Islamic economics, finance, and Islamic banking. In addition, the International Islamic University "Rafah" established in 2002 the Rafah Center for Islamic Business, and in 1985 the Islamic Centre Sheikh Zayed was established, which currently offers programs in Islamic banking and finance for bachelor's, master's, and doctoral degrees. In Malaysia, the International Islamic University established the Institute of Islamic Banking and Finance in 2005, which offers master's and doctoral degrees in Islamic finance. In 2006, the Central Bank of Malaysia established the International Centre for Education in Islamic Finance (INCEIF), and in 2008 it established the International Shari'ah Research Academy for Islamic finance (ISRA). Furthermore, one of the most important educational achievements in Malaysia was the establishment of the Financial Accreditation Agency in 2012, whose tasks include issuing educational standards and accrediting programs in the field of Islamic finance. In Palestine, the College of Shari'ah affiliated to An-Najah National University in Nablus established the Department of Shari'ah and Islamic Banking in 2006, which offers a bachelor's degree in Shari'ah and Islamic banking (Figure 2.1).

After the 2008 financial crisis and in the context of reconsideration of the ethical aspect in managing economic and financial affairs, the peak of interest in Islamic finance and its educational and academic programs increased significantly (Belouafi and Belabes, 2013), and a new phase began in designing courses and academic programs in economics and Islamic finance in many universities through the creation of specialized courses and programs in the

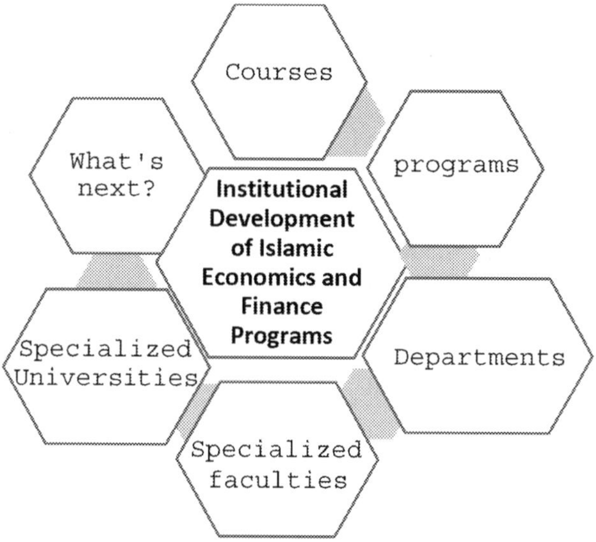

Figure 2.1 Institutional development of Islamic economics and finance programs.

aforementioned field. In this context, Libyan universities witnessed the establishment of scientific departments specializing in Islamic economics and finance, including Al-Asmaria University and its branches in 2008 and 2011, the University of Tripoli, as well as the University of Zawia and the Misrata Academy. In Jordan, specifically at Yarmouk University, the College of Shari'ah and Islamic Studies established, in 2001, the Department of Economics and Islamic Banking, which offers master's and doctoral degrees in economics and Islamic banking, followed by a bachelor's degree in the same specialty in 2016, noting that master's and doctoral degrees had been granted since 1985 by the Department of Fiqh and Islamic Studies and before it by the Centre for Islamic Studies. In 2009, the faculty of business and finance of the International University of Islamic Sciences established the Department of Islamic Banking, which offers bachelor's, master's, and doctoral degrees in Islamic banking. In 2008, the faculty of business and finance of Ajloun National University established the Department of Islamic Banking, which offers bachelor's degrees in Islamic banks. In 2010, the faculty of economics and administration at Zarqa University established the department of Islamic Banking that offers bachelor's and master's degrees in Islamic banking. Likewise, the faculty of Shari'ah at the University of Jordan established in 2010 the Department of Islamic Banking, which offers bachelor's degrees in Islamic banking.

In Spain, the business school IE, in cooperation with King Abdulaziz University, established in 2009 the Spanish Centre for Islamic Economics and Finance. The center's activities are based on four pillars, including academic development in the field of Islamic economics and finance. In Qatar, the College of Islamic Studies established in 2010 the Centre for Islamic

Economics and Finance, in order to provide a rich environment for students, faculty members, and visiting professors, enabling them to participate effectively and achieve tangible progress in this field. In Bahrain, the College of Administration and Business at the University of Bahrain has established the Department of Islamic Banking, which offers bachelor's and master's programs in Islamic banking and financial transactions. In Syria, the faculty of Shari'ah at the University of Damascus established the Department of Islamic Economics, where it teaches courses related to economics, its doctrines, contemporary financial transactions, Islamic financial institutions, and comparative Islamic economics.

In Iraq, the faculty of Islamic sciences of the University of Baghdad established in 2012 the Department of Contemporary Islamic Financial and Banking Sciences, and the College of the Imam A'Adhum of the Sunni Endowment Diwan established in 2018 the Department of Islamic Finance and Banking Sciences. In Kazakhstan, the National Kazakh University of Al-Farabi established in 2019 the Al-Farabi Kaznu Islamic Finance Scientific and Educational Center, which offers Islamic finance programs for bachelors, master's, and doctoral degrees. In Turkey, Istanbul University established in 2014 the Department of Islamic Economics and Finance, as well as Sabahattin Zaim University in 2016 through the College of Business and Administrative Sciences, as well as for Sakarya University (Orhan, 2017) and Karatay University in Konya. In 2019, Marmara University established the Institute of Islamic Economics and Finance as a scientific and educational institution that is the first institution of this specialty in Turkey and plans to open master's and doctoral programs in Islamic economics and finance. In Britain, which is considered the center of Islamic finance in Europe, Durham University has established the Durham Centre for Islamic Economics and Finance, which offers master's and doctoral programs in Islamic finance.

In addition to the institutional development of Islamic economics and finance at departments and institutes in the aforementioned countries, where there are also university institutions that provide programs and courses in Islamic economics and finance under a conventional umbrella, many Islamic and non-Islamic countries (Morocco, Tunisia, Algeria, UAE, Kuwait, Oman, Indonesia, India, France, and others) have witnessed the establishment of programs and courses in Islamic economics and finance in their curricula at the bachelor's, master's, and doctoral levels, and this in itself is an achievement that also gives program content design great importance in achieving the desired educational goals.

Building knowledge content in Islamic economics and finance programs

The process of designing the content of academic programs in Islamic economics and finance is subject to a scientific methodology based on mastering the knowledge material, the quality of the selected references, the quality of learning outcomes, the comprehensiveness of topics, and keeping up new developments in order to design, develop, and improve distinct knowledge and skill content as necessary. In addition, the process of designing the content of Islamic economics and finance programs is based on highlighting the Islamic value and ethical dimensions and their essential position in the formulation of the knowledge and skill outputs and the content of the teaching materials. From this point of view, there is an adoption of Shari'ah, moral values, and Islamic heritage as the main determinants of the content and composition of the courses.

Building learning outcomes in Islamic economics and finance programs

The course consists of four pillars, which are learning outcomes, scientific material, teaching strategy, and assessment methods. The academic program includes learning outcomes, course lists, and faculty members. The learning outcomes are what the learner should acquire in terms of knowledge, skills, and values and be able to apply them. Learning outcomes represent the scientific identity of the academic program and form the main titles of its contents. In this context, it can be said that the formulation of learning outcomes is a minimized picture of the formulation of the scientific content of academic programs in Islamic economics and finance. The design of learning outcomes for the program and the courses are intended to be simple and can be measured and evaluated. In this regard, it is important to know the classification or Bloom's taxonomy pyramid to facilitate the process of formulating the related action verbs, as the learning outcomes are built within the framework of the learning areas, which are understanding, knowledge, skills, and values that the learner is expected to acquire. The learning outcomes are formulated through imperative verbs or noun phrases, and in this case, we say "upon successful completion of this course the student should be able to…"

The focus of learning outcomes around the student-centered approach is the most important and widely used, as the learning objectives are constructed from the teacher's point of view and the learning outcomes are constructed from the learner's point of view. The duration of the program is the determinant of the number of outputs; therefore, the greater the duration, the greater the output. The principles of formulating learning outcomes at the level of courses and programs in Islamic economics and finance should not only address what is dictated by the needs of the education sector and the labor market but also implant Islamic and societal values and *Shari'ah Maqasid* related to justice and wealth preservation, as well as the status of ethics as a knowledge and value component without which economic and financial transactions cannot be straightforward. From this point of view emerges the importance of the Islamic dimension in determining learning outcomes

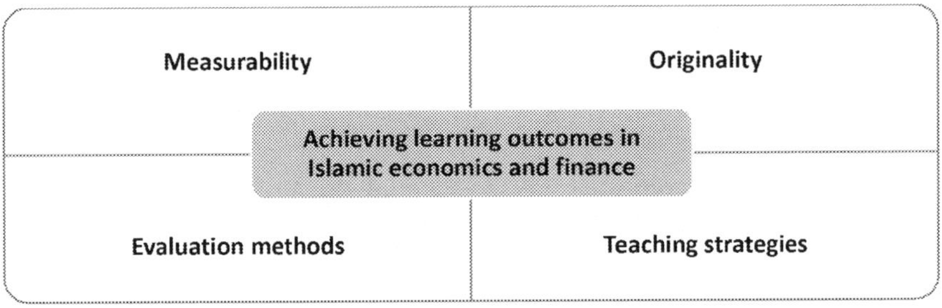

Figure 2.2 Achieving learning outcomes in Islamic economics and finance.

by highlighting the value of Islamic heritage and the history of Islamic economics; the importance of the role of Islamic economics in solving economic problems, reforming the financial system, and Islamic financial institutions; the moral and social impact of Shari'ah on financial transactions; and the importance of earning, spending, and developing wealth through legitimate means. This means that the learning outcomes are also educational with reference to Islamic morals and values (Figure 2.2).

In the same context, the course outcomes are derived from the program outcomes, which means that the outcomes of all the courses are branches of the program outcomes, where the learning outcomes of the courses are linked to the main program outcomes and thus the course outcomes serve the program outcomes. The learning outcomes of the course are originally fixed and do not change from one teacher to another, but the objectives may differ from one teacher to another, and with their differences, they should achieve the same outcomes. In addition, the teaching strategies and evaluation methods of all kinds are considered to serve the learning outcomes, and here, it is important to make a difference in achieving optimal learning outcomes in their knowledge, skill, and value dimensions, and for the student to obtain the necessary knowledge, skills, and scientific tools.

The achievement of learning outcomes is the standard for evaluating the teaching process, and it is considered as a competitive tool between Islamic economics and finance programs in the various colleges and universities concerned with this matter. The evaluation of students and the department is what ensures the achievement of knowledge, skill, and value learning outcomes. It is at the core of the teaching process, and it is a measure of its success as the outcomes can be converted into key performance indicators. The learning outcomes of academic programs in Islamic economics and finance should be presented and discussed in the scientific department in order to identify and improve the quality of learning outcomes. In this context, it is highlighted that there should be standards and procedures for evaluating, improving, and developing academic programs through program performance indicators and questionnaires.

Content and composition of academic courses

The preparation of program and course content depends on several knowledge sources, which can be presented as follows:

- Textbooks and scientific books in the intended field, including books in economic and financial sciences, Shari'ah and historical sciences, literature, and technological development, with a focus on books that deal with the Shari'ah and economic dimensions in a methodological style.
- Relevant programs and courses in local and international universities, with the most prominent trends or basic courses approved by colleges and the weight of the category of courses and topics covered in each program, as well as keeping up with the content of competing programs and courses and making benchmarking comparisons with courses and programs in Islamic economics and finance.
- Research topics published in refereed journals, workshops, and scientific conferences related to the program and intended courses, and to find out the literature, trends, and backgrounds, as there is a link between the development of educational materials with the production of scientific research. It is also important to take into account the role of the outputs of scientific research and to keep up with the scientific and practical development in the fields of the Islamic finance industry and to include them in the vocabulary and courses.
- Reports related to the program and intended courses, including reports of Islamic, international, and regional financial institutions, reports of jurisprudence and Shari'ah institutions, reports of financial and statistics authorities, relevant ministries, and chambers of commerce.
- Government programs in subjects related to courses, such as the program for developing the financial sector in the Kingdom of Saudi Arabia.
- Websites related to Islamic economics and finance and their related articles and reports, as well as text and scientific book publications.
- Standards for academic accreditation and the quality of education and what they contain for principles and guidelines in preparing learning outcomes and the scientific content of the teaching plan, teaching strategy, and evaluation methods.
- Outputs of the department's meetings on teaching and research and internal discussion sessions related to developing teaching programs and courses.

In addition to these sources, it is worth noting the important role of the Shari'ah and educational environment in promoting economic and financing programs, as the institutions of the Islamic Fiqh Academy, the AAIOFI, the IFSB, the Islamic Development Bank, and Islamic banks have an important contribution in this field. Furthermore, the expertise, experience, knowledge, and skills of a faculty member are the main drivers of the teaching process and the success of the program, as the faculty member represents the original source of knowledge through his endeavor to transmit knowledge to students. A faculty member with a Shari'ah background must have knowledge competence in economics and finance, and a faculty member with an economic or financial background must have the knowledge component in Shari'ah sciences. It is also important to divide the references that will be provided to the student into major, support, and free readings in order to let him set priorities in understanding and mastering the courses.

The design of the program and the formulation of the main vocabulary of the scientific content stems from an important situation that education in Islamic economics and finance is a mixture between Shari'ah sciences and economic and financial sciences, and both fields are specializations, since each one owns its principles and foundations. In addition, the competitive advantage among educational institutions imposes an elaborate scientific design for teaching programs and courses, which serves the quality of education and the knowledge economy.

The classification or division of courses into categories is very important to determine the knowledge map of the program, which is shown in Table 2.1 and it is based on the example of classification made by Haneef and Amin (2010) and Belouafi and Belabes (2013). Belouafi (2014) indicated that it is important to identify the main components of the program structure in Islamic economics and finance: Is it a category of Shari'ah materials or technical materials related to Islamic and conventional finance, or is it a combination of both? In this regard, it can be said that the composition is a balanced mix of these categories, and this mixture should include the aspects of Shari'ah. Therefore the Shari'ah materials related to Islamic economics and finance should be strongly present. Moreover, the Shari'ah aspect is an essential knowledge component in the technical courses in Islamic economics and finance by focusing on Islamic concepts relevant to the economic and financial heritage with its contemporary attribute. For instance, the originality of the

Table 2.1 Matrix of teaching courses identification and balance

Category of courses	*Principals concepts*	*courses type*	*Programs level*
• Shari'ah and legal • Islamic finance • Islamic economy • Islamic heritage • Conventional economics and conventional finance • Pre-requisite courses	• AlRizk: الرزق • AlKasb: الكسب • AlInfek: الإنفاق • AlAmwal: الأموال • AlBaraka: البركة • Al Riba: الربا • AlRochd: الرشد	• Compulsory or elective • Theoretical or applied • General or specialized • Arabic or other language	• Bachelor's degree • Research or Executive Master • PhD

function of finance in Islam is to achieve the Shari'ah purposes of earning, circulating, and developing wealth. The most important aspect of the originality is the revival of Islamic economic concepts and their re-inclusion in the knowledge paradigm, including the concepts of spending, investment, livelihood, rationality, and others. In this regard, it is important to use and employ Qur'anic terms in the content of educational curricula (Machouche, 2018). The conceptual construction of the program's materials is extremely important in highlighting the Islamic knowledge model in economics and finance, which is an integral model with reference to the sources of Shari'ah from the Quran and Sunnah. For example, Islamic finance is based on standards that take into account the rules and purposes of Shari'ah and includes behavioral and value-based dimensions (Belouafi and Belabes, 2013).

In this context, the courses are roughly divided into six categories, as indicated in the matrix above, and their weight is determined according to the type of courses and the levels of program. The Shari'ah and fundamental categories represent the largest portion and include, in particular, the courses of financial Fiqh, its rules and purposes, the courses of principles of Islamic economics, principles of Islamic finance, history of Islamic economics, Islamic financial system, zakat, and donations. On the other hand, the titles of courses are very important, as it is preferable that the titles be meaningful, agreed upon, and reflect the content of the program and courses, bearing in mind that there are differences in titles from one college to another and from one university to another, even though the content does not change. In this context, it is very important to define the titles of the courses that should reflect the content, be complementary to each other, and achieve the objectives of the knowledge and skills component of the program. In addition, overlap and repetition between titles of courses should be avoided.

In the same context emerges the importance of choosing compulsory courses as a basic component of Islamic economics and finance programs, and this is subject to several considerations, the most important of which is the focus on the basic knowledge and skills that the student must acquire. In this regard, the compulsory courses in Islamic finance should include all the Shari'ah aspects related to wealth and technical aspects related to the Islamic financial system, financing, and investment practices; Islamic financial products; Islamic financial markets; corporate finance from an Islamic perspective; financing and investment in endowments; and Fintech. It is also important to choose theoretical, applied, general, and specialized courses according to the program levels. Naturally, the content of the courses varies according to the educational degree: bachelor's or postgraduate studies, or according to specialization in the master's program, either Executive Master or Research Master. On the other hand, the condition of the Arabic language for these programs emerges because the distinction of Islamic finance depends on the extent of its Islamism in form and content and because the main sources of knowledge and skills are in Arabic (Belouafi, 2014). In addition, there is a necessity of teaching the courses in Islamic economics and finance in Arabic because of the enormity and importance of ancient and modern scientific sources and references.

In the formulation of the scientific content of graduate studies programs, the scientific background of the students should be taken into account: Does the student have a Shari'ah or an economic/financial background and the effect of that on the teaching process? This disparity is more evident in postgraduate studies that attract a greater number of varying levels and different educational specializations, and scientific courses are often taken alongside basic courses that do not fit and do not meet the actual need of all those enrolled in these teaching programs. In this context, it is important to include prerequisite courses in Shari'ah for students of economics and finance and prerequisite courses in economics and finance for the students of Shari'ah. In the same context, the inclusion of prerequisite courses comes within the framework of the diversity of the master's student and the diversity of their specialization, which could also include the specialization in law, engineering, and the variation of their knowledge levels in Shari'ah and economic fields. Likewise, there could be an Islamic economics or finance program for Shari'ah specialty and another for economists or financiers, or in other words, establishing two branches of specialization in Islamic finance, one for specialists in Shari'ah sciences and another for specialists in finance and banking. Finally, the content of courses in Islamic economics and finance can differ fundamentally if the entity is a business college or Shari'ah college, because the graduates are either economists or Shari'ah.

Conclusion

The history of teaching Islamic economics and finance began decades ago, during which it witnessed scientific and institutional developments and achievements, the most important of which was the establishment of academic programs, scientific departments, and colleges that specialized in Islamic economics and finance. Academic programs in Islamic economics and finance seek to build knowledge and skill capacities in the field of Islamic economics, Islamic finance, financial Fiqh, its principles, rules, and Shari'ah purposes. In this context, the design of an academic program in Islamic economics and finance is the core of the learning process that qualifies for graduate students specializing in this field. The design is based on a scientific methodology starting with the learning outcomes that represent the scientific identity of the academic program content and are intended to transfer knowledge and skills to the student in a scientific way through the courses, teaching strategies, and evaluation methods. On the other hand, the knowledge, skills, and value content of academic programs in Islamic economics and finance is built by identifying sources of knowledge, preparing a list of courses, and then the content and vocabulary of the courses. In this regard, the importance is in focusing on the optimal combination between Shari'ah and technical courses, taking into account the originality factors, compulsory courses, language, and levels of education.

Notes

1 What is meant here is bachelor's, master's, and doctoral degree programs.
2 Surat Al Maeda, 48.
3 The Islamic Fiqh Academy Decision No. 138 (4/15) of 2004 regarding the Islamization of educational curricula referred to two important issues that fit within the core of the topic of this research. The first includes revising the educational curricula prevailing in the Islamic world and developing them in a way that combines Islamic authenticity with contemporary, in order to preserve the Islamic character and to link to the scientific heritage written in Arabic. The second is the formulation of educational topics and courses within the framework of the Islamic perception, by highlighting the Islamic vision (belief, Shari'ah, and method of life) in covering the content.

References

Belouafi, A., & Belabes, A. (2012). Introduction in Islamic Finance in Western Higher Education: Developments and Prospects. Palgrave MacMillan.

Belouafi, A., & Belabes, A. (2013). Islamic financing programs and courses in Higher Education Institutions: Features and Trends. Journal of Humanities and Social Sciences. Volume 28. Imam Mohammad Bin Saud Islamic University. Saudi Arabia, May 2013.

Belouafi, A. (2014). Islamic Finance in Higher Education Institutions in the Arab Gulf States: A Comparative Analytical Study. ISRA International Journal of Islamic Finance. Volume 5. The second issue. December 2014.

Haneef, M.A., & Amin, R.M. (2010). Teaching Islamic Economics in Malaysian Universities: Lessons from the Department of Economics. IIUM: Kuala Lumpur.

Machouche, S.T. (2018). Identifying Educational Ways to Use Quranic Terms in Designing School Science Textbook. Journal of Contemporary Islamic Thought (Islamic Knowledge). 24th year. Issue 94, Fall 2018.

Mohammad, E.M.A. (2008). Curricula and Formulation of Islamic Macroeconomic Theory. Contemporary Islamic Macroeconomics Series. Khartoum, Sudan.

Orhan, Z.H. (2017). Curriculums of Islamic Economics and Finance Postgraduate Programs in Turkey. IKAM Reports 1. Research Notes 1.

3

SWOT ANALYSIS ON RESEARCH METHODOLOGIES AND TECHNIQUES ADOPTED IN ISLAMIC ECONOMICS AND FINANCE

Irfan Syauqi Beik and Tita Nursyamsiah

Introduction

Islamic economics and finance have developed rapidly throughout the world. The Islamic economic and finance industry has thrived in both Muslim and non-Muslim countries. The development is due to the high global demand for products that comply with sharia principles. The high global demand is for Islamic financial products and halal industrial products, such as halal food and beverages, halal cosmetics, halal pharmaceuticals, modest fashion, travel and media, and Muslim-friendly travel. According to the State of the Global Islamic Economy Report 2020/2021, in 2019, it is estimated that total Islamic financial assets reached $2.88 trillion, and the total expenditure of the global Muslim population in the halal industry sector reached $2.02 trillion (Dinar Standard, 2020). This figure is predicted to increase along with the increase in the world's Muslim population. Besides the commercial finance sector, the Islamic social finance sector has developed to support the economy. Islamic social finance broadly comprises traditional Islamic institutions based on philanthropy, such as zakat, *sadaqah* and waqf, which are based on mutual cooperation such as *qard* and *kafala*, as well as contemporary Islamic nonprofit microfinance institutions that use the profit made primarily to cover costs and support their operations. Islamic social finance has proven to be effective in supporting sustainable development goals (SDGs), including reducing poverty and income inequality (Widodo, 2019), ending hunger (Abduh, 2019), and facilitating educational and health institutions for the poor. Programs managed by Islamic philanthropic institutions have also facilitated many educational programs such as scholarships for low-income families as well as health programs with hospitals established and financed by zakat, *sadaqah*, and *waqf* funds and procurement of medical devices during the COVID-19 pandemic.

DOI: 10.4324/9781003252764-5

The positive development of Islamic economics and finance encourages the development of research related to Islamic economics and finance. Generally, research is a search for knowledge (Kothari, 1985). In addition, research is also defined as a scientific and systematic search for related information on a particular topic. The existence of research is expected to support industrial development in the Islamic economic and financial sector and contribute to the development of Islamic economics. In this case, the research applied to Islamic economics and finance is not only intended for industrial purposes but also for academic development. Also, research applied in Islamic economics and finance can be the recommendations for policymakers to support the environment of Islamic economy. Research applied in Islamic economics and finance can be conducted by various methods and techniques. The methods applied in Islamic economics and finance include quantitative, qualitative, and combination of them. Research methods and techniques are part of the research methodology. Research methodology in Islamic economics and finance needs to be developed in order to promote knowledge and provide benefits to industry and society. Therefore, this study aims to analyze the strategy of developing a research methodology that is applied through Islamic economics and finance by using SWOT analysis.

Literature review

Research and research methodology

The term "research" refers to a pursuit of knowledge (Kothari, 1985). A scholarly and methodical search for relevant knowledge on a certain topic can also be defined as research. Research is, in reality, a form of scientific study. Research is a phrase that should be used in a technical meaning because it is an academic activity. As a result, research is a unique contribution to the current body of knowledge that contributes to its progress. It is the search for truth through study, observation, comparison, and experimentation. In a brief, research is the pursuit of information through an objective and systematic technique of obtaining a solution to a problem. Research is also the systematic approach for generalization and the creation of a theory. As a result, the term "research" refers to a procedure that is methodical.

According to Kothari (1985), though each research project has its own particular goal, we may categorize research aims into the following general categories:

- To obtain a better understanding of a phenomena or to gain additional insight into it (studies with this goal in mind are known as exploratory or formulative research studies);
- To properly depict the features of a certain person, circumstance, or group (studies with this goal in mind are referred to as descriptive research studies);

- To assess the frequency with which something occurs or is linked with something else (diagnostic research studies are those that focus on this object);
- To see if a causal link between variables can be proven (these kinds of investigations are referred to as hypothesis-testing research studies).

Research methodology is a method for solving a research problem in a systematic way. It may be thought of as a science that studies how scientific research is carried out. Research methodology refers to a philosophically cohesive set of theories, concepts, or ideas as they apply to a specific subject or field of investigation (Gounder, 2012). Methodology is more than just a set of procedures; it also includes the logic and philosophical assumptions that underpin a study's use of the scientific method. Many different methods are employed in different forms of research, although the word is typically used to refer to research design, data collection, and data analysis. The goal of research methodology is to educate: Why has a research study been conducted? How has the research problem been identified, and how and why has the hypothesis been formed? What data has been collected, and what approach has been used? Why was a certain data analysis approach used? When we discuss research methodology in relation to a research problem or study, we generally get answers to these and other questions (Gounder, 2012).

In simple terms, research methodology is used to provide a clear picture of what the researcher is investigating. Research methodology provides the proper platform for the researcher to map out the research work in relevance and make solid plans in order to plan at the right time and advance the research activity. Furthermore, research methodology encourages the researcher to get involved and become active in his or her subject of study. The goal of the research and the research topic will not always be the same; it will vary depending on the aims and flow of the research, but this may be accomplished with the use of appropriate methodology (Gounder, 2012). Research methodologies can be quantitative and qualitative. In an ideal world, thorough research would include qualitative and quantitative methodologies, but this isn't always achievable owing to time and budget restrictions. In academic research, research methodologies are commonly employed to examine hypotheses or theories. A good design ensures that the study is both valid and trustworthy, in that it explicitly examines the hypothesis and excludes unnecessary factors, and that the results are consistent every time (Gounder, 2012).

Research topics applied in Islamic economics and finance

Research in Islamic economics and finance has been carried out, both with qualitative, quantitative, and combined methods. Several research topics related to Islamic economics and finance can be broadly grouped into Islamic economics, Islamic finance, and Islamic governance and morality. Islamic economic issues can be categorized into economic philosophy and perspectives, economic and monetary policy development, and the impact of economic conditions on Islamic economic policies. At the same time, topics related to Islamic finance consist of Islamic banks, risk management, financial management, financial assets, and consumer behavior, while Islamic governance and morality topics consist of corporate governance, contracting and legal enforcement, and philanthropic and inclusive finance. Among the three categories of subjects addressed, Islamic finance is the most developed. It is due to a long-standing focus on Islamic principles in the creation of Islamic financial services, as well as significant government policy targeted at investing in and growing institutions like Islamic banks. In addition, the number of articles indexed by Scopus and other respectable journals on the development of mathematical model research findings in Islamic economic and financial research has grown, although it is still modest. The most researched topics are Islamic banking and Islamic (macro) economics.

SWOT analysis

SWOT analysis is a tool used in businesses for strategic planning and management. It may be used to develop both organizational and competitive strategies. SWOT analysis is a two-dimensional method that covers four areas. It is divided into four sections: strengths, weaknesses, opportunities, and threats. Opportunities and threats are external elements and attributes of the environment, whereas strengths and weaknesses are internal factors and attributes of the organization. SWOT analyses are commonly drawn in a four-quadrant box, which enables a summary to be structured according to the four section headings. A SWOT analysis, with four elements in a 2 × 2 matrix, is shown in Table 3.1.

Many aspects may be mentioned that influence the preference and utility of SWOT analysis. According to Gürel and Tat (2017), the following are some of the characteristics that might be considered advantages:

- SWOT analysis is a method of looking at problems from a wide perspective and offering comprehensive solutions. The SWOT analysis does not focus on specific details or issues, but they are the subject of later investigations. In this way, a SWOT analysis is a road map that leads from the broad to the detailed.

Table 3.1 The components of SWOT analysis

Strengths	The characteristic that gives value to something and distinguishes it from others.
Weaknesses	A bad and unfavorable characteristic.
Opportunities	Circumstances in the external environment that enable an organization to benefit from its strengths, overcome its weaknesses, or counteract environmental hazards.
Threats	A situation that puts an activity's completion in jeopardy. It alludes to a precarious position. As a result, it possesses a negative trait that should be avoided.

- SWOT analysis is an interactional analysis-based macro-evaluation approach. SWOT analysis helps you to focus on the good and negative aspects of an organization's internal and external surroundings, in other words, the factors that provide plus and minus value, all within the framework of a linked worldview.
- Organizational management may benefit from a SWOT analysis to find profit opportunities. Threats may be dealt with and eliminated by understanding their weaknesses. Strategies for differentiating a company from its rivals may be devised using a SWOT analysis of the company and its competitors.
- SWOT analysis develops a thinking paradigm for organizational management as a strategy and analytical tool. This approach emphasizes the points at which decisions are made and enables for the agenda to be set during the phases of data gathering and interpretation. In other words, a SWOT analysis sets the groundwork for strategic decisions.
- SWOT analysis is compatible with other theories and strategic decision-making approaches. SWOT, for example, encompasses a number of different forms of analysis, such as Porter's Five Forces Model, Delphi Panel, Norton Balanced Score Card, and others.
- SWOT analysis promotes group discussion of strategic challenges and the creation of strategies. It enhances the sharing of knowledge by utilizing novel interactive techniques such as brainstorming and group meetings.
- SWOT analysis aids organizational management by beginning a conversation about the organization's future and aspirations by moving beyond everyday difficulties and the current state.
- Individual, corporate, national, and global levels of analysis can all benefit from a SWOT study. It may be beneficial to educational institutions, non-profit organizations, countries, governments, and intercultural projects.

SWOT analysis can also be referred to as a "Two-by-Two Matrix" as shown in Table 3.2. "SO" strategy is a mechanism that uses internal strengths to take advantage of external opportunities. "WO" strategy is a strategy that aims to overcome internal weaknesses by taking advantage of external opportunities. "ST" strategy is a strategy that utilizes internal strength in reducing

Table 3.2 SWOT matrix

	Strengths	*Weaknesses*
Opportunities	Strategy that uses internal strengths to take advantage of external opportunities	Strategy that aims to overcome internal weaknesses by taking advantage of external opportunities
Threats	Strategy that utilizes internal strength in reducing the impact of external threats	Strategy with the aim of reducing internal weaknesses and avoiding external threats

the impact of external threats. "WT" strategy is a strategy with the aim of reducing internal weaknesses and avoid external threats. The strategy resulting from the combination of SWOT can not only be used for an organization or industry, it can also be used in determining strategies or policies in a country (Wheelen and Hunger, 2012).

SWOT analysis in research methodology applied in Islamic economics and finance

Internal factors

Internal factors are factors derived from research methodology applied in Islamic economics and finance. Internal factors are divided into two aspects, namely, strengths and weaknesses. The aspect of strength is the factors that become advantages of research methodology applied in Islamic economics and finance. Weakness aspects are factors that can hinder the development of research methodology applied in Islamic economics and finance.

Strength

SPIRITUAL VALUE OF RESEARCH METHODOLOGY APPLIED IN ISLAMIC ECONOMICS AND FINANCE

The selection of the theory that underlies the research is part of the research methodology, especially in determining the hypothesis. Islamic economic and financial theory derives from the Qur'an and hadith (Nasrifah, 2016). It causes research in the field of Islamic economics and finance to have spiritual value. It also demonstrates a fundamental distinction between Islamic and conventional economics and finance research methodologies.

JUSTIFICATION FROM ISLAMIC JURISPRUDENCE

The fundamental difference between Islamic economics and finance research with conventional economic and financial research lies in the justification of Islamic jurisprudence (*fiqh*). In conducting research related to Islamic economics and finance, the theory of Islamic jurisprudence becomes the theoretical basis used. It is done to ensure that the study conducted is within the sharia principle, particularly for financial products. Islamic jurisprudence helps researcher to answer the research problem.

THE VARIOUS METHODS APPLIED

Islamic economics and finance research methodology can use various methods, ranging from quantitative, qualitative, or mixed methods. Quantitative research is a type of study that uses statistical, logical, and mathematical techniques to create numerical data and concrete facts, while qualitative research is a type of research that seeks to explore people's thoughts and feelings in the human and social sciences.

Weakness

DOMINATION OF CONVENTIONAL THEORY

The weaknesses of the Islamic economics and finance research methodology mainly refer to conventional economics. It happens because Islamic economics is less developed and popular among academics and researchers. As a result, traditional economic theory is still the primary reference. In comparison to conventional economics, Islamic economics has a different epistemological foundation, which is based on revelation (Furqany and Haneef, 2020). However, Furqani and Haneef (2012) agreed that not all conventional theories should be dismissed; rather, this should be addressed in the near term while seeking to evaluate Islamic economic theory in a way that incorporates both Islamic principles and Islamic practical realities/cases.

LACK OF SECONDARY DATA RELATED TO ISLAMIC ECONOMICS AND FINANCE VARIABLES

In quantitative research methods, secondary data is one type of data that is widely used. The secondary data will later be processed and analyzed, which in turn will produce conclusions. However, the available secondary data relating to Islamic economics and finance is still minimal. For example, data on the gross domestic product (GDP) of the halal industry is still not well-publicized in several countries, including Indonesia. In fact, secondary data has an important role in the development of research methodologies in the field of Islamic economics and finance, especially when conducting empirical research. Secondary databases in the subject of Islamic economics are suitable for good research results because of their speed and inexpensive cost (Hassan, 2007).

LACK OF RESEARCH TOPIC APPLIED IN ISLAMIC ECONOMIC THEORY

Currently, research related to Islamic finance is mainly performed because of the need for the Islamic finance industry. Research related to Islamic economics, especially those aimed at building a theory of Islamic thought, is still less frequently conducted. The existence of theory resulting from Islamic economic research is expected to enrich Islamic economic theory, which is still not widespread.

External factors

External analysis was carried out to identify the factors outside the research methodology in Islamic economics and finance, namely, the opportunity aspect and threats. Opportunity aspects are external factors that can support the development of research methodology applied in Islamic economics and finance. Threat aspects are external factors that hinder the research methodology applied in Islamic economics and finance.

Opportunity

THE RAPID DEVELOPMENT OF THE ISLAMIC ECONOMIC AND FINANCE INDUSTRY

The Islamic economic and finance industry has rapidly increased. The Islamic finance industry, including Islamic banks, Islamic capital market, and *takaful*, experienced positive growth in 2019 (IFSB, 2020). In addition, the Islamic social finance sector continues to experience positive developments. The benefits of Islamic social finance make this sector more developed. This is due to the increasing literacy and interest of the community to participate in Islamic social finance. In addition to Islamic commercial and social finance, the halal industry has also developed quite well (Dinar Standard, 2020).

DEVELOPMENT OF ISLAMIC ECONOMICS AND FINANCE EDUCATIONAL AND RESEARCH INSTITUTIONS

Due to a renewed interest in the development of an Islamic economic system in Muslim countries and the resulting proliferation of Islamic banks, as well as a significant global consumer base interested in Islamic banking products, Islamic economics and finance education has seen recent growth. The growth of the Islamic financial industry has prompted the establishment of Islamic economics studies programs, such as Islamic economics and Islamic banking, as well as other sharia-based courses. Islamic economics and finance education develops not only in Muslim countries but also in non-Muslim countries such as the United Kingdom. There are several universities that have opened special programs in Islamic economics, including one at Durham University (Meirison, 2017). This indicates an increase in Islamic economics and finance educational institutions around the world. In addition, at higher education institutions there are usually research institutions, because higher education institutions also play a role in research development.

POTENTIAL HUMAN RESOURCES

According to World Population Review (2021), Islam is the world's second-largest religion after Christianity, with roughly 1.9 billion Muslims worldwide. Some can become scholars and researchers in the subject of Islamic finance and economics. These scholars and researchers are also supported by the development of research and higher education institutions in Islamic economics and finance.

Threat

CRITICISMS FROM ECONOMISTS REGARDING THE RESEARCH METHODOLOGY OF ISLAMIC ECONOMICS AND FINANCE

As part of the research methodology, Islamic economic theory has been criticized by conventional economists. Some economists criticize Islamic economics for not having a strong foundation. In addition, Islamic economics is considered too based on religious doctrine and irrelevant to today's modern developments. Kuran (1983) stated that to be regarded a genuine alternative to neoclassical (or even Marxist) economic theory, Islamic economic philosophy is too simple and missing in too many important aspects. The Islamic literature's only significant contribution to the knowledge of economic growth is the insights it gives on the significance of behavioral norms in maintaining social cooperation. These lessons, however, are difficult to extract, since they are buried in a slew of grandiose claims about the scope of Islamic literature (Kuran, 1983).

LACK OF RESEARCH GRANTS FOR SCIENTIFIC DEVELOPMENT, INCLUDING ISLAMIC ECONOMICS AND FINANCE METHODOLOGY

Research grants are an essential component in education, especially in research that uses primary data. In some developing countries, access to research grants, especially in Islamic economics and finance, is still relatively limited. In Indonesia, the largest Muslim country, productivity in the field of science is caused by the difficulty of seeking support to finance research projects, as well as a budgeting and financial reporting system that is not flexible.

Development strategy of research methodology applied to Islamic economics and finance

After analyzing the four criteria, namely strengths, weaknesses, opportunities, and threats, it is important to continue to formulate a strategy for developing research methodology applied in Islamic economics and finance. Strategy formulation considers the four criteria used. The strategy that has been acquired must minimize weaknesses and overcome threats by taking advantage of existing opportunities and strengths. Based on the SWOT matrix in Table 3.3, six alternative strategies are formulated.

Increasing cooperation with the Islamic economics and finance industry to conduct joint research

The development of the Islamic economy and finance industry indirectly encourages research in Islamic economics and finance. Increasing research collaboration between the Islamic economics and finance industry is one strategy

Table 3.3 Alternative strategy based on the SWOT matrix.

Internal factors / External factors	*Strength*	*Weakness*
	a Spiritual value of research methodology applied in Islamic economics and finance (S1) b Justification from Islamic jurisprudence (S2) c The various methods applied (S3)	a Domination of conventional theory (W1) b Lack of secondary data related to Islamic economics and finance variables (W2) c Lack of research topic applied in Islamic economic theory (W3)
Opportunity	*SO strategy*	*WO strategy*
a The rapid development of the Islamic economic and finance industry (O1) b Development of Islamic economics and finance educational and research institutions (O2) c Potential human resources (O3)	Increasing cooperation with the Islamic economics and finance industry to conduct joint research (S1, S2, S3, O1) Strengthening Islamic economics and finance research conducted by academics (S1, S2, S3, O2, O3)	Collaborating with the Islamic economics and finance industry to create a data center (W2, O1) Providing incentives to academics to conduct research aimed at building Islamic economic theory (W1, W3, O2, O3)
Threat	*ST strategy*	*WT strategy*
a Many criticisms from economists regarding the research methodology of Islamic economics and finance (T1) b Lack of research grants for scientific development (T2)	Innovating research methodology applied in the field of Islamic economics and finance with various methods and techniques (S1, S2, S3, T1)	Strengthening and developing existing Islamic theory (W3, T1)

used to develop research methodologies in Islamic economics and finance. The research methodology of Islamic economics and finance is expected to contribute to industry and society on the importance of spiritual values that conventional economics do not have. This research collaboration can enrich the knowledge of Islamic economics and finance methodologies and strengthen cooperation between academics, researchers, and practitioners.

Strengthening Islamic economics and finance research conducted by academics

The development of educational and research institutions in Islamic economics and finance has led to more research being carried out in these fields. Increased research in Islamic economics and finance by universities and research institutions is expected to enrich knowledge to support Islamic economics and finance research methodologies.

Collaborating with the Islamic economics and finance industry to create a data center

The difficulty of accessing secondary data is one of the weaknesses in Islamic economics and finance research methodology. Secondary data is expected to assist researchers in conducting this type of empirical research. Empirical research is usually cheaper than research that requires primary data. The Islamic economics and finance industry is expected to support research by facilitating research to access secondary data. If needed, the Islamic economics and finance industry can create a data center that can make it easier for researchers to access secondary data published by companies.

Providing incentives to academics to conduct research aimed at building Islamic economic theory

Currently, conventional economic theory is still widely used as a theoretical basis in Islamic economics and finance research. Mainstream theory is allowed as long as the theory does not conflict with sharia principles. Therefore, it is necessary to develop Islamic economic theory that can be used and become the basis of Islamic economics and finance research methodology. Research for the development of Islamic economic theory can be done by involving academics.

Innovating research methodology applied in Islamic economics and finance with various methods and techniques

Research in Islamic economics and finance can be carried out with various methods, ranging from quantitative, qualitative, or a combination of the two. On the other hand, there are several criticisms related to Islamic economics, one of which considers Islamic economics irrelevant to today's current conditions. Therefore, it is necessary to innovate research methodologies on Islamic economics and finance, especially research methodologies aimed at developing Islamic economics.

Strengthening and developing existing Islamic theory

Islamic economic theories developed through this research method are still relatively small. On the other hand, some economists think that the existing Islamic theory cannot support modern development. Therefore, it is necessary to strengthen and develop existing Islamic economic theory. Strong Islamic economic theory is expected to be the basis for research in Islamic economics and finance.

Conclusion

The progressive development of Islamic economics and finance supports the advancement of Islamic economics and finance research. Various methods and techniques can be used to conduct research in Islamic economics and finance. The research methodology includes research methods and techniques. This study is an attempt to apply SWOT analysis to research methodology applied in Islamic economics and finance. In conducting a SWOT analysis, it is necessary to identify internal and external factors. Internal factors include strengths and weaknesses. The strength aspects of the research methodology applied in Islamic economics and finance include: (1) spiritual value of research methodology applied in Islamic economics and finance; (2) justification from Islamic jurisprudence; and (3) the various methods applied. Weakness aspects of the research methodology applied in Islamic economics and finance include: (1) domination of conventional theory; (2) lack of secondary data related to Islamic economics and finance variables; and (3) lack of research topic applied in Islamic economic theory. In addition, external factors also need to be identified. External factors include aspects of opportunities and challenges. Aspects of opportunities in the research methodology applied in Islamic economics and finance include: (1) the rapid development of the Islamic economic and finance industry; (2) development of Islamic economics and finance educational and research institutions; and (3) potential human resources. Aspects of challenges include: (1) many criticisms from economists regarding the research methodology of Islamic economics and finance; and (2) lack of research grants for scientific development.

References

Abduh, M. (2019). "The role of Islamic social finance in achieving SDG number 2: End hunger, achieve food security and improved nutrition and promote sustainable agriculture," *Al-Shajarah*, 2019 (Special Issue Islamic Banking and Finance 2019), pp. 185–206.

Dinar Standard (2020). *State of the Global Islamic Economy Report 2020/21*.

Furqani, H. and Haneef, M.A. (2012). "Theory appraisal in Islamic economic methodology: Purposes and criteria," *Humanomics*, 28(4), pp. 270–284. doi: 10.1108/08288661211277335.

Furqany, H. and Haneef, M. A. (2020). "Usul Al-Iqtisad approach in developing the foundations of Islamic economics discipline," in Necmettin Kizilkaya (ed.) *Methodology of Islamic Economics Problem and Solutions*. UK: Routledge.

Gounder, S. (2012). "Chapter 3: Research methodology and research questions." In S. Goundar (Ed.), *Cloud Computing*. Research Gate Publications.

Gürel, E. and Tat, M. (2017). 'SWOT analysis: A theoretical review," *The Journal of International Social Research*, 10(51), pp. 994–1006.

Hassan, A. (2007). "Secondary Databases and their Use in Research in Islamic Economics," *7th International Conference on Islamic Economics*, pp. 137–161.

IFSB (2020). *Islamic Financial Services Industry Stability Report 2020*.

Kothari, C. (1985). *Research Methodology Methods and Techniques*. Second ed. New Delhi: New Age International (P) Ltd.

Kuran, T. (1983). "Behavioral norms in the Islamic doctrine of economics a critique," *Journal of Economics Behavior and Organization*, 4, pp. 353–379.

Meirison, M. (2017). "The development of Islamic economics in various parts of the world." *Jurnal Ekonomi dan Bisnis Islam*, 2(2).

Nasrifah, M. (2016). "Sistem Ekonomi Islam Dalam Al-Quran & Hadist," *Iqtishodiyah*, 2(2), pp. 67–86.

Wheelen, T. and Hunger, J. (2012). *13th Strategic Management and Business Policy toward Global Sustainability*. Upper Saddle River, NJ: Pearson Education.

Widodo, A. (2019). "The Role of integrated Islamic commercial and social," *Journal of Islamic Monetary Economics and Finance*, 5(2), pp. 263–286.

4

METHODOLOGIES AND SMART TECHNIQUES RECOMMENDED IN ANALYZING *MAQASID AL-SHARI'AH* FOR ISLAMIC ECONOMICS AND FINANCE

Irfan Syauqi Beik, Randi Swandaru and Priyesta Rizkiningsih

Introduction

The fundamental difference between Islamic finance and conventional finance lies in the concept and practice of its operational activities. In contrast to conventional financial institutions, Islamic financial institutions are economic systems that carry out their operational activities following *Shari'ah* principles that prohibited *maysir*, *gharar*, and *Riba*. Therefore, Islamic financial institutions are considered a financial system that solves economic problems caused by interest. It is further strengthened by research results stating that Islamic financial institutions are more resilient than their counterparts during crises. Islamic financial instruments are divided into two parts: Islamic commercial financial instruments and Islamic social finance instruments. Islamic commercial finance began in 1963, when the first Islamic bank in the world was established, namely, Mit Ghamr Bank in Egypt, and then was followed by Dubai Islamic Bank in 1975. Not only Dubai but other countries have started following Egypt by establishing Islamic banking in their countries, such as Pakistan, Iran, and Sudan (Nagaoka, 2012). As conventional financial products continue to develop, the Islamic community also needs Islamic financial institutions other than banking. It is one of the reasons for the development of other Islamic financial institutions, such as insurance companies, capital markets, microfinance institutions, pension funds, and halal markets. Although the development of non-bank Islamic financial institutions is slower than banking, these institutions are also among the factors that increase the growth of Islamic finance. Based on the Islamic Finance Development Report (2020) data, it is estimated that the total assets of Islamic finance will reach $3,693 billion in 2024.

 DOI: 10.4324/9781003252764-6

In contrast to Islamic commercial financial instruments, which began to be widely known in the 20th century, Islamic social financial instruments have been known since the era of the Prophet Muhammad through the management of zakat, which *Rasulullah SAW* had carried out as the leader of the Islamic state (Fauzia, 2013). The collection and distribution of zakat have been conducted properly to help the *ummah* moving out of poverty. In fact, during the time of Umar bin Khattab, zakat management already had been instituted (Fauzia, 2013). However, the management of zakat since the Prophet's era has experienced dynamic development wherein during the present age, non-government organizations are also allowed to manage zakat professionally. Along with the increasing number of Muslims in the world, the potential for zakat is also increasing. In a report issued by the World Bank and Islamic Development Bank, the potential for zakat in some Muslim countries can reach 3–4% of gross domestic product (GDP) every year. Although the realization of zakat itself is still low, it can be concluded that Islamic social finance also has an important position in the Islamic economy (Figure 4.1).

According to Chapra (2000), Islamic economics is defined as "the branch of science that helps to realize human welfare through the allocation and distribution of resources that are scarce according to maqasid." It means that the objectives of Islamic financial management, both commercial and social, should not deviate from the goals of *Shari'ah* to achieve benefits (*Maqasid al-Shari'ah*). Dusuki and Abozaid (2007) argue that if Islamic financial institutions only use *Shari'ah* for *Maqasid al-Shari'ah* as a legal form of financial products, the practice of Islamic financial institutions will be similar to conventional financial institutions. To ensure that Islamic financial institutions are

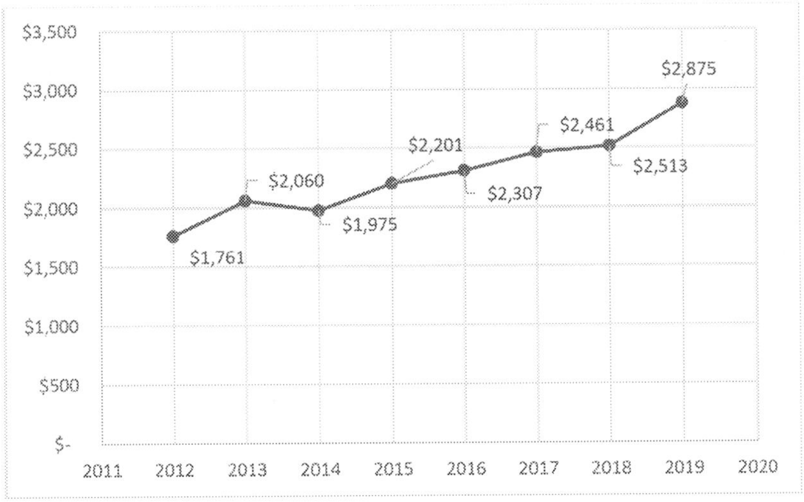

Figure 4.1 Development of Islamic commercial finance assets, 2012–2019.

Source: Mohamed et al. (2020).

in accordance with the *Maqasid al-Shari'ah*, the performance measurement tools need to be adjusted to its aspects. However, Islamic financial institutions still adopt performance measurement tools from conventional financial institutions. As a result, in Islamic commercial financial institutions, such as banks, there is an opinion that poor Islamic banking performance could be due to a mismatch between the objectives of Islamic banks and their measuring tools. Similarly, Mergaliyev *et al.* (2021) also said that measurement using *Maqasid al-Shari'ah* is very important because it affects Islamic banks' good or bad performance. Moreover, many criticisms have also emerged, because Islamic financial institutions are considered unsuccessful in achieving the objectives of *Shari'ah*.

Not only Islamic commercial financial institutions but also Islamic social financial institutions experienced the same challenge. The poor performance of zakat institutions could be because their performance measurement is not based on *Maqasid al-Shari'ah*. The purpose of zakat will only be achieved if it is in accordance with *Maqasid al-Shari'ah*. It also reinforces the importance of measuring the performance of Islamic social financial institutions based on *Maqasid al-Shari'ah*. However, the implementation of *Maqasid al-Shari'ah* as a measurement tool is also extensive since many scholars use this concept to measure things outside of Islamic law, such as in Islamic economics.

This chapter will discuss *Maqasid al-Shari'ah* framework and measurements method in Islamic commercial and social financial institutions: banking, capital markets, and *takaful* (Islamic insurance). Meanwhile, the measurement of *Maqasid al-Shari'ah* on zakat and waqf will be discussed as the proxy of social financial institutions. Finally, the measurement of *Maqasid al-Shari'ah* in sectors other than Islamic commercial finance and Islamic social finance will also be discussed.

Islamic banking

Starting as an interest-free institution financing small projects, using a profit-loss sharing model in the early 1970s, the Islamic banking sector has undergone amazing development in the last half century. According to the Islamic Finance Development Report 2020, there are more than 526 Islamic banking institutions in 74 countries, with total assets of nearly US$1.99 trillion, dominating 69% of global Islamic finance assets (Mohamed *et al.*, 2020). Despite its origin as the countermovement to the socioeconomic failure of socialism and capitalism in Muslim countries, five decades of flourishing upsurge, to some extent, has cost the true spirit of IBF. The lack of Islamic knowledge is the main factor of its loss in creating suitable institutions and organizations that can fulfill the *Maqasid al-Shari'ah* in IBF daily operational activities. This inadequate knowledge has led the industry to copy the conventional product and sometimes dilute the *Shari'ah* requirements.

In contrast to conventional products that merely consider economic performance, Islamic financial products must comply with the legal form of *Shari'ah* and promote the inclusion of social welfare. Moreover, some scholars contend that the replication of conventional practice entails several dilemmas. The *Shari'ah* non-compliance practice may impair reputation risk that may lead to systemic risk and instability (Qattan, 2006). A closer study of Islamic banks worldwide shows that Islamic banks do not have genuine and rigorous effort to eradicate poverty and promote equitable wealth redistribution. Hence, many studies have attempted to discuss, measure, and evaluate the performance of Islamic banking under the *Maqasid al-Shari'ah* framework. Those studies can be categorized into two big groups of research. First, there are studies that criticize Islamic banks that have deviated from the *Maqasid al-Shari'ah* or current financial systems that are incompatible with the objective of *Shari'ah*. These studies emerged and developed in the mid-2000s and have slowly faded in recent years. Most of them are composed of qualitative methodology, using content analysis and logical deduction to provide the findings and analysis.

Meanwhile, the second group of studies emerged in the latter stages and has become more popular in recent years. These studies focus on conceptualizing and measuring the performance of Islamic banks empirically in various Muslim-populated countries. This kind of research is developed using the quantitative method, and it benefited from the data disclosure from Islamic banks. The following discussion will further elaborate on these two groups of studies. Kahf (2006) is one of the pioneers in the first group of studies that lay down the discussion on Islamic banks under the light of *Maqasid al-Shari'ah*. He elaborates on the urgency of *Maqasid al-Shari'ah* in the prohibition of *Riba* and its impact on modern Islamic finance. He argues there are three required conditions for Islamic contracts to deliver the objective of *Riba* prohibition. First, the Islamic financing contract should be asset-based. Second, the underlying asset must be of the kind that is liable to produce a return. Thirdly, the profit margin and the transaction have to be originally designed for what it is for in the first place. Moreover, some studies argue about the incompatibility of the current financial system to deliver the *Maqasid al-Shari'ah*. The fiat money system is detrimental to the realization of *Maqasid al-Shari'ah*. They argue that the Islamic economy is inherently a barter system. Hence, to accommodate the exchange of goods and services and avoid the dilemma related to barter, they argue that it is necessary to use gold as money. Similarly, Dangulbi *et al.* (2012) argue that Islamic banks should operate beyond the fractional reserve banking (FRB) system, because it is counterproductive to the attainment of Shari'ah. The FRB allows the concentration of wealth and power in the hands of few people. It becomes the main socio-economic challenge to achieve justice and well-being.

A study by Al-Mubarak and Osmani attempts to analyze the modern Islamic banking products under the *maslahah* and *Maqasid al-Shari'ah* framework. It argues that the attainment of macro maqasid by Islamic banking products, such as assisting economic flow in society, is not sufficient. It also requires the fulfillment of the micro maqasid whereby the individual financial transaction should be permissible and should not be overlooked for the sake of the greater good. Further, they recommend several meticulously revised products, such as *Bai' al-inah*, *Bai' Bithaman Aajil (BBA)*, and *sukuk ijarah*, because they are not aligned with the *Maqasid al-Shari'ah*. Similarly, Dusuki and Abozaid (2007) also share the potential conflict between the attainment of macro and micro maqasid in justifying Islamic financial contracts. They also add that the lack of comprehension and tools mastery in implementing maqasid is the hindrance to achieve the objective of Islamic law in Islamic banking and finance. Further, the approach to achieve *Maqasid al-Shari'ah* becomes more practical. Zakariyah (2015) examines the approaches of classical scholars and argues that it needs harmonization between legality and morality to attain *Maqasid al-Shari'ah*. It also requires awareness both in legal and moral obligations from Muslim at the micro level. Likewise, it needs commitment from policymakers to enforce Islamic law in its legal and moral dimension at the macro level. Then, Ishak and Asni (2020) conduct an exploratory study by interviewing six members of *Shari'ah* advisory council (SAC) and *Shari'ah* committees (SC) of Islamic financial institutions to determine the role of *Maqasid al-Shari'ah* in applying *fiqh muamalat* in modern Islamic banking in Malaysia. The study shows that several practices, like replicating conventional products into Islamic banks, are needed to sustain the industry in the modern financial system. Under those circumstances, *Maqasid al-Shari'ah* is applied to harmonize between rulings in *fiqh al-muamalat* and banking environments.

The second group of research focuses on conceptualizing and measuring the performance of Islamic banks empirically in various Muslim populated countries. A study conducted by Mohammed *et al.* (2008) is one of the first that proposed a measurement for Islamic banks' performance under the *Maqasid al-Shari'ah* framework. This study utilizes Sekaran's operationalization method to develop the tools (Sekaran, 2000). In this regard, the concept (C) that wants to be captured and comprehended is being broken down into observable characteristics, called dimensions (D). Then, the dimension is broken down into several observable measurements, called elements (E).

This study benefits from the construction of *Maqasid al-Shari'ah* by Ibn 'Ashur (1998) and Abu Zaharah (1997). In this regard, *Maqasid al-Shari'ah* is separated into three broad areas, which are *tahdhib al-fard* (educating the individual), *iqamah al-`adl* (establishing justice), and *jalb al-maslahah* (promoting welfare). Those three broad ideas are perceived as the concept of *Maqasid al-Shari'ah*. The study further develops the dimensions and elements before asking for verification from Shari'ah experts from the Middle East and Malaysia. Table 4.1 summarizes the operational measurement concept of *Maqasid al-Shari'ah* for Islamic banks.

Further, this study applies the above measurement to six Islamic banks. The result shows a mixed performance from the selected Islamic banks. It shows an inconsistency of Islamic banks to achieve the overall *Maqasid al-Shari'ah*. Later on, several studies adopt this methodology for their research. Mohammed *et al.* (2015) apply this method to 24 banks consisting

Table 4.1 Operational measurement concept of *Maqasid al-Shari'ah* for Islamic banks

Concept	*Dimensions*	*Elements*	*Performance ratio*
C1. Education/ *tahdhib al-Fard* (30%)	D1. Advancement of knowledge	E1. Education grant (24%)	R1. Education grant/total income
		E2. Research (27%)	R2. Research expense/total expense
	D2. Instilling new skills and improvements	E3. Training (26%)	R3. Training expense/total expense
	D3. Creating awareness of Islamic banking	E4. Publicity (23%)	R4. Publicity expense/total expense
C2. Justice /*al-'Adl* (41%)	D4. Fair dealings	E5. Fair returns (30%)	R5. profit/total income
	D5. Affordable products and services	E6. Affordable price (32%)	R6. Bad debt/total investment
	D6. Elimination of injustices	E7. Interest-free product (38%)	R7. Interest-free income/total income
C3. Welfare/ *al-Maslahah* (29%)	D7. Profitability	E8. Profit ratios (33%)	R8. Net profit/total asset
	D8. Redistribution of income and wealth	E9. Personal income (30%)	R9. Zakah/net Income
	D9. Investment in vital real sector	E.10 Investment ratio in real sector (37%)	R10. Investment deposit/total

Source: Mohammed et al. (2008).

of 12 Islamic banks and 12 conventional banks. The result shows that Islamic banks perform well under this measurement compared to when they are being measured under the conventional standard. Likewise, Jazil and Syahruddin, who examined the maqasid performance of six selected Islamic banks in Indonesia and Malaysia, show that no bank can achieve high performance in all the ten performance ratios, except on interest-free income ratio and performance indicators.

Similarly, Amaroh and Masturin utilize this model to run a multiple linear regression to measure the performance of Islamic banks in Indonesia. The results show that profit-sharing financing positively influences *Maqasid al-Shari'ah*-based performance, but risk-taking behavior has a negative impact. Meanwhile, cost efficiency does not influence the *Maqasid al-Shari'ah*-based performance of Islamic banks.

A similar approach is conducted by Mohammed *et al.* (2015) to develop the Maqasid-Based Performance Evaluation Model (MPEM) for Islamic banking.

Table 4.2 Dimensions, element, and measurement for MPEM

Dimensions	*Elements*	*Ratios*
Preservation of faith	Freedom of faith	*Muḍārabah* and *Mushārakah* investment/total investment Interest-free income/total income
Preservation of life	a Preservation of human dignity b Protection of human rights	Corporate social responsibility (CSR) expenditure/total expenses *Zakāh* distribution/net asset
Preservation of intellect	a Propagation of scientific thinking b Avoidance of brain drain	Investment in technology/total asset Number of employees left/total number of employees
Preservation of progeny	Care for family [in case of public limited company (PLC)]	Market value/book value Research expense/total expense Training and development expense/total expense Net income/total asset Credit risk Tax paid/profit before tax
Preservation of wealth	a Well-being of society b Minimizing income and wealth disparity	Investment in the real economic sector/total investment Investment in SMEs/total investment Investment in agriculture/total investment

Source: Mohammed et al. (2015).

However, this study is distinguished from the Mohammed *et al.* (2015) study in its construction of *Maqasid al-Shari'ah* derived from Al-Ghazali's dimensions and Ibn 'Ashur's element, as shown in Table 4.2. Recently, the same technique was applied in a research to produce another measurement of *Maqasid al-Shari'ah* performance in Islamic banking. This study differs in its combination of Imam al-Ghazali's and Abu Zahrah's frameworks in *Maqasid al-Shari'ah.*

In parallel with the previous model, Bedoui and Mansour (2015) published their work on performance and *Maqasid al-Shari'ah*'s pentagon-shaped ethical measurement in the same year. This study adopts Al-Ghazali's work (1937) to create a pentagon-shaped performance scheme structure. They argue that this model recognizes ethical performance, such as promoting human welfare, preventing corruption, and enhancing social and economic stability beyond financial gains. Further, at the same research, they offer an extension of this model into an octagon-shaped model by incorporating Al-Najjar's work (2006). It consists of the following objectives, such as human life preservation

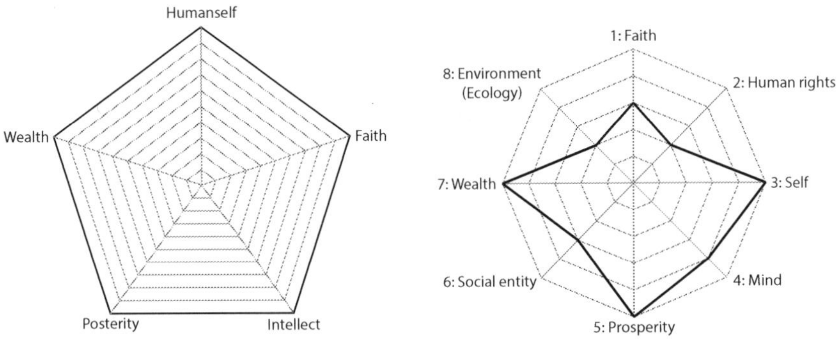

Figure 4.2 Pentagon- and octagon-shaped ethical measurement model.

Source: Bedoui and Mansour (2015).

(faith and human rights); human self-protection (self and mind); safeguarding the value of society (prosperity and social entity); and safeguarding the physical environment (wealth and environment). Figure 4.2 represents both pentagon- and octagon-shaped ethical measurement models.

The most extensive measurement of Islamic banks' performance under the *Maqasid al-Shari'ah* framework has been done recently by Mergaliyev *et al.* (2021). It examined 33 full-fledged Islamic banks from 12 countries between 2008 and 2016. It also utilized Al-Najjar's (2006) framework to create the *Maqasid al-Shari'ah* evaluation framework (Figure 4.3). There are 20 dimensions, 29 elements, and 139 indicators in this index, as represented by the

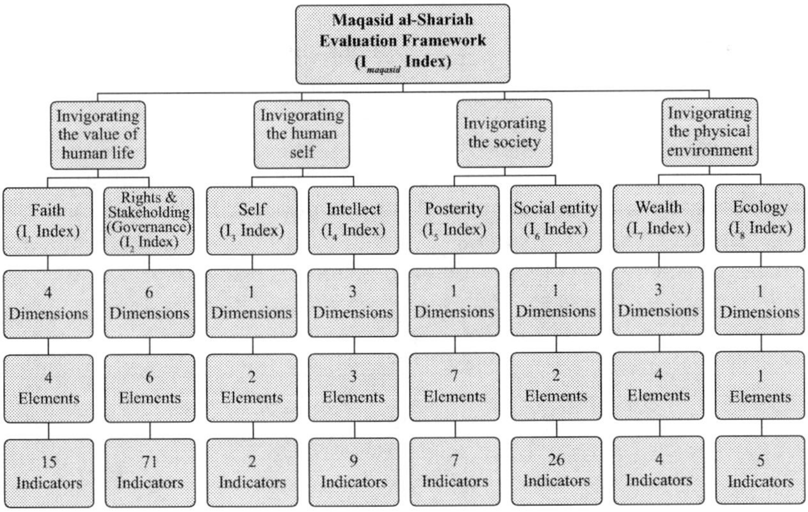

Figure 4.3 Maqasid al-Shari'ah evaluation framework.

Source: Mergaliyev et al. (2021).

following figure. After having the maqasid index for each bank, the study runs a linear regression model with several independent variables, such as political and socioeconomic context variables, time-varying ownership structure variables, time-varying board of directors' variables, time-varying *Shari'ah* supervisory board variables, and control variables. This study finds that the Muslim population indicator, CEO duality, *Shari'ah* governance, and leverage variables positively impact the disclosure of maqasid performance. However, the effect of GDP, financial development, and human development index of the country, its political and civil rights, institutional ownership, and a higher share of independent directors have an overall negative impact on the maqasid performance.

Islamic capital market

The research on the Islamic capital market and its relationship with *Maqasid al-Shari'ah* can be categorized into three major groups. The first group is a theoretical study that scrutinizes *usul fiqh* application, *Shari'ah* prohibition, and ideal models for capital market instruments conveying the *Maqasid al-Shari'ah*. The second group consists of studies that conduct *Maqasid al-Shari'ah* analysis upon capital market products. The last group develops models and measurements on *Maqasid al-Shari'ah* performance and behavior of economic agents in the capital market. A study by Aziz and Noh (2013), one among the first groups, highlight the urgency of *usul fiqh* mastery in structuring *sukuk* to avoid any *Shari'ah* non-compliance risk. Forex financial speculation is counterproductive to the realization of *Maqasid al-Shari'ah* as it may lead to corruption, inflation, economic inequality, and climate change. Therefore, the product innovation in the capital market instruments should go beyond legalistic terms and emphasize the substance of Islamic financial contracts (Dusuki, 2009). Further, the credit enhancement feature in *sukuk*, like liquidity facility and purchase undertaking, conflicts with the objectives of *Shari'ah* and shares the same economic result with the conventional bond. The second group of studies focuses on analyzing the substance of *Maqasid al-Shari'ah* in capital market products. Ab. Aziz *et al.* (2013) scrutinize several principles and concepts, such as *maslahah*, *mafsadah*, hardship elimination, *sad al-zara'i*, and *al-Istihsan* in *sukuk ijarah* structure. Moreover, Mohammed Fisol *et al.* (2019) use the Al-Ghazali maqasid framework for analyzing Islamic public equity funds. The same approach is used by Fisol and Saad (2020) to examine Sukuk Prihatin, the first Malaysian digital *sukuk*.

The last research group consists of studies that develop models and measurements upon *Maqasid al-Shari'ah* in the capital market. For instance, Swadjaja *et al.* (2019) propose an Islamic wealth management model based on *Maqasid al-Shari'ah* for *Shari'ah* stock investments in the capital market, as shown in Figure 4.4.

Another study by Febriadi et al. (2020) analyzes the investor decision-making behavior in *Shari'ah* mutual funds investment using the *Maqasid al-Shari'ah* framework. This study adopts Al-Ghazali's five pillars safeguarding principles to

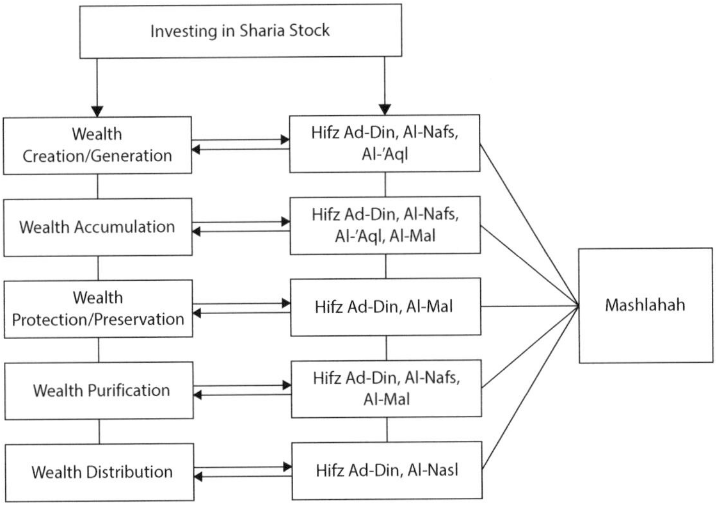

Figure 4.4 Islamic wealth management based on *Maqasid al-Shari'ah*.

Source: Swadjaja et al. (2019).

develop 31 questions. After passing the validity and reliability test, 45 respondents were asked to fill out the questionnaire. The result shows there are four variables, such as faith, soul, and sense, that have a significant influence on investor decision-making. Meanwhile, the offspring variable is observed to be insignificant.

Islamic insurance (takaful)

The size of the Islamic insurance (takaful) industry is only about 2% of the total share of Islamic finance assets, worth US$51 billion in 2019. The industry operates by 336 institutions in 47 countries. The limited size of this specific business aligns with the number of researchers that discuss takaful in light of *Maqasid al-Shari'ah*. Abdullah (2012) is one of the pioneers that discussed takaful and its relation to *Maqasid al-Shari'ah*. Using qualitative methodology, he draws the connection between the risk management in takaful practice with the attainment of *Maqasid al-Shari'ah*. He argues that risk management in takaful services offers life protection, wealth preservation, and dignity safeguarding against any misfortune, which aligns with the universal objective of *Shari'ah*. Similarly, Abdul Aziz and Mohamad (2013) highlight several features in takaful that converge with *Maqasid al-Shari'ah*, such as self- and family protection, asset protection, mutual protection, investment, retirement, and education. Further, Dikko and Ghani (2015) identify several issues and challenges of developing the takaful industry in Nigeria, such as inadequate legislation, human resource quality, and takaful product characteristics provided in the market. Sabirzyanov and Hashim (2015) provide much further elaboration on issues that hinder the development of takaful for attaining *Maqasid al-Shari'ah*. They argue that the takaful industry may face liquidity, market, and credit risk due to the small and illiquid Islamic capital market compared to the conventional one. In addition, they also mention operational risk, *Shari'ah* non-compliance risk, legal risk, and other pertinent issues for the takaful industry.

Islamic social finance (zakat and waqf)

Zakat and waqf are Islamic social funds that have become an alternative to eradicate poverty. In addition to this noble goal, the measurement of zakat or zakat institutions as well as waqf and waqf institutions are still very limited; if anything, the measurement still focuses on the financial conditions of an institution. However, as the institution that brings the spirit of Islam, proper measurement is needed that can accommodate these Islamic values at a higher level. Employing *Maqasid al-Shari'ah* in evaluating Islamic financial institutions can depict the true objective of Islamic values. In the zakat sectors, where the appropriate performance assessment is still limited, a more than a financial assessment method is also essential, as zakat also has social purposes, which are alleviating the poverty level and distributing income. This research discusses the possibility of measuring zakat institutions' performance towards the *Maqasid al-Shari'ah* approach. The result shows that one of the possible methods to assess zakat institutions' performance is by using *Maqasid al-Shari'ah*, which categorized into two scopes: (1) The individual or micro scope, which employs the Ghazali or Syatibi approach, focusing on five basic necessities (faith, human self, intellect, posterity, and wealth); (2) The macro scope, using the Taimiyah or Qayyim approach, which focuses on justice and equality in wider society. In addition, further research is still needed to be conducted in order to be able to derive more detailed assessment categories for zakat institutions (Figure 4.5).

Moreover, a study by Mustafida et al. (2020) that compares zakat distribution programs in the year 2015–2017 according to five necessities of *Maqasid al-Shari'ah* in BAZNAS (BAZIS) DKI Jakarta, Indonesia and

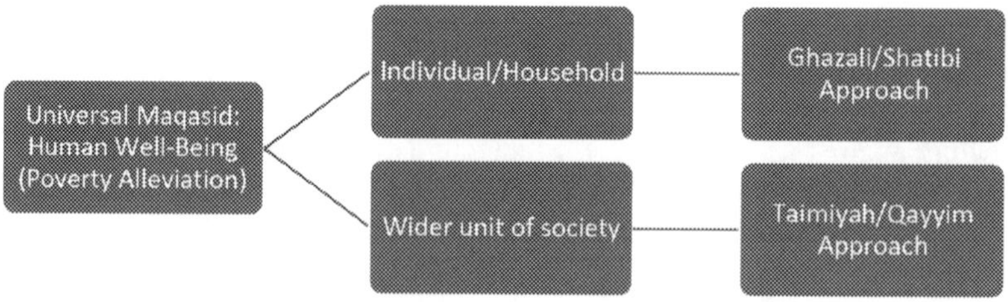

Figure 4.5 The scope of maqasid theory for assessing human well-being as a higher objective of zakat institutions.

Source: Kasri (2016).

Lembaga Zakat Selangor (LZS), Malaysia, shows that BAZNAS (BAZIS) DKI Jakarta's program focuses on the preservation of life and faith, while LZS's program has already fulfilled *Maqasid al-Shari'ah* holistically. Further, they argue that in order to increase the zakat program based on *Maqasid al-Shari'ah*, a zakat commission with an appropriate regulatory framework should be established. Therefore, this commission can maintain and strengthen the *Maqasid al-Shari'ah* objective in the zakat institution activities. Kamaruddin and Hanefah (2021) examine the impact of zakat on *Maqasid al-Shari'ah* and sustainable development goals (SDGs) by taking samples of Malaysian zakat institutions. A binomial logic was used to evaluate the significance of the zakat impact. The finding shows that zakat impact according to both *Maqasid al-Shari'ah* and SDGs variables is high, and it also showed that non-corporatized zakat institutions in Malaysia have a higher zakat impact on both standards.

On the zakat fund collection side, Isnaeni and Qodri (2019) analyze the effect of Islamic social marketing based on *Maqasid al-Shari'ah* and the impact of *Maqasid al-Shari'ah* in the *muzaki* (zakat payer) decision to pay zakat. By examining 360 samples of *muzaki* in Jambi Province, Indonesia, and analyzing using the structural equation method (SEM), the result shows that *Maqasid al-Shari'ah* has impacted the Islamic social marketing employed by zakat institutions. This is reflected in zakat institutions that refer to *Maqasid al-Shari'ah* when doing social marketing in their product, location, promotion, process, and personnel. On the other hand, there is no significant effect of *Maqasid al-Shari'ah* values on the zakat payer decision, even though *muzaki* have a good understanding in *Maqasid al-Shari'ah*, but it is not reflected in zakat paying behavior. In addition, in the waqf sector, a study from Mohamed Fisol et al. (2021) examines waqf property management through the *Maqasid al-Shari'ah* approach by using content analysis as well as a qualitative method. In this research, they investigate whether alteration of waqf properties in order to maximize their purpose is allowed in *Shari'ah* scholars' perspective through the *Maqasid al-Shari'ah* approach. The result found that alteration of waqf property in order to make it more beneficial for *ummah* is in line with the *Maqasid al-Shari'ah* principle of obtaining benefit and avoiding harm.

Others (non-financial industry)

As *Maqasid al-Shari'ah* is the main objective of sharia, its value should be inherent in all aspects of life besides the financial industries described in the previous section. A *Maqasid al-Shari'ah* value is also found in the halal industry, as studied by Waluyo, who examined the halal product law in Indonesia. He found that the law consists of three aspects of *Maqasid al-Shari'ah*, which are: (1) protection of religion; (2) protection of soul; and (3) legal protection towards the halal product. Moreover, the *Maqasid al-Shari'ah* approach is also observed in the research of Muslim-friendly hotels. This research analyzes

MS 2610:2015 Muslim Friendly Hospitality Services Requirements, Crescent Rating Standard, and Salam Standard. The results show that these standards are emphasizing faith protection through performing prayer and fasting; safeguarding lives by only serving and consuming halal food; protecting the mind by avoiding alcoholic beverages; and safeguarding the lineage by separating individuals based on gender in some facilities at the hotels, for instance, swimming pools and spas. In addition, these standards are still needed to improve the fundamental criteria, such as safeguarding lives and property, to become a holistic *Maqasid al-Shari'ah* measurement tool.

Conclusion

Maqasid al-Shari'ah as the goal of *Shari'ah* should be an essential part in order to clearly measure Islamic values in the industry. According to the analysis, *Maqasid al-Shari'ah*-based measurement is still not spread evenly in all sectors. The most developed sector that employs *Maqasid al-Shari'ah* as its basis for performance measurement is the Islamic banking industry. Meanwhile, the application of *Maqasid al-Shari'ah* measurement in other sectors is still in the exploratory stage. Hence, further research in *Maqasid al-Shari'ah* tools to appropriately assess Islamic values should be conducted. In addition, the measurement should focus not only on the macro side of *Maqasid al-Shari'ah* but also on the micro side, to make sure the whole objective of *Shari'ah* is achieved.

References

Ab. Aziz, M. R., Mohd Sahid, M. N., & Ibrahim, M. F. (2013). The Structure of Sukuk Ijarah: An Initial Analysis from The Perspective of Maqasid Al-Shari'ah. In *The 5th Islamic Economic System Conference*.

Abu Zaharah, M. (1997). *Usul al-Fiqh*. Dar al-Fikr al-'Arabi.

Al-Ghazali, A. H. (1937). *Al-Mustafa*. Dār al-Fikr.

Al-Najjar. (2006). *Maqasid al-Shari'ahbi-abadjadıdah*. Dar al-Gharb al-Islamı.

Aziz, M. R. A., & Noh, M. S. M. (2013). Tools of Usul al-Fiqh in Realizing Maqasid al-Shari'ah in Sukuk Structures in Malaysia: An Initial Analysis. *International Journal of Education and Research*, *1*(10), 1–10.

Chapra, M. U. (2000). *The Future of Economics: An Islamic Perspective*. The Islamic Foundation.

Dangulbi, S. M., Salleh, A., Meera, A. K., & Aziuddin, A. (2012). Fractional Reserve Banking and Maqasid Al-shariah: An Incompatible Practice. *SSRN Electronic Journal*, 1–17.

Dikko, M., & Ghani, A. A. (2015). Maqasid Al Shari'ahand Takaful Operations: Issues and Challenges in an Emerging Industry. *Journal of Law, Policy and Globalization*, *43*(11), 30–33.

Dusuki, A. W. (2009). Challenges of Realizing Maqasid al-Shari'ah (Objectives of Shariah) in Islamic Capital Market: Special Focus on Equity-Based Sukuk. *USM-ISDEV International Islamic Management Conference on Islamic Capital Market, October*, 1–30.

Dusuki, A. W., & Abozaid, A. (2007). A Critical Appraisal On The Challenges Of Realizing Maqasid Al-Shariaah In Islamic Banking And Finance. *IIUM Journal of Economics and Management*, *15*(2), 999–1000.

Fauzia, A. (2013). *Faith and the State: A History of Islamic Philanthropy in Indonesia*. Brill.

Fisol, W. N. bin M., & Saad, M. A. bin. (2020). Rebuilding the National Economy By Issuance of the First Malaysia Digital Sukuk (Sukuk Prihatin) and Its Distribution Through Fintech Services: a View From the Perspective of Maqasid Al-Shari'Ah. *International Conference on Contemporary Issues in Islamic Finance (e-ICCIIF 2020)*, *27*(1), 2771–2778.

Ibn 'Ashur, M. al-T. (1998). *Maqasid al-Shari'ah al-Islamiyyah (al-Misawi)*. al-Basa"ir.

Kahf, M. (2006). Maqasid al Shari 'ah in the Prohibition of Riba and their Implications for Modern Islamic Finance. *IIUM International Conference on Maqasid Al Shari'ah*, 184–203.

Mohamed, S., Goni, A., Alanzarouti, F., & Taitoon, J. Al. (2020). *Islamic Finance Development Report 2020: Progressing Through Development*.

Mohammed, M. O., Razak, D. A., & Taib, F. M. (2008). The Performance Measures of Islamic Banking Based on the Maqasid Framework. *IIUM International Accounting Conference*, 1–17.

Mohammed, M. O., Tarique, K. M., & Islam, R. (2015). Measuring the Performance of Islamic Banks Using Maqasid Based Model. *Intellectual Discourse*, *23*, 401–424.

Nagaoka, S. (2012). Frontier of Islamic Economics and Finance: New Challenges Critical Overview of the History of Islamic Economics: Formation, Transformation, and New Horizons. *Asian and African Area Studies*, *11*(2), 114–136.

Qattan, M. A. (2006). Shari'ah Supervision: The Unique Building Block of Islamic Financial Architecture. In *Islamic Financial Architecture Risk Management and Financial Stability* (pp. 273–287). IRTI-IDB.

Sabirzyanov, R., & Hashim, M. H. (2015). Takaful (Islamic Insurance), Risk Management and Maqasid Al- Sharī'ah. *İslam Ekonomisi ve Finansı Dergisi*, *1*, 105–144.

Sekaran, U. (2000). *Research Methods for Business: A Skill Building Approach*. John Wiley & Sons.

Zakariyah, L. (2015). Harmonising legality with morality in Islamic banking and finance: A quest for Maqasid al-Shari'ah paradigm. *Intellectual Discourse*, *23*(January), 355–376.

5

MAINSTREAM METHODOLOGIES FOR ANALYZING FIQH IN GOVERNING ISLAMIC ECONOMICS AND FINANCE

Yoseph Ataa Alsawady, Mohamed Cherif El Amri and Mustafa Omar Mohammed

Introduction

Fiqh, or the knowledge of Islamic legal ruling derived directly or indirectly from evidence in Islamic texts (Nyazee, 2013, p. 50), forms the basis of the emerging discipline of Islamic economics and finance. Specifically, Fiqh is divided into the following two major categories: (1) *Fiqh al-'ibadat*, which is concerned with acts of worship; and (2) *Fiqh al-mu'amalat*, which is concerned with dealings among individual humans, including economic relations and financial transactions (Saleem, 2013, p. xi). On the other hand, Usul al-Fiqh, known as Islamic jurisprudence (Nyazee, 2013, p. 19), is the discipline concerned with deriving Fiqh rulings – a discipline steeped in its own unique methodology. The literal meaning of the word "Fiqh" carries important epistemological implications for any discipline based on it. This Arabic word literally means "understanding" and "discernment" (Nyazee, 2013, p. 37), which pre-supposes the existence of a certain true reality comprehensible to the human intellect. In fact, it even arguably pre-supposes a certain consciousness and intention, which is expected to be understood.

Despite this unique foundation of the relatively new discipline of Islamic economics and finance, from a methodological perspective, the focus has been leaning toward the second part of this discipline's name ("economics and finance"), rather than the first ("Islamic"). Indeed, scholars of economics and finance have dominated the new discipline. They have brought with them their mainstream methodologies and techniques of analysis, based on the scientific method, only to be faced with several challenges. To date, this discipline has been largely defined by the application of the rulings of Fiqh to the conventional (secular) discipline of economics and finance, retaining the basic structure and assumptions of a social science (Addas, 2008, p. vii). Basically, these

 DOI: 10.4324/9781003252764-7

mainstream methodologies of economics and financial analysis have created debates such as the deductive vs. inductive basis of Islamic vs. mainstream or conventional economics and finance, respectively. Islamic economics and finance, being a faith-based discipline, accepts certain fundamental principles detailed in revelation, excluding these matters from the domain of valid analysis and debate.

So, what is the domain of applying these mainstream methods and techniques of analysis, if any, within the discipline of Islamic economics and finance, especially with reference to Fiqh? This study attempts to answer this basic question. Specifically, it has the following three objectives: (1) to analyze the relevant philosophical underpinnings, especially epistemological differences between Islamic and conventional economics and finance; (2) to analyze the nexus in practice between mainstream economic methodology on the one hand and Fiqh on the other (as the foundational sciences underlying Islamic economics and finance); and (3) to recommend the proper use of mainstream methodologies and techniques for the analysis of Fiqh issues in Islamic economics and finance, based on the above analysis.

To achieve these objectives, this study adopts a qualitative research method based on thematic and case analysis of material extracted from secondary literature on the topic of research methods in the discipline. Specifically, the study surveys these secondary sources; analyzes them to identify philosophical underpinnings, themes, and categories in the approach to the discipline, as well as practical examples; and provides recommendations based on this analysis.

Significance and related literature on methodology

Islamic finance and economics is neither Fiqh nor is it a secular social science (Yasin and Khan, 2016, p. 45). Rather, it is a discipline in between – primarily a social science but with basic assumptions and axioms derived from Islamic sources, especially Fiqh principles. Therefore, considering the unique methodology of Islamic economics and finance is important, with reference to the various mainstream methods originally developed for secular or conventional social sciences – mainly economics.

Significance of the methodology debate

Research and debate on methodology is a very broad and difficult to define area even within mainstream or conventional economics. Indeed, although work on the methodology of economics started in the 19th century, it only took off in the 1980s as a mature area of inquiry and debate. Although the focus of this study is on the struggle of Islamic economics and finance to distinguish its own identity via adopting, adapting, or innovating its own appropriate methodology, it is worth noting that mainstream economics itself has had a similar crisis, as it attempts to distinguish itself methodologically from natural science.

An important, though subtle, distinction here is between "methodology" and "methods." Although they may often be used interchangeably (including in this study), "methodology" most rigorously refers to the broad epistemological approach to discovering truths within a certain discipline or area of inquiry. On the other hand, "methods" typically refers to the detailed tools of analysis deployed under the broader umbrella of methodology (Blaug, 1992, p. xii). For example, the falsification approach to establishing the validity of a hypothesis via generating predictions that can (at least in principle) be proven false via empirical testing is a well-established methodology to generate knowledge in economics (Blaug, 1992, p. xiii). On the other hand, collecting data via surveys, for example, is a research method.

In Islamic economics and finance, the problem of methodology falls squarely within the domain of the so-called modern calls for the Islamization of science. The dichotomy born in the West between science (viewed as a secular, value-neutral endeavor) and religion is at the heart of this debate. The modern discipline of Islamic economics and finance is part of this effort to "reintegrate science and religion."

Review of related works

Muhammad Akram Khan has observed that "[t]he literature on methodology of Islamic economics is either superfluous, or ambiguous or confusing" (Khan, 2017, p. 35). Notwithstanding this statement, however, there have been recent efforts to elucidate this domain of inquiry and present concisely the various views on the matter. One of the most recent references in this area is the 2020 book edited by Professor Necmettin Kizilkaya of Istanbul University titled *Methodology of Islamic Economics: Problems and Solutions* (Kizilkaya, 2020). A thematic categorization and review of the opinions expressed in this publication, which are relevant to the current study, would suffice to get the necessary overview of the ongoing debate on methodology in Islamic economics and finance, with specific reference to the applicability of mainstream methods used by economists. For example, Zubair Hassan dismisses the possibility of developing a methodology for this discipline comparable to mainstream economics and finance, due to the fundamental differences between the two disciplines (Kizilkaya, 2020, Chapter 1). Similarly, Asad Zaman highlights the difference between the two disciplines, especially regarding the focus of Islamic economics on unobservable and normative aspects, which are not the domain of science (Kizilkaya, 2020, Chapter 2).

Several scholars have started at the most abstract, philosophical level, examining the epistemology of Islamic economics and finance. For example, Abdulkader Mahomedy has emphasized the role of rationalism (Kizilkaya, 2020, Chapter 12), whereas Ismail Cebeci has observed the ontological distinction in Western thought between economics and morality as separate disciplines compared to Islamic thought, where they are merged into one (Kizilkaya, 2020, Chapter 14). Masudul Alam Choudhury has also started from a grand "Tawhidi knowledge-centered world view" as "a distinct epistemological foundation for explaining all socio-scientific phenomena".

Notably, the literature often refers to the fundamental objectives of Islamic economics and finance as a discipline. This, then, has implications for the applicability of mainstream research methods. For example, Hakan Saribas has considered the main objective to be "to discover the Sunnah of Allah". Monzer Kahf has further clarified the difference in objectives by clarifying that economics, generally including Islamic economics, aims in the first place to understand human behavior, whereas Fiqh aims at providing normative rulings to guide this behavior (Kizilkaya, 2020, Chapter 7). On the other hand, Seif I. Tag el-Din takes a Maqasid (objectives of Shariah) perspective and applies this to the discipline – with strong normative connotations (Kizilkaya, 2020, Chapter 8).

Most crucial, however, to the current study is the work of scholars who have attempted to determine a nexus between the faith-based juristic science of *Usul al-Fiqh* on the one hand and the social science of economics on the other hand. The work of Muhammed Akram Khan in this domain is highly relevant, and his views are elaborated further and built upon in this study. He argues that mainstream research methods can be useful in the domain of checking understanding and interpretation of revelation (Khan, 2017). Furthermore, Waleed Addas, in his comprehensive book titled *Methodology of Economics: Secular vs. Islamic*, attempts a similar analysis of this nexus (Addas, 2008).

Also relevant in this context is the work of Hafas Furqani and Aslam Hanif, who propose the term "Usul Al-Iiqtisad" as "an integrative approach to deal with the sources of knowledge: the Quran and Sunnah, the intellectual reasoning and fact observation". Whereas Necmettin Kizilkaya has argued that in fact the methods of Islamic sciences are most appropriate for Islamic economics, Monzer Kahf has emphasized that the two are not too different, since Fiqh methodology is also based on a sort of mathematical logic and empiricism. Nevertheless, despite these similarities, he asserts the need to introduce a higher level of humanism and to purify these disciplines from biased postulates.

The brief overview of the literature above reveals the lack of clarity regarding the appropriate role of mainstream economics and finance methodologies in analyzing Fiqh issues, especially as they relate to Islamic economics and finance. Furthermore, although there is a significant body of literature investigating the subject of methodology in this discipline, much of it is abstract and philosophical or impractical. There is a dearth of literature providing clear, practical recommendations on the appropriate application of mainstream methodologies within this discipline, which is the major aim of this study.

Related disciplines and their methodologies

Three distinct but interrelated disciplines are worth clearly identifying, so that reference is possible to their various methodologies. These include the following:

- Mainstream economics and finance, also referred to as conventional or secular economics and finance (as compared to the faith-based discipline under consideration in this study), is methodologically grounded in the social sciences. It accepts the scientific method of the enlightenment, and it has proven to be the most amenable of the social sciences to mathematization and adaptation of some of the methods of the natural sciences.
- Usul al-Fiqh, or principles of Islamic jurisprudence, despite dealing with economic matters (under Fiqh al-Mu'amalat) is methodologically different from economics in terms of its focus on the individual rather than the collective, as well as its normative nature vs. the generally positive nature of economics.
- Islamic economics and finance, as a relatively new discipline emerging only during the 20th century, is struggling to accommodate the changing realities of life and advances in various areas of inquiry, not least in economic thought and practice, which has necessitated a departure from the traditional methodologies of Fiqh. Although the traditional discipline of Fiqh that developed up to the 17th and 18th centuries represents a "great treasure," which is at the base of modern work, it is no longer sufficient due these changes in realities (Yasin and Khan, 2016, p. 43).

Philosophical foundations

A continuum exists in the literature from outright rejection of mainstream methods and techniques of analysis with a call to adopting methods tailored to Islamic economics and finance on the one hand, to a wholesale acceptance of all conventional methods and a denial of any uniqueness of this discipline on the other hand. Most views fall someplace in between these two extremes, but even then, a well-defined and agreed-upon approach to the criteria and conditions of applicability is not in place – most approaches remain vague. For example, one view holds that:

> Conventional theories and tools of analysis might be accepted as long as they are not in conflict with the logical structure of the Islamic worldview, they are not against the explicit or implicit injunctions of Islam, or they do not contradict with the principles of Islamic teachings, and should be evaluated within an Islamic framework and using Islamic criteria.
>
> (*Ismail, 2016, pp. 21–22*)

In fact, the debate goes deeper than this. At its core, it is really an ontological debate between those who view Islamic economics and finance as a unique academic discipline and those who view the Islamic economic system and financial principles as one area of inquiry and analysis within the broader disciplines of economics and finance. A more radical criticism of the independent disciplinary classification comes from Masudul Alam Choudury, who has stated that,

> The use of the term 'Islamic economics' is an imitation of contemporary intellectual fashion. It reflects the classification of educational disciplines left to us by the Occidental world. Such classification is devoid of the integrated beginnings of intellectual thought in which all Muslim scholars once immersed themselves in the search for knowledge.
>
> (*Choudhury, 2018, p. 264*)

Mainstream methods of economic analysis

At the most general level, economic methods are divided into the following two categories: theoretical and empirical. Thus, economic work is generally divided into these two broad categories. Another important distinction, mostly within the domain of empirical research, is between qualitative and quantitative methods. The student of modern secular social science generally and economics specifically will be no stranger to this distinction and the relevant qualitative vs. quantitative methods (e.g., case-study vs. regression analysis, respectively). It is worth noting that there is an ongoing debate regarding these methods in conventional economics, as the question of mathematization of economics has received much critical scrutiny as to its merits vs. its weaknesses.

Today, the debate is ongoing among scholars of Islamic economics and finance regarding the correct approach to methodology in their discipline vis-à-vis mainstream economic methodology. Many, such as Hasan, argue that Islamic economics and finance should leverage the already existing methods developed for secular or conventional science, without attempting to re-invent the wheel. On the other hand, others such as Choudhury have argued that the basis of the two sciences is too distinct to allow for simple adoption of methods. The unique foundations of Islamic economics and finance require unique methodological approaches. Nevertheless, the reality is that "[d]espite the differences in axiomatic foundation between Islamic economics and conventional economics, over the years, Islamic economics has borrowed substantially from mathematical models developed in the neoclassical economics sphere."

Sources and epistemological approaches

To shed some light on this debate, an examination of the epistemological basis of Islamic economics and finance and a comparison of the results with the basis of conventional economic sciences could be useful. Conventional economics, as a social science, relies mostly on an inductive approach based on human intellect and observations (data collection). On the other hand, Islamic economics adds a more deductive reliance on religious revelation, namely the Quran and Sunnah (or Prophetic traditions) as primary sources of knowledge.

However, the above is not to say that conventional economics is a perfectly inductive science devoid of any presuppositions or that Islamic economics is entirely deductive. Social science is based on the following three components: "the definitions or terminologies, the postulates or axioms, and the hypotheses" whereby "[t]he axioms and presumptions of a theory are taken for granted and are not considered liable for verification" (Yasin and Khan, 2016, p. 44). In fact, economics is full of both presuppositions and assumptions, which are often never tested, and some are rarely even contemplated. Indeed, the general phenomenon of "value impregnation in scientific analysis" has been especially noted in economics, which has been described by more than one observer as "deeply rooted in a belief system and ideology."

In Islamic economics, the space of presuppositions is arguably broader and of a different nature, although with much room left for induction where human rationality is needed (for interpretation, interpolation, and extrapolation of rulings). For example, until recently, "the fundamental premise of the 'rational economic actor' has remained unchanged" in economics. For the purpose of economic theorizing, this rationality has been taken as the purely instrumental type of rationality, to use the terminology of the famous German sociologist Max Weber. On the other hand, Islamic economics presupposes humans to be "value-rational," another Weberian term meaning that their beliefs and values do in fact factor into their economic decision-making calculus.

Fortunately, however, as writers on methodology in Islamic economics have observed, "modern economics too is cognizant of heterogeneities in behaviour of economic agents". Similarly, a new axiology to define the values of interest for theorizing is needed in the domain of Islamic economic and finance. This axiology would be based on axioms and assumptions more refined than the typical individualistic utility maximizing *homo economicus* of neoclassical economics. For example, the "*homo Islamicus*" has been proposed as an alternate unit of analysis, acting with both individualistic and collective goals and incentives based on a specific code of ethics.

At a more concrete and detailed level in Islamic economics, basic non-controversial details clearly laid out in primary sources of Islamic Fiqh, such as the prohibition of *riba* (interest or usury) and the rate of zakat (compulsory alms levied roughly as 2.5 percent of wealth), can be considered part of the presuppositions space. Crucially, this space of presupposition is taken to lie outside the realm of testing via the mainstream methodologies and techniques of economics and finance. It should be noted that the traditional Islamic discipline known as Usul al-Fiqh, or principles of Islamic jurisprudence, identifies the following four primary sources: Quran, Sunnah, Ijma' (or scholarly consensus) and Qiyas (analogy). It also identifies secondary sources, such as the following: Maslahah Mursalah (considerations of public interest) and Istihsan (equity in Islamic law) (Kamali, 2013). This classification of sources is important in determining the exact role that can be played by conventional research methodology.

Nevertheless, modern observers have noted a "turn" in the epistemology of Usul al-Fiqh in the 20th century toward placing a higher weight on *kulliyyat* ("universal ethical principles") vs. *juz'iyyat* ("specific injunctions of the texts"). The new approach, it is argued, favors "public interest (Maslahah) [one of the secondary sources mentioned above] as the chief criterion for developing fresh legal rulings in the light of new sociopolitical conditions" (Johnston, 2004, p. 233). Underlying all the above is the process of ijtihad, literally exertion, whereby the specialized jurist, scholar, or expert applies the principles of Usul al-Fiqh to arrive at specific Fiqh rulings.

Rational analysis and induction

Accepting Islamic economics and finance as a distinct modern discipline, inheriting its basic principles from Usul al-Fiqh, and identifying with the social science of economics, it becomes crucial to determine the areas of applicability of the tools of social science within the context of Usul al-Fiqh. This is a question regarding the intersection of conventional economics and finance on the one hand and Usul al-Fiqh on the other.

Some of the most interesting literature in this context is the work of Muhammad Akram Khan. He has argued that the best methodology would be to "understand the primary sources in a contemporary context; formulate hypotheses based on that understanding and present these hypotheses for validation through testing" (Khan, 2017, p. 35). In more detail, he has argued for the following approach: (1) examining the basic religious texts (Quran and Sunnah); (2) identifying basic principles and references in texts with economic implications; (3) developing an understanding of the interpretation of these references; (4) formulating a hypothesis based on this understanding; (5) collecting and analyzing data to test this hypothesis using methods and techniques of conventional economics; (6) confirming or rejecting this hypothesis; (7) based on the result, confirming or rejecting the interpretation; and (8) if confirmed, maybe formulating a theory, but if rejected, developing a new interpretation and repeating. Based on this approach, the domain of applicability of conventional economic methodology would be in the grey area of interpretation and understanding of revelation.

In fact, from the perspective of Usul al-Fiqh, this logic can be extended beyond simple interpretation to cover all areas that include rational analysis or mental exertion (in short, all areas of ijtihad), especially related to the secondary sources of Fiqh. The common thread among these secondary sources is some analysis of costs and benefits (or *mafsadah* and *maslahah*, respectively, in Fiqh terminology) and some judgment regarding the greater good, which can be a very tangible area for economic inquiry.

A good example of a secondary source entirely based on such cost-benefit analyses is *maslahah mursalah* (or considerations of public interest). Under this source of Fiqh, a judgement by the *mujtahid* (reasoning jurist performing ijtihad) is necessary regarding the greater public good benefiting society at large. However, some schools of Fiqh, such as the Shafi'is (Kamali, 2013, p. 277), have rejected this and similar sources, citing the subjectivity of such judgement calls. It is precisely in such cases that a rigorous, social scientific approach using the analytical methods of modern economics and finance can be most appropriate. Thus, in summary, mainstream methodologies and techniques of economics and finance can be useful in situations requiring human rationality (or ijtihad), which, in the domain of Usul al-Fiqh, include the following: (1) interpretation of primary sources; and (2) extension of the same logic via secondary sources. The role of these methodologies and techniques would be to minimize the subjectivity involved in the analysis.

The best analogy for the above is a comparison between the domains of legal practice and policy-making. In fact, a novel approach to Usul al-Fiqh could be to make the following categorizations: (1) Quran and Sunnah as sources of basic unchangeable law; (2) Ijma's and Qiyas as sources of legislation, potentially changeable depending on circumstance; and (3) secondary sources as sources of policy, which are more fluid and changeable depending on context and circumstance.

Similarly, although Islamic economics is often considered more normative, in fact both Islamic and mainstream economics include positive (descriptive) and normative (prescriptive) elements, since both attempt to understand reality via rational analysis and then to guide behavior on the basis of this analysis. However, Milton Friedman has argued that as economic knowledge progresses toward higher levels of perfection, the discipline of economics itself will take on a more positivist approach, away from any normative, value based judgements, as results will become more scientific (Friedman, 1953, p. 148). The same could be said of ijtihad as the mainstream scientific methods are harnessed by specialized *mujtahids*.

Cases of mainstream scientific approaches to Fiqh issues

Several practical applications of the approach outlined above are possible. Cases and examples are described below.

Validating interpretation of revelation

Firstly, with regard to Muhammad Akram Khan's approach to testing understanding of revelation, he presents examples of Quranic verses with their interpretations and proposed hypotheses to test these interpretations. A good example is the Quranic Verse Q. 2:276, which clearly states that "God deprives riba of all blessings (yamhaqu Allah al-riba)." Various interpretations of this verse can lead to multiple hypotheses, which can be tested to confirm the correctness of these interpretations. Examples of such hypotheses proposed by Khan include the following:

> **Hypothesis 1:** *Average rate of return on capital invested as interest-bearing loans tends to decline in the long-term, other things remaining the same.*
>
> **Hypothesis 2:** *Aggregate value of assets of moneylenders whose major source of income is interest earned on consumption loans which tends to decline in the long-term, other things remaining the same.*
>
> **Hypothesis 3:** *Average rate of return on the cost of goods sold on deferred payment basis that includes interest in the sale price on the delayed payment tends to decline in the long-term, other things remaining the same.*
>
> **Hypothesis 4:** *On an average, development projects financed by international donors as interest-bearing credit lead to lower than planned rates of net present value and internal rate of return, other things remaining the same.*
>
> (*Khan, 2017, p. 55*)

Evidence-based ijtihad

Secondly, with regard to the broader approach of arriving at sound, evidence-based policies and decisions using secondary sources of Usul al-Fiqh, many examples exist in practice. In fact, this approach is already applied, especially where there is no straightforward answer. Indeed, the International Islamic Fiqh Academy (IIFA), a body of the Organization of Islamic Cooperation (OIC), frequently invites scholars in various disciplines, including economics and finance, to present specific topics to help the Shariah scholars of the IIFA to arrive at a specific ruling. Nevertheless, keeping in mind the potential fallacies of rational analysis in a vacuum and the potential for discovering non-intuitive realities, the importance of applying more rigorous mainstream research methodologies and techniques as standard practice becomes apparent. These would be applied via well-defined research projects designed to answer specific questions (beyond simple expositions of a specific topic by invited experts).

A good example of this is a simple Fiqh ruling regarding a pressing current topic – namely, the use of zakat funds (Islamic obligatory alms) to provide vaccines, which has arisen during the COVID-19 pandemic. In this regard, the IIFA has ruled that this is permissible in principle. This is based on the broad interpretation of "fi sabeel 'Illah," or "in the way of God," as one of the utilizations of zakat explicitly mentioned in the Quran, and on the basis of a maslahah mursalah approach. However, a more detailed economic analysis from a Maqasid (objectives of Shariah) viewpoint might reveal a different story, showing that the net effect, for example, could be to provide governments with an incentive not to deploy resources, which would otherwise be used for the vaccine, in the hope of accessing zakat funds. Such an analysis and determination would require a social scientific approach and are beyond the domain of simple intuition or common sense.

Juristic councils and institutional fatwas

More broadly, there is a modern trend toward institutional fatwas issued by juristic councils. The IIFA, mentioned above, is perhaps the most prominent international example of such a body. Here, the idea is that a council of experts, including Shariah scholars but also experts in the specific scientific discipline that might be relevant to the question under deliberation, would be part of a single deliberative process. As compared to historical fatwas (authoritative ruling) by individual scholars (*muftis*), this new method would allow a collective exertive deliberation (ijtihad) to occur, producing a kind of pseudo-*ijma'* (or consensus, at least within the council) and taking on a sense of being binding (since ijma' is considered a primary source of Islamic law), which can only be abrogated by another, similar institutional fatwa. Notably, the IIFA is a worldwide juristic counsel, whereas similar institutions exist at the regional and national levels, as shown in Table 5.1 (Alahmad, 2014, p. 25).

Table 5.1 Different types of juristic councils

	Global Islamic juristic councils
International (Worldwide)	International Islamic Fiqh Academy
	Islamic Fiqh Council in the Muslim World League
International (Regional)	European Council for Fatwa and Research (ECFR)
	Assembly of Muslim Jurists of America
	Sharia Scholars Association of the Gulf Cooperation Council
	Assembly of Scholars of Countries of al-Sham
National (Examples)	General Presidency of Scholarly Research and Ifta [Saudi]
	Dar al-Ifta al-Massriyyah [Egypt]
	Islamic Fiqh Academy (India)
	Fatwa Committee of the National Council for Islamic Affairs Malaysia
	Islamic Religious Council of Singapore
	Dar al-Ifta (Palestine)
	The Presidency of Religious Affairs (The Republic of Turkey)
	Jordanian General Ifta Directory

Source: Alahmad (2014, p. 27).

These concepts of institutional fatwa and informed decisions based on subject-matter experts are captured in the official objectives of the IIFA. For example, these include the following:

> To achieve intellectual harmony and integration between jurists from recognized schools of Islamic Jurisprudence and experts in various fields of knowledge and human sciences in order to elucidate the position of Shariah towards the issues of contemporary life. To promote collective Ijtihad on questions and issues of contemporary life and choose legal rulings that are in line with the interests of Muslims, as individuals, communities, or States, in full harmony with the legal arguments and the ultimate purposes of Shari'ah.
>
> (*OIC, n.d.*)

Inter-discipline ijtihad

In addition to this model of juristic councils, including scientific experts, there are other models allowing cross-disciplinary collaboration on ijtihad. An example is the many seminars and workshops often arranged by Fiqh institutions, to which subject matter and scientific experts are invited to present papers on specific topics in order to inform the jurists. Illustrative examples from the medical field include inviting biomedical experts to the 1993 IIFA expert meetings, which were convened to deliberate on the emerging challenge of HIV/AIDS (Ghaly, 2013, p. 675). For example, the medical question regarding the effectiveness of male contraceptives in protecting wives of HIV-positive males from infection had serious juristic implications regarding the inevitability of divorce (Ghaly, 2013, p. 691).

More recent examples are numerous. From the same medical field, these include the following: the efforts by the IIFA in collaboration with the Islamic Organization for Medical Sciences (IOMS) to define a Shariah-based standpoint on the genomic revolution, overturning early reservations (Ghaly, 2013), as well as the 2020 Second Medical Fiqh Symposium convened by the IIFA entitled "The Novel Coronavirus (COVID-19): Medical Treatments and Shariah Rulings". Furthermore, the attendance by Muslim jurists at international symposia on the topic in question is another method of sensitizing these jurists. A relevant example from the struggle in the early 1990s to respond to the emerging challenge of AIDS was a symposium convened by the World Health Organization (WHO) in 1991, to which seven Islamic religious scholars were invited (Ghaly, 2013, p. 705)

Other uses of mainstream methodologies in Islamic eco-finance

There are several other examples of different uses of mainstream research methodologies found in the Islamic economics and finance literature. These range from testing and appraising theories to comparing performance of

Islamic economic systems and their institutions with their conventional counterparts. For example, Metwalli used rigorous mathematical models to analyze Islamic fiscal policy, especially taking into account the role of zakat. Another example of applying mainstream research methods is the use of an event-study method to analyze the effect of Ramadan on the Islamic financial industry, which showed a significant impact (Mitchell et al., 2014). Similarly, conventional quantitative methods have been used extensively to compare the performance of Islamic financial institutions with respect to their conventional counterparts, such as the study by Qian and Velayutham on Malaysian banks (Qian & Velayutham, 2017).

Extended applications of mainstream methodologies

Further extensions of mainstream methodologies moving backwards up the chain of Usul al-Fiqh sources are present in the literature. The acceptability of such extensions is debatable and varies from one instance to another. Examples include the following: (1) applications that appear to test basic non-debatable presuppositions that well-defended and stated unambiguously in revelation; and (2) extensions into the realm of esoteric philosophy. There are a number of examples of possible research that would infringe on the domain of Islamic presuppositions and therefore be inappropriate applications of the mainstream methodologies. These include, for example, the division of inheritance among heirs as well as the zakat rate of 2.5 percent (generally), which have been clearly stipulated in the Quran and Sunnah, respectively.

Nevertheless, under the broad headings of inheritance and zakat, there is much room for applying the mainstream methodologies, such as ensuring the best interpretation of the method to calculate zakatable wealth, which is an area of ijtihad and difference among the various schools of Fiqh (e.g., whether real estate is zakatable on the principal value or only the return). Finally, Masudul Alam Choudhury has attempted to apply mathematical methods to derive, develop, and empirically apply the Quranic methodology of the "unity of knowledge," deriving from the monotheistic concept of Tawhid (or Oneness). Although this is an interesting approach with great potential, the appropriateness of applying complex mathematical methodologies to such meta-level matters could be and has been questioned.

Analysis of mini-cases

Ultimately, all the examples presented above are related to ijtihad. In some cases, such ijtihad could lead to an institutional fatwa representing a limited form of scholarly consensus or ijma', which might be called pseudo-ijma'. In any case, the space for scientific analysis via applying mainstream methodologies and techniques of economic analysis to Fiqh issues is clearly positioned squarely within the domain of ijtihad.

A sort of maslaha-mafsadah analysis based on a Maqasid perspective, similar to cost-benefit analysis, would provide a more rigorous foundation for ijtihad (Shaharuddin, 2010). It would allow an informed, evidence-based, and more objective ijtihad, which might be more likely to attain the status of ijma'. Beyond simple descriptive knowledge sharing on the topic of relevance, as is currently largely the case in the juristic councils and symposia described above, applying rigorous mainstream economic methods of analysis (e.g., quantitative methods such as regression modeling) could facilitate a more scientific quantification of maslahah vs. mafsadah, helping to both interpret Shariah rulings mentioned in primary sources as well as to extend them to new cases.

The rigorous application of mainstream methods is especially relevant given that empirical testing has risen in importance during the 20th century with the advent of computers and big data. Nevertheless, major challenges remain, the most notable of which is the availability of data. This is especially true of Islamic economics and finance, given that there are few if any pure applications of this discipline's theories globally. Indeed, there is no fully and perfectly Islamic economic system in all its details in place anywhere in the world today.

However, it is encouraging to note that many foundational economic theories were put in place before any systematic testing was possible. These include such theories as those developed by Adam Smith and David Ricardo, where validation happened much later and over a long period (Yasin and Khan, 2016, p. 44). This gives hope for the possibility of using some mix of Fiqh-based axioms and mainstream economic principles to establish the necessary theoretical infrastructure for Islamic economics and finance, which could be then validated using mainstream empirical methods of economics. Furthermore, the availability of secondary databases relevant to research in Islamic economics and finance is on the rise, providing further avenues for the application of empirical methods (Hassan, 2008).

Conclusion

This study has examined the extent of the adoption of mainstream methodologies and techniques in analyzing Fiqh issues in Islamic economics and finance. Specifically, the study has discussed analytically the philosophy and epistemology related to both Islamic and conventional economics and finance, the application of mainstream economic methodology compared to Islamic Fiqh, and the study has provided recommendations related to the proper use of mainstream methodologies and techniques for the analysis of Fiqh issues in Islamic economics and finance. The study has concluded that the mainstream methodologies and techniques of economics and finance can be applied to analyze Fiqh issues in the domain of human rationality and evidence-based ijtihad. The role of these methodologies and techniques should be minimized where subjectivity is involved in the process of ijtihad. Future research could focus on analyzing complex cases where mainstream methodologies and techniques are used to address Fiqh issues.

References

Addas, W. A. J. (2008). *Methodology of Economics: Secular vs. Islamic (First)*. International Islamic University Malaysia Press.

Alahmad, G. (2014). *Ethics of Research Biobanks: Islamic Perspectives in an International Context*. KU Leuven.

Blaug, M. (1992). *The Methodology of Economics or How Economists Explain* (2nd ed.). Cambridge University Press.

Friedman, M. (1953). The Methodology of Positive Economics. In *Essays in Positive Economics* (pp. 145–178). University of Chicago Press.

Ghaly, M. (2013). Collective Religio-Scientific Discussions on Islam and HIV/AIDS: I. Biomedical Scientists. *Zygon*, *48*(3), 671–708.

Hassan, A. (2008). Secondary Databases and Their Use in Research in Islamic Economics. *Thoughts on Economics*, *23*(2), 41–68.

Ismail, N. (2016). Scrutinizing The Epistemology of Islamic Economics: A Historical Analysis. TSAQAFAH, 12(1):19.

Johnston, D. (2004). A Turn in the Epistemology and Hermeneutics of Twentieth Century. U·ūl al-Fiqh, Islamic Law and Society, 11(2), 233–282. doi: https://doi.org/10.1163/1568519043231787 64

Kamali, M. H. (2013). *Principles of Islamic Jurisprudence*. Ilmiah Publishers.

Khan, M. A. (2017). Methodology of Islamic Economics from Islamic Teachings to Islamic.

Kizilkaya, N. (Ed.). (2020). *Methodology of Islamic Economics: Problems and Solutions*. Routledge.

Mitchell, M. C., Rafi, M. I., Severe, S., & Kappen, J. A. (2014). Conventional vs. Islamic Finance: The Impact of Ramadan Upon Sharia-Compliant Markets. *Organizations and Markets in Emerging Economies*, *5*(1), 105–124.

Nyazee, I. A. K. (2013). *Islamic Jurisprudence* (3rd ed.). Federal Law House, Rawalpindi. OIC. (n.d.). *Subsidiary Organs*.

Qian, D. J., & Velayutham, S. (2017). Conventional Banking and Islamic Banking : Do the Different Philosophies Lead to Different Financial Outcomes? *Journal of Wealth Management & Financial Planning*, *4*(June), 3–14.

Saleem, M. Y. (2013). *Islamic Commercial Law*. John Wiley & Sons Singapore Pte. Ltd. Published.

Shaharuddin, A. (2010). Maslahah-Mafsadah Approach in Assessing the Shari'ah Compliance of Islamic Banking Products. *International Journal of Business and Social Science*, *1*(1), 129–136.

Yasin, Hafiz Muhammad, & Khan, A.-Z. (2016). *Fundamentals of Islamic Economics and Finance (First)*. Islamic Research & Training Institute.

6

METHODS OF TEACHING, LEARNING, AND RESEARCH IN ISLAMIC FINANCE

The case of International Islamic University Malaysia (IIUM)

Rusni Hassan, Nurdianawati Irwani Abdullah, Akhtarzaite Abdul Aziz and Safinar Salleh

Introduction

International Islamic University of Malaysia (IIUM) was established on 20 May 1983 by the government of Malaysia. IIUM's vision is to be a leading international educational excellence center dedicated to restoring the Muslim ummah's dynamic and progressive role in all fields of knowledge and intellectual discourse. The mission is built on four pillars: Integration, Islamization, Internationalization, and Comprehensive Excellence or better known as Triple ICE (IIICE). The university uphold the philosophy that knowledge must be pursued as an *ibadah* (worship) and *amanah* (trust) which *Allah (swt)* has placed upon human being; which is based on the first five verses of *Surah al-'Alaq*:

> Read! In the name of your Lord Who has created! He has created man from a germ-cell! Read! And your Lord is the Most Generous, Who has taught by pen. He has taught man what he did not know.
>
> (*al-Qur'an, 96:1–5*)

These five verses emphasize the fact that knowledge must be acquired, internalized and disseminated in the name of *Allah (swt)* and that this knowledge should be acquired through the pen, intellect and divine revelation. Knowledge based upon the harmony of revelation and reason would surely elevate men to a position of honor and high status. IIUM integrates Islamic values and world-view into its humanities, scientific and technical curricula, befitting its university slogan "The Garden of Virtue and Knowledge". IIUM aspires to restore the roles of Muslims in education and knowledge creation.

DOI: 10.4324/9781003252764-8

IIUM also plays a very important role in acquisition and in contributing to the improvement of quality of life for all mankind.

To ensure delivery of quality tertiary education, IIUM employs accomplished scholars and committed professionals. As of 31 December 2018, there are 2,000 on the academic staff, with 14 *kulliyyahs* (faculties), three institutes, and two centers. IIUM has been offering academic programs that are of high quality and meet international standards. IIUM alumni have gone on to work in prominent positions across the globe, to be respected academics, to be social activists, and to be pillars of society, among other things. Recently IIUM has launched the Sejahtera Academic Framework for The Future (SAF) to provide an environment that is transformative, and that develops both the knowledge, skills, attitudes, and most importantly, values that further enhance IIUM's role as prominent player in higher education across the world.

This chapter looks into the role of IIUM as a pioneering education institution in Islamic finance education. IIUM embarked on Islamic finance education as early as the 1990s with the offering of Islamic finance courses and subjects. However, there is no published literature highlighting the role of IIUM in these aspects, thus making this paper exploratory in nature. Using qualitative methodology, this paper examines the Islamic finance teaching and learning environments in IIUM especially in four (4) faculties (known as *kulliyyahs*): Ahmad Ibrahim Kulliyyah of Laws (AIKOL), Kulliyyah of Economics and Management Sciences (KENMS), Kulliyyah of Islamic Revealed Knowledge and Human Sciences (KIRKHS), and IIUM Institute of Islamic Banking and Finance (IIiBF). These are the main *kulliyyahs* that provide courses and subjects on Islamic finance. The source of information is mainly from the university website and the researchers' knowledge comes from professors and senior lecturers involved directly with the teaching and learning of Islamic finance in the respective *kulliyyahs*. The researchers have been teaching Islamic finance for more than 20 years and have also been involved in pioneering the Islamic finance courses in the university, thus making the information reliable.

The chapter is structured with the introduction of IIUM as the pioneering higher institution in Islamic finance, followed by methodologies adopted in teaching and learning Islamic finance courses. Subsequently, the strength of IIUM as Islamic finance education provider will be presented in the form of findings, before the paper proceeds with recommendations and a conclusion.

IIUM as among the pioneering higher learning institutions in Islamic finance

IIUM aims to become a leading international center of educational excellence in all disciplines of knowledge, including Islamic finance. Being an Islamic university, IIUM's approach in education is inspired by the worldview of Tawhid and the Islamic philosophy of the unity of knowledge. The curriculum in all programs offered by the *kulliyyah* must be reflective of this vision of holistic

Islamic education. As such, Islamic subjects or courses must be offered as being the core component of all the programs designed by *kulliyyah*.

This vision translates well in the Islamic finance programs/courses offered at IIUM. The Islamic subjects are highly significant to Islamic finance programs/courses, since Shari'ah is the fundamental component of Islamic finance. Other main components of Islamic finance education are economics and management, and also legal. These components are represented by different *kulliyyahs* in IIUM, which pioneered Islamic finance programs/courses.

IIUM has integrated Islamic courses in the course structure of every student so that Islamic values will be a core foundation in the students' worldview. To achieve this target, IIUM has developed a structure of courses required by the university, which focuses on promoting Islamic values and lifestyle. Among the courses are: Ethics and Fiqh for Contemporary Issues, and The Islamic Worldview, Knowledge and Civilization. These two courses are the core courses that every student must take. These courses introduce the students to how world is viewed in the lens of Islam and how Muslims should live in this world as a vicegerent of Allah (Khalifah) while engaging themselves in their environment and surrounding. Fundamentally these are the concepts underlying the concepts of sustainable development goals (SDG), and they were adapted by the financial world, which currently promotes the environmental, social and governance criteria in investments.

Faculties or kulliyyah offer Islamic finance courses at IIUM

IIUM has been a pioneering higher education institution offering Islamic finance programs/courses globally since the 1990s. Currently, there are four main *kulliyyahs* offering Islamic Finance Programs. They are the Kulliyyah Economics and Management Sciences (KENMS), Ahmad Ibrahim Kuliyyah of Law (AIKOL), Kulliyyah of Islamic Revealed Knowledge and Human Sciences (KIRKHS), and IIUM Institute of Islamic Banking and Finance (IIiBF). This part provides the overview of the *kulliyyahs* and the Islamic Finance courses offered by each.

Kulliyyah of Economics and Management Sciences (KENMS)

The Kulliyyah of Economics and Management Sciences (KENMS) was one of the first two faculties formed at the inception of the IIUM in 1983. Unique among other economic faculties in various universities in Malaysia, KENMS integrated the Islamic worldview and values in the courses, which is called Islamization. This is in line with the vision of the *kulliyyah,* which is "to be a leading faculty of international excellence for teaching, research and consulting services integrating conventional economics, accounting, business and finance-related areas with Islamic values and ethics" (KENMS, 2021).

KENMS is a rebranding from the original name, Kulliyyah of Economics. It started its voyage by establishing the Department of Economics in 1983, with only seven lecturers and 68 students focusing on Islamic economics. Among the earliest courses offered by the *kulliyyah* was integrated Islamic worldview into the courses, which eventually developed the foundation of Islamic economics in the university.

Later, two more departments were established, the Department of Business Administration in 1984 and the Department of Accounting in 1987. The latest addition for the *kulliyyah* is the Department of Finance, which was formally introduced on November 4, 2010 as the Islamic banking and finance industry were gaining momentum, making the *kulliyyah* feel the urge to establish full-fledged Islamic finance courses.

KENMS offers four undergraduate programs, which are Bachelor of Economics, Bachelor of Business Administration, Bachelor of Accounting, and Bachelor of Islamic Finance. The *kulliyyah* also offers master's programs in economics, accounting, finance, and marketing, with three doctoral programs in economics, business administration, accounting, and finance. Starting off with only one subject on the theory and practices of Islamic banking and institutions in 1990, various Islamic finance courses have later been developed and offered by all departments based on their niche areas.

Ahmad Ibrahim Kulliyyah of Laws (AIKOL)

Another faculty that was established together with KENMS in 1983 was the Ahmad Ibrahim Kulliyyah of Laws. The vision of the *kulliyyah* is to become the best law school in the region with the highest standards of academic and intellectual excellence, with particular focus on the harmonization of civil law and *Shari'ah* law (the terms *Shari'ah* law and Islamic law will be used interchangeably).

The *Kulliyyah* began its first degree program, Bachelor of Laws (LL.B) (Honours) as a single major track, with 3 teaching staff and 59 undergraduate students. In 1986, the *kulliyyah* started offering its Master of Comparative Laws (MCL) and Ph.D. programs. Then it introduced the double-degree program Bachelor of Laws (LL.B/Shari'ah) (Honours) in 1989. In the year 2000, the *kulliyyah* was renamed the Ahmad Ibrahim Kulliyyah of Laws (AIKOL), in honor of the late Emeritus Professor Tan Sri Ahmad bin Mohamed Ibrahim, the founding dean of the *kulliyyah* (*Ahmad Ibrahim Kulliyyah of Laws*, 2021).

AIKOL has three departments, which have been set up since May 1994 (*Ahmad Ibrahim Kulliyyah of Laws*, 2006), the Department of Islamic Law, the Department of Civil Law, and the Department of Legal Practice (previously known as Department of Private Law). All departments provide core and elective courses for all the undergraduate and postgraduate programs.

In July 1997, AIKOL established the Harun M. Hashim Law Centre to conduct continuing legal education programs and to coordinate the research and consultancy services of its academic staff. The Law Centre offers certificates, diplomas, postgraduate degrees, and specialized training courses in various disciplines of law to the Malaysian and international community in the course of promoting lifelong learning. Besides KENMS, AIKOL is also a pioneer in the teaching and learning of Islamic finance in Malaysia, as it started offering an Islamic finance course among its undergraduate programs in 1994 and added the course in the postgraduate program in 1999.

Kulliyyah of Islamic Revealed Knowledge and Human Sciences (KIRKHS)

The Kulliyyah of Islamic Revealed Knowledge and Human Sciences (KIRKHS) was established in 1990. It is now the largest faculty in the university, with over 6,000 students and some 215 full-time academic staff. Currently, the Kulliyyah comprises 11 departments offering various programs at both undergraduates and postgraduate levels. Its formation represents a drive to integrate the human sciences and revealed knowledge disciplines. One of the departments of the *Kulliyyah* is the Department of Fiqh and Usul al Fiqh. The Department was established in 1998 as an independent academic unit within the KIRKHS. The Department has offered undergraduate and postgraduate programs in Fiqh and Usul al-Fiqh. They are the Bachelor of Islamic Revealed Knowledge and Heritage (Honours) (Fiqh and Usul al-Fiqh), Master of Islamic Revealed Knowledge and Heritage (Honours) (Fiqh and Usul al-Fiqh), and Doctor of Philosophy in Fiqh and Usul Fiqh.

The programs offered by the department fulfil the ultimate goal of the *kulliyyah* to become a leading center for integration of revealed values with human knowledge. In the context of Islamic finance, the programs served as the Shari'ah foundation for the development of the industry. The programs introduce students to the study of Islamic jurisprudence and Islamic legal theory. The wide range of courses offered by the department equipped the students with the ability to analyze various views and arguments, to provide an evaluation of proof-values underlying each juristic pronouncement, an appreciation of divergent positions, and most importantly contextualization of juristic discourses with the view of providing solutions to juristic needs of Muslims globally.

IIUM Institute of Islamic Banking and Finance (IIiBF)

IIiBF was officially established in January 2005 as a center of excellence for education and research in Islamic banking and finance. It was specially established as a postgraduate *kulliyyah* with the aim of educating and producing professionals and scholars in Islamic banking and finance. IIiBF's focus is to integrate the required components of Islamic finance knowledge and thus produce Islamic banking and finance graduates that are knowledgeable in Shari'ah and related modern disciplines pertaining to the fields of law, economics, finance, management, accounting, and information technology. IIiBF students are given thorough groundings in both theoretical and applied research on Islamic banking and finance with industry exposure so as to develop their creative skills in devising new and comprehensive Islamic financial instruments and products for the public and the industry at large. The vision of IIiBF is to be the premier global center of excellence for teaching, research, publications, and consultancy in Islamic banking and finance. Their mission is to enhance Islamic banking and finance education and research globally through the provision of capacity building and advisory services underpinned by path-breaking strategic initiatives, development, and innovation.

Islamic finance programs and courses offered

Guided with the vision and mission, IIUM has undertaken the greatly needed task of introducing Islamic banking and finance education by offering of courses and Programs by the four main *kulliyyahs*. This was begun as early as 1990 and 1994, by KENMS and AIKOL, respectively. Later, KIRKHS complemented the efforts by introducing Islamic banking and finance-related courses that were highly demanded by students. Subsequently, IIiBF was established specifically to provide postgraduate programs enabling the undergraduate students from the three other *kulliyyahs* to pursue an Islamic banking and finance specialization.

Kulliyyah of Economics and Management Sciences (KENMS)

KENMS has always been a pioneering *kuliyyah* in developing the Islamic economic and finance curriculum and is striving to be on a par with its peer universities in the global setting. A significant change is in the curriculum of the university, where there were only 11 Islamic courses offered by the *kuliyyah* as a whole in the year 1990 and 30 Islamic courses in 2021. These changes are partly due to the establishment of a Bachelor of Science in Islamic Finance in 2010.

Three departments in KENMS offer Islamic banking and finance-related courses, namely the Department of Economics (DOE), Department of Accounting (DOA), Department of Business Administration (DBA), and Department of Finance (DOF) (*KENMS*, 2021). DOE is the first department established in the *kulliyyah* in 1983, pioneering the courses on Islamic economic and finance. It offers economic and finance courses blended with Shari'ah principles (Maqasid Shari'ah) in line with the vision and mission to produce graduates with the knowledge of conventional economics who are also well-versed in Islamic values integrated into Islamic economics.

With the aims to produce competent business graduates imbued with Islamic values with a broad education in business within the areas of management, finance, marketing, information technology, and international business (BBA, 2021), the DBA offers a Bachelor of Business Administration (BBA) in Islamic banking and finance. One unique nature of this program is that the students are equipped with additional knowledge of Islamic finance where they are required to enroll in the subjects offered by the DOF. Among the required subjects are Management from an Islamic Perspective, Theory and Practices of Islamic Banking and Insurance, Introduction to Islamic Transaction, Islamic Financing Operations, Transaction of Islamic Banking and Finance, and Islamic Banking Product and Services.

DOA offers elective courses with an Islamic perspective, such as Accounting for Islamic Banks, Zakat Accounting, and Accounting, Auditing & Governance of Islamic Financial Institutions. This program has been granted maximum exemption of examination papers by the Association of Chartered Certified Accountants (ACCA), Malaysian Institute of Certified Public Accountants (MICPA), Chartered Institute of Management Accountants (CIMA), Institute of Chartered Accountants in England and Wales (ICAEW) and the CPA (Australia).

The DOF was established in 2010 to cater to the demand for Islamic banking and finance experts in the industry. It offers a Bachelor of Science in Islamic Finance, commonly known as ISFIN. DOF is one of the pioneers in developing a global curriculum for Islamic finance education along with Bank Negara Malaysia. DOF offers courses on Islamic finance, including Foundation of Islamic Finance, *Qawa'id al-Fiqhiyyah* (Legal Maxims) for Islamic Banking and Finance, ICT for Islamic Financial Institution, Islamic Capital Market, Waqf Management, Accounting for Islamic Finance and Auditing, and Governance for Islamic Finance. ISFIN students may opt to do a minor either in marketing, management or Islamic economics.

Ahmad Ibrahim Kulliyyah of Laws (AIKOL)

AIKOL offers an integrated curriculum where Islamic law is taught in parallel with civil law. This curriculum was devised by the late Prof. Ahmad, who is a legendary figure in Malaysian legal education, as a part of his effort to harmonize and incorporate Shari'ah principles and values into the civil law system of Malaysia (AIKOL, 2012). In all academic programs offered by AIKOL, students learn different areas of law from both the legal and Shari'ah perspectives. With this harmonized approach, law graduates from AIKOL are equipped with basic Shari'ah knowledge.

At undergraduate level, students from intake Semester 1, 2020/2021 taking the single major track for the award of Bachelor of Laws (LLB) (Hons.), must complete 168 credit hours. On the other hand, for the double degree track leading to the of Bachelor of Laws (LLB) (Hons.) and Bachelor of Laws (Shari'ah) (Hons.), students must complete 210 credit hours (*Bachelor of Laws [Honours]*, 2021).

Both programs combine civil law and Islamic law subjects, which are divided into the core and elective courses to be completed by undergraduate students. The main differences between LLB and LLB (Shari'ah) Honors Programs are:

- The former normally takes four academic years to complete whilst the latter requires one additional one academic year;
- The number of Islamic law subjects in the latter is more than the former; and,
- In the latter, almost all Islamic law subjects are taught in the Arabic language whereas in the former, Islamic law subjects are taught in the English language.

The integrated curriculum offered by AIKOL is comprehensive. Civil law course teaches the undergraduate students the substance of law and practicing skills in all areas, including the Malaysian legal system, law of contract, law of torts, family law, constitutional law, criminal law, land law, company law, commercial law, equity and trust, law of probate, international law, evidence, civil procedure, criminal procedure, civil litigation, criminal trial advocacy, professional ethics, conveyancing practices, alternative dispute resolution, and others. At the same time, Islamic law courses develop the students' basic understanding on the Shari'ah methodologies, principles, and rules through different subjects including Usul al-Fiqh, the Islamic legal system, Islamic law of transactions, Islamic family law, Islamic criminal law, Islamic law of succession, Islamic law of banking and takaful, and others.

For LLB (Shari'ah) students, their Shari'ah knowledge is further enhanced with additional Islamic subjects such as the Quran and hadith on law, Islamic legal texts, Islamic law of worship, Islamic constitutional law, law on zakat, Islamic law of evidence, Islamic judicial system, Shari'ah advocacy and moot court, comparative fiqh, causes of juristic differences, Islamic legal maxims, Maqasid Al-Shari'ah, Siyasah Al-Shar'iyyah, and Islamic financial and banking transactions.

Even though there are not many Islamic finance subjects offered in the LLB and LLB (Shari'ah) Honours Programs, knowledge of Islamic finance is complemented with other subjects. Hence, the existing courses provide sufficient basic exposure of the principles and practices of Islamic finance to undergraduate students to be qualified as Shari'ah or legal practitioners in Islamic finance.

At postgraduate level, AIKOL offers Master of Comparative Laws (MCL) (by coursework only, by coursework and dissertation, and by research only) and Ph.D. (by research) programs in which students may pursue their study in Islamic finance. In MCL, the subject of Islamic law of banking and securities is offered as one of the Shari'ah courses that may be taken either as a compulsory or elective subject. The subject provides in-depth discussion and comparative analysis on the laws, Shari'ah principles, practices, and issues of Islamic banking, securities, and takaful.

In addition, other related subjects such as Islamic jurisprudence, Islamic law of obligation, comparative law of property, and comparative law of banking are also offered to enhance students' knowledge and understanding in Islamic finance. AIKOL also has many experts who can supervise research students to do master or Ph.D. by research in Islamic finance (AIKOL Postgraduate Handbook 2014–2015).

Besides AIKOL, the Harun M. Hashim Law Centre also offers an LL.M. in Islamic Banking and Finance. This program is mainly offered to professionals seeking to improve and broaden their knowledge in Islamic finance and to enhance professional competency. It provides them with a broad knowledge of Islamic banking and finance law, both at the conceptual and operational levels, strengthened by the analyses of actual practices from the local and international perspectives. This program offers an integrated curriculum comprised of law, Shari'ah, and practical subjects such as law research methodology, law of banking and negotiable instruments, foundations of Shari'ah, Islamic law of transactions, Islamic finance contract, Islamic law of insurance (takaful), Islamic banking and documentations, Islamic capital market and documentations, practical lending and banking securities, and contemporary issues in banking law.

Kulliyyah of Islamic Revealed Knowledge and Human Sciences (KIRKHS)

KIRKHS was established in 1990 and the largest faculty in IIUM, with over 6,000 students and some 215 full-time academic staff. Its formation represents a drive to integrate the human sciences and revealed knowledge disciplines. The program offered by KIRKHS at undergraduate level is the Bachelor of Islamic Revealed Knowledge and Heritage (Fiqh and Usul al-Fiqh). Generally, it combines both Islamic legal rulings (fiqh) in various fields as well as the Islamic Jurisprudence (Usul al Fiqh) dealing with the methodology of deducing those rulings. The fiqh subjects taught comprise all important aspects, including Personal Matters, Family Laws, Inheritance, Waqaf and Zakat, Criminal Laws, International Relation, Islamic Commercial Laws, Islamic Financial Contracts, Islamic Banking and Capital Market, Comparative Law, Islamic Judiciary, The concept of Halal and Haram, and Contemporary Juristic Issues.

On the other hand, the Islamic jurisprudence component (Usul al Fiqh) deals with the methodology of deducing rules from the authorized sources. Some subjects taught under this category include Principles of Islamic Jurisprudence, Evidence of Legal Rules, Maqasid of Shari'ah, Issues in Islamic Rulings, Methods of Legal Deduction, Islamic Legal Maxims, and Ijtihad and Ifta'. The study of Usul al Fiqh or Islamic jurisprudence is closely related to the current development in the Islamic finance industry, as it provides the required skills to understand the Shari'ah basis in all modern Islamic finance products and to perform ijtihad in the area.

Table 6.1 Islamic finance related courses offered by KIRKHS

No	*Fiqh courses*	*Usul al-Fiqh courses*
1	Islamic Commercial Laws	Principles of Islamic Jurisprudence
2	Islamic Financial Contracts	Evidences of Legal Rules
3	Islamic Banking and Capital Market	Maqasid of Shari'ah
4	Comparative Law	Issues in Islamic Rulings
5	Contemporary Juristic Issues	Methods of Legal Deduction
6		Islamic Legal Maxims
7		Ijtihad and Ifta'

Starting from 2009, the *kulliyyah* has introduced practical training by sending the students to various institutions as an elective. Some of the institutions attended by the students are Islamic finance-related institutions like Islamic banks and takaful companies. In 2018, the *kulliyyah* also introduced the Final Year Project, whereby the students are required to provide a mini-thesis on a particular selected topic. One of the favorite areas is Islamic finance, where the students are trained to conduct research in this area.

Table 6.1 shows the subjects offered by the department that are related to Islamic finance.

Aligned to its mission on integration of Islamic revealed knowledge and human sciences and to produce graduates that are able to internalize the worldview of Islam in each and every aspect of their lives, including Islamic finance, KIRKHS's courses are concentrated to Islamic discipline, which is a fundamental component of Islamic finance. Graduates of KIRKHS joining Islamic financial institutions is expected to drive the Islamic values in the workforce and thus strengthen the Shari'ah aspects of Islamic finance.

IIUM Institute of Islamic Banking and Finance (IIiBF)

Distinctive to the other three *kulliyyahs*, IIiBF is established as a postgraduate *kulliyyah* specifically for Islamic banking and finance. With the vision to be the premier global center of excellence for teaching, research, publications, and consultancy in Islamic banking and finance, the programs offered by IIiBF are designed to produce graduates with interdisciplinary knowledge required in Islamic finance.

IIiBF offers three main types of postgraduate programs: the postgraduate Diploma in Islamic Banking and Finance, Master of Science in Islamic Banking and Finance (MScIBF), which is offered either in English or Arabic, and Ph.D. in Islamic Banking and Finance (PIBF). The objective of the MScIBF and PIBF programs is to produce high potential talents with pertinent knowledge and skills to meet the global demand for experts and professionals in Islamic banking and finance. The curriculum in the programs is designed to develop and enhance theories and practices of Islamic banking and finance within the sphere of Maqasid al-Shari'ah.

Table 6.2 Courses offered by IIiBF based on Islamic finance domains

No.	*Domains/categories*	*Example of courses*
1.	Shari'ah	• Islamic Commercial Law • Principles of Islamic Jurisprudence
2.	Economics and Islamic Economics	• Principles of Economics • Islamic Economics
3.	Accounting and Risk Management	• Principles of Accounting and Finance • Financial Management Analysis • Accounting for Islamic Financial Institutions
4.	Legal and Governance	• Legal Issues and Framework of Islamic Banking and Finance • Ethics and Governance of Islamic Financial Institutions
6.	Products and Services	• Takaful and Re-Takaful (Islamic Insurance) • Islamic Banking Products and Operations

The postgraduate programs offered by IIiBF combine various domains of knowledge related to Islamic finance, such as Shari'ah, economics and Islamic economics, accounting and risk management, legal and governance, and Islamic banking and finance products and services. The courses and domains are illustrated in Table 6.2.

Research and publication are an integral part of postgraduate programs offered in IIiBF. Students at MScIBF are required to do research project in addition to the courses undertaken for the completion of the program. For PIBF, it is a full research program where students have to write a thesis on topics related to Islamic banking and finance. The research areas that the students in both programs may cover include, but are not limited to, Fiqh Mu'amalat, regulatory and governance, performance and efficiency of Islamic banks and takaful, economics policy and analysis of Islamic banking and finance, takaful and re-takaful, Islamic wealth management, risk management, Islamic social finance, waqaf and zakat, as well as Islamic fintech.

Apart from that, IIiBF also offers professional courses for industry practitioners who are interested in upskilling their knowledge. Among the short courses available at IIiBF are: Certificate in Islamic Banking and Finance (CIBF), Certificate of Fiqh al-Mu'amalat and Waqf (CIBFW), Certificate in Islamic Banking and Finance for Legal Practitioners (CIBFL), and Certificate of Shari'ah for Takaful Practitioners (CSTP). These professional courses abridge the academics and industry practitioners whereby the modules combined fundamental knowledge and practical aspects of Islamic banking and finance. Trainers and course leaders are carefully chosen from academics and industry practitioners who have substantial knowledge in both aspects.

Methods of teaching, learning, and research in Islamic finance programs at IIUM

The methodologies used for the teaching and learning Islamic banking and finance are different according to the nature of subjects and level of studies. Generally, for IIUM undergraduate Islamic banking and finance courses, the methods commonly used are lectures, case studies, and presentations. For the postgraduate level, apart from the previous methods, seminars and colloquiums are also conducted for a more independent and self-learning experience. These methods are very crucial for postgraduate students for their research activities and thesis writing.

Lectures and presentations

The term "lecture" comes from the medieval Latin word "lecture," which means "to read aloud." As a result, a lecture was comprised of an oral reading of a text accompanied by a discussion. A lecture is a form of teaching in which the teacher offers an oral presentation of facts or principles to students, with the class taking notes. It normally entails little or no class involvement throughout the class time, such as questioning or debate. When a teacher speaks and students listen, a lecture happens. Finally, Monroe (1991) believes that the lecture method may require structured disclosure of information and presentation to students. Table 6.3 shows some classified advantages and disadvantages of lectures.

Similar to any other teaching method in every university in this world, KENMS, AIKOL, KIRKHS, and IIBF also offer regular lectures for their courses. However, unique to the status of its being one of the older public universities in Malaysia, IIUM generally has a regular class with a range of 30 to 50 students at most in one lecture. A larger-capacity lecture theater could accommodate at most 150 students. Lecture rooms and theaters are accommodated with classrooms fully equipped with multimedia systems to enhance students' learning experiences. The classroom system is to ensure that no student will be left behind in any lecture.

Special lectures, which require complex facilities such as digital requirements, are also available in the *kulliyyahs*, equipped with advanced computing facilities. To accommodate needs for subjects which require specific software, the *kulliyyahs* provide those facilities in either the general computer laboratory or in the lecture rooms.

During the almost 2 years of the COVID-19 pandemic, most of the lectures have been utilizing internet-based lectures, which adopt online applications such as Zoom or Google Meet. Online meetings for classes have been a norm for most universities in Malaysia, and IIUM has not been excluded from such norms. To facilitate the students with internet problems, a recorded lecture has been provided. This applies both to undergraduates and postgraduate students.

Table 6.3 Advantages and disadvantages of lectures

Advantages	*Disadvantages*
The proper perspective and orientation of a subject can be presented and the general outline of scope of the subject can be brought out.	It is waste of time to repeat the matter already present in books.
Many facts can be presented in a short time in an impressive way.	The teacher to make the lecture impressive may care more for manner and style but very little for matter or content.
The lecture can stimulate very good interest in the subject.	If the lecture is very fast, the pupil cannot easily take notes and will not have any written record of the salient points made out
Greater attention could be secured and maintained, as interest leads to attention.	A lecture delivered in a style not easily understood by pupils will serve no purpose
Spoken word has greater weight than mute appeal by books.	In the process of lecturing, the learners are more passive than be active in class
The language may be made suitable to all the members of the audience.	The problem-solving attitudes of pupils may disappear in the lecture method
A lecture can present a number of facts belonging to different subjects and it can also facilitate inter-disciplinary approaches to topics.	There is no cooperation and interaction between the teacher and pupils in the lecture process

Source: Kaur, G. (2011).

Depending on the level of year of learning, the nature of lecture and also the subjects vary to nurture the students without giving them pressure and shock in the early years of studies. First-year students usually will attend normal lectures that are basically similar to the school way of teaching. Even so, the lecturers, who are professionally trained, will provoke the thinking of the students and introduce the basics and foundation of the courses they will be taking earlier on.

In the case of IIUM, almost all subjects require lectures and classroom activities like group discussions and presentations. By having discussions, presentations, and two-way communications, lectures will not be only mere dictation, but an important method to disseminate course content, hence eliminating the disadvantages as mentioned above.

Case study

The case study method enables a student to closely examine the data within a specific context. In most cases, a case study method selects a small geographical area or a very limited number of individuals as the subjects of study. Case studies, in their true essence, explore and use case study as a research method to investigate contemporary real-life phenomena through detailed contextual analysis of a limited number of events or conditions and their relationships. Yin (1984, p. 23) defines the case study research method "as an empirical inquiry that investigates a contemporary phenomenon within its real-life context; when the boundaries between phenomenon and context are not clearly evident; and in which multiple sources of evidence are used."

In the case of IIUM, some of the Islamic finance-related subjects might depend on case study method to examine the application of principles taught in lectures on the contemporary real issues and phenomena. In IIiBF for example, case study method is used in all courses taught where the lecturers presented the real Islamic banking and finance cases to be deliberated and analyzed. Students are also assigned to do projects and assignments that empirically investigate the real issues faced by the industry.

Course assessments

For the assessments, the lecturers in the four *kulliyyahs* used various ways to evaluate their students. Among them are quizzes, mid-term tests, assignments (either individual assignments or group assignments), seminars, and presentations depending on the knowledge and skills required for each subject.

Most courses involve some form of continuous assessment of students. This means that marks obtained for projects, assignments, quizzes, and mid-term examinations during the year are taken into account in deciding final marks. KENMS, KIRKHS, and IIiBF, for instance apply a 60:40 ratio of carry marks and final exams. On the other hand, AIKOL's carry marks and final exam are normally set at 40:60, respectively. Carry marks include quizzes, project assignments, mid-term examinations, and class participation, depending on the requirement of the course, and vary with the courtesy of lecturers.

However, postgraduate students of IIiBF are also heavily assessed for their research and presentation skills through class seminars conducted at the end of the semester. Students are required to prepare "journal article-like" papers to be presented and assessed by the lecturers. Most of the papers are later submitted for publication in journals or presented at international conferences.

Seminars, colloquiums, and conferences

Seminar, colloquiums, and conferences are good avenues especially for postgraduate students to present their views and get feedback from an audience with multiple backgrounds. This will broaden their perspective and improve their level of confidence and communication and research skills. For example, the Department of Fiqh and Usul al Fiqh of KIRKHS conducts annual colloquiums for postgraduate students to present and discuss their topics of interest, especially those related to their theses.

In IIiBF, seminars are conducted in almost all courses where students are required to present their research projects at the end of the semester. Interestingly, for the course of Islamic fintech, the students are required to undergo a boot camp, which is a short-term, intense training session designed to prepare students for the practical reality of financial technology in Islamic banking and finance. An annual Ph.D. colloquium is held for PIBF students to present research findings and to report on their study progress.

Supporting the university's theme as the Garden of Knowledge and Virtue, all the four *kulliyyahs* have committed to organize conferences, symposiums, roundtable discussions, and other knowledge-sharing platforms as part of the *kulliyyahs'* annual plan of activities. At least one conference is organized annually in the respective *kulliyyahs*. These are the platforms for academicians, researchers, and students to present their research findings. The industry practitioners from local and international institutions are invited as keynote speakers, panelists, and presenters to share the updates on Islamic finance. The academicians and students are thus not devoid of the practical aspects and remain relevant to the industry.

Research

In promoting and assisting research among students and lecturers, IIUM has introduced the Research and Innovation Unit in every *kulliyyah*. This unit functions as a strategic developer in order to promote, facilitate, and monitor research and publication in the respective *kulliyyahs*. It also disseminates relevant research-related information, research opportunities, and policies to *kulliyyah* researchers; and is a liaison between the Research Management Centre (RMC) and the *kulliyyah*. This unit administers review of research proposals at the *kulliyyah* level, and coordinates with the RMC on monitoring research progress of internal and external grants. As record keeper, this unit updates the *kulliyyah* database on research, publication, and consultancy; assists staff in accessing and uploading necessary material in various research management systems; and prepares reports on *kulliyyah* research and publication activities.

Most of the research done by students is from the postgraduate level varying to their research for Ph.D. or master's topics in respective *kulliyyahs* and departments. Table 6.4 illustrates the most sought research areas among researchers in Islamic banking and finance.

Industry engagement

Industry engagement is also one important element of the education program curriculum and design especially for a fast-moving industry like Islamic finance. Students are always exposed to the current development in the industry by engaging with the industry players. For the undergraduate level, an internship program has been made compulsory to students in all four *kulliyyahs,* offering Islamic banking and finance courses in IIUM. Students will choose the institutions related to their study to do internships according to their field of interest.

Table 6.4 Islamic banking and finance research areas in IIUM

Accounting	• Accounting and Islamic Accounting • Corporate Governance and Accountability • Public Sector and Information Management • Sustainability • Financial Reporting • Quantitative and Managerial Accounting
Management	• Management from Islamic Perspective • Operation Research and Decision Theory • Human Resource Development / Training Management • Marketing and Consumer Behaviour • Quality and Healthcare Management • International Business • Strategic Management
Economics	• Islamic Economics • Economic Development, Social Work and SMEs • Public Finance and Financial Economics • International Economics and Globalisation • Environmental, Agricultural and Health Economics • Labour Economics and Human Resource Development • Applied Econometrics
Finance	• Corporate Governance • Finance and Banking / Islamic Finance and Banking • SMEs and Microfinancing • Capital Market / Islamic Capital Market • Corporate Finance • Financial Crime • Risk Management
Shari'ah and Legal	• Fiqh and Usul Fiqh • Maqasid Shari'ah Shari'ah Analysis on Islamic Banking and Finance • Shari'ah Standards and Resolutions on Islamic Banking and Finance • Legal and Regulatory Framework of Islamic Banking and Finance • Dispute Resolutions in Islamic Banking and Finance • Shari'ah Governance • Islamic Social Finance • Zakat and Waqaf

IIBF has also organized guest speaker series, legal seminars, and pitching sessions. For example, among their events are the Industry Discussion Series and Special Talk with numbers of prominent scholars as the speakers. These industry engagements are really important for building a good network between the faculties and industries. It will also good for the students to have practical and industry exposure. Other than that, it also opens up for industry linkages, networking, and also job opportunities for the graduates.

IIUM strength in teaching, learning, and research in Islamic finance

IIUM is a leading international center of educational excellence that aims to restore the dynamic and progressive role of the Muslim Ummah in all branches of knowledge and intellectual discourse. Through this vision, the university has thus pioneered the teaching, learning, and research in Islamic finance during the last three decades. Led by the four kulliyyahs – AIKOL, KENMS, KIRKHS, and IIiBF – the university has made a remarkable contribution to the Islamic finance education. Among the factors that make IIUM the leader in Islamic finance education are the strong foundation of Islamic knowledge in IIUM curriculum that supports Islamic finance education; comprehensive domains/discipline in Islamic finance programs; the ecosystem in Islamic finance education; and various methodologies adopted for effective teaching, learning, and research in Islamic finance.

Strong foundation for Islamic knowledge in the IIUM programs curriculum

IIUM's vision, mission, and philosophy on education provide a good background on Islamic knowledge, which is essential for Islamic banking and finance education. Islamic banking and finance as a new discipline in contemporary Islamic scholarship requires deep understanding of fiqh discipline to separate the permissible from the non-permissible, as well as to ascertain the position of the Shari'ah in the overall operation of Islamic financial institutions. Quoting Fahim Khan (2002) in commenting on the foundation of Islamic economics, which is the main component of Islamic finance education, that the "roots of Islamic economics (viz-a-viz Islamic finance) should, by definition, lie in fiqh. Islamic economics as a distinct discipline will be justified only if we can show that fiqh literature, that provides understanding of Islamic texts, leads us to different roots for understanding the economic behaviors of man. Consequently, Usul al-fiqh became an important methodology in developing Islamic economics." Thus, it was not a surprise that in the early phase of Islamic finance, it was dominated by the scholars and writers with a background in Islamic sciences, in particular fiqh discipline (Haneef, 1997, Monzer Kahf, 2003, El-Shaikh, 2011).

The importance of Usul Fiqh in the teaching and learning of Islamic banking and finance is acknowledged by the *kulliyyah* at IIUM when offering their courses. All *kulliyyah* have offered the subject of Usul Fiqh as a required course for Islamic banking and finance programs, either at undergraduate or postgraduate level. Indeed, this was the pioneering course offered by the *kulliyyahs* in 1990, and this practice continues now.

Table 6.5 Number of Islamic finance courses based on domains

Kulliyyah	*Number of courses on IF operations*	*No of courses on Shari'ah/ Muamalat*	*No of courses on economics*	*No of courses on legal and governance*	*Total*
KENMS	24	10	29	3	66
AIKOL	2	13	–	20	35
KIRKHS	5	41	–	3	49
IIiBF	9	3	7	3	22

Comprehensive components or domains for Islamic finance programs

Islamic finance is a unique discipline of knowledge that has evolved from different disciplines to meet the financial sector expectations. As a social finance discipline, Islamic finance education consists of different domains, which are (1) Islamic finance operations; (2) Islamic science and Mu'amalat; (3) economics, accounting, and management sciences; and (4) legal, regulatory, and governance. The courses offered by the four *kulliyyahs* at IIUM are aligned to the required components of the disciplines (Table 6.5).

Comprehensive ecosystem in Islamic banking and finance programs

True to its vision and mission to provide comprehensive excellence in the education system, IIUM has planned well in providing a good and complete ecosystem in Islamic banking and finance education. Relying on the strength of each *kulliyyah,* i.e., KENMS, KIRKHS and AIKOL, the undergraduate IBF programs are offered to students in the respective *kulliyyahs.* Without undermining the focus of each *kulliyyah*, the programs and courses offered are aligned accordingly. For example, courses in KENMS are aligned to economics, accounting, risk management, and the like; in AIKOL, the Islamic banking and finance courses are aligned to legal and regulatory aspects; and KIRKHS offers courses that specifically focus on Shari'ah components. These complement well the required domains or discipline of Islamic banking and finance. Following that, IIiBF provides the opportunity for graduates from bachelor's degree programs in the respective *kulliyyahs* to pursue specialization in Islamic banking and finance. Thus, the courses offered at IIiBF comprehensively cover all the related domains/disciplines. In other words, all three *kulliyyahs* provide training grounds for all related sciences required in the Islamic banking and finance curriculum, which are Shari'ah, legal, and economics, whereas IIiBF integrates all sciences under one program at postgraduate level, either for master's or Ph.D. level. This provides a conducive Islamic banking and finance education ecosystem that one can find in a higher learning institution.

Conclusion

Based on almost three decades of experience in teaching and learning Islamic banking and finance, the main strength of IIUM in developing potential leaders, experts, and practitioners of Islamic banking and finance is found in its integrated curriculum, which combines both civil or modern and Islamic education. As a result, many IIUM graduates are directly involved in Islamic banking and finance industry, not only in Malaysia but also globally. Not only that, the IIUM lecturers represent the majority of the Shari'ah Committee members in Malaysian Islamic financial institutions. As of 2021, there are 17 IIUM lecturers who are serving as Shari'ah Committee members in Islamic banks and takaful companies (BNM, 2021). This represents 11% of the total number of Shari'ah committee members in Malaysian Islamic financial institutions. Direct involvement of the lecturers in the industry enhances their knowledge of the quality of teaching and learning of Islamic finance courses in IIUM.

References

El-Shaikh, S. (2011). Islamic economics and finance, then and now: A Fiqhi-conomic perspective on its doctrines and debates. International Journal of Economics, Management and Accounting, 19(1), 77–120.

Haneef, M. A. (1997). Islam, the Islamic worldview, and Islamic economics. IIUM Journal of Economics and Management, 5(1), 39–65.

Hasan, Z. (2018). Methodology of Islamic economics: Is the subject worth discussing? Munich Personal RePEc Archive. https://mpra.ub.uni-muenchen.de/85824/

Kahf, M. (2003). Islamic economics: Notes on definition and methodology. Review of Islamic Economics, 13, 23–47.

Kahf, M. (2019). Islamic economics' methodology and Fiqh. In *Methodology of Islamic Economics* (pp. 161–180). Routledge.

Kaur, G. (2011). Study and Analysis of Lecture Model of Teaching. International Journal of Educational Planning & Administration, 1(1), 9–13.

7

IMPACT OF THE SHIFT FROM REAL ECONOMY TOWARD THE FINANCIAL ECONOMY IN DERIVING NEW RULES (ISTINBĀT) IN MU'AMALĀT

Sheikh Ricky Bains and Sheikh Faizal Ahmad Manjoo

Introduction

Fiqh-al-Mu'āmalāt is a crucial area of Islamic law that embraces a wide spectrum of topics. This corpus of law came into existence through a scientific methodology of deriving law primarily utilizing an interpretative framework as articulated by *Uṣūl al-fiqh*, from which we make *isṭinbāt*. *Uṣūl al-fiqh* has been developed and refined over the centuries. It is the mechanism used to identify solutions or issue Islamic rulings on a given problem, because often the primary sources, i.e., Quran and Sunnah, are limited in the number of clear texts. Interpretative tools are required to extrapolate the rulings and often extensive juristic tools need to be used, such as market custom (*'urf*). With the advent of the financial economy after World War II in the 1960s in particular, many concepts were developed in the Western economies which required a new approach to determine the legitimacy of such products in *fiqh*. These financial concepts received legal legitimacy by enactment of law, but in themselves are abstract concepts and are not tangibles as such. Hence, from an Islamic perspective, the need to create a legal construct became a herculean task for the *fuqahā* as many of these products did not exist at the time of the Prophet (*saw*), such as cryptocurrency, shares, bonds, and derivatives. These are intangible assets which dominate the financial economy and are adopted in many Muslim jurisdictions. Therefore, *Uṣūl al-fiqh* is to be given priority in determining the legitimacy of these financial instruments. Hence, some fundamental principles of *Uṣūl al-fiqh* will be explained and applied in this area. This chapter aims at:

- Identifying the main problems in *Fiqh al-Mu'āmalāt* for the financial economy that warrant a methodology to find solutions.
- Depicting a broad picture of *Uṣūl al-fiqh*.

DOI: 10.4324/9781003252764-9

- Application of *Uṣūl al-fiqh and al-Qawā'id al-Fiqhiyya* by providing some examples of modern-day financial instruments.

To appreciate the discussion, first a brief analysis of the implications of the shift from a real economy towards a financial economy would be analyzed, followed by a holistic approach to the methodology of *Usūl al-Fiqh* and *al-Qawa'id al-Kulliyah al-Fiqhiyyah* as implementary genres in legal theory to deduct law for modern-day issues. The chapter also provides practical guidelines for the researcher looking for a sharia-based solution to a new legal issue.

Implications for the emergence of the financial economy

Islamic law was developed during an era where the real economy was prevailing. The focus of transactions was mostly on commodities that had an intrinsic value. (Usmani, 2002) For instance, a camel had value because it was a camel, and that camel would have a value be it in Arabia or India. It remains a commodity due to its inherent and innate value. However, during the 1960s with the advent of globalization, the American corporations extended their activities in Europe primarily. Their banks followed them to offer their services. As the banks' performance was better, the shift in investment towards those financial intermediaries increased. Financial intermediaries are institutions that develop a stream of products to attract money from those economic agents who have excess liquidity, and channel the finance towards those economic agents who would need such money. In other words, they hold funds from lenders to make loans to borrowers. In doing so the financial intermediaries would develop financial products in the form of a financial instrument. A financial instrument is any financial contract that gives rise to a financial asset of one entity and a financial liability or equity instrument of another entity (IPSAP, 2020). In essence financial assets, financial liabilities, and equity instruments are technically mere paper or electronic documents. For example, buying shares would create a financial asset which technically is a bundle of rights (Manjoo, 2005), including the right to claim dividend by virtue of one's equity in the balance sheet of the company. The company receives money as asset and the shareholder receives equity in the company. Both are intangible concepts. The subject matter of such contracts is an intangible asset as evidenced legally in the share certificate. If the law does not recognize what is written on the share certificate, then the share certificate has no value. In other words, a legal construction is needed. Alternatively let us take the case of an option whereby someone pays a premium in exchange to have a priority right to opt to buy something. This option creates a financial liability on the person who promises to give that option and gives the purchaser the right to exercise that right on the seller of the option. The buyer of the option has a financial asset, i.e., the right to opt to purchase the subject matter of the contract. Both are intangible financial liabilities and assets, respectively. A financial instrument is either cash; evidence of an ownership interest in an entity; or a contractual right to receive, or deliver, cash or another financial instrument. These types of instruments are intrinsically un-Islamic in most cases because they contain prohibitive contractual elements such as *ribā* and *gharar* (Muhammad, *et al.,* 2016). Islamically, this is not acceptable. Therefore, there are some specific Islamic ethos that need to be reflected in these financial instruments.

The main issue with these intangible assets or liabilities or equity is that they are playing a crucial role in holding the world economy. For example, the derivative market is ten times the world GDP; some estimate the market at $1.2 quadrillion; and yet it is nothing but a contract depending on another contract. The Bank of International Settlement (1995) defines it as "a contract whose value depends on the price of underlying assets, but which does not require any investment of principal in those assets." These scenarios warrant that we seek alternative definitions and rulings from an Islamic perspective, as Muslims who constitute 24% of the world population need these alternatives to integrate in the globalized world. From a *fiqhī* angle these instruments are pure paper or electronic documents that have no value in themselves. The value they carry is based on what is written in them. This in turn is crucially based on the legal construction. It is that legal construction that will reveal the legality or illegality of these instruments as financial commodities, liabilities, or contracts from an Islamic perspective.

This creates a problem from a *fiqhī* perspective because this approach is two-edged: first *fuqahā* must understand the legal side of these instruments. These can be determined from various sources: acts of parliaments, case laws, or even based on prevailing customs of a given industry. Thereafter they can make a *fiqhī* construction of said products by engaging with the Islamic legal sources that are used to construct the validity of these instruments. In the past *fuqahā* would first determine the legality of a product by: (1) either that the *Sharī'ah* has defined it, (2) by deduction from *fiqh*, or (3) premised on '*urf*. In the past the *fuqahā* would apply some *Uṣūl* (juristic principles) to make *istinbāt* in determining if the subject matter of the contract is valid or not. Those subjects existed physically and had an intrinsic value; most of these contracts had to do with the real economy. However, in a financial economy, the scenario is completely different because firstly the law creates the financial instruments, as they have no value without a legal construction. Even if people would accept these instruments, they might not be legal, i.e., if the *'urf* accept it, the court or government might reject it. A simple example is digital currency like Bitcoin, which has not been accepted as a legal tender so far by most countries. Consequently, it becomes a daunting task for *fuqahā* to make pronouncements over these financial instruments.

Impact of the shift

To appreciate the above discourse, it is important to grasp the underpinning juristic methodology used by *fuqahā*. In Islamic law the *fuqahā* (of the past) would identify something as *māl mutaqawwim* (commodity of economic value) based on some principles, such as: the product is not haram, or the transaction does not involve prohibitive elements such as *gharar, ghabn fāḥish, ribā,* and *istiḥkār*. After they investigate these general contractual elements, they will issue a ruling on the subject matter of the contract based on very specific rulings pertaining to such transactions. It is important to understand that besides the legality of the subject matter of the contract, the contract itself, under Islamic law, is different from conventional law of contracts. For instance, the *fuqahā* would look at the essential elements of the contract (called the *arkān* of such contract) and not the *naturalia* of the contracts, which are the general conditions for contracts. In other words, they would consider the essential elements that make a transaction valid on its own premise based on Shari'ah rather than developing a general theory of contract. For instance, the validity of a lease contract will be determined based on the Quran and hadith and not on a general principle of contracts as we have in the common law. In other words, the fuqaha would focus on the *essentialia* rather than the *naturalia.*

This new legal phenomenon of financial instruments requires an investigation into the application of *Uṣūl al-fiqh* and *Qawā'id Fiqhiyya* in order to perform *ijtihād* and explore whether we can blend the secular and Islamic legal systems to arrive at a solution to engage with this area of *Fiqh al-Mu'amalāt*. There is another academic discussion regarding the extent to which one can blend two legal systems. All these issues demand that we understand how *Uṣūl al-fiqh* operates and what its limitations and potentials entail. We are dealing with contracts that create financial products, which in themselves are nonexistent, but only come to fruition based on a legal construction. This is completely different from a real economy.

At present, the world has become one globalized village, in particular at the level of trade. Such trade should be urgently redeveloped on the foundation of common standards agreed upon by the international community. To gain acceptability, such standards must be fair and pave the way for the smooth running of global trade and economic growth. This requires a moral benchmark and legal harmonization as a pillar in the process. To achieve a beneficial global economy, from an Islamic perspective and to develop such legal harmonization, jurists have proposed four criteria for rationalistic or benefit-based analysis: (1) making apparent benefit permissible (principles of *ibāha*); (2) forbidding harm and destruction (hadith on the principle of *lā ḍarar wa lā ḍirār*); (3) providing more legal freedom under the fundamental foundations of ease (principle of *taysīr*); and (4) taking the environment of society at the present time as a factor (principle of *zamān* [time] and *'urf* [custom]). In addition, a framework was laid down to address the issue of how these principles of benefit can be applied (Aljloud, 2014, p. 9). The four schools in Sunni jurisprudence stayed away from overruling explicit and specific textual rulings; some jurists allowed the restriction of general rulings, which could be not applied due to benefit analysis. Though previous scholars developed their own *Uṣūl al-fiqh*, nevertheless, some scholars in the twentieth century, including the great Azhari jurist, Abdul Wahhab, went so far as to say that when benefit analysis and other legal proofs were contradictory, then "maximising net benefit is the objective of the law for which rulings were established" and that "objectives should always have priority over and adhere to that opinion" (Aljloud, 2014, p. 93). This was a maxim advocated by all the scholars of legal thought. Hence, to deduct law involves *ijtihad*, as we need to consistently find the balance for benefit.

Usūl al-Fiqh and Qawaid Fiqhiyya

Kamali defines *ijtihad* as "*the total expenditure of effort made by a jurist in order to infer, with a degree of probability, the rules of Shari'ah from their detailed evidence in the sources*" (2006, p. 468). This definition, however, largely covers *ijtihad* based on something explicitly mentioned in a textual reference or *al-ijtihād fī al-naṣṣ* cases dealing with matters which are not explicitly covered in textual sources but are covered by secondary sources such as *Qiyās*, *Istiḥsān*, *Istislāh*, and *'Urf* amongst other rational and contextual interpretive mechanisms (Table 7.1).

Hence, the articulation of *usūl al-fiqh* which we find in many classical manuals is primarily concerned with broadly agreed-upon sources of law such as the Quran, *Sunnah*, *Ijmā'*, and *Qiyās*, as well as other disputed sources of Shariah such as *Istiḥsān*, *Istiṣhāb*, *Aqwāl al-ṣahaba*, and *Istiṣlāh*, *'Urf*, and *Sadd al-Dharā'i*. They also address; questions of legal reasoning, how evidence is reconciled upon contradiction, and topics related to *ijtihad* and *taqlid*. The sources of law as found in the *Uṣūl al-Fqih* works can be classified into three levels: The primary sources, which are the Quran and *Sunnah*, from which the rules are derived, and often *Uṣūl al-fiqh* provides the interpretational mechanism to derive the rules from them depending on the level of *clarity* or *ambiguity* in the text. These are called *Dalālah al-Naṣṣ* (Kamali, 2006, p. 167). Then we have the secondary sources, which are mainly *Ijma'* (consensus of scholars of a given time on a given matter) and *Qiyās* (syllogism or analogical deduction). The third sources are the area of dispute among

Table 7.1 Sources of Islamic law

Textual sources	*Rational/contextual sources*
Al-Qur'an	*Al-Qiyās*
Al-Sunnah	*Al-Istiḥsān*
Al-Ijmā'	*Al-Maslaha al-Mursalah*
Opinions of Companions[1]	*Al-Istiṣhāb*
	Al-'Urf
	Sadd al-Dhara'i

Source: Authors' own.

the *madhāhib*, and it entails juristic tools like '*Urf*, *Istiṣlaḥ*, etc., as mentioned above (Kamali, 2006).

The vast majority of *Usūl al-Fiqh* literature begin by centering their discussion around linguistic principles, in an attempt to understand the primary sources, addressing questions of meaning, clarity, ambiguity, metaphor, and literalism amongst other things.

The importance of these principles is summarized as follows:

- They are essential to *mujtahids* for distinguishing between speculative and definitive meanings and for categorizing these meanings so that whichever is clearer may be given precedence in case of a conflict.
- They provide powerful support for the *mujtahid* in his legal reasoning, especially in the case of conflict between legal proofs of Islamic law.
- They provide understanding of words whose interpretation is a major cause of disagreement among *fuqahā* (Muslim jurists).
- They help in better understanding the legislation of Islam and Islamic law in general.

The points mentioned above demonstrate the importance of *Uṣūl al-Fiqh* to understand methods of textual indications and linguistic principles pertaining to the interpretation of the Quran and Sunnah. This provides the reader with an insight into and appreciation for the systematic methodology and tools used for textual interpretation, as well as legal pluralism amongst classical scholars. They do not, however, offer workable tools for today's student of Islamic finance in dealing with analogous or completely novel financial instruments in an unimaginably different economy, where the legal structures of Islamic finance products are often subject to multifaceted legal interaction both domestically and across borders.

In this vein, Mufti Taqi Usmani makes the following recommendations for the development of *Fiqh* in the modern era.

- Supplementing the study of *Fiqh* with modern commercial issues and encouraging *ijtihad* in those matters that are not *manṣūṣ alayhā* (explicitly referenced in textual evidence); rather, they are found in *Fiqh* texts. Such judgments or even categorizations are a product of *istiqrā'* (legal induction) and *istikhrāj* (legal deduction); hence, they should be evaluated in light of the circumstances those scholars found themselves in and not elevated to the status of textual evidence. Usmani adds, "*the jurist is not simply tasked with judgment, but to provide solutions should they declare something to be impermissible*."
- Secondly, the development of *Fiqh* so that it addresses the needs of the contemporary age. This centers around rulings and their *'illah* (ratio legis); an abundance of rulings can be found that revolve around a particular *'illah*, because the *'illah* could change across time, and so too should the accompanying ruling.

- Lastly, legal texts should be compiled which are in congruence with the modern educational experience which are clearly indexed and easy to navigate for the purposes of research (Usmani, 2014, pp. 259–263).

To clarify, *istidlāl* is the process of grounding a ruling in textual evidence where no precedent exists. For the sake of brevity, we can think of this occurring in two ways: *istiqrā'* (induction) and *istinbāṭ* (deduction). Essentially, *istiqrā'* involves reasoning from specific examples to propose a general rule. *Istiqrā'* is usually associated with extrapolating general rules from different cases where specific facts vary. Conversely, *istinbāṭ* is reasoning based upon a general rule to determine the appropriate outcome in a specific case. Typically, *istinbāṭ* is applied in reasoning from *nuṣūṣ* (textual evidence), which forms a rule of general application.

Some other guidelines from a contemporary scholar, Yusuf al-Qaradawi, identify a set of criteria for contemporary legal interpretations. He writes that before one proceeds to engage in any interpretation, one must ensure that one has understood the legal case at hand in sufficient detail and with all its facets; the new case must not be covered by any definitive texts, speculative texts should not be elevated to the status on definitive, new insights into legal mechanisms and interpretive frameworks should be welcomed, and there should be a move to performing communal *ijtihad* (Qaradawi, 1996).

Thus, *ijtihad* is necessary in every time and every place. The challenges presented by the economy shifting from a real to a financial economy gave rise to a plethora of *nawāzil* or *wāqi'āt*, i.e., novel cases which require *ijtihād* to arrive at a *ḥukm al-shar'I* (legal judgement). Al-Shatibi (2006) discusses *ijtihad,* which continues and never ceases, as that which is connected to *taḥqīq al-manāṭ* (ascertaining the legal ratio), which will be discussed later. Ibn al-Qayyim stresses that the importance of historical and geographical context stating "*... The faqīh is the one who reconciles between what is incumbent (wājib) and the reality on the ground (al-wāqi'). Hence, every time and place have its own ruling, and people of a particular generation are better placed than their predecessors*" (Qayyim, 1996, p. 220).

For now, it is vital to appreciate that *ijtihad* is something which is inevitable, despite the prevailing attitude of dismissing its feasibility. al-Ṣan'ānī quotes ibn al-Wazīr express the sentiment that *ijtihād* has, in the consciousness of students and scholars alike, been perceived to be an impossible feat, which is at odds with the approach of the *Salaf* (first three generations of Muslims), who managed to find a middle ground between a *laissez-faire* interpretation and overly restrictive modes of *ijtihad.* To sum up, Islamic rulings pertaining to Islamic finance and economics will fall into two broad categories:

- Judgments or opinions expressed in the textual sources, which directly address a particular commercial issue. This might include a specific transaction mentioned in primary sources, namely Quranic verses and Prophetic traditions, arrived at through secondary sources, such as *Ijmā'* and *Qiyās* or lastly, tertiary sources which are often rational tools used to arrive at a ruling in a particular context, such as *istiṣḥab* and *'urf.* These judgments can be gleaned from *fiqh* manuals, legal commentaries, and works that catalogue legal edicts.

- The second type are those judgements that have been arrived at after exhausting the Fiqh literature and tools offered by the traditional *Uṣūl al-Fiqh* framework. This is through a careful consideration of *al-Qawa'id al-Kulliyah al-Fiqhiyya,* which are broad legal maxims alongside *ḍawābiṭ*, which are governing principles in certain sub-fields of law. These *qawā'id* and *ḍawābiṭ* are often formulated from a broad investigation of the *Sharī'ah* and its overarching objectives or *maqāṣid* (see Nyazee, 2016).

So, the *Nuṣūṣ*, *Ijmā'*, and *Qiyās* provide a sure means of binding our rulings to the apparent will of the Legislator, God, and the teachings of his Prophet, Muhammad. The second type provides the student and scholar with the interpretive tools necessary to deal with the developments in a fast- paced, ever-changing field like Islamic finance. Therein, it opens the possibility of providing judgments informed by the Shariah as well as solutions that are balanced and comprehensive, which remaining faithful to the spirit of the textual sources.

Nyazee writes on the relationship between *Uṣūl al-Fiqh* and *Qawāi'd al-Fiqhiyya* stating:

> In reality, the very early Hanafis did not make any distinction between the two types when dealing with the law and during the derivation of rules. Jurists like Jassas and al-Dabbusi began separating the two sets as the combined form presented many complexities of method. It is interesting to note that these jurists did not call these separated rules Uṣūl al-Fiqh. There is no separation in al-Karkhi's book, but he dealt with a few rules. His student al-Jassas separated the first set and called his book al-Fusul fi al-Uṣūl, while al-Dabbusi referred to his book as Taqwim al-Adillah. Sarakshi following al-Dabbusi called his book Kitab al-Uṣūl. There is no definition of fiqh or Uṣūl al-Fiqh in these books. **Everything was an asl[2] for these jurists**. The combined form made things difficult, but most of the power lay in this combined approach.
>
> (*Nyazee, 2016 p. 21*)

Furthermore, Ibn Taymiyya writes, "*all specific cases (juziyyāt) must be underpinned by comprehensive foundational principles (kulliyyāt) in order to be based on sound judgment. Otherwise, one remains ignorant of the specific cases and oblivious of the comprehensive foundational principles (kulliyyāt), thereby perpetuating grave error*" (2004, p. 83). Ibn Nujaym goes as far as to claim that these qawā'id *are* in-fact the tools used by the *mujtahid* whilst performing *ijtihad* (Ibn Nujaym, 1985, p. 15), and others such as Qarāfi insists that those who issue judgments in *Nawāzil* without recourse to *Qawā'id* inevitably end up victims to contradictions and inconsistencies. It is this "combined approach" that Nyazee and many before him advocated, which is essential in the derivation of rulings in novel cases, particularly given the complexity of modern financial instruments. But what are the means of tying the judgment in a completely novel and unprecedented legal matter to the textual sources? One of the primary methods which is unanimously agreed upon is that of *Qiyās* (analogical reasoning).

Qiyās in Fiqh al-Mu'amalat

Qiyās provides a systematic form of analogical reasoning that allows the jurists to investigate rulings within legal textual evidence and apply these rulings to analogous unprecedented scenarios through a shared *'illah* (the underpinning cause for the ruling). The importance of this source of the *Uṣūl al-Fiqh* genre cannot be overstated. al-Shafi famously equates *ijtihad* with *qiyas*, although the majority of jurists deem *ijtihad* to be much broader (Ghazali, 1993, p. 281). Nevertheless, *Qiyas* is one of the primary methods of addressing *Nawāzil*[3] (Al-Baghdādī, 2001).

The lexical meaning of *Qiyās* is: Measuring or estimating one thing against another.

In legalese it would mean: "The assignment of a *ḥukm* of an existing case found in the texts of the Quran, the *Sunnah* or *Ijmā'* to a new case whose *ḥukm* is not found in these sources on the basis of a common underlying attribute called *'illah* of the *ḥukm.*" In other words when a new problem crops up, it warrants an Islamic ruling, and if there is no clear answer for it in the texts, then the jurists will identify a similar case to it from Quran, *Sunnah* or *Ijmā'*. Following the identification of a similar case, then the jurists construct a syllogism to extrapolate a ruling. *Qiyās* involves four main concepts: the *maqīs* also known as *far*;[4] the *maqīs 'alayhi,* also called *al-aṣl*;[5] the *'illah,* the cause upon which the ruling was given for the *maqīs 'alayhi*; and finally the *ḥukm*, i.e., the ruling for the *maqīs 'alayh* and to see if the same *ḥukm* can be transferred to the new case, i.e., the *maqīs*. Each of these four elements needs to meet certain criteria (Figure 7.1).

Methods of determining the 'illah

For *Qiyās* to be valid, the identification and discovery of *'illah* (ratio legis) must go through three stages (Nyazee, 1994):

- *Takhrīj Al-Manāṭ*.
- *Tanqīh Al-Manāṭ*, and
- *Taḥqīq Al-Manāṭ*.

First the *mujtahid* or *faqīh* will have to identify the appropriate *'illah* from the Quran, *Sunnah,* or *Ijmā'* from an existing matter. He might identify multiple *'ilal.*[6] "*Takhrīj*" means to derive or extract, and "*manāṭ*" means

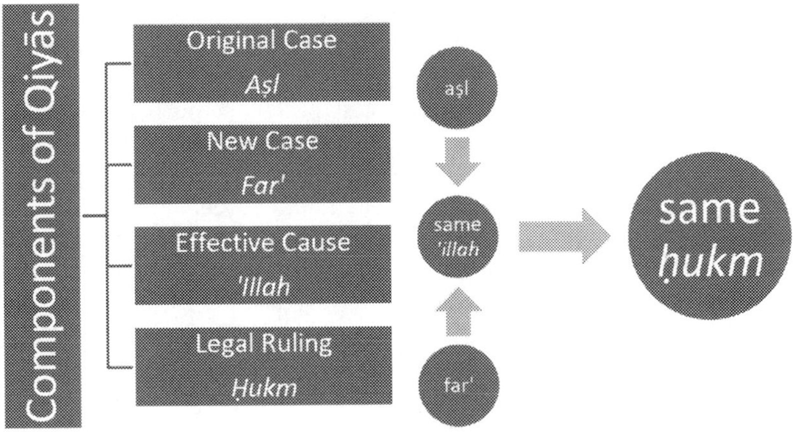

Figure 7.1 (a) Essential components of analogical reasoning. (b) Ratio legis in *Qiyās* and formulating a new ruling.

Source: Authors own.

An example of *Qiyās* in *Fiqh al-Mu'āmalāt* is the prohibition of *bay'* (buying and selling) during Friday prayer time. Does this prohibition extend to doing agricultural work, which is not mentioned in the verse? The same ruling will apply because the *'illah* is diverting one's attention or focus from the remembrance of Allah at time of the Friday prayer. The purpose of Qiyas is not to originate a rule of law but *qiyas* is rather a *muẓhir* (exposer) and not a *muthbit* (originator). Muslims believe that only Allah is the Originator of law. Therefore, the fuqahā' have identified various categories of *Qiyās*.

something on which another thing is suspended or hung. The *mujtahid's* job is to determine which quality or attribute (*waṣf*) present in both the *aṣl* and the *far'* is most appropriate or relevant. So, he might come up with an array of *'ilal*. There are many techniques used to identify the *'illah*; it might be mentioned in the text itself, sometimes it needs to be deducted, and at times there is indication in the text. From these *'ilal* the *mujtahid* needs to carry out what's called *taḥqīq al-manāṭ*. After discovering the underlying cause for the *ḥukm* in the *aṣl*, the jurist turns towards the underlying cause in the new case. This is the verification of the *'illah* in the *maqīs 'alayhi*, known as *taḥqīq al-manāṭ*.

> Taḥqīq al-manāṭ is increasingly important especially amongst contemporary legal reformers such as Bin Bayyah, who clarifies the process of taḥqīq al-manāṭ as "identifying problems as they appear in the real world (al-wāqiʿ), paying close attention to their real-life circumstances, in order to then apply the ruling (ḥukm) of the original case. The difference between this process and al-Qiyās (analogical reasoning) is that the former one does not join something to an original case (so as to bring it within its purview), but instead one applies the ruling based on the ʿillah which has now acquired the status of a universal.
> (*Bin Bayyah, 2015, p. 9*)

This is again the focal point of attempts at *ijtihād* today. *Tanqīh al-manāt* and *takhrīj al-manāt*, whilst both processes of discovering the *'illah* or legal ratio, do so with the legal text exclusively, as opposed to *tahqīq al-manāt*, which is where the "real-life circumstances" or, for the purposes of our discussion, financial instruments are the object. Ibn Taymiyya provides the example of knowing that interest-bearing transactions, whether *ribā al-faḍl, ribā al-nasī'ah*, or loans which provide an additional benefit to the lender, are impermissible. This impermissibility is inferred from textual evidence, which speaks about *ribā.* What the jurists require is knowledge of the types of transactions and contracts, which are governed by such texts. This is essentially what *taḥqīq al-manāṭ* is.

The methods mentioned above are not restricted to any one *madhab* and transcend their respective legal frameworks of interpretation. The scholars, both classical and contemporary, draw up boundaries for what are considered judgments so definitively established by textual evidence, namely Quran and *Sunnah*, that they are not susceptible to change. These texts that are definitive in terms of their interpretations and transmission are known as *qaṭ'ī al-dalālah wa al-thubūt*. Any legal matters which fall outside of this category are where there is interpretive freedom for the jurist. The maxim states, "There is no ijtihad in the face of clear textual evidence" *lā ijtihāda ma'a al-naṣṣ*. This represents the starting point of where the jurists attempt to draw boundaries of legitimate and farfetched interpretations. Jurists argue that it is not permissible after having established that something is definitively permissible or impermissible to investigate their legality, nor are they suitable for *ijtihad*; anyone who differs from such a ruling is categorically mistaken. As far as probabilistic interpretations are concerning *dalālah dhanniyya*, then the scope for interpretive flexibility is much broader. This might be due to the type of hadīth that form the basis of a ruling being singular (*khabar wāhid*) as opposed to mass-transmitted (*mutāwatir*), or the interpretation may be based on *Qiyās* and the process of drawing an analogy usually entails some subjectivity.

Role of 'Urf in Fiqh al-Mu'āmalāt

'Urf, or customary practice, is from the tertiary sources of Uṣūl al-Fiqh. However, this does not mean that its function is not substantial; in fact, its consideration is pivotal. Firstly, it is important to acknowledge that commercial dealings which fall under the slightly broader category of *mu'āmalāt* are rational (*ma'qūl al-ma'nā*). Hence, it is possible for the jurist to discover the "legislative intent"[7] of the legislator (*al-shāri'*), who in this case is Allah. Commercial law is inextricably linked to business practice and custom, which falls under the rubric of *'ādāt*, and *'ādāt* are essentially based on some rationale. al-Shatibi surmises a relevant *qā'idah* as follows: "*Ritual acts ('ibādāt) of worship are fundamentally devotional (ta'abbudī) where there is no point in investigating the legislative intent (ma'nā) whereas commercial and civil*

matters (mu'āmalāt) are based on some identifiable rationale". Furthermore, the methods and means with which commercial transactions and dealings are conducted are much more susceptible to change and development over time, with the added variables of economic systems, conditions, commercial customs, and changing markets. This is recognized by jurists and traditionists alike. al-Bukhari dedicates a relevant chapter of his Sahih to matters pertaining to the law of sales containing a number of *ahādith* which illustrate that certain *ahkām* (rules) were based on commercial custom, Ibn Hajar comments in his Fath al-Bāri that the objective of this section is "*to establish the reliance on custom (al-'Urf).*"

Ibn Taymiyya similarly expresses that *'ādāt* are those essential matters which people have grown accustomed to, the basis of which is permissibility. He then specifically states that *bay'* (sales), *hibah* (unilateral contracts), *ijārah* (leasing), etc., are 'ādāt that are essential for daily life. The Shar'iah is based on certain ethical standards; thus it forbids that which has a corrupting effect, obligates that which is necessary, dislikes that which in inappropriate, and recommends that which has overwhelming benefit. This highlights the heightened significance and urgency of *ijtihad* in *mu'āmalāt* and matters pertaining to Islamic finance.

Qaṭ'ī and Dhannī

How then are we to know which rulings are not susceptible to change, and cannot be adapted according to custom? A *naṣṣ* (clear textual evidence) is categorized according to the probability of it being authentically transmitted as well as whether it uses language which might be interpreted in multiple ways. A *naṣṣ* whose authenticity or transmission is beyond doubt is referred to as *qaṭ'ī al-thubūt* (definitively established). The opposite is *ẓannī al-thubūt* (speculatively established), meaning a *naṣṣ* whose transmission does not yield absolute certainty. Similarly, interpretation of a text could be *qaṭ'ī al-dalālah* (definitive in its indication), in other words, not open to interpretation, or *ẓannī al-dalālah* (speculative in its indication) i.e., suspectable to multiple meanings (Kamali, 2006, pp. 1–15; Zysow, 2013).

Table 7.2 illustrates the four categories any *naṣṣ* would fall into, hence making clear for the jurist or researcher which rulings are based on evidence which

Table 7.2 Qaṭ'ī and Dhannī interpretation and authentication

	Transmission	*Indication*	*Subject to Ijtihād?*
1	Qaṭ'ī al-Thubūt	Qaṭ'ī al-Dalālah	NO
2	Qaṭ'ī al-Thubūt	Ẓannī al-Dalālah	YES
3	Ẓannī al-Thubūt	Qaṭ'ī al-Dalālah	YES
4	Ẓannī al-Thubūt	Ẓannī al-Dalālah	YES

Source: Authors' own.

does not lend itself to interpretation and those rulings which are arrived at or deduced from evidence which is not categorical. Speculative or probabilistic interpretations represent the vast majority of textual evidence as opposed to the first category, which is sparse. Hence, differences of opinion are a salient feature of Islamic law in general and considered to be a strength of the legal tradition, as it provides an invaluable resource for students of *fiqh*, reflecting a culture of legal pluralism and fertile ground for *ijtihad* in unprecedented circumstances, conditional, of course, that novel interpretations do not contradict any *dalīl qaṭ'ī* and are formulated in accordance with a systematic application of *qawā'id* and *ḍawābiṭ shari'iyya.* Zarkashi (1992) states "*Know that Allah does not establish all rulings in the shariah on the basis of dalālah qaṭ'īyyah, rather he makes most ẓannīyah thereby broadening its scope (li al-tawsī').*"

An important note here is that a textual interpretation may be *ẓannī.* However, if jurists should achieve consensus on it, then it is elevated to being *qaṭ'ī* such that it becomes unchangeable and outside of the remit of *ijtihad.* Similarly, *ẓannī* textual evidence might be the basis for certain *qawā'id* or *dawābit.* These *qawā'id* or *dawābit* which are inferred from a wide range of comprehensive sources are considered to be *qaṭ'ī*, despite being derived from disparate *Ẓannī* sources, such as the principle *"al-Umūr bi maqāsidihā"* (matters are determined according to their intentions)." Consider the following textual evidence:

> and if anyone leaves home as a migrant for Allah and His Messenger and is then overtaken by death, his reward from God is sure. God is most forgiving and most merciful.
>
> (*al-Qur'an, 4:100*)

> He (Allah) will not call you to account for oaths you have uttered unintentionally, but He will call you to account for what you mean in your hearts…
>
> (*al-Qur'an, 2:225*)

> Actions are judged by intentions.
>
> (*Sahih al-Bukhari, Hadith No. 1*)

The first verse is explicit about how those who had migrated would be rewarded in accordance to their noble intentions should they pass away before having migrated. The second *ayah* is clear about Allah taking people to account for what the people intend rather than what they might say. These two ayahs would be considered to be *qaṭ'ī* in terms of their transmission. However, extracting the legal maxim that all matters are determined according to their intentions is a case of extension or interpretation, which is why the *dalālah* would be considered to be *ẓannī.* The final text is a hadith, although more explicit in wording. The meaning is more general, such that it would encompass a multitude of scenarios. It is a solitary narration, which means it is *ẓannī al-dalālah,* and hence the potential for interpretation is applicable. However, although these texts are *ẓannī* in isolation, when this evidence is taken together, the sheer number of texts which convey a common theme or meaning elevate this common theme or maxim to being *qaṭ'ī*.[8]

Al-Shatibi argues that the broad principles gathered through a broad inductive survey of a great amount of *ẓannī* evidence on a similar theme, when considered together, are able to yield certainty or *qaṭ'* (Hallaq, 1997, pp. 164–180). Hallaq writes, "This certainty is engendered by virtue of the fact that these principles have been attested to by a wide variety of pieces of evidence, which, in their totality, lead to certitude, although when taken individually they do not rise above the level of probability" (ibid, p. 166). This again stresses that it would be a mistake to conceive of *Uṣūl al-Fiqh* as providing the basis for legal rulings and reasoning, thus yielding more certainty, and *Qawā'id Fiqhiyya* playing second fiddle. They are both indispensable to the interpretive process.

Al-Khinn (2000) provides a detailed study of each of the sources of Islamic law and discusses their proof value and ultimately whether they are considered to be *qaṭ'ī* or *ẓannī*. A selection of some of his findings are provided below, which might act as a guide for researchers in Islamic finance:

- The Qur'an has been mass transmitted (*tawātur*), hence it is *qaṭ'ī al-thubūt*.
- Aspects of the Sunnah have also been transmitted via *tawātur* and therefore are *qaṭ'ī al-thubūt*.
- With regards to *khabar wāhid* (solitary narrations), those which have been unanimously accepted by the jurists are also *qaṭ'ī* in their indication.
- *Ijma' Sarih* is a *qaṭ'ī* evidence when transmitted via *tawātur,* otherwise it is *ẓannī.*
- *Ijma'* that takes place after being debated still affords definitiveness.
- *Ijma'* could rest on *ẓannī* evidence; however, it would still be considered *qaṭ'ī.* Qiyas is *qaṭ'ī* if the *'illah* is specifically mentioned in the textual sources or if there is a consensus on the analogical deduction. All remaining types of qiyas are *ẓannī.*

The categorization of *Qaṭ'ī* and *Ẓannī,* and the *Usūl al-Fiqh* discourse allow us to draw up boundaries for interpretation and clarify for us when something is categorically established as prohibited according to the Quran and *Sunnah*. Any legal system rests on a delicate balance between providing both certainty or consistency and flexibility. *Usūl al-Fiqh* and *Qawā'id Fiqhiyyah,* when taken together, have the potential to provide precisely that balance. What follow are examples of rulings that are based on evidence that is *qat'ī al-dalālah* and *qaṭ'ī al-thubūt*, hence unchangeable, and a ruling that is based on text that is *qaṭ'ī al-thubūt* and *ẓannī al-dalālah,* hence open to some adaptation.

> Allah (swt) has allowed trade and forbidden usury.
>
> (*al-Qur'an, 2:275*)

> O you who have faith! Be wary of Allah and abandon [all claims to] what remains of usury, should you be faithful.
>
> (*Quran, 2:278*)

> The Prophet cursed the receiver and the payer of interest, the one who records it and the two witnesses to the transaction and said: 'They are all alike.
>
> (*Sahih al-Muslim, Hadith No. 1598*)

> A dirham of riba which a man receives knowingly is worse than committing adultery thirty-six times.
>
> (*Sunan Ahmad, Hadith No. 3375*)

The first two verses quoted would be considered to be *qaṭ'ī al-thubūt,* as they are Quranic, and *qaṭ'ī al-dalālah,* as they are general (*āmm*) and clear (*sarīh*), with no ambiguity about their meaning. The hadith that follow would be considered to be *ẓannī al-thubūt,* as they are what traditionists term *khabar wāhid* (solitary narrations); however, the textual indications are clear in their meanings. Lastly numerous scholars, including al-Nawawi, Ibn Taymiyya, and al-San'āni, state that there is an *ijmā'* (consensus) on the impermissibility of engaging in usurious transactions, be it a small or large amount of interest. A consensus of this type would be considered to be definitive and forms a binding precedent. Hence, this relatively small number of sources alone establishes the impermissibility of *ribā* and rules out attempts to exercise any interpretive license.

The example of *Gharar* is based on evidence which is *qaṭ'ī al-thubūt* yet *ẓannī al-dalālah,* namely the verses: "Do not consume your property wrongfully, nor use it to bribe judges, intending sinfully and knowingly to consume parts of other people's property" (Quran, 2:188) and "You who believe, do not wrongfully consume each other's wealth but trade by mutual consent. Do not kill each other, for God is merciful to you" (Quran, 4:29). The exegetes often interpret the phrase "not consuming property wrongfully" to mean *gharar* or other exploitative business practices. The hadith "The Messenger of Allah (saw) prohibited the *gharar* sale, and the *hasah* sale" (Tirmidhi) is far clearer in its indication. Hence, it would be considered *qaṭ'ī al-dalālah*; however, due to the fact it is a solitary narration, it is *ẓannī al-thubūt.*

So where does that leave us with regards to *gharar*? Does that mean that *any* uncertainty in a transaction is impermissible? How do we determine what is or isn't *gharar*? How is *gharar* measured? The textual sources, namely Quran and *Sunnah,* do not provide us with details. This is where *Qawā'id Fiqhiyyah* plays a key role. The prohibition of *gharar* is to ensure there is transparency between all parties conducting business. This prevents deceit, aims to target asymmetric risk, and removes any injustice. Al-Dabbūsī writes that "a matter that is not to be litigated before a *qādi* is not affected by a minor uncertainty (*jahālah*) nor by an excess of it with respect to vitiation." In other words, *gharar* is left to be judged on a case-by-case basis. Anything which is likely to lead to dispute is relevant for *gharar* (Nyazee, 2016, p. 151). This offers a flexible approach to evaluating modern financial contracts and whether they would be deemed impermissible or otherwise. This approach also means that the concept of *gharar* would be evaluated in light of prevailing customs in commercial law, as will be seen later. Ibn Taymiyya articulates that the concept of *gharar* being understood this way means that it falls under the legal maxim "a widespread benefit is given precedence over a small amount of harm." For him, benefit is maximized by allowing trade rather than stifling it, and the harm which might come from *gharar yasīr* (a small amount of uncertainty) is negligible.

Researching Nawāzil in Islamic finance

After having expounded some of the key theoretical discussions and principles which underpin legal discussion in *Uṣūl al-fiqh*, this section provides practical steps which the jurist, practitioner, or researcher might take in evaluating modern financial instruments.

- Understand the legal problem at hand - The maxim states that *al-ḥukm 'ala shay far'un 'an tassawwurihī*. This means that jurists or lawyers should consult with specialists, particularly in *fiqh* councils, and industry professionals.
- Investigate this new case in light of the Quran and *Sunnah*. This requires consulting works of Quranic exegesis, books of *Sunnah*, and their commentaries.
- Investigate this new case in light of the opinions of the companions. Consult books of *Sunnah* (prophetic narrations), *Āthār* (traditions), as well as books dedicated to compiling their views and judgments.
- Investigate this new case in light of the *madhāhib*. This includes the four imams, as well as those *madhabs* which did not necessarily survive, such as al-Thawrī, al-Ṭabarī, and Abū Thawr.
- Investigate this new case in light of fatwā collections, both contemporary and classical, e.g., Fatwā Alamgīrī.
- Investigate this new case in light of verdicts issued by *fiqh* councils and symposiums.
- Investigate this new case in light of academic scholarship (Figure 7.2).

Whilst the discussion from this chapter provides a glimpse of key elements of *Usūl al-Fiqh* and *Qawā'id Fiqhiyyah*, along with some general guidelines for researching unprecedented matters, a word of caution seems appropriate. *Ijtihād* is not a mechanical process which one can't slowly progress toward such as a mathematical problem. The framework for how to approach novel matters is largely based on the process highlighted above, which refers to primary sources and legal authorities throughout the ages, to produce a ruling

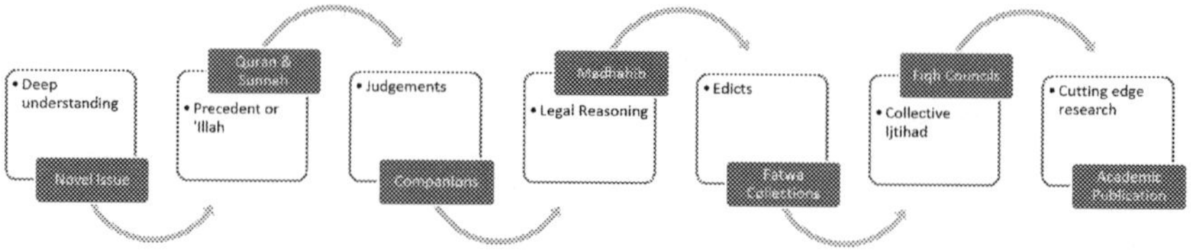

Figure 7.2 Step-by-step guidelines in researching Islamic finance.

Source: Authors' own.

which is coherent within the shariah system. The move towards any given argument is often persuasive, not conclusive. Thus the student of Islamic finance and economics needs to learn the process of valid legal reasoning by appealing to and balancing what has been presented.

Application of the Usūl al-Fiqh and Qawā'id Fiqhiyyah

Selling of stocks not yet transferred in one's name in the stock market system

The importance of the stock market is paramount in a modern financial economy. It is a very fast and volatile market. However, the issue is whether one can sell a stock one bought but which has not been transferred in one's name in the electronic system. The *fiqhi* issue is whether one can sell something one does not possess, as this leads to *gharar* because of the uncertainty in delivery the commodity being sold. This issue has been addressed above using the mechanism of *Istiḥsān* as a juristic tool. It was shown that the system to ensure the actual transfer of the stocks is very advanced. The rationale or *'illah* in hadith that stipulates you should not sell something that you do not have (*la tabi' mā laysa 'indak* is to eliminate *gharar*. But when the system is technologically very advanced, such level of *gharar fāḥish* (excessive uncertainty) does not manifest. Therefore, based on the principle of deeper analogy (*Istiḥsān*) such a sale has been allowed if the owner of the stock wants to do so despite the system has not transfer it on his name yet (Kamali, 2006). This principle is formulated in the aforementioned *qā'idah:* "a matter that is not to be litigated before a *qādi* is not affected by a minor uncertainty (*jahālah*) nor by an excess of it with respect to vitiation." (This is not short-selling, which is a different issue.)

Dealing in derivatives and Islamic solutions

A derivative is a financial instrument whose value is derived from the value of another asset, which is known as the underlying asset. When the price of the underlying asset changes, the value of the derivative also changes. A derivative is not a product. It is a contract that derives its value from changes in the price of the underlying asset from another contract. Hence, derivatives are highly premised on uncertainty (*gharar*). The majority of fuqaha have declared derivatives haram (with the exception of few who allowed it on the basis of necessity due to its importance in hedging risk) (Kunhibava, 2010). There are various types of derivatives. As an example, let us take the case of forward contracts used in agriculture, where parties enter a contract of sale to be effective in the future. So, in such an instance there is a contract within a contract. This is not allowed in Islam because we cannot sell something that does not exist yet (*Bay' al-Mādūm* issue). Secondly, the parties will only pay the actual difference in the prices in practice, which again goes against the spirit of *Fiqh al-Mu'āmalāt*. Both parties will exchange in the future which reflects *gharar fāhish*. All these are not allowed. However, due to the importance of hedging in the modern day, especially in the financial economy, Shariah scholars have developed substitutes for such instruments: *Bay' al-Salam*. This is the case where one purchaser will pay the entire price upfront (spot payment), and the seller is to deliver the specified quantity and quality of a specified fungible commodity, at a specified time and price. Logically, by applying qiyas, this should not have been allowed, as one is still entering a sale of something that one does not possess, or which might not be in existence yet. However, because of the hadith allowing such sale based on some conditions which the Prophet laid down, the hadith will have precedence over qiyas. So, by observing the conditions mentioned above, this mitigates the risk of *gharar* caused by *bay' al-mādūm*. The point is that understanding the derivative contract warrants a legal construction, which then allows fuqaha to provide a solution. So based on qiyas, forward contracts ought not be allowed, but in the presence of hadith, the qiyas is overturned. This is in line with the application of the principles of *Usūl al-Fiqh* to find solutions.

Determining the nature of shares

Shares are also a new commodity which Muslims have to deal with. The case law that laid the foundation in understanding the nature of shares is *Borland's Trustees v Steel* (1901 1 Ch 2791), where Farwell states that:

> a share is the interest of the shareholder in the company measured by a sum of money, for the purpose of liability in the first place, and of interest in the second, but also consisting of a series of mutual covenants entered into by the shareholders inter se in accordance with [s 14]. The contract contain in the articles of association is one of the original incidents of the share. A share is not a sum of money.... But is an interest measured by a sum of money and made up of various rights contained in the contract, including the right to a sum of money of a more or less amount. (Emphasis added)

This judgement negates the literal construction of the word "share" as understood by many Muslim jurists. It is apt to be misleading in relation to the present-day registered company. The purchase of shares in a company does not mean that the shareholder has a share in the property of the company, nor can a shareholder even be said to have an equitable interest in the company's property.

Hence, a share is a bundle of rights that shareholders deal with. Can this be a commodity? In determining what is commodity the fuqaha have identified three steps as mentioned above, either *Sharī'ah* has mentioned it as a commodity, or the definition is derived using *Uṣūl al-fiqh,* or it is based on market practice, which is known as *'urf*. For *'urf* to be valid, some conditions need to be met: e.g., it must not be against Quran and sunnah, it must be an existing prevailing practice, etc. Given that share contains a bundle of rights that accompany it and not necessarily the assets of the listed company, then based on *'urf* it can be considered as an asset class (Manjoo, 2005). So here *'urf* has been used to construct the legality of shares. Some relevant *qawā'id* which have been formulated for such questions, and based on *'Urf* include the following; "*Ādah* is considered when there is no clear text on the matter"; "'*Urf* will be taken into consideration in all things as long as there is no express statement/clause going against it"; "What is known by virtue of *'urf* is like an agreed condition"; and "What is customary practice amongst traders is like an agreed condition."

Takāful (Islamic insurance)

Insurance policy is another financial instrument whereby an insurance company guarantees an indemnity to the insured upon materialization of an insured risk in exchange of a premium to be paid by the insured. Such a contract contains *gharar*, as we do not know when the risk will materialize and how much will be the quantum of damages to be indemnified. There is also an element of riba in it as more money is received compared to what was paid for, and finally it can be argued that there is also certain element of *maysir,* as the insurance company, based on the law of probability and actuarial science, will bet that most probably the risk will not materialize and hence therefore, they decide to underwrite it. This legal construction helps the fuqaha to formulate a solution. These prohibitive elements (*gharar, ribā, and maysir*) occur in bilateral contracts (*'aqd al-mu'āwaḍah*), which leads to exploitation. For example, *ribā* is prohibited based on the verse "*Allah has permitted sale and forbidden ribā*" (Surah al-Baqarah, 2:275). This is from a primary source of Islamic law. Ribā is defined as an excess paid over an exchange contract for which there is no counter value. The prohibition of *gharar* is mentioned in the Sunnah. Again, the Sunnah is a primary source of law. Even *maysir* is prohibited based on Quranic verse (Surah al-Baqarah, 2:219). So, the fuqaha amended the structure of insurance policy and adopted a blend between an insurance for profit and mutual insurance. The clients will instead donate a contribution to the risk pool, which will be managed by the takaful operator. This donation is unilateral contract as compared to a unilateral contract.

Hence, the action emanates voluntarily from a single person and such action does not attract the prohibitive elements. The way the solution was formulated is based again on Quran and *Sunnah*. When the participants donate to the pool, the pool becomes a legal entity (AAOIFI Shari'ah's Standards 26/2). It is from that entity that participants in the pool are compensated for the loss accrued from materialization of an underwritten risk. This is based on the *takāful* agreement. Again, this example shows that a legal construction of the insurance policy is necessary in order to further develop a solution.

Conclusion

This chapter showed that in a modern-day financial economy, many products are developed that are based on the concept of financial instruments. These are widespread in the economy, and Muslims need them, but due to some prohibited elements in these products, alternatives are required for Muslim customers. To achieve this, legal constructions for these financial instruments are necessary in order to find solutions that are acceptable legally and Islamically. To achieve this, the Shariah scholars have to go back to Uṣūl al-Fiqh, wherein the sources of law are embedded. The other complementary approach is to utilize the maxims and legal mechanisms afforded by Qawā'id Fiqhiyyah. The examples of stocks, derivatives, shares, and insurance provide a glimpse of the way these juristic principles and their methodologies can be applied in today's time.

Notes

1 The Opinions or Legal Verdicts of the Companions could fall under rational rather than contextual sources. For an overview of the differing perspectives see Kamali (2006, pp. 313–322).
2 A foundational principle.
3 Novel legal case or unprecedented matters.
4 The subject matter that needs a ruling.
5 The thing upon which deduction is made by using syllogism.
6 Plural of 'illah.
7 Also a term used for statutory interpretation UK Law.
8 Note, these three texts represent a small sample of the textual evidence which allude to the legal maxim in question. For more examples please see.

References

AAOIFI Shari'ah Standard 26. http://aaoifi.com/ss-26-islamic-insurance/?lang=en

Al-Baghdādī, A. B. (2001) al-Faqīh wa al-Mutafaqqih. Riyadh: Dar ibn al-Jawzi.

Al-Ghazali, A. H. (1993) al-Mustasfa fi Uṣūl al-Fiqh. Beirut: Dar Kutub al-Ilmiyyah.

Aljloud, S. A. (2014) "Ijtihād and Ikhtilāf: Re-interpreting Islamic Principles in Contemporary Times" *Arab Law Quarterly*, 2014, Vol. 28, No. 1 (2014), pp. 85–98.

Al-Khinn M. (2000) Abhāth hawla Usūl al-Fiqh al-Islāmī. Damascus: Dar al-Kalim al-Tayyib.

Al-Shatibi, A. I. (2006) al-Muwāfaqāt fī Uṣūl al-Sharī'ah. Ed. by 'Abd Allah Darraz. Cairo: Maktabah Dar al-Hadith.

Bank of International Settlement (1995).

Hallaq, W. (1997) A History of Islamic Legal Theories: An Introduction to Sunni Uṣūl al-fiqh. Cambridge: Cambridge University Press.

Ibn Nujaym, Z. (1985) al-Ashbāh wa al-Nazā'ir. Dar al-Kutub al-'Ilmiyyah: Beirut

Ibn Qayyim, S. (1996) I'lām al-muwaqqi'īn 'an rabb al-'alamīn, ed. by Muḥammad 'Abdalsallām Ibrāhīm, 4 vols. Beirut.

Ibn Taymiyya, T. (2004) Minhaj al-Sunnah al-Nabawiyah Dar al-Hadith: Cairo vol. 5.

IPSAP (International Public Sector Accounting Pronouncements) (2020). Financial instruments: Disclosures (IPSAS 41). New York: International Federation of Accountants (IFAC).

Kamali, M.H. (2006) Principles of Islamic jurisprudence. Islamic Text Society: Cambridge.

Kunhibava, S. (2010) Derivatives in Islamic finance. Research Paper No.7/2010. Kula Lumpur: ISRA.

Manjoo, F. A. (2005) Reviewing the concept of shares: Towards a dynamic legal perspective. Jeddah IRTI.

Nyazee, I. K. (1994) Theories of Islamic law, the methodology of ijtihad. Kuala Lumpur: One Word Press.

Nyazee, I.A.K. (2016) Islamic legal maxims (Qawa'id Fiqhiyyah). Islamabad: Center for Excellence in Research.

Qaradawi, Y. (1996) Al-ijtihād fī al-sharī'ah al-islāmiyyah. Kuwait: Dar al-Qalam.

Usmani, T. (2002) An introduction to Islamic finance. Karachi: Maktabah Ma'ariful Quran.

Usmani, M.T. (2014) Maqālāt al-Uthmāni. Karachi: Ma'ārif al-Qurān.

Zarkashi, M.B. (1992) al-Bahr al-muhit fi Uṣūl al-fiqh Wizarat al-Awqaf. Kuwait: Wizarat al-Awqaf.

Zysow, A. (2013) The economy of certainty: An introduction to the typology of Islamic legal theory. Atlanta: Lockwood Press.

Part 2

SMART TEACHING METHODS FOR ISLAMIC ECONOMICS AND FINANCE

8

DEVELOPING PEDAGOGICAL METHODOLOGIES IN TEACHING ISLAMIC ECONOMICS

Imran H. Khan Suddahazai and
Sheikh Faizal Ahmad Manjoo

Introduction

The discipline of Islamic economics as an established body of study in Western academia is a recent innovative development, a tangible outcome, resulting from the desire of the revivalist Islamization of knowledge movements to gain parity and redress against the onslaught of materialistic economic policies as instituted by their former colonial masters. The contemporary study of economics in accordance with the classic or bible of the field, Joseph A. Schumpeter's *The History of Economic Analysis*, which established in essence the accepted history of economic thought and analysis, by dating the birth of analytical economics to the 18th century. Here the gatekeepers to the discipline of economics decided to attribute ideas related to the development of economics solely to Western European proponents by completely disregarding the contribution of Islam and Muslim civilization to the field of economics (Ali and Thompson, 1999). A possible reason for this omission, which does not necessarily legitimize the omission, is due to the variance in the epistemological and ontological foundations of Western secularist functionalism and Islamic worldview, based upon the notion of "tawhid" and divinity. Furthermore, any extant discussions and awareness of the subject of economics, especially in the late 18th century were based upon classical commentaries by such luminaries as Abu Yusuf, Ibn Salam Ibn Taymiyah, Al-Ghazali, etc., which were entirely based upon Shari'ah and fiqhi orientation. Although there were obvious exceptions to this perspective, such as Ibn Khaldun, referred to as the father of the social sciences, whose approach was primarily sociological, his magna corpus *al-Muqaddimah* represents a systematic examination of society and established the benchmark for the scientific study of society. Arguing from this Khaldunian framework, it is presented that those certain aspects of the current economic system are in coherence with Islamic principles. This is because Islam does not reject the secular or

DOI: 10.4324/9781003252764-11

physical mundane world but unequivocally attempts to provide guidance in regulating and managing it as a collective society.

Islamic pedagogical paradigm

In order to explicate the Islamic notions of pedagogical approaches to teaching Islamic economics, it must be recognized that the process of education as deciphered from the classical Islamic sciences and tradition is based upon a *transformation* in the learners' behavior. This implies that the learner's behavior is changed as a result of the knowledge, they acquire, analyze, and apply. From an Islamic lens, it can be understood that the dialogical nature of the sacred revelations reveals the essence of the educational process as a series of conversations, questions, and answers revealing Allah (swt) to be an educator, a teacher to His Prophets. This suggests that education conceived from a dialogical process is a continuous narrative. The conversation pertains to the purpose, relationship, and responsibility of the human being as Allah's (swt) Khalifa upon the earth. The essence of this relationship is imbued in the revelation and content of the Quran, whereby Muhammad (s), from a human perspective, embodies the divine educational model. As a role model, Muhammad (s) is acknowledged to be a perfect example of a leader, or *imam*, who goes before his people in the capacity of teacher (Quran, 2:151). The Quran explicitly declares that in the personhood of the Prophet "*is an excellent example (uswah hasanah)...*" (Quran, 33:21). Adair (2010) argues that in contemporary parlance, Prophet Muhammad (s) is a "*role model.*" The designation of Role implies "*... by origin a part taken by an actor in a play, but in our wider use it means a person's characteristic or expected function ...*" whilst a "*'Model' is a person who is regarded by others as an outstandingly good example of a particular role*" (Adair, 2010, p. 1). According to Gregg, when this notion of role model is applied to "*God, the Prophets, the saints and teachers ... it might be termed a 'Sacred Other ... from whose perspective a believer sees themselves and perceives the discourse for creating and performing one's self*" (Gregg, 2005, p. 112).

In normal human relations, this epitomizes the relationship between a teacher and a student. The notion of responsibility is in upholding the ethical and moral virtues in the relationship. Sahin (2013) states that the Quranic notion of *tarbiya* encapsulates a method that entails the holistic development of an individual through a systematic process of nurturing, care, and guidance (17:24; 22:5; 26:18). It is the "*gradual, stage by stage developmental process informing an organism's growth until the complete actualization of its potential*" (Sahin, 2013, p. 182).

Although the focus upon pedagogy appears to be a new development in recently produced Islamic educational literature, there exists a rich and well-developed notion of pedagogy in the Muslim tradition. The Quranic narrations reiterate the literal and metaphorical methods of the Prophets to guide and educate society through purification (*tazkiyah*) (2:151), pedagogical practices that encompass contemplation (*tafakkur*), remembrance (*tadhakkur*), reflection (*tadabbur*), understanding (*tafaqquh*), gathering insight (*tabassur*), discerning between matters (*tawassum*), and considering all perspectives (*nazar*) before deriving the instructive lesson (*i'tibar*) from the episode itself. Seminal work by Makdisi (1981) further demonstrates that the methods of education utilized in contemporary secular institutes such as the lecture (*qira'at*), note writing, (*ta'liqat*), disputation (*tariqat an-nazar*), dialectics (*jadal*), and discourse (*munazara*), were being utilized in Muslim educational institutions several hundred years before medieval European universities adopted them.

In a continuation of this tradition of knowledge exchange and sharing, it is recommended that the reader familiarize themselves with the contemporary research on pedagogical approaches. This will facilitate their teaching of economics by introducing them to new methods and applications that have been empirically tested, validated, and analyzed for their usefulness (Ahmed, 2009). This includes an informed awareness of the most significant philosophical school of sciences, such as the behaviorist[1] and constructivist[2] schools and their respective approaches to pedagogy.[3]

From a behaviorist perspective, this pertains to the influence of ideas derived from the work on classical conditioning and its variants by Skinner (1953). The notion of *classical conditioning* is classified as an unconscious method of learning, whereby conditioned responses are paired with specific stimuli to create learnt behavior.[4] This has also been discussed by classical Muslim scholars, from Ibn Sina's discussions on the relationship between memory formation and the unconditioned and neutral stimulus to Al-Ghazali's early promulgation of Pavlov's experimentations in describing the role of the imagination and its ability produce physical responses in the human body. Meanwhile, from the Constructivist perspective, closely related to the notion of *tarbiya*, the educators must begin to appreciate ideas related to human learning and knowledge formation as a construction and reflection of the social environmental context of the learner. Therefore, knowledge is not passed on from teacher to student but is systematically developed upon antecedent cognitive structures that the student is seeking to develop, augment, or change. Learners are guided towards relying upon prevailing knowledge, experiences, and perspectives to grasp new learnings, a process that is assisted by the environment and the engagement with teachers and peers (Sahin, 2013).

This point further validates the argument around universal truths and knowledge existing in all traditions and approaches.[5] Therefore, it is imperative that Muslim educators utilize all available lenses to conduct an in-depth examination of their own actions, training methods, and recommended styles of teaching upon the learners and the learning process. The traditionalist Muslim pedagogical models as exemplified through the classical madrasah institutes[6] have always utilized "*... a fluidity within knowledge acquisition that is discussed in the context of the interplay between memorization and orality and the clarity of thought from a pedagogical perspective on the role of the text ... the use of the written word in supporting knowledge acquisition.*"

This is a unique relationship, specific to the Islamic tradition via a cultural Arabic heritage, which perceives a seamless transmission of knowledge with consideration to prophecy, belief, and the justification of it through an oral history, the spoken word committed to memory. The inevitable consequence of this is that the interplay between memorization, orality, and the written word enables the acquisition of knowledge through a spiritual lens. The great theologian, Al-Ghazali (d. 1111) argued that students would become aware of and be able to distinguish between the knowledge required to transition to the hereafter and the knowledge base that would allow them to conduct their affairs within the secular world (Sheikh and Ali, 2019).

This inimitable Islamic pedagogical approach finds validity in many of the contemporary cognitive perspective on theories of learning, such as cognitivism, which explores the learners' mental capacities. For instance, Chomsky (1962) observed that a certain high level of learning could only be attained via a consolidation of conditioning that is informed with an insight into the internal mental state of the learner, which encompasses an appreciation for mental constructs such as beliefs, memories, and emotions (Chomsky, 1962).

This is also supported both implicitly and explicitly by Bandura's social learning theory, which attempts to blend both behavioral and cognitive theories within a social context (Bandura, 1989). His discussions on the notions of observational learning, whereby a students' behavior changes due to observations they have made of others (Bandura, 1989), confirms the traditional practice of *taqlid* (imitation) from the classical Muslim tradition. The point of this was not to induce blind imitation or a pure form of indoctrination but to lead the student through a process of self-development and realization, until the point they could, through the concept of self-efficacy, take positive action to actively formulate their own independent perspectives. The plethora of great early scholars from the golden era of Islam is an example of this approach.

In seeking to recommend and explicate upon recommended pedagogical approaches towards teaching economics from an Islamic perspective, a firm appreciation of the Islamic *Weltanschauung* (worldview) is essential. The ontological reality of Islam, as encapsulated in the notion of unity (*tawhid*), is established upon a holistic perception of life that originates from a single source, the Creator. Therefore, fragmented and discursive approaches that seek to isolate and study phenomena as a series of independent processes contradict the Islamic worldview.

For instance, the conventional economics perspective is solely based upon a logico-scientific foundation, which defines the narrative of conventional or secular economics, and consequently, research pertaining to that narrative as being acceptable due to its theoretical or empirical validity, or totally rejected if not derived from the logico-scientific epistemological base.[7] This approach is perceived from an Islamic worldview to not be erroneous but incomplete and justifies the argument for Islamizing the social sciences due to this inherent epistemological bias. Hence, Islamic economics must develop an inherent awareness and narrative that is based upon the comprehension of the *tawhidic* worldview. This is, however, only possible if the concept of knowledge (*'ilm*), and its epistemology is conceived in duality. This deems the logico-scientific knowledge to formulate an aspect of the Islamic epistemological foundation, the secular, mundane. The other aspect is the divine, revealed knowledge, which interacts with the secular through a dialectical process that is mutual, reciprocal, balanced, and harmonious to arrive at a holistic and comprehensive understanding (*tawhid*) (Murata, 2001). In order to operate from this philosophical pedagogical method, the educator is recommended to adopt a critically reflective approach that is in line with the classical notions of education or *tarbiya*.

Critically reflective pedagogy

The notion of reflection here suggests that the educators are aware of the broad range of pedagogical methods available to them to utilize in accordance with the contextual circumstances and situation. The review of literature in the field advocates that educators firstly develop a holistic picture of their teaching practice, which is not solely constructed from tangible quantifiable outcomes such as exam or assessment results, but from the process leading to these ends.[8] The idea presented is that the reflective practitioner engages in a continuous dialogue with both their students and themselves with regards to their pedagogical practice and the students' experience of learning. This is supported by the educator's intimate knowledge, theoretically and practically, of the subject matter.

In applying Rahman's (1988) "double hermeneutical" method to the contemporary notion of critical pedagogy, it becomes comparable to the classical Islamic understanding of *tarbiya*. This pedagogical ideal can be further gleamed from an examination of the classical Islamic educational literature (Ibn Abd Al-Bur, d. 1044; Al-Mawerdi, d. 1058; Al-Baghdadi, d. 1070; Al-Ghazali, d. 1111; Al-Zarnugi, d. 1194; Ibn Jamaa'h, d. 1241), which sought the outcome of the educational process to be the creation of reflective practitioners.[9]

This approach is particularly useful for the teaching of economics from the Islamic perspective, as it suggests that pedagogical practices seeking to liberate individuals from indoctrinating banking models of education are in adherence to the Prophetic model. Freire's (1970) assertions on the purpose of pedagogy for humanization over dehumanization resonate profoundly with the ethos of Islamic pedagogical practice. His definition of violence as "… *any situation in which some individuals prevent other from engaging in the process of inquiry* …" (Freire, 1970, p. 85) could be used to define simultaneously the concept of justice in Islamic education and economic practice. Freire (1970), in seeking liberation for the oppressed, preaches liberation for the oppressor also, as it is a dialectical relationship, and the two parties are in a mutual and reciprocal relationship, just as it is in any economic transaction. Therefore, cross-cultural ideas that are considered to be revolutionary and paradigm-shifting, such as Freire's (1970) conception of critical pedagogy, find support in this general understanding of classical Islamic pedagogical practice.

As a suggestion for the educators seeking to engage further in self-reflective examination is the notion of *reflexive* practice. This approach is not based just on the practice but the *practitioner,* which naturally assumes the impact and influence of the broader individual, societal, and universal contexts within which practice transpires. This can be summarized as a query posed by both the reflexive teacher and the reflexive learner, as to how their own classroom behavior can then be analyzed in more depth: "*What did I do that was right or wrong, that worked or did not work?*" Rather the query would become more invasive, intimate, and introspective: "*Why do I do that which was right or wrong, that worked or did not work?*" and "*How did my past and current experience of life and work influence me in behaving in the particular way I did or in suggesting the particular courses of action I took?*"

Group research interactive teaching (GRIT)[10]

This is an overarching approach that effectively combines a number of pedagogical methods in individual learning within a group scenario. The learners are systematically walked through a series of stages to initially acquaint themselves with an ideal (*X*), to engage with it, and then apply it or teach it once they can demonstrate some elementary command over the divergent discourses and perspectives on that ideal (*X*). There are five defined stages, which the educator walks the learners through, with varying methods being employed in accordance with and consideration of the contextual situation of the class. This could include the prior experience and knowledge of the learners, the difference in learning abilities of the learners, or availability of expertise and facilities alongside the demands as in aims and objectives of the course (Figure 8.1).[11]

In order to demonstrate the workings of this framework, the subsequent section provides an idealized vision of how core topics within Islamic economics can be taught using the GRIT approach, alongside recommended introductory reading for each suggested pedagogical method.

	Teaching Phase	**Purpose**	**Pedagogical Methods**	**Assessment**
Stage 1	Engagement	Developing Topical Interest	Demonstration; Discussion; Questioning	Students are engaged in dialogue on the topic
Stage 2	Instruction	Introducing Core Knowledge	Didactic; Discussion; Lecture; Questioning	Students able to address set tasks from lecture
Stage 3	Collaboration	Formation of Working Groups	Autodidactic; Deductive/ Inductive; Inquiry Based; Project Orientated	Students able to collaborate and delegate shared responsibilities
Stage 4	Application	Presentation of Research	Active; Autodidactic; Demonstration; Experiential; Role Playing	All Group Members Participate in the Research and Presentation Phase
Stage 5	Evaluation	Feedback	Discussion; Reflection	Successful Completion of Module Learning Outcomes and Objectives

Figure 8.1 The structural framework of the GRIT pedagogical method.

Pedagogical teaching illustration

Critically reflective pedagogical approaches in exploring the worldview of the homo economicus and the homo Islamicus

Stage 1: Engagement

This is the introductory stage, whereby students are introduced to the topical subject matter. The introduction acts as a foundational conduit for further exploration and engagement.

Pedagogical approaches

A combination of methods – conversations, discussions, questions, and group work – can be used alongside presentations: visual (video: news, current affairs); auditory (radio, podcasts, etc.); print (newspaper, journal articles); and social media.

Conversational

This approach can be wonderfully summarized in the example provided by Colander: "*...when Ptolemy I, the king of Egypt, wanted to learn geometry, Euclid told him that it would take long hours of study and memorization. When the king demanded a shortcut, Euclid responded 'there's no royal road to geometry'. To that I would add, there's no 'relating road' to learning economics*" (2004). This essentially implies that the sound practice of teaching is related more to the notion of motivation than relating to students on an individual, personal level. Colander argues that issues related to teaching are "*getting our students to exercise their mind... Some things just need to be done over and over again to learn, and others need to be memorized*" (Ibid). This does not imply that teachers merely preach to the students, as per the old instructional models of learning. It suggests that teachers utilize conversational tones to communicate with their students rather than long monotonous lectures that merely teach facts. The literature suggests that the most effective way in which students learn is by enabling them to discuss issues related to economics in a class or group setting, investing their time in reading about and around the economy, then feeding that back through class-based assessments, such as presentations and weekly quizzes on topical issues covered in the media arising from current affairs. This method resonates with the classical Muslim approach in first contemplating (*tafakkur*), reflecting (*tadabbur*), and understanding (*tafaqquh*) the issue by collating research and gathering insight into the issue (*tabassur*), which allows them to discern between arguments (*tawassum*) as they take all perspectives into consideration (*nazar*) before learning from the process as an instructive lesson (*i'tibar*).

The educator should seek to introduce the topic by relating it directly to the experience of the students. The session could begin with a brief introduction on the study of conventional economics based upon the premise of the idealistic "economic man," the *homo economicus*, the economic agent of modern economics thought, whose purpose is to enjoy or maximize utility. From the Islamic perspective or Islamic economics there is an equivalent economic man, identified as the *homo Islamicus,* the Islamic man. This man is characterized as a paradigm of righteousness imbuing Prophetic qualities within his own micro-foundation (Hafas, 2015).

Questions, discussion, and group work (Brookfield, 2005)

The students in the class can be organized into two groups to address specific questions related to the *homo economicus* and the homo Islamicus. These broad questions should garner their interest and uncover their understanding from the discussion thus forth.

Group 1: Questions such as: What is the reality of the *homo Islamicus* in the real world? Is the ideal of the *homo Islamicus* attainable?

Group 2: Questions such as: Can the *homo economicus* be altruistic? Does the *homo economicus* take into consideration moral or religious values?

Assessment

This can be conducted through group feedback led by students. An indicator of the successful completion of this stage is student interest in the topic through active participation, sharing ideas and perspectives with their peers in the class discussion. Experience demonstrates that engaged and informed students will provide responses which acknowledge that:

Group 1: The nature of the *homo economicus*, as being characterized by greed and selfishness, is more akin to reality then the idealistic *homo Islamicus*.

Group 2: The *homo economicus* is responsible for the destruction of the environment, due more to his insatiable appetite for consumption based upon his experience of pleasure or pain than any philosophical worldview.

Any students not engaging with the class can be given special attention to engage their interest, confidence, and self-efficacy in a more private personal conversation. These students can then be monitored for their progress. The time attributed to this stage is dependent upon the course, module time, and period duration. This stage could last years for extremely complex studies and projects to months for research projects to weeks for course modules or even hours and minutes for shorter courses. The total period of this stage is at the discretion of the educators and how quickly they are able to engage their students.

Stage 2: Instruction

This is a developmental stage, whereby students are introduced to the core concepts and aspects of their course. This stage establishes the foundational premises upon which the subject will be examined and taught.

Pedagogical approaches

Didactic; presentations as in Stage 1; delivery of a lecture followed by engagement with the students via an open discussion on core points.

Lecture (Bligh, 1998)

This can begin by exploring the conventional definition and understanding of economics. Students should be provided with examples and visual representations of the argument surrounding the concepts of maximization of utility and their influence upon the individual decision-making process. The lecture can discuss the works of Bentham and Mill, for instance, to provide a historical account and awareness of the heritage on the discourse of contemporary economics. Students should become familiar with the development in ideas such as the idea from classical economics that utility or usefulness implies "*the greatest happiness principle*," or as Mill advocated, "*utility is not only a pleasure, but pleasure itself with exemption from pain*." To demonstrate the impact of these early ideas, the development of utilitarianism could be mentioned, and references provided to those students who desire to examine this further. These ideas and formulations could then be contrasted with modern understanding of individual preference. This implies that an individual will always select the best option or what is in their interest, if presented with an option or choice. Therefore, the concept of utility is now understood to imply that individuals as rational beings will act in their best self-interest (Ibid, p. 6). Thus, the notion of utility has transformed from a mere representation of pleasure in the absence of pain to an instrument to measure and quantify human happiness and satisfaction through the acquisition, possession, or desire of material goods and services (Furqani, 2015, p. 81).

Reflection[12]

Students should then be asked to reflect upon the information provided and tasked to compile a synopsis of the notes made during the lecture.

Discussion

This should then take place during the tutorial sessions, which examine the critique surrounding the *homo economicus* as existing to maximize his own self-gratification at the expense of others in a zero-sum game and that in real life, human beings are irrational and unpredictable.

Assessment

This is conducted through a discussion on the reflective notes of the students during the tutorial discussions. Students will have been expected to take notes, reflect upon the lecture, and share those notes with their tutorial group and tutor. The educator can assess to gauge the level of participation, engagement, and understanding of the student during these sessions. Further guidance can also be provided at this stage, as well as identifying good practice and progress.

In this example, Stage 2 shall be repeated, as it is presenting the Islamic aspect to economics through a didactic approach.

Stage 2a: Instruction for dual application

This is a developmental stage, whereby students are introduced to core concepts and aspects of their course. This stage establishes the foundational premises upon which the subject will be examined and taught.

Pedagogical Approaches: Didactic; presentations as in Stage 1; delivery of a lecture followed by engagement with the students via an open discussion on core points.

Lecture: This can begin by exploring the Islamic definition and understanding of economics. Students should be provided with examples and visual representations of the argument surrounding the arguments of the epistemological bias in economics methodology, the secular as opposed to the Islamic worldview. The lecture can then discuss the Islamic worldview and the concept of *maslahah* rather than maximization as the ends for *homo Islamicus*. Then the definitions and understandings of *maslahah* could be explored, from its connotations of a guarantee of provisions and protection by Allah to its use in fiqh and spiritual practice. The three main characteristics of the *maslahah* from the Shari'ah perspective can also be introduced. First, *maslahah* is not just limited to *maslahah dunyawiyyah* (worldly affairs), but also to *maslahah diniyyah* (religious purposes) as well. All decisions of the existing law should be based on the Qur'an and Sunnah. Secondly, *maslahah* is not limited to the externalized physical, but is equally applicable to the metaphysical realm, or the inner spiritual dimension. Thirdly, the determination of *maslahah* is not limited to this existence or life but is applicable in the hereafter.

Arguments around the acceptance and rejection of maximization should also be introduced to demonstrate the diversity in Islamic economics, with some authorities rejecting the use of maximization, whilst others accommodate it with stipulations.

At this stage, students can be asked reflective questions to ponder upon and discuss in their tutorial groups. Questions as posed by Furqani, for instance (Furqani, 2015, p. 81):

- What is to be maximized, utility or *maslahah*, the choice between pain-pleasure or beneficial-harmful?
- What for is the maximization, the choice between self-satisfaction-pleasure or self-actualization-transformation?
- What are the instruments or means required to achieve them?

Demonstration[13]

An example of a *mujtahid* can be utilized to demonstrate his *ijtihad* to make a legal decision; the considerations of the consequences he would have to consider.

Reflection

Students should then be asked to reflect upon the information provided and tasked to compile a synopsis of the notes made during the lecture.

Discussion

This should then take place during the tutorial sessions, which examine the critique surrounding the *homo Islamicus* and the maximization of *maslahah* and its application to not only human concerns, but also environmental issues. Consideration here should be given to the consumption of halal and tayyib goods and services (*al-Qur'an*, 2:168), explicit warning against wanton extravagance and expenditure (*al-Qur'an*, 6:141; 17;27), the call for generosity (*al-Qur'an*, 25:67), rejection of hedonism (*al-Qur'an*, 89:20), etc.

Assessment

This is conducted through a discussion on the reflective notes of the students during the tutorial discussions.

Students will have been expected to take notes and reflect upon the lecture and share those with their tutorial group and tutor. The educator can assess to gauge the level of participation, engagement, and understanding of the student during these sessions. Further guidance can also be provided at this stage, as well as identifying good practice and progress.

Stage 3: Collaboration

This is a transitory period for the students, as they are developing into informed and engaged learners. At this stage, learning is essentially student-centered, with an emphasis on group work and use of variety of resources.

Pedagogical approaches

A combination of methods to be deployed: Autodidactic/Didactic; Enquiry based learning; Group Work Scaffolding; Presentations as in Stage 1; Delivery of a Lecture followed by engagement with the students via an open discussion on core points.

Enquiry-Based Learning (EBL)[14]

This is a student-led type of learning where the process of enquiry is driven by the students through group work. Having become familiar with the issues in the field in Stages 1 and 2, students begin to identify their own areas of interest and developing questions. The educator acts a guide and facilitator to aid the students with relevant knowledge and research directions alongside ensuring the students take responsibility for what and how they learn. In this case, EBL is used in conjunction with didactic instruction to provide guidance to new students to the field. More advanced students can dispense with this type of guidance and begin to work on their own research directions and interests.

Group work

Students can be split into groups, depending on the number of students. In this example there are two working groups for analytical demonstration.

Didactic instruction

A premise is presented to the groups, alongside reading material and references with regards to their particular areas of enquiry and interest leading from the premise.

THE PREMISE HERE COULD BE[15]

The reason as to why economics emerged as an academic discipline is to theorize the issue of resolving the problem of scarcity, which man faces in satisfying his basic economic needs and wants for his daily life. Often these are referred to as the basic economic needs of man: food, clothing, and shelter. But the reality is that in our modern time more economic needs can be added to this list, such as education and health. One of the premises of this theory is that man's wants are unlimited while the resources to produce these myriad needs and wants are limited. The resources needed to produce the services and commodities that man needs are known as the four factors of production, i.e., land, labor, capital, and entrepreneurship.

These two concepts, basic economic needs and factors of production, logically have a universal value. However, from an Islamic economics point of view it ought to be viewed differently and taught differently.

Objective

To work independently in your groups to research and discuss why, from the Islamic economics point of view it ought to be viewed differently and taught differently.

Autodidactic[16] or Independent Group Work

The students in the class can be organized into two (or more) groups. From past experience, the groups have managed to independently develop their research from the initial guidance and provide research discussions, such as the following examples:[17]

Group 1

From the Islamic economics point of view, it should be viewed differently and taught differently. The reason is because there is an Islamic element of attaining economic justice, which warrants a close look at these concepts. As far as Muslims are concerned, there are restrictions as to the extent man can satisfy his needs. There is the concept of *homo Islamicus* as compared to *homo economicus*. These two concepts have a major impact on the theory of consumption, production, and distribution, regarding allocation of the factors of production and also theory of expenditure. Muslims cannot consume whatever they wish, nor they are allowed to indulge in excessive consumption and shopping sprees, (i.e., *isrāf*) or to be spendthrifts (*tabzīr*). This automatically influences what is to be produced, unlike in a capitalist system, where profit maximization drives production. Muslims need to appreciate that the entire theory of waste management and circular economy is an integral part of Islamic economics. This is where the narrative discourse comes into the curriculum. Islam has an entire concept on expenditure, and this must be inculcated in Muslims so that an economy develops that takes into account the circular economy and waste management, both at a micro- and macroeconomic levels. The Quran emphatically rebuts those who want to spend the way they wish. The Quran describes their behavior: "*They are those who spend neither wastefully nor stingily*" (25:67). They spend moderately. Moderation in spending is considered as a virtue. At this point it is interesting to note that the word "economics" emanates from the Greek word *oiko nomía,* which means "household management." But the famous hadith *al-iqtisād fi nafaqati nifs al-ma'īshah*, moderation in spending is half or livelihood, highlights the theory of spending in Islam, which should be a very good yardstick in addressed the issue of scarcity. The word *iqtisād* is deeper than mere economizing. In Islam, despite being well-off financially, we must not waste and indulge. The rationale for this is that the resources can be used in satisfying more of what society needs in such a way that it meets the *maqāasid al-Shari'ah*, i.e., protection of deen, life, progeny, intellect, and assets. This is why some economists have developed the maqāsid index to evaluate the way industries are developed. It should be inline in meeting these higher objectives. This is a major point of divergence when teaching economics. The combination of the various theories should tally with achieving these higher objectives.

Unlike capitalism, which focuses on consumerism at the expense of the entrepreneur becoming richer, Islam will encourage various approaches to entrepreneurship. Employees can become partners like in a *mudharabah* commercial arrangement context. Even in farming there are various ways employees are treated as partners. This approach mitigates the greed of entrepreneurs. Instead, it develops a system of cooperation rather than exploitation, as advocated by Marx for instance against capitalism.

Optimizing consumerism is not a solution to economic problems in Islam. Moderation is meant to optimize the use of the factors of production, which in turn is guided by Quran and Sunnah. One can argue that the entertainment industry and the gambling industry, for instance, contribute a lot towards the GDP of certain countries! The question is whether the GDP is always an appropriate measure for happiness of a nation or is it a camouflage of the real economic problem where people will be losing/wasting money via gambling. Hence, another way to resolve the issues of the theory of production, consumption, and distribution of commodities and services will be done within a given parameter so that an ethos can be attained. The *homo economicus* approach is to incline towards the utility theory (deriving satisfaction from consumption). On the other hand the *homo Islamicus* concept of satisfying one's utility would be different because the concept of pleasure is not only mundane, but it also has a continuation in the hereafter. The Muslims, when they obey the law, have hope for reward in the hereafter. In other words, by fasting and not consuming food, there is another level of satisfaction in our market behavior. So when teaching these fundamental principles, Islamic economics must take into account where the Muslim world ought to be. If a poor Muslim country will develop non-permissible industry or allocate resources to produce more luxuries than necessities, it will be difficult to remove the yoke of poverty.

Group 2

In order to differentiate the teaching of Islamic economics from conventional economics we are focusing on the *infāq* (philanthropic) sector. This is an altruistic and unique feature of Islamic economics. It is geared to legally channel resources in fulfilling the needs of the poor, unlike the laissez-faire economy, which operates on the price mechanism whereby a person will decide to buy something depending on the size of his pocket, as the market adjusts the price through the law of supply and demand. If he can afford what he wants, that is fine, or else he will be deprived, especially the lower strata of society. Under the state-owned economy, the state or government makes a unilateral decision about what to produce for whom, etc. Again, people cannot acquire many things they wish for. Under the mixed economy, the production of commodities and services is partially controlled by the government. In Islamic economics, though, there is a tendency for a laissez-faire economy based on the hadith *innallah huwa al-musa'ir* (very Allah is the controller of the price), which does not negate certain levels of control. In Islam we have the concept of *hisbah* (market control via accountability), which needs to be reactivated, as it stops not only market malpractices but also moral decadence. Again, this should be taught in order to inculcate the need to protect the market and moral behavior. These concepts, if implemented, will change consumer and producer behavior. Commodities that are more needed will be produced and there will be mitigation of Pareto optimality. Pareto efficiency or Pareto optimality is a situation where no individual or preference criterion can be better off without making at least one individual or preference criterion worse off or without any loss thereof. Without a marketplace, there is no place to sell what is being produced. Islam brings in a seminal concept of *hisbah* to ensure ethical behavior permeates the marketplace. This of course needs to be contextualized in the modern-day virtual market. This demands incorporation in the curriculum. Looking at the philosophy of the Quran, Allah says that "*in their wealth there is the right of the poor and destitute*" (51:19). Hence, it is mandatory to share with the poor exclusively. This falls outside the ambit of taxation we normally witness in monetary and fiscal policy. In Islam, priority is given in uplifting the poor. Therefore, the Quran says that by giving them money, there is more money in circulation, i.e., more velocity of currency in the economy, in the words of Willaim Petty. So the curriculum for Islamic economics should be geared toward activating this unique branch of alleviating poverty and help the people to satisfy their needs. In Islamic economics, methodologies should be developed to enhance the collection and distribution of this money for the *infāq* sector.

Scaffolding[18]

In order to support the weaker students, identified in the previous two stages, they are paired with individuals or within groups that will actively ensure these act as their support and mentoring network.

Assessment

This is conducted through group presentations and reports. Contributions of all members can be discerned by the requirement for individualized elements within the presentation and group report.

Stage 4: Application

This is an advanced stage of economic analysis and practical application of ideas. At this stage students are introduced to more advanced theories and ideas, which they can develop independently as an applied solution to real world issues.

Pedagogical approaches

A combination of methods – autodidactic, demonstrative, experiential, lecture, modeling, group work – can be used alongside presentations: visual (video, financial news); auditory (radio, podcasts, etc.); print (newspaper, journal articles); and social media.

Lecture

A significant seminal debate that must be introduced to the students at this stage is normative versus positive economics. Students should be taught to recognize that normative economics is attached to a set of values that will differ from person to person. Hence, positive economics tends to dominate the discourses. People like Friedman, Robbins, etc. advocate positive economics. However, from an Islamic perspective, normative economics plays a more important role, as these are underpinned by Islamic axioms (such as *'adl* and *ihāsan*, *khilāfa*, *Risālah* and *Rubūbiyyah*), which are well-entrenched in the Quran and Sunnah.

Autodidactic

Students will be expected to reflect upon the developing Muslim economies and their awareness and role for such concepts as *khilafah, falah, maqāasid al-Shari'ah*, *'adl*, etc. How are these traditionally entrenched and embedded relevant to current economic life? If these are taught properly, can Islamic countries develop their own economic idiosyncrasies, considering that even in conventional economics we have heterodox economics which accommodates various approaches in resolving economic problems.

Demonstrative/Modeling[19]

The teaching of macroeconomics, which works mainly in mathematical modeling, must be actively demonstrated by the educator through the prism of Islam and the way it should be implemented, although it must be admitted that there exist two significant challenges in teaching macroeconomic theories. First, it is usually too advanced for the third-world Muslim majority countries; hence, alternative theories have to be identified. Secondly, the resources to teach them might not be available both financially and socially. This is an important area for development as the emerging Muslim economies will require a new approach towards teaching Islamic macroeconomics in a globalized world.

Assessment

This is conducted through a discussion on the reflective notes of the students during the tutorial discussions. Students will have been expected to take notes and reflect upon the lecture and share those with their tutorial group and tutor. The educator can assess to gauge the level of participation, engagement, and understanding of the student during these sessions. Further guidance can also be provided at this stage, as well as identifying good practice and progress.

Stage 5: Evaluation

This is the final stage of the GRIT process, and its purpose is to provide both the educator and the learner with an idea of the student's learning experience.

Pedagogical approaches

DISCUSSION AND REFLECTION

The literature argues that in the real world, economists have a limited awareness about the economy. Expecting students to have a high understanding is unrealistic as the discipline of economics is based upon an approach to examining issues, which encompass a certain level of uncertainty. Therefore, presenting the discipline as being fixed upon certain principles does not correlate to the real-world experience of economists. Colander argues that "*...economists, only understand about 20% about the economy... Business-people often only understand 10% of a problem before they make a decision*" (2004). Henceforth, students should become accustomed to making decisions with limited information and be content with only grasping a partial element of an intricate subject matter. Accordingly, the assessments should reflect this reality and be cognizant of the overarching structure of the course and subject matter. The assessments could range from multiple-choice tests, short essays, exams, and portfolio work, depending on the complexity of the topic, the class potential and size, and the expertise of the faculty members themselves. This would then correlate with the grading scheme, which some research suggests should not be based upon a curve, as it creates competition amongst students as opposed to cooperation.

From an Islamic perspective, there is nothing to suggest from the literature derived from the fields of education and economics that assessments are contradictory to the Islamic worldview. Ibn Jamaah (b. 639), a renowned educator from the classical Islamic era, recommended that students be regularly tested on the material they have learnt in previous classes by being able to conduct a discussion on it in front of their peers and being able to handle questions about the topic. This, he advised, would ensure the students retain the knowledge and understanding of the material.[20]

Assessment

It is recommended that students be assessed through these methods as a minimum: presentations, group reports, examinations.

Reflections on pedagogical approaches

The pedagogical framework discussed above is an innovative and novel solution, in that it provides Islamic economics educators with an alternative approach to countering a significant point of concern in the field. A common finding from the research suggests that the lecture format, rather than a dialogical or discussion-based approach, remains the predominant method of teaching economics. This is despite the fact, for instance, that in the United States, the National Council on Economic Education has been working alongside the American Economic Association, via its Committee on Economic Education, since the 1950s to further the latest pedagogical practices for teaching economics in academia and schools. Additionally, the *Journal of Economic Education*, founded in 1969, was created with the explicit purpose of addressing the educational practices of economics by continually advocating novel and innovative methods of student participation in the learning process.

The general practice of pedagogy within the field of economics appears to be at this stage at odds with the general practice across further and higher education, which entails greater learner-led approaches, rather than simple didactic instructional learning. Observers in the field argue that academic economists tend to perceive themselves as being primarily being responsible for research in economics rather than conducting research on education in economics. Colander (2004), as a reflective voice of a cohort of scholars, argued that economists must transition their approaches to take ownership of their roles as teachers and then also maintain a research agenda by undertaking research in correlation to economics education, along with keeping up to date with and contributing to economics education journals. However, in the same breath he also urges a cautious warning to those teaching that they must not get stuck in the "*education school dilemma*" (Colander, 2004). This implies that in essence it is the content, and not the delivery, which defines the qualities of a good teacher. There is at present a tremendous concentration on the delivery rather than the content of education; thus, conferences and publications have become geared towards discussing the endless stream of new teaching and learning approaches.

Lowman encapsulates the contentions of this argument wonderfully, when he observes,

> ...what all the great teachers appear to have in common is love of their subject, an obvious satisfaction in arousing this love in their students, and an ability to convince them that what they are being taught is deadly serious.
>
> (*Lowman, 1984, p. 1*)

This implies that "... *the primary goal of undergraduate courses in economics is to enable students to think like economists.*" Thereby research is heavily focused towards understanding how economics courses taught in further and higher educational institutions can enrich the application and appreciation of economic analysis (Ibid). This point formulates the bedrock of the GRIT framework in that it seeks to stimulate interest in the students by developing their knowledge and appreciation of economic application. This could encompass a dedicated focus upon issues ranging from poverty alleviation to economic growth with an additional proviso of understanding of how this can be achieved in line with the guidance of the Shari'ah through practical real life case studies examined through a project-based approach.

A further point of reflection and learning for Muslim educationalists and policy makers is enumerated by research, which demonstrates that the field of conventional economics was profoundly impacted by the decline in recruitment of economics students in the 1980s and 1990s, which highlighted a fundamental weakness in the practice of teaching economics.[21] At that time, academic economists did not understand the market for potential students of economics. The consequence of this realization was the formation of newly inspired economics teaching proposals which were expressively intended to increase recruitment and retention. The discussions centered around issues centrally concerned with the content of the economics curricula in terms of its emphasis on "fundamental" concepts, and awareness of other nonessential and often what appeared to be distinct material from other fields.[22] This can be highlighted with the emergence and infusion of social media and globalized news coverage to bring significant issues of concern to the living consciousness of students, such as the various economic, financial, monetary, and fiscal policies and crises that directly impact economic thinking and discussions. Subsequently, this has led to an increase in recruitment to the economics discipline and study, as its appeal and relevance to undergraduate and postgraduate students becomes more cognizant and important.[23]

In relation to the teaching of Islamic economics, the above-cited example becomes ever-salient when considering, for example, the recent downturn in the recruitment of Islamic economics students and courses in the UK. Therefore, Islamic economics educators must take note of the teaching dimension and seek to engage the learners. At present a critique of the pedagogical practices and curricular developments of Islamic economics courses suggests that there is no practical guidance and demonstration on how knowledge derived from divine sources can be coherently utilized within a logical reasoning and empirical testing framework. This is in essence an essential aspect of conventional economics as well as formulating an inherent feature of Islamic economics (Khan, 1984). This implies that that there is no novelty in the methodology of Islamic economics other than being informed by the Islamic worldview.

The literature argues that education qualified by the "Islamic," e.g., Islamic economics, is principally a contemporary endeavor, an antithetical rejoinder to the secularized experience of post-colonialist education. A significant impact of this approach has resulted in a metameric perspective on knowledge, leading to the formation of two distinct approaches,[24] the Islamic divine and the secularist atheistic. Khan observes, "*If the hypotheses of Islamic economics must be derived from our understanding of the Qur'an and Sunnah… (then) What is the need for evaluating these hypotheses against the same criteria from which they have been derived?*" (1984, p. 39). In essence, "*How could a hypothesis be against these sources if it has been derived from them?*" (Ibid). Additionally, the blanket use of *Sharīʿah*, to imply that injunctions derived from the Qur'an, Sunnah, and fiqh are all divine, when in reality it is the Quran and Sunnah that claim divine origin, whilst the science of fiqh is a testament to the lived

Muslim tradition and experience, which cannot be classified as an exclusive divine revelation. Therefore, it is open to human critique and alteration.

> While fiqh can be consulted in order to come up with solutions, contemporary reality in terms of human knowledge and technology cannot be ignored... Doing this may not only require expanding the scope of Maqasid al-Shari'ah in framing new laws for the present time, but may also need revisiting the usul al-fiqh that has remained unchanged since the 11th century CE...
>
> (*Ahmed, 2009, p. 179*)

The overarching repercussions of this binary scheme of education has been described as the "*crisis within the Muslim psyche*" (Sahin, 2013, p. 177), due to the epistemological bias in knowledge formation, within which the "*malaise of the Ummah*" can be framed.[25] The implications of this inadvertently fragmented perspective of knowledge have led to the development of the "foreclosed" as opposed to the "reflective" mindset, thereby leading to what Sahin describes as a "*largely reactionary framework*" whereby "*...education has been categorized as 'Islamic' in order to distinguish it from secular education...*" (Sahin, 2013, p. 177). This has led Muslim scholars, especially under the guise of the Islamization ethos, to misinterpret and misconstrue the secular humanistic approaches to only inform as to what Islam is not; a form of negational educational theology, employed to define the very notion of what it is that Islamic education addresses. Conversely, even in seeking reform, Muslim educators have simply sought to borrow or integrate secular concepts without exploring their conceptual and hermeneutical implications with regards to the Islamic *Weltanschauung* (Nasr, 1991), or simply sought to prescriptively apply reform-centered Shari'ah-based injunctions, derived from newly uncovered approaches such as *Maqasid,* to the extant educational programs (Ibn Ashur, 2013).

A reflection on this demonstrates that commentators on Islamic economics have yet to fully realize the ethos of a virtuous engagement with the process of economics, *et in ipso*. In credulously attempting to applicate Islamic antecedents from the juristic and theological propositions to economic concepts, the visions of Islamic economics appear to become confined to a monolithic narrative, preserved via the sanctimony of an imagined homogenous past banded together by law and theology with little appreciation for the consequences of the socio-eco-political processes that have led to this understanding.

Accordingly, this has resulted in a reaction against Western secular economics, based upon assumed divergences and epistemological flaws, rather than the development of a holistic perspective, informed and evolved through a process of critical reflection, analysis, and examination of the lived Muslim experience with reference to its sacred sources. This requires that the interpretation of the lived experiences of the Muslim tradition and civilization is recognized as an agency of the human mind, which is neither infallible nor beyond critique.

Further, this implies that in the first instance, Muslim economists must appreciate the disparity between " ... *secularism, as an aggressive anti-religious position, and 'secularity' as an inclusive political principle within modern western democracies*" (Sahin, 2013, p. 178). This will prevent the discourse on Islamic economics from being reduced to a reactionary gesture by finding definition and meaning in its polarized and contrary stance to economic secularity, rather than addressing the ideological particularities of economic secularism.

Conclusion

This chapter has engaged with and derived from secularity, its lived experiences, and advice with regards to the interaction in human learning between the student, the teacher, and the content. Secularity, in this case, is the vagaries of the mundane, ordinary aspect of our worldly existence. The Islamic *Weltanschauung* entails through necessity a recognition of the divine revealed knowledge, as the *ayahs* (signs) are the *hidayah* (guidance) for deriving and utilizing the knowledge of the *duniya,* the secular.

As argued above, the attempt to simply Islamize Economics as a distinctly exact science has not only been questioned, but significant critical shortcomings in the epistemological and conceptual designs of the content and its eventual delivery have been identified, leading many to ponder as to where the "Islamic" was in the economics (Nasr, 1991). The concern of this chapter has been not to explore that aspect of the debate but to look at best practice with regards to delivery or pedagogy of the economics teaching material and to learn from the proficiencies of the prominent educational perspectives. The Group Research Interactive Teaching (GRIT) method was shared as a best practice model, which has been adopted for use in an undergraduate teaching program in Islamic economics. This model engages with traditional Muslim and contemporary pedagogical approaches along with retaining a strong focus on content and expertise in knowledge by using a variety of innovative teaching methods. These encompass working in groups; scaffolding for weaker students; working independently; utilizing technology to learn, teach, and communicate; and experiential learning opportunities alongside traditional didactic approaches such as lecturing and task-based activities. The teaching or pedagogical practice must reflect the context and content that it primed to deliver. Hence the onus is on the Islamic economics practitioner to be aware of the broad range of methods and approaches available to them and the opportunity to avail them. However, as a final point of consideration, it is only with time and subsequently the experience it brings that individual will find their perfect approaches that balance with their own personality characteristics alongside greater self-awareness and knowledge. It must be remembered that when we speak of time, it means not simply the notches on a calendar, but the dedicated quality, value, and proficiency afforded to an activity, which becomes seamless and innate with the repetition of practice of that activity and the reflection upon that practice.

Notes

1 See: Skinner, B. F. (1953). *Science and Human Behaviour*. New York: Macmillan.
2 See: Bishop, E. (2012). *Foundations of Constructive Analysis*. ISHI Press International.
3 See: Dr. Mary Anne Weegar (2012) "A Comparison of Two Theories of Learning – Behaviourism and Constructivism as applied to Face-to-Face and Online Learning" https://g-casa.com/conferences/manila/papers/Weegar.pdf.
4 See: Chapter 12 with regards to economics application: Editor(s): Frances K. McSweeney, Eric S. Murphy (2014). *The Wiley Blackwell Handbook of Operant and Classical Conditioning*. Hoboken: John Wiley & Sons.
5 For more on perennialism and its influence on Islamic thought see works of Seyyed Hossein Nasr.
6 Here, reference is being made to the classical madrasas of the 9/10/11th centuries.
7 Explore McCloskey, D. (1994). *Knowledge and Persuasion in Economics*. Cambridge: Cambridge University Press.
8 See alternative schooling practices such as Steiner and Montessori.
9 For a more comprehensive examination of classical Muslim educational institutes, educators, and curriculums with rich descriptive accounts of the teachers, their relationship with students, and the pedagogical methods utilized for learning and dissemination, see doctoral projects by Khaled Al-Khaledi (2002) and Khalid Fahad Al-Oadah (1998).
10 A critically reflective pedagogical approach pioneered by Dr. Imran H Khan Suddahazai, head of the Islamic education department at the Markfield Institute of Higher Education (MIHE), which has been adopted for use by the Islamic Economics and Finance Department.
11 This methodology was first trialed through a series of pilot programs and then subsequently developed within the B.A. Islamic Educational Program at MIHE.
12 Recommended background reading in B. Bassot (2016).
13 For a successful example of this pedagogical application, see study by A. U. Muhammad, D. Bala, K. M. Ladu (2016).
14 An intriguing and reflective insight into this approach is provided by H. G. Petrie (2011).
15 These are examples taken from the classes on Islamic economics by Sheikh Dr Faisal Manjoo.
16 For those interested in autodidectism from the Islamic perspective, examine Avner Ben-Zaken's (2011) *Ḥayy Ibn-Yaqẓān: A Cross-Cultural History of Autodidacticism*. Baltimore: John Hopkins University Press.
17 The following responses by Group 1 and Group 2 are actual responses provided by students in formal presentations in class, during the MA Islamic Economics and Finance class of 2020/21.
18 For an excellent introductory text into the notion of scaffolding and ideas around its implementation, see a text that is aimed at early childhood education but is nevertheless relevant in terms of introducing core concepts that can be developed and implemented contextually at all levels of education. The recommendation is: Berk, L. E., Winsler. A. (1995). Children's Learning: Vygotsky and Early Childhood Education: Vygotsky & Early Childhood Education, Vol. 7: National Association for the Education of Young Children.
19 Readers may want to further explore the notions such as "Agent Based Modelling: Recommend Introductory Text" by Hamil and Gilbert (2016).
20 An *Ijaza* (certificate of knowledge) was issued to students on the completion of their studies. This is equivalent to the awarding system of degrees and certifications in the contemporary parlance.

21 For a detailed study on this please refer to Dearden et al. (2010) and Walker and Zhu (2011).
22 See also: Ormerod (2003) and Helburn (1997).
23 For a detailed study on this please refer to Dearden et al. (2010) and Walker and Zhu (2011).
24 *ulum shar'iyyah* and the rational, *'ulum 'aqliyyah.*
25 Professor Faruqi was murdered (Shahid, 1986).

References

Ahmed, H. (2009). "The methodology of Islamic economics." In M.N. Siddiqi (Ed.), *Encyclopaedia of Islamic economics*, Vol. 1 (pp. 177–185). London.

Ali, A., Thompson, H. (1999). "The Schumpeterian Gap and Muslim Economic Thought." Journal of Interdisciplinary Economics Vol 10, Issue 1.

Bandura, A. (1989). "Perceived Self-efficacy in the Exercise of Personal Agency." *The* Psychologist: Bulletin of the British Psychological Society Vol. 2, pp. 411–424.

Bassot, B. (2016). *The Reflective Practice Guide: An Interdisciplinary Approach to Critical Reflection.* London: Routledge.

Berk, L. E., Winsler. A. (1995). *Children's Learning: Vygotsky and Early Childhood Education*. Vygotsky & Early Childhood Education v. 7.

Bligh, D.A. (1998). *What's the Use of Lectures?* 5th Ed. Intellect Books, GB.

Brookfield, S. D. (2005). *Discussion as a Way of Teaching: Tools and Techniques for Democratic Classrooms.* 2nd Ed. Hoboken: John Wiley & Sons, Inc.

Chomsky, N. (1962). "Explanatory Models in Linguistics." In Nagel, E., Suppes, P., and Tarski, A. (Eds.) *Logic, Methodology and Philosophy of Science*. Stanford: Stanford University Press.

Dearden, L., Fitzsimons, E., Wyness, G. (2010). *The Impact of Higher Education Finance on University Participation in the UK.* BIS Research Paper No 11, Department for Business, Innovation and Skills [Online].

Furqani, H. (2015). "Individual and Society in an Islamic Ethical Framework: Exploring Key Terminologies and the Micro-Foundations of Islamic Economics." Humanomics Vol. 31(1), pp. 74–87.

Gregg, G.S. (2005). *The Middle East: A Cultural Psychology*. New York: Oxford University Press.

Hafas, F. (2015). "Individual and Society in an Islamic Ethical Framework: Exploring Key Terminologies and the Micro-Foundations of Islamic Economics." Humanomics Vol. 31(1), pp. 77–82.

Helburn, S. (1997). "ECON 12 and the New Social Studies: Love's Labour's Lost?" The Social Studies, 88 (6), pp. 268–276.

Ibn Ashur, M.A. (2013). *Treatise on Maqasid Al-Shariah.* Hendon: IIIT.

Khan, T. (1984). *Islamic Economics: A Bibliography.* Jeddah: Islamic Research and Training Institute, Islamic Development Bank.

Makdisi, G. (1981). *The Rise of Colleges: Institutions of Learning in Islam and the West.* Edinburgh: Edinburgh University Press.

Muhammad, A. U., Bala, D., Ladu, K. M. (2016). "Effectiveness of Demonstration and Lecture Methods in Learning Concept in Economics among Secondary School Students in Borno State." Nigeria: Journal of Education and Practice Vol. 7(12).

Murata, S. (2001). *The Tao of Islam: A Sourcebook on Gender Relationships in Islamic Thought.* Lahore: Suhail Academy.
Nasr, V (1991). "Islamization of Knowledge: A Critical Overview." Islamic Studies Vol. 30(3), pp. 387–400.
Ormerod, P. (2003). "Turning the Tide: Bringing Economics Teaching into the Twenty-First Century." International Review of Economics Education Vol. 1(1), pp. 71–79.
Rahman, F. (1988). "Islamization of Knowledge: A Response." The American Journal of Islamic Social Sciences (AJISS) Vol. 5(1), pp. 3–11.
Sheikh, U., Ali, M. (2019). "Al-Ghazali's Aims and Objectives of Islamic Education" Journal of Education and Educational Development [Online].
Skinner, B. F. (1953) *Science and Human Behaviour* New York: Macmillan
Walker, I, Zhu, Y (2011). "Differences by Degree: Evidence of the Net Financial Rates of Return to Undergraduate Study for England and Wales." Economics or Education Review Vol. 30(6), pp. 1177–1186.

9

APPLICATION OF SCL, PBL, AND MM IN TEACHING ISLAMIC ECONOMICS AND FINANCE

Irfan Syauqi Beik and Laily Dwi Arsyianti

Introduction

Education is essential in Islam to understand and being one who received wisdom as stated in the Quran Surah al-Baqarah verse 269: "He gives wisdom to whom He wills, and whoever has been given wisdom has certainly been given much good. And none will remember except those of understanding." One meaning of the word *Ulil Albaab* indicates people not only have a brain, but also are granted to know how to use in correct way. It implies that Allah has given human a brain, and lets human use it in any way human wants. However, human needs to look at the sky and all His creatures, not only drilling verses in the Quran. Thus, human needs to understand all His creatures, why all are created, to read the beauty of its vastness. Wisdom can be achieved through understanding things. Understanding things can be excelled at by gaining knowledge, continuous learning, and acquiring education. One famous hadith stated, "*When a man dies, his good deeds come to an end except three: ongoing charity, beneficial knowledge, and righteous offspring who will pray for him*" (narrated by *Sahih al-Muslim*). Thus, education becomes one of most valuable investments in Islam. The rapid growth of digital technology generates new skills and creates new challenges to education systems and individuals. The Statistical, Economic and Social Research and Training Centre for Islamic Countries or SESRIC (2016) pointed out that the aim of education, especially in Organisation of Islamic Cooperation (OIC) countries, is to "*ensure inclusive and equitable quality education at the primary, secondary and tertiary levels and promote life-long learning opportunities that advance knowledge and skills needed for gainful employment, entrepreneurship, innovation and sustainable development.*" OIC countries have held eight meetings of the Islamic Conference of Ministers of Higher Education and Scientific Research (ICMHESR) to address related issues and challenges across the Islamic world in educational and scientific development.

DOI: 10.4324/9781003252764-12

The current stance of education in OIC countries derives from two general conclusions: first, large disparity among OIC member countries; second, the members lag far behind developed countries in particular. The total adult literacy rate in OIC member countries reaches 74.5% while developed countries reach 98.1%. OIC member countries' governments on average spend 3.5% of their GDP for education expenditure, while the rest of world spends 4.9% according to the SESRIC report (SESRIC, 2016). However, this amount reflects more portions compared with the government expenditure, in total, for OIC member countries. In the Islamic economic and finance industry, according to the Islamic Finance Country Index, Malaysia has dominated the index since 2011. Its neighbor country, Indonesia, which is now in the upper-middle-country group according to the World Bank, has tried to catch up by being at the top in 2019, and moving slightly down to be the runner up in 2020. In particular, the index also captures education in the Islamic economic and finance industry (Cambridge Institute of Islamic Finance, 2020). Education and the industry should be linked intensely so that both can achieve the goals of what have been thought in Islam, i.e., *Maqasid al-Shari'ah*. In term of research exposure, Malaysia is still at the top of the chart in the Islamic economics and finance industry. Meanwhile, for education, Indonesia is ranked 1 due to the number of Islamic economics-related study program offered in Indonesia (INCEIF Refinitiv, 2020). How this research, education, and industry exposure can be connected and strengthen each other to give more contributions to global development, especially in the OIC countries that still have education gaps compared to the rest of the world, will be discussed in this chapter.

Therefore, this chapter covers practical solutions, justified models, and methods of application in today's reality in Islamic economics and finance education, especially in the rising countries that try to improve the Islamic economics and finance industry. The structure of this study is based on a program launched by the Ministry of Education and Culture of the Republic of Indonesia in general, and how it can be applied in the Islamic economics and finance education system.

Practical solutions

The rapid advancement in science and technology has accelerated changes in various aspects of life. Many jobs are lost, while various types of work have arisen. In this very dynamic phase, universities must respond as quickly as possible to catch up what has happened in the industry. Learning transformation is, thus, highly needed to be able to equip and prepare higher education graduates to become a superior generation. Student-centered learning (SCL) is basically a method in education in which the students are the core who actively build their competencies to meet what they need through programs offered by education institutions. Meanwhile, the lecturer as a facilitator, supervisor, mentor, or coach works cooperatively with relevant partners in the industry to achieve learning outcomes for students that meet the industry demands (Singh, 2011). Creativity and innovation are the keywords to ensure sustainable development. Students who are currently studying at the universities must be prepared to become true learners who are skillful, flexible, and agile. Independent Learning is one of programs launched by the Minister of Education and Culture of the Republic of Indonesia. It teaches graduates to be tough, relevant to the needs of the times, and ready to be leaders with passion. The program prepares students to have three semesters of study outside their Islamic economics and finance major. Opportunities are created to open broader areas for students to enrich and improve their insight and competence in the real world according to their passions and ideals.

Project-based learning (PBL) allows students to learn by doing and applying their ideas (Krajcik and Blumenfeld, 2006). The program immerses students in the notion that learning can happen anywhere, and the universe of learning is limitless, not only in classrooms, libraries, and laboratories, but also in villages, industries, workplaces, research centers, and the communities. Through immense interaction between universities and the real world, the university will be presented as a springboard for the development of the nation, in particular in the industry of Islamic economics and finance. PBL interplays three core elements dynamically, namely: teachers' collaboration with industry consultants, classroom enactment by carrying out new practices, and teachers' reflection on implementation to advance knowledge (Kokotsaki, Menzies, and Wiggins, 2016). The so-called Independent Learning – Merdeka Campus program allows students to implement either (1) following the entire learning process in the study program at the institutions according to the study period and study load or (2) following the learning process in the study program to fulfill part of the study period and study load, and the rest of that study period and study load will be fulfilled by participating in a learning process outside their Islamic economics and finance major. These basically are the implementation of SCL, PBL, and mind mapping (MM) methods.

Through Merdeka Campus, students have the opportunity to spend 1 semester or the equivalent of 20 credit hours studying outside their Islamic economics and finance major or study program at the same university and a maximum of 2 semesters or the equivalent of 40 credit hours studying the same Islamic economics and finance major or study program at different universities, learning in different study programs in different universities, and/or learning in industry, outside the classroom. Learning in the Merdeka Campus provides challenges and opportunities for development of creativity, capacity, personality, and student needs, as well as develop independence in seeking and finding knowledge through realities and dynamics in the industry, such as fulfilling skill requirements, solving real problems, engaging in social interaction, expanding the collaboration, building self-management, and achieving demands, targets, and achievements.

In order to prepare students to face changes in the social, cultural, and working world and rapid technological advances, student competencies must be more prepared to adapt to the needs of the times. They must link and match not only with the industrial world but also with a rapidly changing future. Universities are required to be able to design and implement innovative smart learning processes so that students can achieve learning outcomes that include relevant aspects of attitude, knowledge, and skills optimally. The program is expected to be the answer to these demands. Merdeka Campus is a form of learning in higher education where students act independently and are flexible so as to create a learning culture that is innovative, not restrictive, and matches the student needs. Various forms of learning activities take place outside of institutions, including internships/work practice in the industry or other workplaces, service projects to the community in the village, teaching in the education unit, participating in student exchange, conducting research, conducting entrepreneurial activities, making independent projects, and participating in humanitarian programs. All these activities must be carried out with the guidance of the lecturer as their supervisor. Merdeka Campus is expected to provide industry-contextual experiences that will enhance students' competencies as a whole, ready to work, or create new jobs.

In order to achieve the solution, MM technique is believed to be an effective tool in delivering knowledge, especially in social science (Parikh, 2016). Hopper (2016) depicted MM as visually organized information showing relationships among pieces drawn on the map. It facilitates learning through remembering, encouraging creativeness of students, materializing abstract concepts, drawing impressive techniques, and allowing students to contribute with joy (Çoban and Selçuk, 2017). The technique is believed to help student better understand topics in their lectures and mind map their carrier path.

Justified model

Universities accommodate rights for students to take credit hours outside institutions for a maximum of 2 semesters or the equivalent of 40 credits. Students can also take credits in different study programs at the same university for 1 semester or the equivalent to 20 credits. Therefore, universities must develop academic policies or guidelines to facilitate activities learning outside the study program as well as widen and create cooperation with industry partners. As for the faculty, they need to prepare a list of faculty-level courses that can be taken cross Islamic economics and finance major students as well as prepare widen cooperation with relevant partners. Lastly, certainly, the study program needs to develop or adapt the curriculum to the campus implementation model independently.

As for the stakeholders in peer higher education, they need to facilitate students who will take cross-university courses by listing, offering, and conducting equivalence courses that can be taken by students outside the study program and abroad, as well as their requirements. Alternative online courses must be prepared in case there are courses or credit hours that have not been fulfilled from outside study programs and outside universities. The students themselves need to consult their academic advisors about the relevant courses/programs that meet their needs to be taken outside their Islamic economics and finance major or study program. Therefore, they need to register for program activities outside their study program and complete the requirements, including participating in the selection, if any. Partners in the industry need to create cooperation with relevant universities or faculty of specific Islamic economics and finance majors or study programs and carry out activities outside the study program in accordance with the existing provisions cooperation agreement.

Methods of application in today's reality

The independent learning program allows students to explore and experience the real life of the Islamic economics and finance industry. The methods include student exchange, internship/working experience, teaching or research assistant, research, humanitarian project, entrepreneurial activity, independent study, and building a thematic village/community development program.

Teaching assistant in an education unit

Despite being a number one provider in Islamic economics and finance education, the literacy rate on Islamic economics and finance is still low in Indonesia, i.e., 16.3% (Bank Indonesia, 2021). This industry still has a huge job to educate their people; hence, the literacy can be improved. One way to spread the Islamic economics and finance knowledge is through a teaching assistant program carried out by Islamic economics and finance students. The quality of primary and secondary education in Indonesia is still very low. (In Programme for International Student Assessment [PISA] 2018, Indonesia ranked 7 from the bottom.) There are many and varied problems, both in formal and non-formal education units. Learning activities in the form of teaching assistance are carried out by students in educational units such as elementary, secondary, or above. The school where the teaching assistant practices can be located can be in a city or in remote areas.

A teaching assistant is basically teaching a large population an introductory curriculum (Gardner and Jones, 2011). It fits primary, secondary, and the first 3 years of the undergraduate program. Teaching assistance programs in educational units allow students to grab opportunities to deepen their knowledge of how to become a teacher in an education unit. This program is expected to improve the distribution of education quality and relevance to primary and secondary education with higher and developmental education era. The university needs to prepare cooperation with education unit partners and get permission from relevant stakeholders in destination units. The program should allow opportunities to participate in both formal and non-formal education units. Education unit data can be obtained from the Ministry of Education and Culture or the local education office. The need for the number of teaching assistants and the subjects are based on the needs of each regional education office.

Supervisors need to be assigned to provide assistance, training, monitoring, and evaluation of teaching activities in the education unit. Equalization or recognition of credit hours of teaching activities in the education unit also needs to be set. The process can be done through an electronic system built by the university. Together with the supervising lecturers, the mentors in the destination education unit manage to monitor and evaluate the activities attended by students while at the same time providing scores to be recognized as student credits. After getting approval from academic advisors, the students immediately carry out teaching assistance activities in the education unit under the guidance of the supervising lecturer. They are required to fill out the logbook as well as prepare activity reports and submit reports in the form of presentations. Teaching assistant experience suggests that students who participate in the program obtain benefits similar to those who participate in research assistant programs (Schalk, McGinnis, Harring, Hendrickson, and Smith, 2009).

Conducting research or being a research assistant

Silva, da Cunha Aguiar, Leta, Santos, Cardoso, Cabral, Rodrigues, and Castro (2004) emphasized that research assistant programs have been underappreciated in the developing countries. Furthermore, academic research was predicted to face lack of generational scientific researchers in the upcoming 10 years. Universities should set programs involving students in conducting research. Conducting research or being in research assistant program is believed to achieve a student's refinement of critical thinking abilities and clarification of their career goals (Wood, 2019). For students who have a passion for being researchers, independent learning can be realized in the form of research activities at research institutes or study centers. Through research, students can develop critical thinking, a very important thing required for various scientific divisions at the higher education level. With the ability to think critically, students will deepen, understand, and be able to conduct better research methods. At the same time, the research institutes sometimes lack research assistants when working on research projects in the short term (1 semester up to 1 year). Research assistants have two optional roles: either they assist the principal investigator or conduct part of the methods used in the research, for example, the focus group discussion.

The objectives of conducting research or being in a research assistant program include improving the quality of student research, strengthening the topically pooled research talent, gaining research competence through conducting research directly at the research institutes or study centers, and improving the ecosystem and the quality of research in study centers and research institutes of Indonesia by providing research resources and regeneration of researchers in Islamic economics and finance area since early stage. Universities need to collaborate with partners from research institutes or allow their research centers to hire research assistants to be involved in their projects. This will give students the right to take part in the selection to evaluate research programs in both off-campus research institutes and on-campus research centers. A supervisor in the internal study program still needs to be assigned to provide guidance, supervision, and together, with researchers in institutions or research centers, provide value through technical guidelines for learning activities through research. A supervisor also conducts final evaluation and equalization of research activities into relevant credit hours and sustainable programs. Students are predicted to refrain from the university research career path (Silva *et al*, 2004). Universities, through the academic advisory lecturer, should encourage students to enroll in a research assistant program. Therefore, students have the opportunity to carry out research activities in accordance with the direction of the research institute or research center. Allowing students to conducting their own projects can enhance the quality of their research experience and endeavor to produce publication-worthy materials (Wood, 2019).

Student exchange

Currently, there are many student exchanges with full credit transfers with international university partners. However, there is still a lack of programs accommodating national level university partners in credit transfers. Student exchanges are organized to form the knowledge of cultural diversity, views, religions, and beliefs, as well as work together and have social sensitivity and concern for community and environment. A global citizen is one who has cultural strength from their own country while at the same time being able to perform as multicultural citizen of the world. Thus, the educated individual is supposed be able to interact and has network of individuals from multiple countries at multiple levels (Atalar, 2020). The objectives of student exchanges include study across both domestic and overseas campuses, and living with a family at the destination campus. Students' insights about the different cultures and brotherhood will be developed stronger. Students can build friendships cross regions, ethnicities, cultures, and religions. Lastly, the program aims to organize knowledge transfer to cover disparities in education, both among domestic universities, as well as overseas. The concerned Islamic economics and finance study program (SP) should develop or adapt an accommodative curriculum for students taking courses in other study programs. The SP also should define and offer courses that can be taken by students from outside the SP, thus meeting the quota of participants from outside the SP and setting the equivalent of credit hours that can be taken from other SPs. Following the preparation, Islamic economics and finance study programs should make agreements with partner universities concerning the learning process, credit recognition and assessment, and financing schemes. Cooperation can be done in the form of bilateral, consortium (association), cluster (based on accreditation), or zoning (based on region).

Bohman and Borglin (2014) found that motivation of students joining student exchange programs are cultural aspects and cultural awareness, including for personal or professional experiences. However, students must obtain the academic advisor's approval before participating in this program and must participate in program activities with the existing academic guidelines in both face-to-face and online learning programs. Therefore, they can maintain good learning outcomes. As for the lecturers, automatic agent-based intelligent systems would help them in academic advising (Abdelhamid, Ayoub, and Alhawiti, 2015). Considering the increasing number of students and decreasing teacher/lecturer per student ratio in OIC countries (SESRIC, 2016), the system would help much to relax their burden. The system should include academic timetabling, as well as carrier path and life goals of students. This also would help student exchange programs from outside universities.

Internship or working experience

Silva, Lopes, Costa, Seabra, Melo, Brito, and Dias (2016) found that study programs that offer internship programs tend to significantly enhance employability of their graduates. Their results indicate a work-based learning system is an effective strategy to bridge theoretical knowledge and practice as well as enhance graduate employability. Students in the current system have lacked work experience in the industry, so they are not ready to work. The existing system that provides internship programs in a short period (less than 6 months) is stipulated to provide not enough experience and industrial competence to fulfill the demands. Companies that accept internships also stated that short-term apprenticeships are useless, and even interfere with industrial activities. Therefore, it is the university's challenge to reorganize and restructure the curriculum to fit the industry. Organizing internship programs in the university is important (Franco, Silva, and Rodrigues, 2019). Furthermore, they found that industrial involvement in the program gives much greater influence in student perspectives to acquire new knowledge. Therefore, the internship program should include at the least one to two semesters, providing sufficient experience to students and direct learning in the workplace (practical learning). During internships, student will develop hard skills (complex problem solving, analytical skills, and any other relevant skills), as well as soft skills (professional/work ethics, communication, cooperation, any other relevant skills). Cockayne (2021) stated that globalized labor markets demand industry most privileged workers supposed to be as agile as possible, or at least, as mobile as capital. Meanwhile, the industry can get talent when it fits, and the talent can be directly recruited, thereby reducing the cost of recruitment and initial training/induction. Students who already know the workplace will be more stable entering the world of work and career. Through this activity, universities are required to update teaching materials, learning methods, and research topics in higher education to be more relevant.

Learning activities carried out in collaboration with partners that include corporations, nonprofit foundations, multilateral organizations, government institutions, and start-up companies. To start the collaboration, universities need to set an agreement with partners, including the learning process, semester credit recognition, and assessment. The program should be developed by both the university and partners, in the sense of competencies that will be obtained by students, as well as the rights and obligations to both parties during the internship process. Supervisors in both university and industry partners need to be assigned and if necessary, the university supervisor makes a visit to the internship site for monitoring and evaluation. They need to compile a logbook and conduct assessment of student achievement during the internship. Monitoring of the internship process can be done through the help of an automatic internship monitoring system built by the university. The automated system is also a medium of communication among the student, university supervisor, and industry partner supervisor. During the internship, the industry partner is advised to provide rights and guarantees in accordance with laws and regulations including health insurance, work safety, internship fees, and any other relevant interns' rights.

After obtaining approval from academic supervisor, the student registers or applies and participates in the internship selection according to the provisions of the internship place and gets an internship supervisor. Students need to fill in the logbook, prepare activity reports, and submit reports to industry partner supervisors and supervising lecturer. Although Franco *et al.* (2019) found that university orientation of internship programs was the least influential on students' perspective on acquiring their new knowledge, students need to be debriefed before joining internships, mentored, and guided during internship process, before finally carrying out evaluations and assessments on the results of the internship.

Humanitarian project

Indonesia has experienced many natural disasters, in the form of earthquakes, volcanic eruptions, tsunamis, hydrological disasters, and many other kinds. Universities have been involved to help overcome disasters through humanitarian programs. Students are engaged voluntarily, however only in short term. Many local and international institutions (UNESCO, UNICEF, WHO, and *amil* institutions, both public and private, like BAZNAS-National Board of Zakat) conduct pilot projects for development in Indonesia and other developing countries as well as in-depth studies in humanitarian projects. Ngo and Chase (2020) found this project motivated them in sustainable practices, social changes, and appreciation of their profession.

The objectives of the humanitarian project program include preparing excellent students who uphold human values in carrying out duties based on religion, morals, ethics, and humanitarian disciplines; and training students to have social sensitivity when exploring the existing problems and provide solutions according to the interests and needs of their respective expertise. Universities need to make cooperation documents with partners both domestically (local government, Red Cross, BAZNAS, and *waqf* administers) and foreign agencies (UNESCO, UNICEF, WHO, UNOCHA, UNHCR).

Together with partner institutions, universities appoint assistant lecturers to provide assistance, supervision, assessment, and evaluation of humanitarian project activities done by students.

Partner institutions need to ensure the humanitarian activities that students participate in are in accordance with the agreement as well as the fulfillment of student rights and safety while participating in humanitarian project. Students can conduct humanitarian projects with their partners not only in the form of field projects like humanitarian logistics projects (Özpolat, Chen, Hales, Yu, and Yalcin, 2014), but also setting up free and open access software to assist disaster management, microfinance, and local election monitoring.

Entrepreneurial activities

Based on the Global Entrepreneurship Index (GEI) in 2018, Indonesia only scored 21% entrepreneurs from various occupation backgrounds or a rating of 94 among the 137 surveyed countries. Meanwhile, according to research from the IDN Research Institute, in 2019, 69.1% of Indonesian millennials had an interest in entrepreneurship. Unfortunately, the entrepreneurial potential for the millennial generation has not been well managed so far. Independent Campus encourages students' entrepreneurial interest development with appropriate learning activity programs. The objectives of the entrepreneurial activity program include shaping students who have an interest in entrepreneurship to develop their business early and guiding them through personal development, social skills, business and market innovation, dealing with unemployment problems that result in unemployment intellectuals from scholars. Therefore, entrepreneurship learning activities should be set up to be both intrinsically and extrinsically specified in the curriculum of the Islamic economics and finance study program. The requirements are set in the guidelines of the academic certificate issued by the university.

In addition, the university ought to ensure that students in entrepreneurship programs should compile a syllabus of entrepreneurial activities that can fulfill 20 credits per semester or 40 credits per year. The program can be a combination of courses from various study programs offered by the faculty at the university or outside the university, including courses or micro-credentials offered through online and offline learning. For the assessment of the entrepreneurship program, an assessment rubric can be arranged or a measure of the success of learning achievement. For example, if a student succeeds in creating a startup at the end of the program, then the students get an A with 20 credits/40 credits. During the entrepreneurship program, students are guided by mentors from their university or mentors of successful entrepreneurs. Islamic economics and finance needs to encourage real-sector development and match it with the growing Islamic financial sector. Students who are actively participating in entrepreneurial courses and events are gaining their entrepreneurial intention, so as to higher institutions who channel the students with such activities. Hence, universities are encouraged to have incubation centers, while for those who lack opportunity to launch it can cooperate with other incubation or business acceleration centers. This learning system is supposed to have training facilitation, coaching, and debriefing from mentors or business actors.

Supplement tools of simulation-based studies are proven to be an amusing way of learning and able to stimulate students to think critically (Zulfiqar, Sarwar, Aziz, Ejaz Chandia, and Khan, 2019). With the guidance of the incubation center or entrepreneurship mentors or coaches, students prepare proposals for their entrepreneurial activities.

Independent study or project

There are many students who have passion for realizing great works competed at the national and international level or the work of an innovative idea. Ideally, independent study or projects are to accomplish the existing curriculum taken by students or as a complement. Universities or faculties can create independent studies to complete topics that are not covered in the lecture schedule but are still available in the syllabus of the Islamic economics and finance study program. Independent project activities can be done in the form of cross-disciplinary group work. The objectives of the independent study or project include realizing student ideas in developing innovative products, organizing research and development (R&D)-based education, and improving student achievement in national and international competitions. The integration of independent study activities into courses is calculated based on the contributions, participations, and roles of students as evidenced in activities under the coordination of the supervisor. Eventually, the programs challenge the students in their careers upon graduation despite the growing need for professionals (Stewart and Willy, 2020), to some extent, in the Islamic economics and finance industry.

Universities should provide a team of co-lecturers for independent projects that are submitted by the student team according to expertise. An independent project team is encouraged to develop interdisciplinary students. The team benefits from integrating the competition into instructional courses, independent study, as well as volunteer club activity (Stewart and Willy, 2020). The outcome of the project or independent study activities is to produce materials to be entered in national- or international-level competitions. Chua and Koh (2017) highlighted that modules for the project are better equipped with internal design competitions to enhance student learning outcomes and to make learning process more attractive.

Village or regional empowerment (VE)

Village empowerment is a form of education to provide a learning experience for students to live in the middle of a community outside their campus. Students are directly identifying local economy potentials as well as the problems. Hence, students are expected to empower village or regional potentials and formulate solutions to existing problems in the village. These activities are expected to improve soft skills, partnerships, cross-disciplinary/ cross-competence students' collaborations, and student leadership in managing programs' development in rural areas. To this point, already running the VE program, only the Semester Credit Unit has not been able or can be recognized in accordance with the independent campus program, which credit the recognition equivalent to 6–12 months or 20–40 credits, with implementation based on several models. It is also hoped that after the VE implementation, students can write down the things they do and the results in the form of assignments. MM technique can be effective to apply the visual information. Preparing notes, weekly plans, daily plans, session plans, text or presentation, exams, and special education programs are among the activities to organize MM (Parikh, 2016).

The implementation of VE can be carried out in very underdeveloped, underdeveloped, and low-income villages, whose talents do not yet have the ability to plan with such large funding facilities. Effectiveness of using village funds to drive economic growth still needs to be improved, one way is through students who can become the talents that empower village funds. Continuous learning, periodic adjustment and maintenance, learning, and redesigning concepts from operating experience are definitely important in empowering villages (Duffy, 2008). The objectives of the program are to build a real village empowerment so that students implement what they have been taught at the earlier stage. Student attendance for 6–12 months can provide opportunities for students to take advantage of science, technology, and skills they have in collaboration with many stakeholders' interests in the field.

According to Arsyianti, Lubis, Ayyubi, Hidayat, Nurzaman, Samidi, Nasution, and Permata (2019), activities for an Islamic economics field study involve village empowerment; students can promote halal and healthy lifestyles. To the extent of increasing Islamic economics literacy, this program can promote the existing Islamic financial institutions; planning the community financial matters; introducing digitalization in Islamic economics and finance; promoting Islamic social finance that includes zakat, *waqf*, *sadaqa*, and Islamic microfinance; as well as inspiring the community to live up to the Masjid economic management program. Students can do research as well while they are conducting the programs for village empowerment, for example, by using the Zakat Village Index (ZVI) on how the village is qualified to receive a zakat empowerment fund.

There are several models in the implementation of VE:

- Universities create competency packages that will obtained by students in the regular VE program. Then students are given an opportunity to apply for a VE extension for a maximum of 1 semester or the equivalent to 20 credits. Students can obtain the benefits of the Holistic Coaching and Village Empowerment Program. The extended VE activities can be in the form of community empowerment projects in villages and research for student' final assignments.

- Universities work together with partners in carrying out VE based on opportunities and conditions of the. The number of students participating in this program depends on the needs of the village by using the MM method. Students will have 6–12 months on site or the equivalent of a maximum of 20 credits. Calculation of the equivalent of 20 credit hours can be transformed into several subjects' courses that are relevant to the competence of graduates. Performance appraisal can be identified from reports and the portfolio or rubric exams of VE activities. For conformity with the achievement of graduate competencies, it is necessary to prepare a proposal or activity plan that can represent areas of expertise. Field supervisors must represent the study program tutor for the final semester of each study program.
- The implementation of this activity is prioritized to educate the community. For students outside the education study program, like Islamic economics and finance, they can carry out teaching in accordance with the field of expertise in the context of community empowerment, as mentioned earlier. All VE teaching activity is to help formal and non-formal teaching.
- Students are given the freedom to explore and determine appropriate VE programs that will be implemented with partners. In compiling the program, students must pay attention to the curriculum related to activities and in consultation with their academic advisor or supervisor.

Evaluation

In general, the equalization of Merdeka Campus activities is divided into two forms, namely free form and structured form.

Free form allows independent learning activities for 6 months and is equivalent to 20 credits without taking any classroom courses online or offline. The 20 credits are obtained in the form of competence obtained by students during the independent learning program, both in hard skills and soft skills in accordance with the desired learning outcomes. For example, in Islamic economics and finance fields, examples of hard skills as part of learning outcomes are the ability to formulate complex problem-solving in the perspective of Islamic economics and finance and scientific knowledge. Examples of soft skills are the ability to communicate in a professional work environment, the ability to cooperate in a team, and the ability to carry out professional ethics. Learning achievements and the assessment can be expressed in these competencies. In addition to the assessment, experience or improved competencies during the internship can also be written in the form of a portfolio as certificate accompanying a diploma.

On the other hand, structured form allows independent learning activities to be structured according to the curriculum. The 20 credits are stated in form of equality with the courses whose competencies in line with the internship. In addition to these two forms, hybrid forms, combinations can also be designed between free-form and structured.

Quality assurance unit at the university that organizes Merdeka Campus should recognize a formal mechanism to evaluate and monitor students periodically and must have the program of "*right to study three semesters outside the study program.*" To ensure the quality of the program, monitoring and evaluation are carried out starting from the preparation, implementation, and assessment stages. The assessment or evaluation is a series of activities to improve quality, performance, and productivity in carrying out industrial-linked programs.

Conclusion

Education has become one of most valuable investments in Islam. SCL, PBL, and mind mapping methods are tools for better education. In Islamic economics and finance fields, even in the OIC member countries, the literacy and inclusive rate are still low. Therefore, allowing students to explore more freely and involving them in shaping their competencies are believed to have better effectiveness, thus the achievement of competency in Islamic economics and finance education. The focus of the evaluation is the individual student, namely, achievements in the implementation of internships or other forms of independent learning programs. Evaluation reflects what has and has not been achieved by students during the activity. Furthermore, independent learning programs are aimed to improve student competencies.

References

Abdelhamid, Y., Ayoub, A. and Alhawiti, M., 2015. Agent-based intelligent academic advisor system. *International Journal of Advanced Computer Technology*, *4*(2), pp. 1–6.

Arsyianti, L.D., Lubis, D., Ayyubi, S.E., Hidayat, S.E., Nurzaman, M.S., Samidi, S., Nasution, A., Permata, A., 2019. *Panduan Pelaksanaan Kuliah Kerja Nyata – Tematik (KKN-T) Ekonomi Syariah (Guidance for Islamic Economics Thematic Field Study)*. Komite Nasional Keuangan Syariah (KNKS), Jakarta.

Atalar, A., 2020. Student exchange: The first step toward international collaboration. In *Successful Global Collaborations in Higher Education Institutions* (pp. 63–71). Springer, Cham.

Bank Indonesia. 2021. Laporan Ekonomi dan Keuangan Syariah 2020 [Islamic Economic and Finance Report 2020]. Jakarta, Indonesia.

Bohman, D.M. and Borglin, G., 2014. Student exchange for nursing students: Does it raise cultural awareness? A descriptive, qualitative study. *Nurse Education in Practice*, *14*(3), pp. 259–264.

Cambridge Institute of Islamic Finance. 2020. *Global Islamic Finance Report 2020*. Cambridge Institute of Islamic Finance, United Kingdom.

Chua, Y.L. and Koh, Y.Y., 2017. Internal competition in engineering education—a case study of project design competition in UNITEN. *Advanced Science Letters*, *23*(2), pp. 708–711.

Çoban, S. and Selçuk, E., 2017. The effect of mind mapping technique on students' achievements in music lesson and on their attitudes towards the mind mapping technique. *Eğitim ve Bilim*, 42(190). DOI:10.15390/EB.2017.6856.

Cockayne, D., 2021. Entrepreneurial education: The role of internships in higher education in North America. *ACME: An International Journal for Critical Geographies*, *20*(1), pp. 81–98.

Duffy, J., 2008. Village empowerment: service-learning with continuity. *International Journal for Service Learning in Engineering, Humanitarian Engineering and Social Entrepreneurship*, *3*(3), pp. 1–17.

Gardner, G.E. and Jones, M.G., 2011. Pedagogical preparation of the science graduate teaching assistant: Challenges and implications. *Science Educator*, *20*(2), pp. 31–41.

Hopper, C.H., 2016. *Practicing College Learning Strategies*, 7th Edition, ISBN 9781305109599, Ch. 7. Cengage Learning EMEA.

INCEIF Refinitiv. 2020. INCEIF Refinitiv Islamic Finance Knowledge Outlook Report 2020. Kuala Lumpur, Malaysia.

Kokotsaki, D., Menzies, V. and Wiggins, A., 2016. Project-based learning: A review of the literature. *Improving Schools*, 19(3), pp. 267–277.

Krajcik, J.S. and Blumenfeld, P.C., 2006. Project-based learning. *The Cambridge Handbook of the Learning Sciences*, pp. 317–334.

Özpolat, K., Chen, Y., Hales, D., Yu, D. and Yalcin, M.G., 2014. Using Contests to Provide Business Students Project-Based Learning in Humanitarian Logistics: PSAid Example. *Decision Sciences Journal of Innovative Education*, *12*(4), pp. 269–285.

Parikh, N.D., 2016. Effectiveness of teaching through mind mapping technique. *The International Journal of Indian Psychology*, *3*(3), pp. 148–156.

Schalk, K.A., McGinnis, J.R., Harring, J.R., Hendrickson, A. and Smith, A.C., 2009. The undergraduate teaching assistant experience offers opportunities similar to the undergraduate research experience. *Journal of Microbiology & Biology Education*, *10*(1), pp. 32–42.

Singh, N., 2011. Student-centered learning (SCL) in classrooms—A comprehensive overview. *Educational Quest–An International Journal of Education and Applied Social Sciences*, *2*(2), pp. 275–282.

Stewart, S.W. and Willy, D.M., 2020. The collegiate wind competition – Undergraduate education through student competition. *Journal of Physics: Conference Series*, *1452*(1), p. 012022.

Wood, S., 2019. Undergraduate research Assistant leadership for rigorous, high quality research. *Frontiers in Psychology*, *10*, p. 474.

Zulfiqar, S., Sarwar, B., Aziz, S., Ejaz Chandia, K. and Khan, M.K., 2019. An analysis of influence of business simulation games on business school students' attitude and intention toward entrepreneurial activities. *Journal of Educational Computing Research*, *57*(1), pp. 106–130.

10

CHALLENGES AND PROSPECTS IN ADOPTING IDEAL METHODOLOGIES IN TEACHING ISLAMIC FINANCE

Ayman Mohammad Bakr, Mohamed Cherif El Amri, Mustafa Omar Mohammed and Ensari Yücel

Introduction

In the last few decades, Islamic finance has gained interest among Muslims and non-Muslims. Suffice it to say that "Islamic banking has become a very fast-growing element of global capital markets and international banking system in the last twenty years." Muslims consider Islamic finance as an alternative to conventional finance and a way to eliminate interest, which is akin to usury (Ribā), in line with the commandments of Islam. Non-Muslims, on the other hand, attempt to seize the opportunity to tap a market that has a huge potential and continuous growth. This fact is underpinned by the 2016 World Islamic Banking Competitiveness Report by Ernst & Young where, with the exception of Turkey, it reported that participation[1] banking continues to drive high growth over conventional ones and continues to capture market share in all key markets. According to the same report, the expected growth of the participation banking profit pool across QISMUT[2] in 2020 is almost three-folds larger than the value recorded in 2014; that is, US $27.8 billion in 2020, up from US $10.8 billion in 2014. Its rich database of detailed contracts that observe Shari'ah makes it a very practical science applicable to all financial facets of life. Hence that explains the boom in the Islamic financial industry since its inception in the 1970s, the proliferation of Islamic financial institutions, and the rapid development of its tools and solutions.

In as much as Islamic economics and finance grew in significance, delivering its laws, concepts, and principles became equally important. The need for well-versed scholars and practitioners in the field is key to its development. Notwithstanding, the field of Islamic economics and finance is vast and governed by a great body of laws that are retrieved or deduced, both directly and indirectly, from the Qur'ān and Sunnah. One can safely say that

 DOI: 10.4324/9781003252764-13

the composition of Islamic finance is not less in volume and complexity than the composition of its conventional counterpart, and in certain instances Islamic finance exceeds its counterpart. An implication of this is to compare the development of Islamic finance subject delivery and its methodologies to how the conventional finance is being delivered to students. For instance, in a study conducted by Olokoyo and Oyewo (2014), they found that there is empirical evidence that students' interest in financial management is significantly influenced by four factors, of which "teaching method" is one. While carrying out similar research on subjects delivered in the field of Islamic economics and finance seems logical and very important, nonetheless the significance of "teaching method" in delivering Islamic finance courses should be recognized from the onset. This research should guide the development of "teaching methods" for such courses in a way that acknowledges their own unique characteristics and recognizes the differences from the courses of their conventional counterparts. Rather than starting from scratch, the foundation of these "teaching methods" should be based on existing teaching theories whereupon one can build on the approaches and understand how technology levels can affect the whole teaching environment and experiences during the delivery of such courses.

A succinct review of the extant teaching theories should shed lights on the direction the "teaching methods" of Islamic finance should adopt. In brief, the current teaching theories can be organized into four quadrants based on two major parameters – the approach and the tech level. Under each parameter fall two broad method categories. The approach parameter looks at whether the methodologies followed in teaching are teacher-centered or student-centered. The former methodology assumes the students are empty vessels that are ready to be filled with the knowledge provided by the teacher. In that methodology, everything revolves around the teacher as he/she presents, demonstrates, guides, and assigns work to students. The latter methodology involves students in the learning process. Teachers act as facilitators and mentors as they guide students' participation and involvement. On the other hand, the tech level parameter describes the level of technology utilized for teaching. On one end of the tech level spectrum is the high-tech methodology, which extensively utilizes technology in the delivery of information. On the other end of the tech level spectrum is the low-tech methodology, in which the use of technology in the delivery of information is negligible. Figure 10.1 illustrates the four outcomes of the various parameter combinations:

Several studies on the teaching methods used for courses of conventional economics and finance have shown the preference of the student-centered approach over the teacher-centered one. For example, several studies maintained the superiority of the student-centered Problem-Based Learning (PBL)[3] teaching method over the traditional teacher-centered approach in courses related to economics. Likewise, several studies demonstrated the enabling effect of PBL and its ability to improve students' competencies in courses related to business and finance. As an example, most of the methods

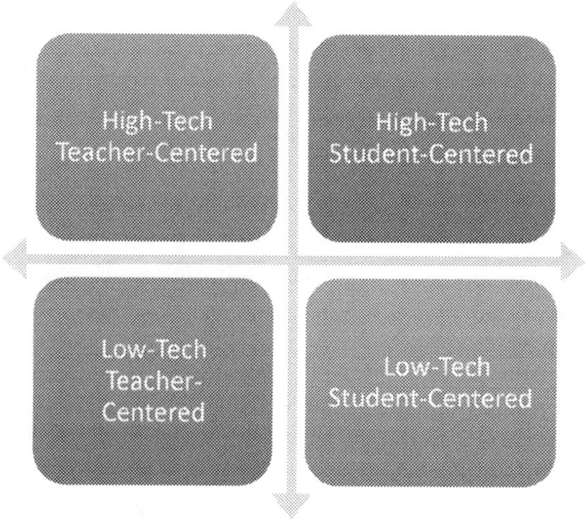

Figure 10.1 Four quadrants summarizing teaching theories depicting the teacher-centered vs. student-centered approach and high-tech vs. low-tech level.

Source: Adapted from teach.com.

recommended by Olokoyo and Oyewo (2014) in teaching financial management courses are geared towards a student-centered approach. This includes discussion groups and studying beyond the classroom. Comparably, other studies have favored the integration of technology in the delivery of finance and economics courses over traditional classes that do not use technology. For instance, in a study conducted by Zhai, the researcher finds that the class that was subjected to the use of information technology for the practical teaching of finance and economics had a higher mastery level of the topic than the class that was exposed to traditional face-to-face teaching of finance and economics.

The aforementioned argument indicates the importance of combining a student-centered approach with a high-tech level in order to achieve an optimal level of a class outcome. In other words, economics and finance classes should be geared towards achieving the upper right quadrant of Figure 10.1. Courses of Islamic finance can greatly benefit from such teaching methods in order to attain desired class outcomes. However, Islamic finance courses are very challenging because they involve detailed laws extracted from the Qur'ān, Sunnah, and Ijmā' whereby the student is required to learn the elements of each type of contract, its conditions, the various jurisprudential opinions related to it, its salient contemporary applications, and features of hybrid contracts and their applicability in today's world. There is no exaggeration if one classifies Islamic finance as a subject that falls under the "detailed law subjects" category. Detailed law subjects are not easy to deliver, and therefore, the methodologies used to teach such subjects in general will significantly affect the whole learning experience. But one needs to identify the methodology challenges in teaching Islamic finance courses before the optimum method(s) are found and applied.

The rest of this chapter is divided into four other sections organized in the following manner. Subsequent to the introduction, the second section reviews the related literature on the methodological challenges of teaching Islamic finance to identify methodological challenges and gaps existing in the current literature. These challenges and gaps are then analyzed in the third section, and prospects are pinpointed and presented. The third section proposes a holistic approach to handle methodological challenges in teaching Islamic finance. The fourth section concludes the chapter with a summary of the findings and analysis of the topic. This is followed by the fifth section, which offers suggestions in light of this study and proposes the way forward for future research.

Methodological challenges of teaching Islamic finance

There is a scarcity of articles and monographs of literature discussing the subject of pedagogy in Islamic finance in general and teaching methods in particular, let alone discussing their challenges. The few works available on the topic have been mostly disjointed and lacked the in-depth inspection of the methodological challenges in teaching Islamic finance. Some are even largely descriptive and prescriptive in nature. These few works can be divided into two broad categories. The first category relates to studies that focus on the methodological challenges associated with the curriculum of a typical Islamic finance course. The second category consists of research papers that discuss challenges linked to academic talent development. While most of the studies from both categories are able to identify some of the methodological challenges in teaching Islamic finance, the fact is that these studies have handled the subject in dribs and drabs rather than taking a holistic approach. Moreover, these studies have barely discussed the issue of teaching Islamic finance from the perspective of learning theories and instructional design. But be that as it may, the purpose of this review is to extract the methodological challenges of teaching Islamic finance from extant work, as well as identify gaps that need to be filled in literature.

Methodological challenges associated with the curriculum

Islamic finance lends itself to the field of Islamic law. Fiqh al-Mu'āmalāt,[4] which makes the largest share of the content of a typical Islamic finance course, is in fact a subset of the Shari'ah. Like any other legal course, Islamic finance is characterized by detailed law and therefore is very heavy in content and very difficult to digest in the very short duration of the course, let alone relating it to the practical world. This fact is underpinned by a study that showed students facing difficulties in understanding the terms and types of contracts in Islamic Mu'āmalāt law, as well as finding difficulties in memorizing evidence of the Islamic transaction contracts from Qur'ān and Sunnah (Halim *et al.*, 2018). This dual issue, being difficult to digest and lacking industrial pragmatism, has been identified in the literature, albeit in various depths and degrees, and many dealing with one of the issues while missing the other.

In his monograph on teaching Islamic economics, Siddiqi (2005, p. 35) embarks on giving teaching guidelines to address teaching challenges for topics related to Islamic finance. For example, he describes a method to deliver certain concepts when he says:

> The teacher should elaborate upon this point [the difference between debt-creating modes like murābaḥa and interest-bearing debts] by describing conventional banking as well as Islamic banking in detail.
> (*Siddiqi, 2005*)

While such teaching methods can help address the issue of digesting the material, the method is prescriptive in nature and lacks dimensions of a pedagogy paradigm shift that understands modern learning theories and methodologies. In contrast, in an attempt to address the heavy content challenge, Halim *et al.* (2018) proposed a diversified method in teaching which, along with lectures and tutorials, includes interactive lectures, PBL, and learning by playing which they called the Mu'āmalāt Interactive Game. Although their diversified method in teaching yielded positive results, nonetheless their study lacked the methodology to address the detachment of academic work from the real industry.

The latter issue has been frequently expressed in literature. Many Islamic finance courses from reputable universities are rich in the Islamic finance knowledge, but are poor on the practical side, which is required for working in the industry and innovating through technology (Jamil & Seman, 2019, p. 78). In response to such an issue, Zou (2021, p. 263) maintained that there is a need for industry and university research cooperation in the economic management specialty to introduce the latest technology and industrial scenarios and materials into the curriculum teaching, which in turn will have the effect of improving the quality of economic management professional training. This is in direct agreement with the reasoning of Ahmad, Mawar, and Ripain (2017, p. 646) and Jamil and Seman (2019, p. 78), who believe that cooperation and collaboration between academia and industry is necessary to direct curricula and research towards the skills and expertise needed by industry. In contrast, Haneef (2018, p. 60) argues that due to pressure from "practical industry demand," some Islamic banking and finance programs have not given sufficient attention to the Islamic worldview and its constituent elements; instead they've been a reflection of neoclassical economics of profit maximization and maximizing shareholder wealth rather than addressing the goals and objectives of Islamic economics. A reconciliation is obviously required between both views. A cursory look into this discrepancy reveals that the selected teaching methods should not ignore either of the opinions; the curriculum must be balanced in terms of its knowledge content and industrial practicality.

Methodological challenges linked to talent development

In this category, most of what has been mentioned in the literature lacks thorough inspection on the issues of human capital development and has failed in general to devise proper teaching methods to address human-related challenges. The list mainly was constrained by challenges of talent availability and development. Haneef (2018, p. 60) quotes the findings of a study conducted by the International Council of Islamic Finance Educators (ICIFE), where one of them shows that the domain of Islamic finance is seriously underrepresented by the available talent of academics.

One of the reasons for this shortage might be due to shortages in specific Islamic finance programs. Shahzad, Ur Rehman, Saeed, and Ehsan (2019, p. 75) recommend integrating Islamic finance in the curriculum of Deeni Madaris (Religious Seminaries) to cover an understanding of modern Islamic finance transactions. They recommend special training programs for human development for both the students and teaching faculty of the Deeni Madaris. This is in line with the findings of another study by Salh and Mohammed, which ascribes the skill issue to a shortage of centers and training courses in the Islamic finance field on the one hand, and on the other hand, to unqualified staff in the Islamic finance industry who lack sufficient Islamic financial knowledge.

While the above studies identified challenges related to human and talent development, such studies remained silent on the methodological challenges that need to be addressed in order to have an adequate supply of talented academics who are capable of delivering Islamic finance in the most optimum way. There is a myriad of questions that remain unanswered. What are the characteristics of a well-rounded academic in the Islamic finance field? How can similar academics be developed? What does it take, and what technologies are needed for achieving such development? What are the methodologies required? Are there any methodological challenges? Why has the status quo not addressed these challenges?

Perhaps the case study conducted by Lavoie and Moghul (2014) was the most thorough in this category of the literature and answers some of the above questions. According to them, learning theory and instructional design have not gained significant public attention within the Islamic finance industry, since the focus remained on the curriculum and the credentials of the instructors. Instead of focusing on the faculty qualifications, Lavoie and Moghul (2014) articulate that the educators of Islamic finance should monitor developments in educational methods and technologies to ensure that practitioners learn in the best way. However, the focus should not be on technology alone. Technological advancements and innovations – represented by the emergence of the web, internet, Learning Management Systems (LMS), mobile technologies, and Massive Open Online Courses (MOOCs) – have provided increased

Table 10.1 Gaps in the literature of methodological challenges in teaching Islamic finance

No.	*Gaps in literature*
1	Scarcity of research dealing with the subject of pedagogy in Islamic finance in general and teaching methodologies and their challenges in particular.
2	Studies on the topic are generally disjointed and lack in-depth discussion on teaching methodology challenges while some are largely descriptive and prescriptive in nature.
3	The literature handles the topic of Islamic finance teaching methods in dribs and drabs instead taking a holistic approach.
4	The literature barely discusses the issue of teaching Islamic finance from the learning theories and instructional design perspective.

access, affordability, convenience, and availability for higher education. Yet, these online courses, for instance, are often pre-existing courses designed for the traditional passive learning mode (Lavoie & Moghul, 2014, pp. 130–131). What is needed is a "pedagogical paradigm shift which challenges the utilization of technology for efficiency and the missed opportunity for effectiveness" (Lavoie & Moghul, 2014, p. 131). In other words, the faculty of Islamic law and finance is not prepared for such a pedagogy paradigm shift and thus, according to the authors, they need to be developed using student-centered methodology to design and deliver active student-centered learning courses.

Nonetheless, due to lack of research in the application of learning theories to the field of teaching Islamic finance, further understanding of the methodological challenges is blurred. Careful analysis of the identified gaps in literature, coupled with the examined challenges, can shed further light on the topic. This will be the subject of the next section. Table 10.1 summarizes the identified gaps extracted from the literature review while Table 10.2 summarizes the methodological challenges in teaching Islamic finance.

Table 10.2 Methodological challenges in teaching Islamic finance

No.	*Methodological challenges*
1	Islamic finance teaching methods need to address its heavy content and the difficulty of grasping and digesting information.
2	Teaching methods should not lead to detachment of education from industry pragmatism and separation of academia from latest technologies in the industry.
3	Teaching methods must ensure that the curriculum is balanced in terms of its knowledge content and industrial practicality.
4	Shortage of talent exerts pressure on finding proper teaching methods to deliver Islamic finance courses.
5	Development of faculty and teachers requires more than the traditional ways of training. The development should incorporate special teaching methods to prepare the faculty for a pedagogy paradigm shift.

Analysis of the challenges and the prospects

In this section, the authors analyze the methodological challenges identified in the second section and summarized in Table 10.2. Due to lack of research on the applicability of learning theories to teaching Islamic finance, the analysis assumes that mainstream teaching approaches are being applied in teaching Islamic finance. The analysis produces a two-parameter gauge under the student-centered approach to determine the best method for delivering the curriculum. In addition, the analysis leads to proposing a tri-perspective holistic approach for addressing the methodological challenges of teaching Islamic finance.

On the onset of the analysis, it is worth mentioning that learning theories show preference to student-centered teaching approaches over teacher-centered ones and favor a high-tech level in the delivery of courses over a low-tech level. Lavoie and Moghul (2014, p. 104) report that pedagogy is undergoing a shift in the United States and elsewhere, evolving from teacher-centered learning methods to student-centered active learning. Following this global pedagogy shift, the analysis henceforth will be based on the assumption that the desired methodology to be followed in teaching Islamic finance should be student-centered, high-tech active learning. Despite the positive results achieved by Halim *et al.* (2018) when applying diversified student-centered methods to their sample utilizing high levels of technology, one should bear in mind that research in the application of learning theories to the methods for teaching Islamic finance is yet to be conducted in order to validate such positive results. This issue is a direct consequence of Gap 4 from Table 10.1, identified in the literature review from the previous section.

Out of the five methodological challenges listed in Table 10.2, the first three challenges are related to the curriculum of a typical Islamic finance course. The first challenge, "Islamic finance teaching methods need to address its heavy content and address the difficulty of grasping and digesting information," can be addressed by actively involving students in the learning process. Essentially, teachers should follow a student-centered active learning approach. They need to design their teaching sessions accordingly. Tools such as PBL and the use of technology such as Halim *et al.*'s (2018) Mu'āmalāt Interactive Game can help achieve the desired results. Challenge 2, on the other hand, is linked to ensuring industrial exposure in the curriculum of Islamic finance. Challenge 3 is also linked to ensuring industrial exposure in the curriculum but also relates to ensuring sufficient knowledge content. This allows the researchers to devise two new parameters within a student-centered approach. The first is the level of industrial exposure and the second is the level of knowledge content. The former involves exposing students to industrial practices and latest technologies used, while the latter involves providing the students with sufficient knowledge in the domain of Islamic finance. Such an arrangement results in four outcomes within a student-centered approach, depicted in Figure 10.2.

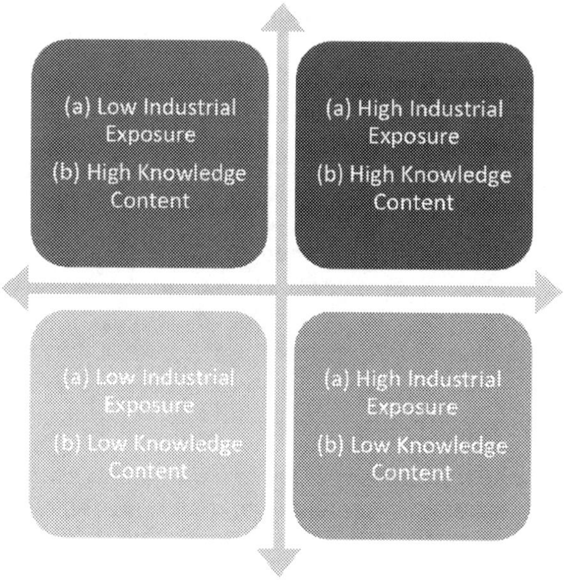

Figure 10.2 Four quadrants summarizing curriculum content methods within the student-centered approach depicting horizontally (a) High Industrial Exposure vs. Low Industrial Exposure, and vertically (b) High Knowledge Content vs. Low Knowledge Content.

Ideally, a student-centered approach in Islamic finance should aim for high industrial exposure and high knowledge content, that is to say, the methods should be designed to have a curriculum that targets the upper right quadrant in Figure 10.2. Notwithstanding, such an arrangement is subject to time constraints and level of access to the industry.

The other two challenges in Table 10.2, Challenge 4 and Challenge 5, are linked to academic talent development. Since they do not come from an education background, the faculty academics delivering Islamic finance are not prepared to design a student-centered class setting (Lavoie & Moghul, 2014). This is in essence Challenge 5. Developmental trainings, thus, should not be a mere coverage of use of technology and just introducing the latest education methods for the sake of it. Traditional trainings will fail to produce the intended results that make talent academics capable of designing a student-centered class setting. While applying a student-centered approach in the training of the academics themselves is deemed necessary, the faculty should as well be exposed to the latest learning theories and instructional design that will enable them to design student-centered courses.

That being said, this chapter proposes a tri-perspective for teaching methods in Islamic finance; one that adopts a more holistic approach to the teaching experience and contributes to the pedagogy paradigm shift. A tri-perspective that does not just seek the best curricular teaching methods, but one that

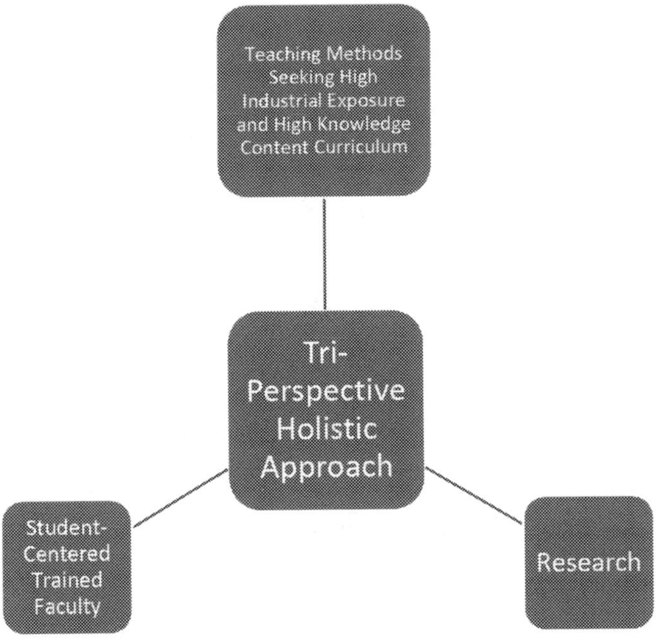

Figure 10.3 Tri-perspective holistic approach to address methodological challenges in teaching Islamic finance.

looks at all its dimensions: the curriculum, the industrial pragmatism, the faculty preparedness, and theoretical research. Such a model will help address Gap 3, "The literature handled the topic of Islamic finance teaching methods in dribs and drabs rather than taking a holistic approach." It will set the context for addressing methodological challenges faced in teaching Islamic finance. Moreover, this model can help in addressing the methodological challenges faced in teaching Islamic economics courses in general. Figure 10.3 illustrates this tri-perspective model.

To recap, the analysis produces a two-parameter gauge within the student-centered approach, which looks at the extent to which the methods used for the curriculum incorporate industry practices and the extent of knowledge coverage. This feeds into a tri-perspective holistic approach that addresses methodological challenges in teaching Islamic finance.

Conclusion

Since its establishment in the 1970s, Islamic finance has continued to gain interest, not only from Muslims but also from non-Muslims. The past half century was sufficient to create tremendous improvements and developments in its domain. A direct implication of this fact is the growing demand for highly adept professionals and practitioners qualified to serve the Islamic finance industry and capable of accommodating the changes required in the field. This exerts high pressure on the field of education, as adequate programs that suit the resulting situation urgently need to be sought and proper teaching methods need to be adopted.

In this chapter, a critical lens was applied to the literature to extract methodological challenges in teaching Islamic finance. Four gaps were identified: research in Islamic finance pedagogy is scarce, available research is fragmented and lacks in-depth coverage of methodological challenges, the topic of Islamic finance teaching methods is handled in dribs and drabs, and the literature barely touches upon the learning theories in the context of Islamic finance. Additionally, five challenges were identified: teaching methods need to acknowledge the heavy content of Islamic finance and address its difficulty; teaching methods should not lead to the detachment of education from the industry practicalities; teaching methods need to ensure that the curriculum is balanced in terms of its knowledge content and industrial practicality; shortage of talented academics; and the challenge of developing faculty to ensure the flow of a pedagogy paradigm shift.

The identified gaps and challenges were analyzed with the assumption that teaching Islamic finance follows the global pedagogy shift towards a student-centered approach. The analysis has yielded a two-parameter gauge within the student-centered methodical approach. This gauge studies the extent to which the curriculum of an Islamic finance course has exposure to the industry on the one hand, and the extent of knowledge content on the other hand. The analysis also culminated in proposing a tri-perspective approach to address methodological challenges in teaching Islamic finance.

Suggestions and the way forward

Gap 1, retrieved from Table 10.1, indicates the scarcity of available studies and therefore suggests that there is ample space for research in the domain of pedagogy in Islamic finance and its teaching methodologies. The findings in this chapter suggest that further research needs to be carried out with three main issues in mind. First, the tri-perspective model depicted in Figure 10.3 can help guide the research to address teaching method challenges from a holistic approach. This will have the effect of avoiding handling the topic of Islamic finance teaching methods in dribs and drabs, which is identified herein in this chapter as Gap 3. Secondly, more in-depth studies and discussions on methodological challenges faced in teaching Islamic finance are required. This will be in immediate response to Gap 2, which states that the current research is largely descriptive, rather than having the desired depth of study. Thirdly, there is negligible number of studies that have discussed learning theories in the context of teaching Islamic finance. The literature has barely touched on the issue and this chapter has identified this as Gap 4. The research in learning theories and instructional design from the perspective of teaching Islamic finance will be of profound importance, as this will help identify the most optimum learning theories for teaching Islamic finance. In essence, it will validate the assumption that pedagogy in Islamic finance follows the paradigm shift witnessed in the world and that the student-centered approach is the most optimal.

Notes

1 Participation banking is another terminology that is synonymous with Islamic banking.
2 QISMUT: **Q**atar, **I**ndonesia, **S**audi Arabia, **M**alaysia, **U**nited Arab Emirates, **T**urkey.
3 PBL is a student-centered teaching method introduced by Howard Barrows, a professor of neurology at McMaster University in Canada. The method pursues changing students' passive learning role into an active one whereby they take part in understanding the problem, collecting data, and analyzing them.
4 Fiqh al-Mu'āmalāt is the Arabic term that commonly refers to the jurisprudence of Islamic transactions and business contracts.

References

Ahmad, N. W., Mawar, M. Y., & Ripain, N. (2017). The Exploration Study on Employability of Islamic Banking and Finance Graduates. *Proceeding of the 4th International Conference on Management and Muamalah*, 639–647.

Jamil, N. N., & Seman, J. A. (2019). The Impact of Fintech on the Sustainability of Islamic Accounting and Finance Education in Malaysia. *Journal of Islamic, Social, Economics and Development (JISED)*, *4*(17), 74–88. Retrieved from www.jised.com.

Lavoie, D. R., & Moghul, U. F. (2014). Redistributive Pedagogy: A Case Study in Islamic Finance Education and Student-Centered Learning. *Albany Government Law Review*, *7*(2), 101–153.

Siddiqi, M. N. (2005). *Teaching Islamic Economics*. Jeddah: King Abdulaziz University, Scientific Publishing Center.

Zou, D. (2021). Discussion on the Integration Strategy of Industry and Education of Finance and Economics Specialty in University. *Advances in Social Science, Education and Humanities Research*, *551*(ERMM), 263–266.

11

IMPACT OF E-LEARNING TECHNIQUES IN CONDUCTING THE PROFESSIONAL SHARI'AH AUDIT TRAINING AND EMPLOYABILITY PROSPECTS DURING THE COVID-19 PANDEMIC

Muhammad Iqmal Hisham Kamaruddin and Mustafa Mohd Hanefah

Introduction

The 2019 coronavirus disease (COVID-19) pandemic is a new tragedy in human civilization. It was first identified in December 2019 in Wuhan, China and spread rapidly, resulting in an ongoing global pandemic. As COVID-19 is primarily spread between people during close contact, either via coughing, sneezing, or talking, social distancing became the leading prevention approach adopted by most countries, which have introduced restrictions on movement and lockdown orders, including Malaysia. Malaysia introduced several phases of movement control orders, also known as lockdowns, from 18–31 March, followed by 1–14 April, 15–28 April, 29 April–11 May, 12 May–9 June, 10 June–31 August, and the latest is from 1 September–31 December 2020. Since the introduction of lockdown, people are required to restrict their activities by working from home, and almost all economic sectors were closed except for essential services. Included in the essential services are food, healthcare, water, energy, security and defense, solid waste and public cleansing, communication, banking and finance, e-commerce, and logistics (Bernama, 2020a). As education sectors do not fall under the essential services category, all activities related to education were suspended. Apart from the normal classes, students and teachers cannot attend related physical education activities such as tuition, extra classes, sports training and co-curricular activities (Roslan, 2020).

DOI: 10.4324/9781003252764-14

Moreover, other education programs, including tertiary education, as well as professional trainings and programs were also affected.

Therefore, the online platform has been utilized as a medium for learning processes for all educational levels starting from kindergarten to tertiary and professional education. However, there is a concern about the issues and challenges faced, especially by students or participants in the e-learning processes via online platforms (Rashid et al., 2020). Even during this challenging period, a group of experts from USIM was involved in conducting a professional *shariah* training program known as the Certified Professional Shariah Audit (CPSA) program for bankers and students in Malaysia. In this chapter, the effectiveness of the e-learning approach and employability prospects related to the training program conducted during the pandemic to the students from various Malaysian universities throughout Malaysia are discussed.

Literature review

In this section, several issues related to the effectiveness of the e-learning approach in conducting a professional *shariah* audit training program and employability prospects during COVID-19 are discussed. This includes the impact of COVID-19 on the educational sector in Malaysia, mainstreaming professional *shariah* audit training programs via the e-learning approach, and employability prospects during COVID-19.

Impact of COVID-19 on the educational sector in Malaysia

Malaysia, like the rest of the world, was affected by this health crisis. The first closure of all educational institutions started on 18 March 2020, due to the implementation of the MCO. The enforcement involved all preschools; government and private schools, including daily schools; boarding schools; international schools; expatriate schools; *tahfiz* centers; colleges; and other primary, secondary, and university educational institutions (Roslan, 2020). The total number of schools affected due to this closure was 10,220 schools, consisting of 7,780 primary schools and 2,440 secondary schools. This involved a total 4,987,401 students, consisting of 208,131 preschool students, 2,741,837 primary school students, and 2,037,433 secondary school students. A total of 416,743 teachers were also affected, consisting of 236,993 teachers from primary schools and the remaining 179,750 teachers from secondary schools. For the tertiary education level, the total number of higher education institutions affected was 455, consisting of 20 public universities, 51 private universities, 10 foreign university branches, 39 university colleges, and 335 colleges. This involved at least a total of 1,323,449 students, consisting of 567,625 public university students, 633,344 private higher education institutions, 96,362 polytechnics students, and the remaining 26,118 were community colleges students. In addition, the closure of higher education institutions also affected a total of 67,616 academic staff: 31,626 academic staff from public universities, 25,961 academic staff from private higher education institutions, 7,263 academic staff from polytechnics, and 2,766 academic staff from community colleges. The number for students, teachers, and academic staff in the educational sector constitutes more than 20% of the total 32.73 million of Malaysian population in February 2021 (Bernama, 2021).

In order to continue the learning process, many educational institutions in the world, including Malaysia, decided to convert the teaching from the traditional one (face-to-face) to e-learning. At the same time all on-campus activities were canceled or postponed until the crisis could be controlled (Sarea *et al.*, 2021). Among the online platforms used for education purposes in Malaysia during the crisis period were Microsoft Teams, Google Classroom, Zoom, Cisco Webex, and custom made e-learning management systems. The Ministry of Education in Malaysia has collaborated with tech giants such as Google, Microsoft, and Apple to revamp its year-old e-learning platform known as DELIMa (Xiung, 2020). These e-learning platforms enable the teachers and trainers to interact with their students and participants virtually through live or recorded lectures, chatting, training, online exams and quizzes, and assignments. E-learning platforms also allow students to arrange time flexibly, reduce the cost for textbooks, and lower the threshold for accessing educational resources. It makes e-learning platform a great supplement to conventional teaching methods (Abu Karim, 2020).

It is expected that the COVID-19 pandemic will benefit participants, as there will be lower-cost education due to the online transition. This shift to online education will enable students to save costs and time, which in turn will profit them. However, education, including professional training during the current crises, might face several challenges that might affect the quality of outcomes. This includes the students' evaluation process, the faculty members' self-efficacy, digitizing the professional training program, and the lecturing time and teaching methods (Sarea *et al.*, 2021).

Mainstreaming the professional shariah audit training program via the e-learning approach

Currently, most education institutions all around the world are investing in e-learning platforms regardless of educational program types. The integration between the internet and professional training program is seen as a helpful way for the trainers to assess the participants electronically and provide e-feedback (Sarea *et al.*, 2021). This caused boundless growth of e-learning in general and in the professional training programs for accounting and auditing, including training programs for *shariah* audit in particular. In this case, using technology in education enables trainers to get constructive and timely feedback from participants about the effectiveness of the teaching and learning methods used in delivering the material. Besides, participants also appreciated the use of e-assessment and feedback techniques in teaching accounting subjects.

There is a phenomenological study by Perry (2012) on the experiences of students and site supervisors involved in professional clinical training online. In this study, online students viewed themselves at least as well-prepared as the students who are going through the traditional face-to-face training. Surprisingly, some of the online students even reported that their experience in online training was superior as compared to other students who were going through the traditional face-to-face training. From the trainer perspective, a study conducted by Sarea *et al.* (2021) of 102 accounting trainers in the Gulf Cooperation Council countries reveals that they have a positive perception toward the transformation to e-learning due to COVID-19. In this case, accounting trainers not only manage to change their teaching methods to cope with the COVID-19 situation, but e-learning also improves the trainers' efficiency in managing their time. This happened as the time spent for the preparation has dropped. In order to have good e-learning for professional training programs, including *shariah* audit, Murphy *et al.* (2007) highlight several criteria that need to be fulfilled. This includes the ability of respective training institutions to establish standards, monitor participant progress, review outcomes, and assure quality. E-learning for professional training programs must have sufficient contact and interaction between trainers and participants by utilizing various online platform tools to boost the understanding of the participants during the learning process.

In addition, it is believed that e-learning takes place as long as one of the interactions between participants and trainers, participants and other participants, and participants and course content is operative at a high level. Besides, to design and evaluate any e-learning program, there is a need to understand how the e-learning module tools are used (configuration), the instructional methodology, the presentation enhancements, the participant interactions, and learning applications from different schools of learning theory impact participant performance, learning outcomes, and participant satisfaction (Bradley, 2011). Similarly, another study conducted in Malaysia found that course design, trainer characteristics, participant characteristics, and institutional factors were considered as four determinants of e-learning results and satisfaction. Course design in e-learning refers to course information, course organization, instructional objectives, and course layout. Meanwhile, trainer characteristics in e-learning refer to pedagogical, technological, and personal challenges faced by trainers in delivering the e-learning sessions. On the other hand, participant characteristics in e-learning refer to interpersonal relationships among trainers, participants, and their peers during e-learning sessions. Lastly, institutional factors in e-learning refer to such factors as culture, policy, funding, and technological infrastructure issues, which require adequate internet, strong operational e-learning policies, technical skills, and knowledge among trainers. Improving all four determinants will result in boosting e-learning satisfaction.

Apart from focusing on the learning satisfaction, another concern is on the beliefs and intentions of trainers to use and integrate the technology in education. In this case, training institutions were supposed to provide adequate professional development and support for trainers to acquire technology and pedagogical skills to conduct e-learning sessions. This will indirectly help trainers to shift from traditional learning to online learning effectively. Moreover, although trainers are skilled in term of using the computer and exploring online platforms, having positive attitudes toward e-learning and perceived support from administrators in implementing e-learning, the current workload and lack of time become the major barriers that prevent trainers from giving their full commitment in e-learning sessions (Alsadoon, 2009). This includes existing administration work in the training institutions as well as other scopes such as conducting research, publications, and community engagements.

Finally, although mainstreaming professional *shariah* audit training programs might be useful in terms of flexibility, trainers may be concerned about the participants' learning and knowledge (Humphrey & Beard, 2014). In this case, the lack of physical interaction between trainers and participants was the main criticism of e-learning (Sarea *et al.*, 2021). Besides, the lack of an effective learning process because of the sudden transition to e-learning might lead to unexpected consequences that might affect the participant's future professional prospects (Aguguom *et al.*, 2020).

Employability prospects during COVID-19

It is an undeniable fact that employability prospects will become more challenging due to COVID-19. For instance, employment opportunities sharply decreased due to the rise in number of closed businesses, due to their inability to survive during COVID-19. According to the Malaysian Computer and Multimedia Industry Association, about 40% of new technology companies are expected to be closed due to COVID-19 (Bernama, 2020b). In addition, about 650,000 micro-businesses cannot operate due to lockdown orders and inability to pay their employees (Mohd Amin, 2020). The latest unemployment rate in Malaysia rose to 5.3% in May 2020, and the rate of unemployment increased to about 826,000 persons (Zulkapli, 2020). This figure is believed to have continuously risen to two million people, and the unemployment rate has soared to 10% or even 15% (Hoh, 2020). By taking into account the new fresh graduate numbers, amounting to between 300,000 and 350,000 yearly, this will become another challenge for graduates to compete with existing unemployed employees. This can be seen in a recent survey conducted on the employment prospects in the future in Malaysia, showings that final-year students from public universities believe that the employment prospects in the future after COVID-19 is low.

Meanwhile, in the financial sector, several main industry players at the international level are making job cuts due to COVID-19. This includes Lloyds Bank in United Kingdom with 780 job cuts, Wells Fargo in United States with 700 job cuts, Barclays in the United Kingdom with 1,140 job cuts, UniCredit in Italy with more than 6,000 job cuts, and Commerzbank in Germany with 10,000 job cuts (Hamilton, 2020). In addition, HSBC also accelerated 35,000 job cuts globally due to COVID-19 (Makortoff, 2020). In Malaysia, although there is no official statement on job cuts due to COVID-19 in the financial sector, the implementation of the moratorium and other factors relating to COVID-19 have an impact especially on the profit falls by these industrial players, including for Islamic financial institutions that might impact on the retrenchment and job cuts near in the future (Lee, 2020).

Therefore, the shortage of workforces, including *shariah* auditors, in the Islamic finance industry due to COVID-19 will impact the growth of the Islamic finance industry itself. As such, the development of *shariah* auditor talents, especially for undergraduate students, is becoming one of the important solutions to overcome the scarcity of talents as well as to support the growth in the Islamic finance industry. The scarcity can be filled by competent and skillful *shariah* auditors who possess professional certification and skills.

Methodology

Data collection procedure

As mentioned previously, only USIM and UIAM at present are offering *shariah* audit as part of their curriculum. However, under the National Graduate Employability Program, USIM was awarded a grant from the Ministry of Higher Education to conduct the Certified Professional Shariah Auditor (CPSA) training program for final-year students at Malaysian public universities. This is part of the government initiative to equip final-year students with adequate knowledge and skills as an additional value for them to be employed after their graduation. In general, the CPSA program covers the technical skills and understanding on *shariah* audit and review processes for the Islamic finance industry (IBFIM, 2019). This program is developed based on academia-industry collaboration between USIM and IBFIM to ensure that the program is offered with the highest quality and meets all industry requirements at the same time (Kamaruddin & Hanefah, 2017). It is expected that by enrolling in the CPSA program, participants will able to learn and apply *shariah* audit and review skills in Islamic financial institutions to ensure *shariah* compliance and assurance to all stakeholders.

The CPSA program consists of six modules related to *shariah* audit. The modules cover various aspects on *shariah* audit practices starting from *shariah* principles, *shariah* governance, accounting and reporting for Islamic financial transactions, *shariah* risk management, *shariah* audit planning, *shariah* audit programs, *shariah* audit fieldwork, and *shariah* audit communication. The module outline for CPSA program is summarized in Table 11.1.

Normally, the training is fully conducted face-to-face, as was done in 2019. However, due to COVID-19, the e-learning approach was adopted to conduct the training. For this, training videos and online class sessions were fully used

Table 11.1 CPSA module outline

Module	*Descriptions*
Fundamentals of *Shariah* for Islamic Finance	This module covers *shariah* concepts and principles in the Islamic finance industry.
Fundamentals of Governance and Auditing	This module covers governance and auditing in the Islamic finance industry.
Accounting and Reporting for Islamic Financial Transactions	This module covers *shariah*-based accounting and reporting for Islamic financial transactions.
Shariah Risk Management and Internal Control	This module covers *shariah* risk identification and mitigation in Islamic finance industry.
Shariah Audit Planning and Program	This module covers *shariah* audit processes and programs based on scope, plan, and processes in the Islamic finance industry.
Shariah Audit Fieldwork and Communication	This module covers on *shariah* audit fieldwork and communications in the Islamic finance industry.

Source: IBFIM (2019).

by all module trainers. Both pre-recorded and online class sessions were conducted through Microsoft Teams for all six modules. Pre-recorded training videos that cover every topic for every module were made by trainers and uploaded to Microsoft Teams at the beginning of the training programs for self-learning purposes. Next, a series of online class sessions were scheduled five times for each module at the weekend. This training program was executed from July to August 2020.

In order to explore and identify the effectiveness in adopting e-learning approaches to conduct the professional *shariah* audit training program and also employability prospects during COVID-19, a survey questionnaire was designed and used in the training. The questionnaire is divided into three sections. The first section collects the demographic profile of the participants. The second section collects data about the effectiveness of participating in the e-learning training program to enhance *shariah* audit knowledge and skills. Finally, the last section solicited the results of the training on employability prospects 6 months after the training programs.

Before the final distribution of the survey, a copy of the instrument was distributed to a number of academicians and experts to give their feedback on the wording, the content, and the appropriateness of the questions; the coverage of the dimensions of the current COVID-19 outbreak as perceived by the researchers; the simplicity of the questions; and the presentation. Amendments made to the final version and the actual survey were disseminated to the participants of the CPSA training program under the GE 2020 program initiative.

For instrumentation purposes, the first section on the demographic profile covered background information of the participants, including gender, university, region, academic background, and *shariah* audit education. Meanwhile, for the second section, five questions covered the level of the knowledge learned for each module, which are: (1) strengthening the fundamental knowledge; (2) empowering the knowledge understanding, (3) obtaining the value added; (4) gaining in-depth knowledge; and (5) acquiring technical skills. In order to measure such prospects, this study employed a 5-point Likert scale ranging from "(1) = strongly disagree" to "(5) = strongly agree." Finally, the last section on the employability prospects was asked by identifying participants' employment status within 6 months after the training. This includes employment status, industry placement, job position, and starting salary.

For analysis purpose, qualitative data were analyzed by using thematic analysis where the data were grouped into several themes. Meanwhile, for quantitative data, a descriptive analysis technique was applied to analyze the collected data. This technique was used to explore the participant perception regarding challenges and prospects faced by joining the professional *shariah* audit training program via e-learning during COVID-19. This technique was chosen as it had been used widely in the similar previous studies (Sarea *et al.*, 2021).

Data collection sample

In total, all 296 participants from various Malaysian public universities answered the survey. Table 11.2 summarizes the background information of these respondents.

Based on Table 11.2, the gap between male and female students is quite huge (51.4%), where 72 males responded compared to 224 female respondents. This is not surprising, as about 70% of Malaysian universities' students consist of more female students than male students. These students come from 13 different universities in Malaysia, where the highest percentage is USIM (32.8%), followed by UUM (7.1%), UIAM (6.8%), UNISZA (6.8%), UMK (6.8%), UPSI (6.8%), UMS (6.3%), UITM (6.1%), UMT (6.1%), UKM (5.7%), UM (4%), and the lowest are from UNIMAS (2.4%) and UPM (2.4%).

In term of regions, one-third of the students reside in the central region of Malaysia (33%). This was followed by students who reside at the eastern region (27.7%), northern region (20.3%), and southern region (16.6%). Besides, there were also about 2.3% of the students who came from the Malaysian Borneo region (Sabah and Sarawak). For academic background, responses showed mixed backgrounds, where 36.5% of the students had Islamic banking/finance backgrounds. Meanwhile, students with accounting backgrounds consist of 23% of the respondents, closely followed by both *shariah*/*usul fiqh*/law and *muamalat*/Islamic economics with 21% and 19.5% of the respondents, respectively. From these figures,

Table 11.2 Respondents' background information

Details	*Frequency*	*Percentage (%)*
Gender		
Male	72	24.3
Female	224	75.7
University		
Universiti Sains Islam Malaysia (USIM)	97	32.8
Universiti Islam Antarabangsa Malaysia (UIAM)	20	6.8
Universiti Teknologi Mara Malaysia (UITM)	18	6.1
Universiti Malaya (UM)	12	4.0
Universiti Kebangsaan Malaysia (UKM)	17	5.7
Universiti Utara Malaysia (UUM)	21	7.1
Universiti Sultan Zainal Abidin (UNISZA)	20	6.7
Universiti Malaysia Terengganu (UMT)	18	6.1
Universiti Malaysia Sabah (UMS)	19	6.3
Universiti Malaysia Sarawak (UNIMAS)	7	2.4
Universiti Malaysia Kelantan (UMK)	20	6.8
Universiti Putra Malaysia (UPM)	7	2.4
Universiti Pendidikan Sultan Idris (UPSI)	20	6.8
Region Area		
Northern Region (Perlis, Kedah, Penang & Perak)	60	20.3
Southern Region (Negeri Sembilan, Melaka &	49	16.6
Johor)	82	27.7
Eastern Region (Kelantan, Terengganu & Pahang)	98	33.0
Central Region (Selangor, Kuala Lumpur &	7	2.4
Putrajaya)		
Malaysian Borneo Region (Sabah, Sarawak & Labuan)		
Academic Background		
Accounting	68	23.0
Shariah/Usul Fiqh/Law	62	21.0
Islamic Banking/Finance	108	36.5
Muamalat/Islamic Economic	58	19.5
Shariah Audit Education Prior the Program		
Yes	88	29.7
No	208	70.3

about 88 students (29.7%) have learned *shariah* audit while the remaining 208 (70.3%) students did not undergo any formal *shariah* audit course prior to the program.

Findings and discussions

This section discusses the empirical findings on the effectiveness in adopting the e-learning approach for the professional *shariah* audit training program due to COVID-19. Besides, this section also covers on the employability prospects after enrolling the training program during COVID-19. There are two major findings based on these objectives, namely (1) effectiveness of the training program via the e-learning approach; and (2) employability prospects after the training program during COVID-19.

Effectiveness of the training program via e-learning approach

Based on Table 11.3, the majority of the participants emphasized that they were able to master the *shariah* principles knowledge and skills for *shariah* audit via the e-learning approach. Remarkably, 98.7% of participants agree (69.3% strongly agree and 29.4% agree) that they are able to strengthen the fundamental knowledge for *shariah* principles via the e-learning approach. The similar agreement also goes for empowering the knowledge understanding (98%), obtaining the value-added (97.6%), gaining the in-depth knowledge (98.7%), and acquiring the technical skills (98.3%). The remainder (between 1.3% and 2.4%) agree moderately on each item, and interestingly no one disagreed on any of the items asked in the questionnaire. Hence, from the findings, it can be concluded that the participants are able to master the *shariah* principles knowledge and skills for *shariah* audit via the e-learning approach.

Next, as can be seen from Table 11.4, the highest agreement by participants on mastering the *shariah* governance knowledge and skills for *shariah* audit via e-learning is in gaining the in-depth knowledge, which is about 98.6% (67.9% strongly agree and 29.7% agree). This is followed closely by strengthening the fundamental knowledge (97.3%), acquiring the technical skills (97.3%), empowering the knowledge understanding (96.6%), and the least is obtaining the value-added (95.3%). The remaining votes are on moderate agreement between 2.4% and 3.7% for each item. Thus, from the results, it can be concluded that the participants are able to master the *shariah* governance knowledge and skills for *shariah* audit via the e-learning approach.

Table 11.3 Shariah principles knowledge and skills

Items	*Agreement (agree and strongly agree)*	*Neutral (moderate)*	*Disagreement (disagree and strongly disagree)*
Strengthening the fundamental knowledge	5 = 205 (69.3%) 4 = 87 (29.4%)	3 = 4 (1.3%)	2 = 0 (0%) 1 = 0 (0%)
Empowering the knowledge understanding	5 = 210 (71%) 4 = 80 (27%)	3 = 6 (2%)	2 = 0 (0%) 1 = 0 (0%)
Obtaining the value-added	5 = 202 (68.2%) 4 = 87 (29.4%)	3 = 7 (2.4%)	2 = 0 (0%) 1 = 0 (0%)
Gaining the in-depth knowledge	5 = 224 (75.7%) 4 = 68 (23%)	3 = 4 (1.3%)	2 = 0 (0%) 1 = 0 (0%)
Acquiring the technical skills	5 = 222 (75%) 4 = 69 (23.3%)	3 = 5 (1.7%)	2 = 0 (0%) 1 = 0 (0%)

Note: Strongly Agree = 5; Agree = 4; Moderate = 3; Disagree = 2; Strongly Disagree = 1

Table 11.4 Shariah governance knowledge and skills

Items	*Agreement (agree and strongly agree)*	*Neutral (moderate)*	*Disagreement (disagree and strongly disagree)*
Strengthening the fundamental knowledge	5 = 184 (62.2%) 4 = 104 (35.1%)	3 = 8 (2.7%)	2 = 0 (0%) 1 = 0 (0%)
Empowering the knowledge understanding	5 = 195 (65.9%) 4 = 91 (30.7%)	3 = 10 (3.4%)	2 = 0 (0%) 1 = 0 (0%)
Obtaining the value-added	5 = 182 (61.5%) 4 = 103 (34.8%)	3 = 11 (3.7%)	2 = 0 (0%) 1 = 0 (0%)
Gaining the in-depth knowledge	5 = 201 (67.9%) 4 = 88 (29.7%)	3 = 7 (2.4%)	2 = 0 (0%) 1 = 0 (0%)
Acquiring the technical skills	5 = 191 (64.5%) 4 = 97 (32.8%)	3 = 8 (2.7%)	2 = 0 (0%) 1 = 0 (0%)

Note: Strongly Agree = 5; Agree = 4; Moderate = 3; Disagree = 2; Strongly Disagree = 1

From Table 11.5, participants mostly agree that they are gaining an in-depth knowledge of Islamic financial transactions (98.3%, 71.6% strongly agree and 26.7% agree) and strengthening the fundamental knowledge (98.3%, 65.5% strongly agree and 32.8% agree) by mastering the Islamic financial transaction knowledge and skills for *shariah* audit via the e-learning approach. This is followed closely by empowering the knowledge understanding (98%), obtaining the value-added (97.6%), and the least is acquiring the technical skills (96.6%). The remaining votes are on moderate agreement between 1.7% and 3.4% for each item. In other word, participants are able to master the Islamic financial transaction knowledge and skills for *shariah* audit via the e-learning approach.

Table 11.6 exhibits the participants' agreement on the prospects of mastering the *shariah* risk management knowledge and skills for *shariah* audit

Table 11.5 Islamic financial transaction knowledge and skills

Items	*Agreement (agree and strongly agree)*	*Neutral (moderate)*	*Disagreement (disagree and strongly disagree)*
Strengthening the fundamental knowledge	5 = 194 (65.5%) 4 = 97 (32.8%)	3 = 5 (1.7%)	2 = 0 (0%) 1 = 0 (0%)
Empowering the knowledge understanding	5 = 202 (68.2%) 4 = 88 (29.8%)	3 = 6 (2%)	2 = 0 (0%) 1 = 0 (0%)
Obtaining the value-added	5 = 189 (63.8%) 4 = 100 (33.8%)	3 = 7 (2.4%)	2 = 0 (0%) 1 = 0 (0%)
Gaining the in-depth knowledge	5 = 212 (71.6%) 4 = 79 (26.7%)	3 = 5 (1.7%)	2 = 0 (0%) 1 = 0 (0%)
Acquiring the technical skills	5 = 196 (66.2%) 4 = 90 (30.4%)	3 = 10 (3.4%)	2 = 0 (0%) 1 = 0 (0%)

Note: Strongly Agree = 5; Agree = 4; Moderate = 3; Disagree = 2; Strongly Disagree = 1

Table 11.6 Shariah risk management knowledge and skills

Items	*Agreement (agree and strongly agree)*	*Neutral (moderate)*	*Disagreement (disagree and strongly disagree)*
Strengthening the fundamental knowledge	5 = 203 (68.6%) 4 = 90 (30.4%)	3 = 3 (1%)	2 = 0 (0%) 1 = 0 (0%)
Empowering the knowledge understanding	5 = 209 (70.6%) 4 = 84 (28.4%)	3 = 3 (1%)	2 = 0 (0%) 1 = 0 (0%)
Obtaining the value-added	5 = 203 (68.6%) 4 = 88 (29.7%)	3 = 5 (1.7%)	2 = 0 (0%) 1 = 0 (0%)
Gaining the in-depth knowledge	5 = 222 (75%) 4 = 72 (24.3%)	3 = 2 (0.7%)	2 = 0 (0%) 1 = 0 (0%)
Acquiring the technical skills	5 = 216 (73%) 4 = 74 (25%)	3 = 6 (2%)	2 = 0 (0%) 1 = 0 (0%)

Note: Strongly Agree = 5; Agree = 4; Moderate = 3; Disagree = 2; Strongly Disagree = 1

via the e-learning approach. The results show that most participants are mastering the *shariah* risk management knowledge and skills by gaining the in-depth knowledge, which is 99.3% (75% strongly agree and 24.3% agree). In line with both are strengthening the fundamental knowledge and empowering the knowledge understanding with 99% agreement, respectively. This is followed closely by obtaining the value-added (98.3%) and the least is acquiring the technical skills (98%). On the other hand, the remaining votes are on moderate agreement between 0.7% and 2% for each item. Therefore, it can be interpreted that participants are able to master the *shariah* risk management knowledge and skills for *shariah* audit via e-learning.

As seen in Table 11.7, the agreement in mastering the *shariah* audit planning and program knowledge and skills for *shariah* audit via e-learning are

Table 11.7 Shariah audit planning and program knowledge and skills

Items	*Agreement (agree and strongly agree)*	*Neutral (moderate)*	*Disagreement (disagree and strongly disagree)*
Strengthening the fundamental knowledge	5 = 197 (66.6%) 4 = 96 (32.4%)	3 = 3 (1%)	2 = 0 (0%) 1 = 0 (0%)
Empowering the knowledge understanding	5 = 203 (68.6%) 4 = 90 (30.4%)	3 = 3 (1%)	2 = 0 (0%) 1 = 0 (0%)
Obtaining the value-added	5 = 196 (66.2%) 4 = 95 (32.1%)	3 = 5 (1.7%)	2 = 0 (0%) 1 = 0 (0%)
Gaining the in-depth knowledge	5 = 202 (68.2%) 4 = 87 (29.4%)	3 = 7 (2.4%)	2 = 0 (0%) 1 = 0 (0%)
Acquiring the technical skills	5 = 187 (63.2%) 4 = 94 (31.8%)	3 = 15 (5%)	2 = 0 (0%) 1 = 0 (0%)

Note: Strongly Agree = 5; Agree = 4; Moderate = 3; Disagree = 2; Strongly Disagree = 1

Table 11.8 Shariah audit fieldwork and communication knowledge and skills

Items	*Agreement (agree and strongly agree)*	*Neutral (moderate)*	*Disagreement (disagree and strongly disagree)*
Strengthening the fundamental knowledge	5 = 197 (66.6%) 4 = 95 (32.1%)	3 = 4 (1.4%)	2 = 0 (0%) 1 = 0 (0%)
Empowering the knowledge understanding	5 = 205 (69.3%) 4 = 89 (30.4%)	3 = 2 (0.7%)	2 = 0 (0%) 1 = 0 (0%)
Obtaining the value-added	5 = 194 (65.5%) 4 = 95 (32.1%)	3 = 7 (2.4%)	2 = 0 (0%) 1 = 0 (0%)
Gaining the in-depth knowledge	5 = 206 (69.6%) 4 = 86 (29.4%)	3 = 4 (1.4%)	2 = 0 (0%) 1 = 0 (0%)
Acquiring the technical skills	5 = 195 (65.9%) 4 = 94 (31.8%)	3 = 7 (2.4%)	2 = 0 (0%) 1 = 0 (0%)

Note: Strongly Agree = 5; Agree = 4; Moderate = 3; Disagree = 2; Strongly Disagree = 1

dominant. The results indicate that most participants are able to strengthen the fundamental knowledge and empower the knowledge understanding, which are 99%. Contrarily, the minority (5%) have moderate agreement, especially on acquiring the technical skills. Hence, it can be concluded that participants are able to master the *shariah* planning and program knowledge and skills for *shariah* audit via e-learning.

Table 11.8 shows that majority of the participants (99.3%) agree that their understanding on *shariah* audit fieldwork and communication knowledge and skills for *shariah* audit via the e-learning approach is much higher. Secondly, most participants also agreed that they are able to strengthen the fundamental knowledge and gaining the in-depth knowledge, which is 98.6% of agreement for both items. Next is the agreement on obtaining the value-added and acquiring the technical skills, with 97.6% of agreement, respectively. The remaining vote is on moderate agreement between 0.7% and 2.4% for each item. These results highlight the prospects on mastering the *shariah* audit fieldwork and communication for *shariah* audit knowledge and skills via the e-learning approach.

Overall, our results suggested that all modules for the professional *shariah* audit training program can be delivered via e-learning. However, based on the results, there is an issue especially on acquiring the technical skills of the professional *shariah* audit training program via e-learning, as most of the moderate agreement made by participants is on this item. This is similar to the concern by Humphrey and Beard (2014) and Sarea *et al.* (2021) on e-learning, which is the lack of physical interaction between trainers and participants. Besides, the results also consistent with the previous study by Kamaruddin and Hanefah (2017), where comprehensive *shariah* audit training can enhance *shariah* audit knowledge of the participants.

Employability prospects after the training program during COVID-19

Apart from the effectiveness in conducting the professional *shariah* audit training program via e-learning, this study also aims to examine the employability prospects within 6 months after the training during COVID-19. Based on the survey, Figure 11.1 shows the employment status for all 296 participants within 6 months after the training program.

Based on Figure 11.1, out of 296 participants, a total of 204 participants (69%) had found employment. Meanwhile, a total of 43 participants (15%) have continued their studies at the master's level, 22 participants (7%) have become entrepreneurs or self-employed, and 4 participants (1%) more participants are still waiting for placement. The remaining 23 participants (8%) are still unemployed.

For industry placement, Figure 11.2 shows that a total of 31 participants (10%) had obtained employment in the auditing sector. This was followed by finance-related sectors such as the banking sector (29 participants, 10%), *takaful* (14 participants, 5%), financial advisory (12 participants, 4%), and the capital and real estate market (3 participants, 1%). A total of 64 participants (22%) are in the education sector, including 43 participants who have continued their studies at the master's level and 21 participants (7%) in government agencies. Meanwhile, the remaining 98 participants (11%) were in other sectors, and 24 participants (8%) were not related (unemployed and waiting for placement).

For job positions, Figure 11.3 indicates a total of 22 participants (7%) were offered jobs as auditors, 21 participants (7%) as accountants, 17 participants (5%) as *takaful*/financial advisors/real estate agents, 16 participants (5%) as financial officers, and another 15 participants (5%) as bank officers.

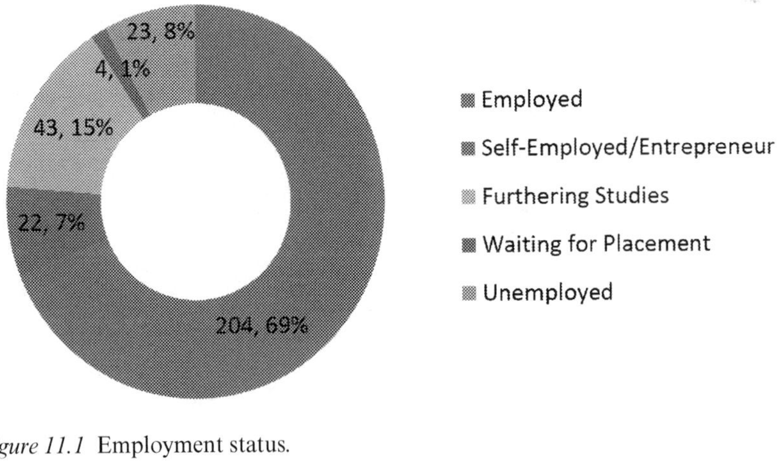

Figure 11.1 Employment status.

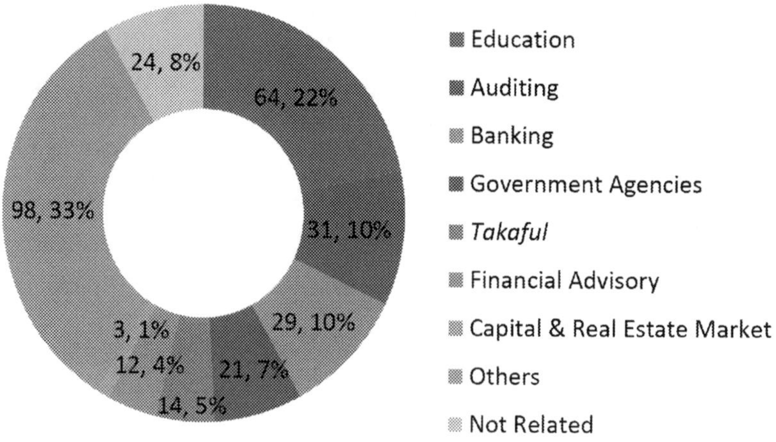

Figure 11.2 Industry placement.

Forty-three participants (15%) are postgraduate students, 19 participants (6%) are government officials, and 18 participants (6%) have become entrepreneurs or self-employed. A total of two participants (4%) were offered jobs as financial service agents and one participant (2%) was offered a job as administrative officer. The remaining 99 participants (15%) were offered various positions, including consultant, media host, and even protégé, and 26 participants (9%) were not related (unemployed and waiting for placement).

Lastly, on starting salary, Figure 11.4 highlights that a total of 115 participants (38.85%) were offered jobs with a starting salary between RM1,000 and RM1,499. This was followed by 47 participants (15.88%) who were offered jobs with starting salaries between RM1,500 and RM1,999 and between RM2,000

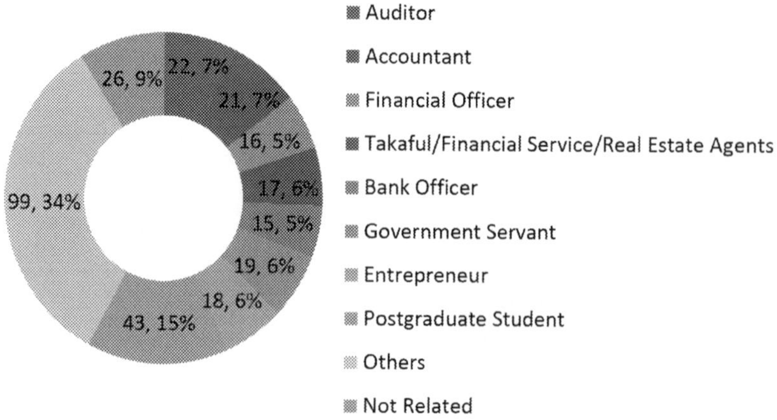

Figure 11.3 Job position.

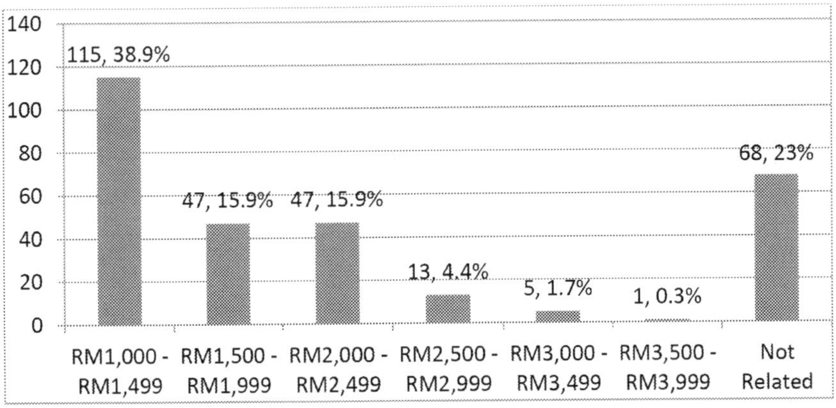

Figure 11.4 Starting salary.

and RM2,499, respectively. Meanwhile, a total of 13 participants (4.39%) were offered jobs with a starting salary between RM2,500 and RM2,999. A total of five participants (1.69%) were offered jobs with a starting salary between RM3,000 and RM3,499 and one participant (0.34%) was offered a job with a starting salary exceeding RM3,500. The remaining 68 participants (22.97%) did not have a starting salary offer; they consist of 43 full-time postgraduate students, 23 people who are unemployed, and two others who are still in the status of waiting for placement.

Conclusion

This study was carried out during the current pandemic COVID-19, and the findings are very helpful to all interested parties including education policy makers, professional trainers, educators, and others. As online classes have become the alternative to face-to-face methods during the COVID-19 pandemic, this study shows that conducting professional training programs via e-learning is able to give relevant knowledge and skills to participants, thus portraying its effectiveness. Meanwhile, on employability prospects, despite economic slowdown due to COVID-19, the results indicate that most of the participants are still able to find placement and are employed. This study has a number of limitations. The respondents were from the CPSA training program conducted by USIM and IBFIM. Future studies should explore respondents from other training and education programs. A larger sample would likely give better understanding about the effectiveness of the e-learning approach in conducting professional training programs. COVID-19 is a challenge to all, especially the educators and trainers. Nevertheless, the pandemic has brought about a number of innovations in the field of education and training. Lessons learned during COVID-19 will be useful to face future challenges as pandemics occur.

Acknowledgements

The authors would like to thank the Ministry of Higher Education Malaysia (MOHE) and University Sains Islam Malaysia (USIM) for financial assistance under the National Graduate Employability Program 2020 – Certified Professional Shariah Auditor (GE CPSA 2020).

References

Abu Karim, M. (2020). Online Platforms Erase Barriers to Learning. *New Straits Times*, 8 July.

Aguguom, T., A., Ajayi, A., & Dare, O. E. (2020). COVID-19 and Accounting Education in Sub-Sahara Africa. *European Journal of Business, Economics and Accountancy*, *8*(3), 1–11.

Alsadoon, E. A. (2009). *The Potential of Implementing Online Professional Training Development for Faculty in the College of Education at King Saud University* (Master's Dissertation, Ohio University).

Bernama (2020a). Five Additional Made to the List of Essential Services during Phase 3 of MCO. *Malay Mail*, 15 April.

Bernama (2020b). COVID-19: Sejumlah 40 Peratus Syarikat Baru Teknologi Mungkin Tutup Operasi. *Berita Harian*, 6 April.

Bernama. (2021). Populasi Rakyat Malaysia Kini 32.73 Juta. *Berita Harian*, 10 February.

Bradley, W. E. (2011). A Conceptual Framework for the Design and Evaluation of Online Learning Modules in Professional Training and Academic Education in Business. *The Business Review, Cambridge*, *18*(1), 20–27.

Hamilton, A. (2020). 2020 Review: 10 Largest Bank Job Cuts This Year. *Fintech Futures*, 24 December.

Hoh, K. S. (2020). MEF: 2 Million Malaysians Lose Jobs. *The Sun*, 24 April.

Lee, L. (2020). REFILE-UPDATE 1-Q3 Profit for Malaysia's Top Banks Falls as Pandemic Takes Tolls. *Reuters*, 27 November.

Makortoff, K. (2020). HSBC Accelerates 35,000 Job Cuts Amid COVID-19 Profit Plunge. *The Guardian*, 3 August.

Mohd Amin, K. A. (2020). 650,000 Majikan Bagai Telur di Hujung Tanduk. *Sinar Harian*, 24 July.

Rashid, C. A., Salih, H. A., & Budur, T. (2020). The Role of Online Teaching Tools on the Perception of the Students during the Lockdown of Covid-19. *International Journal of Social Sciences & Educational Studies*, *7*(3), 178–190.

Roslan, S. H. (2020). COVID-19: Semua Sekolah Diarahkan Tutup, Kebajikan Pelajar Mesti Diambil Kira. *Astro Awani*, 19 March.

Xiung, J. (2020). Education Ministry Relaunches Digital Learning Platform with Help from Apple, Google and Microsoft. *Malay Mail*, 16 June.

Zulkapli, R. (2020). Kadar Pengangguran Negara Meningkat kepada 5.3 Peratus pada Mei. *Astro Awani*, 14 July.

12

EFFECTS OF TEACHING AND LEARNING THROUGH ZOOM APPLICATION

Ramadhani Mashaka Shabani, Mustafa Omar Mohammed, Ensari Yücel and Mohamed Cherif El Amri

Introduction

The prevailing COVID-19 pandemic, which started as an epidemic in 2020, has drastically and adversely affected the education sector, particularly in terms of delivery modes for classes. Educational institutions are forced to accept the hard reality that it is no longer feasible to conduct classes face-to-face. Most of the institutions in least-developed countries and some in developing countries were forced to close down due to lack of online facilities. Meanwhile, education institutions in the developed and high-developing countries resorted to technology to meet their educational needs. These institutions have taken full advantage of their development in technology, and continue to offer and popularize online classes.

The platform of the online classroom, including teleconferencing, is not a new technology; rather, it has become popular due to the necessity of learning within the prevailing environment today. Several applications are in use; some are old, and others are new. These applications can be accessed through various devices such as laptops, desktop computers, tablets, Android devices, and iPhones. The old applications were developed in tandem with the development in communication technology. On the other hand, the new applications catering to the needs of the "new normal" classroom applications drastically increased during the pandemic, which began in 2020. Other applications were also forced to change and improve their service to adapt to the "new normal" to attract more users.

In developed countries, many universities integrate their classroom platforms into their websites, and others use third-party applications. This is integration is made possible due to the availability of expertise for developing the platforms, which in turn has reduced cost and risk of using third-party

DOI: 10.4324/9781003252764-15

applications. Despite these improvements, many of these integrated platforms cannot compete with the old classroom platforms that were developed before the COVID-19 pandemic, because the old platforms were already tested, used for a long time, and received regular updates for improvements. Prior to the pandemic, Skype and Zoom were popular applications for online classes and teleconferencing, compared to other applications like G Suite, GoToMeeting, Microsoft Teams, and Google Meet.

The use of the Zoom platform is divided into two parts. The first part is the application itself that provides the required services to the user. This includes creating the application, configuring for updates, availability of internet connection, privacy, and security. The second part is the use of the application. The knowledge of operating the application is vital, and since the learning process on the platform is long distance, which is different from face-to-face learning, self-management becomes imperative.

Despite its numerous advantages, Zoom application has some challenges, though over time many of these challenges have been addressed. For example, from the beginning Zoom had limited capacity to accommodating a maximum of 100 users in one session, but this limit has been increased over time. Secondly, users need to have devices with good specifications and must have a strong internet connection so that they can communicate comfortably. Thirdly, there was insufficient information about all features of the application to educate users about the platform. These problems were apparent at the beginning of 2020, when several institutions and universities started popularizing the use of Zoom application. These institutions had relative difficulties teaching their staff and students about use of Zoom application due to insufficient information about its features. Furthermore, several users experienced unstable Internet connections, there were problems with interpersonal communication through the devices among users, and there was high risk of hacking that interfered with the communication.

The primary objective of this chapter is to analyze the impact of teaching and learning by using the Zoom application. Specifically, it analyzes the impact of using the Zoom application on the user side and the technical issues that arise. To achieve these objectives, the study has adopted library research in the form of literature review relying on extant literature, bulletins and reports on Zoom application, and its use at different levels.

The chapter is structured as follows: After the introduction, the second section provides an overview of online classes, their origin, growth, and types of applications used. The third section reviews work on Zoom application and its features. In the fourth section, the advantages of using Zoom application for teaching and learning are discussed, followed by the fifth section discussing the challenges faced by the users of the Zoom application. The sixth section provides an analysis of the impact of Zoom application related to teaching and learning. The seventh and final section presents the conclusion and recommendations.

Overview of e-learning

The history of online learning can be traced back over 170 years ago before the invention of the internet. It originated in Great Britain, where correspondence was used to deliver materials and receive completed assignments. Since then, online teaching has continued to grow, hitherto offering various learning modes. In the 1950s, before the invention of the internet, the use of television and slide projector–based classes was considered the first online classes, offered by the University of Illinois in the United States, whereby students began to lean through computer terminals interlinked on the network. The University of Illinois developed a teaching system in the form of PLATO, which stands for "Programmed Logic for Automatic Teaching Operations." In this system, several students were taught individually through the computer. In 1979, Apple developed *Lemonade Stand*, which was a video game that simulated the idea of business activities in which the player chose the goods to buy, advertised them and sold to others, and finally saw the amount of profit earned.

The University of Toronto was the first university ever to offer a full-fledged online course in 1984, followed by the Electronic University Network that was developed using DOS and Commodore 64 in 1986. Three years later a full-fledged online university, the University of Phoenix, offered bachelor's and master's degree through online platform. This laid the foundation and created interest for developing various platforms for online learning. In 1993, Jones International University developed a web-based system and became the first university to use it, and in 1994, it began offering real-time online classes in its CALCampus with real-time participation and instruction in the form of synchronous learning. Within a span of 4 years, until 1998, the Virtual University of California offered about 700 online classes.

Today, online classes have become the future, and the need has become even more real following the COVID-19 pandemic that began in 2020. The education sector, with its erstwhile face-to-face classes, faced a lot of challenges in delivering the classes to the students. They had no option but to take full advantage of the development in technology and embrace online classes in delivering lessons during this challenging time. The online platforms have become popular due to the necessity of learning within the dictates of the environment we have today. The massive growth of online classes has happened within the last decade, from 2010 to 2020. Up to the end of 2019, before the pandemic, overall online courses worldwide had reached 13,500, provided by 900 universities. In 2019 alone, about 2,500 courses were launched by 450 universities online. Figure 12.1 shows the growth of online classes between 2012 and 2019.

Bates (2020) predicted that there would be fast growth of online learning between 2020 and 2025, as many universities are shifting from traditional modes to online classes due to the spread of the pandemic. As stated earlier, several applications are being used to cater to online classes. These applications are accessible through various devices such as laptops, desktop computers,

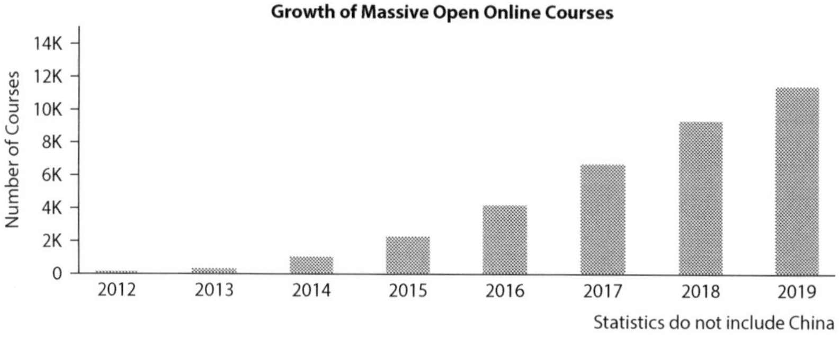

Figure 12.1 The growth of online courses (2012–2019).

Source: Shah (2019).

tablets, Android devices, and iPhones. Popular among these applications are Zoom, Skype, G Suite, GoToMeeting, Microsoft Teams, and Google Meet, among others. The choice of the classroom application depends on different factors, including the user interface, ability to accommodate many participants at one time, and subscription fee. As time goes by, application providers have continued to improve the features of their applications to respond to the demands of the users. For example, Google Meet was previously called Google Hangout, and it was accessibly only by subscription. But in May 2020, Google Hangout canceled its subscription model and offered its service free, and, at the same time, it changed its name to Google Meet. Furthermore, the service was improved from the limit of 25 participants to 100, and from a 60-minute time limit to 24 hours.

Zoom application and its features

Zoom application

Zoom is a videotelephone software application created by Zoom Video Communications, Inc. It offers free plans for video messaging services for 100 participants with a 40-minute time limit. Users can upgrade to a paid plan by subscribing to any of the three levels. For example, the highest level allows up to 1,000 participants at one time and has a 30-hour time limit. Participants do not need an account to download and use the Zoom program, unlike Skype and Adobe Connect. The Zoom application can generate an electronic meeting invitation with a live connection that only needs a click to access the meeting, and it can be edited and improved to create clarity for the type of subject the modulator is performing (Gray et al., 2020). Users can interact with others by using different features available on the Zoom application.

The Zoom conference platform has performed well during the COVID-19 pandemic and it is reported to have made a profit of $663.5 million for the 3 months ending 31 July 2020, beating analysts' expectations of $500.5 million.

This shows that Zoom has become the first choice for many users. Zoom is accessible from Android devices, iPhones, Windows computers, and macOS computers. The minimum requirement for Windows computers is Windows 7 and macOS X is macOS 10.10 with at least 2.5 GHz for a single screen connected to 2.0 Mbps bandwidth and 2.8 GHz for multiple screens connected up to 6.0 Mbps bandwidth, while audio chatting requires 60–80 kbps bandwidth. The application provides high-quality video, audio, and screen sharing with a secure connection (with a Pro account) of up to 300 users, which can have up to 25 users on video windows on the screen. Zoom also provides chat, polling, presentation indicators and screen sharing, and break-out rooms.

Features of Zoom application

Zoom users integrate by using inbuilt features, some of which are free and others are available for subscription with a determined fee. The salient features of Zoom include:

Screen and application sharing

This allows the users to share screens, specific windows, or applications. When teaching or learning, the users can share PowerPoint presentations, allowing other users access not only for sharing but also to ask for the control of the presentation slides.

Whiteboard feature

Some subjects cannot be learnt from the presentation slides alone, so the Zoom application provides the whiteboard feature to complement such need. The whiteboard has functions where teachers can write or draw on the white area created by Zoom. Additionally, teachers can add text, signs, or photographs to the completed share screen feature (Lathifah & Lestari, 2020).

Raise hand feature

Students and the trainer can interact using features like the raise hand. This feature allows the participant to call the attention of the current presenter. In multiple participants, the feature gives the priority to the person who clicked the raise hand feature first.

Participants manage features

The application allows 25 participants to be seen on the window during the meeting regardless of how many participants are there. By using participants manage, features the modulator can see all participants, and manage or mute any participants.

Chat room platform feature

This platform is divided into two parts. The first one is the chatroom platform available during the meeting where the participants can chat, ask questions, and share different materials during the meeting or class. The second chat room platform is a general chat room that is available outside the meeting, whereby a person can chat with anyone available on his/her saved contacts. This works the same way as the WhatsApp chat platform, although one can create a group chat of 500 for a free account and 5,000 for a premium account.

Co-annotation and remote control

By using this feature, the host may access the attendees by using the remote control function. This is useful because it allows the participant to use their mouse or pointer to show or select any object displayed in the shared screen by the host, for example, to click on the right answer or object (Cuaca Dharma et al., 2017).

Polling quiz feature

This is a function that helps one to ask various questions to, for example, students (participants). The host can use this to get feedback on the comprehension and attention of students in a comparable class to an iClicker. It can also be used to evaluate the progress of students (participants), since one can record the responses with each student's identification. The host user type must be the licensed Zoom desktop client for Windows, macOS, and/or Linux. The polling can be a planned meeting or an instant meeting with Zoom ID. In conclusion, Zoom has over time improved its application to the extent that it contains almost all features for classroom sessions that a normal class would have. The difference is the absence of physical contact among participants, since all the interactions are online.

Teaching and learning through Zoom application

The Zoom application is multi-tasking. It is useful for webinars, meetings, conferences, training, teaching, and learning. As of 2020, several companies are increasingly using Zoom to conduct their organizational meetings, and orientation seminars (webinars) have become popular, connecting participants worldwide through this application. Teaching and learning through Zoom have been well-conducted and have become largely the main application for online classes. Today, online education has incorporated many different terms, such as e-learning, mixed learning, online learning, online classes, and others. Students regularly debate these terms and sometimes get confused in their interpretation of online learning. Singh and Thurman (2019) define online learning as "*learning experienced through the internet/online computers in a synchronous classroom where students interact with instructors and other students and are not dependent on their physical location for participating in this online learning experience*." This definition has become largely associated with the development of various online class platforms, and the present study has adopted this definition. Accordingly, Zoom application that has become popular has its features embodied in this definition, and students will have no problem perceiving online education from this perspective.

According to Rahayu, the activities of online learning involve three categories, which are communication, materials, and the study process. Communication is the first activity after joining the class, where teachers and students get to interact with each other, and it involves welcoming each other, pre-learning small talks, private discussions with lectures, questions and answers among students and lecturers, question and response between students, and group discussions. The second category is sharing materials among teachers and students, involving slides and screen materials, downloading workout questions, and submitting exercise answers. The last category is the study process that involves answering polling questions, lecturing by slide sharing and whiteboard, response learning, question and answer, and group work in the classroom. Other applications are also used simultaneously, for example, often lectures are organized through social media applications such as WhatsApp, and materials are generally transmitted via WhatsApp and other social media through file sharing. WhatsApp increases the effectiveness of Zoom application learning, although on Zoom application, you can find the chat room that works the same as WhatsApp. Fadda et al. (2020) explained that students are comfortable using WhatsApp in organizing the class. Students are reported to say that WhatsApp is effective, since it acts as the medium for collecting materials, providing links to different websites to collect information and review materials. Meanwhile other students have unfavorable views about some of the WhatsApp groups, which they see as redundant.

Merits of using Zoom

Zoom application has become popular due to the various advantages users have experienced. The comfort of using the application and the success in delivering learning materials by the host and receiving them by the participants has driven many users to opt for Zoom. Other indicators as to why people prefer to use the Zoom application are shown by how Zoom Video Communications, Inc. could make huge profits during the COVID-19 pandemic compared to their earnings before the pandemic.

Cuaca Dharma et al. (2017), in their study on the advantages and disadvantages of Japanese online learning using Zoom, found that the Zoom application is suitable for online learning according to its features, but is limited to the classes which involve conversation learning. This view was supported by Haqien and Rahman (2020) who find that in comparison to a research application performing written communication tasks according to the theory of educational communication, the Zoom meeting was better because communication among individuals was done orally in the application of the Zoom meeting, although such success for university students in Jakarta and Depok was reported to be low. Lathifah and Lestari (2020) analyzed how Zoom conferences can increase the communication skills of students based on the perspective of educators and teachers. In the study conducted on the teachers, trainers, and educators, it is found that 80% of teachers continued to use assignments to enhance the skills of students compared to 67% of teachers, trainers, and educators before the start of the pandemic. The study conducted by Arahman on undergraduate students' ability to understand mathematical concepts found a significant effect on students of the online training with Zoom applications for statistics. Archibald et al. (2019) used the Zoom application as a tool to collect qualitative data and found it convenient due to its relative ease of use, cost-effectiveness, data management functions and safety options, and viability in collecting quality data. Other advantages of Zoom application include simplicity in use, ease for planning meetings, equipment with telephone options, interactive features, video recording, and free basic package.

Simple to use

It is believed that despite the challenges found in the Zoom application, it is simple to use by both host (teacher) and participants (students). After downloading and installing the application, the host is required to click on the New Meeting button on the left side of the app dialogue and invite other participants or click on the Meeting button on the top of the app and choose to schedule the next meeting. The host is supposed to have an account to start or schedule a meeting, but the participants can join the meeting without having an account.

Easy and ad hoc planning for meetings

Ad hoc planning for meetings, webinars, or classes does not need much effort. After clicking the Meeting button at the top of the application, the host can choose whether to schedule on Google Calendar, Outlook Calendar, or any other calendar that is suitable for the user. Also, the host may add the title of the meeting or class, set the date and time, choose to generate the meeting ID or use the personal ID, and decide if the host or participant or both will be visible to the camera. So it is just a few steps and the schedule is saved to allow the host to share the link with the participants. The schedule can be for an individual or the whole class.

Accessing by one-click notification or invitation link

After the meeting is scheduled and an invitation is sent to the participants, the participants can save the schedule on their calendar and receive the notification a few minutes before the meeting begins. The participants are required to click on the notification to join the meeting or click on the link itself, and they may choose to join with video or audio if is allowed by the host.

Telephone option for audio

One can instantly join computer audio if one is participating in a webinar. A switch to phone audio can be made by clicking the Up arrow next to Audio Settings. To make a phone call, one has to go to the Phone Call tab. Note that if the call out add-on is installed, one can join the conference by Zoom calling one's phone number. This is useful when users do not have a mic or speaker on their computer, do not have a smartphone (iOS or Android) with them when they are outside, or can't connect to a network for video or VoIP (computer audio).

Interactive features for easy meetings or classes

Zoom application has built-in tools that allow the host and participants to interact with each other through screen share, chat room, live video, sharing materials, whiteboard features, raise hand features, and participant management tools, among others. All these features make the users feel like they are in one place.

Video recording option

This is a very interesting option because it allows the lesson or meeting to be recorded. This enables the participants to view the record later. So, this is useful for those who skip part of the lesson or were not able to attend the lesson on time. It also allows the participants to clear doubt whenever they could not understand the material during the live or synchronized session.

Free basic package for 100 participants

One does not need to pay to use the basic package of Zoom application for up to 100 participants. Although the premium package is available, Zoom application can be used for free scheduling in 40 minutes for 100 participants. In this way the class can be scheduled in a 40-minute interval with breaks in between. This enables users who cannot pay for a subscription to use the application for free.

In summary, the advantages of the Zoom application are obvious in the high number of users and attendance of participants, a level of likeness that is evenly distributed in all material presented by speakers, and a very high level of satisfaction with services. Students are as comfortable studying online by Zoom application as in the normal class.

Challenges of using Zoom application

Supervisor involvement

Zoom application is used at all levels of learning, from kindergarten to universities. There are hardly any features in the Zoom application that are suitable for kindergarten and different from those in the universities. The interaction between teachers and students is through microphones and camera that can be turned on and off. Suppose a student joins a class and his/her status appears as "online" but he/she engages in activities other than following the class. Even if the camera is turned on, the ability of the Zoom application to display participants is limited to 25 participants. The idea of a large class is better because it enables a lecturer to manage a large number of participants at once, but the limitation is on how to control every participant. Nagel and Kotzé examined teaching in a large online class and they argue that the supervising such a class is unrealistic. Education is increasing and mixed modes of conducting classes include gradually more components of e-learning. The shortage of educators is compensated for by extending the limits of classes to allow up-to-date online courses.

The learning quality does not always have to be lower in supervised schools. If people are engaged in online activities and take charge of the consistency of their engagement, then they can learn more. So for the effectiveness of the online class, students' commitment is important. For adult students, it is probably possible to commit themselves to Zoom classes, but what about children? Not all students observe and follow the complete planning of the class discussions (Agustina & Mustika, 2020). They added that the role of parents in complementing the application is highly decisive to their children's commitment. Parents find it challenging to accompany their children to follow the discussion schedule. It is reported that the number of students who do not take an intermittent exam and do not do homework in an online class is increasing. Students find it difficult to focus on Zoom classes due to distractions, lack of commitment, and emotional tension. Agustina and Mustika (2020) suggested that schools have to be adjusted to include different forms of learning platforms, such as YouTube videos and interpersonal communication through WhatsApp, for students and their parents. The support of the supervisor or parents for the students is important in helping them follow the schedule of classes and other class activities.

Privacy and technical issues

Running Zoom application requires not only devices but also the internet, security, and privacy. During the beginning of the COVID-19 outbreak, the number of Zoom application users increased to over 200 million as of April 2020, compared to 10 million uses in December 2019. The growth of the number of users normally attracts hackers who attempt to interfere with the user information (Çubukçu & Aktürk, 2020). Threatening actors have worked hard to produce attacks that profit from new defects caused by a COVID-19 pandemic. The spectrum includes phishing, scams and hoaxes for fraud, and cybercriminals (Maor, 2020). Maor (2020) added that according to the research done by insiders, it is discovered that hackers exchanged 2,300 record databases, and approximately 500,000 video conference account details were sold to the dark net.

The unwanted, interruptive interference in a video conference call, usually by internet trolls "Zoom bombing," also hacks different information, ranging from login credentials to host keys, usernames, and conference IDs. In Zoom bombing, hackers use the zWarDIal tool to interfere with the meeting by auto-generating the meeting ID and joining the meeting. They always share offensive comments or materials that distract other members. It is surprisingly easy for hackers to infiltrate conferences with just a 9-11 number ID to join a session by zWarDIal. In one case, a high school from Massachusetts noted: "Someone was able to hack one of the school meetings easily and flashed swastika tattoos, the emblem of the German Nazi party."

Another issue is information linkage. Zoom allows login by using third-party accounts like Google and Facebook. This leads to confusion between users, and Zoom has been accused of sharing user credentials to third-party accounts. A study shows Zoom's iPhone app sent information to Facebook on users' smartphones, even users with no Facebook profiles. At least two federal cases were brought against the firm, first by a California citizen who claimed that Zoom had ignored the new Consumer Privacy Act by revealing information to Facebook without giving proper notification or the option to disqualify customers. The processing or sending of data to Facebook does not involve Zoom. Zoom's privacy policy indicates that the enterprise can capture users' "Facebook profile information (when you use Facebook to log-in to our Products or to create an account for our Products)." However, there's nothing explicit about sending Zoom users' data to Facebook when a user has no Facebook account at all.

Internet connection

Availability of a strong internet connection is recommended during Zoom classes for good quality of video and sound. The minimum requirement is at least 2.0 Mbps bandwidth for a single screen and 6.0 Mbps bandwidth for multiple screens. Audio chatting requires 60–80 kbps bandwidth. Restricted access to the internet for instructors and educator applicants is the main challenge to online learning. An unstable internet connection creates stress for many students that in turn affects their decision to attend and participate in class, but more stress is caused by superficial IT mastery (Hassan et al., 2020). Meanwhile Haqien and Rahman (2020) also found that a lecture that was conducted using Zoom Meeting was considered ineffective because users often faced the problem of poor network or internet signal for students who did not use WiFi. This had later an impact on the quality of the video signal they received. Agustina and Mustika (2020) consider that learning from home using the Zoom application is a burden to some parents. Apart from paying tuition fees and other necessary cost, parents also are obliged to pay for the internet. Dhawan (2020) found that electricity supply and reliable internet service remain major problems in many Indian cities, which persistently face regular power supply problems.

Devices and digital awareness

While the Zoom application is increasingly becoming popular, not all users know how to use it, because the online class is dictated by its learning environment during the COVID-19 pandemic period. Universities and schools took positive measures to ensure that their teachers and students are comfortable with online learning through Zoom. They provide them with training to ensure that the classes are conducted well. Zoom has also provided a guideline for online classes since 2020, although it is similar to another form of conference. The guidelines comprise five aspects on how to: (1) sign in for the first time, (2) download the Zoom client, (3) schedule a meeting, (4) join a class or meeting and (5) ensure best practices while in a Zoom class/meeting.

Analysis of the impacts of Zoom application for teaching and learning

The significance of technology cannot be denied in today's life, especially during the COVID-19 pandemic. Lockdown and curfew as well as the imposition of social distancing have created a new way of living, especially in workplaces and schools. Zoom application has become a handy tool for interaction among people at work, meetings, and learning platforms. Although some people face difficulties using Zoom, the researchers agree that using the application is easy for teaching and learning. However, the issues of internet connection, security, and privacy still pose challenges. Nevertheless, there is progress in maximizing security and privacy on Zoom application. Below is the analysis of Zoom on teaching and learning.

Cases of selected impacts

After signing into the Zoom application, the participant should turn off the camera and mic if he or she is not the person delivering the talk. This helps to improve the quality of the signal coming and going from the device. For the presenter, the camera can be turned on, he/she has to focus on the camera, and it's better to position the camera at eye level. To reduce background noises, it is recommended to turn on the mic only when one speaks. This gives the presenter a better sound that is audible to the other participants. When the presentation requires the presenter to appear on the shared screen, it is advised that the setup of the background should be a solid color or a virtual background, which is available on the Zoom application.

For the classes that require much attention and follow-up with the students, like kindergarten and primary school, it is better to have a class of a small number of students, preferably a number of participants that can be seen on screen. For the meeting or webinar class, it is not necessary to have a limited number of participants than those limited by Zoom themselves. Teachers and student should prepare their materials in a simple way that enables sharing to the Zoom screen. For example, PowerPoint is the popular way of sharing slides. Also, students can request control of the presented slides and browse on their own without skipping if the presenter is fast in the presentation. The participants can use a third-party application to notify the class whenever there is a problem of electricity or internet, since WhatsApp is good for organizing meetings, asking questions, and collecting links for different sites (Fadda et al., 2020). Kids' parents can help to follow the schedules as well as join with them in class. To draw attention to the students, the teacher can use random questions to check on the students to see if they are active and focusing on the class.

Supervising examinations through the Zoom application can be difficult, because what can be visible during the Zoom class is only the faces of 25 participants and not the faces of all the participants attending on the platform. This can create opportunities for other participants to use outside materials during the examination. Another impact is on the students when the examination requires a lot of writing, and writing on a computer requires experience of typing with speed. Given a time constraint, not all students can finish the exam on time. Teachers can use the poll feature as a way of giving examinations through Zoom. The advantage of the poll is the question pop-up, and student can choose the answers and submit their responses. Other forms like Microsoft Form or Google Form can be integrated into Zoom and used for supervising exams. Zoom application is useful, and people are required to accept the challenge and adapt to the new way of learning. Zoom can develop an application more suitable for education than meeting, which is different from the current one. Zoom can collaborate with educators to design a new application that can include inherent features and self-learning materials and can be accessed directly from the application without using sharing screen features. The materials can be developed based on the idea of the Microsoft Encarta software developed by Microsoft.

Zoom accessories for safety and privacy

No one would like his or her privacy to be violated and made public. This is the big challenge of internet technology. Whereas others are trying to develop a system to make life easy and facilitate it for society, there are those who are trying to interfere with this system and the information it has stored. The increasing number of Zoom users has attracted hackers to interfere with the system either through the information the users stored or by interrupting their meeting. The zWarDIal tool has become a threat to the data of Zoom users. The tool can autogenerate a user ID and guess passwords. Before the COVID-19 pandemic, users were able to join a meeting by clicking on the button, but due to interferences, users must also log in to the meeting after logging into their account. Furthermore, users can join a meeting by logging in to the meeting without logging in to the user ID if they are not the hosts.

To avoiding information leakage, it is recommended a user create a user ID directly from the Zoom client instead of logging in using a third-party platform like Google or Facebook. Sharing a user ID or password is not recommended, because anyone with your user ID and password can run the meeting. Also, the security of information can be enhanced by using recently updated software for firewalls, antivirus software, and encryption techniques. Creating new security features can also be availed by hiring "white hackers." These are hackers who become loyal to the company after hacking it, and they will help to show their bugs. This technique was used by Google in 2015 when it hired the teenager who hacked them.

The issue of the internet is less a problem in developed countries than in developing countries. It is basically the problem of availability and price. Normally, internet with high speed and large bandwidth leads to good quality of video and sound. For developing countries, such internet quality is expensive, and therefore it becomes challenging to manage classes every time. The use of Zoom data leaps with more callers. Group meetings with Zoom range from 810 MB to 2.4 GB per hour or from 13.5 MB to 40 MB per minute. Overcoming this challenge may require a small application with small bandwidth to be developed. But the problem will still persist as the quality of video and audio will not be satisfactory.

Çubukçu and Aktürk, (2020) argued that the Zoom application is not the only software that can be used in teaching and learning. There are similar and more secure platforms, such as GoToMeeting, Skype, AnyDesk, and Google Meet. Furthermore, a learning management system is believed to be more secure. For example, in Turkey, primary and high school education use the EBA platform. Universities in Turkey have choices of platforms. More than one LMS or webinar is helpful for the diversification of protection and privacy threats (Çubukçu & Aktürk, 2020).

Conclusion

This chapter has analyzed the impact of teaching and learning using the Zoom application from the perspective of users and the technical aspects. Zoom application is found to be suitable for the teaching and learning process in high-level learning such as universities. For primary school and kindergarten, it is less effective because it needs more effort from parents to supervise their children. Privacy and security are other problems facing almost all online platforms, and Zoom is no exception. Presently, Zoom is using AES

256-bit GCM encryption, which is supported from the Zoom 5.0 version and above. To ensure the accessibility of Zoom applications at all levels, the availability and price of high bandwidth should be considered, especially when such applications are offered in developing countries or to poor users. There are increasing works that continue to examine issues in the application of Zoom and ways of overcoming these issues to enhance the effectiveness of the application. Future research on Zoom application could focus on technical issues related to security, privacy, database, and storage, and ways of preventing hackers from interfering with the application.

References

Çubukçu, C., & Aktürk, C. (2020). The rise of distance education during COVID-19 pandemic and the related data threats: A study about Zoom. *Iğdır University Journal of Social Sciences*, *Ek2*, 127–143.

Dhawan, S. (2020). Online learning: A panacea in the time of COVID-19 Crisis. *Journal of Educational Technology Systems*. https://doi.org/10.1177/0047239520934018.

Gray, L. M., Wong-Wylie, G., Rempel, G. R., & Cook, K. (2020). Expanding qualitative research interviewing strategies: Zoom video communications. *Qualitative Report*, *25*(5), 1292–1301.

13

RATIONAL OUTLOOK OF TEACHING AND LEARNING ISLAMIC ECONOMICS AND FINANCE THROUGH THE ZOOM APPLICATION

Ahmed Aref

Introduction

Over the past 2 years, there has been a rapid shift from physical interpersonal meetings to virtual meetings. The rapid change has been brought about due to the novel COVID-19 virus, which led to a pandemic. The result of that was an enforced social distancing as a means of protection against the virus. With heightened social distance rules, individuals and businesses had to look for an alternative solution to face-to-face meetings. The virtual solution came knocking in the form of the Zoom application, which allows seamless video communication. Zoom has provided individuals and businesses an opportunity to meet one another in a safe and comfortable environment or at a location chosen by each individual.

Naturally, all aspects of communication were affected, including learning and teaching. In general, learning is divided into two broad categories. The first category is skills, learning which includes technical learning of programming languages and computer skills such as Microsoft Office proficiency. The second category is beneficial learning, and its ultimate purpose is for us to acquire helpful knowledge about the self, values, intrinsic motivation, authenticity, and life purpose. The result would be to awaken the heart to pursue behaviors that align with our purpose, mission, vision, and what makes life meaningful. In this regard, beneficial learning guides our skills learning. The more beneficial knowledge that we would acquire would enliven our hearts to pursue the right skills learning. Practical learning should lead to self-respect and others' respect, and that should lead to cooperation between people from different backgrounds, and it would foster creativity, disruption, and wealth creation.

The chapter will reflect on how key teaching elements have been impacted, such as learning environment, clear and shared outcomes, varied content and

 DOI: 10.4324/9781003252764-16

instruction methods, practice, feedback, et cetera. Furthermore, the chapter will reflect on teaching methods and how they have been impacted, such as the teacher-centered method, learner-centered method, content-focused method, and interactive/participative method. Both teaching and learning have shifted toward the virtual space, where students and teachers use applications, such as Zoom, to communicate. As mentioned, this chapter will analyze how the shift toward online platforms such as Zoom, in particular, has impacted teaching and learning from an Islamic economic finance perspective.

Importance of learning from Islamic perspective

Learning is a basic human right; it happens every day and collectively through interactions and repetitions. Emotions create feelings during interactions, which creates a learning experience for our souls. Similarly, we learn about economics and life using our own past experiences and advice from the Holy Book. Individuals study the Holy Book's teachings and implement them in their modern context to attain their personal and business goals while adhering to the Holy Book. Learning brings you closer to the Almighty as "*It is those of His servants who have knowledge who stand in true awe of Allah. Indeed, Allah is almighty, most forgiving*" – Surah Fatir, 35:28 (Hisham 2020). This indicates that it is best practice for yourself to pursue knowledge. Given that we are constantly learning, we should ensure that learning benefits us and makes us more whole.

The purpose of beneficial learning is to acquire beneficial knowledge about the self, values, intrinsic motivation, and be faithful to the purpose of aligning your mission and vision with the true awakening of your heart. Beneficial learning leads to self-respect and enlightens you to respect others who may come from a different background. It fosters creativity and the distribution and creation of wealth, which not only benefits yourself and your family but your community as a whole. Keeping this in mind, beneficial learning guides us toward learning new skills. The more beneficial knowledge we absorb, the more we awaken our hearts to the true beauty of living and becoming whole.

Learning from a historic Islamic perspective

In ancient times, the knowledge spread was slow. Tribes stuck to what they knew and greeted anybody who threatened their way of life with hostility. As time progressed and knowledge favored tribes who utilized them to sustain and improve their way of life, individuals became more open toward learning. From an Islamic perspective, learning in the past was facilitated to enlighten Muslims in a "*kuttāb*." These locations varied; they were mosques, homes, even open spaces. There is no specific date as to when these venues were initially used. However, it is estimated that they were used in the middle of the eighteenth century. Learning in Islam allows one to become a complete person in all aspects of life, both social and spiritual (Landau, 1986).

Although education became more structured with the use of the "*kuttāb*," it still spread at a slow rate and was only a communal activity. Communication technology at the time did not allow a rapid spread of information, as messages were either spread through horseback or by the footsteps of man. Thus the spread of knowledge was limited by the technology of the time. As time progressed and communication technology improved, the spread of information became more accessible. A faster flow of information resulted in individuals becoming more civilized; it sparked man's curiosity to seek knowledge and interact with people from different backgrounds. It allowed man to organize in finances with Islamic economic principles.

The invention of modern transportation bridged the gap between both teacher and student from different geological areas. At this point, teaching was still conducted primarily through face-to-face physical interactions. However, these meetings became more convenient and feasible.

The dawn of computing technology gave birth to the internet. Messages were shared instantly, and soon there were video conferencing applications available. Video conferencing changed the way we communicated; for the first time, we could both see and hear the individual, a substitute for face-to-face meetings. Zoom seems to be leading the way regarding video conferencing. It was downloaded 485 million times in 2020, and the number of annual meeting minutes has reached over 3.3 trillion (Dean, 2021). Zoom allows individuals and business to "*bring their teams together in a frictionless environment*" to achieve more (Video Conferencing, Web Conferencing, Webinars, Screen Sharing, 2021). As demonstrated through history, factors such as language and geographical gaps have almost disappeared with improved technology and transportation. Zoom has culminated in bridging communication gaps between individuals to provide the most complete solution to face-to-face interactions to date. This has allowed the teachings of the Holy Book and Islamic economic finance to spread more efficiently.

Concerns and limitations in teaching and learning Islamic economics and finance through the Zoom application

Although Zoom has bridged geographical gaps between individuals, it only bridges those gaps if the user has access to a good internet connection and electricity. It limits communication with individuals who are from rural communities or communities where there is no relevant infrastructure. It provides the spread of information rapidly; it also allows the spread of misinformation at an equally rapid rate to benefit individuals with ulterior motives. Individuals acting in self-interest may not work in the interest of humanity as a whole and, as a result, take us further away from the teachings of Islam and Islamic economic finance. Zoom may negatively impact your family duty as the business has now been brought into individuals' homes, their dining areas, and perhaps their rooms, a private space reserved for the individual and his family. Individuals may pay less attention to their family because they may struggle to switch off. After all, there is no physical barrier between work and home.

The most incredible substitute for physical face-to-face contact exists in the form of video calling or conferencing. However, video conferencing or calling platforms, including Zoom, are also no substitute for physical face-to-face contact, as they do not provide the sense of connectedness one feels when speaking to someone face-to-face. This has caused specific individuals to be isolated and not feel the love and touch of a fellow human, destabilizing their souls. Zoom ensures interactive learning. However, the teacher may not be able to provide personalized one-to-one attention to students. This negatively impacts individuals with a lack of discipline. This lack of discipline may result in some individuals not studying content in a constructive manner, ultimately being less informed in the principles of Islamic economic finance and general academic content. Hence, although Zoom has allowed for the instant spread of information, it has also slowed the spread of information due to individuals not being disciplined enough to efficiently receive the information.

Once again, teachers use body language to ensure engaging lessons. In the absence of this, students are not as engaged on Zoom when compared to physical face-to-face lessons. Some students find it challenging to receive lectures online where they are constantly looking at a screen. Furthermore, distracting activities increase when using Zoom, as students can minimize the app and browse the internet, et cetera.

Impact analysis of teaching and learning Islamic economic and finance through the Zoom application

Zoom has its concerns. However, it has enabled individuals and businesses to conduct seamless communication, allowing ideas to be shared instantly. This will enable individuals to ensure that Islamic economic principles are being practiced within their organization through providing education of these principles to staff members and analyzing if the daily activity falls in line with the recommendation of the Holy Book. Ensuring that the Islamic economic principles are followed would allow an individual to attain wholesomeness in his daily business activity and bring him closer to achieving general wholesomeness in his life.

The year 2020 has allowed learning to become more universal and accessible. It has fostered an environment for opportunities around worldwide networking and cross-cultural interactions. Teachers and students from different continents can share their experiences and views more inclusively regarding teaching and learning. Teaching and learning have been affected at all levels, including at the very highest levels of universities. While some universities have moved toward distance learning, where lectures are administered online, they still administer some lectures in a traditional lecture hall. The recent pandemic has forced all activity to shift toward online lectures instead of traditional face-to-face lectures. In turn, the teaching of Islamic economic principles was administered online as businesses and academic institutions shifted teaching to an online platform.

Businesses and academic institutes have had to resort to synchronous and asynchronous learning to adapt to a changing learning environment. Synchronous learning occurs when a group of individuals learns at the same time. Asynchronous learning is the opposite and occurs in isolation, where the student and teachers do not engage in real time. Zoom was used to administer synchronous learning through the application by allowing real-time interaction between teachers and students. Teachers administered lectures, and students interacted by asking questions concerning the content, in this case, the principles of Islamic economic finance. Although social distancing measures were enforced in light of COVID-19, students still benefited from this by enjoying real-time interaction with teachers, giving a personal face-to-face feel without being physically present, and allowing lessons to be administered in the convenience of their own home. This has allowed students to study Islamic economic finance regardless of their location, which would bring an individual closer to achieving wholesomeness in business and personal life.

Zoom was utilized more in a synchronous learning environment as opposed to the asynchronous learning environment. Zoom allows an individual to record a video conference; however, the convenience of accessing these recordings prevents them from being utilized in a more asynchronous learning environment. There are more suitable platforms that use asynchronous learning methods where content is accessible for the student, which has allowed the principles of Islamic economic finance to be accessible at the convenience of the student. The student can now keep a schedule that could allow the student to pursue other Islamic teachings from the Holy Book, fulfilling his soul. This is achieved by increasing spare time during the day by cutting down travel time, among other things. Greenler from the Center for Integration of Research, Teaching, and Learning reviews key elements of successful online facilitation, such as allowing sufficient time, being clear with instructions, soliciting feedback, and reducing cognitive load. She then describes how to match learning outcomes to the correct tools such as breakout rooms, whiteboards, chats, and emoticons, among others, in a 12-minute video. The video should provide some guidance when teaching online to keep students more engaged in the content, enhance their knowledge, and provide a better standard of living in the long run. The recommendations could be used for both synchronous and asynchronous techniques.

Further expanding on the impact on teaching elements, reveals the following.

Learning environment

The physical space of learning appears not in a physical classroom or lecture hall, but instead, wherever the student wants it to be; it could be his living room, a coffee store, et cetera. The routine of students has changed; no longer is it get up and go to lectures. Now students get up, conduct their routines, and then begin learning in their homes. Regarding building positive relationships with fellow students and teachers, this has become more difficult as there is no face-to-face contact to truly bond with someone. Online learning has become less personal to all parties; this takes away the spark and romance of learning within an institute.

Clear and shared outcomes

The learning outcomes must be communicated, so the student is fully aware of the consequences of his actions. Online learning has not changed the outcome of learning as much as other elements. Students and teachers know the importance of education, and online learning has helped students contact teachers more frequently. The reason is that students often have the email address or WhatsApp contacts of teachers. Online video platforms have also enabled students to write exams at home, provided their video camera is on and recording; this is a massive shift from traditional sit-down exams.

Varied content and methods of instruction

Due to online learning, content appears in many forms; it could present itself in a video, a voice recording, an interactive game, et cetera. Students can record Zoom lectures and replay them to drive home the message of the teacher. The method of instruction has shifted to using online mediums and video calling, which utilize apps such as Zoom, as opposed to classrooms and lecture halls.

Practice and feedback

Students now can take mock tests and complete online interactive activities relating to the content to practice the principles of whatever they are learning. Regarding feedback, this has been positively influenced by online learning and Zoom video calls. Students can contact educational institutes and often get answers to their questions within a matter of minutes; they can also get virtual face-to-face feedback through Zoom for a more personalized feeling.

Stimulation of complex thinking

Students are encouraged to use their complex thinking abilities when tackling tasks through teaching and repetition. Online learning has benefited students, as they can use the knowledge they obtain to solve complex problems in interactive activities and games. No longer are students just interacting with a piece of paper.

Philosophy

The teaching and learning process of a teacher and student being in one place has now been transformed. Teachers and students can be in different parts of the globe, and sometimes there may be no physical contact between teacher and student.

Classroom management

Before online teaching, teachers had to discipline students to maintain discipline and not disturb the rest of the class. Now it is the student who needs to maintain discipline as he receives the lesson in isolation. This has eased the classroom management process for the teacher and allowed the teacher to use his energy more constructively. The only thing the teacher must now manage is the constructive engagement between students and learning material. This will have a positive effect on the student.

Motivation

Great teachers always encourage students to be enthusiastic about their learning experience. In face-to-face interaction, this can be achieved without using words; body language is a great communicator of enthusiasm, and teachers use this to motivate students. This has made it difficult for teachers to encourage students to not use body language to influence other students. Teachers use words to encourage scholars, and thus scholars have had to look upon themselves to find the motivation to stay focused during lessons, with reduced levels of motivation received from the teacher.

Inclusivity

Teachers must engage with all students at an equal level to ensure all students who receive the content can understand what is being taught. Zoom has it more difficult for teachers to include all students in a lesson as it is less personal than traditional physical face-to-face learning.

Think-pair-share

This entails three steps: students must develop a discussion question, students should partner up, and students should then discuss their responses and encourage each other to share their ideas with the class. Zoom has changed this method as instead of physically paring students, they can now be put into break rooms on Zoom where they can develop questions, discuss responses, and present to the class in the main meeting room once done.

Reflecting on Zoom affecting teaching methods

Teacher-centered method

Emphasis on the teacher is one of the fundamental elements that is now being shifted toward students' basic learning elements. Teachers have become more like facilitators, overseeing the learning journey of students.

Learner-centered method

Learners are being centered when learning as online platforms are developed and centered around optimizing the user experience, which is the learner instead of the teacher.

Content-focused method

Content is no longer in the form of paper; it is now optimized to engage the learner constructively with the learning material through a combination of video conferences, games, and online quizzes.

Interactive or participative method

Although students may not physically interact with fellow students, they remain connected through video calling, messaging, et cetera. These tools allow interaction and participation between students. Furthermore, as touched on, educational games allow for real-time teamwork among students. For the next generation of kids growing up, online synchronous and asynchronous learning is all they know. They are being conditioned to think that this is how the world is meant to learn, as this may be the first learning environment they encounter. Apart from Islamic economic principles being shared over Zoom, the general teaching of the Holy Book has also shifted toward using online platforms to maintain social distancing, to protect humanity from the COVID-19 virus.

In the face of the COVID-19 pandemic, governments and higher education institutes have done a great job in shifting lectures online to ensure continuity. However, this excluded the students who do not have access to Zoom. These institutes should implement coordinated mechanisms, allowing mutual advancement in developing greater resilience in the higher education sector in the face of future crises. It is essential to involve students, teaching, and non-teaching staff in designing the responses that emergencies require to reach out to all students, as the message from the Holy Book is for all of humanity. There needs to be national and global cooperation to form policies that protect the teacher, student, and non-teaching staff to maintain high standards across the board of education.

The COVID-19 pandemic has found governments and educational institutions lacking efficient infrastructure across the globe, restricting the student's ability to learn online. Governments and academic institutes worldwide must develop infrastructure to allow students to have the facilities to learn online, regardless of the external situation. Apart from ensuring measures to reach all students during future crises, these institutes must develop regulations in line with the law to prevent the spread of misinformation and protect both teachers and students when conducting lessons online. It is vitally essential then that nobody is taken advantage of in an inappropriate way when on a one-to-one video conference. This would go against the Holy Book's teachings, so it is very important that measures are taken to protect the integrity of people in these relatively uncharted waters. This could be the difference between behaving in line with Islamic economic finance principles or behaving out of line with such principles, which would go against the Holy Book recommendations for a fruitful and fulfilled life. One of the COVID-19 situation's benefits is prioritizing humanity's well-being, which aligns with the Islamic eco-finance principles. New humanistic values need to be prioritized and included in learning. The first step is to have values clarification teaching methods to harmonize the community efforts toward well-being.

The purpose of values clarification is to help students become aware of and identify their values and those of others; secondly, to help students communicate openly and honestly about their values; and thirdly, to help students use rational thinking and emotional awareness to examine their personal feelings, values, and behavior patterns. The values clarification strategies commonly used in teaching are role playing, games, simulations, contrived or real value-laden situations, introspection or in-depth self-analysis exercises, sensitivity activities, small group discussions, and group dynamics.

Regarding the job sector, non-teaching staff in the educational sector were most adversely affected by students learning through Zoom. The reason is that there was no face-to-face interaction during the pandemic, which resulted in no students being on campus and thus no need for certain staff members to fulfill their roles. The lack of demand for non-teaching staff, compounded with a difficult financial situation, saw such staff lose jobs, as students were forced to stay home to receive lectures via Zoom. It remains to be seen if these non-teaching staff roles will ever be required again, as there is a general shift toward online teaching and learning in the short and certainly the long term. The shift toward online teaching and learning will bring a glimmer of hope for non-teaching staff in selected industries. There will be a rise in the demand for individuals working in the information technology sector, as key skills are required to ensure the smooth running of online teaching and learning.

Learning will become more accessible for students in the future due to the shift toward online learning. The supply of education is no longer restricted to the number of seats available in institutions; instead, the supply of education is restricted by only an individuals' ability to receive the online lesson through access to the internet and a device that allows for such activity.

Ultimately the supply is available to all mankind, provided they have access to such facilities. The demand for education will also increase due to more students realizing it is important and available. Students are no longer restricted by geographical and social limitations. This massive increase in the supply of teaching and learning brought about by online learning, coupled with an increase in demand for education, will see fees decrease. Factors such as reduced overhead costs for these institutions will further drive down the price of education, thus increasing the demand further as the financial barrier is further reduced.

Zoom has positively impacted cross-cultural relations as it bridged the gap between scholars from different nations and backgrounds. Although these scholars may share a different school of thought, Zoom provides an open platform for healthy debate to consider each school of thought. This could be the present-day neutral zone where there is no intent of hostility. This allows scholars to consider all aspects of a topic and not just their school of thought. Such thought brings mankind closer to unity. Zoom allows scholars of all walks of life to sit together at the table and brainstorm ideas to create a universal understanding for humanity, irrespective of nationality or background.

Indeed, the offerings from the educational institutes will have to change considering Zoom. Before COVID-19, there was a strong emphasis on face-to-face learning for undergraduates, where distance learning was favored more by postgraduates due to other commitments in life such as a having job. More emphasis will now be placed on online as opposed to face-to-face learning as online learning provides students with the flexibility of their time. As touched on, these educational institutes will have to offer both synchronous and asynchronous learning methods. This could give rise to new institutions forming that solely focus on online learning. Furthermore, with the next generation of children taking lessons from Zoom, they become more conditioned to accept online learning as a normal format. Thus, educational institutes will have strong offerings centered around online learning if they want to remain relevant in the long run.

Policy recommendations for governments and educational institutes considering online learning for the future

Policymakers need to protect the integrity of the current educational system so that the only direction it may take is improving. This will have to center around strong administration measures, which clearly define operational plans and regulations to ensure the integrity of the educational sector.

Financial security must be ensured. There has to an emergency fund available for future unpredicted circumstances to mitigate the negative consequences of such circumstances. From a government perspective, this can be achieved through funneling a small portion of tax each month or year into an emergency educational fund. From an educational institute perspective, a small portion of fees must be set aside for an emergency fund. Further, these institutes can welcome donations from alumni to assist with the emergency fund.

Infrastructure development across governments and educational institutes must be centered around providing resources to the student to study. This includes improving the internet infrastructure to ensure all students have access to the internet, subsidizing electronic devices to learn online.

Framework to guide online teaching and learning for the future

- Education must be non-discriminatory to allow for equal opportunities regardless of color or background.
- Access to education must be fair and ensure that all students are catered to regardless of external circumstances.
- Legal and administrative policies must be followed to ensure the sustainability and continuation of education regardless of external circumstances.
- There must be reviews of the implemented framework to ensure it remains relevant for the time.
- Governments and educational institutes must work closely together to maintain and improve the execution standards of education.

Fostering a universal learning community

The Quran has bestowed up humanity for the greater good and well-being of all mankind. We should respect it and conform to its recommendations in daily life. Everyone should benefit from the teaching shared in the Holy Book, regardless of the situation they face, even if we are faced with a pandemic that threatens the lives of humanity. The message of Islam applies to all who are open to receiving it, regardless of color or nationality.

COVID-19 has taken away a lot from our everyday lives, while the one thing COVID-19 has done for humanity is to unite us. It has brought us together, regardless of traditions, customs, social norms, and nationalities, to join in ensuring the survival of our fellow brothers and sisters. We united by sharing our resources to the best of our ability to ensure that the hungry did not go hungry and the sick did not remain sick. The unity falls in line with the beauty of Islamic economic principles. The goal is to ensure the fulfillment and increase prosperity across all segments of life for all humanity.

Human beings form their reality within their mind; this leads to differences in perception of reality. This difference in perception causes us to not see eye to eye at certain times; this remains true for the Holy Book. There are differences in interpretation that lead us to behave differently. Regarding of Islamic economic finance, COVID-19 has provided a golden opportunity to put aside our differences and unite for the greater good of all mankind.

Regardless of our interpretation of the spoken word, the average follower of each understanding wants to ensure the greater well-being of humanity. COVID-19 threatened our well-being, which has caused the average follower to align and help people in need. Humanity's alignment with one another has shown that regardless of interpretation, followers have united to help one another consciously or subconsciously as per the Holy Book guidance. The Creator says, "*Help one another in acts of piety and righteousness. And do not assist each other in acts of sinfulness and transgression. And be aware of Allah. Verily, Allah is severe in punishment*" (Quran 5:2).

Teaching and learning, which includes diversity, entail being intercultural, and this will foster a greater understanding between different schools of thought. This would allow for collaboration protocols to develop a unique and universal approach to Islamic economic finance, which bridges the gap between all mankind. In recent years, applications such as Zoom have ensured that teaching and learning continue to occur regardless of external circumstances.

The current video platforms have forced an internal reflection upon how teaching and learning will be administered in the future. Learning has always remained an integral part of human development, and although video conferencing calls for new protocols concerning the past, it will be subject to change in the future.

The future will see learning consistently go beyond the traditional classroom; teachers will have to encourage students to maintain discipline and take risks to achieve their goals. Along the way, Islamic principles must not be abandoned; risk-taking must comply with the recommendations of the Holy Book (The future of learning and teaching: Big changes ahead for education).

The future well-being of humanity depends on new generations learning about the Holy Book and its principles to enjoy a fulfilled life. While the learning environment will change in the future, the core Islamic principles will be a message for humanity in the present and future.

Conclusion

Technology has afforded humanity the ability to communicate worldwide with anyone who has access to the required communication channels. There is a constant evolution of how we contact our daily tasks in life, and teaching and learning are no different. We have seen a shift from physical face-to-face learning to virtual learning using applications such as Zoom, which allow humanity to see each other in real-time while not physically being present. Learning is a beneficial activity, as it advances our understanding of our surroundings; with all aspects of life shifting toward online activity, learning will follow such a path. Regardless of the era we live in, learning always shapes our minds, and we must protect it and adapt to change to ensure it remains relevant at all times. The teachings of Islam and Islamic economic principles will continue to be taught and have the same meaning regardless of whatever platform is used. It is a message that speaks directly to one's soul and as such, although teaching and learning may change, the urge and responsibility to spread the beauty of Islam will remain constant, as it has done in the past, present, and future.

References

Landau, J. M. 1986. "Kutta Åb." In *Encyclopedia of Islam*. Leiden, Netherlands: E.J. Brill.

Hisham, U., 2020. *3 Reasons Why We Should Seek Knowledge*. [online] Muslim.sg. Available at: https://muslim.sg/articles/seek-knowledge-islam-quotes-hadith-cradle-to-grave [Accessed 16 April 2021].

14

IMPACT ANALYSIS OF TEACHING AND LEARNING ISLAMIC ECONOMICS AND FINANCE THROUGH ZOOM CLOUD MEETING

Irfan Syauqi Beik and Qurroh Ayuniyyah

Introduction

The COVID-19 pandemic that has hit Indonesia since March 2020 has brought multidimensional impacts, including on the health, economic, and education sectors. From the health sector, data from the Ministry of Health of the Republic of Indonesia and the Healthy Living Community Movement (called GERMAS) on July 3, 2021 showed that the number of confirmed positive COVID-19 patients increased significantly by 27,913 people with a total of 281,677 active cases. At most, 13,282 recoveries and 493 fatalities were recorded within a span of 24 hours. As of July 3, there have been more than two million positive confirmed cases of COVID-19 in Indonesia with 2.66 percent of mortality rate, placing this country at the top of confirmed positive cases in ASEAN, and it ranks 17 in the world.

In order to slow down the spread of the virus, the government of Indonesia has implemented "large-scale social restriction," which later was amended to "enforcement of limitation on community activities." In general, this policy adjusted forms of activities and operating hours for essential and nonessential sectors during the COVID-19 pandemic. This includes office and workplace activities; teaching and learning activities; traditional and modern markets; restaurants; construction; religious activities; art, social, and cultural activities; offline meetings and seminars; public transportation; and other activities in public areas such as public facilities, public parks, tourist attractions, and many more. In education sector, schools and universities, especially in red zone areas, are required to conduct online lectures or distance learning systems during this period to avoid physical meeting, which has the potential to increase the spread of this virus. Through this system, teachers, lecturers, and students are encouraged to improve their knowledge and skills in technological usage

DOI: 10.4324/9781003252764-17

to support the implementation of online lecture systems. In doing so, online meeting applications are needed as proper media to facilitate communication between lecturers, teachers, and the students (Fitriyani et al., 2020).

One application that is widely used for teaching and learning activities is Zoom Cloud Meeting, usually referred as Zoom (Guzacheva, 2020). Accordingly, this application is user-friendly and easier to use compared to other similar applications. Zoom is a proprietary video teleconferencing software program developed by Zoom Video Communications. There are two plans offered by this application, namely, free and premium plans. The former supports up to 100 people to participate at the same time and the meeting duration is limited to 40 minutes only. Meanwhile, the latter allows up to 1,000 concurrent participants for meetings lasting up to 30 hours (https://zoom.us). The application employs written, oral, and video as a medium of communication in order to provide a variety of practical, relatively low-cost, and user-friendly functions to enable online meeting activities (Scanga *et al.*, 2018). In comparison with number of users of other similar online meeting applications, Zoom has been a leading application with a significant increase in the number of its users by 183 percent since mid-March 2020. There are 257,853 users of Zoom as of March 20–26, 2020, which is followed by Skype with 71,155 users, and Hangout Meets with 10,454 users. Rank numbers 4 and 5 go to Cisco Web Meeting and GoToMeeting with 8,748 and 977 users respectively in the same period (Statqo Analytics, 2020). This is depicted in Table 14.1.

It is interesting to note from Table 14.1 that originally the number of Skype users ranked highest from 28 February to 12 March. However, the number of Zoom users dramatically jumped by more than ten times from 8,985 to 91,030, making this application as the most used software among others. The figures keep on drastically increasing by almost three times in the period of 20–26 March. In addition, the remaining four aforementioned applications have also had an inclining trend during the period of 28 February to 26 March 2020. This chapter aims at analyzing the determinants of the level of importance and satisfaction of university students in using Zoom as the most-used online meeting application in their online learning activities.

Table 14.1 Number of users of five top online meeting platforms in Indonesia, March 2020

		Number of users			
No.	*Name of application*	*28 February–5 March*	*6–12 March*	*13–19 March*	*20–26 March*
1.	Zoom	8,791	8,985	91,030	257,853
2.	Skype	60,614	60,641	65,875	71,115
3.	Hangout Meets	1,448	1,554	7,917	10,454
4.	Cisco Web Meeting	3,983	4,123	8,257	8,748
5.	GoToMeeting	479	505	696	979

Source: Statqo Analytics (2020).

Specifically, this chapter has two objectives. First, the study attempts to examine the experience of university students in using Zoom in their online learning activities. Second, this study analyzes the comparison of the performance of Zoom with other similar applications. This study observes 124 respondents who are students from universities in Indonesia and at the same time have experience in using the application for at least 2 months. This study employs several methods. To achieve the first objective, three methods are used, which include Importance Performance Analysis (IPA), gap analysis, and Customer Satisfaction Index (CSI). Meanwhile, the t-test method is used to realize the second objective. This chapter is divided into five sections: introduction, literature review, research method, results, and analysis, as well as conclusions.

Literature review

The use of video conferencing or online meeting applications in distant learning process has an advantage to help students in their learning activities as they can have interactive communication with their teachers and lecturers from different places. Learning media in fact has a great impact on the effectiveness of students' learning process. In other words, the use of online meeting applications shall have significant role in enhancing students' development if it is done properly. Currently, there are many products that provide video conferencing service that facilitate lecturers, teachers, and students in conducting their online learning activities. One of the applications that has been used widely by users, including those from various universities in Indonesia, is Zoom (Statqo Analytics, 2020). Therefore, the existence of this application shall have impact on the process of online learning activities.

There are quite number of studies that analyze the role of online meeting applications, including Zoom, in the distant learning activities during the pandemic. For instance, Rizaldi and Fatimah (2020) conclude that the Zoom Cloud Meeting application is an effective tool in online learning by taking the case study of mechanics and thermostatics courses. This application is able to facilitate educators and students to conduct online class activities during the COVID-19 pandemic. This is also in line with the findings from Rosyid *et al.* (2020). According to them, the effectiveness of learning activities using Zoom are in terms of time, place, and supporting tools. However, the drawbacks of this application are poor internet network, large internet quota consumption, and the size of the Zoom application. Similarly, Laili and Nashir (2020) show that the effectiveness of Zoom in English learning processes are due to several factors, including internet network, built-in feature of its application, and the level of understanding of the students themselves.

Monica and Fitriawati (2020) also attempt to examine the effectiveness of Zoom in online learning activities by taking the case study of ARS University in Indonesia. The study shows that in general, online learning activities using Zoom are effective. By using interview method, the application has good feedback according to the students. Lathifah and Lestari study the impact of Zoom in improving students' mathematical communication skills from the perspectives of teachers. The results show that 80 percent of teachers still use assignments as a tool to determine students' mathematical communication skills. In addition, this study finds 67 percent of students' mathematical abilities have decreased compared with before the pandemic. The application of the problem-based learning model with a realistic mathematics approach on Zoom Meeting-based learning is expected to improve the communication skills of elementary school students.

Fajrin and Tiorida (2020) measure the factors that influence behavioral interest in using video conferencing applications in webinar activities, with predictor factors including performance expectancy, effort expectancy, social influence, and facilitating conditions. This study uses purposive sampling methods on 165 respondents with multiple linear regression analysis. It shows that performance expectancy was the single most significant factor influencing behavioral interest in using this technology. Despite numerous studies conducted by various researchers on the impact of Zoom on learning activities, studies that use 15 different variables to assess the effectiveness of this application based on users' perception and satisfaction are still lacking. This study, therefore, is a humble attempt at bridging this gap.

Research methodology

Data and variables

This study selects 124 respondents who are students from several universities who have used Zoom for at least 2 months in their online learning process. The questionnaires are used to gather the information relevant for this study, including the following elements.

- General information regarding gender, marital status, level of formal education attained by the students, and background of their formal education.
- Economic status comprising their monthly income accruals from many sources, including fee/salary from jobs outside of being students, allowance from their parents, and scholarships, as well as their average monthly spending.
- Information on their experiences in using Zoom comprising the importance and satisfaction on several variables given. This also includes their comparison between Zoom and other similar applications.

There are 15 variables used in this study that can be found in Table 14.2.

The data and variables are analyzed using four methods, including Importance Performance Analysis (IPA), gap analysis, Customer Satisfaction Index (CSI), and t-test. The following section presents the explanation of each method.

Table 14.2 Variables

Variable	*Meaning*
A1	The easiness of using the application
A2	The simplicity of the application
A3	The completeness of the application
A4	Audio feature
A5	Screen or visual feature
A6	Recording feature
A7	Virtual background feature
A8	Filter feature
A9	Beta studio feature
A10	Size of the application
A11	Internet data usage
A12	Effectiveness on the study
A13	Price of premium subscription
A14	Number of participants
A15	Internal control function

Importance Performance Analysis (IPA)

Irawan (2002) stated that customer satisfaction indicators are tangibles, reliability, responsiveness, assurance, empathy, and product facilities. These dimensions are made in the form of a questionnaire which measures customer's satisfaction. Definitions of these attributes are as below:

- Tangible: physical performance, equipment, personnel, and communication material.
- Reliability: ability to provide promised services accurately.
- Responsiveness: willingness to assist customer and to give fast information and services.
- Assurance: knowledge, workers' hospitality, and ability to create trust on customer.
- Empathy: workers' willingness in serving and showing concern to the customer without any discrimination.
- Product facilities: providing supporting facilities, such as a present or discount.

Customer satisfaction assessment using the Important Performance Analysis (IPA) model aims at measuring the importance-level of work implementation. It is a technique which is used to measure attributes or dimensions from various importance levels with customers' expected performance, and it is useful in building effective marketing strategy. IPA analysis also becomes a foundation for management in their decision-making process aimed at enhancing a company's or product's performance and maintaining the customer's satisfaction. The obtained data will be analyzed by the IPA method in order to find out which product is considered the most important one by the customer.

Table 14.3 Assessment of performance and importance levels

Scores	*Performance (X)*	*Importance (Y)*
1	Not satisfied	Not important
2	Less satisfied	Less important
3	Satisfied enough	Important enough
4	Satisfied	Important
5	Very satisfied	Very important

In this method, the performance giving the customer satisfaction is symbolized with X, while Y shows importance level of the customer. To assess the performance and importance level of customer, the Likert scale is used. This scale allows the respondents to express the intensity of their feelings toward a certain characteristic of a product. The Likert scale shows customer responses on available choices, which are made in order starting from lower priority to higher priority. These scales consist of not important/satisfied, less important/satisfied, important/satisfied enough, important/satisfied and very important/satisfied. These five scales are depicted in Table 14.3.

These importance and performance levels will be analyzed by comparing the scores of performances and the scores of importance level. This comparison will determine the priority list of the factors affecting customer satisfaction. The formula used is as depicted below.

$$T_{ki} = \frac{X_i}{Y_i} \times 100\%$$

where:

T_{ki} = Compliance level
X_i = Assessment score for performance
Y_i = Score for importance assessment

The horizontal axis (X) will be filled with performance scores and the vertical axis (Y) will be filled with importance scores. In a simplified formula, each factor will influence customer satisfaction using the following formulas:

$$\bar{X}_i = \frac{\Sigma X}{n}$$

$$\bar{Y}_i = \frac{\Sigma Y}{n}$$

where:

$\bar{X}_i$ = average score for performance
$\bar{Y}_i$ = average score for importance level
n = number of respondents

Furthermore, after the values of $\bar{X}_i$ and $\bar{Y}_i$ are obtained, a Cartesian diagram is made. This diagram is also reflecting the values of $\bar{\bar{X}}$ and $\bar{\bar{Y}}$.

$$\bar{\bar{X}} = \frac{\sum_{i=1}^{n} \bar{X}}{k}$$

$$\bar{\bar{Y}} = \frac{\sum_{i=1}^{n} \bar{Y}}{k}$$

where:

$\bar{\bar{X}}$ = average score of performance of all components or attributes of services' quality
$\bar{\bar{Y}}$ = average score of importance level of all components or attributes of services' quality
k = the number of attributes of services' quality which affect customer satisfaction

This diagram is divided into four quadrants, and each shows a different condition. The strategies that can be made are based on the position of each attribute in these four quadrants. The details are as depicted below (Rangkuti, 2005):

- Quadrant I (top priority): it contains variables which are considered important by the customers, but in reality, are still not satisfying them. The strategy used in this area is to improve the performance of all variables that fall in this quadrant.
- Quadrant II (maintain the achievement): it comprises variables which are considered important and satisfying to the customers. The variables under this quadrant should be maintained as all these variables make the product is superior based on customers' perspectives.
- Quadrant III (low priority): it contains variables which are considered not important and not satisfying by the customers. Improvement on the variables under this quadrant will not significantly affect customers' perception.
- Quadrant IV (excessive): it contains variables which are considered not important by the customers, but satisfying them, and these variables are felt to be excessive. The variables under this quadrant should be reduced for the purpose of cost efficiency. For the details of this IPA diagram, let us take a look at Table 14.4.

Table 14.4 IPA diagram

Quadrant I Top priority	Quadrant II Maintain achievement
Quadrant III Low priority	Quadrant IV Excessive

Gap analysis

According to Rangkuti (2005), a gap occurred when the "*quality of service received by the customers is higher than the desired service or lower than the adequate service they expect. The former will lead to high satisfaction, while the latter can cause disappointment.*" Gap analysis is used to determine the gap between the actual and the ideal qualities. The former is indicated by perceived quality with its indicators, while the latter is indicated by expectations with its indicators. Technical gap determination is obtained by calculating the difference between perceived quality and its expectations. This can be found in the following formula.

$$Q = P - I$$

where:

Q = level of the quality gap
P = value of current perceived or actual quality/performance
I = value of ideal quality or expectation and need to be developed/importance

If the value of Q is positive ($Q \geq 0$), it indicates that the actual quality can fill out the ideal quality expected by the customers. On the other hand, the negative value of Q ($Q < 0$) indicates that the actual quality received by the customers has not met their expectations.

Customer Satisfaction Index

Irawan (2002) opines that CSI measurement is needed since its result can be used as indicator determining future targets. It is also needed by top management to determine certain goals in order to increase customer satisfaction. Dickson as cited in Phebruanti (2004) stated that there are four steps in calculating the CSI:

Calculating *mean importance score* (MIS) and *mean satisfaction score* (MSS). These values are obtained from average importance level and average performance of each respondent:

$$MIS = \frac{\sum_{i=1}^{n} Y_i}{n}$$

$$MSS = \frac{\sum_{i=1}^{n} X_i}{n}$$

Determining *weighted factor* (WF), which is the percentage of MIS value per attribute on total MIS of all attributes.

$$WF = \frac{MIS}{\sum_{i=1}^{n} MIS_i} \times 100\%$$

where:

n = number of importance attributes
i = i^{th} service attribute

Determining Weighted Score (WS)

This score is obtained from multiplication between *weighted factor* (WF) and *mean satisfaction score* (MSS).

$$WS_i = WF_i \times WSS_i$$

where:
i = attribute of service

Calculating CSI

Customer satisfaction scale used in the index interpretation is from zero to one or zero to one hundred. CSI formula is as follows:

$$CSI = \frac{\sum_{i=1}^{n} WSI_i}{5} \times 100\%$$

The whole customer satisfaction can be seen from criteria of customer satisfaction mentioned in Table 14.5.

t-test

In general, t-test is used to compare the average values of the two data sets. It is a type of inferential statistic used to determine if there is a significant difference between the means of two groups, which may be related in certain features. This study tests hypotheses with one sample statistic. This is used to compare the satisfaction of Zoom usage with other similar applications. The respondents are asked to score 15 statements (as presented in Table 14.6) using a scale of 1–5 based on their agreement with each statement on the variables (Table 14.7). The limit values are equal to 2.5. The hypotheses are as follows.

H_0: The satisfaction in using Zoom is at most other similar applications ($\bar{x} \leq 2.5$).
H_1: The satisfaction in using Zoom is greater than other similar applications ($\bar{x} > 2.5$).

Table 14.5 Satisfaction index values

No.	*Index value (%)*	*Note*
1	00.00–34.99	Not satisfied
2	35.00–50.99	Less satisfied
3	51.00–65.99	Satisfied enough
4	66.00–80.99	Satisfied
5	81.00–100.00	Very satisfied

Source: Phebruanti (2004).

Table 14.6 Statements

Variable	*Meaning*
B1	Zoom is easier to use than other similar applications
B2	Zoom is simpler than other similar applications
B3	Zoom has more complete features than other similar applications
B4	Zoom has better audio feature than other similar applications
B5	Zoom has better screen or visual feature than other similar applications
B6	Zoom has better recording feature than other similar applications
B7	Zoom has better virtual background feature than other similar applications
B8	Zoom has better filter features than other similar applications
B9	Zoom has better beta studio features than other similar applications
B10	Zoom has better size than other similar applications
B11	Zoom has better internet data usage than other similar applications
B12	Zoom is more effective in supporting online lectures than other similar applications
B13	Zoom has better price of premium subscription than other similar applications
B14	Zoom has better number of participants than other similar applications
B15	Zoom has better internal control functions than other similar applications

Table 14.7 Degree of agreement

Scores	*Degree of agreement*
1	Not agreed
2	Less agreed
3	Agreed enough
4	Agreed
5	Very agreed

Results and analysis

Demographic characteristics of the respondents

Table 14.8 depicts the information on demographic characteristics of the respondents. The demographic factors comprise gender, age, marital status, educational background, types of university, study program, occupation, total monthly income, total monthly spending, and total monthly spending on internet usage. In terms of gender, Table 14.8 shows that male students dominate the characteristics of the respondents by more than a half. Based on the age of respondents, it is observed that majority of respondents are between 16

Table 14.8 Respondents' demographic characteristics

Demographic characteristics		*Number*	*Percentage (%)*
Gender	Male	71	57.30
	Female	53	42.70
Age	16–20 years old	52	41.94
	21–25 years old	41	33.06
	26–30 years old	12	9.68
	30–35 years old	8	6.45
	36–40 years old	7	5.65
	More than 40 years old	4	3.23
Marital status	Married	29	23.40
	Not married	95	76.60
Current level of education	Diploma	1	0.80
	Bachelor's degree	85	68.50
	Postgraduate degree	38	30.60
Types of university	Public university	12	9.70
	Private university	112	90.30
Study program	Islamic economics and finance	82	66.10
	Non-Islamic economics and finance	42	33.90
Occupation	Full time student	43	34.68
	Teacher/lecturer/educator	40	32.26
	Employee	21	16.94
	Business owner	16	12.90
	Housewife	4	3.22
Total monthly income[a]	Less than IDR 500,000	39	31.50
	IDR 500,000–IDR 1,000,000	29	23.40
	IDR 1,000,001–IDR 2,000,000	16	12.90
	IDR 2,000,001–IDR 3,000,000	7	5.60
	IDR 3,000,001–IDR 4,000,000	15	12.10
	IDR 4,000,001–IDR 5,000,000	6	4.80
	More than IDR 5,000,000	12	9.70
Total monthly spending[a]	Less than IDR 500,000	45	36.30
	IDR 500,000–IDR 1,000,000	32	25.80
	IDR 1,000,001–IDR 2,000,000	18	14.50
	IDR 2,000,001–IDR 3,000,000	7	5.60
	IDR 3,000,001–IDR 4,000,000	8	6.50
	IDR 4,000,001–IDR 5,000,000	6	4.80
	More than IDR 5,000,000	8	6.50
Total monthly spending on internet usage[a]	Less than IDR 20,000	2	1.60
	IDR 20,000–IDR 50,000	14	11.30
	IDR 50,001–IDR 80,000	31	25.00
	IDR 80,001–IDR 100,000	35	28.20
	More than IDR 100,000	42	33.90

[a] As of July 3, 2021, IDR 500,000 equals to USD 34.58.

and 20 years old (41.94 percent), followed by those who are between 21 and 25 years old (33.06 percent) and between 26 and 40 years old (21.78 percent). Only few of them are more than 40 years old (3.23 percent). In relation to marital status, it is observed that more than three-fourths of the respondents are not married.

The findings of the age and status of the respondents are strengthened by their educational background. The majority of the respondents are still working toward their bachelor's degree (68.50 percent). The postgraduate students are 30.60 percent. Only 0.80 percent of them are pursuing a diploma degree. In addition, more than 90.00 percent of the respondents are from private universities, including Bogor Ibn Khaldun University, Tazkia Institute, Pertamina University, Sahid Islamic Institute, and STIE Triguna. Only less than one tenth of them are from public universities, such as IPB University and Brawijaya University. Besides, most of the respondents are majoring in Islamic economics and finance study programs. In terms of occupation, the majority of the respondents are full-time students (34.68 percent), followed slightly by teacher/lecturer/educator (32.26 percent). Besides, 16.94 percent of the respondents work as employees and 12.90 percent of them have their own businesses. Only 3.22 percent of the respondents are also housewives.

With regards to total monthly income, as a majority of the respondents are full-time students, more than one-third of them earn less than IDR 500,000, followed by those who earn between IDR 500,000 and IDR 1,000,000 (23.40 percent). The remaining respondents have a total monthly income more than IDR 1,000,000. These findings are also substantiated by the fact that most of the total monthly spending of the respondents is less than IDR 1,000,000. However, it is interesting to note that more than one-third of the respondents spend more than IDR 100,000 per month on internet costs. This shows that the internet has become an essential need for students, specifically during pandemic time, to support their online lecture activities.

Discussion on Importance Performance Analysis (IPA)

Based on IPA analysis, there is one variable that falls under quadrant I, nine variables fall under quadrant II, and the remaining five variables are in quadrant III. No variables are under quadrant IV. This is depicted in Figure 14.1.

Specifically, the detail explanation of IPA results is as follows.

First, quadrant 1, called a "primary areas to improve" area

This quadrant is an area that contains variables that are considered important by the users, but in reality, these factors cannot meet their expectation. In other words, the level of satisfaction obtained from the variables is low. In this study, A11 or internet data usage of Zoom falls under this quadrant. This means Zoom is high-cost in terms of internet data usage. Based on the company's official website, Zoom requires internet speed (bandwidth) of around 600 kbps–1.8 Mbps for video teleconferencing with one person (1:1), depending on the quality of the displayed video. If the speed of 1 Mbps can consume about 450 MB of data per hour, it means that one hour of using Zoom can consume around 270 MB–810 MB of internet data. Meanwhile, for group

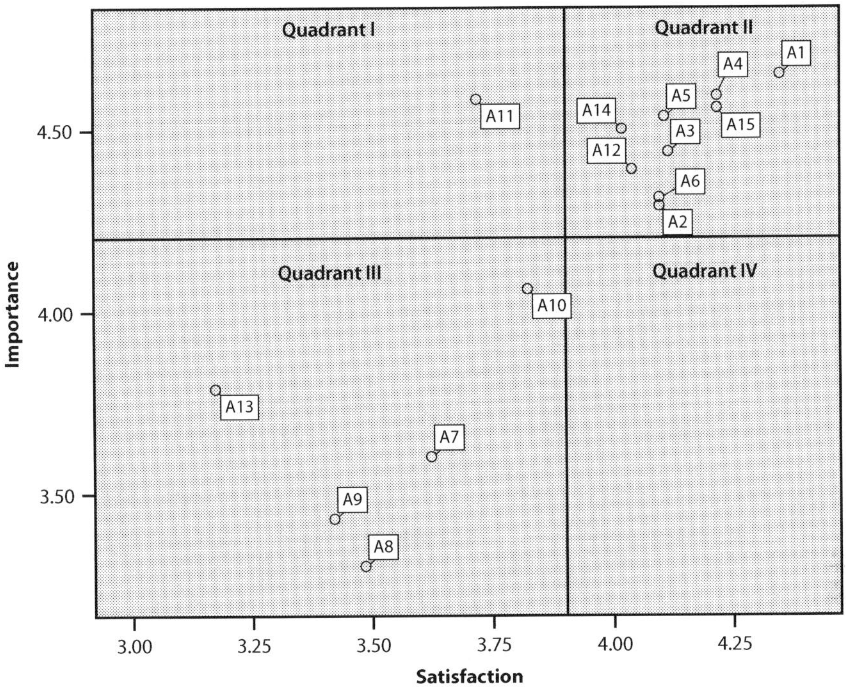

Figure 14.1 IPA diagram.

video teleconferencing, Zoom requires a bandwidth of 800 kbps–3 Mbps. In other words, the data used for online lectures can reach up to 360 MB to 1.35 GB per hour.

However, the data consumption varies between users based on several factors. These include Zoom's features being used during meetings, the duration of the video conference, internet speed, the number of people involved, the quality of the video viewed, the device used, and many more.

Second, quadrant 2, called a "primary area to maintain" area

This quadrant comprises factors that are important for the customers and the application can fulfill their expectations. Variables under this quadrant deliver high satisfaction to the customers. It is interesting to find that the majority of the variables being observed fall under this quadrant. These are A1 or the easiness of using the application, A2 or the simplicity of the application, A3 or the completeness of the application, A5 or the screen or visual feature, A6 or the recording feature, A12 or the effectiveness on the study, A14 or number of participants, and A15 or internal control function. The easiness of using Zoom (A1) and its simplicity (A2) have become main selling points. One of the instances of the easiness of the Zoom application is that the users do not have to log in using a certain email to join an online meeting. This makes it easy for the users to start, join, and collaborate across any device. The completeness of the application (A3) in terms of its features and activities, supported by this application, also delivers high satisfaction to the users. This includes meetings, marketplaces, video webinars, phone systems, and other online meeting activities. Besides, the screen or visual (A5) has good performance, as this application brings HD video that supports up to 1,000 video participants and 49 videos on screen. In addition, concurrent participants can share their screen simultaneously and co-annotate for a more interactive meeting. This helps the attribute deliver high satisfactions to its users.

Similarly, the recording feature (A6) also has a good impression to the users. This feature helps the host and cohosts to record the meetings locally on their respective devices. Besides, the record can be stored to the cloud with a searchable transcript. Our respondents also feel that Zoom is an effective tool to be used in their online learning activities (A12), as this variable delivers good performance that meets their expectation. This might be one of factors with the highest number of users of Zoom among other similar online meeting applications, as evident in Table 14.1. The number of participants that can join in one meeting using this application (A14) is perceived to deliver good performance based on our respondents. As mentioned earlier, this application supports up to 1,000 video participants through the premium subscription of the host. In addition, internal control functions (A15), such as mute and unmute speaker or stop and open video, give high satisfaction to its users.

Third, quadrant 3, called a "secondary area to improve"

It contains five variables, including virtual background feature (A7), filter feature (A8), beta studio feature (A9), size of application (A10), and price of premium subscription (A13). These five variables are considered less important by the users, and in fact their performances are not too special. This finding indicates that the five variables become the second priority to be improved after internet data usage (A11), which places in the first quadrant.

Discussion on gap analysis

Gap analysis is used to examine the observed variables and whether or not they meet the expectation of the users. It is simply obtained by subtracting the value of performance with the value of importance of each variable.

Table 14.9 presents the score of gaps for each variable. Positive scores show that the variable is able to meet users' expectation while negative scores reflect otherwise. From the 15 observed variables, the gap scores show that only two

Table 14.9 Scores of gap analysis

Variables		*Performance*	*Importance*	*Gap*[a]
The easiness to use the application	A1	4.35	4.65	–0.30
The simplicity of the application	A2	4.10	4.29	–0.19
The completeness of the application	A3	4.12	4.44	–0.32
Audio feature	A4	4.22	4.59	–0.37
Screen or visual feature	A5	4.11	4.53	–0.42
Recording feature	A6	4.10	4.31	–0.21
Virtual background feature	**A7**	**3.63**	**3.61**	**+0.02**
Filter feature	**A8**	**3.49**	**3.31**	**+0.18**
Beta studio feature	A9	3.43	3.44	–0.01
Size of the application	A10	3.83	4.06	–0.23
Internet data usage	A11	3.72	4.58	–0.86
Effectiveness on the study	A12	4.04	4.39	–0.35
Price of premium subscription	A13	3.18	3.79	–0.61
Number of participants	A14	4.02	4.50	–0.48
Internal control function	A15	4.22	4.56	–0.36

[a] Positive value of gap reflects that the variable can meet users' expectation.

attributes meet users' expectations, namely, the virtual background feature (A7) and the filter feature (A8). Meanwhile the remaining variables have not been able to fulfill users' expectation according to this analysis.

Discussion on the Customer Satisfaction Index (CSI)

The Customer Satisfaction Index (CSI) reflects the level of Zoom users' satisfaction as a whole by taking into account the level of importance and the performance value on the observed variables towards the application being used. Table 14.10 depicts the value of CSI. Based on data processing results as delineated in Table 14.10, it found that the Customer Satisfaction Index (CSI) value is 0.79. This result indicates that the users' satisfaction using Zoom for their online lectures is categorized as "satisfied." This means in general users are satisfied with the overall performance of this application.

Discussion on t-test

The one-sample statistics t-test is used to prove the satisfaction of the online lecture using Zoom as compared with other similar applications. The scale used is five levels, so it uses a value limit of 2.5 to accept or not to accept the null hypothesis as mentioned in method section. Table 14.11 shows the result of one-sample statistics. From Table 14.11, it is concluded that the null hypothesis (H_0) is not accepted and the alternative hypothesis (H_1) is accepted. This result indicates that Zoom has better performance in terms of 15 variables under consideration according to the respondents as compared with other similar online meeting applications.

Table 14.10 Score of customer satisfaction index

Variables		*Performance*	*Importance*	*WF*	*WS*	*CSI*
The easiness to use the application	A1	4.35	4.65	7.36	32.01	0.79
The simplicity of the application	A2	4.10	4.29	6.80	27.92	
The completeness of the application	A3	4.12	4.44	7.05	29.03	
Audio feature	A4	4.22	4.59	7.28	30.69	
Screen or visual feature	A5	4.11	4.53	7.19	29.55	
Recording feature	A6	4.10	4.31	6.84	28.02	
Virtual background feature	A7	3.63	3.61	5.73	20.79	
Filter feature	A8	3.49	3.31	5.26	18.35	
Beta studio feature	A9	3.43	3.44	5.46	18.71	
Size of the application	A10	3.83	4.06	6.44	24.69	
Internet data usage	A11	3.72	4.58	7.26	27.00	
Effectiveness on the study	A12	4.04	4.39	6.96	28.10	
Price of premium subscription	A13	3.18	3.79	6.01	19.09	
Number of participants	A14	4.02	4.50	7.13	28.65	
Internal control function	A15	4.22	4.56	7.24	30.52	
Total		**58.55**	**63.07**		**393.14**	
Average		**3.90**	**4.20**			

Abbreviations: CSI, Customer Satisfaction Index; WF, weighted factor; WS, weighted scores

Table 14.11 One-sample statistics

Variables	*N*	*Mean*	*Standard deviation*	*Standard error mean*
B1	124	4.05	0.927	0.083
B2	124	3.89	0.964	0.087
B3	124	3.97	0.836	0.075
B4	124	3.89	0.885	0.080
B5	124	4.10	0.834	0.075
B6	124	4.02	0.841	0.075
B7	124	3.85	0.963	0.086
B8	124	3.72	0.898	0.081
B9	124	3.64	0.849	0.076
B10	124	3.77	0.955	0.086
B11	124	3.10	1.299	0.117
B12	124	3.88	0.993	0.089
B13	124	3.02	1.122	0.101
B14	124	3.60	1.160	0.104
B15	124	4.01	0.915	0.082

Conclusion

The COVID-19 pandemic that has hit Indonesia since March 2020 has impacted the education sector as the learning system has been changed into an online form. To support this online learning system, Zoom has been widely used by the universities in conducting their activities. By observing 124 students from universities in Indonesia who have experience in using this application for at least two months, this study attempts to analyze the determinants of the level of importance and satisfaction of this application. The study employs four methods, including Importance Performance Analysis (IPA), gap analysis, Customer Satisfaction Index (CSI) and t-test methods in analyzing 15 variables under consideration. This study suggests several findings. Firstly, based on IPA method, it is found that internet data usage is the top priority that should be improved. Secondly, the gap analysis shows that only two variables, namely virtual background and filter features, have met the users' expectation. Thirdly, according to CSI value, respondents are satisfied in general with the Zoom application in supporting their online lecture activities. Lastly, when compared with other similar online meeting applications, the t-test of one sample statistics shows that Zoom has better performance.

References

Fajrin, M. U. & Tiorida, E. (2020). Faktor yang Memengaruhi Minat Perilaku Penggunaan Teknologi (Studi: Pengguna Aplikasi Video Conference selama Physical Distancing). Proceeding of The 11th Industrial Research Workshop and National Seminar Bandung, 26–27 Agustus 2020, 977–984.

Fitriyani, F., Febriyeni, M., & Kamsi, N. (2020). Penggunaan aplikasi Zoom Cloud Meeting pada proses pembelajaran online sebagai solusi di masa pandemic Covid-19. *Edification*, *3*(1), 23–34.

Guzacheva. (2020). Zoom technology as an effective tool for distance learning. *Bulletin of Science and Practice*, *6*(5), 457–460.

Irawan, H. (2002). *Sepuluh Prinsip Kepuasan Pelanggan*. Jakarta, Indonesia: PT Elex Media Komputindo.

Laili, R. N. & Nashir, M. (2020). The use of Zoom Meeting for distance learning in teaching English to nursing students during Covid-19 Pandemic. Proceedings in UHAMKA International Conference on ELT and CALL (UICELL), 17–18 December, Jakarta, Indonesia, 236–244.

Monica, J. & Fitriawati, D. (2020). Efektivitas penggunaan aplikasi *Zoom* sebagai media pembelajaran *online* pada mahasiswa saat pandemi Covid-19. *Jurnal Kommunio: Jurnal Ilmu Komunikasi*, *11*(2), 1630–1640.

Phebruanti, I. (2004). *Analisis Tingkat Kepuasan pengunjung Taman Safari Indonesia, Cisarua Bogor* [Bachelor's Thesis]. Departemen Sosial Ekonomi Industri Peternakan, Fakultas Peternakan. IPB University, Bogor, Indonesia.

Rangkuti, F. (2005). *Marketing Analysis Made Easy* (Marketing and Case Analysis Technique Using Excel and SPSS). Jakarta, Indonesia: PT, Gramedia Pustaka Utama Publisher.

Rizaldi, D. R. & Fatimah, Z. (2020). Penggunaan aplikasi Zoom Cloud Meeting pada mata kuliah mekanika dan termostatistika saat pandemi COVID-19. *Kappa Journal*, *4*(2), 225–232.

Rosyid, N. M., Thohari, M. I., & Lismanda, Y. F. (2020). Penggunaan aplikasi Zoom Cloud Meetings dalam kuliah Statistik Pendidikan di Fakultas Agama Islam Universitas Islam Malang. *Vicratina: Jurnal Pendidikan Islam*, *5*(11), 46–52.

Scanga, L.H., Deen, Y. M. K., Smith, S. R., & Wright, K. (2018). Special issue on innovation 2018 Zoom around the world: Using videoconferencing technology for international trainings. *Journal of Extension*, *56*(5). https://archives.joe.org/joe/2018september/iw1.php

Part 3

SMART RESEARCH METHODS FOR ISLAMIC ECONOMICS AND FINANCE

15

METHODOLOGIES AND SMART TECHNIQUES RECOMMENDED IN ANALYZING QUR'ANIC PRINCIPLES FOR ISLAMIC ECONOMICS AND FINANCE

Ahmed Aref

Introduction

Religious teaching is perceived as old-school thought and not applicable to modern, globalized life. This perception is creating a gap between human needs and economic behavior. This chapter aims to show how big data and machine learning can direct our perception toward aligning our financial behavior with our human needs from the lens of Quranic principles. The rise of artificial intelligence (AI) is a breakthrough in the art of merging contemporary technology and the needs-fulfilling economic principles.

Current perception shapes our reality and how to elevate it

There are approximately 7 billion people that reside within this world, yet the irony is that we often feel incredibly alone and distant from other human beings. We have been conditioned to believe that all we need is the Creator and nothing else. Yet, the Creator gave us families, friends, work colleagues, and people who can serve us. There is a deeper wisdom within these relationships. Each one teaches us something about ourselves, our place within the world, and their purpose within our lives. Every one of us at some point in our lives will experience a degree of hardship or pain that hurts us. Therefore, it is important to explore the significance of helping others from a humanistic-economic context. Helping each other is a way to overcome the grief that we may experience; it can empower us to have an impact and create a legacy. The greatest human beings who walked or walk the earth offer wisdom, compassion, kindness, and mentorship. These people believed in the Creator, namely Muhammad, Jesus son of Mary, Moses, Abraham,

DOI: 10.4324/9781003252764-19

Noah, and Adam. May peace be upon them all. The words of the Creator have been sent to all humanity to support the integrity of humans. Integrity means to be true to your ideals and contextually voice it in your life and business decisions. The words of the Creator guide us toward a set of values and principles. These values and principles serve to nurture the human body and ensure food and drink are beneficial for the optimized functioning of organs. These values and principles serve biological needs, such as sleep and nutrition, by organizing sleeping times and recommending what types of food are beneficial to humans. In addition to rest and nutrition, these values and principles also serve financial needs, ranging from buying and selling to regulating economic activity. These values and principles were followed throughout the centuries and are meant to preserve the human soul in its adversities and trials. It provides a path to fulfilling common needs. It uplifts spirits regarding the required intrinsic motivation to work, survive, and thrive according to shared values and universal principles to meet our common needs.

The above requires a holistic understanding of the self, which refers to the mind, body, and soul. In addition to understanding the self, it provides a sense of economic human behaviors and habits during prosperity and hardship. Through the scripture and smart technologies, there can be an understanding of how the complicated relationships between financial and relational values and principles affect human behavior. Our current behavior resulted mainly from the social proofing of others around us, the contemporary communal family traditions and customs, primarily based on our ancestors' habits. Each human being teaches his siblings what his family holds dear to them and how these values and traditions were preserved in the past and preserved at present. These values and traditions are ingrained in our subconscious values system, guiding us in the present and future. These values and traditions could be social, economic, hereditary, political, et cetera, and the adherence to these traditions represents the good, and its violations represent the bad.

The traditions and economic behavior prevalent in markets are reflections of the community and in particular to dynastic family values. If the values are family-centered, it will affect the utilization of the profits generated in the market at large for the family members. For example, if the values are inclined toward aesthetics, paintings, and finely decorated buildings, et cetera, and if these values are communal-centered, then the effect would be to have institutions that serve the community's needs, such as Waqf or endowments. People, in general, yearn for support by establishing connections with others. This trickles down from life to business as we find syndicates, private networks/groups, and societies, where decision-making or brainstorming happens and the economic interests are debated and agreed upon. At present, there are commercial chambers, rotary clubs, and other private groups.

The above realities have prevailed for centuries. It is crucial to be mindful of if we want to extract further and enact the principles derived from the Quran and what follows in Islamic eco-finance further. The first thing we need to achieve is understanding of the causes and objectives of the current situation regarding human economic behavior and habits. The realization of a cultural gap between the West and East will be important when determining practical methodologies to govern Islamic eco-finance moving forward. The reason for this is because economic behavior in the West is conducted differently than in the East. The current frame of reference for the perception of the self, the world, and work in the West has dominated the whole globe, including the Islamic eco-finance principles of increasing assets under management to mainly serve the shareholder's monetary needs as a foundational principle, irrespective of the true Quranic principles underlying Islamic eco-finance and its true socioeconomic mission.

Creators' words of wisdom

> It is Allah who has subjected to you the sea so that ships run upon it at His command, and so that you may seek His bounty and be thankful. (12) He has subjected to you whatsoever is in the heavens and the earth; all is from Him. Surely, there are signs in this for people who contemplate. (13)
>
> (*al-Qur'an 45: 12–13*)

> People, We have created you from a male and a female and made you into nations and tribes that you might know one another. The noblest of you before Allah is the most righteous of you. Allah is the Knower, the Aware.
>
> (*al-Qur'an 49: 13*)

> Have they never thought to themselves that Allah did not create the heavens and the earth and all that is between except with truth, and for a stated term? Yet most people disbelieve that they will ever meet their Lord.
>
> (*al-Qur'an 30:8*)

> Nay! Man will be a witness against himself [as his body parts (skin, hands, legs, etc.) will speak about his deeds.
>
> (*al-Qur'an 75:14*)

> And also in your selves. Will you not then see?
>
> (*al-Qur'an 51:21*)

> And We have sent you (O Muhammad SAW) not but as a mercy for the 'Alamin (humankind) and all that exists.
>
> (*al-Qur'an 21:107*)

Qur'anic principles were detailed, repeated to support the continuous human improvement and best possible functioning in their different, diverse, and evolving life and work facets and in all their life stages.

> Who has created death and life, that He may test you which of you is best in deed. And He is the All-Mighty, the Oft-Forgiving.
>
> (*al-Qur'an 67:2*)

> Verily! Allah will not change the good condition of a people as long as they do not change their state of goodness themselves (by committing sins and by being ungrateful and disobedient to Allah.)
>
> (*al-Qur'an 13:11*)

The above principle of each functioning autonomously in the best way possible is reflected in western culture as self-determination theory (SDT). Deci and Ryan developed the self-determination theory of motivation, toppling the dominant belief that the best way to get human beings to perform tasks is to reinforce their behavior with rewards (controlled motivation). Islamic eco-finance existed to bring Quranic principles, including psychological needs of autonomous competence and relatedness, into life. Islamic eco-finance in that regard is not a theory and cannot be viewed as an industry in the same way there is a gold, metal, or FMCG industry. Islamic eco-finance, which is currently a branch of economics, is the only way to guide humans to fulfill all the holistic human needs, which will result in economic prosperity and achieving what we need and desire for our well-being. Past scholars from the East have worked independently to determine how to extract Quranic principles and analyze them: great scholars like Ibn Hanbal, Al-Sahtibi, Ibn Taimiah, Ibn Al-Qayem, and Ibn Khaldun and Al-Ghazaly, peace be upon them. They have contributed to state various methodologies to deliver the best possible theory to advance the whole of humanity's well-being.

All of these great scholars have reviewed the work of their like-minded predecessors and contributed their views to that of their predecessors, especially Ibn Khouldon, by incorporating sociology. Evidence shows that each scholar has a context influenced by his era, which he addresses in his writing. This chapter aims to provide a contextual, all-inclusive, visionary methodology regarding the implementation of Islamic eco-finance through the lens of the last holy book using big data, machine learning, and AI. The Creator's words remain the most holistic and authentic words since the sun's dawn on the earth, till it extinguishes the world. I can assume that the coordination occurring in this book of the current scholars' talent is more than necessary to face the unprecedented challenges of the spread of ignorance about the principles and novelty of the last message that can transform people's lives on Earth.

> Whoever relieves a believer's distress of the distressful aspects of this world, Allah will rescue him from a difficulty of the difficulties of the Hereafter. Whoever alleviates [the situation of] one in dire straits who cannot repay his debt, Allah will alleviate his lot in both this world and in the Hereafter. Whoever conceals [the faults of] a Muslim, Allah will conceal [his faults] in this life and the Hereafter.
>
> (*Sahih al-Muslim*)

It is one of the principles of our faith to help our fellow human beings with our emotions, utilizing our intellectual and financial means to serve others to achieve our fulfillment first and benefit others and gain their loyalty. There are genuinely breakthrough skills in the economic and business worlds (emotional and social intelligence) and leadership concepts (servant leadership), which allow us to be our essential self and act according to our values. Human lives remain vague, and we feel heedless if not attended by service to humanity. The following verse of the Quran is often cited to encapsulate the Islamic idea of social welfare:

> It is not righteousness that you turn your faces towards East or West; but it is righteousness to believe in Allah and the Last Day, and the Angels, and the Book and the Messengers; to spend of your substance, out of love for Him, for your kin, for orphans, for the needy, for the wayfarer, for those who ask, and for the ransom of slaves; to be steadfast in prayer, and practice regular charity, to fulfil the contracts which we have made; and to be firm and patient, in pain or suffering, adversity, and throughout all periods of panic. Such are the people of truth, the God-fearing.
>
> (*al-Qur'an 2:177*)

In the Qur'an, Allah (SWT) says: "*Help one another in acts of piety and righteousness. And do not assist each other in acts of sinfulness and transgression. And be aware of Allah. Verily, Allah is severe in punishment*" (al-Qur'an 5:2). From the above words of wisdom, we can find helpful practices of emotional and social intelligence skills introduced by Daniel Goleman and endorsed by the United Nations, allowing us to tap into several leadership styles depending on the context. For example, we are kind to others.

> O Aisha, Allah is gentle and He loves gentleness. He rewards for gentleness what is not granted for harshness and He does not reward anything else like it.
>
> (*Sahih al-Muslim*)

It is important to remember that in our daily lives, we will encounter many people and we are not always aware of what storm they may be going through.

The simple act of being kind can sometimes be life-changing to someone. One of the ways this can be done is through exchanging positive conversations or even simply smiling at someone. You can contribute by providing monetary help to people through structured endowments, caring for fellow humans who are contributing their time and skills to create a propseperous economy.

Finally, we need to sharpen the saw for the rest of our lives by seeking forgiveness and repairing. This is an act of purification and a greater chance of our decisions to have an impact on our and other lives. We must remember that we must help ourselves first, before helping others. When we repent, we are cleansed. Repentance acts like a polish for the heart, the same way we polish our cars. We know when we do this we make it shinier than when it is when left untouched. Then comes the intentional behavior of repairing the current dysfunctionalities of the past toward ourselves and others. When we invite ourselves to pause, fixing ourselves has an introspection toward what we miss and how to invite new behaviors into our lives to fulfill these needs. Secondly, the repairing toward others enables others to learn about their common needs, be literate in emotion education, and be better communicators to have purposeful relationships. The above should happen in schools, universities, et cetera. The vision toward a fulfilling ending can be visualized and shaped by merging the big data application to advance our understating of the Islamic eco-finance. We need to also include the core human need of self-fulfillment into our universal perception, which will address a huge gap existing in the lives of the wealthy and general community.

The globalized polar world

Self-fulfillment has never been a goal in economics. Measuring value has been the ultimate goal while creating holistic value is absent. Talking about numbers is the sole focus in business. On the other hand, the common needs for purpose, self-fulfillment, and the economic impact on communities have to focus when discussing business and economics. Islamic eco-finance principles in the East cannot exist in isolation from the predominant Western values and regulations governing all the financial and economic institutions. The central banks worldwide operating under the same economic rules, which hedge against losing money, seek incremental gains (interest rates) in financial markets, and gain from foreign exchange differentials. These activities are not value-creating. Islam has a unique dispensation on the theme of wealth, its ownership, distribution, and social relationship. Islam enjoins wealth creation not for its own sake. The theme of Islamic dispensation of wealth is treated as a deeply moral study of self and society. The true nature of wealth in Islam requires social preferences and market exchange mechanisms that are ethicized by human consciousness of the Moral Law. Islam gives precise moral injunctions as to what are and are not acceptable kinds of wealth. They point out how individual preferences on wealth formation ought to be utilized within the social meaning.

We need to move from the fear of loss or losing status into positive psychology of self-fulfillment and establish an economic growth strategy. The common theme worldwide is the over-simplistic choice of profit to a small portion of humanity as the sole value determinant and another principle of achievements or results and performance to achieve identity. Both represent the dominant language in Western and Eastern economics and businesses. This over-simplistic, narrow view of the self limits the fulfillment of well-being of the beneficiaries themselves from economic activities and the executives, employees, financial institutions, and communities. According to Shaikh Yusuf Talal DeLorenzo, well-known and respected Shari'ah advisor, Islamic scholar, and author of the three-volume "*Compendium of Legal Opinions on the Operations of Islamic Banks*," the first English reference on the fatwas (religious rulings) issued and published by the Institute, business, in the Qur'anic sense of "profitable trade" or tijarat'un rabihah is business that brings blessings to those who conduct it. Profits are important as ends, but how those profits are earned is even more important, that is, if our profits were obtained with clean or unclean hands. Indeed, the reason for the emphasis on proper transaction is that the last message accords great importance to the economic welfare of society.

Economic taxonomy

The profit-first narrow focus ignored the values of diversity that some businesses adhered to in the Eastern and Western worlds. Some business owners, such as Bob Chapman in the manufacturing industry and Barry Wehmiller, who have billions of dollars, are running purpose-driven businesses. These businesses enforce values of respect, dignity, diversity inclusion, and maintain a culture of togetherness. They express a great deal of care toward their employees, their customers, and creating holistic value in their communities. We can expand on these values by focusing on the universal common needs that we all seek from our authentic sources. Using big data, AI, and machine learning will be helpful in the merging of original Eastern and Western business values regarding the economic context. It would aid in forming both the content (what) and the process (why) of goals.

One of the most important objectives of the values-led message is to realize greater justice in human society. According to the last message, a society where there is no justice will head toward decline and destruction ultimately as revealed in "*Indeed We have sent Our Messengers with clear proofs, and revealed with them the Scripture and the Balance (justice) that mankind may keep up justice*" (al-Qur'an 57:25). Justice requires a set of rules or shared moral values, which everyone accepts and faithfully complies with. The financial system may be able to promote justice or balance, in addition to being strong and stable, if it satisfies at least four conditions based on moral values. One of the recommendations would be that the financier should also share in the risk, so as not to shift the entire burden of losses to the entrepreneur. Another suggestion is that there should an equitable share of financial resources mobilized by financial institutions which could become available to the poor to help eliminate poverty. This will expand employment and self-employment opportunities and thus help reduce inequalities of income and wealth.

To fulfill the first condition of justice, the last words of wisdom require both the financier and the entrepreneur to have an equitable share in profit and loss, which is what typically happens with angel investors. For this purpose, one of the basic principles of Islamic finance is "no risk, no gain." This should help introduce greater discipline into the financial system by motivating financial institutions to assess the risks more carefully and to effectively monitor the use of funds by the borrowers. The double assessment of risks by both the financier and the entrepreneur should help inject greater discipline into the system, and go a long way in reducing excessive lending.

Islamic finance, in its ideal form should help raise the share of equity and profit-loss-sharing (PLS) in businesses substantially. Greater reliance on equity financing has supporters, even in mainstream economics. Professor Kenneth Rogoff of Harvard University states that in an ideal world, equity lending and direct investment would play a much bigger role. Greater reliance on equity does not necessarily mean that debt financing is ruled out. This is because the financial needs of individuals, firms, or governments cannot be made amenable to equity and PLS. Debt is therefore indispensable, but should not be promoted for nonessential, wasteful consumption and unproductive pursuits. The first condition will help eliminate a large number of derivative transactions that involve nothing more than gambling by third parties who aspire to claim compensation for losses that have been suffered only by the principal party and not by them. The second condition of justice will help ensure that the seller (or lessor) also shares a part of the risk, to be able to get a share of the return. Once the seller (financier) acquires ownership and possession of the goods for sale or lease, he/she bears the risk. This condition also puts a constraint on short sales, thereby removing the possibility of a steep decline in asset prices during a downturn. However, the moral principles have made an exception to this rule in the case of salam, where the goods are not already available in the market and need to be produced or manufactured before delivery. Thus, financing extended through Islamic modes can expand only in steps with the rise of the real economy, thereby helping curb excessive credit expansion. The third and fourth conditions will not only motivate the creditor to be more cautious in evaluating the credit risk, but also prevent an unnecessary expansion in the volume and value of transactions. This will prevent debt from rising above the size of the real economy and also release a substantial volume of financial resources for the real sector. This will help expand employment and self-employment opportunities and the production of need-fulfilling goods and services. The discipline that Islam wishes to introduce in the financial system may not materialize, unless governments reduce their borrowing from the central bank to a level that is in harmony with price and financial stability.

One may object that all these conditions will perhaps end up shrinking the size of the economy by reducing the number and volume of transactions. This is not likely to happen because of several reasons; speculative and derivatives transactions are generally known to be zero-sum games and have rarely contributed positively to total real output. Hence a decline in them is also not likely to hurt the real economy. While a restriction on such transactions will cut the commissions earned by the speculators during an artificially generated boom, it will help them avert losses and bankruptcy that become unavoidable during the decline that leads to a financial crisis.

The injection of a greater discipline into the financial system may tend to deprive the subprime borrowers access to credit. Therefore, justice demands that some suitable innovation be introduced in the system to ensure that even small borrowers are also able to get adequate credit while sharing in profits as a return. Such borrowers are generally considered to be subprime and their inability to get credit will deprive them of realizing their dream of owning their own homes and establishing their microenterprises.

Thus, we can see that the Islamic financial system is capable of minimizing the severity and frequency of financial crises by getting rid of the major weaknesses of the conventional system. It introduces greater discipline and rational behaviors into the financial system by requiring the financier to share in the risk. It links credit expansion to the growth of the real economy by allowing credit primarily for the purchase of real goods and services, which the seller owns and possesses and the buyer wishes to take. It also requires the creditor to bear the risk of default by prohibiting the sale of debt, thereby ensuring that he evaluates the risk more carefully. Islamic finance can also reduce the problem of subprime borrowers by providing credit to them at affordable terms.

Common methodology

Islamic eco-finance should be perceived as a connection point between various disciplines such as philosophy, ancient civilizations, sociology, psychology, economics, et cetera. Its ultimate goal is to shape the views of the self, world, and work. These various disciplines require bold choice and courage to establish an inclusive methodology and universal perception to achieve our individualistic and collective well-being.

A seven-step methodology in deriving the Qur'anic principles to support modern eco-finance is as follows. The first step is to perceive and assess the reality as our perception is a pre-condition to reach our goals. Secondly, to precisely define the purpose of our existence, form a strategic intent to reshape economic relationships and the impact we strive to achieve in life. Thirdly, determine the well-being outcome, including self-fulfillment as a need and the work ethic as a priority value. Fourth, to choose a starting point from the current reality. Fifth, to set a values-based direction. Sixth, to form a holistic identity by connecting the values, beliefs, and perceptions. Seventh, to build conceptual habits and behaviors that support achieving our well-being outcomes.

Following the above methodology will help us attain a narrative of legitimacy and fairness in economic proposals. In reaching a consensus and agreement with the Western world, we would first need the help of smart techniques when using big data, AI, and machine learning to analyze the worldwide (in the East and West) history of economic relationships: the history of currencies, establishments of banks, bilateral trade agreements, motives of having capital markets, the inception of the first corporation, et cetera. It is essential to understand the historical data of these financial and economic systems to figure out recurring patterns or assess situations that lead to specific outcomes.

Professionals from Islamic eco-finance need to be objective when reading the relationships and results derived from the smart techniques, and they need to understand the findings. The understanding will ensure that all parties interests are considered. It will promote relationships embedded in trust, and it will showcase the existence of other options that could satisfy both parties' interests. We will know what works, what does not work, and the reasoning behind each alternative. The economic world would not have been connected had it not been for the development of IT technological advancement, which allowed connectivity of worldwide stock exchanges. Connectivity based on a narrow view of a few values, without considering the broader spectrum of moral values and the common needs of all parties, leads to a financial crisis.

The new, connected economic world based on common needs and shared moral values will be far more resilient. The new system will not threaten the current beneficiaries. It will provide them with equitable financial gains, in addition to the most important "lost purpose" in their lives. In reality, the real owner of our souls and wealth is the Creator. Man only owns wealth by proxy as guardian for which purpose he has been made guardian (Khalifah) of the Creator on Earth. Unlike capitalism and socialism, which believe that man – in his quest for wealth – must deal with the scarcity of resources, the last message views the concept of wealth differently, as wealth is considered a bounty of God and thus it is not scarce, for Allah (swt) says: "*God is rich but you are poor*" ([al-Qur'an 47:38).

What is scarce is the ability of mankind to utilize the bounties of God. The situation is worsened by their inability to explore new resources due to the limitation of knowledge and perceptions. The words of Creator regard wealth as a means of human fulfillment in his endeavor to attain al-Falah or prosperity that leads to a good life, in this world and after. Therefore, the quest for wealth is not condemned. Yet each human being is bound to work as a means to earn his livelihood, as Allah says: "*He it is Who made the earth smooth for you, therefore go about in the spacious sides thereof, and eat of His sustenance, and to Him is the return after death.*" (al-Qur'an 67:15). Needless to say, humanity must follow all the commandments of their Creator, as those who fail to do so are condemned. However, in their quest for livelihood, they must observe that all economic activities must not bear any elements that contravene the values and principles. Therefore, man should manage wealth by the values and principles which help us fulfill our holistic needs. Good wealth management is important because any possessions or assets would not grow without proper planning and implementation. In contemporary terminology, it is known as financial planning. Comprehensive financial planning encompasses several critical areas such as wealth creation (e.g., working or earning a living); wealth accumulation (e.g., investment, inheritance, saving); wealth protection (e.g., retirement planning, collective insurance); and wealth-conscious distribution (e.g., Waqf/endowments, crowdfunding and planned giving), and productive wealth (e.g., human development, supporting research, supporting ideas through startups).

Nevertheless, this explanation is the generic concept of financial planning, and it must be refined to ensure that the concept can be recognized as moral financial planning. However, the process of refinement does not require an abandonment of the existing generic concept. The concept can be recognized as moral financial planning by adding a clause that it must comply with the values and principles which help us fulfill our holistic needs. What is important is to ensure that whatever activities or behaviors we follow regarding wealth creation, wealth accumulation, wealth protection, wealth distribution, or productive wealth. We must comply with the search for holistic needs, creating an impact and earning our legacy. Therefore, instead of dealing with profit-based insurance, humans should opt for collective insurance; instead of investing in harmful/non-productive shares, they should only buy shares or stocks that are beneficial to our common needs and preserve our wisdom. Investment in endowments reflects people with great hearts who are charitable.

For people who have an extremely high sense of self-awareness, excessive self-consciousness will occur within them, i.e., they will have values consciousness. Therefore, when they plan for something, they should consider this criterion and as such, their financial planning should also stretch to cover their spiritual values. Thus, by having proper financial planning and implementation, conscious humans will strike a balance between fulfilling their needs and wants and executing spiritual obligations. Adherence to spiritual teachings, in this context, will prevent any hostility that often occurs among people while engaging in economic activities, especially when wealth and money are considered the most important elements in society.

This ill-feeling has been spelt out by the Last Messenger when he says, "*The heart of an old man remains young in two respects: his love for the world (its wealth, amusements and luxuries) and his incessant hope*" (as narrated by Abu Hurairah). For this reason, wealth in Islam may function as a means of trial and test to find out the true values we are attaching to wealth. Is it inclined toward creation, protection, accumulation, distribution, or production? The more significant imbalance between those facets, the more significant the direction for correct economic behaviors. As the Creator says, "*And as for man, when his Lord tries him, then treats him with honour and makes him lead an easy life, he says: 'My Lord honours me.' But when He tries him (differently), then straitens to him his means of subsistence, he says: 'My Lord has disgraced me'*" (al-Qur'an 89:15–16).

Nonetheless, moral values highly encourage their beholders to be financially stable, for the reason that poverty or hardness among faith-based or humans in general may lead them to infidelity. Despite this encouragement, rational economic behaviors should be our guide to achieve common needs and be heart-fulfilling. We should resist directing all our behavior toward wealth accumulation and distributing only to others who commit their loyalties to us. The former can lead to more inclusive, resilient communities. The latter would create social levels. AI has been applied as an advanced data processing tool for scriptural Bible studies. There are some projects which use natural language processing, image recognition, and advanced data processing. For example, Ecce (Explanatory Core Concept Extraction, also Latin for "behold") uses natural language processing to find topics and verses related to a search phrase. It draws in data from the English Standard Version, Nave's Topical Index, and the Treasury of Scripture Knowledge to cross-references to train a model relating each entry to possible input terms. Another example is "Theologies of the Digital Project." This project aims to explore the following question: "What can we learn from reading the Bible with machines?" The team's role is to build a text-generation model that will take a short passage from the Bible as input-to-output narrative commentary on the passage. We begin with the assumption that machines can be significant partners in reading corpus, as they do with the Bible by learning from existing commentary data and introducing novel reflections on a given passage. These machine-generated reflections on Bible passages can teach us about the existing tendencies in Bible commentary and raise new questions and insights on the corpus.

AI and big data can shape a universal humane culture and prosperity

We face a world that can feel like a pyramid full of social levels. Trust-building is key to fostering collaboration, healing ourselves, repairing the effect of our previous actions, moving us forward, and flattening social structures. Networks should be based on shared values, common purpose, and common vision. To create a different reality, we need to be courageous and reflect on our habits and behaviors that are formed based on our narrow focus on locality and family. We ultimately need to expand our perspective of the self, the world, and work to create new mental and social habits. We need different behaviors and habits, and we need to take advantage of technological advancements that can help us progress and elevate together toward fulfillment. The universal culture would require us to build cross-cultural relationships in business where we seek to understand without making assumptions, embrace an open mindset, keep our word, assume positive intent, get involved, and start with "who you know." The best place to start is with others you know inside and outside your organization, business, and social organizations. Finally, attend multicultural networking events to broaden your perspectives. The current AI and big data's current smart techniques help us broaden our perspectives on history, common needs, nuances of human psychology, and emotions. It will create a universal culture based on recognizing each other's talent, where interdependence and work ethic are favored, rather than favoring blood relations only.

History reveals that big events such as industrial revolutions were not started by a small group of families or people located in one area. It was ignited by one man who sincerely believed in something and spoke about it with a passion for materializing a reality he had dreamed of. He experimented with new aspects of social life and work processes and finally succeeded in scaling his idea in the socioeconomic context. The Scripture has shown us that the wisest spiritual people had achieved their life mission together with people other than their relatives and families. This contributed to their more incredible goodness, which helped them to achieve their fulfillment. These were the lessons we learned from the past. Moving forward, we can depend on big data and AI to explore two things; immoral behaviors and people's good behavior. Our role would then be to initiate new economic relationships and conditions based on good behavior at the local level and expand on it on a universal scale. Achieving this will help us finding meaning for our siblings, family, and ourselves.

Conclusion

Financial institution fiduciaries and the owners and associates have aligned their interests around financial gains only. All the common needs between humans are not reflected in economic behaviors and decisions. Heightened perception of the self, the world, and work in light of humanity's common needs through AI and machine learning are much needed. AI and machine learning can act as interpreters to human economic behavior throughout human history, through the Quran to derive human economic principles that fulfill common needs. Our families and siblings are deserving of decision-makers to be courageous and shift our perspectives from our centuries-long traditions and customs toward what matters most to us now. This shift will allow us to pursue meaning in life and having our legacy, and this will help our heirs to enjoy fulfillment for the majority of their lives.

16

HARMONIZATION OF MAINSTREAM TECHNIQUES WITH MAQASID BASED METHODOLOGY FOR ISLAMIC ECONOMICS AND FINANCE RESEARCH

Yussuf Charles Yussuf, Mohamed Cherif El Amri and Mustafa Omar Mohammed

Introduction

This chapter attempts to explore the need for harmonizing the mainstream techniques with Maqasid-based methodology for Islamic economics and finance research. This is because Islamic economics and finance is a young field of study, which does not offer a complete set of tools for economic analysis. Thus, in contemporary Islamic economics and finance, the research in the field adopts mainstream techniques as tools of analysis that apply pure mathematical postulations, which are adopted from positive conventional economics (logical empiricism). This is also attributed to the fact that we are living in a world of narrower specialization governed by monodisciplinary styles in diverse fields of human life ranging from economics, finance, physical science, etc., in which Islamic economics and finance have fallen into a similar trap. Monodisciplinary research is where just one discipline is employed to solve the inherent problem. While earlier scholars were polymaths who had many fields of specialization, for instance, [Muslim scholar first], then Archimedes apart from the contribution he made in physics he had other remarkable contributions with interest in mathematics, astronomy at the same time he was known as an engineer and inventor (Rafikov and Akhmetova, 2020). Aristotle, apart from being a renowned philosopher, had an interest in poetry, biology, and physics.

The monodisciplinary design, which is the result of narrower specialization, was partly driven by the Enlightenment and the Industrial Revolution during the 20th century. However, this narrower specialization in physical, social, natural,

 DOI: 10.4324/9781003252764-20

and human sciences slowly departed from religious values (Zaman 2013). The departure from religion creates conflict with Islamic economics, as it was believed every phenomenon can be solved and answered using science, based on logical empiricism or logical positivism, completely ignoring the religious worldview. This tendency, according to scholars, comes with imperfection, as it offers limited solutions that may lead to creating rather than solving social, economic, and financial problems, hence causing recurring economic and financial crises (Rafikov and Akhmetova 2020).

According to Russell (1910), logical empiricism should reflect the scientific concept of an observable phenomenon that can be tested or touched, or if it cannot physically be observed at least it should be deduced through its visible implication. Thus, the science of so-called logical positivism dealt with hypotheses about this world that have observable implications; therefore, the concept of God, religion, and the hereafter, which have no observable implications, are considered meaningless. Here is where the contradiction with the Islamic economics and finance starts.

Hence, making the idea of logical positivism as adopted by the mainstream techniques is in full contrast with the Quranic position. The Quran encompasses guidance for those who believe in the unseen or unobserved phenomena (Zaman, 2013). Thus, ethical and moral values are completely overlooked from the mainstream techniques; for instance, the application of a pure positive worldview for analyzing financial and economic behavior, which is applied to various policies, has created repeated financial turmoil, including during the Great Recession of 2008. The 2008 financial crisis was partly attributed to a lack of moral concern in financial matters, such as excessive gambling and trading on debt and virtual assets. Also, the positive worldview of the Enlightenment considers religion to be a fantasy of imagination which is nonexistent (Chapra, 2001). This led to completely ignoring religious ethical values while relying purely on science.

Traditionally the idea of logical empiricism, commonly known as logical positivism, was influenced by Ernst Mach between 1838 and 1916 (Rafikov and Akhmetova, 2020), which started with the Vienna Circle, which suggested that for knowledge to be scientific it must be based on testable and verifiable physical experiences (Caldwell, 1994). Hence, positivism's idea avoids the position of value judgment that is expressed through emotional attitude, such that the philosophical study of being and knowing (metaphysics) was considered to be close to stupidity. Moreover, logical positivism denies the invisible (unseen) while Islamic economics and finance recognize this concept; hence, these conventional ideas are in disagreement with Islam (Zaman, 2013).

This further led to the debate on the right methodology to be adopted for Islamic economics and finance that would place importance on religious ethical values; however, up to recently, it has remained among the contested areas for over four decades (Rafikov and Akhmetova, 2020). In 1976, the First International Conference on Islamic Economics held in Jeddah proposed the idea of developing an applicable methodology for Islamic economics and finance that would not only differ from a secularist conventional mainstream methodology but also would be in line with the traditional Islamic philosophical theory of knowledge (Abdullahi, 2004). However, Auda J. (2010) presupposes that up until recently the Islamic methodology including its counterpart, the conventional economics methodologies, are based on the Greek system of reasoning. Thus, it is asserted that the contemporary social sciences, in general, have been influenced by Greek philosophy, which then was transmitted to Muslims who were educated in Western countries during the time of the Enlightenment (Rafikov and Akhmetova, 2020).

But according to Newman and Friedman (1954), the approach of logical positivism has one major flaw that makes it more rigid and unrealistic. This does not mean this idea is completely wrong; it has its potentiality in economics and finance as a social science. But the lack of realism and the ignorance of religion in the mainstream methodologies where the theories are transformed into policies and models cause some of them not only to be unfeasible and impractical in real life but also to contradict religion. Consider for example the origin of modern human beings, based on science, who evolved from Africa as *Homo erectus/sapiens* who lived between 1.9 million and 135,000 years ago and spread out over the whole world. Other mainstream economic models are compounded by pure statistical and mathematical modeling, such that the focus is placed on the process of hypothesizing the phenomenon and on the attractiveness and integrity of statistical manifestations rather than the practicality in real life (Rafikov and Akhmetova, 2020).

Consequently, with the application of a limited number of variables to be used for economic forecasting, economists regularly fail to determine and foresee the crises. That is why Lawson contends that the practitioners of the mainstream methodology of economics and finance failed to comprehend that the future is simply incomprehensible and thus it is not possible to make an accurate prediction. Mainstream techniques adopt the same idea of logical positivism, which trusts in the verifiable observation that can be seen and realized with factual data presentation, while the opposite is considered as irrational, unscientific, superstitious, and unreliable (Zaman, 2013). Hence the rejection of the unseen that forms an integral part of Islamic economics necessitates the need to adopt a mixed approach, at least for the moment where there is no independent methodology that accurately fits Islamic economics and finance. This requires a deeper understanding of Maqasid al-Shari'ah and adoption of a systematic methodology based on the integrated approach, as the former will cater to the need of religious values such as faith and the unseen while the latter will be accommodated as an auxiliary for analyzing concepts in mathematical terms where Islamic economics cannot stand on its own. If there is too much reliance on the latter, according to Auda J. (2010), the holistic nature of the phenomenon tends to be overlooked, leading to an inaccurate conclusion.

Nevertheless, the preceding study shows that most research that applies mainstream techniques in Islamic economics and finance relies on purely mathematical models which are adoptive of conventional economics models

(Rusydiana, Sanrego, and Rahayu 2021), thus being unable to account for the value judgment based on the moral and the unseen, including the main values of Maqasid al-Shari'ah, such as religion, human life, genealogy, intellect, and property.

Therefore, the present chapter discusses the need for an integration of methodology from natural and human sciences and attempts to suggest a multidisciplinary methodology that blends the Maqasid al-Shari'ah/purposes of Islamic law for proper application to the field of Islamic economics and finance. Thus, the scope of this paper is limited to the methodology from the perspective of integrated knowledge between Maqasid al-Shari'ah and the mainstream techniques. So far, there is hardly any study that maps the need for blending the Maqasid methodology with the mainstream techniques in Islamic economics and finance. Therefore, this study becomes integral to fill the research gap.

The chapter is library research based on a literature survey and contents analysis, where the literature on the mainstream techniques is reviewed to explore its contributions made in Islamic economics, particularly in the use of mathematical models to build Islamic economic theories. The literature that pinpoints the challenges associated with the mainstream techniques to Islamic economics and finance is also explored.

The chapter is organized as follows. Firstly, is the introduction, followed by a general elaboration of Maqasid al-Shari'ah. The third section discusses the significance of mainstream techniques to Islamic economics and finance, the fourth section discusses the main issues associated with mainstream techniques to Islamic economics and finance, and the fifth section analyzes the issues and examines the need for harmonizing the mainstream techniques with Maqasid-based methodology. The final section concludes the chapter.

Maqasid al-Shari'ah and its methodological role in Islamic economics and finance research

Methodology with reference to science refers to the process and procedures used in collecting and analyzing information on a particular phenomenon. In Arabic terminology, it is characterized by the word "manhajiyyah," which implies a clear and easygoing path (Rafikov and Akhmetova, 2020). According to Rafikov and Akhmetova (2020), it is also mentioned in the Quran as the word "Shir'ah," which also means a pathway to a watering place. Islamic economics and finance are derived from the Quran and Sunnah. Hence Kahf (2020) postulates that to articulate Islamic economic methodology, Islamic economists must understand the component of the Islamic economic system and be equipped with enormous knowledge of Islamic history and literature. Islam lays down an ethical foundation by spelling out values and non-values, as well as what is and what is not desirable from a moral, spiritual, and social point of view.

The purpose of Islamic law, hereinafter the Maqasid al-Shari'ah, originates from the Arabic word "Maqsada," which denotes an objective or aim of an action, whereas the word "Shari'ah" originates from the Arabic word "Shara," which in legal terms means to establish Islamic law. Thus, Shari'ah is defined as an approach of values and ethics covering all aspects of life ranging from personal, social, political, and the way economic activities are organized, such that in Islam, moral and spiritual aspects are indispensable to political and economic life (Dusuki and Abdullah, 2007). Hence, the combination of the two words "Maqasid al-Shari'ah" refers to the purpose or objective of Islamic law.

Imam Abu Hamid al-Ghazali (1058–1111) defined the objective of Islamic law to promote and protect the well-being of an individual as well as the community, whereas according to Imam al-Shatibi (720–790 A.H./1320–1388 C.E.), the Shari'ah objective rests on freeing human beings from the grip of their whims so that they become true servants. Therefore, the prime objective of Shari'ah, hereinafter the Maqasid al-Shari'ah, is to foster and protect human welfare against any detriment, which stems from safeguarding their faith (din), the soul (nafs), intellect (aql), posterity (nasl), and wealth (Mal).

The Maqasid contains a set of principles that lay down the foundation and standards for establishing welfare both worldly and in the hereafter. Moreover, these principles can be used to set the criteria for the acceptability of action or conduct. The notion of Maqasid al-Shari'ah has been used as an authentic framework for generating acceptable models, theories, and approaches in various angles of human lives (Omar and Sari, 2019).

Consequently, Maqasid al-Shari'ah is construed as one of the essential principles necessary for attaining social good (Mergaliyev et al., 2019); thus, integrating Maqasid-based methodology in mainstream Islamic eco-finance research will provide a pathway to the inclusion of unobservable elements of the unseen that are left behind by the mainstream methodology. Friedman (1979) postulates that mainstream methodology based on positive economics in principle is free from an ethical and moral position, and its sole assignment is the arrangement of the system of generalizations to create correct predictions. Thus, the ethical foundation is the main departing position of Islamic economics from conventional economics (Hasan, 2016). However, this does not mean Islamic economics has to completely ignore conventional ideas, though Islamic economics is cautious of ethical concern, and also acknowledges the role of science in general, especially the cause-and-effect relationship with realistic model construction (Hasan, 2016). Thus, comprehending one concept of Maqasid al-Shari'ah or Maslah (the public good) according to Shari'ah may lead to a theoretical understanding of sciences, economics, and technologies (Dusuki and Abdullah, 2007). What really matters for adopting scientific models in Islamic economics is that it shouldn't cause impediments in accomplishing the objectives of Islamic economics and finance, which is based on Falah (Abdullahi, 2018).

To the best knowledge of the authors, this is the earliest study to explore the integration of the Maqasid-based methodology with the mainstream techniques in Islamic economics and finance research. The focus should be on application and understanding both mainstream techniques, as postulated by the idea of logical positivism, and also focus on the traditional approach enriched with religious values such as Maqasid al-Shari'ah toward multidisciplinary or interdisciplinary approaches. Therefore, this study is crucial to define the new research directions in the field of Islamic economics that are targeted to realize the multidimensional objectives. This includes fulfilling both the economic requirement as well as social and moral requirements of the purpose of Islamic law. Also, the study is essential in the Islamic economics and finance literature by exploring the need for the inclusion of Maqasid al-Shari'ah in the mainstream methodology. This is vital for research works in Islamic economics and finance in contributing to the attainment of moral, ethical, and social spheres realized through the Maqasid al-Shari'ah.

The mainstream techniques and their significance for Islamic economics and finance research

The role of mainstream techniques in Islamic economics and finance so far cannot be underestimated as they played a great role in this field. Mainstream techniques have been applied in determining the financial performance of various economic agents in Islamic economics and finance literature. A recent study shows that Islamic banking and finance is the hottest and the most interesting topic in Islamic economics literature, where the application of mathematical models in the majority of this research is used in modeling the profit and loss sharing scheme (Rusydiana, Sanrego, and Pratomo, 2021). These models (mathematical applications) have been presented, even using complex numbers including, matrices, vectors, mathematical operations, and symbols that are used to explain the situations of the Islamic economic and financial problems.

Further studies show that between 1980 and 2020 most of the researches published in Islamic economics and finance with the application of the mathematical techniques (indexed by dimension) were from Malaysia, which had the highest number with 23 publications, followed by Indonesia with 15 research works with mainstream techniques. Pakistan, Saudi Arabia, the United States, Oman, Iran, and the United Kingdom had a total of 11, 9, 6, 4, 2, and 2 publications, respectively (Rusydiana, Sanrego, and Pratomo, 2021).

On the other hand, other research works that employed the mainstream techniques as indexed by Scopus again put Malaysia and Indonesia on the top of the list. Malaysia had a total of 27 publications, followed by Indonesia having 21 publications. The rest were conducted in Pakistan, Saudi Arabia, the United States, Oman, and Iran, each of these having 10, 9, 5, and 2 publications, respectively (Achour *et al.*, 2020). Thus, from these statistical figures, it is evidence of how important mainstream techniques are for Islamic economics and finance research.

As postulated in the preceding section, Islamic economics acknowledges the role of sciences in development, including the use of mathematical modeling.

Hence, in building, accomplishing, and application of these factors in Islamic economics and finance, Hasan (2016) contended that in Islamic economics there is no need to reject everything from conventional economics; however, efforts must be made to incorporate them to fit into Islamic economics by eliminating only critical issues that conflict with Islamic norms.

This statement is further supported by Furqani and Aslam Haneef (2012), that Islamic economics methodology need not begin from scratch, but then again in using them an attempt could be employed to make them consistent with Islamic economics norms. For instance, Mergaliyev *et al.* (2019) employed the Maqasid index to measure the ethical performance of Islamic banking. This is in addition to the application of traditional techniques that are used in assessing financial and economic performance. The challenge with too much reliance on financial and economic performance with the mainstream techniques is that moral and ethical concerns might be ignored because the trade-off exists between the interest of shareholders to maximize economic and financial returns, and moral issues as represented by the purpose of the Islamic law.

As Samuelson, for instance, comprehended that the application of mathematical procedures could simplify the clarity and interpretation of the ideas (Backhaus 2012), the mathematical method has some benefits because the application of symbols is more useful when used in deductive analysis and undoubtedly is more favorable to conciseness and defining the problem statement more precisely (Bello and Chiang, 1970).

Through the application of mathematical procedures, Choudhury (2008) made a remarkable impact on the field of Islamic economics and finance when these were to be taken into consideration. Several of Choudhury's works in this field are authored in mathematical languages. As cited from Chiang (2005), the aim of the mathematical method in economics is not different from the non-mathematical approach, as the aim is to derive a set of conclusions from a given set of postulates. Nevertheless, Zaman and Asutay (2009) have contended that the development in Islamic and finance must go beyond theoretical mainstream economics, but the logic of fiqh, which is founded on Quran and Sunnah, should be contemplated.

Though the mainstream technique is of importance, integration is necessary because moral and ethical issues cannot be accurately determined or represented using mathematical techniques. Furthermore, all mathematical models may not reflect economic realities, and thus they must be converted into econometric models to confirm their real-world application.

Issues in adopting mainstream techniques for Islamic economics and finance research

This section discusses, based on the literature survey, the salient issues associated with the adoption of mainstream techniques for research in Islamic economics and finance. As discussed in the preceding sections, secular conventional scholars who developed mainstream research techniques completely deny the role of faith and therefore devoted themselves to creating a new way to understand the world devoid of any reference to God. Thus, the secular scholars dismissed all traditional beliefs and re-constructed thought based on the modern premise (Zaman, 2013). Mainstream techniques are based on the idea of logical positivism, which rejects the unseen and faith, and considers morality as irrational, contrary to the position of Islam where morality is a central part of Islamic economics (Zaman, 2013). But Zaman posits that science also contains many unseen and invisible elements, for example the concept of atoms, the force of gravity, and the concept of electrostatics.

Therefore, several scholars, for example Tag El-Din, have condemned mainstream economics for rejection of religion, faith, and ethical economic behavior in the theoretical formulation. While Abdullahi (2018) postulates that the overuse of mainstream mathematical techniques in economics has its weakness when it is exclusively applied to Islamic economics because moral and ethical phenomena, which are inherent to the nature of Islam, are neglected; thus cannot be presented in terms of mathematical formulation or numbers rather through value judgment. Similarly, Rashid (1991) contends that the claim of conventional economics being value-neutral can be described as hypocrisy, because no social science discipline can be thought of to be value-neutral.

Malinvaud presupposes that conventional economics has borrowed all types of tools of analysis from the physical sciences with the main objectives of analyzing and understanding economic phenomena and suggests the likely actions, independent of God, that are necessary to improve market failures resulting from unemployment and high inflation. However, according to Chiang (2005), mathematical models are merely oversimplified and abstract forms of economic theory that do not always come to be true and valid at all times.

Conventional economists have always claimed that economics shall be positive independent from value judgment. Thus, the use of the mainstream technique is not only rejected in incorporating the ethical and moral phenomena but also failed to accurately predict the reality about the future (Friedman, 1979). Hence there have been critics and calls from various angles from both Islamic economic scholars and mainstream economists to minimize the overuse of neoclassical economic prescriptions by policymakers due to inherent flaws (Abdullahi, 2018).

Among the critics of conventional economics is Friedman, who argues that traditional economics is a positive science that has the predictive ability. This predictive nature of economics failed to accurately forecast and prevent the past global financial crisis of 2008. This crisis aided in widening the cracks in the traditional economics methodology, hence suggesting the need for a fundamental restructuring of this very old field. Consequently, some scholars opined that it should be abandoned and a new alternative system shall be introduced. This is because the theoretical assumptions that are built in the mainstream techniques are short of the reality from the actual world phenomenon (Palasca, 2013).

Even though the mathematically oriented economists see an advantage, other economists see disadvantages; for instance, Boulding (1970) believes that the use of mathematical interpretation and manipulation of the data to fit the mathematical requirements might lead an obstacle to the advancement of knowledge as the interest of the real world might be lost. Another critic, Alatas, sees the reliance on the overuse of mainstream techniques for Islamic economics makes it incapable of serving as an alternative to the conventional mainstream economy, as he sees modern Islamic economics and finance position itself in the shadow of its counterpart, conventional economics. Zarqa (2003) noted that the main difference between Islamic economics and other systems is that Islam recognizes that a human being (true Muslim) has a strong tendency toward selfish altruism by pursuing both self-interest as well as the consideration for others, and apart from being materialistic also shows spiritual inclinations, which is deficient in its conventional economics counterpart. The next section analyzes the issues discussed and examines the extent to which harmonizing the mainstream techniques with Maqasid-based methodology could minimize some of the issues related to the adoption of conventional techniques for Islamic eco-finance research.

Analysis of the issues and the way forward toward harmonization

This section analyzes the main issues in the mainstream techniques and then investigates the need for harmonizing the mainstream technique with the Maqasid-based methodology for Islamic economics and finance research. As is postulated by several scholars, Islamic economics is still a young field of study compared to conventional economics. The field is not yet built-in with complete tools of analysis for economic as well as social phenomena. As explained, the mainstream methodology has played a significant role in research related to Islamic economics and finance. It is also recognized and argued that Islamic economics as a field of study is not yet fully enriched with all set of tools of analysis, and thus cannot afford to discard everything from conventional economics and finance. Harmonization of both techniques will offer an unbiased conclusion by taking into consideration both economic phenomena that can be tested empirically as well as social postulation that requires value judgment.

Friedman postulates that positive economics is independent of ethical positions, and its sole task is based on generalizations to make probable predictions, and to accomplish this task, the mainstream techniques rely on measurable physical data to make such predictions. Economic behavior under Islamic economics is value-loaded, and the reference is always made to the ethical foundations of the Islamic system. Thus, to account for a phenomenon based moral and ethical positions, researchers in Islamic economics need to adopt a methodology that will complement the missing elements from the mainstream techniques. This is because in Islamic economics, the ethical consideration is always endogenous to the socioeconomic system; this permits the consensus between individual and social preferences (Choudhury, 1990).

Several studies show that the contemporary Islamic economics and finance research which applies mainstream techniques is merely deductive of conventional economics models with purely mathematical postulation (Rusydiana *et al.*, 2021). Hence these research works failed to account for Islamic norms, ethics, and moral positions, including the Maqasid al-Shari'ah, which are based on value judgment. For this reason, these values cannot be accurately accounted for by using absolute mathematical equations. Thus, the need for harmonization emanates from the idea of the unity of knowledge and as a composite to attaining multiple goals through multidisciplinary approaches.

Researchers in Islamic economics and finance need not worry about the application of mainstream techniques. Some scholars attempt to oppose mainstream techniques, calling for their total rejection, and instead adopt a new methodology that corresponds to the nature of Islamic economics which focuses on the unseen and unobservable phenomena. Devising an axiomatic research technique for research in Islamic eco-finance is a good idea, but for the time being this field of research is not equipped with a full set of tools for economic analysis, and thus it will be a very bad idea to make a complete rejection of the mainstream technique. Rather than complete rejection, adopting mixed approaches based on the multidisciplinary design will lead to attaining multiple goals that accommodate both needs, i.e., economic need as well the inclusion of value-based judgment. It is normal for any field of study to borrow some techniques from other fields of study to accomplish its goal. This is similar to the case of conventional economics, which borrowed some mathematical postulation from physical sciences. Islamic economics as a young field of study can borrow tools of analysis from other fields, however, taking into consideration that the fundamentals of religion and the ethical economic postulations are not compromised in the process of harmonization, and the Maqasid al-Shari'ah-based methodology will offer the way forward. Muqorobin (2016) contended that in the short run, Islamic economics can't ditch the conventional economic analytical methodology. The Islamic economics approach is deep-rooted in the Quran and Sunnah; thus, ethics and economics under Islamic economics cannot be separated (Abu-Saud, 1993). Therefore, the harmonization of mainstream techniques with the Maqasid-based methodology will offer the inclusion of important elements that are deficient in the mainstream techniques.

According to Saleem (2010), the other way round is to look at the main sources of knowledge in Islamic economics, which are the Qur'an and the Sunnah. Islam presents to human beings clear guidance on the unseen attributes that they need to focus on without negligence. This guidance is forever until the Day of Judgement (Quran 5:3) (Zaman, 2013). Furthermore, Azid and Asutay (2007) argue that professionals in the contemporary world as well as in academia are bound to accept the truth that they may have to take into consideration the role of religion if they need to understand the economic system properly. Similarly, Al-Alwani calls for the integration of the revelation, which is based on the unseen, with the existential knowledge based on observation, which he sees as a necessity to bring the balance in a proper understanding of the world reality. Hence, researchers in Islamic economics and finance must strive for a broader understanding of various sciences (mainstream techniques) as well as the revealed knowledge to propel this knowledge gap toward integrated and multidisciplinary knowledge for understanding the world.

Thus, integration or harmonization is essential to account for other values that are integral to the objectives of Islam. Maqasid al-Shari'ah involves the preservation of individuals as well as social interests, which are normative. Therefore, the harmonization of conventional techniques with Maqasid-based methodology is imperative to understanding the extent of the preservation and promotion of the holistic objectives of Islamic Shari'ah. This makes the mainstream techniques relevant to accommodate its analysis in the preservation of faith (Hifz al deen), life (Hifz al Nafs), intellect (Hifz al Aql), progeny (Hifz al Nasl), and wealth (Hifz mal). As discussed previously, there are several studies in Islamic economics and finance that now integrate mathematical models with Maqasid-based methodology (Larbani and Mohammed, 2011). Therefore, research on Islamic eco-finance that integrates conventional techniques with Maqasid-based methodology may produce policy prescriptions and financial solutions that are human-friendly and not only organization-centric (Rafikov and Akhmetova, 2020). Hence, such integration or harmonization will offer an inclusive recommendation and solution.

Conclusion

The study is about the harmonization of mainstream techniques with Maqasid-based methodology for research in Islamic eco-finance. To achieve the intended objective, library research has been employed based on the survey of various related literature on mainstream techniques and the Maqasid al-Shari'ah. A review of the literature reveals that the mainstream research technique is largely reductive and relies on positive observable models with purely mathematical postulation devoid of the normative aspects of research. On the other hand, the Islamic approach is deep-rooted in the Quran and Sunnah. It is value-laden yet balanced with observable phenomena. This approach incorporates the moral, ethical, and practical dimensions of research, giving equal emphasis to both the unseen or latent and observable phenomena. Several examples of Islamic eco-finance research have adopted the conventional techniques for their analyses. These mainstream methods, while focusing on positive observable models, are deficient to meet the moral and ethical aspects that are normally integral to research from an Islamic perspective.

Yet research tools in eco-finance are not fully developed for robust analysis, and thus there is a need for Islamic researchers to complement them with mainstream techniques. This calls for the harmonization of mainstream techniques with the Islamic approach especially the Maqasid-based methodology. Such approach will harness the potential of both techniques to complement one another. The harmonization will take into consideration the imperatives of Maqasid al-Shari'ah that generally involve the achievement of individual as well as societal interests at both positive and normative levels. Specifically, the harmonization with Maqasid will incorporate the preservations of fine essential elements (faith, soul, intellect, progeny, and wealth), which have far-reaching research recommendations and thus policy implications.

Hence, researchers in Islamic economy and finance must strive for a broader understanding of various science as well as the revealed knowledge to propel this knowledge gap toward integrated and multidisciplinary knowledge for understanding real-world phenomena. Consequently, a clearer understanding of Maqasid al-Shari'ah and adopting a systematic method based on the integrated approach are essential, as Maqasid in this sense will cater for the need of inclusion of value judgment such as religion, faith, and the unseen while the mainstream technique will be accommodated as an auxiliary for analyzing concepts in mathematical terms, such as the concept related to wealth as one of the Maqasid values. Therefore, following the fact that research tools for Islamic economics and finance are not as matured as their mainstream counterparts, there is a need to adopt this integrated approach that would eliminate the inherent controversial issues in Islamic economics and finance research. Therefore, harmonizing mainstream techniques with Maqasid-based methodology for Islamic eco-finance research will provide a pathway to the inclusion of unobservable elements of the unseen that are left behind by the mainstream methodology.

References

Abdullahi, S.I. 2004. "Role of mathematics in zakat assessment and collection." Unpublished Thesis Submitted to the Department of Economics Usman Danfodio, University Sokoto, Sokoto, Nigeria.

Abdullahi, Shafiu Ibrahim. 2018. "Contribution of Mathematical Models to Islamic Economic Theory: A Survey." *International Journal of Ethics and Systems* 34(2): 200–212.

Abu-Saud, Mahmoud. 1993. "The Methodology of the Islamic Behavioral Sciences." *American Journal of Islam and Society* 10(3).

Achour, Brahim, Ibrahim Foughali, Liya Ur Rahman Liyakath Alikhan, and Nur Jamaludin. 2020. "Article Review of the Critical and Empirical Research in Islamic Economics." *Islaminomics: Journal of Islamic Economics, Business and Finance* 10(1):39–44.

Backhaus, Jürgen Georg. 2012. Handbook of the History of Economic Thought: Insights on the Founders of Modern Economics.

Bello, Ivan and Alpha C. Chiang. 1970. "Fundamental Methods of Mathematical Economics." *Econometrica* 38(5).

Boulding, K.E. (1970). *Economics as a Science*. McGraw-Hill, New York, NY.

Caldwell, Bruce. 1994. Beyond Positivism: Economic Methodology in the Twentieth Century.

Chapra. 2001. *What Is Islamic Economics*. 2nd ed. Jeddah: Islamic Research and Training Institute-IRTI.

Chiang, A.C. 2005. *Fundamental Methods of Mathematical Economics.* New York: McGraw-Hill International Editions.

Choudhury, Masudul. 1990. "The Humanomic Structure of Islamic Economic Theory: A Critical Review of Literature in Normative and Positive Economics." *Journal of King Abdulaziz University-Islamic Economics* 2(1).

Choudhury, Masudul Alam. 2008. "Operation of Dual Monetary Policy for Stabilization Role in Indonesia: An Islamic Political Economy Approach." *International Journal of Applied Business and Economic Research* 6(1).

Dusuki, Asyraf Wajdi and Nurdianawati Irwani Abdullah. 2007. "Maqasid Al-Shari'ah, Maslahah, and Corporate Social Responsibility." *American Journal of Islamic Social Sciences* 24(1).

Furqani, Hafas and Mohamed Aslam Haneef. 2012. "Theory Appraisal in Islamic Economic Methodology: Purposes and Criteria." *Humanomics* 28(4).

Hasan, Zubair. 2016. "Nature and Significance of Islamic Economics." *Economic and Social Thought* 3(3).

Kahf, M. (2020), "Relevance, Definition and Methodology of Islamic Economics," available at: http://monzer.kahf.com/papers/english/methodology_malaysia.pdf (accessed 22 May 22, 2021).

Larbani, Moussa and M.O. Mohammed. 2011. "A Decision Making Tool for Allocating Investible resources Based on Maqasid al-Shari'ah Framework." *Islamic Economic Studies Journal, IRTI* 19(2). ISSN: 1319/1616.

Muqorobin, Masyhudi. 2016. Journey of Islamic Economics in the Modern World.

Newman, Peter and Milton Friedman. 1954. "Essays in Positive Economics." *Economica* 21(83).

Omar, Mohd Noor and Norhanim Mat Sari. 2019. "Maqasid al-Shari'ah Philosophy in Monetary Regime towards Inclusive Sustainable Growth." *International Journal of Islamic Economics*.

Palasca, S. 2013. "Mathematics in Economics. A Perspective on Necessity and Sufficiency." *Theoretical and Applied Economics* 20(9).

Rafikov, Ildus and Elmira Akhmetova. 2020. "Methodology of Integrated Knowledge in Islamic Economics and Finance: Collective Ijtihād." *ISRA International Journal of Islamic Finance* 12(1):115–129.

Rashid, Salim. 1991. "An Agenda for Muslim Economists: A Historico-Inductive Approach." *Journal of King Abdulaziz University-Islamic Economics* 3(1).

Russell, B. 1910. "Knowledge by Acquaintance and Knowledge by Description." *Proceedings of the Aristotelian Society* 11. Oxford: Blackwell Publishing.

Rusydiana, Aam, Yulizar Sanrego, and Solihah Rahayu. 2021. "Modeling Islamic Economics and Finance Research: A Bibliometric Analysis." *International Journal of Islamic Economics and Finance (IJIEF)* 4(1):149–176.

Rusydiana, Aam Slamet, Yulizar Djamaluddin Sanrego, and Wahyu Ario Pratomo. 2021. "Mathematical Modeling on Islamic Economics and Finance: A Scientometric." *Library Philosophy and Practice* 2021(February):1–23.

Saleem, Muhammad Yusuf. 2010. "Methods and Methodologies in Fiqh and Islamic Economics." *Review of Islamic Economics* 14(1).

Zarqua, Muhummad. 2003. "Islamization of Economics: The Concept and Methodology." *Journal of King Abdulaziz University-Islamic Economics* 16(1):3–42.

17

STANDARD METHODOLOGY FOR RESEARCH IN ISLAMIC ECONOMICS AND FINANCE

Ascarya and Indra

Introduction

There is still an unfinished debate about Islamic economics (including finance) as a social science, similar to conventional economics (including finance). Even conventional economics with capitalism has still been criticized as a social science, since conventional economics focuses on self-centered views, self-interest, or selfishness, where there is no place for selflessness or social interest. As Muhammad Yunus put it in Yunus and Heiden (2020), "But I ask the question: what is social there? It is very hard to see anything social in economics because all you are doing is for yourself. You want to make money – that's all." The prolonged debate has also still been ongoing on the methodology of Islamic economics, such as: Should it be deductive, inductive, or both? (Chapra, 2001; Bendjilali, 2009); should it be normative, positive, or both? (Yasin and Khan, 2016); should it be based on falsification, verification, or both? (Addas, 2008); should it be applied to Muslims only or to all human behavior? (Bendjilali, 2009); and can we use the methodology of conventional economics, with or without reserve? (Khan, 2018). In conclusion, as also mentioned by Abdullahi (2018), Islamic economics has yet to have a universally accepted research methodology.

Nevertheless, we will follow the summary of Khan (2018), where the methodology of Islamic economics and finance is both deductive and inductive, both normative and positive, both based on falsification and verification, applicable to all human behavior, integrating divine knowledge received from revelation with knowledge acquired through observation, experimentation, and human thinking, so that Islamic economists need to develop distinct approaches to transform divine sources of Islam into a social science, as proposed in Figure 17.1.

First, clear understanding of Islamic economic teachings from Al-Qur'an and Al-Hadith in the contemporary reality, involving extensive innovative thinking (*ijtihad*), should be developed. *Second*, the understanding of divine

DOI: 10.4324/9781003252764-21

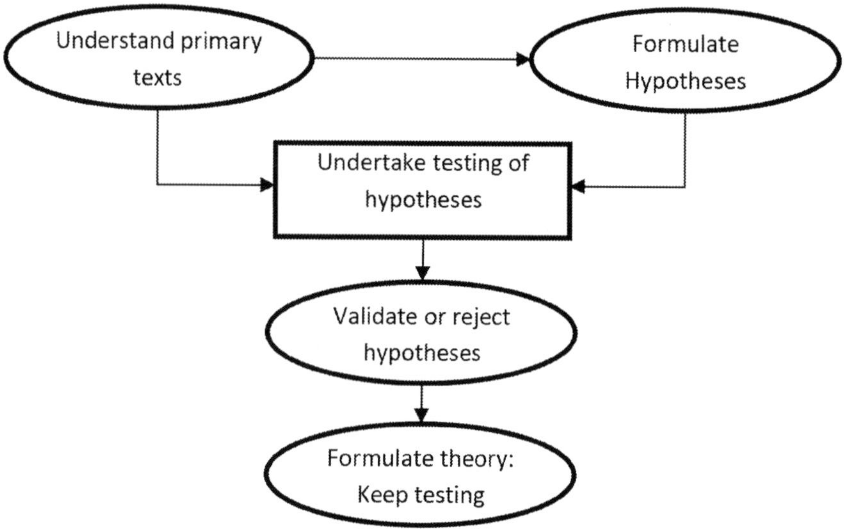

Figure 17.1 Theory building in Islamic economics and finance.

Source: Khan (2018), redrawn and modified by authors.

sources should be transformed and formulated into hypotheses. *Third*, the hypotheses should be formatted in such a way that is amenable to validation through the process of verification or falsification. *Fourth*, hypotheses testing through an extensive process of consultation, discussion, verification, or falsification, using collected data. *Fifth*, the formulated theory based on hypotheses would be examined continuously to confirm or falsify them, and would be accepted as theory after repeated trials for extended periods. *Sixth*, if the formulated Islamic economics theory could not be refuted, it would become Islamic law. Therefore, we could use the methodology, tools, and methods used by conventional economics and other social sciences.

The standard methodology for research in Islamic economics and finance discussed in this chapter will include qualitative methods as well as quantitative methods, where the quantitative methods will include methods for various types of data, including cross-section, time series, and pooled or panel, where the summary can be seen in Table 17.1.

Qualitative method

Descriptive qualitative method

Descriptive method is a research method that describes the characteristics of the population, situation, or phenomenon under study of uncontrollable variables. This method focuses more on the "what" (and could include "where" and "when") of the research subject than the "why" and "how" of

Table 17.1 The standard methodology for research in Islamic economics and finance

Qualitative	*Cross-section data*
Descriptive qualitative Ethridge (2004); Fox and Bayat (2007) **Content analysis** Krippendorff (1989, 2004, 2012, 2018); Rosengren (1981); Stemler (2000, 2015) **Etc.**	**Ordinary least squares** Wooldridge (2016) **Simultaneous equation (2SLS)** Wooldridge (2016) **Probit/logit regression** Wooldridge (2016) **Etc.**
Time series univariate	**Time series multivariate**
ARMA, ARIMA Box and Jenkins (1970) **ARCH, GARCH, TARCH, TGARCH** Engle (1982, 2001); Bollerslev (1986, 2010) **Etc.**	**All cross-section data methods** **Error correction model (ECM)** Engle and Granger (1987); Enders (2010) **Autoregressive distributed lag (ARDL)** Pesaran and Shin (1998); Pesaran, Shin, and Smith (2001) **Etc.**
Static panel data	**Dynamic panel data**
General Baltagi (2008); Wooldridge (2002; 2010) Gujarati and Porter (2009); Hsiao *et al.* (1999) **Fixed effect** Hsiao (2003); Wooldridge (2013) **Random effect** Gardiner *et al.* (2009)	**General** Baltagi (2008); Roodman (2009); Wooldridge (2002, 2010) **First-difference GMM** Bhargava and Sargan (1983); Arellano and Bond (1991) **System GMM** Arellano and Bover (1995); Blundell and Bond (1998)

the research subject (Ethridge, 2004). According to Fox and Bayat (2007), descriptive research method is "aimed at casting light on current issues or problems through a process of data collection that enables them to describe the situation more completely than was possible without employing this method." Descriptive method could be quantitative or qualitative, where in Islamic economics (including finance) this method is mostly used for qualitative research, so that oftentimes it is called descriptive qualitative.

The descriptive qualitative method has been used widely, especially in the early times of the Islamic economics and finance (IEF) revival in the 1970s, 1980s, and even in the 1990s for some countries like Indonesia, where quantitative data on IEF was still very limited or nonexistent, where studies at those times aimed to explore population, situation, or phenomena to discover and describe the characteristics of the subjects under study. As illustrated in Figure 17.1, when something has never been explored or studied, we cannot jump to sophisticated research on "why" and "how" without knowing "what" the subject under study is.

Even though descriptive the qualitative method sometimes is considered as a nonscientific research method (see Figure 17.2), it could provide more holistic approach involving various sources of data producing rich data

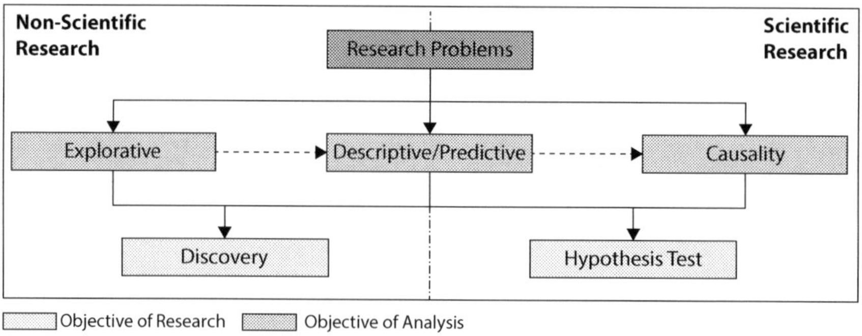

Figure 17.2 The spectrum of research.

collection resulting in deeper understanding on the subjects under study, including various perspectives, point of views, and behaviors. Data collected is mostly qualitative, which requires qualitative methods of analysis, including inductive exploration to develop theories. The evidence in Islamic economics research could be seen in the early volumes of *Journal of Research in Islamic Economics* in 1983–1984 and *Journal of King Abdulaziz University: Islamic Economics* in the 1990s.

Some of the descriptive qualitative method advantages include: (1) it could effectively analyze non-quantified topics and issues; (2) it opens the possibility to observe the phenomenon in a completely natural and unchanged environment; (3) it provides the opportunity to integrate the qualitative and quantitative methods of data collection; and (4) it would be less time-consuming than quantitative experiments.

However, there are also some disadvantages of this type of descriptive qualitative research method, such as: (1) it could not test or verify the research problem statistically; (2) the results might reflect a certain level of bias due to the absence of statistical tests; (3) most of these descriptive studies are not "repeatable" due to their observational nature; and (4) these descriptive studies could not be used to identify causes behind described phenomenon. There are three types of descriptive research methods, including observation, case study, and survey. The most common descriptive research method is the survey, which includes questionnaires, personal interviews, phone surveys, and normative surveys. Case study has also been used frequently in Islamic economics research.

Content analysis

The content analysis method is arguably the most important method in social science. The term "content analysis" has been in *Webster's Dictionary of the English Language* since 1961, defined as "analysis of the manifest and latent content of a body of communicated material (as a book or film) through classification, tabulation, and evaluation of its key symbols and themes in order to ascertain its meaning and probable effect" (Krippendorff, 2004), since content analysis has been used in research since the eighteenth century in Scandinavia (Rosengren, 1981). In his earlier paper, Krippendorff (1989) defined content analysis, combining qualitative and quantitative content analysis, as a research technique for making replicable and valid inferences from data to their context. Questions to be addressed in content analysis include:

- Which data are analyzed?
- How are they defined?
- What is the population from which they are drawn?
- What is the context relative to which the data are analyzed?
- What are the boundaries of the analysis?
- What is the target of the inferences?

Krippendorff (1989, 2012) wrote that the content analysis procedures consist of six steps, including design, unitizing, sampling, coding, drawing inferences, and validation, as depicted in Figure 17.3. The first step, design, is a very important step where the researcher designs a conceptual framework combining context, data, and analytical construct. The design should spell out the observational conditions under which the inferences made could be considered valid in representing what they claim to represent. The second step, unitizing, will identify the units of analysis of available data from various scientific literature, official data, authoritative news, etc., which would make the drawing of a statistically representative sample from a population possible. The third step, sampling, is where a sample will be drawn from the previous step to choose representative samples, which is not indigenous of content analysis.

The fourth step, coding, will describe the recording or classifying units in terms of categories of the chosen analytical construct, evaluated by two criteria, namely, reliability and relevance. The fifth step, drawing inferences, is

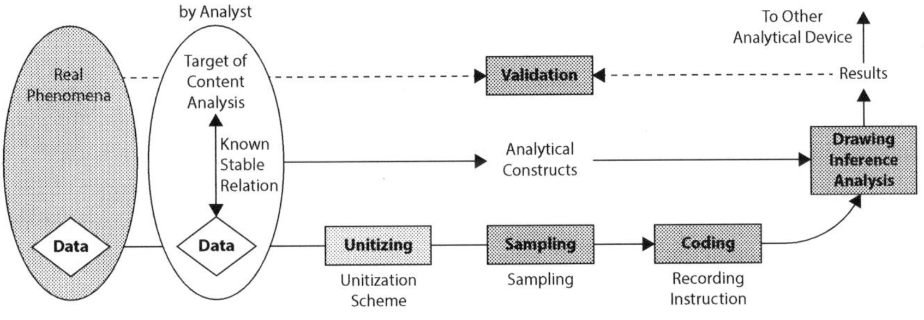

Figure 17.3 Procedures of content analysis.

Source: Krippendorff (1989, 2012), redrawn by authors.

considered the most important step, applying the stable knowledge about how the variable accounts of coded data are related to the phenomena to generate results, where steps involved are oftentimes not obvious. The final step, validation, is essential for every research, although it will be limited in content analysis, where validating evidence is not readily available.

Content analysis method has some inherent limitations. First, the nature of its qualitative research would make it difficult to be statistically significant. Second, the content analysis method suffers from replicability. Third, the findings of the content analysis method could not be generalized beyond the given data.

Content analysis has been evolving in the digital era with the emergence of new media (especially social media) and big data. Stemler (2015) believed that content analysis can be the most powerful tool in the researcher's kit in the era of big data. Meanwhile, Krippendorff (2018) introduced the content analysis method for analyzing the textual fabric of contemporary society, where data are treated not as physical events but as communications that are created and disseminated to be seen, read, interpreted, enacted, and reflected upon according to the meanings they have for their recipients. Interpreting communications as texts in the context of their social use distinguishes content analysis from other empirical methods of inquiry.

Cross section data method

Linear regression model (OLS Method)

The linear regression model is widely used in social and economic research because it allows researchers to determine and analyze the effect of one or more independent variables on dependent variables. In general econometric literature, there are at least two types of linear regression models, namely simple linear regression and multiple linear regression. A regression model that involves only one dependent variable relying on one independent variable is called a simple linear regression model. However, simple linear regression models are often insufficient to explain the behavior of an economic indicator. In the consumption-income relationship, for example, it is assumed explicitly that only income affects consumption. But in fact, economic theory is rarely that simple. Besides income, there may be several other variables that affect consumption, such as wealth or the price of other similar goods. Therefore, the regression model can be expanded by using a larger number of independent variables. A regression model involving one dependent variable that depends on more than one independent variable is called a multiple linear regression model.

Multiple regression analysis can be used to build a better model for predicting the dependent variable because it allows us to involve many observed factors that influence the dependent variable. Adding more factors to the model makes the variation of the dependent variable more explained. Multiple regression analysis is generally used for ceteris paribus analysis. It allows us to explicitly control many other factors that simultaneously affect the dependent variable. This is important both for testing economic theory and for evaluating the effects of a policy when we have to rely on non-experimental data. Generally, the multiple linear regression model can be written as:

$$Y = \beta_0 + \beta_1 X_1 + \beta_2 X_2 + \cdots + \beta_k X_k + u \tag{17.1}$$

where:

Y is a dependent variable
X_i are the independent variables, $i = 1,\ldots, k$
β_0 is an intercept
β_i are the parameter associated with X_i
u is an error term

Multiple linear regression analysis can be performed by first calculating the coefficient, $\hat{\beta}$ which is an estimator for the parameter β. The general method that can be applied to estimate these parameters is ordinary least squares (OLS). Suppose the estimated regression equation for (17.1) is given as follows:

$$\hat{Y} = \hat{\beta}_0 + \hat{\beta}_1 X_1 + \hat{\beta}_2 X_2 + \cdots + \hat{\beta}_k X_k \tag{17.2}$$

The basic principle of OLS is to minimize the sum of squared error, which is expressed as:

$$\sum_{i=1}^{n} \left(\hat{Y} - \hat{\beta}_0 - \hat{\beta}_1 X_1 - \hat{\beta}_2 X_2 - \cdots - \hat{\beta}_k X_k\right)^2 = 0 \tag{17.3}$$

The minimization problem (17.3) can be solved by determining the first-order condition for (17.3) which is expressed as:

$$\sum_{i=1}^{n} \left(\hat{Y} - \hat{\beta}_0 - \hat{\beta}_1 X_1 - \hat{\beta}_2 X_2 - \cdots - \hat{\beta}_k X_k\right) = 0$$

$$\sum_{i=1}^{n} X_1 \left(\hat{Y} - \hat{\beta}_0 - \hat{\beta}_1 X_1 - \hat{\beta}_2 X_2 - \cdots - \hat{\beta}_k X_k\right) = 0$$

$$\vdots$$

$$\sum_{i=1}^{n} X_k \left(\hat{Y} - \hat{\beta}_0 - \hat{\beta}_1 X_1 - \hat{\beta}_2 X_2 - \cdots - \hat{\beta}_k X_k\right) = 0$$

This problem will solve for the $\hat{\beta}_0$ coefficient, which is called the OLS intercept estimate, and the coefficients $\hat{\beta}_0, \hat{\beta}_1, \hat{\beta}_2, \cdots, \hat{\beta}_k$ which are known as the OLS slope estimates.

The key assumptions of the OLS method can be stated simply through conditional expectations:

$$E\left(u|X_1, X_2, \ldots, X_k\right) = 0 \tag{17.4}$$

Equation (17.4) requires that the explanatory variables are uncorrelated with the unobserved error term. According to Wooldridge (2016), this also means that we have correctly calculated the functional relationship between the variables described and the explanatory variables. Any problem that causes u to correlate with one of the independent variables causes (17.4) to fail to be satisfied. This assumption is important because it is a prerequisite that the estimator produced by OLS is unbiased.

Simultaneous equation model (2SLS Method)

An economic system can usually be explained in terms of the behavior of various economic agents. The equilibrium is produced in the economic system when these behaviors can be reconciled. For example, economists might describe market mechanisms through demand behavior, supply behavior, and equilibrium levels of employment and wages. The market-clearing process will feed back wage rates into the supply-and-demand equation. It then creates a simultaneous equilibrium. It implies that each equation that makes up the behavior and the equilibrium cannot be treated separately.

This issue will lead us to the discussion of simultaneous equation systems. Simultaneous equation systems represent a set of relationships between variables in several interrelated equations. Thus, one cannot estimate the parameters of one equation without taking into account the information provided by other equations in the system. In a simultaneous equation model where there is a dependence between several variables in a system of equations, it implies that each equation cannot be treated separately as a single equation model. The application of the OLS method will produce biased and inconsistent estimates (Wooldridge, 2016). This bias is due to the endogenous variables in the model, which are independent variables correlated with an error term. This issue is called an endogeneity problem caused by simultaneity. This arises when one or more of the explanatory variables is jointly determined with the dependent variable, typically through an equilibrium mechanism.

As an illustration, consider the following simultaneous equation model:

$$Y_1 = \alpha_0 + \alpha_1 Y_2 + u_1 \tag{17.5}$$

$$Y_2 = \beta_0 + \beta_1 Y_1 + \beta_1 X_1 + \beta_2 X_2 + u_2 \tag{17.6}$$

In the equation system above, every shock in the equation (17.5) represented by Δu_1 will cause a change in Y_1. Since Y_1 is the explanatory variable in equation (17.6), any change in Y_1 will have an impact on Y_2. So that the shock of Δu_1 will cause a change in Y_1, and a change in Y_1 will affect Y_2, so changes in Y_2 will also be responded to by Y_1. In this case, the fact that Δu_1 affects Y_2 meaning that $\operatorname{cov}(Y_2, u_1) \neq 0$, or there is a correlation between the error term in equation (17.5) and the explanatory variable, Y_2. The same case can be shown that $\operatorname{cov}(Y_1, u_2) \neq 0$. In the case of equation (17.5), it can be shown that:

$$\hat{\alpha}_1 = \frac{cov(Y_2, Y_1)}{var(Y_2)} = \alpha_1 + \frac{cov(Y_2, u_1)}{var(Y_2)} \tag{17.7}$$

Since $\operatorname{cov}(Y_2, u_1) \neq 0$, then $E(\hat{\alpha}_1) \neq \alpha_1$, so the OLS estimator $\hat{\alpha}_1$ is a biased estimator.

Since OLS is biased and inconsistent when applied to a structural equation in a simultaneous equations system, we need an alternative approach to solve this problem. In the general econometric literature, one approach that can be applied to overcome bias caused by simultaneity in a simultaneous equations system is two-stage least squares (2SLS). The 2SLS method uses information available from the equation system specification to generate a unique estimate for each structural parameter. This method applies two sequential stages. In the first stage, 2SLS includes the establishment of instruments, while the second stage includes a variant of the instrumental-variables estimation. For an illustration, we provide the procedure of the 2SLS method to estimate structural parameters in a simultaneous equations system.

Consider the previous simultaneous equation model:

$$Y_1 = \alpha_0 + \alpha_1 Y_2 + u_1 \tag{17.8}$$

$$Y_2 = \beta_0 + \beta_1 Y_1 + \beta_1 X_1 + \beta_2 X_2 + u_2 \tag{17.9}$$

The reduced form of the equations system (17.8) and (17.9) can be expressed as:

$$Y_1 = \pi_{11} X_1 + \pi_{12} X_2 + v_1 \tag{17.10}$$

$$Y_2 = \pi_{21} X_1 + \pi_{22} X_2 + v_2 \tag{17.11}$$

In the first stage, the reduced form equation (17.11) is estimated by using OLS. It can be performed by regressing Y_2 on all exogenous variables (X_1 and X_2) in the equation system. From this stage, the fitted values of the endogenous variable $\hat{Y}_2$ are obtained. The fitted value $\hat{Y}_2$ by construction be independent and uncorrelated with u_1 and u_2. In the second stage, the structural parameter in equation (17.8) is estimated by replacing the variable Y_2 with the first-stage estimated variable $\hat{Y}_2$. This stage will produce a consistent and unbiased estimator of Y_2 parameter α_1. If exogenous variables are included in equation (17.8), 2SLS would also estimate those parameters consistently.

Logit and probit models

In some cases, researchers often apply regression models with qualitative dependent variables to answer the problems they face. Qualitative variables are generally nominal and consist of several categories. Models of this type are sometimes called qualitative response models, because the dependent variables are discrete, rather than continuous. The simplest qualitative dependent variable is generally expressed in terms of a binary variable which consists of only two categories. This model will not only lead us to a different estimation approach but also to the interpretation of the model parameters. This model is generally applied to a situation describing the dependence between variables in the context of conditional probabilistic. Thus, the relationship between dependent variables and independent variables must be interpreted in terms of probabilistic.

In the general econometric literature, some methods that can be applied to estimate parameter models with qualitative or binary response variables are the linear probability model, logistic regression, and probit regression. The linear probability model is simple to estimate and use because it applies the ordinary least square approach. But it can be shown that it has some disadvantages. The two most important drawbacks are that the fitted probabilities value obtained by the model can be less than zero or greater than one and the partial effect of any explanatory variable is constant (Wooldridge, 2016). These weaknesses of the linear probability model can be overcome by using more advanced binary response models, namely logistic regression and probit regression.

A general form of the binary response model can be expressed as:

$$\mathrm{P}(y=1|\mathrm{x}) = F(z) = F(\beta_0 + \beta_1 X_{1i} + \beta_2 X_{2i} + \cdots + \beta_k X_{ki}) = F(\beta_0 + x\beta) \quad (17.12)$$

where F is the function whose values lies strictly between 0 and 1, $0 < F(z) < 1$, for all real number z. In the logit model, F is expressed in the form of a logistic function as follows:

$$F(z) = \frac{e^z}{1+e^z} \quad (17.13)$$

Based on equations (17.12) and (17.13), the specification of the logit regression model can be expressed as:

$$F(z) = \frac{e^{(\beta_0+\beta_1 X_{1i}+\beta_2 X_{2i}+\cdots+\beta_k X_{ki})}}{1+e^{(\beta_0+\beta_1 X_{1i}+\beta_2 X_{2i}+\cdots+\beta_k X_{ki})}} = \frac{1}{\left(1+e^{-(\beta_0+\beta_1 X_{1i}+\beta_2 X_{2i}+\cdots+\beta_k X_{ki})}\right)} \quad (17.14)$$

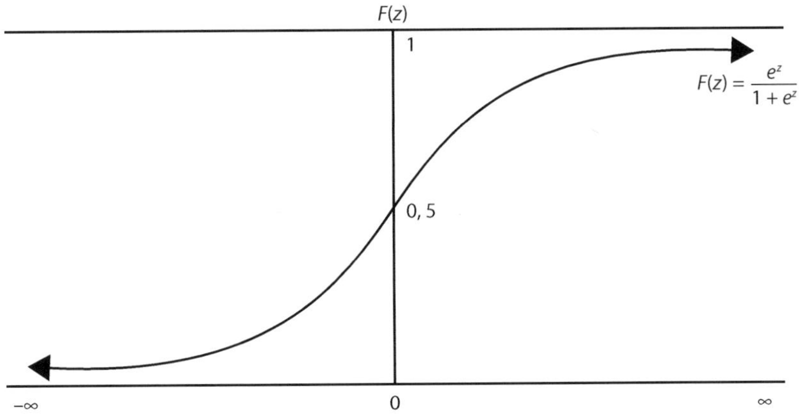

Figure 17.4 Graph of logistic function.

From equation (17.14), it can be shown that:

$$z = F^{-1}(z) = ln\left(\frac{p}{1-p}\right) = \beta_0 + \beta_1 X_{1i} + \beta_2 X_{2i} + \cdots + \beta_k X_{ki} + u_i \qquad (17.15)$$

The F function has a nonlinear form and is an increasing function. The predicted value of F will be guaranteed to lie between 0 and 1. This is because, when z ranges from $-\infty$ to ∞, P or F will always be between 0 and 1. The logistic function is plotted in Figure 17.4.

The basic idea of the probit model is the same as the logit model. The logit model uses the logistic distribution function, while the probit model uses the normal distribution function. The probit model can be developed based on a latent variable model. Consider the regression equation as follows:

$$z = F^{-1}(z) = \beta_0 + \beta_1 X_{1i} + \beta_2 X_{2i} + \cdots + \beta_k X_{ki} \qquad (17.16)$$

If there is a critical value (threshold) z_i^* that is lower or equal to z_i, then the probability that $y = 1$ will be even greater, and the opposite is true. This condition can be written as follows:

$$y = \begin{cases} 1; \ z_i \geq z_i^* \\ 0; \ z_i < z_i^* \end{cases} \qquad (17.17)$$

The probability that $z_i \geq z_i^*$ can be calculated from the standard normal cumulative distribution function as follows:

$$Pr(y=1) = p = F\left(z_i \geq z_i^*\right) = F\left(\beta_0 + \beta_1 X_{1i} + \beta_2 X_{2i} + \cdots + \beta_k X_{ki}\right) \qquad (17.18)$$

where $Pr(y=1)$ explains that the probability that $y = 1$ for a certain value of X, and z_i is the normal standard variable where $z_i \sim N(0,\sigma^2)$. Furthermore, the functional form of the probit regression model can be expressed in the standard normal form of cumulative distribution function as follows:

$$p_i = F(z_i) = \frac{1}{\sqrt{2\pi}} \int_{-\infty}^{z_i} e^{-z^2/2} dz \tag{17.19}$$

or

$$p_i = F(z_i) = \frac{1}{\sqrt{2\pi}} \int_{-\infty}^{\beta_0+\beta_1 X_{1i}+\beta_2 X_{2i}+\cdots+\beta_k X_{ki}} e^{-z^2/2} dz \tag{17.20}$$

In equation (17.18), the value of p_i represents the probability that y = 1. It is represented by the area under the normal standard curve from $-\infty$ to z_i. In this case, the value of p_i will always lie between 0 and 1. The comparison of logit and probit curves is presented in Figure 17.5.

Furthermore, because the F function has a nonlinear form, we can apply the maximum likelihood estimation method to estimate the parameters in the logit and the probit models. The interpretation of the estimation results of binary regression (logit and probit) cannot be performed directly. To analyze the effect of the independent variable on the dependent variable in the logit and probit models, we can use the marginal effect. Marginal effect measures

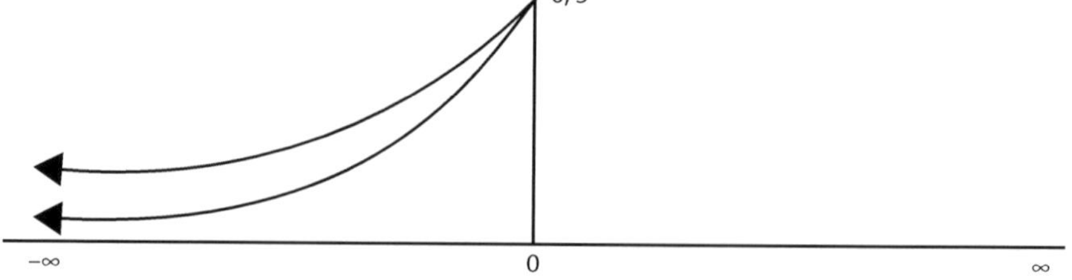

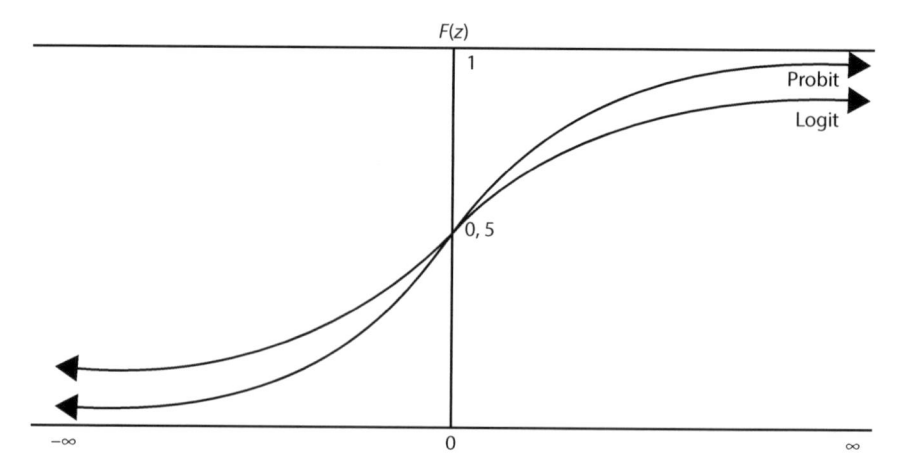

Figure 17.5 The comparison graph of logit and probit function.

the instantaneous effect of independent variables on dependent variables. The marginal effect from the logit model can be expressed as:

$$m_j = \frac{\partial p}{\partial X_j} = \frac{\beta_j}{F'\left[F^{-1}(\beta_0 + x\beta)\right]} = \frac{\beta_j}{F'(p)}; j = 1,2,\cdots k \quad (17.21)$$

while the marginal effect from the probit model can be formulated as:

$$\begin{aligned} m_j &= \frac{\partial P(y=1)}{X_j} = \beta_j F(\beta_0 + \beta_1 X_{1i} + \beta_2 X_{2i} + \cdots + \beta_k X_{ki}) \\ &= \beta_j F(\beta_0 + \mathbf{x}\beta);\ j = 1,2,\cdots,k \end{aligned} \quad (17.22)$$

Time series univariate method

ARMA/ARIMA model

The ARMA/ARIMA model is a type of linear model that can represent stationary and non-stationary time series. This method was developed by George Box and Gwilym Jenkins (1970). ARMA/ARIMA is a class of univariate models that do not include the independent variable in their specification. This model can produce accurate short-term forecasts by utilizing historical patterns in the data.

The ARMA/ARIMA method does not assume a certain pattern from the time series data to be predicted. This method applies an iterative approach to identify the most feasible and adequate model from the general class of models. This method will produce several possible models to be selected and used for forecasting time series data. Some possible models are then verified against the historical data to see if the model accurately describes the data. The model is said to be suitable if the residuals are relatively small and randomly distributed. If the specified model is inadequate, the process is repeated using another alternative model designed to improve the previous model. This procedure is repeated until the most adequate model is obtained. Furthermore, the most adequate model among the possible models can be used for forecasting.

The ARMA model is a combination of the autoregressive (AR) model and the moving average (MA) model, which is specified as:

$$X_t = \varphi_1 X_{t-1} + \varphi_2 X_{t-2} + \cdots + \varphi_p X_{t-p} - \theta_1 e_{t-1} - \theta_2 e_{t-2} - \cdots - \theta_q e_{t-q} + e_t \quad (17.23)$$

where:

X_t = the time series variable at time t

X_{t-i} = time series variable at time lags $t - i$, i = 1,..,p

e_t = the error term at time t

e_{t-i} = the error term at time lags $t - i$, i = 1,..,q

$\varphi_1,\ldots,\varphi_p$ and $\theta_1,\ldots,\theta_q$ = the coefficients to be estimated

Model (17.23) is also called ARMA (p,q), where p is the order of the autoregressive part and q is the order of the moving average part. This model implies that the forecast results will depend on current and past values of the series, X_t, and current and past values of the residual, e.

The ARMA/ARIMA method applies an iterative model-developing strategy consisting of model identification, parameter estimation, and model verifying. The model identification is performed to determine whether the time series data is stationary and to obtain several possible initial models. The series is said to be stationary if they appear to vary about a fixed level. Meanwhile, a nonstationary of the series is indicated by the appearance of the series, which tends to increase or decrease over time. In the ARMA/ARIMA model, if the series is not stationary, it should be transformed to a stationary series by differencing procedure. For example, suppose that the series X_t is not stationary, but the first difference of X_t, $\Delta X_t = X_t - X_{t-1}$, is stationary. In this case, we can extend the ARMA (p,q) model into an autoregressive integrated moving average model that is denoted by ARIMA (p,d,q). Here, d denotes the amount of differencing that makes the series stationary. For this case, d is equal to one. Meanwhile, if the original series is stationary, or $d = 0$, we can simplify the ARIMA (p,d,q) models to the ARMA (p,q) models.

Once we have obtained a stationary series, the next step is to determine the form of the initial model represented by the possible number of autoregressive orders, p, and moving average orders, q. In this case, we can identify the appropriate autoregressive order (p) by using the pattern of the sample partial autocorrelation and the moving average order (q) by using the pattern of the sample autocorrelation. At this point, we usually have several possible initial models to be verified. The initial model should be regarded as tentative. Once tentative models have been identified, the parameter for those models must be estimated.

Before performing the model for forecasting, we have to verify all tentative models for adequacy. An overall test of model adequacy can be represented by a chi-square (χ^2) test based on the Ljung-Box Q statistic. This test is based on the sizes of the residual autocorrelations as a group. The Ljung-Box Q statistic is written as:

$$Q = n(n+2)\sum_{i=1}^{m} \frac{r_i^2(e)}{n-i} \tag{17.24}$$

where:

$r_i(e)$ = the residual autocorrelation at lag i
n = number of residuals
i = time lag
m = number of time lags to be tested

The Q statistic in equation (17.24) is approximately distributed as a chi-square random variable with n-k degrees of freedom where k is the total number of parameters estimated in the model. If the *p*-value associated with the Q statistic is small (i.e., less than 0.05), the model is considered inadequate. Once an adequate model is obtained, forecasts for one period or several periods ahead can be performed.

Volatility model (ARCH, GARCH, TARCH, TGARCH)

Time series data, especially in the financial sector, often shows dynamic volatility over time. This is illustrated by a condition in which volatility is high at certain periods and low at other periods. This behavior forms a volatility clustering. In this case, the time series data have non-constant variance and show a heteroscedasticity pattern. In many empirical cases, the data can experience volatility clustering, which makes the conditional variance inconstant over time. The volatility clustering can be caused by various factors, such as: (1) the number of shocks that occurred in a particular industry; (2) oil price shocks; (3) crash of the stock market; (4) the global financial crisis; (5) change of government regime.

An empirical illustration of volatility clustering is presented in Figure 17.6. It can be seen that the volatility of the S&P 500 Index fluctuated quite highly during 1990–1992. However, from 1993 to 1996 the volatility tended to be stable. Furthermore, the volatility of the S&P 500 Index data again experienced a significant spike in 1997. This surge was inseparable from the various events that occurred at that time. As is well known, in the period 1997–1998 the global economy, especially in Asian countries, was under severe pressure due to the financial crisis. This then impacts economic and financial indicators in various countries, including the S&P 500 Index.

There are several volatility models available in the literature. The volatility model can be built in the framework of the multivariate model or the univariate model. In this case, the volatility model is discussed in the framework of

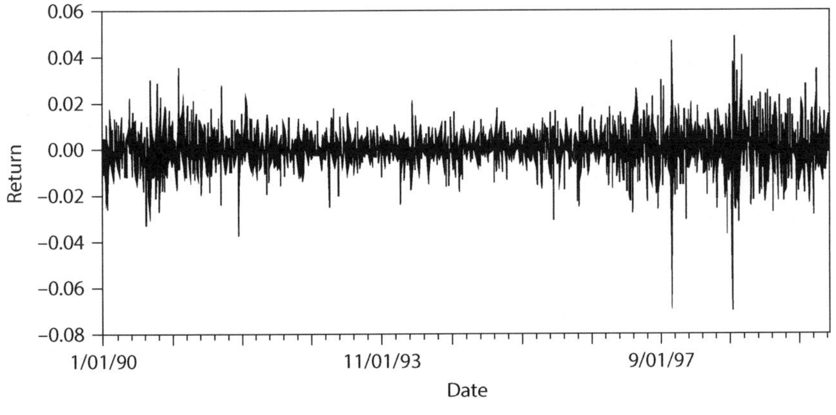

Figure 17.6 The volatility of S&P 500 Index.

the univariate model. The univariate volatility model was first introduced by Engle (1982), who developed the autoregressive conditional heteroscedasticity (ARCH) model. This model was later developed into the generalized autoregressive conditional heteroscedasticity (GARCH) model (Bollerslev, 1986), the exponential generalized autoregressive conditional heteroscedasticity (EGARCH) model, and the threshold generalized autoregressive conditional heteroscedasticity (TGARCH) model. The first two volatility models (ARCH and GARCH) assume that volatility moves symmetrically. However, volatility seems to react differently to good news (positive shock) and bad news (negative shock), with the latter having a greater impact. This phenomenon is referred to as the leverage effect. These properties play an important role in the development of volatility models. In this section, the asymmetric effect will be accommodated by the last two models (EGARCH and TGARCH).

The structure of the volatility model consists of two equations, namely the mean equation and the conditional variance. The mean equation is an equation that represents the mean data series over time. In the case of the univariate volatility model, the specified mean equation is generally represented by the ARMA/ARIMA model. Meanwhile, the conditional variance is an equation that represents the behavior of the residual variance that is inconstant over time. The residuals on the conditional variance equation are generated by the mean equation.

As an illustration, suppose that the mean equation is given in the form of the ARMA model (p,q) as follows:

$$X_t = \varphi_1 X_{t-1} + \varphi_2 X_{t-2} + \cdots + \varphi_p X_{t-p} - \theta_1 e_{t-1} - \theta_2 e_{t-2} - \cdots - \theta_q e_q + e_t \quad (17.25)$$

And suppose that the variance of error generated by the mean equation (17.25) is heteroscedastic. Furthermore, to accommodate the heteroscedasticity of the error, several conditional variance equations can be applied as follows:

ARCH (q). In the ARCH (q) model, the conditional variance, σ_t^2, only depends on the previous squared error or the squared error at time lags $t-j$, ε_{t-j}^2. The term of ε_{t-j}^2 is also called as ARCH component. So, the constant q in the ARCH (q) model refers to the order of the ARCH component. The ARCH (q) model can be written as:

$$\sigma_t^2 = \alpha_0 + \sum_{j=1}^{q} \alpha_j \varepsilon_{t-j}^2 \quad (17.26)$$

where $q = 0, 1\ldots$ are integers, $\alpha_0 > 0$, $\alpha_j \geq 0, j = 1, \ldots q$, are model parameters.

GARCH (p,q). The GARCH (p,q) model is an extended version of ARCH (p). The GARCH (p,q) model does not only depend on the squared error at time lags $t-j$, ε_{t-j}^2, but also on the previous conditional variance or the conditional variance at time lags *t–i*, σ_{t-i}^2. The latter component is also called a GARCH component. The GARCH (*p,q*) model is expressed as:

$$\sigma_t^2 = \alpha_0 + + \sum_{j=1}^{q} \alpha_j \varepsilon_{t-j}^2 + \sum_{i=1}^{p} \lambda_i \sigma_{t-i}^2 \tag{17.27}$$

where *p, q* = 0, 1… are integers, $\alpha_0 > 0$, $\alpha_j \geq 0$, $\beta_i \geq 0$, $i = 1, \ldots p$, $j = 1, \ldots q$, are model parameters.

EGARCH (*p,q*). The EGARCH (*p,q*) model is a method that can capture the asymmetric effect on the volatility of the time series data. In this model, the existence of the leverage effect or the asymmetric effect can be identified from the value γ_j. The asymmetric effect exists when $\gamma_j \neq 0$, and it does not exist if $\gamma_j = 0$. In the EGARCH (*p,q*) model, the ARCH component has two terms consisting of sign effect, $\varepsilon_{t-j}/\sigma_{t-j}$ and magnitude effect, $|\varepsilon_{t-j}/\sigma_{t-j}|$. The sign effect shows that there is a difference in the effect between positive and negative shocks in period *t–j* on the current variance. Meanwhile, the magnitude effect shows the magnitude of the volatility effect in period *t–j* on the current variance. The EGARCH (*p,q*) model is expressed as:

$$\ln \sigma_t^2 = \alpha_0 + \sum_{j=1}^{q} \left\{ \alpha_j \frac{\varepsilon_{t-j}}{\sigma_{t-j}} + \gamma_j \left(\left| \frac{\varepsilon_{t-j}}{\sigma_{t-j}} \right| - \left(\frac{2}{\pi} \right)^{1/2} \right) \right\} + \sum_{i=1}^{p} \beta_i \ln \sigma_{t-i}^2 \tag{17.28}$$

where *p, q* = 0, 1… are integers, $\alpha_0 > 0$, $\alpha_j \geq 0$, $\beta_i \geq 0$, $\gamma_j \geq 0$, $i = 1, \ldots p$, $j = 1, \ldots q$, are model parameters.

TGARCH (*p,q*). In the TGARCH (*p,q*) model, the asymmetric effect can be captured by the coefficient of the dummy variable $I_{\varepsilon_{t-j}}$, γ_j. From the model, it is seen that a positive ε_{t-j} (or good news) contributes $\alpha_j \varepsilon_{t-j}^2$ to the conditional variance, whereas a negative ε_{t-j} (or bad news) has a larger impact $\left[\alpha_j + \gamma_j I_{\varepsilon_{t-j}}\right] \varepsilon_{t-j}^2$ with $\gamma_j > 0$, to the conditional variance. The model uses zero as its threshold to separate the impacts of past shocks. The TGARCH (*p,q*) model is expressed as:

$$\sigma_t^2 = \alpha_0 + \sum_{j=1}^{q} \left[\alpha_j + \gamma_j I_{\varepsilon_{t-j}}\right] \varepsilon_{t-j}^2 + \sum_{i=1}^{p} \beta_i \sigma_{t-i}^2 \tag{17.29}$$

Where:

$$I_{\varepsilon_{t-j}} = \begin{cases} 1\,;\ \varepsilon_{t-j} \leq 0 \\ 0\,;\ \varepsilon_{t-j} > 0 \end{cases}$$

where *p, q* = 0, 1… are integers, $\alpha_0 > 0$, $\alpha_j \geq 0$, $\beta_i \geq 0$, $\gamma_j > 0$, $i = 1, \ldots p$, $j = 1, \ldots q$, are model parameters.

Time series multivariate method

Error correction model (ECM)

The initial test for time series data is stationarity. If there is a group of variables that is not stationary, it will be interesting to study further whether these variables are cointegrated. If these variables are cointegrated, long-term relationships can be identified. Meanwhile, most time series data are not stationary at their level. If these variables are estimated by regression, spurious regression will occur. Thus, the alternative is to regress the variables when the variables are stationary, for example, in the first difference. But often the use of first difference data makes researchers lose long-term information, which is actually very important.

As a result of the problems mentioned above, a new approach called cointegration emerged which was first introduced by Engle and Granger in 1987. Engle and Granger (1987) stated that a linear combination of two or more variables might be stationary I(0), although the individual variables are not stationary I(1). If this linear combination is stationary then the linear relationship can be called cointegration, and if the form is an equation then this is a cointegration equation and the parameters are cointegration parameters that reflect the long-term relationship.

Furthermore, non-stationary variables can be used to estimate the model with an error correction mechanism, or ECM. Even though they are not stationary, these variables in fact are cointegrated. This implies that there is an adjustment process that prevents mistakes in the long run from getting bigger and bigger. Engel and Granger (1987) have proven that cointegrated variables like this have error correction. Error correction mechanisms are widely used in economics with the simple idea that the proportion of equilibrium in one period will be corrected in the next period. According to Engle and Granger (1987), a time series vector x_t will have an error correction representation if it can be expressed as:

$$A(B)(1-B)x_t = -\gamma z_{t-1} + u_t \tag{17.30}$$

where u_t is a stationary multivariate noise, with $A(0) = \text{I}$, $A(1)$ having finite elements, $z_\tau = \alpha' x_\tau$ and $\gamma \neq 0$.

Suppose there are two variables y_t and z_t; here are the steps that must be done in estimating the ECM model. The first stage is to test the stationarity of each research variable to determine the degree of integration. Because by definition, cointegration requires that these variables be integrated in the same order. If the two variables are stationary at the level, then there is no need to take the next step for ECM estimation, because the standard time series method can indeed be applied to stationary variables.

The second step that must be done is to estimate the following long-term equilibrium relationships:

$$y_t = \beta_0 + \beta_1 z_t + e_t \tag{17.31}$$

where β_0 is the intercept and β_1 is the long run coefficient. After the long-term regression process with OLS, the next step is to test the residuals. If the residual turns out to be stationary, the next step is to estimate the ECM model, with the following general form:

$$\Delta y_t = \alpha_1 + \alpha_2 \Delta z_t + \gamma e_{t-1} + \varepsilon_t \tag{17.32}$$

where α_2 is the short-term coefficient and γ is the adjustment coefficient, which is often called the error correction term (ECT). The last step that must be done is to test whether the ECM model formed is appropriate or not. Diagnostic testing should be done to test whether the error is white noise or not. And the last thing to note is that the value of the speed of adjustment or ECT in this case must be in a value between –1 and 0 ($-1 < \gamma < 0$).

Autoregressive Distributed Lag (ARDL)

For some time, cointegration techniques received a lot of attention, especially to determine the existence of relationships between variables at their level. Two main approaches have been widely used, namely, the two-stage residual testing procedure by Engle and Granger in 1987 and the Johansen cointegration approach in 1991. All of these methods focus on cases where the variables used are integrated in first order. Meanwhile, Pesaran and Shin (1997) introduced a cointegration approach using the autoregressive distributed lag (ARDL) model. The following is an augmented autoregressive model for ARDL distributed lag (p, q) according to Pesaran and Shin (1997):

$$y_t = \alpha_0 + \alpha_1 t + \sum_{i=1}^{p} \varnothing_i y_{t-i} + \beta' x_t + \sum_{i=0}^{q-1} \beta_i^{*\prime} \Delta x_{t-1} + u_t \tag{17.33}$$

$$\Delta x_t = P_1 \Delta x_{t-1} + P_2 \Delta x_{t-2} + \cdots + P_s \Delta x_{t-s} + \varepsilon_t \tag{17.34}$$

where x_t is a variable with a dimension of k in the integration of one I(1) which is not cointegrated between them, u_t and ε_t are interference/errors with zero means, constant variance and covariance and not serial correlation. P_i is the $k \times k$ coefficient matrix of the autoregressive vector process at stable x_t.

It is also assumed that the roots of $1-\sum_{i=1}^{p} \varnothing_i z^i = 0$ are outside the unit circle and that there is a long-term stable relationship between y_t and x_t.

$$\varnothing(L,p)y_t = \sum_{i=1}^{k} \beta_i(L, q_i)x_{it} + \delta' w_t + u_t \qquad (17.35)$$

where:

$$\varnothing(L,p) = 1 - \varnothing_1 L - \varnothing_2 L^2 - \cdots - \varnothing_p L^p \qquad (17.36)$$

$$\beta_i(L, q_i) = \beta_{i0} + \beta_{i1}L + \cdots + \beta_{iq_i}L^{q_i},\ i = 1,2,\ldots,k \qquad (17.37)$$

L is the lag operator so that $Ly_t = y_{t-1}$ and w_t are vectors $s \times 1$ of deterministic variables such as intercept, seasonal dummy, trend, or exogenous variables with fixed lag. *First*, equation (3.8) is estimated using the OLS method for all possible values of $p = 0, 1, 2, \ldots, m$, $q_i = 0, 1, 2, \ldots, m$, $i = 1, 2, \ldots, k$; that is, the ARDL model is different from the total $(m+1)^{k+1}$. The maximum amount of lag, m, is chosen by the researcher, and all models are estimated for the same sample period, namely $t = m + 1, m + 2, \ldots, n$.

In the *second* stage, the researcher can choose to determine one model from the total number of models $(m+1)^{k+1}$ using four model selection criteria: $\bar{R}^2$ criterion, Akaike information criterion (AIC), Schwarz Bayesian criterion (SBC), or Hannan-Quinn criterion (HQC). The computer program will calculate the long-run coefficient and asymptotic standard error for the selected ARDL model. The long-run coefficient for y_t response to one-unit change x_{it} is estimated by:

$$\hat{\theta}_i = \frac{\hat{\beta}_i(1,\hat{q}_i)}{\hat{\varnothing}(1,\hat{p})} = \frac{\hat{\beta}_{i0} + \hat{\beta}_{i1} + \cdots + \hat{\beta}_{i\hat{q}_i}}{1 - \hat{\varnothing}_1 - \hat{\varnothing}_2 - \cdots - \hat{\varnothing}_{\hat{p}}},\ i = 1,2,\ldots,k \qquad (17.38)$$

where $\hat{p}$ and $\hat{q}_i$, $i = 1,2,\ldots,k$ is the estimated value of p and q_i, $i = 1,2,\ldots,k$. In the same way, the long run coefficients associated with deterministic or exogenous variables with lag are still estimated by the formula:

$$\hat{\varphi} = \frac{\hat{\delta}(\hat{p}, \hat{q}_1, \hat{q}_2, \ldots, \hat{q}_k)}{1 - \hat{\varnothing}_1 - \hat{\varnothing}_2 - \cdots - \hat{\varnothing}_{\hat{p}}} \qquad (17.39)$$

where $\hat{\delta}(\hat{p}, \hat{q}_1, \hat{q}_2, \ldots, \hat{q}_k)$ is the OLS estimate of δ in for the selected ARDL model.

Cointegration testing using the bound test or ARDL approach has several advantages. First, the testing procedure is simple when compared to the

Johansen-Juselius cointegration test. This is because the use of a bound test is enough to test the cointegration relationship that is estimated using OLS when the lag of the model has been identified. Second, the bound test does not require pre-estimate testing, such as unit root testing for the variables to be used in the model. This test can be used without depending on the regressor integration order at I(0), I(1), or cointegration with each other. Third, this test is relatively more efficient for small and limited data samples. For the two variables y_t and z_t, the ECM conditionals are as follows:

$$\Delta y_t = c_0 + \delta_1 y_{t-1} + \delta_2 z_{t-1} + \sum_{i=1}^{p-1} \lambda_i \Delta y_{t-i} + \sum_{i=0}^{p-1} \xi_i \Delta z_{t-i} + \varepsilon_t \tag{17.40}$$

The procedure that must be done in testing the cointegration with the bound test is as follows:

- Equation (3.14) is estimated using OLS, which is intended to determine the existence of a long-term relationship between variables by applying the F test. This F test is used to see the joint test for long-term coefficients. The hypotheses tested are:

H_0: $\delta_1 = \delta_2 = 0$

H_1: $\delta_1 \neq \delta_2 \neq 0$

We can determine whether there is a long-term relationship (cointegration) by comparing the F-statistic value with its critical value. There are two asymptotic critical limit values to test for cointegration when the independent variable is integrated in I(d) where ($0 \leq d \leq 1$). The lowest value (lower) assumes the integrated regressor is at I(0) while the highest value (upper) assumes the integrated regressor is at I(1). If the F-statistic is more than the highest critical value, then the null hypothesis about the absence of a long-term relationship can be rejected. Conversely, if the F-statistic is below the lowest critical value, the null hypothesis cannot be rejected. Finally, if the F-statistic is between the lowest and highest critical values, there is no conclusion. The critical value in question is not an ordinary value, but a critical value that has been calculated by Pesaran and Shin (1997).

If in the first stage a long-term relationship has been found, the next step is to estimate the ARDL model as follows:

$$y_t = c_0 + \sum_{i=1}^{p} \delta_1 y_{t-i} + \sum_{i=0}^{q_1} \delta_2 z_{t-j} + \varepsilon_t \tag{17.41}$$

Panel data method

Panel data refers to a data structure in which the cross-section is observed repeatedly over time. A cross-section is generally an entity that can be an individual or household, company, region, or country. The application of estimation methods that utilize panel data is becoming increasingly important in both the theoretical and applied micro-econometric literature. This popularity is a consequence of this method, which can answer various problems that cannot be solved by pure cross-sectional and pure time series models. Compared to pure time series and cross-sectional models, the panel data model has several advantages, namely (1) increased precision of regression estimates; (2) the ability to control for individual fixed effect; and (3) the ability to model temporal effects without aggregation bias.

The panel data estimation method is differentiated based on the model construction or the regression equation formed. If the regression equation involves the lag of dependent variable on the regressor, it is known as a dynamic model, otherwise, it is called a static model (Wooldridge, 2002; Baltagi, 2008). The differences in model specifications will lead to different estimation approaches. The estimation method for the static panel data model and the dynamic panel data model will be described below.

Static panel data

There are several approaches to the static panel data method, including pooled least square (PLS), fixed effect model (FEM), and random effect model (REM). The PLS parameter estimation method applies the ordinary least square method as in pure time series or pure cross-section models. The PLS method assumes homogeneity among individuals or assumes that individual effects are fixed or common across entities. Meanwhile, the REM and FEM methods assume heterogeneity among individuals or assume that any differences across individuals. The two methods are distinguished based on the presence or absence of a correlation between the error component and the independent variable.

Suppose a simple panel data regression equation is given as follows:

$$Y_{it} = \beta_0 + \beta_1 X_{it} + \varepsilon_{it} \tag{17.42}$$

where Y and X denote dependent variable and independent variable, respectively, that are observed for $i = 1,\ldots,N$ individuals over $t = 1,\ldots,T$ periods, β is a parameter to be estimated, and ε denotes error term. In practice, T can be the same or differ across individuals. A balanced panel refers to a data set in which each individual has the same number of periods, while in unbalanced panel data, at least one individual has a different number of periods.

The estimation method for the parameter in the panel data model (17.34) can be classified based on the error component specification, namely, the one-way error component model and two-way error component model. In the one-way approach, the composite error component can be written as $\varepsilon_{it} = \lambda_i + u_{it}$, while in the two-way approach the composite error is $\varepsilon_{it} = \lambda_i + \mu_t + u_{it}$. In this case, λ_i is the unobservable individual-specific effect, μ_t is the unobservable time-specific effect, and u_{it} is the remainder disturbance. It is assumed that u_{it} is not correlated with X_{it}.

The FEM is suitable when differences among individuals may reasonably be viewed simply as parametric shifts in the regression function. This situation can be reflected by the existence of the correlation between individual effects and independent variables, or $\text{cov}(X_{it}, \lambda_i) \neq 0$. In general in econometric literature, there are at least two approaches that can be applied to estimate the parameters in the FEM, namely within-group estimator and least square dummy variable estimator. Meanwhile, in the REM, the individuals are drawn from a larger population, and then it may be more suitable to view the individual-specific terms in the sample as randomly distributed effects across the full cross-section of agents. So, in the REM, it is assumed that individual effects and independent variables are uncorrelated, or $\text{cov}(X_{it}, \lambda_i) = 0$. The common approach that can be applied to estimate the parameters of the REM is the generalized least square estimator.

The question now is how to choose an appropriate method in the panel data model among the existing methods. In this case, we can apply several statistical test procedures to choose a proper estimation method in the panel data model. The Chow-F statistics can be used to check whether individual effects are common or differ across individuals. In this method, the null hypothesis assumes the individual effects are common (PLS), and the alternative hypothesis assumes heterogeneity among individuals (FEM). Meanwhile, the Breusch-Pagan Lagrange Multiplier statistics provide a test of the REM against the PLS model, where the null hypothesis is the PLS estimator and the alternative hypothesis is the REM estimator. Furthermore, the Hausman statistics can be applied in comparing directly the FEM estimator and the REM estimator. The Hausman test of the null hypothesis assumes no correlation between individual effects and independent variables, or this constitutes to REM model. The summary of best model selection can be seen in Figure 17.7.

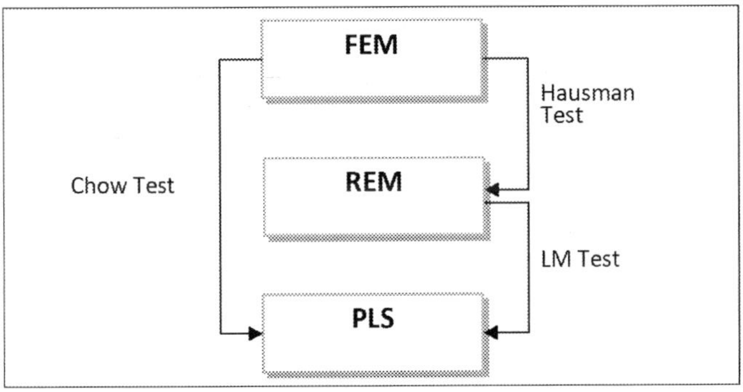

Figure 17.7 Selection of the best panel data model.

Dynamic panel data

Many relationships among economic variables are dynamic. This dynamic relationship is characterized by the existence of a lag in the dependent variable between the regressors. As an illustration, consider the two cases of the dynamic panel data model as follows:

Fixed effect model:

$$y_{it} = \mu_i + \delta y_{i,t-1} + x_{it}'\beta + u_{it}; \quad i = 1,\ldots,N; \quad t = 1,\ldots T \tag{17.43}$$

where δ is a scalar parameter, x_{it}' is expressing the matrix of exogeneous variables of size 1 x K, β is expressing the matrix parameter of size K x 1, μ_i is an individual effect, and u_{it} is a random error where $u_{it} \sim IID\left(0,\sigma_u^2\right)$.

Random effect model:

$$y_{it} = \delta y_{i,t-1} + x_{it}'\beta + u_{it}; \quad i = 1,\ldots,N; \quad t = 1,\ldots T \tag{17.44}$$

where u_{it} is assumed to follow the one-way error component model: $u_{it} = \mu_i + v_{it}$, $\mu_i \sim IID\left(0,\sigma_\mu^2\right)$ represents the individual effect, and $v_{it} \sim IID\left(0,\sigma_v^2\right)$ is the random error.

In the static model, it can be showed that FEM or REM provides consistent and efficient estimators. However, in the dynamic models (17.35) and (17.36), the situation is substantially different. Since y_{it} is a function of μ_i, then $y_{i,t-1}$ will also be a function of μ_i. Moreover, since μ_i is a function of u_{it}, there will be a correlation between the regressor $y_{i,t-1}$ and u_{it}. This will cause the least square estimator (as used in the static panel data model) to be biased and inconsistent, even if v_{it} is not serial correlated. To overcome this problem, Arellano and Bond (1991) suggest a generalized method of moments (GMM) approach which is an extension of the instrumental variable method. In GMM estimators, we weight the vector of sample-average moment conditions by the inverse of a positive definite matrix. When that matrix is the covariance matrix of the moment conditions, we have an efficient GMM estimator.

In dynamic panel data modeling, there are at least two GMM approaches that can be applied, namely the first-difference GMM (FD-GMM) and the GMM system. FD-GMM was developed by Arellano and Bond (1991); therefore some literature refers to it as AB-GMM. The FD-GMM estimator uses a specification of the first-difference equation. This transformation will eliminate the individual effect and allow the endogenous lag variable in the second and previous periods as the correct instrument variable, assuming the random error is not serially correlated. This condition can be checked through an autocorrelation test on the residuals in the form of first differences.

However, the FD-GMM estimator may contain bias on limited samples; this occurs when the lagged level of a series is weakly correlated with the next first difference so that the available instruments for the first-difference equation are weak (Blundell and Bond 1998). Simulations conducted by Blundell and Bond (1998) show that the FD-GMM estimator can be constrained by the downward finite sample bias, especially when the available observation period is relatively short. To overcome the weaknesses of FD-GMM, Blundel and Bond (1998) developed the System-GMM. The basic idea of using the System-GMM method is to use the lagged level of $y_{i,t}$ as the instrument variable in the first differences equation and to use the lagged differences from $y_{i,t}$ as the instrument variable in the level equation (Blundell and Bond 1998). Thus, this approach does not only utilize the condition moment and the instrument variable matrix from the first difference model found by Arellano and Bond (1991). Blundell and Bond (1998) combined the condition moments from the first difference and the condition moments from the level, as well as the instrument variable matrix from the first difference and the instrument variable matrix from the level.

In the dynamic panel data model, we can employ three statistical test procedures to check the adequacy of the model. Arellano and Bond (1991) suggested the m_1 and the m_2 statistics test to verify whether the estimates suffer from the serial correlation. These procedures can be applied to check the consistency of the estimator. First, consistency using the Arellano-Bond test. The consistency is indicated by significant results from m_1 statistic and insignificant results from m_2 statistic. Furthermore, in the GMM, the estimator can produce consistent estimates only if the moment conditions used are valid. Although there is no method to test if the moment conditions from an exactly identified model are valid, one can test whether the overidentifying moment conditions are valid. In this case, we can apply the Sargan test of overidentifying conditions (Arellano and Bond, 1991). Second, instrument validity using Sargan test. In the Sargan test, the null hypothesis states that the overidentifying restrictions are valid. Rejecting this null hypothesis implies that we need to reconsider our model or our instruments. Third, the unbiased test. It can be shown that the parameter estimation in the dynamic panel data model using the FEM and PLS approaches will produce an estimated parameter where OLS will cause upwards bias and FEM will cause downwards bias. Therefore, an unbiased estimator in the dynamic panel data model should lie between the range of estimate FEM and estimate OLS.

References

Abdullahi, S.I. (2018). Contribution of mathematical models to Islamic economic theory: a survey. *International Journal of Ethics and Systems, 34*(2), 200–212.

Addas, W.A.J. (2008). *Methodology of economics: Secular vs. Islamic.* Kuala Lumpur: International Islamic University Malaysia Press.

Arellano, M., Bond, S. (1991). Some tests of specification for panel data: Monte Carlo evidence and an application to employment equations. *Review of Economic Studies, 58*(2), 277.

Baltagi, B.H. (2008). *Econometric analysis of panel data* (4th ed.). Chichester: John Wiley & Sons.

Bendjilali, B. (2009). The scope of alternative methodologies: Deductive, inductive and empirical approaches. In M.N. Siddiqi (Ed.), *Encyclopedia of Islamic economics*, Vol.1. London, pp. 165–170.

Bhargava, A., Sargan, J.D. (1983). Estimating dynamic random effects models from panel data covering short time periods. *Econometrica*, *51*(6), 1635–1659.

Bollerslev, T. (1986). Generalized autoregressive conditional heteroskedasticity. *Journal of Econometrics*, *31*(3): 307–327.

Bollerslev, T. (2010). Chapter 8: Glossary to ARCH (GARCH). In Bollerslev, T., Russell, J., & Watson, M. (eds.). *Volatility and time series econometrics: Essays in honor of Robert Engle* (1st Ed.). Oxford: Oxford University Press, pp. 137–163.

Chapra, M.U. (2001). *What is Islamic economics*. IDB Prize Winners' Lecture Series. Jeddah: Islamic Research and training Institute, Islamic Development Bank.

Enders, W. (2010). *Applied econometric time series* (3rd ed.). New York: John Wiley & Sons, pp. 272–355.

Engle, R. (2001). GARCH 101: The use of ARCH/GARCH models in applied econometrics. *Journal of Economic Perspectives*, *15*(4), 157–168.

Engle, R.F. (1982). Autoregressive conditional heteroscedasticity with estimates of the variance of United Kingdom inflation. *Econometrica*, *50*(4), 987–1007.

Ethridge, D.E. (2004). *Research methodology in applied economics*. Iowa, USA: Blackwell Publishing.

Fox, W., Bayat, M.S. (2007). *A guide to managing research*. Landsdowne, Capetown: Juta Publications.

Gardiner, J.C., Luo, Z., Roman, L.A. (2009). Fixed effects, random effects and GEE: What are the differences? *Statistics in Medicine*, *28*, 221–239.

Gujarati, D.N., Porter, D.C. (2009). Panel data regression models. *Basic econometrics (5th International Ed.)*. Boston: McGraw-Hill, pp. 591–616.

Hsiao, C. (2003). Fixed-effects models. *Analysis of panel data* (2nd ed.). New York: Cambridge University Press, pp. 95–103.

Hsiao, C., Lahiri, K., Lee, L., *et al*., eds. (1999). *Analysis of panels and limited dependent variable models*. Cambridge: Cambridge University Press.

Khan, M.A. (2018). Methodology of Islamic economics from Islamic teachings to Islamic economics. *Turkish Journal of Islamic Economics*, *5*(1), 35–61.

Krippendorff, K. (1989). Content analysis. In E. Barnouw, G. Gerbner, W. Schramm, T.L. Worth, & L. Gross (Eds.), *International encyclopedia of communication* (Vol. 1). New York, NY: Oxford University Press, pp. 403–407.

Krippendorff, K. (2004). *Content analysis: An introduction to its methodology*. London, United Kingdom: Sage Publications Ltd.

Krippendorff, K. (2012). *Content analysis: An introduction to its methodology* (3rd ed.). Thousand Oaks, CA: Sage Publications.

Pesaran, M.H., Shin, Y. (1997). An autoregressive distributed lag modelling approach to cointegration analysis. Paper Proceeding, Symposium at the Centennial of Ragnar Frisch, The Norwegian Academy of Science and Letters, Oslo, March 3–5, 1995.

Pesaran, M.H., Shin, Y. (1998). An autoregressive distributed-lag modelling approach to cointegration analysis. In Econometrics and economic theory in the 20th century: the Ragnar Frisch Centennial Symposium. Cambridge: Cambridge University Press pp. 371–413.

Pesaran M.H., Shin, Y., Smith, R.J. (2001). Bounds testing approaches to the analysis of level relationships. *Journal of Applied Econometrics*, *16*, 289–326.

Roodman, D. (2009). How to do xtabond2: An introduction to difference and system GMM in Stata. *The Stata Journal*, *9*(1), 86–136.

Rosengren, K.E. (1981). Advances in Scandinavia content analysis: An introduction. In K.E. Rosengren (ed.), *Advances in content analysis*. Beverly Hills, CA: Sage Publications, pp. 9–19.

Wooldridge, J.M. (2002). *Econometric analysis of cross section and panel data*. Cambridge, MA: MIT Press.

Wooldridge, J.M. (2013). Fixed effects estimation. In *Introductory econometrics: A modern approach* (5th International ed.). Mason, OH: South-Western, pp. 466–474.

Wooldridge, J. (2010). *Econometric analysis of cross section and panel data* (2nd ed.). Cambridge, MA: MIT Press, p. 252.

Yasin, H.M., Khan, A.Z. (2016). *Fundamentals of Islamic economics and finance*. Jeddah: Islamic Research and Training Institute, Islamic Development Bank.

Yunus, M., Heiden, C. (2020). The future of microfinance. *Brown Journal of World Affairs*, *26*(2), 119–126.

18

RECOMMENDED METHODOLOGY FOR RESEARCH IN ISLAMIC ECONOMICS AND FINANCE

Ascarya and Omer Faruk Tekdogan

Introduction

Choudhury and Hoque (2004) introduced the epistemology of a generalized methodology that configures all relationships in every world system in terms of the unity of knowledge and develops the scope for its application. This feature of interactive, integrative, and evolutionary (IIE) process-oriented circular causation means that all God's creations depend on God and are interdependent to each other, forming evolving circular causal interrelationships among them resulting in a system of guided and evolutionary equilibriums across multiple evolutionary optima that continuously learn and evolve according to the *Shuratic* process (Choudhury & Hoque, 2004). Furthermore, according to Choudhury and Korvin (2002), as the consequence of this evolving circular causation, the more appropriate methods/methodologies of research in Islamic economic and finance would be simulation models instead of optimization models, which comply with the epistemological methodology underlying the continuously evolving universe according to the *Tawhidi* worldview (Reda, 2012).

For example, if we have five variables as depicted in Figure 18.1, each variable has causal interrelationships with the other four variables. Variable A has causal interrelationships with Variable B, Variable C, Variable D, and Variable E.

Even though specific applied methods/methodologies have not been developed featuring the IIE process-oriented circular causation proposed by Choudhury, several conventional methods/methodologies could have/resemble these features, such as vector autoregression (VAR), structural equation modeling (SEM), analytic network process (ANP), and agent-based model (ABM).

For example, the VAR method (and all its variants) treats all variables as a priori endogenous and makes all variables form interdependent relationships (Sims, 1980), which resemble the circular causation of Choudhury's Islamic methodology. Moreover, since the VAR method assumes no specific theory (or a theory), we can insert Islamic economics and finance theories in the

DOI: 10.4324/9781003252764-22

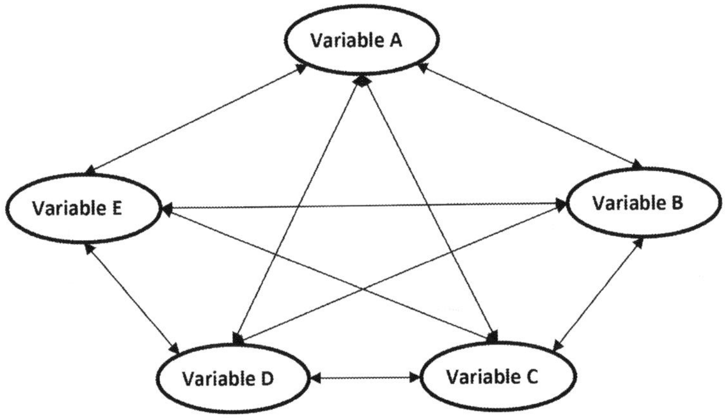

Figure 18.1 Causal interrelationships among all variables.

Source: Authors.

VAR models. Another example, ABM, is a computer program that creates an artificial world of heterogeneous agents and enables investigation into how interactions between these agents, and other factors, such as time and space, add up to form the patterns seen in the real world (Hamill & Gilbert, 2015). ABM, as a simulation model, could also study complex interdependent systems, which resembles the circular causation of Choudhury's Islamic methodology.

The best methodology for research in Islamic economics discussed in this chapter will include methods which have circular causation features as mentioned before, where the summary of the methods and their references can be seen in Table 18.1.

Table 18.1 The best methodology for research in Islamic economics and finance

Vector autoregression (VAR)	*Structural equation modeling (SEM)*
Vector autoregression – VAR Sims (1980); Lütkepohl (2006); Asteriou and Hall (2011); Qin (2011) **Structural VAR** Amisano and Giannini (1997)	**CB-SEM** Jöreskog (1973); Keesling (1973); Hair *et al.* (2010); Hair *et al.* (1998, 2010); Hair *et al.* (2017) **PLS-SEM** Hair *et al.* (2011, 2014); Hair *et al.* (2017)
Analytic network process (ANP)	*Agent-based model (ABM)*
ANP Saaty (1996, 2001, 2004, 2005, 2008); Saaty and Ozdemir (2005); Saaty and Vargas (2006); Saaty and Cillo (2007) **Delphi-ANP** Sakti *et al.* (2019); Ascarya and Sakti (2021); Ascarya *et al.* (2021)	**ABM** Bonabeau (2002); Barr *et al.* (2011); Napoletano *et al.* (2012); Hamill and Gilbert (2015); Chan-Lau (2017); Schinckus (2019)

Vector autoregression

VAR is an equation of n with n endogenous variables, where each variable is described by its own lag, and present and past values of other endogenous variables in the model. Therefore, in the context of modern econometrics, VAR is considered a multivariate time-series that addresses all endogenous variables, because there is no certainty that the variables are actually exogenous, and VAR allows the data to tell what actually happened. Sims (1980) argues that if there is true simultaneity between a number of variables, then those variables should be treated on an equal footing and there should be no a priori differences between endogenous and exogenous variables. According to Achsani *et al.* (2005), a common VAR model can be mathematically described as follows.

$$x_t = \mu_t + \sum_{i=1}^{k} A_i + X_{t-1} + \varepsilon_t \tag{18.1}$$

x_t is a vector of endogenous variables with dimensions (n × 1), μ_t is a vector of exogenous variables, including constants (intercept) and trends, Ai is a coefficient matrix with dimensions (n × n), and ε_t is a residual vector. In a simple bivariate system y_t and z_t, y_t is affected by the present and past values of z_t, while z_t is affected by the present and past values of y_t. Enders (2015) formulates a simple first-order bivariate primitive system that can be written as follows.

$$y_t = b_{10} - b_{12}z_t + \gamma_{11}y_{t-1} + \gamma_{12}z_{t-1} + \varepsilon_{yt} \tag{18.2}$$

$$z_t = b_{20} - b_{21}y_t + \gamma_{21}y_{t-1} + \gamma_{22}z_{t-1} + \varepsilon_{zt} \tag{18.3}$$

With assumptions that both y_t and z_t are stationary, ε_{yt} and ε_{zt} are white-noise disturbances with standard deviations of σ_y and σ_z, respectively, and ε_{yt} and ε_{zt} are uncorrelated white-noise disturbances. Meanwhile, the standard form of the above primitive form can be written as follows.

$$y_t = a_{10} + a_{11}y_{t-1} + a_{12}z_{t-1} + e_{yt} \tag{18.4}$$

$$z_t = a_{20} + a_{21}y_{t-1} + a_{22}z_{t-1} + e_{zt} \tag{18.5}$$

VAR provides a systematic way to capture dynamic changes in multiple time series, and it has a credible and easy-to-understand approach for describing data, predictions, structural decisions, and policy analysis. VAR has four analysis tools, namely, prediction (forecasting), impulse response function (IRF), forecast error variance decomposition (FEVD), and the Granger causality test. Forecasting can be used to predict the present and future values of all variables by utilizing all past information from these variables. IRF can be used to determine the current and future responses of each variable to the shock of a particular variable. FEVD can be used to predict the contribution of each variable to shocks or changes in certain variables. Meanwhile, the Granger causality test can be used to determine the causal relationship between variables.

Like other econometric models, VAR also consists of a series of specification and identification process models. Model specifications include the selection of variables and their lag lengths to be used in the model. Meanwhile, model identification is used to determine the equation before it is used in estimation. There are several conditions that may occur in the identification process. An overidentified condition occurs when the amount of information exceeds the number of parameters estimated. Exactly identified or just identified conditions occur if the amount of information and parameters estimated is the same. Meanwhile, the underidentified condition occurs when the amount of information is less than the estimated parameter. The estimation process can only be carried out if the conditions are overidentified and exactly identified or just identified.

The advantages of the VAR method compared to other econometric methods are (Enders, 2015; Gujarati, 2004): (1) The VAR method is free from various limitations of economic theory that often exist, such as false endogenous and exogenous variables; (2) VAR develops the model simultaneously in a complex multivariate system, so that it can capture all the relationships between variables in the equation; (3) The multivariate VAR test can avoid parameter bias because it excludes relevant variables; (4) The VAR test can detect all relationships between variables in the system of equations by treating all variables as endogenous; (5) The VAR method is a simple method, where there is no need to determine which variables are endogenous and which are exogenous, because VAR treats all variables as endogenous; (6) VAR estimation is simple, because the general ordinary least squares (OLS) method can be used for each equation separately; and (7) The predicted prediction obtained is, in most cases, better than the more complex simultaneous-equation model.

Meanwhile, the weaknesses and problems in the VAR model, according to Gujarati (2004), are: (1) The theoretical VAR model, because it uses less prior information, unlike the simultaneous equation model, where the exclusion and inclusion of certain variables play an important role in identifying models; (2) The VAR model is less appropriate for policy analysis, because of its emphasis on prediction; (3) Choosing the appropriate lag length is the biggest challenge in the VAR model, especially when there are many variables with long lag, causing too many parameters, which consume a lot of degrees of freedom and require a large sample size; (4) All variables must be stationary (together). Otherwise, all data must be converted correctly, such as in the first-differencing way. Long-term relationships are lost when there is a change in data levels, which is necessary for analysis; (5) IRF is at the heart of VAR analysis, which has been the question of researchers.

To overcome the shortcomings of the first-difference VAR and to regain the long-term relationship between variables, the vector error correction model (VECM) can be used, as long as there is cointegration between variables.

The trick is to reincorporate the original equation at the level into the new equation. The general VECM model, mathematically, can be described as follows (Achsani *et al.*, 2005).

$$\Delta x_{t-1} = \mu_t + \prod x_{t-1} + \sum_{i=1}^{k-1} \Gamma_i \Delta x_{t-i} + \varepsilon_t \tag{18.6}$$

Π and Γ are functions of Ai. The Π matrix can be broken down into two matrices λ and β with dimensions (n × r). $\Pi = \lambda\beta T$, where λ is the adjustment matrix and β is the cointegration vector, whereas r is the cointegration rank. Therefore, the bivariate system of VECM can be written as follows.

$$\Delta y_t = b_{10} + b_{11}\Delta y_{t-1} + b_{12}\Delta z_{t-1} - \lambda\left(y_{t-1} - a_{10} - a_{11}y_{t-2} - a_{12}z_{t-1}\right) + \varepsilon_{yt} \tag{18.7}$$

$$\Delta z_t = b_{20} + b_{21}\Delta y_{t-1} + b_{22}\Delta z_{t-1} - \lambda\left(z_{t-1} - a_{20} - a_{21}y_{t-1} - a_{22}z_{t-2}\right) + \varepsilon_{zt} \tag{18.8}$$

Where a is long-term regression coefficient, b is short-term regression coefficient, λ is an error correction parameter, and the phrase in the bracket shows the cointegration between variables y and z.

The process of VAR analysis can be read in Figure 18.2. After the basic data is ready, the data is transformed into a natural logarithm (ln), except for interest rates and profit-sharing returns, to obtain consistent and valid results. The first test to be carried out is the unit root test, to determine whether the data is stationary or still contains a trend. If the data is stationary at the level, then VAR can be performed at the level, including VAR level and even

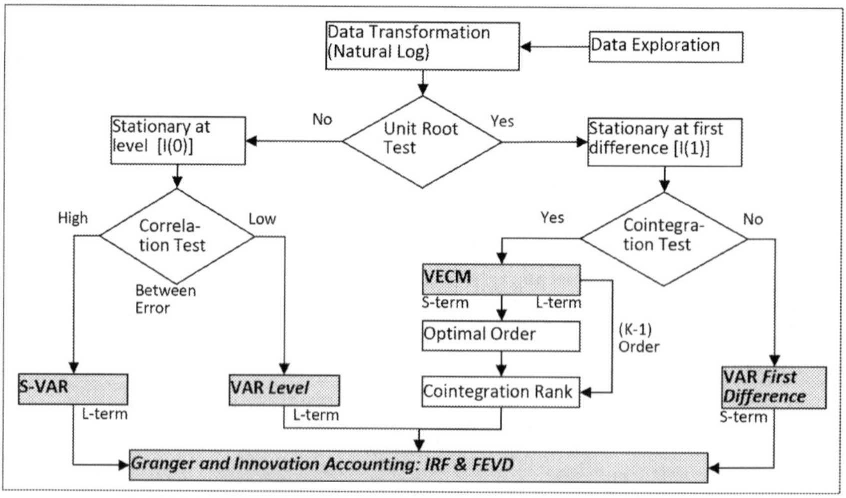

Figure 18.2 Process of vector autoregression.

structural VAR if correlation between error is high. VAR level can estimate the long-term relationship between variables. If the data is not stationary at the level, then the data must be derived at the first level (first difference) which reflects the difference or change in data. If the data is stationary in the first derivative, then the data will be tested for the presence of cointegration between variables. If there is no cointegration between variables, then VAR can only be done on the first derivative, and it can only estimate the short-term relationship between variables. Innovation accounting will not be meaningful for long-term relationships between variables. If there is cointegration between variables, then VECM can be done using level data to obtain long-term relationships between variables. VECM can estimate the short-term and long-term relationships between variables. Innovation in accounting for VAR levels and VECM will be meaningful for long-term relationships.

Structural equation modeling

SEM is a model originally developed by Karl Jöreskog (1973) which is combined with a model developed by Keesling (1973). The model is well recognized as the linear structural relationship (LISREL) model, or sometimes as the JKW model. The SEM is essentially a simultaneous equation as in econometrics. The difference is that econometrics use measured or observed variables while the SEM uses unobservable variable or latent variables. The supporting computer software was developed by Jöreskog and Sörbom and called LISREL, which is considered to be an interactive and user-friendly program.

SEM consists of two main components. First is the measurement model, which measures or estimates the respective latent variables using the concept of confirmatory factor analysis (CFA) or exploratory factor analysis (EFA). It is important to note that one cannot combine indicators arbitrarily to form latent variables. They have to be selected based on underlying theories. Figure 18.3 shows examples of five measurement models of exogenous (ξ = Ksi) and endogenous (η = Eta) latent variables, each with indicators

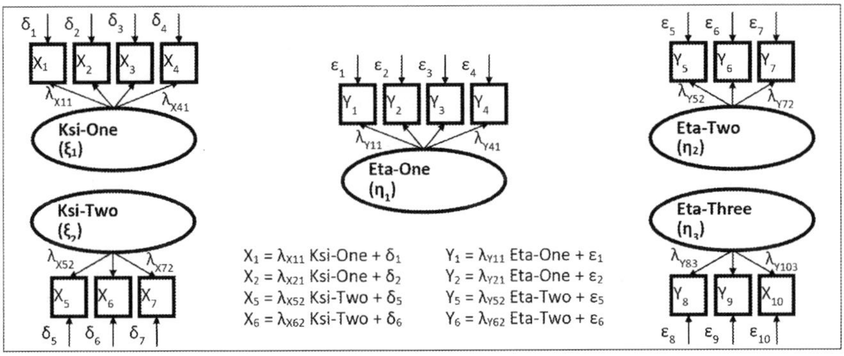

Figure 18.3 Measurement model of latent variables.

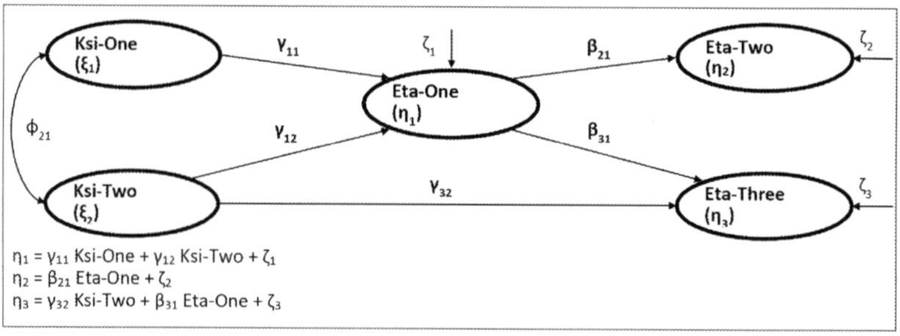

Figure 18.4 Structural model.

(X for exogenous, and Y for endogenous), where the arrows start from the latent variable to the indicators, showing the reflective nature of the indicators to their latent variable. Each indicator forms a measurement equation (see equations in Figure 18.3).

Second is the structural model, which describes the structural relationships among latent variables or unobserved variables or constructs or factors. These variables are measured or estimated indirectly by their respective indicators. Figure 18.4 shows the structural model of the five measurement models in Figure 18.3, where direct relationship from exogenous latent variable to endogenous latent variable is written as γ (gamma), direct relationship from endogenous latent variable to another endogenous latent variable is written as β (beta), and the error term of endogenous latent variable equation is written as ζ (zeta). Each endogenous latent variable forms a structural equation (see equations in Figure 18.4).

There are two types of structural equation models or SEM: covariance-based SEM or CB-SEM developed by Jöreskog and partial least squares SEM or PLS-SEM developed by Wold. These two SEM models are more complementary than competitive. CB-SEM is often referred to as "hard modeling" because it requires some strict assumptions, such as "normality" and a large sample requirement, whereas PLS-SEM is often called "soft modeling" because it requires looser assumptions and can use a small sample.

CB-SEM, or for short – SEM, has three variants: SEM based on AMOS (analysis of moment structures), SEM based on EQS, and SEM based on LISREL (linear structural relationship). SEM is the second generation of multivariate analysis techniques (Bagozzi & Fornell, 1982), which allow researchers to examine the relationships between complex variables to obtain a comprehensive picture of the entire model, unlike ordinary multivariate analysis (multiple regression, factor analysis). The weakness of CB-SEM is that the manifest variable (indicator) can only be reflective, which means that the latent variable describes the indicator, and the indicator cannot be formative, where the indicator explains the latent variable. Meanwhile, PLS-SEM can overcome this weakness because in PLS-SEM it is possible to use indicators that are both reflective and formative.

There are several advantages of the SEM method over the OLS method: (1) it allows for more flexible assumptions; (2) the use of confirmatory factor analysis to reduce measurement error by having many indicators in one latent variable; (3) the attractiveness of the graphical modeling interface to make it easier for users to read the output of the analysis results; (4) the possibility of examining the overall model rather than individual coefficients; (5) the ability to test models using several dependent variables; (6) the ability to model against intermediate variables; (7) the ability to create error term models; (8) the ability to test for coefficients outside of multiple subject groups; (9) the ability to handle difficult data, such as time series data with autocorrelation errors, abnormal data, and incomplete data.

However, there are also some disadvantages of the SEM method. For example, first, the use of SEM is strongly influenced by parametric assumptions that must be met; for example, the observed variables have a multivariate normal distribution and observations must be independent of one another. Second, SEM requires that in forming latent variables, the indicators are reflective, according to the actual fact that indicators can be in the form of formative indicator models. In the formative model, indicators are seen as variables that affect latent variables. According to Bollen and Lennox (1991), formative indicators are not in accordance with classical theory or factor analysis models.

Although SEM could be confirmatory and exploratory, SEM procedures seem to be more confirmatory than exploratory. This is due to the use of one of the following approaches. First, the strictly confirmatory approach means that a model is tested using goodness-of-fit tests to determine if the variance and covariance patterns in a data are consistent with the structural path model specifically made by the researcher. Even if other unobserved models fit the data or are even better, the accepted model is only an affirmative model. Second, the alternative models approach means that researchers can test two or more causal models to determine which model is the most suitable. There are many measures of goodness-of-fit tests that reflect different considerations, and researchers typically report only three or four. Third, the model development approach, where in practice, many studies combine confirmatory and exploratory objectives, that is, a model is tested based on suggestions in the SEM modification indices. The problem with this approach is that the model is unstable or will not fit the new data because it was created based on the uniqueness of the original data set. To overcome this, researchers can use a cross-validation strategy in which a model is developed with a calibration data sample and then confirmed using an independent validation sample.

The steps of research using SEM method could be seen in Figure 18.5, comprised of six phases, namely: (1) phase 1 – specification; (2) phase 2 – identification; (3) phase 3 – estimation; (4) phase 4 – fitness test; (5) phase 5 – re-specification; and (6) phase 6 – analysis of results. The more detailed steps of using the SEM method can be seen in Figure 18.5.

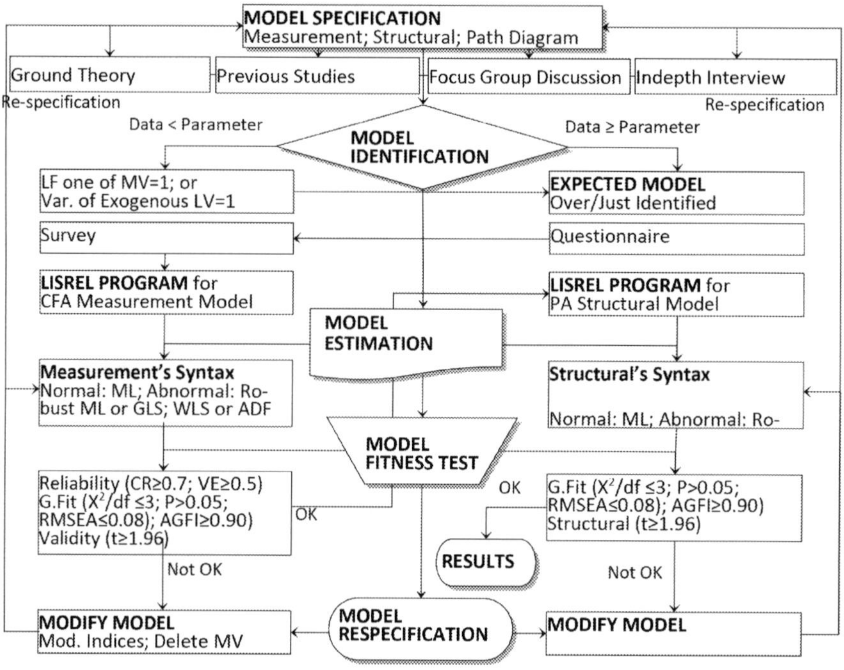

Figure 18.5 Steps of SEM research.

Note: LF: loading factor; SLF: standardized loading factor; MV: measured variables; LV: latent variables; RMSEA: root mean square error of approximation; CR: construct reliability, $CR = (\Sigma SLF)^2/((\Sigma SLF)^2 + \Sigma e_j)$; VE: variance extracted, $VE = \Sigma SLF^2/(\Sigma SLF^2 + \Sigma e_j)$; CFA: confirmatory factor analysis; e_j; measurement error for each indicator or measured variable, $e_j < 0.75$; ML: maximum likelihood; GLS: generalized least square; WLS: weighted least square; MI: modification index; no. of data $= (p + q) \times (p + q + 1)/2$, p = no. of measured variables from all endogenous variables; q = no. of measured variables from all exogenous variables; no. of Parameter $= p + \gamma + \lambda_x + \lambda_y + \theta_\delta + \theta_\varepsilon + \zeta + \Phi$.

Phase 1 – Model specification

Understand the problem or research question in the SEM framework by deepening the related theoretical basis, previous studies, in-depth interviews, and/or focus group discussions with experts. The result is a complete SEM model design (one structural model as well as several measurement models for exogenous and endogenous latent variables) based on a strong theoretical basis and/or robust expert opinion. See for example, Hair *et al.* (1998, 2010).

Phase 2a – Model identification

Test the SEM model design by comparing the number of parameters and the amount of data, to ensure the model is just identified or overidentified (not underidentified). Then, design the SEM questionnaire according to the SEM model design, followed by a survey to a number of respondents who fit the criteria.

The results are: (1) a valid SEM model design; (2) complete SEM questionnaire as many times as needed, which is then compiled to produce SEM data that is ready to be used for estimation. See for example, Hair *et al.* (1998, 2010).

Phase 2b – Survey

Based on the valid SEM model, we develop questionnaires referring to the indicators/manifests used in the measurement models using the Likert scale for each statement representing each indicator. The SEM respondents should at least have some knowledge or understanding on the topic under study. Although the sample size of the SEM depends on the estimation method used, as a rule of thumb it should be between 100 and 200 if we use maximum likelihood estimation method. Another requirement is that the number of sample respondents should be between five and ten times of the number of indicators. See for example, Hair *et al.* (1998, 2010).

Phase 3 – Model estimation

Perform tests of normality assumptions, multicollinearity, and outliers. Then, estimate the SEM model by creating certain computer program syntaxes (LISREL, AMOS, or EQS) with the most appropriate specific method (ML, GLS, or WLS) for measurement models and also structural models (when the measurement model meets the requirements). The results are the test results for normality, multicollinearity, and outliers; result of measurement model; and the results of the structural model (if the measurement model is fit). See for example, Hair *et al.* (1998, 2010).

Phase 4 – Fitness test

Evaluation of the results of the degree of fit or goodness of fit (GOF) from the measurement and structural models includes (a) overall model fit, (b) analysis or fit of the measurement model (measurement model fit), and (c) analysis or structural model fit. The results are the outputs of several goodness of fit indexes, which include: (1) X^2/df; (2) p-value; (3) RMSEA; and (4) AGFI for measurement models and structural models. See, for example, Hair *et al.* (1998, 2010) and Rigdon and Ferguson (1991).

Phase 5a – Model re-specification

When the results of the measurement model are not yet fit, it is necessary to re-specify the measurement model (LISREL has modification indices). Likewise, when the results of the structural model are not yet fit, until optimal results are obtained. The result is a modification of the initial model, which is ready to be re-estimated back to phase 3 and phase 4 to produce a fit model. See for example, Hair *et al.* (1998, 2010) and Rigdon and Ferguson (1991).

Phase 5b – Analysis of results

Analyze the results of measurement models and structural models separately or in an integrated manner, evaluate initial hypotheses, translate the meaning behind the numbers, and compare results with previous studies. The results are critical, in-depth, and complete analyses of the SEM model design under study within a scientific framework.

Analytic network process

Analytic network process or ANP, one of the most important and popular research methods in systems approach and systems thinking, is a multicriteria decision making (MCDM) research method, which changes the qualitative and/or quantitative opinion data input of the relationship (including feedback) between elements/clusters in the ANP model into a quantitative output that represents the priority of the elements within/between clusters. When viewed from the data point of view, ANP is more appropriately classified as a quasi-quantitative method, such as the structural equation modeling (SEM) method.

ANP is a research method developed by Thomas L. Saaty (late) for the first time around the 1970s under the name Analytic Hierarchy Process (AHP), which was recorded in 1980 under the title "Multicriteria Decision Making: The Analytic Hierarchy Process." It was further developed and refined into ANP, which was first recorded in 1996 with the title "Decision Making with Dependence and Feedback," which was subsequently revised in 2001. Saaty continued to make improvements and published in various international journals, and finally published books in 2005 with the titles *Theory and Applications of the Analytic Network Process: Decision Making with Benefits, Opportunities, Costs, and Risks* and *The Encyclicon: a Dictionary of Applications of Decision Making with Dependence and Feedback based on the Analytic Network Process*, volume 1 (2005, co-written with Mujgan S. Ozdemir), volume 2 (2007, co-written with Brady Cillo), volume 3 (2011, written with Luis G. Vargas), until the last book written with Luis G. Vargas in 2006 and revised in 2013 with the title *Decision Making with the Analytic Network Process*.

ANP is a research method with various beneficial characteristics, which is: (1) versatile, because it can be applied in various fields or disciplines; (2) flexible, because the ANP model can be designed almost without limits; (3) effective, because the ANP model can be designed as much as possible; (4) up to date, because it can be used to solve current and future problems; (5) easy to apply, because it does not require many respondents; (6) affordable, because the ANP software, Super Decisions, can be obtained free of charge; (7) scientific, because the processing of input into output must follow a tested mathematical procedure; (8) robust, because the initial data must be consistent and the results can be tested statistically.

ANP is also suitable for research in the field of Islamic economics and finance, because of the nature of the ANP: (1) general, so that there are no certain restrictions that are not in accordance with Sharia; (2) a-theory (does not follow certain theories), so that it can include Islamic economic and financial theories in designing its ANP model; (3) the interdependent relationship between the elements/clusters that form a circular causation is similar to the IIE process-oriented (interactive, integrative, and evolutionary) causal model and continuity proposed by Choudhury and Hoque (2004), which simply means that everything that existed in this universe is a dependent (faqir) creation (makhluq) and only Allah alone is independent as the Creator.

ANP is essentially a general theory of measurement to derive relative priorities on absolute scales, based on discrete and continuous paired comparisons in feedback network structures (Saaty, 2005). ANP is considered as a new approach in the decision-making process, which provides a general framework for treating decisions without making assumptions about dependence of elements in lower levels on elements in higher levels or about independence of elements within the same level. This method presents a number of advantages over other methods of decision-making analysis. In the study aiming to identify a good decision-making method, Peniwati (2005) concluded that the ANP method is relatively superior to other decision-making methods based on a number of different criteria, such as problem abstraction, structure width, structural depth, scientific basis, and validity of the results (see Table 18.2).

ANP requires that the respondents must be consistent in answering the pair-wise comparison questionnaires, with the allowed inconsistency of maximum 10 percent (Saaty, 2005). Nevertheless, ANP does not require significant consensus (such as, Kendall's W rater agreement) among respondents when

Table 18.2 Comparison of decision-making methods

Method	*Scope of problem abstraction*	*Breadth of structure*	*Depth of structure*	*Faithful-ness of judgment analysis*	*Breadth and depth of analysis*	*Scientific and math geneality*	*App. of intangibles*	*Validity of the outcomes*
Analogy	Medium	NA	NA	NA	NA	NA	NA	NA
Brainstorming	Low	NA	NA	NA	NA	NA	NA	NA
Delphi	Medium	Low	Low	Low	Low	Medium	NA	Low
Matrix evaluation	Medium	High	Low	Medium	Medium	Low	Low	Medium
Bayesian analysis	High	Low	Low	Very high	Medium	High	Medium	Medium
AHP	Very high	High	High	Very high	Very high	High	Very high	High
ANP	Very high	High	Very high	Very high	Very high	High	Very high	High

Source: Peniwati (2005), modified by authors.

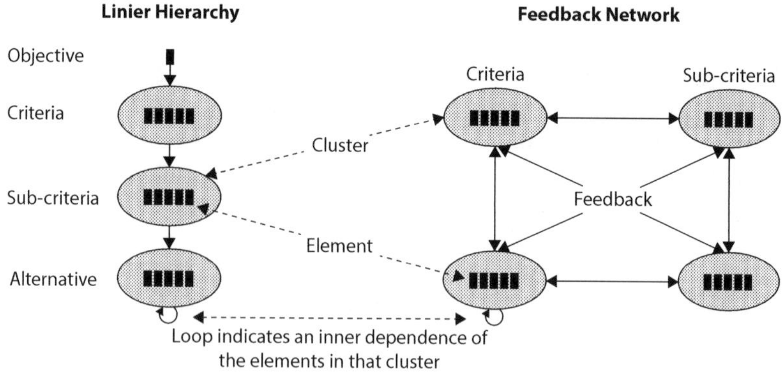

Figure 18.6 Comparison between AHP and ANP structures.

they fill out the questionnaires individually. Furthermore, Figure 18.6 shows the comparison between AHP and ANP structures.

The main advantages of ANP method are in terms of its ability to consider dependent and feedback factors systematically, as well as in accommodating quantitative and qualitative factors. The linkage between criteria in the ANP method is of two types, namely the relation in a set of clusters (inner dependence) and the interrelationship between different clusters (outer dependence). There are three basic principles of AHP/ANP, namely decomposition, comparative judgments, and hierarchical composition or synthesis of priorities (Saaty, 1996). The principle of decomposition is applied to structure complex problems in a hierarchical framework or network of clusters, sub-clusters, sub-sub-clusters, and so on. In other words, decomposition is modeling the problem into the AHP/ANP framework. The principle of comparative assessment is applied to construct pairwise comparisons of all combinations of elements in the cluster as seen from the parent cluster. This pair comparison is used to get the local priority of elements in a cluster as seen from the parent cluster. The principle of hierarchical composition or synthesis is applied to multiply the local priority of elements in a cluster by the "global" priority of the parent element, which will generate global priority of the entire hierarchy and add them to produce global priority for the lowest-level element (usually an alternative).

Based on the above basic principles, the procedure in using the ANP method for research in IEF can be seen in Figure 18.7 comprising three main phases, namely: (1) phase 1 – model construction; (2) phase 2 – model quantification; and (3) phase 3 – results analysis.

Phase-1 is knowledge acquirement intended to gather information and knowledge needed for this study, including: (1) literature review; (2) focus group discussion (FGD); and (3) in-depth interview. There are two types of literature, namely scientific literature from journals and textbooks, and general literature from articles, books, data, and news. This knowledge and information will be used as the basis to conduct small FGD and in-depth

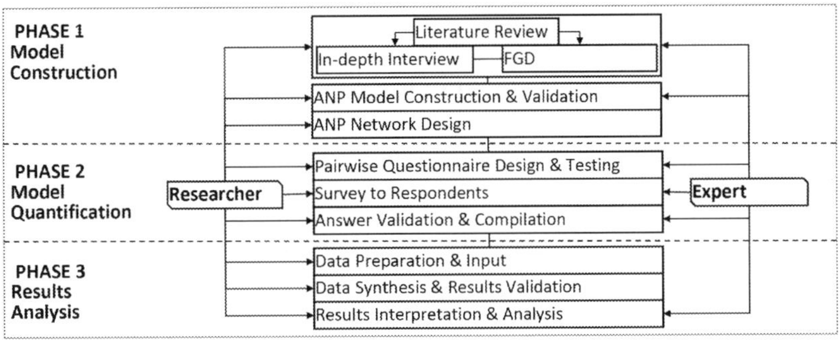

Figure 18.7 Steps of ANP research.

interviews with experts, including academicians, regulators, and practitioners. All of this knowledge will be used to develop the summary of the research problem, construct the ANP model, and design the ANP network with Super Decisions software. The draft of the ANP model needs to be validated by the experts before it can be applied further.

Phase-2 is ANP model quantification to evaluate proposed models, including: (1) designing the ANP pairwise questionnaire based on the ANP network; (2) testing the pairwise questionnaire to make sure of its validity and workability; and (3) surveying expert respondents to fill out the pairwise questionnaire to acquire knowledge from the expert respondents, while maintaining the consistency of their responses. Pairwise comparison uses the fundamental scale of values to represent the intensities of judgments shown in Table 18.3.

Table 18.3 Pairwise comparison fundamental scale of absolute numbers

Intensity of importance	*Definition*	*Explanation*
1	Equal importance	Two activities contribute equally to the objective
2	Weak	
3	Moderate importance	Experience and judgment slightly favor one activity over another
4	Moderate plus	
5	Strong importance	Experience and judgment strongly favor one activity over another
6	Strong plus	
7	Very strong or demonstrated importance	An activity is favored very strongly over another; its dominance demonstrated in practice
8	Very, very strong	
9	Extreme importance	The evidence favoring one activity over another is of the highest possible order of affirmation

Source: Saaty and Vargas (2006).

Phase-3 is ANP results analysis, starting with data preparation and input to mine the data obtained, to input the data to Super Decisions software, to check the consistency again, and to synthesize the whole ANP network producing ANP results. Subsequently, these results need to be validated by the expert respondents and to find the meanings and interpretations behind the numbers. Finally, results are presented, which include the robustness tests and the analysis, to arrive at the recommendations from the study.

The data required for the study using ANP method is primary data obtained from knowledgeable respondents, including experts (academicians, regulators, and observers) and practitioners. Experts usually have ideal/normative views, while practitioners usually have pragmatic views.

Saaty (2005) stated that the ANP method required one FGD. The number of respondents per FGD could range from 3 to 21 respondents with a median of 10 respondents (Nyumba *et al.*, 2018), while Dilshad and Latif (2013) asserted that one FGD needs 6–12 knowledgeable respondents. In addition, 6–8 participants are considered sufficient (Nyumba *et al.*, 2018), while for small FGD it could include only 3–5 persons (Rabiee, 2004). Therefore, if there are plenty of knowledgeable people in the topic under study, it would be better for us to select 6–12 experts and 6–12 practitioners as respondents.

Agent-based modeling

Agent-based computational modeling or ABM is a computational research method that is difficult to study without computer support and is used in studies on complex issues. ABM emerged as a result of studies that were generated in the era of complexity in economics to model interactions of agents (Schinckus, 2019). The arrival of personal computers in the 1980s and early 1990s facilitated ABM to become the most widely used tool to capture the economic complexity based on computerized simulations of interactions of heterogeneous agents, which are endowed with different characteristics that enable them to act under different circumstances (Hamill & Gilbert, 2015; Schinckus, 2019).

A complex system is composed of interacting units and exhibits emergent properties, which is called emergent phenomena in ABM literature. The new paradigm for building macroeconomic models is complexity and ABM is a tool to analyze emergent phenomena (Gatti, Gaffeo, & Gallegati, 2010). In ABM, agents are objects and different agents can implement different rules when they interact with each other. The agents might represent biological organisms, social groupings, asset management firms, or banks, and the dynamic system in which they interact will allow macroscopic behavior to emerge from microscopic rules. These simple rules at the micro-level may lead to complexity at the macro-level that is observable and measurable (Al-Suwailem, 2008; Bookstaber, 2012;). Therefore, ABM is practical for studying problems from the bottom up rather than through rules imposed from the top down. Other than the knowledge of the discipline in which ABM is being applied, knowledge of mathematics, statistics, and computer science is needed to build an agent-based model (Turrell, 2016).

ABM is used in a wide range of fields and is called by different names in different disciplines, such as Monte Carlo simulations in the physical sciences, individual-based models in biology and ecology, and multi-agent systems in computer science and logistics. ABM is useful in policy implications and decision-making, especially in the fields of economics, finance, political science, education, and management science (Al-Suwailem, 2008; Turrell, 2016). During the 1990s, scientists mainly coming from physics or biology began to implement their agent-based methods to economic systems. Accordingly, "econophysics" refers to the importation of physical models into economics, while "econobiology" refers to the biological-based interpretation of economic systems (Schinckus, 2019).

ABM is sometimes referred to as agent-based computational economics (ACE) in the context of economics (Hamill & Gilbert, 2015). In ACE, the initial state of an economic system is defined by the modeler by specifying each agent's initial data, which might include its type attributes, structural attributes, and information about the attributes of other agents. For instance, type attributes may include bank, market, and consumer; structural attributes may include cost function and consumption function. On the other hand, Hamill and Gilbert (2015) put agents' characteristics under four headings: perception, performance, memory, and policy. In short, agents can see other agents in their environment, can move and communicate, can recall their past states, and can have rules that determine their next actions.

The bottom-up approach of ABM contrasts with the top-down approach of neoclassical models (especially dynamic stochastic general equilibrium [DSGE] models) that are based on a neoclassical microeconomic foundation) in which a representative agent is constrained by strong assumptions associated with equilibrium, rationality, and the regularity conditions (Bookstaber, 2012). The representative agent approach rules out the possibility of the analysis of complex interactions. In ABM, individual actions of the agents combine to produce emergent phenomena (behavior), that is, statistical regularities arising from the interactions of individuals that cannot be inferred from the properties of individuals (Stiglitz & Gallegati, 2011). Adam Smith's metaphor of the invisible hand is a good example for emergent phenomena, as interactions of real agents in the economy, whose actions are aimed at satisfying individual needs and attaining individual objectives, combine to produce socially optimal outcomes and this can be examined in ABM (Gatti *et al.*, 2010; Turrell, 2016).

Islamic economics, as stated by Al-Suwailem (2008), is the study of Islamic principles concerning economic behavior. Neoclassical models concern with equilibrium states and ignore moral values and social aspects. Islamic principles are equally concerned with the process and the final states (Al-Suwailem, 2008). In agent-based models, equilibrium is neither assumed nor imposed by the modeler since ABM allows for the market behavior to emerge as a result of the interactions of agents (Gatti *et al.*, 2010). The assumption of rationality is absent in agent-based models where agents' actions are based on behavioral heuristics when making decisions, that is, agents have bounded rationality. The environment of economic agents is too complex for rationality and people often use heuristics when making decisions. ABM allows for generating realistic behavior based on observed behavior (Bookstaber, 2012; Turrell, 2016). Moreover, in agent-based models, agents do not have rational expectations since they do not know how the entire system wherein they operate works (Napoletano, Gaffard, & Babutsidze, 2012).

ABM overcomes the drawbacks aroused from the representative agent paradigm by introducing heterogeneity of agents' characteristics and behavior (Napoletano *et al.*, 2012). Heterogeneous agents have different rules and heuristics, endowments, and objectives which enable agent-based models to incorporate gaming behavior and informational asymmetries (Bookstaber, 2012). ABM is a perfect tool to incorporate a large degree of heterogeneity in models for much richer behavior (Chan-Lau, 2017). On the other hand, contrary to the assumption of DSGE models that mistakes are not repeated, in agent-based models agents can be programmed to correct their behavior following a mistake (Hamill & Gilbert, 2015).

The flexibility of ABM is another benefit over other modeling techniques. It is easy to add more agents and tune the complexity of them by changing their properties, and also easy to change levels of description coexisting in a given model (Bonabeau, 2002). The flexibility of ABM allows for exploring a large number of possibilities efficiently by applying probabilistic rules to each agent to explore alternative scenarios (Turrell, 2016).

Figure 18.8 shows the main steps to build an agent-based model. The process starts with setting the research question and collecting relevant data and information about the real system to identify the causal mechanisms that are likely to be significant in the model. Since this would be a model of the real

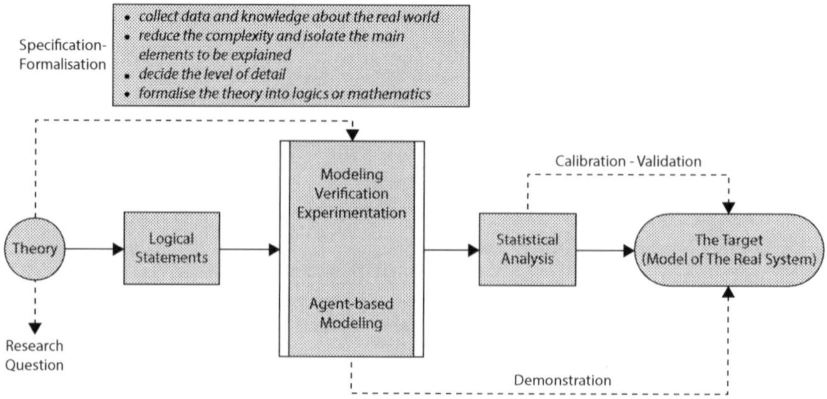

Figure 18.8 Steps of ABM research.

world to explain a phenomenon, the main elements need to be isolated by removing some processes and elements. After formalizing the theory into logics or mathematics or expressing it in a procedural form, the formalized model can be coded/programmed. Verification is a difficult process in ABM since simulations include random number generators and every simulation run is different. This can be tackled by running multiple experiments using a set of test cases. If the model can generate the type of outcome to be explained, it means the computational demonstration is sufficient to generate the macro-structure of interest. For the model to be considered valid, the acceptable extent of the difference between the real and simulated data should be decided by the modeler, which can be done using some statistical analysis (Salgado & Gilbert, 2013).

As well as its benefits, ABM has some drawbacks. An agent-based cannot work if it's built for general purpose; however, it should be built to serve a purpose at the right level of description and detail to serve its purpose (Bonabeau, 2002). Therefore, it is difficult to find answers from a model that tells how bonds are traded for questions about the housing market (Turrell, 2016).

Another drawback concerns the huge range of behavioral rules available for agents in ABM. This gives a lot of freedom to the modeler and can make the model vulnerable to the Lucas critique. This critique points out the fact that policy changes would change how people behave in a way that may not follow historically observed relationships, which would also change the structure being modeled. Therefore, the model would not be useful for policy evaluation (Hamill & Gilbert, 2015; Napoletano *et al.,* 2012; Turrell, 2016).

Modeling with ABM in the social sciences often involves human behavior that can be irrational and complex, which is difficult to quantify, calibrate, and justify (Bonabeau, 2002). An agent-based model can be adjusted to fit the real-world facts by initializing it with empirical data, which is called calibration. Analytical investigation of agent-based models is limited and generally many computer simulations can be needed to analyze them. One can come up with different simulation results because of the randomness issue, which makes it difficult to analyze and validate the results of the simulations (Napoletano *et al.*, 2012).

Building dynamically complete economic models in ABM requires the modeler not to make any further intervention once the initial conditions are set. Therefore, all details about agents' properties and attributes should be specified at the initial stage. In order to achieve robust predictions, intensive experimentation needs to be conducted over a huge variation of initial specifications. This would be computation-intensive and time-consuming. For such large models, this high computational requirement of ABM is a significant matter (Bonabeau, 2002).

Economic and financial modeling needs a new paradigm, which became apparent after the global financial crisis. As recognized by the former president of the European Central Bank, Jean-Claude Trichet, the crisis made it apparent that existing economic and financial models have serious limitations.

They failed to predict the crisis and were incapable of explaining convincingly what was happening in the economy. Trichet emphasizes the need to better deal with the interaction among those heterogeneous agents, which makes ABM a worthy approach for attention (Trichet, 2010).

References

Achsani, N.A., Holtemöller, O., & Sofyan, H. (2005). Econometric and Fuzzy Modelling of Indonesian Money Demand. In Cizek, P., Wolfgang, H., & Rafal, W. (Eds.). *Statistical Tools for Finance and Insurance*. Berlin & Heidelberg, Germany: Springer-Verlag.

Al-Suwailem, S. (2008). *Islamic Economics in a Complex World*. Jeddah, Saudi Arabia: Islamic Development Bank.

Amisano, G., & Giannini, C. (1997). *Topics in Structural VAR Econometrics* (2nd Ed.). New York: Springer.

Ascarya, A., Rahmawati, S., Sukmana, R., & Masrifah, A.R. (2021). Developing Cash Waqf Models for Integrated Islamic Social and Commercial Microfinance. *Journal of Islamic Accounting and Business Research*, forthcoming.

Ascarya, A., & Sakti, A. (2021). Designing Micro-fintech Models for Islamic Micro Financial Institution in Indonesia. *International Journal of Islamic and Middle Eastern Finance and Management*, forthcoming.

Asteriou, D., & Hall, S.G. (2011). Vector Autoregressive (VAR) Models and Causality Tests. *Applied Econometrics* (2nd ed.). London: Palgrave MacMillan, pp. 319–333.

Bagozzi, R.P., & Fornell, C. (1982). Theoretical Concepts, Measurements, and Meaning. In Fornel, C. (Ed.). *A Second Generation of Multivariate Analysis, Vol. II: Measurement and Evaluation*. New York, NY: Praeger.

Barr, J.M., Tassier, T., & Ussher, L. (2011). Introduction to the Symposium on Agent-based Computational Economics. *Eastern Economic Journal*, *37*(1), 1–5.

Bollen, K., & Lennox, R. (1991). Conventional Wisdom on Measurement: A Structural Equation Perspective. *Psychological Bulletin*, *110*(2), 305–314.

Bonabeau, E. (2002). Agent-based Modeling: Methods and Techniques for Simulating Human Systems. *Proceedings of the National Academy of Sciences*, *99*(Supplement 3), 7280–7287.

Bookstaber, R. (2012). *Using Agent-Based Models for Analyzing Threats to Financial Stability* (No. 3).

Chan-Lau, J. A. (2017). *ABBA: An Agent-Based Model of the Banking System* (No. WP17/136).

Choudhury, M.A., & Hoque, M.Z. (2004). *An Advanced Exposition of Islamic Economics and Finance*. New York: Edwin Mellen Press.

Choudhury, M.A., & Korvin, G. (2002). Simulation versus Optimization in Knowledge-Induced Fields. *Kybernetes*, 31(1), 44–60.

Dilshad, R.M., & Latif, M.I. (2013). Focus Group Interview as a Tool for Qualitative Research: An Analysis. *Pakistan Journal of Social Sciences (PJSS)*, *33*(1), 191–198.

Enders, W. (2015). *Applied Econometrics Time Series* (4th Ed.). Danvers, MA: John Wiley & Sons.

Gatti, D. D., Gaffeo, E., & Gallegati, M. (2010). Complex Agent-based Macroeconomics: A Manifesto for a New Paradigm. *Journal of Economic Interaction and Coordination*, *5*(2), 111–135.

Gujarati, D.N. 2004. *Basic Econometrics* (4th Ed.). New York, NY: McGraw-Hill.

Hair Jr., J.F., Black, W.C., Babin, B.J., & Anderson, R.E. (2010). *Multivariate Data Analysis* (7th Ed.). London, UK: Pearson Education.

Hair, J.F., Ringle, C.M., & Sarstedt, M. (2011) PLS-SEM: Indeed a Silver Bullet. *Journal of Marketing Theory and Practice, 19*(2), 139–152.

Hair Jr, J.F., Sarstedt, M., Hopkins, L., & Kuppelwieser, V. G. (2014). Partial Least Squares Structural Equation Modeling (PLS-SEM). *European Business Review, 26*(2), 106–121.

Hair Jr, J.F., Matthews, L.M., Matthews, R.L., & Sarstedt, M. (2017). PLS-SEM or CB-SEM: Updated Guidelines on which Method to Use. *International Journal of Multivariate Data Analysis, 1*(2), 107–123.

Hamill, L., & Gilbert, N. (2015). *Agent-Based Modelling in Economics* (1st Ed.). Hoboken, NJ: John Wiley & Sons, Ltd.

Jöreskog, K. (1973). A General Method for Estimating a Linear Structural Equation System. In A.S. Goldberger and O.D. Duncan (Eds.). *Structural Equation Models in the Social Sciences*. New York, pp. 85–112.

Keesling, J.W. (1973). *Maximum Likelihood Approaches to Causal Flow Analysis*. Dissertation. Chicago: University of Chicago.

Lütkepohl, H. (2006). *New Introduction to Multiple Time Series Analysis*. Berlin and Heidelberg: Springer.

Napoletano, M., Gaffard, J.-L., & Babutsidze, Z. (2012). *Agent Based Models: A New Tool for Economic and Policy Analysis* (No. 3). https://hal-sciencespo.archives-ouvertes.fr/hal-01070338/document

Nyumba, T.O., Wilson, K., Derrick, C.J., & Mukherjee, N. (2018). The Use of Focus Group Discussion Methodology: Insights from Two Decades of Application in Conservation. *Methods in Ecology and Evolution, 9*, 20–32.

Qin, D. (2011). Rise of VAR Modelling Approach. *Journal of Economic Surveys, 25*(1), 156–174.

Rabiee, F. (2004). Focus-group Interview and Data Analysis. *Proceedings of the Nutrition Society, 63*, 650–655.

Reda, A. (2012). A Response to Masudul Alam Choudhury. In Biddle, J.E. & Emmett, R.B. (Ed.) *Research in the History of Economic Thought and Methodology: A Research Annual* (Vol. 30, Part 1). Bingley: Emerald Group Publishing Limited, pp. 101–109.

Rigdon, E.E. and Ferguson, C.E. (1991). The Performance of the Polychoric Correlation Coefficient and Selected Fitting Functions in Confirmatory Factor Analysis with Ordinal Data. *Journal of Marketing Research, 28*, 491–497.

Saaty, T.L. (1996). *Decision Making with Dependence and Feedback: The Analytic Network Process*. Pittsburgh, PA: RWS Publications.

Saaty, T.L. (2004). Fundamentals of the Analytic Network Process – Dependence and Feedback in Decision-making with a Single Network. *Journal of Systems Science and Systems Engineering, 13*(2), 129–157.

Saaty, T.L. (2005), *Theory and Applications of the Analytic Network Process, Decision Making with Benefits, Opportunities, Costs and Risks*. Pittsburgh, PA: RWS Publications.

Saaty, T.L. (2008). The Analytic Hierarchy and Analytic Network Measurement Processes: Applications to Decisions under Risk. *European Journal of Pure and Applied Mathematics, 1*(1), 122–196.

Saaty, T.L., & Cillo, B. (2007). *The Encyclicon: a Dictionary of Applications of Decision Making with Dependence and Feedback based on the Analytic Network Process*. (Vol. 2). Pittsburgh, PA: RWS Publications.

Saaty, T.L., & Ozdemir, M.S. (2005). *The Encyclicon: a Dictionary of Applications of Decision Making with Dependence and Feedback Based on the Analytic Network Process* (Vol. 1). Pittsburgh, PA: RWS Publications.

Sakti, A., Husodo, Z.A., & Viverita, V. (2019). The Orientation of Microfinance Regarding Group-Lending Strategy: Delphi and Analytic Network Process Evidence. *Pertanika Journal of Social Sciences & Humanities*, 27(S2), 197–212.

Salgado, M., & Gilbert, N. (2013). Agent Based Modeling. In T. Teo (Ed.). *Handbook of Quantitative Methods for Educational Research*. Rotterdam, the Netherlands: Sense Publishers, pp. 247–265.

Schinckus, C. (2019). Agent-based Modelling and Economic Complexity: A Diversified Perspective. *Journal of Asian Business and Economic Studies*, *26*(2), 170–188.

Sims, C.A. (1980). Macroeconomics and Reality. *Econometrica*, *48*(1), 1–48.

Stiglitz, J., & Gallegati, M. (2011). Heterogeneous Interacting Agent Models for Understanding Monetary Economies. *Eastern Econ Journal*, *37*, 6–12.

Trichet, J-C. (2010) *Reflections on the nature of monetary policy non-standard measures and finance theory*. Speech by President of the ECB, Opening address at the ECB Central Banking Conference Frankfurt, 18 November 2010.

Turrell, A. (2016). Agent-based Models: Understanding the Economy from the Bottom Up. *Bank of England Quarterly Bulletin*, (Q4), 173–188. http://www2.econ.iastate.edu/tesfatsi/ABMOverview.BankOfEngland.ATurrell2017.pdf

19

ACCEPTABLE METHODOLOGY RECOMMENDED FOR RESEARCH IN ISLAMIC FINANCE

Fauzia Mubarik and Sadia Saeed

Introduction

In the nineteenth century, the struggle of Islamic finance to strengthen its footing in the well-established conventional finance industry paved the ways to sustain it in the existing world through research and development. The rise of research in Islamic finance helped to identify the appropriate methodologies needed to theologically and scientifically apply it in modern-day economics. Islam is an ideology that provides a framework influencing cultural, social, political, monetary, and economic aspects of life. Hence, Islamic finance is one of the constituents of this ideology that developed the Islamic monetary system in the country.

Issues and challenges in research of Islamic finance

The interdict of interest in Islam has actually given vogue to the Islamic financial institutions in the recent past. There is a remarkable growth in Islamic finance, but research and development in Islamic finance is still in the emergent phase and faces certain challenges in context of risk, stability, and effectiveness (Haseeb and Alam, 2018). Nevertheless, the researchers' keen interest to explore, identify, and differentiate the principles of Islamic finance has contributed to the existing literature, such as the sustainability of the separate accounting standards for the Islamic banking system (Mohammed, 2018); overcoming technical, legal, and social hindrances in the penetration of Islamic products within the economy (Gherbi, 2018); and in particular bridging the gap between Islamic finance theories and the conventional business research models (Olorogun, 2018), respectively.

The striking feature that differs Islamic finance from conventional finance is the principle of profit and loss sharing, because Islamic banks share 100% loss with their clients, which is contrary to the principle of conventional finance. This is the most relevant point that has always encouraged the researchers of Islamic finance to empirically model, analyze, and evaluate the robustness of the

DOI: 10.4324/9781003252764-23

Islamic finance theories and models in the existing literature. The traditional way to conduct Islamic finance research is encouraged through ijtihad based on the classifications of revealed and derived sources of Islamic law, where the revealed revelation is Shariah that tends to act as the primary source of Islamic law (Ahmed, 2012) based on which the whole Islamic finance industry functions.

The objective of Islamic finance investment is to function in compliance with Shariah by imposing certain restrictions on the products that cannot be included in the portfolio of assets, and it is clear in its stance of the exclusion of the assets that are prohibited in light of Quran and Sunnah, such as the stocks of those companies that indulge in alcohol, pork, pornography, tobacco, gambling, and any other product or activity that has been declared haram in Islam.

Islamic instruments and models

Before explaining the most readily used methodologies in the field of Islamic finance, some of the Islamic instruments (models) are explained below.

Takaful

Takaful, or Islamic insurance, is one of the services provided in Islamic finance. Insurance in Islamic finance is different compared to conventional insurance. Islamic insurance requires mutual cooperation from their clients instead of direct selling of products for protection and prevention. Takaful is an Islamic tool in the insurance field to mitigate risk based upon two factors: mutual cooperation, known as Tabarru, and the separation of stockholder's funds from participant's funds.

Qualitative methodology is used for examining the compatibility of Shariah-compliant models in Islamic insurance. Factors including market efficiency, operational efficiency, governance, reliability, innovation, and regulatory policies are considered for measuring the operationalization of Islamic insurance models in research (Olorogun, 2018).

Wakalah insurance model

In this model, principal-agent relationship exists between financial insurers and participants. The insurer is an agent and is authorized to manage the funds of participants. Agents decide the level of contribution and eligibility criteria for selecting participants. In case of damage or loss, the insurer decides the amount of payment to be given to the participant. If an insurer finds a deficiency in pool funds, he may ask for an additional contribution from the participant and may take legal action under accounting and auditing organizations for Islamic financial institutions (AAOIFI) against the refusals. The insurer is entitled to a commission in the form of an agency fee for the services provided. The Wakalah model is the most acceptable and operational model in the field of research on Islamic insurance.

Mudharabah investment model

In the Mudharabah investment model, a partnership relationship exists between the insurer and participant. Insurers act as entrepreneurs and participants are the capital providers for investment. The insurer decides the amount of investment, type of investment, allocation of funds, and sole operator of revenues of investment. The profit and loss ratio is determined with the consent of partners. In case of loss without the negligence of the entrepreneur, the participant has to bear it. On the other hand, an insurer is responsible for the entire loss if it occurs due to his negligence.

Wakalah Mudharabah model

This is a combination of agency and investment models. Wakalah is designed for the underwriting field whereas Mudharabah is workable for investment purposes. The insurer provides his expertise for investment. Moreover, he is entitled to manage the funds on behalf of participants and receive performance fees. The liabilities and revenues are divided between parties based on the agreed ratio after deducting performance fees.

Waqf model

Initially, the Waqf fund was initiated by the insurer using donations. It is followed by contributions of participants (see Figure 19.1) who agree to relinquish a certain amount as Waqf money. Waqf money along with Islamic insurance funds are invested in Shariah-compliant products. After deducting performance fees of managing Waqf, profit is sent back to the Waqf program.

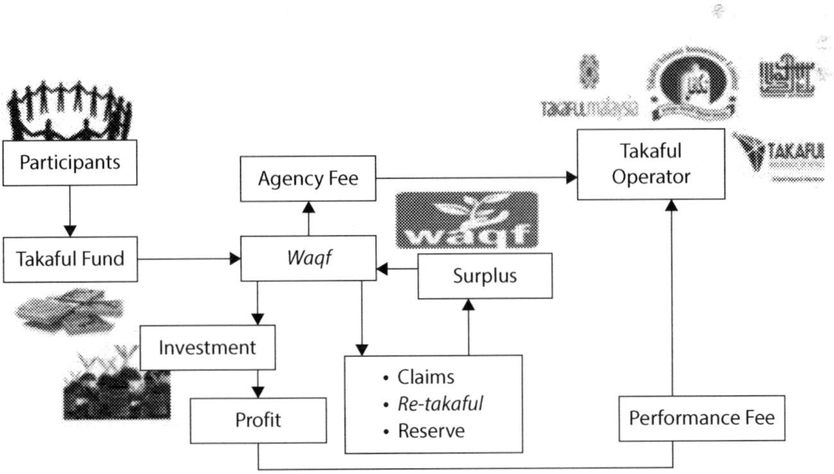

Figure 19.1 Waqf model.

Source: ISRA (2013).

The accumulated amount of Waqf is given to the participants in case of misfortune or loss. The surplus in Waqf may also be used for claims regarding takaful and reserves.

Islamic finance and research methodologies

Despite all the loopholes and the existing problems, different practitioners have endeavored to suggest various methodologies that are readily used in the application of Islamic finance as described below.

Credit scoring model

The credit scoring model usually uses an accessing tool to evaluate the creditworthiness of customers in conventional banking. In light of Islamic banking and finance, Abdou *et al.*, (2014) wrote that the credit scoring model is comprised of two parts: credit and scoring. The word credit refers to buy now and make payments later. Scoring is the ranking of customers in terms of their regular payment. Based on scoring, clients are classified as good customers and bad customers. Good customers make regular payments on time and bad customers fail to make payments regularly in time. The present study advocates that the credit scoring model may be considered as the best model for Islamic banking as a rationale for extending credit to the clients, because of its quality of offering transparency and certainty in the business-client relationship, as well as the demographic and loan-specific information of clients, respectively. This model tends to contain empirical strength to apply statistical techniques such as discriminant analysis, neural networks, and logistic regression, respectively.

Discriminant analysis is used to classify the applications as being accepted or rejected based on the social and economic differences of clients. Prehistoric data of clients are evaluated in the discriminant analysis, which would be otherwise complex and time-consuming if it is done manually. The equation used in discriminant analysis is:

$$Z = \alpha + \beta_1 X_1 + \beta_1 X_1 + \cdots + \beta_n X_n$$

where X variable indicates the independent variables.

It is a technique that classifies the sample (independent variables) into linear compositions of two or more groups. It is assumed that the independent variables tends to possess normal distribution with common covariance but different means among the groups (classes) (Al-Osaimy and Bamakhramah, 2004).

Neural network

The neural network is used to analyze the complex relationship among variables. The model is a network of connected nodes. The layers included in the model are input, hidden, and output. The input layer is comprised of

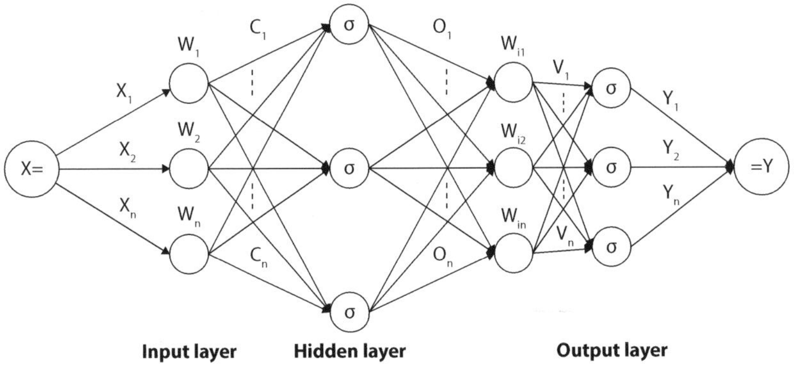

Figure 19.2 Neural network.

predictor variables that give values to the neurons of the hidden layer. After assigning weights to hidden variables, the transfer function is applied to generate the output value. The model is built for accuracy in the prediction of accepted and rejected applications of credit in Islamic finance. The diagrammatic representation of the neural network is shown in Figure 19.2.

Figure 19.2 explains the neural network patterns of the time series data. It is the most recent empirically tested methodology to model and analyze any form of time series data. It is based on four steps of collection and prehandling of the data patterns, identification of neural network structure and architecture, forecastability, and lastly, validation.

Logistic regression

Logistic regression is designed to investigate someone for giving credit or not. It is one of the statistical techniques that use categorical values. The persons falling in the category of 0 are rejected to for a loan because they fail to repay the loan back. On the other hand, persons who are categorized as 1 are selected for a loan. The formula of logistic regression can be written as:

$$Log\left[\frac{p}{(1-p)}\right] = \alpha + \beta_1 X_1 + \beta_1 X_1 + \cdots + \beta_n X_n$$

where the above equation depicts the strong association between the independent variables based on logistic regression.

CAMELS system

Ledhem and Mekidiche (2020) suggested another methodology, the CAMELS system, to investigate the financial performance of Islamic finance and economic growth. CAMELS is an acronym for six parameters: capital adequacy, asset quality, management efficiency, earnings, liquidity, and sensitivity to market risk. The CAMELS approach is an extension of the CAMEL model that includes both systematic and unsystematic determinants for examining the performance and stability of Islamic financial Institutions. The first five factors – the adequacy of capital, quality of assets, the efficiency of management, income, and liquidity – are unsystematic. The last factor is the sensitivity to market risk. This is a systematic component of the model that encounters the risk of the organization. The parameters of the CAMELS system along with their formulas are illustrated in Table 19.1.

The CAMELS approach can easily be analyzed by applying panel regression statistical techniques, including panel regression with fixed, random effect and generalized method of moment (GMM). The estimation is biased using

Table 19.1 The CAMELS system

CAMELS parameters	*Operational definitions used in research of Islamic finance*	*Formulas*
Capital Adequacy Ratio (C)	It is a capital to risk ratio. It is calculated to know that capital is adequate to protect the amount deposited in the bank. The ability of the bank to respond to credit and operational risk	CAR% = Total regulated capital Risk-weighted assets
Asset Quality (A)	It indicates the instability of bank assets due to non-performing loans	AQ = Gross non-performing loan Gross financing
Management Efficiency (M)	It depicts the efficiency of management in reducing costs to increase profit to avoid bank failures	M E = Operating costs Gross profit
Earnings (E)	Earning is the performance indicator and its contribution to generating funds for the company internally	Net profit Margin = Net income Gross income Return on assets = Net income Total assets Return on equity = Net income Shareholders' equity
Liquidity (L)	Liquidity reveals that the bank can reimburse its short-term obligations	Liquidity = Liquid assets Total assets
Sensitivity to Market risk (S)	It demonstrates the effect of market risk, including interest rate risk, foreign exchange risk, and inflation rate risk, on assets, liabilities, and net worth of bank	Sensitivity = Net foreign exchange open position Total capital (regulated)

regression with fixed and random effects in panel data sets because these models neglect endogeneity, individual effects, and the covariance between lagged variables and regressors. Rubi developed three-factor Fama and French models on the Malaysian Stock Market Index intrigued from the concept of Fama-French model. To test the validity and applicability of the Fama-French model in the Malaysian market, the author employed GMM. The GMM technique showed robust results over ordinary least squares (OLS) method of the FF model to test on the Islamic market equities in the case of Malaysia.

Therefore, the most appropriate statistical technique to employ for the analysis of CAMELS approach is GMM, because it takes into account all the neglected components in panel regression (Roodman, 2009).

Islamic fin-tech model

Fin-tech is the combination of two words, "finance" and "technology." Technology and mobile devices are used for the notification of bank transactions and debit/credit account balances. Short messages services are used to convey information relating to debit and credit alerts. Islamic fin-tech gained more popularity during the coronavirus pandemic, and the fin-tech investments increased from $2.9 billion to $80.1 billion in 2019 globally (Ahmad & Al Mamun, 2020) as depicted in Figure 19.3.

The research on Islamic fin-tech in Islamic finance is still at its infancy stage but poses lot of potential theoretical contributions to the existing literature, especially in this era of pandemic. Islamic fin-tech is the technology application in Islamic financial activities, such as investment, lending, hedging, and wealth management based on Shariah guidelines. Basically, the Shariah guidelines compliant with Islamic financial products include risk sharing, profit and loss sharing, exclusion of interest from an investor's return, enforcement upon equity investment rather than debt instruments, and focus on social and economic justice in the Islamic financial system, respectively.

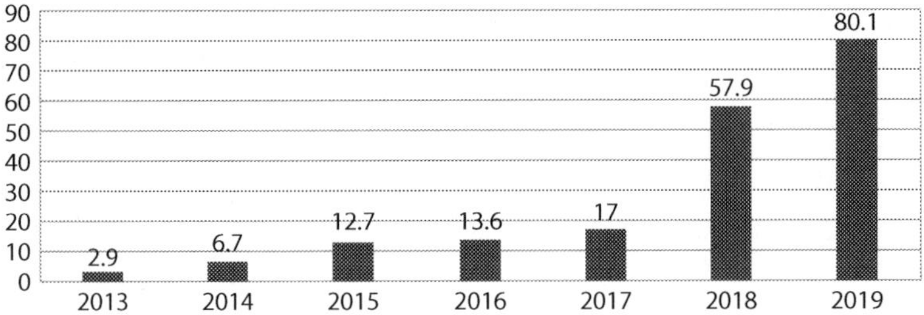

Figure 19.3 Global fintech investments (billion dollar).

Source: The Global Islamic Fin-tech Report (2019)/The UK Islamic Fin-tech Panel (Salaam Gateway).

Technologies including artificial intelligence, big data analytics, quantum computing, mobile payment, open banking, P2P finance, blockchain (distributed ledgers), cloud adoption, and cyber-security are embedded in Islamic fin-tech to provide Islamic banking services to customers, including consumers, businesses, and financial institutions. Therefore, some of the technologies are explained below that could empirically contribute to the existing literature.

Artificial intelligence

Artificial intelligence introduces machines to interact with banking activities and respond to the big data of banks in an intelligent manner. Machines are created and trained that give them the ability to perform a task instead of than humans using machines for performing bank tasks. The best example of artificial intelligence is robots that detect scam transactions and money laundering activities in Islamic finance.

Big data analytics

Big data is the huge amount of unstructured and high-dimensional data continuously produced, saved, and used at high speed. Big data analytics is the analysis of massive data stored in a server and can easily be assessed with one click for Islamic banking transactions.[1]

Quantum computing

Special computers are designed to apply quantum theory principles. These computers have more processing power to solve complex problems quickly, appropriately, and efficiently as compared to conventional computers. Moreover, quantum computing transfers the data safely and secures the saved data to avoid fraudulent transactions.

Blockchain

A blockchain is an information source. It is in the form of a database. A large amount of information regarding Islamic finance transactions and Islamic business activities is stored in it. Bank clients or potential customers have access to this data. This data is available in a specific format, and filtering of specific information can easily be derived from this database. The data chain is termed a ledger and this ledger is disseminated to a server for decentralization.

Cloud adoption

This is a strategy related to the use of the cloud, comprised of software and services required for operating the internet-based database efficiently. The cloud of system software is adopted in Islamic fin-tech to minimize risk and cost (Figure 19.4).

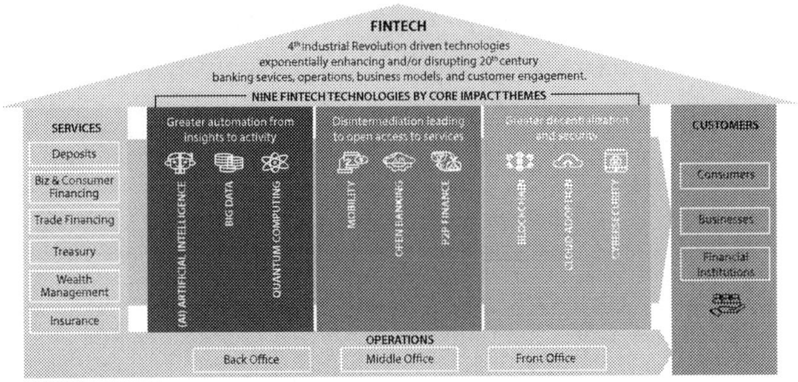

Figure 19.4 Fourth Industrial Revolution-driven technologies.

Source: Islamic Fin-tech Report (2018).

The development of an Islamic index comprising of Shariah-compliant stocks can add another complement in the existing finance industry to investigate the behavior of investors regarding Islamic equity investment (Bordoloi et al., 2020), but the problem remains the same, that is, of recognition, sustainability, and policy implications.

Conclusion

The present study attempts to provide an insight about the most appropriate methodologies that could be employed to empirically explore, model, analyze, and evaluate the Islamic finance theories and models, respectively. Firstly, the authors endeavored to explain the issues and challenges being faced by the Islamic finance industry in the existing global financial industry. Next, some light is laid on the existing Islamic models and their functions. Lastly, to promote, contribute, and enhance the existing Islamic finance theories and models in the existing literature, the authors have attempted to explain the most appropriate financial techniques and methodologies, respectively. In a nutshell, the best way to promote Islamic finance in the existing dominance of traditional finance is simply through research.

Note

1 HEXANIKA is one of the big data analytics tools that can ingest data in multiple formats and can enhance the access of information to customers speedily.

References

Abdou, H. A., Alam, S. T., & Mulkeen, J. (2014). Would credit scoring work for Islamic finance? A neural network approach. *International Journal of Islamic and Middle Eastern Finance and Management*, 7(1), 112–125.

Ahmed, H. (2012). Islamic law, investors' rights and corporate finance, *Journal of Corporate Law Studies*, 12(2), 367–392.

Ahmad, S. M., & Al Mamun, A. (2020). Opportunities of Islamic Fin-tech: The case of Bangladesh and Turkey. *CenRaPS Journal of Social Sciences*, 2(3), 412–426.

Al-Osaimy, M. H.J., & Bamakhramah, A. S. (2004). An early warning system for Islamic banks performance. *Journal of King Abdulaziz University, Islamic Economics*, 17(1), 3–14.

Bordoloi, D., Singh, R., Bhattacharjee, J., & Bezborah, P. (2020). Assessing the awareness of Islamic law on equity investment in state of Assam, India. *Journal of Islamic Finance*, 9(1), 001–012.

Gherbi, E. H. (2018). Factors of influence in the establishment of Islamic banking and finance in Algeria. *Academy of Accounting and Financial Studies Journal*, 22, 1–7.

Haseeb, M., & Alam, S. (2018). Emerging issues in Islamic banking & finance: Challenges and solutions. *Academy of Accounting and Financial Studies Journal*, 22, 1–5.

Ledhem, M. A., & Mekidiche, M. (2020). Economic growth and financial performance of Islamic banks: a CAMELS approach. *Islamic Economic Studies*, 28(1), 47–62.

Mohammed, A. M. (2018). Determinants of implementation of accounting standards for Islamic financial institutions in Iraq: A conceptual framework. *Academy of Accounting and Financial Studies Journal*, 22, 1–6.

Olorogun, L. A. (2018). Compatibility between Islamic insurance theory and its current models of operation. *Academy of Accounting and Financial Studies Journal*, 22, 1–11.

Roodman, D. (2009). How to do xtabond2: An introduction to difference and system GMM in Stata. *The Stata Journal*, 9(1), 86–136.

20

THE BEST METHODOLOGY RECOMMENDED FOR RESEARCH IN ISLAMIC FINANCE

Monsurat Ayojimi Salami, Mustapha Abubakar and Harun Tanrivermiş

Introduction

Despite the fact that Islamic finance became noticeable global practice about four decades ago, Astrom (2013) traced development of Islamic finance back to 1960. At the earlier stage of the current Islamic finance, the majority of the research was conducted through interviewing Shari'ah scholars and contacting series of Arabic text on *Muhamalat*. At that period, studies on Islamic finance were few due to low numbers of Shari'ah scholars. Use of questionnaires for data collection contributed to the increase in the research on Islamic finance prior to availability of secondary data on several databases. Recently, studies have shown that Islamic finance has been bombarded with a series of methodologies, currently creating confusion on which methodologies to adhere to while doing research on Islamic finance. Furthermore, some researchers have gained the advantage of an increase in the use of technology to use artificial intelligence and machine learning techniques for analyzing Islamic finance data. Despite that, the new development in research is a welcome innovation for research in Islamic finance; still, analysis tools need to be used with sufficient knowledge because all has to do with "garbage in garbage out." The big concern is understanding the ability of the underlying assumptions so as to avoid misleading conclusions, and the ability to interpret the findings from the context of Shari'ah that individuals and industry would benefit and be useful to the real economy.

It is worth to note that methodologies are merely analysis tools which allow researchers to analyze data while adhering to underlying assumptions. Before now, not much attention has been drawn to the methodology-related matters in Islamic finance research because the discipline is relatively young as compared to conventional finance. Currently, it has become necessary to recommend best methodologies for research in Islamic finance after evaluating a series of available methodologies. Besides, global recognition of Islamic

DOI: 10.4324/9781003252764-24

finance is increasing substantially. It is also essential that the Islamic finance research methodology should be able to provide in-depth findings that will be useful for the masses. According to the editorial report in one of the Islamic finance journals written by Hashim (2017), the International Monetary Fund (IMF) and World Bank Group have shown impressive interest in Islamic finance. Therefore, recommending best methodologies for research in Islamic finance may reflect how Islamic finance is being practiced globally and how it should be practiced to prevent discrepancies which might arise from deviating from Shari'ah rulings on Islamic finance.

A well-known, peculiar feature of Islamic finance is maintaining justice in its transactional dealings which therefore made the masses' expectation high (Hashim, 2017). The fact is that Islamic finance emerged at an appropriate time when the global conventional finance market crashed and many lost hope in its financial rescue capacity. This triggered an increase in trading Shari'ah-compliant instruments as well as research on Islamic finance instruments. According to a study conducted in 2012, Islamic finance has grown in capital volume as well as organizational structure for more than three decades (Cebeci, 2012). This might have been due to the uniqueness of several Islamic finance instruments and less emphasis on profit maximization. This may also contribute to the reasons that Islamic finance instruments are more appealing to investors with ethical investment ambitions. As a result, Shari'ah scholars continuously check whether financial services and products of Islamic finance institution are not departing from Shari'ah standards. Otherwise, excess/abnormal gain is considered as non-Shari'ah compliance, which is usually given away as charity as one of the Shari'ah purification approaches for the remaining revenue (Bekri, Kim, and Rachev, 2014). At the same time, rigorous and meaningful research is capable of availing the users of Islamic finance findings on how Islamic finance addresses the immediate needs of society and distinguishes itself by addressing the challenges in conventional finance. This has raised challenges of exploring and suggesting best research methodologies that could be employed in doing research in Islamic finance.

Although different research objectives may attract different research designs, research in Islamic finance still has a role to play, especially on how financial puzzles in conventional finance are answered differently. It is also well-understood that different research designs follow different research paradigms. Nevertheless, research in Islamic finance is highly essential to pay special attention to the research design that is clear from misleading conclusions, and the findings are clearly presented from the context of Shari'ah rather than converging with or diverging from conventional findings on the same matter. This emphasizes the need to employ best research methodology in addressing research objectives to avoid bias presentation of the outcomes of research, most especially on the issues relating to *Maqasid al-Shari'ah*, among which are potential contributions of Islamic finance to social development (Cebeci, 2012). Yet, some researchers still consider that more efforts are required for it to contribute to the real economy. The rest of this study is structured as follows. The second section focuses on types of research design methodologies. The third section explains comparative feature in each research design methodology. The fourth section is a discussion and conclusion for this study.

Types of research design methodologies

With the clear fact that Islamic finance is operating in an already-established debt-based economy as created by the capitalism worldview made mainstream, secular discipline methodologies appear attractive for conducting research in Islamic finance. This is not to criticize conventional discipline research methodologies but to provide justification for the use of the research design methodologies. In other words, absolutely all research design used in conventional finance research is used in Islamic finance research as well. As noted earlier, methodologies are mainly analysis tools. Therefore, those research methodologies are broadly grouped into five: qualitative research design, conceptual research design, quantitative research design, mixed method research design, and case study research design. Each of the research designs belongs to different research paradigms. And it is highly essential to adhere to ontological and epistemological assumptions of the type of research paradigm, as they provide guidelines on the interpretation of the research findings.

In a simple term, ontology could be defined as reality. From contextual definition, Islamic worldview as guided by Al-Quran and Hadith defines ontology as reality "based on idea of *Tawhid* (monotheism)" (Rafikov and Akhmetova, 2020), which is an essential element of the worldview. From an Islamic worldview, ontology is classified into the physical world and hereafter (Khalid, 2020). Both ontology and epistemology assumptions guiding research in Islamic finance should be based on *Tawhid* (oneness of Allah) (Hashim, 2018). Therefore, research in Islamic finance is expected to comply with *Tawhid* epistemology and ontology. Note that discussion of *Tawhid* epistemology and ontology is beyond the context of this chapter and they are not the focus of the current study. According to Bienhaus and Haddud (2018), it is essential to combine more elements of ontology and epistemology as required by the type of research design employed. Hence, understanding the ontology of research design is crucial to do research for accuracy and quality of the interpretation of the findings. John and Burns (2014) also argued that ontological and epistemological assumptions should guide selection of appropriate theories for the research. Therefore, best methodologies for research in Islamic finance are expected to meet the need of the masses in the physical world in the manner that would not jeopardize the benefits in the hereafter. Alsharari and Youssef (2017) conducted case study research and were reported to have strictly followed the ontological and epistemological assumptions that underpin the interpretative paradigm for the case study research.

Furthermore, qualitative research design allows the researchers to be part of the research or have influence over the research; therefore, the findings from it are subjective in nature. The conceptual research design enables the researchers to present the process involved in Islamic finance instrument. The conceptual research design is a special type of qualitative research design that presents a set of instructions or processes in a graphic manner. The quantitative research design disallows researchers to have influence on the outcome of the research, which is also known as a positivism research paradigm. Therefore, the findings in quantitative research design are regarded as objective. The researcher in quantitative research is detached from the study outcomes. This implies that the researcher in quantitative research is allowed to report the outcomes of the research according to data predictions without adding their own story (Bienhaus and Haddud, 2018). The mixed research design allows a combination of two different research design paradigms in a single study. In other words, it allows the use of both qualitative and quantitative research designs in a study. Case study research design is a scenario research design that allows research to conduct a study either on a single community or society, or on a series of communities with similar issues. According to Damenu and Beaumont (2017) case study research design is usually used when the researcher seeks to understand either complex issues or objects using detailed contextual analysis while having limited numbers of situations as well as their relationships. One of the main challenges facing case study research is that the outcomes could not be generalized, especially if it is a single case study.

Based on the previous studies, researchers have explored several aspects in Islamic finance, and they have employed several research designs in explaining research objectives. The research design employed ranges from the use of qualitative research approach and/or quantitative research approach (see, for example, Abu Hussain and Al-Ajmi, 2012; Algabry *et al.*, 2020; Cevik and Bugan, 2020; Hassan, 2009; Rosman and Abdul-Rahman, 2015; Trabelsi, 2019) to graphic presentation of findings (see, for example, Abdullah, 2018; Bahoo *et al.*, 2019; Jouti, 2019; Laldin and Furqani, 2018). In some situations, researchers use mixed method research design for their studies (see for example, Ali, 2020; Hudaefi and Noordin, 2019; Migdad, 2017; Tamanni and Besar, 2019). It is worth knowing that different research approaches have different underlying assumptions, and in some cases data restrictions pose challenges to the researchers regarding the approach to be employed in carrying out their studies. Still, there is a need for more enhanced research design methodology to convey adequate messages about the research findings to the users of Islamic finance. This might have been one of the reasons for exploring the best methodologies for research in Islamic finance studies.

Qualitative research design

Qualitative research could be viewed from two ways: first, through the nature of data used in the study, which could either be pure interview; second, through a set of instructions from previous studies, such as conceptual studies.

Researchers mainly embarked on interviews for data collection if the study required more in-depth findings from the Shari'ah perspective. This research area is relatively new and without sufficient numerical data to support the study. In this sense researchers could contact the Shari'ah scholars in the field of that research topic for Shari'ah rulings on the subject matter. Similarly, Shari'ah scholars would provide facts with reference to Al-Quran and Hadith (sayings and practice of the Holy Prophet Muhammed [peace be upon him]) (Ajmi *et al.*, 2019; Mohammad, 2015). In the absence of clear or direct evidence about those issues in the sacred text of Islam, the Islamic scholars provide Shari'ah related evidence through *Ijma* (consensus) from *Qiyas* (analogy), *Istihsan'* (juristic preference) and *Urf* (local custom of people) (Ajmi *et al.*, 2019). Those options allow Shari'ah scholars to view issues from the perspective of situations surrounding the matter since there are not clear meanings from the Islamic sacred texts. Therefore, the outcomes of using qualitative research design are always subjective in nature and unsuitable for generalization purposes. Similarly, Islamic finance also allows dealing with issues according to the situation surrounding the matter rather than emphasizing on generalization at all times.

Several researchers in Islamic finance have used qualitative research design in addressing several research topics; among the most recent studies are evaluation of Shari'ah audit structure, evidence of *Zulm* (injustice/exploitation) in rent-seeking behavior, *Takaful* (Islamic insurance) demand, and more. Algabry *et al.* (2020) investigated effectiveness of internal Shari'ah audit structures and practices among Yemeni Islamic financial industries. The authors conducted interviews with some of the management as well as the Shari'ah Board to conclude that Yemen's internal Shari'ah auditor lacked necessary tools to achieve desired audit objectives, which makes effectiveness of internal Shari'ah auditors unquantifiable.

Beside the use of interviews in data collection for research in Islamic finance, reviews of previous findings are used in qualitative studies. Farooq (2019) examined *Zulm* in the concept of rent-seeking behavior (earned gains without contributing to the real economy) and rentier state. The author used evidence from the previous findings to establish that rent-seeking exists and concluded that appropriate attention is required on the issue since the Islamic position is to uphold a *Zulm*-free society as well, as Quran (2:279) warns against *Riba'*. Despite the fact that *Takaful* began in 1979, Husin and Haron (2020) reported that *Takaful* demand attracts less attention from the corporate sectors and researchers after the review of a series of articles published in Scopus and Web of Science (WoS) on the topic. The authors drew the attention of researchers in Islamic finance to this research gap.

It could be inferred that researchers used qualitative research design to explore more in-depth findings that numerical data may not reveal. It indicates that the researchers contacted either Shari'ah scholars or obtained information from the series of available documents on the issues being examined to employ qualitative research design.

Conceptual research design

The conceptual research design allows sets of instructions or processes to be displayed in a graphic manner, and it is one type of qualitative studies. Conceptual research design is usually based on reviews of previous studies with the purpose of integrating several findings of Islamic researchers together and presenting them in a graphic view to attain a complex approach, such as an Islamic finance ecosystem. Jouti (2019) developed an Islamic social finance ecosystem through integration of several Islamic finance findings. The integration of *Waqf* (Islamic endowments), *Zakat* (compulsory alms), *Sodaqah* (donations), and *Qard hasan* (benevolent loans) is a way among the Islamic finance instruments to fund and invest in Islamic social finance (Jouti, 2019). It ought to have been known that each of the above-mentioned instruments has been separately studied. Eventually, through integration there is a tendency that they could collectively address more complex issues in Islamic finance. In another situation, researchers use conceptual research designs to present sets of instructions within two interconnected Islamic finance instruments to convey the stages involved in the instrument, such as a *Musharaqah Mutanaqisah* contract.

Jouti (2019) examined the sustainability of Islamic social finance ecosystems; the author presented a set of previous findings in a graphic chart to arrive at an idea that could solve social issues in everyday businesses as well as sustain Shari'ah-compliant funding. Similarly, Laldin and Furqani (2018) used a graphic chart to present how a comprehensive framework could be developed for Shari'ah governance in the Islamic finance industry by Bank Negara Malaysia. In addition, Abdullah (2018) investigated *Waqf* and sustainable development goals in the context of *Maqasid al-Shari'ah*. The author used library-based research to conceptualize *Waqf* in a graphic chart as one of the tools for actualizing sustainable development goals in fulfilling the highest objectives of Shari'ah. These show that researchers in Islamic finance are unrelenting in researching simple or complex contemporary issues.

Quantitative research design

Quantitative research design is another type of research design methodology that researchers use to address their research objectives. This research design requires the use of numerical data. There are three relatively different ways in which quantitative data could be obtained. Firstly, primary data could be obtained through a questionnaire. Secondly, secondary data could be obtained from reliable databases such as Bloomberg, DataStream, Bankscope, and others. Thirdly, few numerical data could be obtained from experts in the field based on their experience in the research area and further process using statistical tools to stimulate data based on existing data for more robust predictions. On another occasion, when available secondary data is relatively small for carrying out the objectives of the study, researchers may use statistical tools to address it. For instance, in the study conducted by Salami (2021) on pricing of Islamic financial instruments in Southeast Asia, the author reported to have gotten limited data and used statistical tools on the existing data to stimulate more data while complying with underlying assumptions. Findings from quantitative research design are considered as objective provided that underlying assumptions of the statistical tools used are not violated. However, violation of underlying assumptions of some econometric techniques used has been shown in some Islamic finance studies, and authors even proceeded with interpretations of such misleading findings.

Although there are several ways in which researchers strive to use numerical data to evaluate the soundness of Islamic finance instruments, caution is still required in using econometrical tools in making predictions. Some researchers used conventional findings as a benchmark for evaluating the performance of Islamic finance instruments. Sometimes, convergence arises in the findings of conventional and Islamic finance studies, which usually raises alarms that such Islamic finance instruments are not different from conventional financial instruments of the type or even worse. According to a study conducted by Roberts (1991), researchers were cautioned about relying heavily on annual reports in evaluating an organization's activities, as it does not give a complete picture of disclosure practices. Salami (2021) used secondary data and employed NARDL modeling to investigate pricing effectiveness of Islamic financial instruments in some southeast Asian countries, namely, Malaysia, Indonesia, and Brunei. The author found that some Islamic financial assets examined reflect asymmetry in pricing, which is an indication of unfair pricing. This kind of conclusion may call the attention of Shari'ah scholars in those countries to re-examine pricing of some of the instruments and eliminate non-Shari'ah compliance income, if any, and take action relating to Shari'ah purification measure for the revenue.

Akram and Rahman (2018) used accounting ratios in annual reports to examine credit risk management between Islamic banks and conventional banks in Pakistan. The authors employed multiple regression to conclude that Islamic banks are outperformed in credit risk management relative to conventional banks. However, Abu Hussain and Al-Ajmi, (2012) obtained primary data through questionnaires and found that both Islamic and conventional banks in Bahrain are faced with the challenges of credit, liquidity, and operational risks. In addition, Rosman and Abdul-Rahman (2015) developed questionnaires based on Islamic Financial Services Board (IFSB) Guideline Principles of Risk Management and found that Islamic banks have better-managed operational risks as well as Shari'ah noncompliant risks while they are deficient in risk-related liquidity, commercial, and equity investment. However, the authors reported significant risk managing practices in the Islamic banks from Middle East, Asian, and African countries. Those conflicts in the findings may continuously remind Islamic banks of where more efforts are needed in relation to their risk management techniques.

Mixed method research design

Research design is considered to be mixed method when any of the two different types of research design are simultaneously used in one study. Usually, researchers tend to use combinations of research designs in Islamic finance when available numerical data or Shari'ah scholars for the interview are very small. In some situations, their research objectives too broad to fit into one research design. In other words, this happens when the objectives of the study are beyond what numerical data could explain in a convincing manner. In another instance, there may be disparity between findings using one type of research design and real-life situations. Then the researcher will combine another research design to complement the research findings. Although the mixed method research design is time-consuming due to two stages of obtaining data, it makes more enriching findings possible. However, some researchers even argued against the mixed method research design as it combined two opposing research design paradigms. In Islamic finance research, the concern is not to violate *Tawhid* epistemology and ontology. Using mixed method research design is more common in conducting Islamic finance Ph.D. dissertations to allow in-depth research and comprehensiveness in the interpretation of the findings beyond data predictions.

Ali (2020) used mixed method research design for content analysis and self-administered questionnaires for sixteen Islamic commercial banks in Malaysia. The author discovered that some non-Shari'ah compliance practices in *Tawarruq* (Islamic commodity financing) occurred in the context of Malaysia, which he argued might have been due to the improper sequence of the contract. Also, he found out that the treatment of non-Shari'ah compliant income varies across Islamic banks in Malaysia as Shari'ah decisions are influenced contrarily by the boards of directors of the financial institutions. Tamanni and Besar (2019) used mixed method research design to find out that small Islamic microfinance institutions maintain the objective of serving the poor, while they tend to focus on sustainable objectives when they become larger. Hudaefi and Noordin (2019) used mixed method research design to develop an integrated *Maqasid al-Shari'ah* index for Malaysian Islamic banks.

Migdad (2017) used mixed method research design to examine contributions made by the corporate social responsibility (CSR) of Palestinian Islamic banks toward socioeconomic development. The study reveals that although CSR is highly valued among Palestinian Islamic banks, its contributions are small and only have marginal effects on socioeconomic development of the Palestinian community. The findings from the above studies revealed some sense of comprehensiveness in using mixed method research design.

Case study research design

Case study research design is a special type of design that focuses on issues relating to niche communities or a small sample of the total population. Case study research is usually appropriate for explorative study as it enables researchers to focus on a specific issue relating to community (see, for examples, Farooqi, 2006; Mohammed and Waheed, 2019) or economic variables (see, for examples, Almutriat, 2020; Alsharari and Youssef, 2017). A case study is usually structured to reveal more in-depth information regarding the subject matter as the researchers are expected to obtain direct facts from the affected community through interviews, which could be merged with other relevant evidence from other reports. In general, information about a case study may be obtained through multiple mediums, such as interviews, press reports, company chronicles, organizational brochures, and websites of the organization (Mitter and Hiebl, 2017). Sometimes, multiple information mediums about the case study could be purely non-numeric data or a combination of numeric and non-numeric data. Mohammed and Waheed (2019) conducted a case study about a community in India using combination of primary and secondary data. According to Mitter and Hiebl (2017), multiple case study enables researchers to group their findings into similarity and differences across the case studied. However, findings from a single case study analysis could not be generalized (Dalgleish and Cooper, 2005; Damenu and Beaumont, 2017).

Mohammed and Waheed (2019) investigated interest-free microfinance practices in India, to identify issues and suggest possible solutions. The case study was conducted among the Bait-un-Nasr (BuN) Urban Cooperative Credit Society in Mumbai, India. The authors found that while the performance of BuN was lower compared to the microfinance industry standard, BuN still succeeded in providing interest-free microfinance service in their community in India. Farooqi (2006) studied Islamic social capital and networking among Muslim community life in a village in the Birbhum district of West Bengal province in India. The study was based on the viewpoint of the researcher and concluded that "the strengthening informal co-operative networks through the inputs of technology, financial, and human capital from across different sectors constitutes an essential element in forwarding sustainable development." This implies that researchers use case studies to reach the affected society and publish their needs or success. Researchers may not incorporate suffocated econometric tools in analyzing their findings before revealing their research findings for case studies.

Comparative of features in different Islamic finance research design methodologies

Having enumerated several common research methodologies in Islamic finance, Table 20.1 is the proposed checklist for selecting the best methodologies based on previous studies across different research methodologies.

Furthermore, through recent increase in the use of technology, several methodologies have evolved and even in some cases, some data could be processed and hold some assumptions to stimulate more data. For instance, if the researchers consulted several Shari'ah scholars and found out a certain

Table 20.1 Comparative features of different research design methodologies

Type of research design	*Qualitative research design*	*Conceptual research design*	*Quantitative research design*	*Mixed method research design*	*Case study research design*
New Islamic finance instrument	Interview Islamic scholars	Graphical presentation	Questionnaire	Interviews and questionnaires	Interviews and other reports
Contemporary issues in Islamic finance, e.g., cryptocurrency, green finance, Sukuk on blockchain, smart contracts	Interview Islamic Scholars	Set of instructions or findings	Primary or secondary data, if any	Interview Islamic scholars and obtain data from the affected population	Explorative study on the issue from affected people
Availability of numerical data	Nil	Nil	Yes	Yes, coupled with interview	It may but limited through reports
Nature of data available	Non-numerical data	Set of instructions or findings	Numerical data	Both numerical and non-numerical data	Interviews and limited numerical data
Data justification	Subjective data	Partly subjective data	Objective data	May use subjective information to explain puzzles in objective findings or vice versa	Partly subjective data
Sources of data	Interview	Findings from past studies	Primary or secondary data	Interviews and primary or secondary data	Primary data and reports
Population	Fewer people	Nil	Large samples	Small samples	Small samples

Source: Authors' own extractions.

possible range of figures through their experience on a particular issue, they may use several statistical tools, such as Monte Carlo simulation, to generate sufficient data for carrying out empirical research. This signifies that there are interwoven lines in the use of research designs and appropriate knowledge on how to use methodology. This understanding is necessary and highly essential. It also implies that the ideas of Shari'ah scholars could now be used for furthering quantitative modeling. It may reduce total reliance on single-approach research design, especially on complex or sensitive issues in concluding Islamic finance studies that may result in misleading conclusions. As a result of this, employing one research design might not provide justifiable evidence, as many factors beyond the control of researchers might come into play and affect the final results of different countries. According to Roberts (1991), relying exclusively on accounting ratios somehow could not provide an appropriate picture of disclosure practices of an organization. Therefore, orderliness of best research methodologies in Islamic finance is presented in Figure 20.1.

From Figure 20.1, quantitative research is ranked least because the essence of research in Islamic finance is beyond total reliance on data for making predictions but engages in more in-depth research outcomes. Despite that, making predictions is inevitable in finance due to high uncertainty about the future

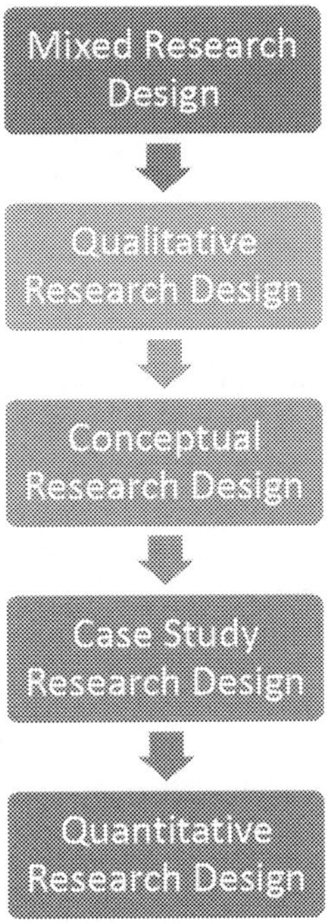

Figure 20.1 Top-bottom orderliness of best research methodologies in Islamic finance.

of the investment, and the direction of the market, as reported in the study by Jadevicius (2020) (which was originally derived from Economist, 2016), still makes the future prediction a tough task. According to Yogi Berra, great baseball-playing philosopher, "it is very tough to make predictions about the future." Contrary to this, researches in Islamic finance is more focused on the evaluation of existing or proposed Islamic financial instruments and eliminate all non-Shari'ah compliant or possible amendment wherever necessary on the instruments. Therefore, the best research methodology in Islamic finance should provide more reliable findings through a combination of research designs rather than results that may have some probability of misleading if the underlying assumption of the methodology is violated.

Conclusion

This study explored several research methodologies being employed in Islamic finance research and classified them into five broad categories, namely: qualitative research design, conceptual research design, quantitative research design, mixed method research design, and case study research design. Each of the research design methodologies has different ontological and epistemological assumptions to be followed regarding interpretation of the outcomes. In Islamic finance, interpretation of the study should comply with *Tawhid* epistemology and ontology. In most cases, selection of research methodology should be capable of addressing the objectives of the research while taking availability of data into consideration. There is emphasis that research methodologies are just tools for analyzing the available data and caution on the underlying assumptions of the research design, which needs to be complied with. The main identified data for carrying out research are either numeric data or non-numeric data or both. It is further discovered that some research designs used sets of instructions or findings from earlier studies that may be integrated to provide solutions to more complex issues in Islamic finance, such as the formation of an Islamic ecosystem through integration of a series of Islamic finance instruments. Therefore, it is more appropriate to abide by the best methodology that would be suitable for explaining the findings in a more comprehensive manner while allowing integration of Shari'ah interpretations. This could only be achieved via mixed method research design. However, extensive use of mixed research design may lower the number of publications on Islamic finance, while it may enhance quality of the research interpretation and convey more in-depth findings.

References

Abdullah, M. (2018) 'Waqf, sustainable development goals (SDGs) and Maqasid al-Shari'ah', *International Journal of Social Economics*, 45(1), pp. 158–172.

Abu Hussain, H. and Al-Ajmi, J. (2012) 'Risk management practices of conventional and Islamic banks in Bahrain', *The Journal of Risk Finance*, 13(3), pp. 215–239.

Ajmi, H. *et al.* (2019) 'Adverse selection analysis for profit and loss sharing contracts', *International Journal of Islamic and Middle Eastern Finance and Management*, 12(1997), pp. 532–552.

Akram, H. and Rahman, K. (2018) 'Credit risk management: A comparative study of Islamic banks and conventional banks in Pakistan', *ISRA International Journal of Islamic Finance*, 10(2), pp. 185–205.

Algabry, L. *et al.* (2020) 'Assessing the effectiveness of internal Sharīʿah audit structure and its practices in Islamic financial institutions: A case study of Islamic banks in Yemen', *Asian Journal of Accounting Research*, 1, pp. 1–21.

Ali, M. M. (2020) 'Survey on Sharīʿah non-compliant events in Islamic banks in the practice of Tawarruq financing in Malaysia', *ISRA International Journal of Islamic Finance*, 12(2), pp. 151–169.

Almutirat, H. A. (2020) 'The impact of intellectual capital in organizational innovation: Case study at Kuwait Petroleum Corporation (KPC)', *Review of Economics and Political Science*, pp. 1–22. https://doi.org/10.1108/REPS-08-2019-0113

Alsharari, N. M. and Youssef, M. A. E.-A. (2017) 'Management accounting change and the implementation of GFMIS: A Jordanian case study', *Asian Review of Accounting*, 25(2), pp. 242–261.

Astrom, Z. H. O. (2013) 'Credit risk management pertaining to profit and loss sharing instruments in Islamic banking', *Journal of Financial Reporting and Accounting*, 11(1), pp. 80–91.

Bahoo, S. *et al.* (2019) 'A model of the Islamic sovereign wealth fund', *Islamic Economic Studies*, 27(1), pp. 2–22.

Bekri, M., Kim, Y. S. (Aaron) and Rachev, S. (Zari) T. (2014) 'Tempered stable models for Islamic finance asset management', *International Journal of Islamic and Middle Eastern Finance and Management*, 7(1), pp. 37–60.

Bienhaus, F. and Haddud, A. (2018) 'Procurement 4.0: Factors influencing the digitisation of procurement and supply chains', *Business Process Management Journal*, 24(4), pp. 965–984.

Cebeci, I. (2012) 'Integrating the social Maslaha into Islamic finance', *Accounting Research Journal*, 25(3), pp. 166–184.

Cevik, E. I. and Bugan, M. F. (2020) 'Regime-dependent relation between Islamic and conventional financial markets', *Borsa Istanbul Review*, 18(2), pp. 114–121.

Dalgleish, F. and Cooper, B. J. (2005) 'Risk management: Developing a framework for a water authority', *Management of Environmental Quality: An International Journal*, 16(3), pp. 235–249.

Damenu, T. K. and Beaumont, C. (2017) 'Analysing information security in a bank using soft systems methodology', *Information and Computer Security*, 25(3), pp. 240–258.

Farooq, M. O. (2019) 'Rent-seeking behaviour and zulm (injustice/exploitation) beyond riba-interest equation', *ISRA International Journal of Islamic Finance*, 11(1), pp. 110–123.

Farooqi, A. H. (2006) 'Islamic social capital and networking', *Humanomics*, 22(2), pp. 113–125.

Hashim, A. M. (2017) 'Editorial', *ISRA International Journal of Islamic Finance*, 9(2), pp. 114–116.

Hashim, A. M. (2018) 'Editorial', *ISRA International Journal of Islamic Finance*, 10(1), pp. 2–5.

Hassan, A. (2009) 'Risk management practices of Islamic banks of Brunei Darussalam', *The Journal of Risk Finance*, 10(1), pp. 23–37.

Hudaefi, F. A. and Noordin, K. (2019) 'Harmonizing and constructing an integrated Maqasid al-Sharīʿah index for measuring the performance of Islamic banks', *ISRA International Journal of Islamic Finance*, 11(2), pp. 282–302.

Husin, M. M. and Haron, R. (2020) 'Takaful demand: A review of selected literature', *ISRA International Journal of Islamic Finance*, 12(3), pp. 443–455.

Jadevicius, A. (2020) 'Make a call: Assessing capital calls velocity for closed end Asia Pacific non-listed real estate funds', *Journal of Property Investment and Finance*, 38(6), pp. 617–625.

John, B. and Burns, J. (2014) 'Qualitative management accounting research in QRAM: Some reflections', *Qualitative Research in Accounting & Management*, 11(1), pp. 71–81.

Jouti, A. T. (2019) 'An integrated approach for building sustainable Islamic social finance ecosystems', *ISRA International Journal of Islamic Finance*, 11(2), pp. 246–266.

Khalid, A. A. (2020) 'Role of audit and governance committee for internal Shari'ah audit effectiveness in Islamic banks', *Asian Journal of Accounting Research*, 5(1), pp. 81–89.

Laldin, M. A. and Furqani, H. (2018) 'Islamic Financial Services Act (IFSA) 2013 and the Sharīʿah-compliance requirement of the Islamic finance industry in Malaysia', *ISRA International Journal of Islamic Finance*, 10(1), pp. 94–101.

Migdad, A. M. (2017) 'CSR practices of Palestinian Islamic banks: Contribution to socio-economic development', *ISRA International Journal of Islamic Finance*, 9(2), pp. 133–147.

Mitter, C. and Hiebl, M. R. W. (2017) 'The role of management accounting in international entrepreneurship', *Journal of Accounting and Organizational Change*, 13(3), pp. 381–409.

Mohammad, M. T. S. H. (2015) 'Theoretical and trustees' perspectives on the establishment of an Islamic social (Waqf) bank', *Humanomics*, 31(1), pp. 37–73.

Mohammed, W. S. and Waheed, K. (2019) 'Interest-free microfinance in India: A case study of Bait-un-Nasr Urban Cooperative Credit Society', *ISRA International Journal of Islamic Finance*, 11(2), pp. 322–337.

Rafikov, I. and Akhmetova, E. (2020) 'Methodology of integrated knowledge in Islamic economics and finance: Collective ijtihad', *ISRA International Journal of Islamic Finance*, 12(1), pp. 115–129.

Rosman, R. and Abdul-Rahman, A. R. (2015) 'The practice of IFSB guiding principles of risk management by Islamic banks', *Journal of Islamic Accounting and Business Research*, 6(2), pp. 150–172.

Salami, M. A. (2021) 'Critical assessment of Islamic financial assets pricing in South-East Asia: Evidence from NARDL modelling', *Journal of Financial Reporting and Accounting*, 1, pp. 1–21.

Tamanni, L. and Besar, M. H. A. H. (2019) 'Profitability vs poverty alleviation: Has banking logic influenced Islamic microfinance institutions?', *Asian Journal of Accounting Research*, 4(2), pp. 260–279.

Trabelsi, N. (2019) 'Dynamic and frequency connectedness across Islamic stock indexes, bonds, crude oil and gold', *International Journal of Islamic and Middle Eastern Finance and Management*, 12(3), pp. 306–321.

21

CHALLENGES IN APPLYING STANDARD METHODOLOGY FOR RESEARCH IN ISLAMIC ECONOMICS AND FINANCE AND THE WAY FORWARD

Ascarya and Atika R. Masrifah

Introduction

The chapter discusses problems on how to address the fundamental and technical challenges in conducting IEF research using standard or best methodologies, which include the following:

First, for certain fields of IEF which have not been (or rarely) studied, we need more exploratory and descriptive studies, which could not only apply descriptive qualitative and content analysis methods but also use: (a) the Likert method, as Haji Muhammad (2015) did with a doctrinal study to conceptualize the Islamic social bank based on cash waqf; (b) the Delphi method, as Lateh *et al.* (2016) did in a study on the formation of Shariah-compliant gold instruments, or Meisamy and Gholipour (2020) did in a preliminary and evaluation study on Iranian Islamic banking to determine its primary challenges and propose respected policies; and (c) a combination of Delphi-Likert, such as a study by Ascarya and Sakti (2021b) to determine the characteristics, design, and propose new sustainable Islamic microfinance model.

Second, for further and more sophisticated studies in these rarely studied fields, as well as for frontier studies, Delphi or Delphi-Likert could be applied as the preliminary studies, where the results will be used as the input for the main studies using other methods, such as structural equation modeling (SEM) and analytic network process (ANP). We could call these: (a) Delphi-SEM method, as with Tamanni *et al.* (2019), who did a study in mainstreaming Islamic social finance to enhance inclusivity and quality of economic growth; (b) Delphi-ANP method, as with Sakti *et al.* (2019), who did a study to determine the dominant orientation of

DOI: 10.4324/9781003252764-25

microfinance providers in serving poor and micro-small enterprises (MSEs) through the use of group-lending approaches, and Ascarya and Sakti (2021a), who did a study to design appropriate micro-fintech models for Islamic microfinance institutions (IMFI), especially Baitul Maal wat Tamwil (BMT) in Indonesia, enabling the BMT to combine Islamic social and commercial microfinance optimally; and (c) a combination of Delphi-Likert and Delphi-ANP, as with, Ascarya and Sakti (2019), who did a comprehensive study to design micro-fintech model for IMFI/BMT by first determining the characteristics, proposing various micro-fintech models, and finally determining the best model.

Third, for certain fields of IEF which also exist in conventional economics and finance (CEF) when the data are readily available or could be obtained, studies could be conducted using quantitative methods (such as autoregressive distributed lag [ARDL], error correction model [ECM], and VAR/vector error correction model [VECM], as well as panel data) or quasi-quantitative methods (such as SEM and ANP). For example: (a) a study on monetary policy transmission under dual financial system in Indonesia (Ascarya, 2014), which applied ECM, ARDL, and VECM simultaneously; and (b) a study on Muslim customer behavior in online halal food purchasing (Al-Banna, 2019), which used a modified technology acceptance model (TAM) and applied SEM method.

Finally, to evaluate performance of Islamic financial institutions (IFIs), commercial or social, oftentimes the traditional/conventional performance indicators could not be used. To overcome these challenges, we could use a non-parametric data envelopment analysis (DEA) method, which could measure institution's performance using various inputs and outputs. Some examples of DEA studies include: (a) Sufian, who measured and analyzed the efficiency (technical, pure technical, and scale efficiencies) of domestic and foreign Islamic banks in Malaysia, using DEA with intermediation approach; (b) Ascarya (2014), who measured and compared the technical efficiency (TE) (including pure technical and scale efficiencies) of leading BMT and conventional cooperatives in Indonesia, using DEA with intermediation approach; and (c) Rusydiana and Marlina (2019), who measured and analyzed financial and social efficiency of 11 Islamic banks in Indonesia during 2013–2018, using DEA with intermediation approach.

Moreover, some examples of two-stage DEA studies include: (a) Rosman *et al.* (2014), who measured the efficiency of 79 Islamic banks in Middle Eastern and Asian countries during the global financial crisis in 2007–2010, using DEA with intermediation approach and data from the BankScope database, while at the second stage this study determined the main determinants of Islamic banking efficiency using the tobit method; (b) Sufian and Akbar Noor Mohamad Noor (2009), who determined 16 MENA and Asian Islamic banks' efficiency changes, using DEA with intermediation approach, while at the second stage this study determined the impact of internal and external factors on Islamic banks' efficiency using tobit regression method; and (c) Lee *et al.* (2019), who measured the cost and TEs of the Takaful industry (including 11 family Takaful companies and 8 general Takaful companies) in Malaysia during 2011–2015, using DEA, while at the second stage this study determined the impact of internal factors (firms' specific and corporate governance) on Takaful companies' efficiency using panel linear regression.

Likert scale

The Likert scale may help to gather expert opinions in qualitative research aimed at determining the importance or screening of items. The Likert scale is common in five or seven points. Two "extremely agree" and "extremely disagree" scales at both ends of a spectrum are used for developing the Likert 5-point scale. The 9-point scales can also be used by defining the intermediate values.

A number of Likert scales, including 2-point, 5-point, 7-point, 9-point, 11-point, and 12-point, were investigated by Diefenbach, Weinstein, and O'Reilly (1993). Lewis found a stronger correlation to t-test results by 7-point scales. It was demonstrated that there was no significantly better scale than the 7-point scale (Figure 21.1).

The mean score of their opinions on each dimension is calculated after the experts have collected opinions. In the absence of consensus, the experts will receive the calculated mean as controlled feedback from the questionnaire. After all those rounds, if a consensus was achieved, based on the average of the final round, the items will be screened.

Likert scale is rarely used as a single method in research, but it usually is used to complement other method, such as in SEM methods. However, sometimes, the Likert scale is used to help in certain exploratory surveys to specific respondents, such as Haji Muhammad (2015) studies an alternative Islamic banking system concept using cash waqf, called Islamic social waqf bank. The questionnaire example can be seen in Table 21.1, which was distributed to 9 out of 15 waqf institutions in Malaysia.

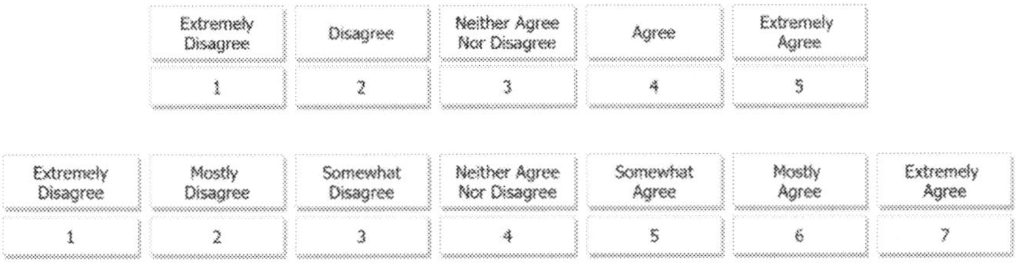

Extremely Disagree
Disagree
Neither Agree Nor Disagree
Agree
Extremely Agree
1
2
3
4
5
Extremely Disagree
Mostly Disagree
Somewhat Disagree
Neither Agree Nor Disagree
Somewhat Agree
Mostly Agree
Extremely Agree
1
2
3
4
5
6
7

Figure 21.1 A 5-point and a 7-point Likert scale.

Table 21.1 The example of a Likert questionnaire

1	*Memorandum of Association (MOA), shall state that the waqf bank shall*	*Response*				
1.1	Normal Islamic banking	1	2	3	4	5
1.2	Shariah and waqf law compliant	1	2	3	4	5
1.3	Promote the culture of giving	1	2	3	4	5
1.4	Accumulate welfare funds	1	2	3	4	5
1.5	Contributing to national economy	1	2	3	4	5

Note: 1 = strongly disagree; 2 = disagree; 3 = neutral; 4 = agree; 5 = strongly agree.

Delphi method

Delphi is considered as a decision-making method of experts' opinions, and was initially developed by Norman Dalkey and Olaf Helmer at Rand Corporation, a research institute in Santa Monica, California, in the 1960s (Dalkey and Helmer, 1963), to forecast the impact of technology on warfare, since at that time there were limited forecasting approaches to be used. The general explanation and guide to conduct the Delphi method could be found, among others, in Hsu and Sanford (2007).

Delphi is a decision-making approach based on multi-stage (two or more) surveys to experts to achieve convergence opinions on certain topics. Tiered surveys are conducted to gain the most reliable consensus of opinion from a group of experts. This is done by using a series of intensive questionnaires with feedback in the form of expert opinion or judgment. Linstone and Turoff (1975) defined Delphi as a method for structuring a group communication process to enable the process to be effective in dealing with a complex problem in a group of individuals as a whole. They concluded, however, that there was no point in bringing the experts together in the conference room. Dalkey and Helmer (1963) developed the Delphi method to eliminate conference rooms for an expert consensus. The group members do not need to meet face to face. Anonymity was required in the context that no one knew who was participating.

Consequently, the main objective of the Delphi method is to achieve the most reliable consensus among a group of experts through a series of intensive questionnaires and controlled opinions (Dalkey and Helmer, 1963, p. 458). When a group of experts reached consensus through this process, researchers could identify and prioritize problems and develop a framework to acknowledge them.

The Delphi method is a scientific method that uses a descriptive approach to explore reliable and valid information about complex problems where they are explicitly assessed by experts. It aims to achieve consensus by implementing a series of questionnaires and feedback to selected experts who have expertise in key areas. This method could describe factors and subfactors that participate in a problem with its ranking score or provide a relative general position for alternatives in a multidimensional area.

The Delphi method would be started with a survey of literature related to the study, including literature on the supporting theories and literature on the previous studies. Based on the literature review, the researcher could construct initial questionnaires to be used in the Delphi process with or without focus group discussion (FGD).

The Delphi method in Round-1 identifies and asks experts from the required key areas to participate. They are anonymized in the sense that they will not be attributed by name to any of their statements. Experts may be asked to give their opinion on an issue in the first questionnaire, which could be open-ended (traditional Delphi) or close-ended (modified Delphi) questionnaires.

In Round-2 structured questionnaires resulting from Round-1 are given to experts, where expert respondents are asked to review the list of elements that have been summarized by researchers based on the responses from Round-1. The respondents will give the rank order to set the initial priority among the collected elements. The result would be the initial consensus, where the value of the agreement and disagreement can be identified.

The ranking score would be presented to the group in the Round-3 third questionnaire and experts with their extreme opinions would be asked to re-evaluate their opinions and give their reasons. At the end of the third round, the researchers would synthesize these reasons, and the third questionnaire should be based on the synthesized reasons.

The new group judgment on the issue, together with reasons for the extreme opinions, would be presented in this Round-4 fourth questionnaire. In view of the reasons given, each group of experts would be asked to re-evaluate his position. They may also be asked to prove with any facts, if necessary, the extreme reasons. Those arguments and the evolving group would be presented in the final round as well as a re-evaluation would be requested. The number of Delphi iterations is highly depended on the level of consensus that researchers are looking for and can vary from two to four. The steps of Delphi method can be illustrated in Figure 21.2.

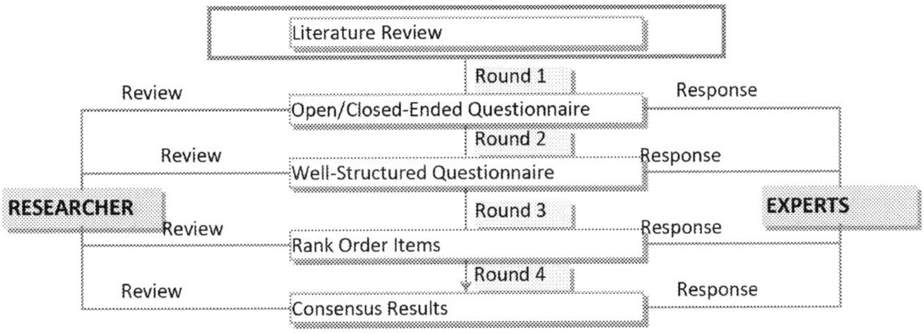

Figure 21.2 Steps of the Delphi method.

Source: Dalkey and Helmer (1963) and Hsu and Sanford (2007), modified by the authors.

Essentially, there is no accurate mechanism for identifying the number of experts to be included in a Delphi study (Williams and Webb, 1994). Although the structure and panel size of the Delphi technique differ, there is a dominant pattern. The panel size may vary depending on the subject matter covered (Mahyudi, 2020), or the time and money provided (Van Zolingen and Klaassen, 2003), and a combination of people with multiple specialties and heterogeneous groups is also suggested (Somerville et al, 2008). Hsu and Sanford (2007) stated that Delphi method required data from at least one FGD. The number of respondents per FGD could range from 3 to 21 respondents with a median of 10 respondents (Nyumba *et al.*, 2018), while Dilshad and Latif (2013) asserted that one FGD needs 6–12 knowledgeable respondents. In addition, Hsu and Sanford (2007) suggested a minimum of 8 respondents, an average of 16 respondents and maximum of 80 respondents.

Another issue with the Delphi method is a scientific method for establishing the level of consensus. In different studies, a variety of methods were proposed. One way to determine the level of consensus among respondents is the calculation of rater agreement using Kendall's Coefficient of Concordance (Kendall's W). The rater agreement is a measure of non-parametric statistic that is used to assess the level of agreement among the respondents (R1–Rn) as raters of a problem in certain cluster, which is known as Kendall's Coefficient of Concordance (W: $0 < W \leq 1$), where $W = 1$ indicates perfect conformity or complete agreement, while $W = 0$ indicates no agreement. To calculate Kendall's W, first rank every answer and sum it up.

$$R_i = \sum_{j=1}^{m} r_{i,j} \tag{21.1}$$

where R_i = total ranks of a factor; m = number of rank sets or judges.

The average value of the total rank is:

$$\bar{R} = \frac{1}{n}\sum_{i=1}^{n} R_i \tag{21.2}$$

where n = number of ranked factors or phenomena.

The sum of squares of deviation (S) can be calculated as follows.

$$S = \sum_{i=1}^{n}\left(R_i - \bar{R}\right)^2 \tag{21.3}$$

So that, the Kendall's W can be calculated as follows.

$$W = \frac{12S}{m^2\left(n^3 - n\right)} \tag{21.4}$$

Table 21.2 The example of a Delphi questionnaire

	Challenges of Islamic banking in Iran	*Ranking*
1	Theoretical challenge	
2	Governmental attitude toward Islamic banking	
3	Lack of competition	
4	Lack of a legitimate solution for delayed payments and rollover	
5	Requesting collateral even in musharakah contracts	
6	Not revising the law (RFBA)	
7	Lack of Shariah supervision	
8	Paying on-account monthly profit to depositors	
9	Lack of accounting and auditing standards	
10	Little research and education	

Source: Meisamy and Gholipour (2020).

To determine the significance of Kendall's W, we could calculate the p-value of each W based on its X^2 and degree of freedom. Finally, the results of the Delphi method show the rank of elements in every question in the whole Delphi questionnaire. The Delphi consensus should fall within a certain range, such as 70 percent (Green, 1982) or 80 percent (Ulschak, 1983), but Scheibe *et al.* (1975) suggested more reliable alternative. The Delphi method is rarely used as a single method in research. Instead, it usually is used to complement other methods, such as in Delphi-Likert, Delphi-SEM, and Delphi-ANP methods. However, sometimes, the Delphi method is used to help in certain exploratory surveys to specific respondents, such as in study by Meisamy and Gholipour (2020), who tried to identify the various impediments facing the Islamic banking industry in Iran and to suggest a prioritized listing of these challenges. This example of Delphi questionnaire can be seen in Table 21.2, which was distributed to 32 Iranian Islamic banking experts.

Delphi-Likert method

As has been mentioned before, Likert and Delphi methods have mostly been used to complement other methods. Nevertheless, both methods could be combined, referred to as the Likert-Delphi or Delphi-Likert method, to explore certain issues, to determine certain characteristics of hypothetical institutions and other frontier research. The Likert method, with five or seven scales, could be used to determine certain agreed-upon important issues or desirable characteristics, while the Delphi method, with its conclusive ranking, could be used to arrive at statistically significant consensus of the issues or the characteristics to provide robust results.

One of these examples is the study by Ascarya and Ali (2021b) who aimed to determine the characteristics of fintech needed and suitable for Islamic microfinance, and then propose a new Islamic microfinance model, combining

Table 21.3 The example of Likert scale results of Delphi-Likert

No.	*Characteristic*	*Expert*			*BMT*			*Fintech*			*All*		
1	Type of micro-fintech to be adopted by IMFI/BMT in commercial area	AG	NE	DI	AG	NE	DI	AG	NE	DI	AG	NE	DI
1.1	Digital banking	7	3	1	11	0	0	5	3	0	23	6	1
1.2	Payment	9	2	0	8	3	0	6	1	1	23	6	1
1.3	Crowdfunding P2P financing	10	1	0	9	2	0	8	0	0	27	3	0
1.4	E-commerce	6	4	1	6	5	0	6	2	0	18	11	1
1.5	Insurtech	2	6	3	3	8	0	3	4	1	8	18	4
1.6	Capital market	3	3	5	3	6	2	4	2	2	10	11	9
1.7	Integrated (various fintech needed)	4	4	3	9	2	0	4	3	1	17	9	4

Abbreviations: AG, agree; DI, disagree NE, neutral.
Source: Ascarya and Ali (2021b).

Islamic social finance and Islamic commercial finance, as well as embracing new fintech, called micro-fintech models, which could ensure the sustainability of IMFI/BMT in Indonesia. The example of a Delphi-Likert questionnaire can be seen in Table 21.3, which is distributed to 11 experts, 11 BMT practitioners, and 8 micro-fintech practitioners. The actual questionnaire consists of 13 questions.

The statistically significant results show desirable characteristics of micro-fintech, where the Likert scale results show the agreement/disagreement of certain micro-fintech characteristics for IMFI/BMT. The example can be seen in Table 21.4.

The results show that the micro-fintech needed by IMFI/BMT to be adopted in commercial sector agreed by all respondents is crowdfunding peer-to-peer (P2P) financing, complemented with payment and digital banking, although

Table 21.4 The example of a Delphi-Likert questionnaire

1	*Type of micro-fintech to be adopted by IMFI/BMT in commercial area*	*Ranking*	*Opinion*				
1.1	Digital Banking		1	2	3	4	5
1.2	Payment		1	2	3	4	5
1.3	Crowdfunding P2P Financing		1	2	3	4	5
1.4	E-Commerce		1	2	3	4	5
1.5	Insurtech		1	2	3	4	5
1.6	Capital Market		1	2	3	4	5
1.7	Integrated (various fintech needed)		1	2	3	4	5

Note: 1 = strongly disagree; 2 = disagree; 3 = neutral; 4 = agree; 5 = strongly agree.

Table 21.5 The example of Delphi results of Delphi-Likert

		Rater agreement (W)							
No.	*Characteristic*	*Expert*	*p-value*	*BMT*	*p-value*	*Fintech*	*p-value*	*All*	*p-value*
1	Type of micro-fintech to be adopted in commercial area	**0.395**	0.000***	**0.489**	0.000***	**0.448**	0.000***	**0.393**	0.000***
2	Type of micro-fintech to be adopted in social area	**0.575**	0.000***	**0.393**	0.000***	**0.584**	0.000***	**0.454**	0.000***
3	Micro-fintech for ZIS to be adopted	**0.407**	0.000***	**0.440**	0.000***	**0.725**	0.000***	**0.400**	0.000***
4	Micro-fintech waqf to be adopted	**0.379**	0.001***	**0.478**	0.000***	**0.618**	0.000***	**0.371**	0.000***
5	Integrated micro-fintech ZIS-waqf to be adopted	**0.416**	0.000***	**0.541**	0.000***	**0.552**	0.000***	**0.367**	0.000***

*** Significant at 1% level.

BMT prefers to implement digital banking first, followed by crowdfunding P2P financing, showing that BMTs feel more comfortable to collect commercial funding by itself first using digital banking to maintain their independence before turning to other sources, such as fintech. Meanwhile, the Delphi results show the significance of each question in the Delphi-Likert questionnaire, consisting of all 13 questions, where the 5 examples can be seen in Table 21.5.

Based on these agreed upon characteristics of micro-fintech for IMFI/BMT, the authors proposed several feasible micro-fintech models for IMFI/BMT, which could be selected by the IMFI/BMT depending on the current characteristics of the IMFI/BMT.

Delphi-SEM method

The SEM method is usually used to test the hypothesis (or hypotheses) supported by certain a theory (or theories) in the framework of causal modeling or path analysis, confirmatory factor analysis (CFA), second-order factor analysis, regression model, covariance structure model, and correlation structure model (Hair *et al.* 2010), which essentially use strictly a confirmatory approach or an alternative model approach. In addition, SEM could also be used in the framework of exploratory factor analysis (EFA) using the model development approach, whereas the supporting theory might not be firmly established, especially for frontier research, and there are very limited or no previous studies

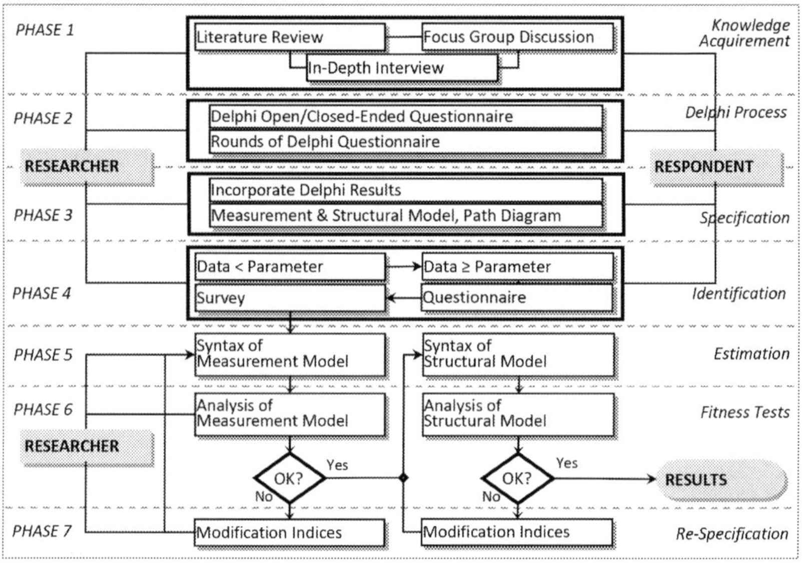

Figure 21.3 Steps of the Delphi-SEM method.

Source: Hsu and Sanford (2007), Hair *et al.* (2010), drawn and modified by the authors.

available to support the model development. Therefore, the Delphi method could be used to provide the scientific basis of the SEM model to be developed. The steps of the Delphi-SEM method could be seen in Figure 21.3.

Figure 21.3 essentially shows the steps of the Delphi method in the beginning (phase 1 and phase 2), as has been explained in Figure 21.2, where the results of Delphi will be used to develop the SEM model (measurement model and structural model) in phase 3. The next steps, phases 4–7, are steps of the SEM method described in the previous chapter. One example is the study by Tamanni *et al.* (2019), who aimed to identify new models for integration of Islamic social finance and Islamic commercial finance toward inclusive growth, which is built on the hypothesis that social and commercial financial integration, represented by ownership integration and operational integration, can play a role in strengthening inclusive growth. Unfortunately, there are no studies specifically which have formulated the three dimensions of integration depicted in Figure 21.4 on the left. Therefore, the authors started the study with the Delphi method to formulate these three dimensions of integration as SEM-latent variables and their respective indicators. Meanwhile, the growth indicators, economic, social, and financial, could be built based on the theory of growth.

Based on the Delphi method, the initial proposed model in Figure 21.4 has been refined and resulted in Figure 21.5 with five integration variables, with additional organization and mandatory integrations, as well as four growth indicator variables, with the breakdown of economic indicators into macroeconomic and microeconomic indicators.

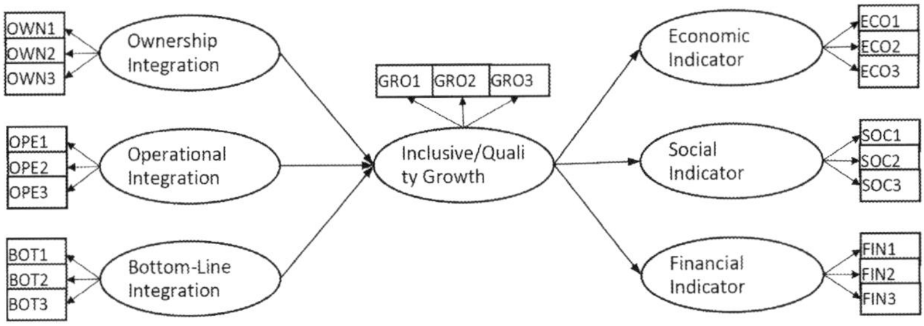

Figure 21.4 Proposed SEM model of Tamanni *et al.* (2019) before the Delphi method.

Source: Tamanni *et al.* (2019), drawn by the authors.

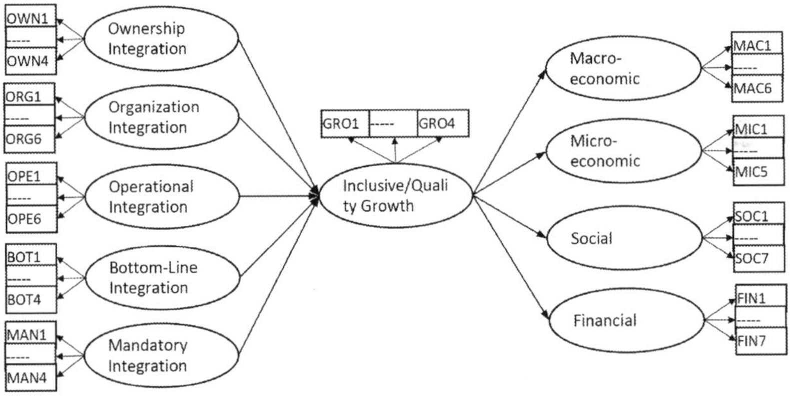

Figure 21.5 Proposed SEM model of Tamanni *et al.* (2019) after the Delphi method.

Source: Tamanni *et al.* (2019), drawn by the authors.

Delphi-ANP method

The ANP method usually is applied in multicriteria decision-making problems in various areas or disciplines. Similar to SEM, the ANP method is usually used in applied, explanatory, or deductive studies supported by a certain theory (or theories), so that the proposed ANP model and network developed can be scientifically justified. Moreover, the ANP method could also be used in more basic, exploratory, or inductive studies, as well as frontier studies, where the supporting theory (theories) has (have) not been developed. In addition, there are very limited or no previous studies available to support the study to develop the ANP model and network. To solve this problem, the Delphi method could be used to provide the scientific basis to develop the ANP model and network. The steps of the Delphi-ANP method could be seen in Figure 21.6.

Figure 21.6 essentially shows the steps of Delphi method in the beginning (step 1 and step 2), as has been explained in Figure 21.2, where the results of Delphi will be used to develop and design the proposed ANP model and

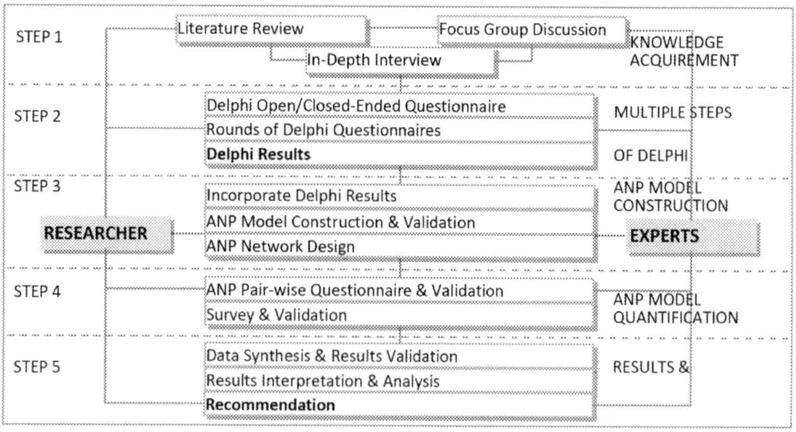

Figure 21.6 Steps of Delphi-ANP method.

Source: Hsu and Sanford (2007), Saaty and Vargas (2006), drawn and modified by the authors.

network step 3. The next steps, 4 and 5, are of the ANP method described in the previous chapter. One example is the study by Sakti *et al.* (2019), who aimed to determine the dominant orientation of microfinance providers in serving poor and micro-small enterprises through the use of group-lending approaches. The complexity in the relationships between causal and mediating factors, together with random environmental noise, causes difficulties in determining intangible and immeasurable parameters. Therefore, the authors started the study using the Delphi method, where the results could be used to develop a proposed ANP model, as can be seen in Figure 21.7.

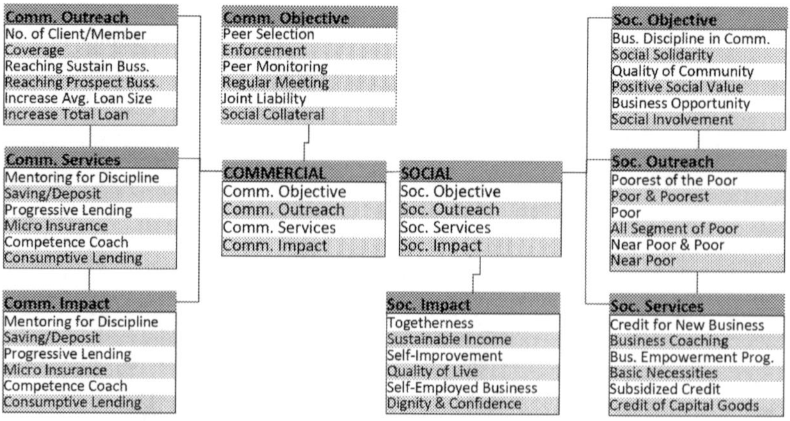

Figure 21.7 Proposed ANP model of Sakti *et al.* (2019) based on Delphi results.

Source: Sakti *et al.* (2019), drawn by the authors.

The above proposed ANP model has been developed based on statistically significant results of the Delphi method, which provides robust scientific basis for the ANP study.

Modified conventional theory

Many areas of IEF, especially in Islamic finance, have their counterparts in CEF, especially in conventional finance, including direct financial markets, such as capital markets (equity and bond) and money markets, as well as indirect financial markets, such as commercial banks, investment banks, insurance, finance companies, microfinance, pawnshops, and pension funds. Moreover, similarities of Islamic economics and conventional economics also exist, such as public finance, macroeconomy, and monetary. Studies of IEF or comparison between IEF and CEF in these areas mostly use econometric research, which could be defined as the quantitative analysis of actual economic phenomena based on the concurrent development of theory and observation, related by appropriate methods of inference. Goldberger (1964) defined econometrics as the social science in which the tools of economic theory, mathematics, and statistical inference are applied to the analysis of the economic phenomena, while Gujarati *et al.* (2004) defined econometrics as an amalgam of economic theory, mathematical economics, economic statistics, and mathematical statistics, illustrated in Figure 21.8, which could be applied for hypothesis testing, forecasting, prediction and policy purpose, or evaluation.

As has been discussed in the previous chapter, the research in IEF could use the methodology of conventional economics (Khan, 2018), including econometrics, which has theoretical econometrics and applied econometrics, so that it could be used for IEF theoretical and applied research. The crucial

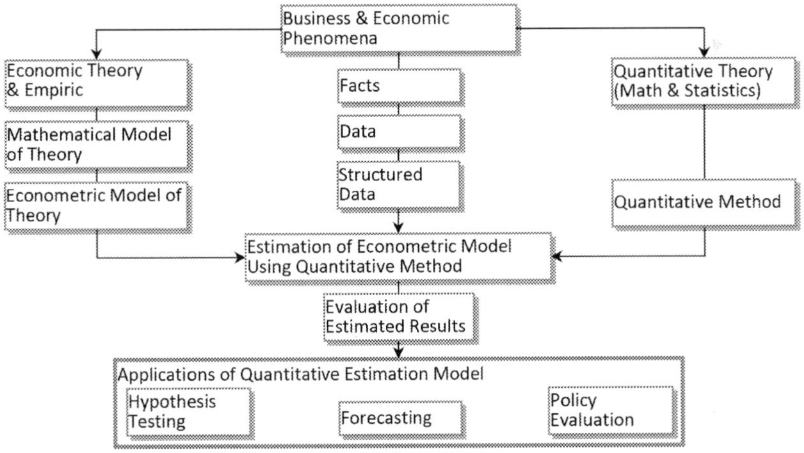

Figure 21.8 The anatomy of econometric modeling.

Source: Gujarati *et al.* (2004), drawn by the authors.

part here is in the first step in stating the theory or hypothesis, which could have not been developed, and/or the previous related studies are very limited or nonexistent. Here, we will discuss examples of IEF studies which modify conventional theories by replacing or inserting Islamic variables.

Modified Monetary Policy Transmission Mechanism

Ascarya (2014) studied the monetary policy transmission mechanism (MPTM), through interest-profit channels, under dual financial systems in Indonesia, in transmitting the monetary policy into real economy and prices. Here, Bank Indonesia, the central bank of Indonesia, introduced several Islamic monetary instruments comparable to conventional monetary instruments which comply with Shariah.

Based on Mishkin (2004) the conventional MPTM through the interest channel to output (IPI, industrial production index as the proxy of GDP) and price (CPI, consumer price index) can be formulated as follows:

$$IPI = f(nCCONS, rCDEP, PUAB, SBI) \quad (21.5)$$

$$CPI = f(nCCONS, rCDEP, PUAB, SBI) \quad (21.6)$$

Therefore, the Islamic MPTM through profit channel to output (IPI) and price (CPI) could be formulated as follows:

$$IPI = f(nICONS, rIDEP, PUAS, SBIS) \quad (21.7)$$

$$CPI = f(nICONS, rIDEP, PUAS, SBIS) \quad (21.8)$$

where rSBI: rate of SBI; rSBIS: return SBIS; rPUAB: rate of conventional interbank money market; rPUAS: return of Islamic money market; rCDEP: interest on conventional deposits; rIDEP: return on Islamic deposits; nCCONS: total amount of conventional consumption spending; nICONS: total amount of Islamic consumption spending; output or IPI: industrial production index; prices or CPI: consumer price index. Therefore, the MPTM under the dual financial system can be illustrated as follows (see Figure 21.9).

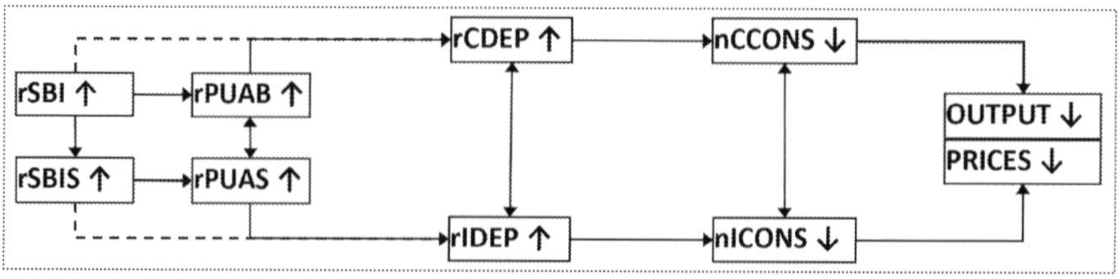

Figure 21.9 Interest-profit channels of MPTM under dual financial systems.

Meanwhile, the econometric model of interest-profit channels of MPTM under dual financial systems could be formulated as follows.

$$\text{IPI} = f(\text{nICONS}, \text{nCCONS}, \text{rIDEP}, \text{rCDEP}, \text{PUAS}, \text{PUAB}, \text{SBIS}, \text{SBI}) \tag{21.9}$$

$$\text{CPI} = f(\text{nICONS}, \text{nCCONS}, \text{rIDEP}, \text{rCDEP}, \text{PUAS}, \text{PUAB}, \text{SBIS}, \text{SBI}) \tag{21.10}$$

All six econometric models then were estimated using the VECM, since the variables were stationary at first difference and there existed at least one cointegration. For robustness tests, these models were also estimated using the ARDL and ECM.

Modified Technology Acceptance Model

Al-Banna (2019) did a study to examine the Muslim customers' behavior in purchasing halal food through online transactions. The author utilized the TAM developed by Davis (1989) and modified it to include Islamic variables, while the SEM method was applied. The original TAM can be illustrated in Figure 21.10.

There are two determinants of attitude toward use of certain technology, including perceived ease of use and perceived usefulness. Perceived usefulness is the degree to which an individual believes that using a particular information system or information technology would enhance his or her job or life performance. Perceived ease of use is the degree to which a person believes that using a particular information system or information technology would be free of effort. Since this is a study about Muslim customer behavior, the author modified the original TAM to include Islamic variables, namely religious knowledge and halal label, which could be seen in Figure 21.11.

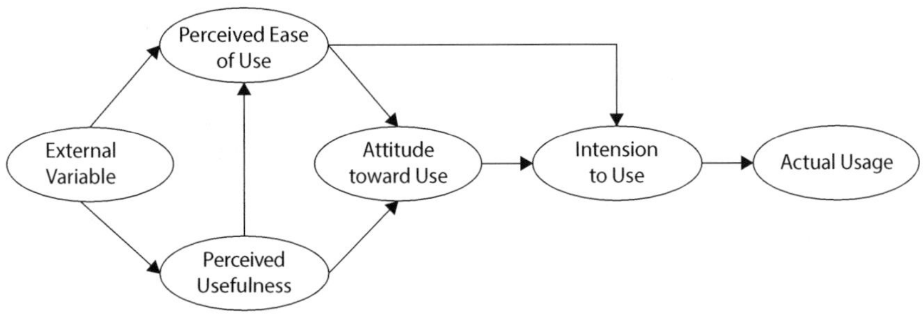

Figure 21.10 Technology acceptance model by Davis (1989).

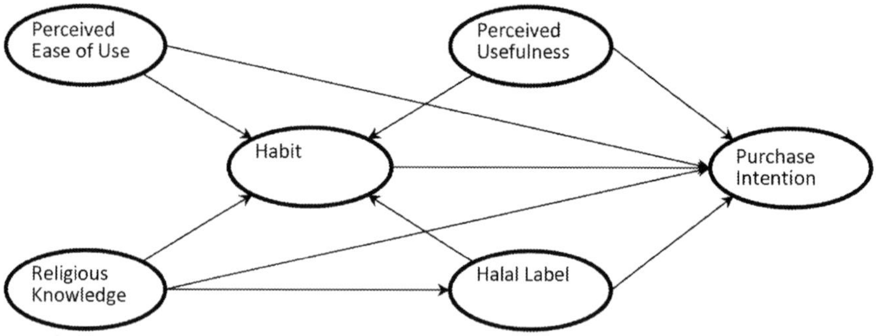

Figure 21.11 Modified technology acceptance model.

All of the additional variables, including habit, religious knowledge, and halal label, were supported by plenty of references, ensuring the scientific formulation of respected hypotheses.

Data Envelopment Analysis

Efficiency consists of two components. TE represents the ability of a business segment to maximize output for a certain quantity of inputs. Allocative efficiency (AE) expresses the ability of a business segment to use inputs in an efficient proportion based on their cost. When two different types of efficiency are combined, economic efficiency, or cost efficiency, or overall efficiency (OE) will be achieved. A company can be considered to be financially sensible if it is able to minimize the cost of production of certain output at the level of common technology and market prices. Tools to measure efficiency could be parametric and non-parametric. The parametric methods have advantages relative to the non-parametric methods of allowing for random error. These methods are less likely to misidentify measurement error, transitory differences in cost, or specification error for inefficiency. However, a disadvantage of the parametric methods is that they impose more structure on the shape of the frontier by specifying a functional form for it. There are three parametric econometric approaches, namely: (1) stochastic frontier approach (SFA); (2) thick frontier approach (TFA); and (3) distribution-free approach (DFA). The parametric approach to measuring efficiency uses a stochastic econometric and tries to eliminate the impact of disturbance to inefficiency.

Meanwhile, the non-parametric approach is used to measure the efficiency using a non-stochastic approach and tends to combine disturbance into inefficiency. One of the non-parametric approaches, known as DEA, is a mathematical programming technique that measures the efficiency of a decision-making unit (DMU) relative to other similar DMUs with the simple restrictions that all DMUs lie on or below the efficiency frontier.

Efficiency measurement, parametric or non-parametric, of financial institutions such as banks can be propositioned from their operations. There are three different approaches to explaining the relationship between bank input and output. Two approaches, namely the production (or operation) and the intermediation approach, apply the firm's classical microeconomic theory. One approach, namely a modern (or asset) approach, applies the modified firm's classical theory by incorporating certain specific features of bank activities, namely risk management and information processing, as well as some form of agency issues that are crucial to explaining the role of financial intermediaries (Freixas and Rochet, 1998).

The approach to production explains banking operations as the production process to depositors and borrowers by using accessible production factors, such as workers and fixed assets. Bell and Murphy (1968) started this approach and regarded banks as producing deposits to depositors and loans to creditors. Consequently, this approach defines input as the number of employees, capital expenditure on fixed assets, and other components, and identifies output as the total amount of all deposit accounts or other financial activities. According to Freixas and Rochet (1998) intermediation approach describes banking activities as an intermediary responsible for turning the money borrowed from depositors into the money lent to borrowers. In other words, typically divisible deposits, liquid, short-term deposits, and lower risk are transformed into typical indivisible, illiquid, long-term, and risky loans. This approach therefore defines input as financial equity, including the deposits collected and the funds borrowed, and output as volume of loans and outstanding investments.

The modern approach aims at improving the two first approaches through integration of risk management, information processing, and agency issues into the company's classical theory. This approach leads to a possible discrepancy of profit maximization behavior between the bank manager and the owner. If bank managers are not risk-neutral, they usually choose a level that is different from the cost reduction level (Figure 21.12).

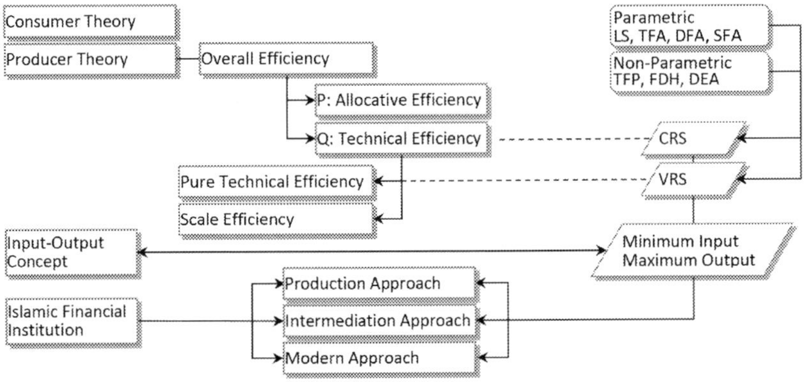

Figure 21.12 Overview theory of efficiency.

DEA is a non-parametric and non-deterministic tool for determining the relative efficiency of production frontiers, derived from empirical data of multiple inputs and outputs of DMUs. DEA can be used to evaluate multiple inputs and outputs without initially assigning weight. The efficiency produced is a relative efficiency based on observed data. Besides producing efficiency value for each DMU, DEA also determines DMUs that are used as reference for other inefficient DMUs (Charnes *et al.*, 1978).

In 1978, DEA was first introduced by Charnes, Cooper, and Rhodes. DEA does not require an a priori assumption about the analytical form of the production function, so it imposes very little structure on the shape of the efficient frontier. DEA allows to compare the relative efficiency of banks by establishing efficient banks as benchmarks and by assessing inefficiencies in input combinations in other banks relative to benchmarks. DEA is a non-parametric, deterministic approach for assessing the relative efficient production frontier.

$$Efficiency\ of\ DMU_0 = \frac{\sum_{k=1}^{p} \mu_k y_{k0}}{\sum_{i=1}^{m} v_k x_{i0}} \tag{21.11}$$

n DMUs to be evaluated; m different inputs; p = different outputs; x_{ij} = amount of input i consumed by DMUj; y_{kj} = amount of output k produced by DMUj.

There are two DEA models that are most frequently used, namely, the CCR and BCC models. The CCR model was developed by Charnes, Cooper, and Rhodes in 1978. Charnes *et al.* (1978) assumed that each DMU operates with constant return to scale (CRS). The CCR model measures the overall efficiency (OE = TE × SE). OE = AE × TE.

$$\max_{\mu_k,\, v_i} \sum_{k=1}^{P} \mu_k y_{k0}$$

$$s.t \sum_{i=1}^{m} v_i x_{i0} = 1$$

$$\sum_{k=1}^{p} \mu_k y_{kj} - \sum_{i=1}^{m} v_i x_{ij} \leq 0 \quad j = 1, \ldots, n$$

$$\mu_k \geq \varepsilon, v_i \geq \varepsilon;\ \mathrm{k} = 1, \ldots, \mathrm{p};\ \mathrm{i} = 1, \ldots, \mathrm{m} \tag{21.12}$$

x_{ij} is the number of input i consumed by DMUj and y_{kj} is the number of output k produced by DMUj.

Maximizing shown in the above formula represents TE or OE (CCR). Efficiency scores are always less than or equal to 1 (≤1). DMUs with an efficiency score of less than 1 mean that they are relatively inefficient, while DMUs with an efficiency score of equal to 1 mean that they are relatively efficient.

The BCC model was developed by Banker, Charnes, and Cooper in 1984. Banker *et al.* (1984) assumed that each DMU can operate with variable return to scale (VRS). BCC model measures the TE. TE can be broken down into pure TE (PTE) and scale efficiency (SE), so that TE = PTE × scale efficiency (SE). Therefore, OE = AE × PTE × SE.

$$\max_{\mu_k,\, v_i} \sum_{k=1}^{P} \mu_k y_{k0} - \mu_0$$

$$s.t \sum_{i=1}^{m} v_i x_{i0} = 1$$

$$\sum_{k=1}^{p} \mu_k y_{kj} - \sum_{i=1}^{m} v_i x_{ij} - \mu_0 \leq 0 \quad j = 1,\ldots,n$$

$$\mu_k \geq \varepsilon, v_i \geq \varepsilon;\ \mathrm{k} = 1,\ldots,\mathrm{p};\ \mathrm{i} = 1,\ \ldots,\ \mathrm{m} \tag{21.13}$$

where, x_{ij}: number of input i consumed by DMUj; y_{kj}: number of output k produced by DMUj.

The maximizing shown in the above formula represents pure TE (BCC). Efficiency scores are always less than or equal to 1 (≤1). DMUs with an efficiency score of less than 1 mean that they are relatively inefficient, while DMUs with an efficiency score of equal to 1 mean that they are relatively efficient.

In general, the efficiency score of the CCR model (technical efficiency or TE) for each DMU will not exceed the efficiency score of the BCC model (pure technical efficiency or PTE). TE will equal to PTE when SE (scale efficiency) is equal to 1. Meanwhile, Jemrić and Vujčić (2002) argued that the BCC model analyzes each DMU "locally" (i.e., compared to a subset of DMUs operating in the same region) rather than "globally."

The DEA method has been vastly developing into various types of DEA. Some of the most important DEA methods in Islamic economics and finance research, include: (a) the original CCR and BCC models; (b) DEA window analysis; and (c) various two-stage DEA methods. The development of various types of DEA methods can be seen in Table 21.6.

Table 21.6 The development of various DEA methods

No.	*Model*	*Year*	*Writer*
1	Data Envelopment Analysis CCR (CRS) Model	1978	Charnes, Cooper & Rodes
2	Non-Radial DEA	1978	Färe & Lovell
3	Malmquist Productivity Index	1982	Caves, Christensen & Diewert
4	Data Envelopment Analysis BCC (VRS) Model	1984	Banker, Charnes & Cooper
5	Free Disposal Hull [FDH]	1984	Deprins, Simar & Tulkens
6	DEA Additive Model	1985	Charnes, Cooper, Golany, Seiford & Stutz
7	DEA Window Analysis	1985	Charnes, Clarke, Cooper & Golany
8	DEA Assurance Region [DEA-AR]	1986	Thompson, Singleton, Thrall & Smith
9	DEA Cross Efficiency	1986	Sexton, Silkman & Hogan
10	DEA Facet Model	1988	Bessent, Bessent, Elam & Clark
11	DEA Super Efficiency	1988/1993	Banker & Gifford; Andersen & Petersen
12	DEA Cone Ratio	1990	Charnes, Cooper, Huang & Sun
13	Fuzzy DEA	1992	Sengupta
14	Dynamic Network DEA	1996	Färe & Grosskopf
15	Hierarchical/Nested Model DEA	1998	Cook, Chai, Doyle & Green
16	Bootstrap DEA (Two-Stage)	1998/2007	Simar & Wilson
17	DEA: Russell Measure [RM]	1999	Pastor, Ruiz & Sirvent
18	Imprecise Data DEA [IDEA]	1999	Cooper, Park & Yu
19	Parallel Model DEA	2000	Cook, Hababou, Tuenter
20	Dynamic DEA	2000	Fare & Grosskopf
21	Slack Based Measure [SBM] DEA	2001	Tone
22	Stochastic DEA	2002	Cooper, Deng, Huang & Susan
23	Three-Stage DEA	2002/2008	Fried, Lovel, Schmidt & Yaisawarng; Shang, Hung, Lo & Wang
24	Meta Frontier DEA	2003	Rao, O'Donnel & Battese
25	Context-Dependent DEA	2003	Seiford & Zhu
26	Hybrid (Radial and Non-Radial) DEA	2004	Podinovski; Tone
27	DEA: Game Cross-Efficiency	2008	Liang, Wu, Cook & Zhu
28	OLS DEA (Two-Stage)	2008	Banker & Natarajan
29	Two-Stage Fuzzy DEA	2011	Kao & Liu
30	Virtual Frontier Benevolent DEA Cross Efficiency model [VFB-DEA]	2015	Cui & Li
31	Hybrid Window DEA	2018	Halkos & Polemis
32	Game Meta-Frontier DEA	2019	Sun, Li & Wang
33	Two-Stage Network-Based Super DEA	2020	Wang & Feng

References

Al-Banna, H. (2019). Muslim customer behavior in halal food online purchasing. *Journal of Islamic monetary economics and finance*, *5*(3), 517–540.

Andersen, P., & Petersen, N. C. (1993). A procedure for ranking efficient units in data envelopment analysis. *Management science*, *39*(10), 1261–1264.

Ascarya, A. (2014). Monetary policy transmission mechanism under dual financial system in Indonesia: Interest-profit channel. *International journal of economics, management and accounting*, *22*(1), 1–32.

Banker, R. D., & Gifford, J. L. (1988). *A Relative Efficiency Model for the Evaluation of Public Health Nurse Productivity*. Pittsburgh: Carnegie Mellon University.

Bell, F. W., & Murphy, N. B. (1968). Economies of scale and division of labor in commercial banking. *Southern economic journal*, *35*, 131–139.

Caves, D. W., Christensen, L. R., & Diewert, W. E. (1982). The economic theory of index numbers and the measurement of input, output, and productivity. *Econometrica: Journal of the econometric society*, *50*, 1393–1414.

Charnes, A., Cooper, W. W., Huang, Z. M., & Sun, D. B. (1990). Polyhedral cone-ratio DEA models with an illustrative application to large commercial banks. *Journal of econometrics*, *46*(1–2), 73–91.

Cook, W. D., Chai, D., Doyle, J., & Green, R. (1998). Hierarchies and groups in DEA. *Journal of productivity analysis*, *10*(2), 177–198.

Cooper, W. W., Park, K. S., & Yu, G. (1999). IDEA and AR-IDEA: Models for dealing with imprecise data in DEA. *Management science*, *45*(4), 597–607.

Dalkey, N., & Helmer, O. (1963). An experimental application of the Delphi method to the use of experts. *Management science*, *9*(3), 458–467.

Deprins, D., & Simar, L. H. Tulkens (1984), Measuring labor inefficiency in post offices. In M. Marchand, P. Pestieau and H. Tulkens (eds.), *The Performance of Public Enterprises: Concepts and Measurements* (pp. 243–264). Amsterdam, North-Holland.

Färe, R., & Grosskopf, S. (1996). Productivity and intermediate products: A frontier approach. *Economics letters*, *50*(1), 65–70.

Freixas, X., & Rochet, J. C. (1998). Fair pricing of deposit insurance. Is it possible? Yes. Is it desirable? No. *Research in Economics*, 52(3), 217–232.

Green, P. J. (1982, March). *The content of a college-level outdoor leadership course*. Paper presented at the Conference of the Northwest District Association for the American Alliance for Health, Physical Education, Recreation, and Dance, Spokane, WA.

Gujarati, D. N., Bernier, B., & Bernier, B. (2004). *Econométrie*. Brussels: De Boeck.

Hair, J. F., Black, W. C., Babin, J. B., & Anderson, R. E. (2010). *Multivariate Data Analysis*. (7th ed.). Upper Saddle River, NJ: Prentice Hall.

Halkos, G. E., & Polemis, M. L. (2018). The impact of economic growth on environmental efficiency of the electricity sector: A hybrid window DEA methodology for the USA. *Journal of environmental management*, *211*, 334–346.

Jemrić, I., & Vujčić, B. (2002). Efficiency of banks in Croatia: A DEA approach. *Comparative economic studies*, *44*(2), 169–193.

Khan, M. A. (2018). Methodology of Islamic economics from Islamic teachings to Islamic economics. *Turkish journal of Islamic economics (TUJISE)*, *5*(1), 35–61.

Lateh, N., Din, G., Osman, M. R., Yaakob, E., & Rejab, S. N. (2016). Application of the Delphi technique in the formation of Shariah-compliant gold instrument (SCGI). In Ab. Manan, S. K., Abd. Rahman, F., & Sahri, M. (Eds.). *Contemporary Issues and Development in the Global Halal Industry* (pp. 81–94). Singapore: Springer.

Mahyudi, M. (2020). Islamic economics as an integrated social science: Novel ideas on its foundations. In Kizilkaya, N. (Ed.). *Methodology of Islamic Economics: Problems and Solutions* (pp. 134–158). New York, NY: Routledge.

Nyumba, T. O., Wilson, K., Derrick, C. J., & Mukherjee, N. (2018). The use of focus group discussion methodology: Insights from two decades of application in conservation. *Methods in ecology and evolution*, *9*(9), 20–32.

Podinovski, V. V. (2004). Production trade-offs and weight restrictions in data envelopment analysis. *Journal of the operational research society*, *55*(12), 1311–1322.

Rosman, R., Wahab, N. A., & Zainol, Z. (2014). Efficiency of Islamic banks during the financial crisis: An analysis of Middle Eastern and Asian countries. *Pacific-basin finance journal*, *28*, 76–90.

Saaty, T. L., & Vargas, L. G. (2006). The analytic hierarchy process: wash criteria should not be ignored. *International journal of management and decision making*, *7*(2–3), 180–188.

Sakti, A., Husodo, Z. A., & Viverita, V. (2019). The orientation of microfinance regarding group-lending strategy: Delphi and analytic network process evidence. *Pertanika journal of social sciences & humanities*, *27*(S2), 197–212.

Scheibe, M., Skutsch, M., & Schofer, J. (1975). Experiments in Delphi methodology. In H. A. Linstone, & M. Turoff (Eds.). *The Delphi Method: Techniques and Applications* (pp. 262–287). Reading, MA: Addison-Wesley Publishing Company.

Sexton, T. R., Silkman, R. H., & Hogan, A. J. (1986). Data envelopment analysis: Critique and extensions. *New directions for program evaluation*, *1986*(32), 73–105.

Somerville, R. S., Hopkins, P. F., Cox, T. J., Robertson, B. E., & Hernquist, L. (2008). A semi-analytic model for the co-evolution of galaxies, black holes and active galactic nuclei. *Monthly notices of the Royal Astronomical Society*, *391*(2), 481–506.

Sufian, F. and Akbar Noor Mohamad Noor, M. (2009), The determinants of Islamic banks' efficiency changes: Empirical evidence from the MENA and Asian banking sectors, *International journal of Islamic and Middle Eastern finance and management*, *2*(2), 120–138.

Thompson, R. G., Singleton Jr, F. D., Thrall, R. M., & Smith, B. A. (1986). Comparative site evaluations for locating a high-energy physics lab in Texas. *Interfaces*, *16*(6), 35–49.

Tone, K. (2001). A slacks-based measure of efficiency in data envelopment analysis. *European journal of operational research*, *130*(3), 498–509.

Ulschak, F. L. (1983). *Human Resource Development: The Theory and Practice of Need Assessment*. Reston, VA: Reston Publishing Company, Inc.

Van Zolingen, S. J., & Klaassen, C. A. (2003). Selection processes in a Delphi study about key qualifications in senior secondary vocational education. *Technological forecasting and social change*, *70*(4), 317–340.

Williams, P. L., & Webb, C. (1994). The Delphi technique: a methodological discussion. *Journal of advanced nursing*, *19*(1), 180–186.

22

CHALLENGES FACED IN ADOPTING STANDARD METHODOLOGIES FOR RESEARCH IN ISLAMIC FINANCE AND THE WAY OUT

Monsurat Ayojimi Salami, Harun Tanrivermiş and Mustapha Abubakar

Introduction

Islamic finance is a discipline that deals with the financing aspect of Islamic economy in accordance with *Shari'ah* rulings. The emergence of Islamic economics dates back to the mid-1970s (Hasan, 2018). Islamic finance activities are therefore expected to strictly handle matters relating to five components of *Maqasid al-Shari'ah* (the higher objective of *Shari'ah*): the protection of religion (*din*), intellect (*'aql*), life (*nafs*), lineage (*nasl*), and wealth (*mal*) (Hosen et al., 2019), and the effectiveness to be verifiable through appropriate research methodologies. Similarly, the methodology in conducting Islamic finance research should be capable of providing reliable information and interpretation from the context of the *Maqasid al-Shari'ah*. To achieve this, perfect integration of contextual knowledge about Islamic finance and methodology for doing research is expected from the persons conducting Islamic finance research to be able to convey required interpretation of the findings from the *Shari'ah* perspective. In support of this, Laldin and Furqani (2018) reported that collaboration between Shari'ah scholars, Islamic finance researchers, and Islamic finance experts enhances formulation of robust *Shari'ah* standard and operation parameters, which the Bank Negara Malaysia (Central Bank of Malaysia) later sent to industry for the feedback on the practicability of the standard.

However, contextual knowledge about Islamic finance and Islamic finance research methodologies are in the hands of two different categories of people. The first category is Islamic finance scholars who are expert in dealing with different contemporary issues arising from Islamic finance, and the second category is the researchers who are interested in Islamic finance research.

DOI: 10.4324/9781003252764-26

Islamic scholars can be defined as experts in understanding and interpretation of the *Quran* and *Hadith* (saying and practice of the Holy Prophet Muhammed [peace and blessings upon him]) who are capable of addressing financial related matters from the context of the Islamic Holy Book. In most cases, Islamic finance scholars constitute *Shari'ah* governance in Islamic organizations. In addition, Abidin, Yasin, and Abidin (2020) described *Shari'ah* governance as experts who guide corporate transactions through the financial and transaction rulings according to the *Quran* and *Hadith*.

Unfortunately, only a minority have knowledge of both required to achieve meaningful Islamic finance research. In other words, the majority of experts in the context of Islamic finance rulings are not equally expert in the methodology of doing research in Islamic finance. The majority of researchers in Islamic finance are from the mainstream secular discipline and provide research methodology training for future researchers in Islamic finance based on statistical interpretation. Hasan (2018) described overuse of mathematical and parametric modeling in Islamic finance research as a disadvantage to the discipline. The understanding that majority in Islamic finance are distinguished but lack integrated knowledge needed in conducting Islamic finance research has posed challenges in the way and manner Islamic finance research are conducted. This constituted one of the challenges in adopting standard methodology for research in Islamic finance. In the quest for standardized Islamic finance research methodology, much research conducted in Islamic finance resembles conventional finance, and their findings are interpreted in a conventional sense. For instance, Gunn and Shackman (2014) concluded that long-term equity investment may slow down economic growth in Muslim countries. The authors' argument was based on the fact that Islamic finance is too inflexible to allow debt investment as alternative investment. This kind of argument does not support fundamental principles of Islamic finance. As long as interest-based transactions are prohibited in Islamic finance, such is no longer a basis for supporting evidence for Islamic finance research findings. Contrarily, Chazi and Syed (2010) revealed that Islamic banks were protected during global financial crisis because they completely abstained from interest-based transactions involving *gharar* (excessive uncertainty). Both payment and receipt of *riba* (interest) are prohibited in Islamic finance transactions (Naifar, 2016). Therefore, such a distinct difference poses challenges in using conventional understanding to interpret findings in Islamic finance research.

Furthermore, Islamic finance researchers are unable to blend the jurisprudence knowledge of Islamic scholars with mainstream secular discipline knowledge due to different worldviews. To fulfill higher objectives of *Shari'ah*, standardization of Islamic finance methodologies has been a subject of debate among Islamic scholars. Some researchers expect a significant difference in the way and manner in which Islamic financial institutions are dealing with matters relating to *Maqasid al-Shari'ah*. They therefore argued in favor of standard methodologies that to carry out research in Islamic finance is essential to convey reliable information to Islamic finance users. However, this has not been achieved ever since the commencement of Islamic finance. Those arguments pointed toward having standard Islamic finance research methodology, which might provide more reliable information beyond prediction from data analysis. For instance, Kamla and Rammal (2013) reported that when Islamic banks are being criticized for financing terrorist organizations, Islamic banks strengthen their report toward their involvement in ethical financing and socially responsible activities to refute the allegation. In addition, another study reveals that a company's annual reports provide reliable information for strengthen research findings (Unerman, 2000). In contrast to those findings, some studies have argued that companies' disclosures are an not accurate reflection of their actual events and practices (Ingram and Frazier, 1980; Ullman 1985). With these series of conflicting findings and arguments, total reliance on prediction from data analysis through methodology may not provide convincing information about how companies are doing. Therefore, contextual interpretation from Islamic finance scholars may be required to bridge the gaps that data analysis might failed to provide or even strengthen the findings.

In addition, it is well acknowledged that Accounting and Auditing Organization of Islamic Financial Institutions (AAOIFI) is an international Islamic financial body that sets a series of standard accounting reports to be adopted in Islamic financial institutions. However, different countries in which Islamic finance is being practiced have different accounting standards that guide their reports as well. This is argued to have posed more challenges, especially to Islamic banking. It ought to have been understood that Islamic financial institutions have to comply with both conventional financial reporting standards and *Shari'ah* requirements as specified by central banks of various countries. It is obvious that Islamic financial institutions have to equally comply with rules and regulations set by conventional financial and *Shari'ah* requirements (Kamla and Rammal, 2013). From a *Shari'ah* requirement perspective, Islamic financial institutions have to pay attention to components of *Maqasid al-Shari'ah* which may vary in proportion across different Islamic finance institutions in different countries. In addition, differences may also arise from the treatment of accounting information based on adaptation or adoption of IFRS across the countries that are practicing Islamic finance. Usually, these differences are ignored when researchers are using annual report data for cross-country studies with those using different IFRS policies. This is because different accounting reporting treats some accounting items in the annual reports differently, which tends to have different final results. For instance, some cross-country studies might have been using different international accounting standard reporting, such as IFRS, either by adoption or adaptation, in which some countries practicing Islamic finance are not excluded. In fact, some differences in treating some accounting items are expected between those countries that adopt IFRS and those that adapt IFRS. Unfortunately, such differences usually ignored by Islamic finance researchers even though it might have significant impact on their findings. Although most researchers ignored differences in the assumption behind adoption and adaptation of international accounting standards being used in the country of their study, this does not indicate that the impact is negligible in their findings, especially for cross-country studies that apply different IFRS policy. However, this may be another challenge which calls for standardization that researchers in Islamic finance need to take note of. This is because it opposes focusing data analysis alone in predicting the contribution of Islamic financial institutions to the real economy and in making decisions on whether the expectations have been attained.

It could be perceived that methodology standardization in Islamic finance research would not allow research findings to reflect uniqueness of Islamic finance practices across different countries. Therefore, without standardization of methodology for research in Islamic finance, there is greater tendency that Islamic finance findings regarding similar subject matter may be different in different countries even within the same region. For example, findings from the Saudi Arabian studies may be different from findings from Kuwait, Qatar, Bahrain, United Arab Emirates, and Oman, even though they are GCC. Sarea and Salami (2021) revealed that Islamic social reporting (ISR) disclosure varies across GCC and most Islamic banks comply with mandatory aspects of ISR disclosure rather than both voluntary and mandatory aspects of the reporting. To some extent, those differences in the findings could be traced to the differences in the policy of adoption or adaptation of international accounting standards they are using. Therefore, standardizing methodology for research in Islamic finance may make the findings from research mislead majority users in making sound investment decisions or justifying the health of Islamic finance. This is because not all the countries that practice Islamic finance have standardized *Shari'ah* rules and regulations, which may bring about some variation in findings. The variations in the findings may also be subject to the weight given to the five components of *Maqasid al-Shari'ah* by independent *Shari'ah* scholars across different Islamic financial institutions in different countries.

The second section discusses categories of challenges facing Islamic finance research methodology standardization, which is further divided into subsections. The third section elaborates and enlists differences in the Islamic finance research that are against adoption of standard methodology for research in Islamic finance. The fourth section focuses on conclusions and discussions.

Challenges faced by Islamic finance research

As noted earlier, the proposition for adopting standard methodology for research in Islamic finance has been an issue of debate among Islamic scholars. This has brought about different views from the researchers. Some Islamic researchers have been agitating for standard methodology for research in Islamic finance with the view that it may enhances comparison as well as set the benchmark of research findings across different Islamic finance-practicing countries. Some Islamic scholars argued against setting standard methodology as their argument in favor of uniqueness of different Islamic activities, which requires completely unique techniques. In addition, Islamic scholars are not in favor of tailoring Islamic finance research to please international investors. This is because the main objective of Islamic finance may be distorted in the process. This argument is consistent with findings in the study by Mohamad, Ahmed, and Badri (2017) that no one method fits for all. Similarly, Razak and Taib (2011) consider use of rental rates as a benchmark for enhancing fairness in home financing. It is obvious that rental rates would vary across locations and the type of buildings to be developed. Both studies emphasize that Islamic finance instruments as well as research require unique approaches for unique matter. In line with this, the challenges faced in adopting standard methodology for research in Islamic finance are further elaborated on in subsections below based on different categories identified in Islamic finance research.

Islamic scholars and contextual understanding of Islamic finance

Once Islamic scholars understand the challenges faced by Islamic banking and finance, it is their responsibility to design *Shari'ah*-compliant instruments that would not undermine the competitiveness, profitability, and viability of the bank in the long run (Dusuki and Abozaid, 2007). Smolo and Hassan (2011) also reveal that it is impossible for the Islamic banking and finance industry to come up with new instruments without referring back to Islamic holy books. Therefore, developing a well-explained standard with fundamental *Shari'ah* requirements for different Islamic instruments or contracts as stipulated by the Islamic Financial Services Act (IFSA) of 2013 is highly essential (Laldin and Furqani, 2018). This may also be another reason that scholars in Islamic finance believe that caution is needed on standardization of methodologies for Islamic finance research, to prevent resemblance of Islamic finance with conventional finance findings in the long run and, furthermore, to prevent jeopardization of the main objective of Islamic finance in fulfilling *Maqasid al-Shari'ah*. Contrary to that, the danger of not having methodology was pointed out in the study by Eldersevi and Haron (2020) that the *Shari'ah* committees of Islamic financial institutions validated Islamic instruments that maximize profit, which compromises Shari'ah principles. With the fact that most *Shari'ah* scholars in Islamic finance are more comfortable contributing to Islamic finance research through interviews, most of the studies involving *Shari'ah* scholars are in qualitative format. Kashi and Mohamad (2017) reported that an in-depth interview was conducted with some *Shari'ah* scholars for them to identify issues in *Musharakah Mutanaqisah* Partnership (MMP) and to prevent the product from converging with conventional home financing. This emphasizes that comprehensive information regarding Islamic finance instruments could only be received through interviews, especially in the absence of quantitative data or when available quantitative data is unable to provide sufficient information required. In this sense, standardizing methodology of research in Islamic finance may pose a series of challenges since prominent Islamic scholars are few in number. Table 22.1 presents some qualitative research conducted with Islamic scholars.

Table 22.1 Qualitative Islamic finance research involving Islamic scholars

Authors	*Research objectives*	*Date sources*	*Country*	*Findings*
Abidin, Yasin, and Abidin (2020)	Interdependence among *Shari'ah* committee	Semi-structured interview	Malaysia	Suggested that the *Shari'ah* committee should deliver their duties as the bank's professionals without heavily relying on remuneration from banks for their living.
Eldersevi and Haron (2020)	Evaluation of resolution issued by Shari'ah Advisory of Central Bank Negara Malaysia (SAC-BNM)	Comparative technique	Malaysia	Found that the resolution issued by the Shari'ah Advisory of Central Bank Negara Malaysia is consistent with *Maslahah* (public interest).
Ahmad (2019)	Poverty alleviation through *Zakat* and *Waqf* institutions	Semi-structured interview	Nigeria	Revealed that improper awareness about *Zakat* and *Waqf* has slowed down the use of Islamic financial instruments in alleviating poverty in the country.
Jabar, Ramli and Sazali (2018)	Focuses on ***Musharakah*** *Mutanaqisah* as provided by Islamic cooperatives (ICs) regarding default and more	Interview	Malaysia	Found that despite a significant record of abandoned housing projects, ICs never take bankruptcy action against customers; instead, they use a negotiation approach to understand the situation and extend term of payment, if there is need for it.
Thaker (2018)	Cash *Waqf*	Semi-structured interview	Malaysia	Proposed that cash *Waqf* may ease financing challenges facing micro- enterprises, as a proposed approach to further encouraging micro-enterprises for their contributions toward poverty reduction, reduced unemployment, and increased standard of living.
Kashi and Mohamad (2017)	Study related to *Shari'ah* aspect and technical issues in implementing MMP.	In-depth interview	Malaysia	Found MMP, BBA, and conventional housing loans to be converging, especially in benchmarking and the default case.

Note: MMP indicates Musharakah Mutanaqisah Partnership. Malaysia is considered one of the leading countries in the Islamic finance industry (IFI) (Laldin and Furqani, 2018).

Sources: Authors' own extractions from previous studies.

Islamic finance researchers and understanding of research methodology

As well acknowledged that research reveals essential information about the objectives of the study, if well conducted together with underlying assumptions of the methodology applied is not violated. As noted earlier, the worldview of most of the researchers in Islamic finance drives the interpretation of their findings. This was due to the earlier need to open the door for academic and support staff from mainstream secular disciplines, while some of them do not have needed knowledge of Islamic jurisprudence (Hasan, 2018). This has made several studies conducted by the researchers in Islamic finance tend more toward academic purposes rather than for industrial use. Furthermore, several kinds of methodology adopted in Islamic finance research are just to verify whether their research objectives are achieved or not. Still, their findings are not tailored in Layman's terms, which made those studies less attractive to the intended users. In other words, their outcomes are less useful for the industrial purposes and individual users. Eventually, most of Islamic finance research remained in publishers' databases and university libraries.

Focus of Islamic finance researchers on econometrics modeling and conventional worldview interpretation

Because Islamic finance covers all aspects of *Shari'ah* compliance business, several researchers have been adopting techniques used in conventional finance to handle research in Islamic finance. Their argument is that once practices of Islamic finance are in compliance with *Shari'ah*, using conventional methodology could be benchmark to avoid double standards in evaluation. However, this has brought about criticism toward Islamic finance research. A series of criticisms has been leveled on findings from Islamic finance studies as they are converging with conventional finance (Godlewski, Turk-Ariss, and Weill, 2013). Another study by Zubairu, Sakariyau, and Dauda (2012) argued that after evaluating social reporting of four Islamic banks in Saudi Arabia over the period 2008–2009, their involvement resembles conventional banks' social responsibility rather than *Shari'ah* requirements. In a recent study, Hasan (2018) argued that Islamic finance researchers have overused the mathematical and parametric modeling to the disadvantage of studies in Islamic finance. For more clarity, Table 22.2 presents some of the recent studies on Islamic finance and the techniques used.

National accounting standards in different Islamic financing practicing countries

With less attention of researchers on national accounting standards used in different countries over adoption of a particular research methodology design may eventually have significant impact on final outcomes of their

Table 22.2 Islamic finance Research and methodologies adopted

Authors	*Research objectives*	*Methodology*	*Findings*
Kamla and Rammal (2013)	Social reporting by Islamic banks	Explicative content analysis techniques	Revealed that Islamic banks disclosure lack detail information regarding poverty eradication or enhancing social justice.
Yıldırım, Yıldırım, and Diboglu (2020)	Sukuk market development and economic growth	Cointegration techniques	Found long run relationship between Sukuk market and economic growth.
Ledhem (2020)	Sukuk financing and economic growth	One-step GMM	Concluded that Sukuk financing is boosting economic growth in Southeast Asia.
Jalil and Rahman (2012)	Sukuk investment using Ijarah and *Musharakah Mutanaqisah*	Mathematical technique	Revealed that Sukuk by Ijarah is more profitable to investors than Sukuk by *Musharakah Mutanaqisah*
Ahroum *et al.* (2018)	*Sukuk* investment using Ijarah and *Musharakah Mutanaqisah*	Rebalancing technique	Found that despite that Sukuk investment is growing still 'buy and hold' is distorting rate of growing of Sukuk investment.
Godlewski, Turk-Ariss, and Weill (2013)	Sukuk vs. conventional bond	OLS regression	Concluded that Sukuk mirrors conventional securities, which raises the criticism on whether *Shari'ah* innovative financial instruments are different from conventional bonds.
Naifar (2016)	Dependence structure between Sukuk and stock market returns	Archimedean copula Model	Found that Sukuk yield only shows significant dependency on stock market return volatility.
Maghyereh and Abdoh (2020)	Sukuk, gold, and Islamic stocks	Quantile cross-spectral dependence technique (QS)	Concluded that gold is not always safe-haven especially during bullish -bearish but may be safe-haven during short term and normal economic condition.
Alkhazali and Zoubi (2020)	Gold and portfolio diversification of Islamic indices	Stochastic dominance (SD) technique	Revealed that by including gold in Islamic stock indices, portfolio maximizes investors' expected utilities.
Kok, Giorgioni, and Laws (2014)	Investigated Islamic banks risk tools –*wa'ad* (contractually binding promise) and *murabaha* (cost plus sale)	Options technique	Found that innovative Islamic risk sharing tools oppose conventional risk transferring tools.

Note: Different research techniques were used to investigate whether their research objectives are achieved or not. However, most Islamic research findings would have contributed to the economy in a more meaningful manner and caught the attention of appropriate end users, provided that contextual interpretations are not misleading.

Sources: Authors' own extraction from previous studies.

studies and somehow resulted into misleading conclusions. Among the challenges in Islamic finance studies are Islamic finance researchers, especially as those that are using accounting ratios tend to use the same view to evaluate Islamic finance studies in different regions and draw conclusions, even though those countries are using different accounting standards. In other words, most of the countries that are practicing Islamic finance have their national accounting standards, which in most cases institutions need to adopt together with international accounting standards as presented in Table 22.3. From Table 22.3, it could be observed that most of the countries adopted IFRS and some adapted IFRS, whilst few countries neither adopt IFRS nor adapt IFRS. It is obvious that there would be some differences in the manner in which some accounting items would be treated across those countries. In addition, Kok, Giorgioni, and Laws (2014) argued that Malaysia is the only country that has clear rules and regulations regarding Islamic finance among

Table 22.3 Accounting standards complied with in different countries that practice Islamic finance

Countries	*International accounting standard policy used in different Islamic finance practicing countries*	*Region*
Saudi Arabia	Adopting IFRS	Arabic speaking countries
Kuwait	Adapting IFRS	
Qatar	Adopting IFRS	
United Arab Emirates	Adapting IFRS	
Jordan	Adapting IFRS	
Bahrain	Adopting IFRS	
Oman	Adapting IFRS	
Egypt	Nil	
Malaysia	Adopting IFRS	Asian
Indonesia	Nil	
Brunei	Adapting IFRS	
Pakistan	Adopting IFRS	
Turkey	Adopting IFRS	
Afghanistan	Adopting IFRS	
Bangladesh	Adopting IFRS	
Iran	Adopting IFRS	
Nigeria	Adapting IFRS	Africa
United Kingdom	Adopting IFRS	Europe

Note: IFRS indicates International Financial Reporting Standards. Adapting IFRS implies that the country is fully implementing all rules and regulations for treatment of accounting items as stated in the IFRS. Adopting IFRS implies that the country only applies some of the IFRS rules and regulations to some accounting items while applying its national financial reporting to other accounting items. Due to this difference, IFRS policies of each country may be necessary to take into account in cross-country analysis, especially for that analysis that requires accounting ratios.

Source: https://www.ifrs.org/use-around-the-world/use-of-ifrs-standards-by-jurisdiction/.

most of the countries that are practicing Islamic finance, while other countries such Pakistan and those in the Middle East rely on individual religion scholars and their interpretations of the Holy Quran. Therefore, differences in treatment of accounting posting are expected, which researchers need to take into consideration, but they are ignored. This argues that research in Islamic finance is not just about having access to data to proceed with analysis but to ensure that other factors that may affect the analysis are taking to consideration.

Research gaps between Islamic finance research and practitioners

As noted, Islamic finance as alternative financing to conventional finance attracts both Muslim and non-Muslim investors. In line with this, the majority of the Muslim transactions in Islamic finance are those who believe that Islam handles every aspect of human life and they are going to be accountable for everything in the hereafter. Hence, demand for *Shari'ah*-compliant products is growing drastically to meet demand from Muslims who are conscious of their affairs to be in accordance with *Shari'ah* (Smolo and Hassan, 2011). In addition, some non-Muslims who also prefer ethical finance have been patronizing Islamic finance as a way out. These imply that expectations from Islamic finance are far beyond what people have already known about conventional finance. According to Cebeci (2012) the users of Islamic finance are expecting clear differences in the way and manner Islamic finance handles financing matters compared to conventional finance. To achieve this, convincing research plays a significant role in revealing whether these expectations are met or not. Thorough Islamic finance research could convey the right messages to the current users as well as potential users of Islamic financial instruments. Usually, many use findings from several Islamic finance research to make inferences on whether Islamic finance fulfills necessary conditions to meet such high expectations. This strengthens the fact that appropriate research methodologies are essential while contextual interpretation of the findings according to the core value of Islamic finance is crucial in Islamic finance research.

Several studies conducted by the researchers in Islamic finance serve academic purposes rather than industrial functions. This remains a serious concern on how to blend Islamic finance research with economic development in an understandable way. In most cases, methodology adopted in Islamic research may be full of econometrics terminology instead of focusing on Layman understanding that would enhance effective use of the findings. In other words, most of the Islamic finance findings are less useful for the industrial purposes. In a similar sense, Islamic finance researchers have been called upon on several occasions to focus on practical implications of their findings and work closely with industrial personnel to enhance economic benefits in their findings.

Differences in the Islamic finance research as against adoption of standard methodology

Based on findings from the above, it is clear that research on Islamic finance may not necessarily have standardized methodology based on several reasons. Firstly, some of the research on Islamic finance needs consultation with Islamic scholars and their information is usually qualitative. Furthermore, uniqueness of research subject matter may not allow standardization of methodology for research in Islamic finance. Secondly, in some situations, research conducted in Islamic finance may require collecting information from certain groups of people. For that unique reason, researchers tend to develop unique research questions for the purpose of collecting information regarding the subject matter. Information collected through self-developed questionnaires may not necessarily have similar research objectives that would require using standardized research methodology.

On the other hand, the research conducted with secondary data may not necessarily attract the same standard methodologies but instead are tailored in relation to research objectives. Sufficient attention is required on the use of accounting ratios from different international accounting standard policies, especially when a study focuses on different countries practicing Islamic finance, such as adoption of IFRS and adaptation of IFRS. Underrating IFRS policy in use may be more severe for cross-country studies if accounting reporting differences based on IFRS policy is not accounted for. Coupled with the series of challenges stated earlier, Islamic banks which constitute a substantial part of Islamic finance have been overwhelmed with a series of rules and regulations to comply with and have their methodology of doing research as well as other Islamic financial instructions. Therefore, they may not abide with methodology standardization for research different from theirs. Table 22.4 presents the summary of different categories involving in Islamic finance research and data sources, which further clarifies the basis for different methodologies in Islamic finance research.

Table 22.4 Basis for different methodologies in Islamic finance research

Categories	*Data source*	*Data*	*Remarks*
Islamic scholars	Primary data	Interview	Methodology standardization of Islamic finance research is not visible under different data approach.
Researchers in Islamic finance	Primary data	Questionnaire	
	Secondary data	Annual report data	
Industry and individual users	Accounting standard	Adoption of IFRS	
		Adaptation of IFRS	

It is clearly shown that available data may drive methodology, not necessarily vice versa.

Sources: Authors' own extraction from previous studies.

Conclusion

This study examines different challenges faced in adopting standard methodologies for research in Islamic finance and the way out. The study has pointed out that challenges arise from several aspects among different individuals in Islamic finance industries having unintegrated knowledge required to do comprehensive research in Islamic finance. The authors pointed out that some Islamic finance experts are knowledgeable contextually while others are researchers in the field of Islamic finance. The inability of some Islamic finance researchers from mainstream secular disciplines to blend the jurisprudence knowledge of Islamic scholars in Islamic finance research serves as a great challenge in differentiating Islamic finance findings from conventional finance findings. Godlewski, Turk-Ariss, and Weill (2013) reported that Sukuk is generally structured along with Western rules of asset securitization, which is against the wishes of Islamic scholars, as they argued against structuring Islamic financing instruments to please international investors. Another study reported that introduction of Sukuk trading in the bond market has made some of their applications subject to criticism in Islamic finance industries (Bekri, Kim, and Rachev, 2014). Another fact is the argument that data analysis is insufficient to reveal reliable predictions of the Islamic financial institutions, and the inability to meet the expectation remains a paradox. This is because of a series of earlier and recent studies (Kamla and Rammal, 2013) that showed that annual reports are not a reflection of actual events and practices of the companies, or the annual reports of Islamic banks also omitted essential information predicting how some Islamic finance institutions are dealing with the five components of *Maqasid al-Shari'ah*. Therefore, this study is against making predictions on Islamic financial institutions mainly based on data available on the annual reports, as it may mislead. This study suggests the way out through integrating knowledge of both Islamic finance scholars and the Islamic finance researchers' expertise rather than focusing on adoption of standard methodologies for research in Islamic finance. It has been a challenge that most of the researchers in Islamic finance had a rationalistic and value-neutral view of the economics because they are educated in the Western tradition (Hasan, 2018). Furthermore, Hasan (2018) considered "fruitful and purposive change in Islamic finance research design and direction as necessary. It is obvious that methodologies are essential for arriving at a more convincing objective of research. However, strong emphasis on methodology or standardizing methodologies may cause more harm than good in conducting research in Islamic finance.

References

Abidin, N. H. Z., Yasin, F. M. and Abidin, A. Z. (2020) 'Independence from the perspective of the Shari'ah committee', *Asian Journal of Accounting Research*, 1, pp. 1–14.

Alkhazali, O. M. and Zoubi, T. A. (2020) 'Gold and portfolio diversification: A stochastic dominance analysis of the Dow Jones Islamic indices', *Pacific Basin Finance Journal*, 60(January), pp. 1–15.

Bekri, M., Kim, Y. S. (Aaron) and Rachev, S. T. (Zari) (2014) 'Tempered stable models for Islamic finance asset management', *International Journal of Islamic and Middle Eastern Finance and Management*, 7(1), pp. 37–60.

Chazi, A. and Syed, L. A. M. (2010) 'Risk exposure during the global financial crisis: the case of Islamic banks', *International Journal of Islamic and Middle Eastern Finance and Management*, 3(4), pp. 321–333.

Dusuki, A. W. and Abozaid, A. (2007) 'A critical appraisal on the challenges of realizing', *IIUM Journal of Economics and Management*, 2(2), pp. 143–165.

Eldersevi, S. and Haron, R. (2020) 'An analysis of maslahah based resolutions issued by Bank Negara Malaysia', *ISRA International Journal of Islamic Finance*, 12(1), pp. 89–102.

Godlewski, C. J., Turk-Ariss, R. and Weill, L. (2013) 'Sukuk vs. conventional bonds: A stock market perspective', *Journal of Comparative Economics*, 41(3), pp. 745–761.

Hasan, Z. (2018) 'The alarming rise in predatory publishing and its consequences for Islamic economics and finance', *ISRA International Journal of Islamic Finance*, 10(1), pp. 6–18.

Hosen, M. N. *et al.* (2019) 'The effect of financial ratios, Maqasid Sharia Index, and Index of Islamic Social Reporting to profitability of Islamic Bank in Indonesia', *Journal of Islamic Economics*, 11(2), pp. 201–222.

Ingram, R.W. and Frazier, K. B. (1980) 'Environmental performance and corporate disclosure', *Journal of Accounting Research*, 18(2), pp. 614–622.

Jalil, M. J. A. and Rahman, Z. A. (2012) 'Sukuk investment comparison of the profits obtained by using principles with long-term tenure', *Qualitative Research in Financial Markets*, 4(2/3), pp. 206–227.

Kamla, R. and Rammal, H. G. (2013) 'Social reporting by Islamic banks: Does social justice matter?', *Accounting, Auditing & Accountability Journal*, 26(6), pp. 911–945.

Laldin, M. A. and Furqani, H. (2018) 'Islamic Financial Services Act (IFSA) 2013 and the Sharī'ah-compliance requirement of the Islamic finance industry in Malaysia', *ISRA International Journal of Islamic Finance*, 10(1), pp. 94–101.

Ledhem, M. A. (2020) 'Does Sukuk financing boost economic growth? Empirical evidence from Southeast Asia', *PSU Research Review*, 1, pp. 1–17.

Naifar, N. (2016) 'Modeling dependence structure between stock market volatility and sukuk yields: A nonlinear study in the case of Saudi Arabia', *Borsa Istanbul Review*, 16(3), pp. 157–166.

Razak, D. A. and Taib, F. M. (2011) 'Consumers' perception on Islamic home financing: Empirical evidences on Bai Bithaman Ajil', *Journal of Islamic Marketing*, 2(2), pp. 165–176.

Sarea, A. and Salami, M. A. (2021) 'Does social reporting matter? Empirical evidence', *Journal of Financial Reporting and Compliance*, 1(1), pp. 1–26.

Smolo, E. and Hassan, M. K. (2011) 'The potentials of mushārakah mutanāqisah for Islamic housing finance', *International Journal of Islamic and Middle Eastern Finance and Management*, 4(3), pp. 237–258.

Ullman, A.A. (1985) 'Data in search of a theory: a critical examination of the relationships among social performance, social disclosure, and economic performance of US firms', *The Academy of Management Review*, 10(3), pp. 540–557.

Unerman, J. (2000) 'Methodological issues: Reflections on quantification in corporate social reporting content analysis', *Accounting Auditing & Accountability Journal*, 13(5), pp. 667–680.

Zubairu, U. M., Sakariyau, O. B. and Dauda, C. K. (2012) 'Evaluation of social reporting practices of Islamic banks in Saudi Arabia', *Journal of Business Ethics and Organization Studies*, 17(1), pp. 1–10.

INDEX

Note: Locators in *italics* represent figures and **bold** indicate tables in the text.

Abbasiyah period 8–9
Abdou, H.A. 306
Abdullahi, S.I. 249
Abidin, A.Z. 349
Abidin, N.H. Z 349
Abozaid, A. 43, 46
absolute numbers **295**
Abu Hussain, H. 319
academic courses, content and composition 24–27
academic programs, design methodology 17–18; content and composition of academic courses 24–27; institutional development 18–21; knowledge content building 21–27; learning outcomes 22–23; process of designing content 21–22
academic programs in Islamic economics and finance 17–18
academic research 31
Accounting and Auditing Organization of Islamic Financial Institutions (AAOIFI) 351
accounting standards **357**
Addas, Waleed 59
Ad hoc planning for meetings 188
AE. *see* allocative efficiency (AE)
agent-based modeling (ABM) 282, **283**, 296–300
ahkām 101
Ahmad Ibrahim Kulliyyah of Laws (AIKOL) 72–75, 77–79, 87
Ajloun National University 20
Akbar Noor Mohamad Noor, M. 328
Akhmetova, E. 245
Akram, H. 319
Aktürk, C. 194
Al-Ajmi, J. 319
Al-Azhar University, Egypt 19
Al-Banna, H. 341
Al-Farabi Kaznu Islamic Finance Scientific and Educational Center 21
al-Ghazali, Imam Abu Hamid 232; dimensions 48; five pillars safeguarding principles 50–51
Ali, M.M. 320
al-ijtihād f ī al-naṣṣ 94
al-Istihsan 50
Al-Khinn 103
Allah (swt) 71
allocative efficiency (AE) 342
al-Muqaddimah 113
Al-Najjar 48
al-Qawa'id al-Kulliyah al-Fiqhiyyah 91, 97
Al-Qayem, Ibn 232
Al-Sahtibi 232
Alsharari, N.M. 315
al-Shatibi, Imam 100, 246
amanah (trust) 71
Amin, R.M. 25
AMOS (analysis of moment structures) 288, 291
analogical reasoning *99*
analytic hierarchy process (AHP) 292, *294*
analytic network process (ANP) 282, **283**, 292–296, *294–295*
An-Najah National University 19
AnyDesk 194
'aql 349
Aqwāl al-ṣahaba 94
ARCH *(q)* model 270
Arellano, M. 278–279

Arellano-Bond test 279
ARMA/ARIMA model 267–269
al-Arqam bin Abi al-Arqam al-Makhzumi 7
Arsyianti, L.D. 148
artificial intelligence (AI) 229, 240–241, 310
Ascarya, A. 328, 340
'Ashur, Ibn 46
Aslam Haneef, M. 248
asset quality **308**
Astrom, Z.H.O. 313
autodidactic or independent group work 125–127
autoregressive conditional heteroscedasticity (ARCH) model 270
autoregressive distributed lag (ARDL) 273–275, 328
ayah 102
Ayyubi, S.E. 148
Aziz, Abdul 51
Aziz, M.R.A. 50

Bai' al-inah 46
Bai' Bithaman Aajil (BBA) 46
Baitul Maal wat Tamwil (BMT) 328
Bait-un-Nasr (BuN) Urban Cooperative Credit Society in Mumbai, India 321
Bank Negara Malaysia 349
Bank of International Settlement 92
banks 32
Bankscope 318
Bay' al-Mādūm 107
Bay' al-Salam 107
BAZNAS (BAZIS) DKI Jakarta 53
Beaumont, C. 316
Belabes, A. 18, 25
Belouafi, A. 18, 25
Berra, Yogi 324
Bible 240
big data analytics 240–241, 310
Bitcoin 92
blockchain 310
Bloomberg 318
Bloom's taxonomy pyramid 22
Bohman, D.M. 143
Bollen, K. 289
Bond, S. 278–279
Borglin, G. 143
Boulding, K.E. 250
Burns, J. 315
business-client relationship 306

Cairo Conference 18
CAMELS system 307–309, *308*
capital adequacy ratio **308**
capital markets 42
Cebeci, Ismail 58, 358
Central Bank of Malaysia 19
Centre for Islamic Economics and Finance 20–21
Certificate in Islamic Banking and Finance (CIBF) 81
Certificate in Islamic Banking and Finance for Legal Practitioners (CIBFL) 81
Certificate of Fiqh al-Mu'amalat and Waqf (CIBFW) 81
Certificate of Shari'ah for Takaful Practitioners (CSTP) 81
Certified Professional Shariah Auditor (CPSA) 169; module online **170**
Certified Professional Shariah Audit (CPSA) program 165
Chapman, Bob 235
Chapra, M.U. 43
Chomsky, N. 116
Choudhury, Masudul Alam 58, 61, 68, 248, 282
Chua, Y.L. 147
Cisco Web Meeting **210**
class-based learning 11
climate change 50
cloud adoption 310–311
Cockayne, D. 143
Colander 130
College of Administration and Business at the University of Bahrain 21
College of Islamic Economics and Finance 19
College of Islamic Studies 20
College of Shari'ah, Palestine 19
College of Shari'ah and Islamic Studies 20
colloquiums 84–85
colonialism and post-colonialism period 9–10
commercial law 100
comprehensive ecosystem in Islamic banking and finance programs 88
conceptual research design 317–318
conferences 84–85
confirmatory factor analysis (CFA) 287
constant return to scale (CRS) 344
consumer behavior 32
consumer price index (CPI) 340
contemplation *(tafakkur)* 115

content analysis 258–260
content design methodology 17
content-focused method 203
conventional economics and finance (CEF) 328
conventional theories 35
corporate social responsibility (CSR) 320
corruption 50
courses: assessment methods 22; content 18; description 18; learning outcomes 22; pillars 22–23; scientific material 22; teaching strategy 22
covariance-based SEM 288
COVID-19 pandemic 29, 65, 67, 164–165; employability prospects after training program 177–179; employability prospects during 168–169; impact on educational sector in Malaysia 165–166; social distancing and 200; training programs during 172–173; *see also* Zoom application, teaching and learning IEF
credit scoring model 306
Crescent Rating Standard 54
critically reflective pedagogy 117–118
Çubukçu, C. 194
curriculum: content methods *160*; development 17
customer satisfaction index (CSI) 211–212, 216–217, 223–224

Dalālah al-Naṣṣ 94
Damascus, Syria 8
Damenu, T.K. 316
Dangulbi, S.M. 45
Darul Arqam 7
data collection 169–172
data envelopment analysis (DEA) 328, 342–346
DataStream 318
Dauda, C.K. 355
debt-based economy 315
decision-making methods **293**
decision-making unit (DMU) 342
Delphi-ANP method 327, 337–339
Delphi-Likert method 333–335, **334–335**
Delphi method 327, 330–333, *331*
Delphi questionnaire **333**
Delphi-SEM method 327, 335–337, *336*
demonstration 8
Department of Economics and Islamic Banking 20
Department of Fiqh and Islamic Studies 20
Department of Islamic Banking 20–21
Department of Islamic Economics 19, 21
Department of Islamic Economics and Finance 21
Department of Islamic Finance and Banking Sciences 21
determining weighted score (WS) 217
development strategy 37; collaborating with Islamic economics and finance industry 39; incentives to academics to conduct research 39; increasing cooperation with the Islamic economics and finance industry 37–38; innovating research methodology 39; strengthening and developing existing Islamic theory 39; strengthening Islamic economics and finance research conducted by academics 38–39
Dhannī 101–105
Dhawan, S. 192
dialectics *(jadal)* 115
Dikko, M. 51
din 349
discerning between matters *(tawassum)* 115
discourse *(munazara)* 115
discriminant analysis 306
discussion 8
disputation *(tariqat an-nazar)* 115
distribution-free approach (DFA) 342
donations 22
Dubai Islamic Bank 42
Durham Centre for Islamic Economics 21
Dusuki, A.W. 43, 46
dynamic panel data 278–279

early phase, Islamic studies and teaching methodologies: Darul Arqam 7–8; *halaqah* 8; Mecca 7–8; Medina 7–8; Nabawi Mosque 8
earnings **308**
econometrics modeling *339*; and conventional worldview interpretation 355
economic inequality 50
economic taxonomy 235–237
educational achievements 17
educational curricula at Al-Azhar University 18

educational methods 8
educational subjects and courses 17
education phase transformation 9
EGARCH *(p,q)* model 271
El-Din, Tag 249
e-learning and employability related to training program conducted in COVID-19 pandemic 164–165; course design 167; data collection 169–172; effectiveness of training program 173–176; employability prospects 168–169; employability prospects after the training 176–179; findings and discussions 172–173; in Malaysia 165–166; professional *shariah* audit training program 166–168
e-learning processes 165, 183–184
ending hunger 29
Engle, R.F. 270, 272
entrepreneurial activities 146–147
entrepreneurship program 146
equalization 142
error correction model (ECM) 272–273, 328
error correction term (ECT) 273
evidence-based ijtihad 65–66
exploratory factor analysis (EFA) 287
exploratory or formulative research studies 30
exponential generalized autoregressive conditional heteroscedasticity (EGARCH) model 270

face-to-face training 167
faculties or kulliyyah offer Islamic finance courses 73–74
Fajrin, M.U. 212
Fama and French models 309
Farooqi, A.H. 321
Fatimah, Z. 211
fatwas 66–67
Ferguson, C.E. 291
field-based learning 11
finance in Islam 26
Financial Accreditation Agency 19
financial assets 32
financial crisis of 2008 19
financial economy 91–92
financial Fiqh 18, 26
financial institution fiduciaries 241
financial institutions development 5
financial management 32
financing terrorist organizations 351
fin-tech model 309–310
fiqh 56–57, 90, 95; economic analysis 61; evidence-based ijtihad 65–66; extended applications of mainstream methodologies 68; inter-discipline ijtihad 67; interpretation of revelation, validating 64–65; Islamic eco-finance 67–68; juristic councils and institutional fatwas 66–67; mainstream scientific approaches 64–68; methodology debate, significance of 57–58; mini-cases analysis 68–69; philosophical foundations 60–64; rational analysis and induction 63–64; review of related works 58–60; sources and epistemological approaches 61–63
Fiqh al-'ibadat 56
Fiqh-al-Mu'āmalāt 46, 56, 90, 107, 155
fiqhī 92
first-difference GMM (FD-GMM) 278
First Makkah Conference on Islamic Economics 18–19
First World Conference on Muslim Education in Mecca 9
Fisol, Mohammed 50
Fitriawati, D. 211
focus group discussion (FGD) 331
forecast error variance decomposition (FEVD) 284
forecasting 284
fractional reserve banking (FRB) system 45
Friedman, Milton 64, 250
F-statistic 275
fuqahā 90, 92–93, 95
Furqani, H. 35, 59, 248, 349

gap analysis 211–212, 216
GARCH *(p,q)* model 270
gathering insight *(tabassur)* 115
generalized method of moments (GMM) 278, 308–309
GERMAS Indonesia 209
ghabn fāḥish 93
Ghani, A.A. 51
gharar 42, 92–93, 104
gharar fāḥish 106
al-Ghazali, Imam Abu Hamid 48, 113, 116, 246
Ghazali approach 52
Global Entrepreneurship Index (GEI) 146
global financial crisis 350

global Islamic juristic councils 66, **66**
Godlewski, C.J. 360
goodness-of-fit tests 289, 291
Google Calendar 188
Google Form 193
Google Meet 182, 184, 194
GoToMeeting 182, 184, 194, **210**
Granger causality test 284–285
Great Recession of 2008 243
Greek cultural heritage 8
gross domestic product (GDP) 35
group-lending approaches 328
group research interactive teaching (GRIT) 118, 133
G Suite 182, 184
Gujarati, D.N. 339
Gulf Cooperation Council 167
Gürel, E. 32

hadith 34
Hair, J.F. 290–291
Hajar, Ibn 101
halal cosmetics 29
halal food 341; and beverages 29; sector 5
halal markets 42
halal pharmaceuticals 29
halal travel 5
Hallaq, W. 103
Hanbal, Ibn 232
Haneef, M.A. 25, 35
Hanefah, Mustafa Mohd 53
Hangout Meets **210**
hard modeling 288
hardship elimination 50
harmonization 250–252
Hasan, Z. 248, 349, 355, 360
Hashim, A.M. 51, 314
Hassan, Zubair 58
Heiden, C. 255
Hidayat, S.E. 148
higher learning institutions in Islamic finance 72–73
HIV/AIDS 67
Holistic Coaching and Village Empowerment Program 148–149
homo economicus 62, 119–120, 125
homo Islamicus 62, 125
Hopper, C.H. 140
Hudaefi, F.A. 320
ḥukm 98
ḥukm al-shar'I 96
humanistic-economic context 229
humanitarian project 145–146
human resources (HR) 5–6, 15
hypothesis-testing research studies 31

ibadah (worship) 71
'ibādāt 100
ibāha, principle of 93
IBF. *see* Islamic Banking and Finance (IBF)
Ibn 'Ashur's element 48
Ibn Jamaah 129
IIUM Institute of Islamic Banking and Finance (IIiBF) 72, 75–76, 80–81, 87
Ijmā' 63, 94, 103
Ijma' Sarih 103
ijtihad 66–67, 96, 255
'illah, methods 98–100
Imam Mohammad Ibn Saud Islamic University 19
Imla method 9
importance performance analysis (IPA) 211–215, *221*
impulse response function (IRF) 284
income inequality 29
independent learning 139
Indonesia 6, 10–12; education providers of Islamic economics and finance *11*; IEF 11; natural disasters 145
industrial production index (IPI) 340
inflation 50
Institute of Islamic Banking and Finance 19
Institute of Islamic Economics and Finance 21
Institute of Islamic Economics in Jeddah 18
institutional development of Islamic economics *20*, 21
institutional developments 17–21
institutional fatwas 66–67
insurance companies 42
Integration, Islamization, Internationalization, and Comprehensive Excellence (Triple ICE (IIICE)) 71
interactive, integrative, and evolutionary (IIE) process-oriented circular 282
interactive or participative method 203
inter-discipline ijtihad 67
interest-free institution financing 44
interest-free microfinance practices in India 321
International Centre for Education in Islamic Finance (INCEIF) 19

International Conference on Islamic Economics 243
International Financial Reporting Standards (IFRS) 351–352, 357, **357**, 359, **359**
International Institute for Islamic Economics 19
International Islamic Fiqh Academy (IIFA) 65
International Islamic University 19
International Islamic University in Malaysia 10
International Islamic University in Pakistan 10
International Islamic University of Islamabad 19
International Islamic University of Malaysia (IIUM) 71–72; Ahmad Ibrahim Kulliyyah of Laws (AIKOL) 74–75, 77–79; case study 83–84; comprehensive ecosystem in Islamic banking and finance programs 88; course assessments 84; faculties or kulliyyah offer Islamic finance courses 73–74; higher learning institutions in Islamic finance 72–73; IIUM Institute of Islamic Banking and Finance (IIiBF) 75–76, 80–81; industry engagement 85–86; Islamic finance programs and courses offered 76–81; Kulliyyah of Economics and Management Sciences (KENMS) 73–74, 76–77; Kulliyyah of Islamic Revealed Knowledge and Human Sciences (KIRKHS) 75, 79–80; lectures and presentations 82–83; methods of teaching, learning, and research 81–86; research 85; seminars, colloquiums, and conferences 84–85; strength in teaching, learning, and research in Islamic finance 87–88; strong foundation for islamic knowledge 87–88
International Monetary Fund (IMF) 314
International Shari'ah Research Academy for Islamic finance (ISRA) 19
investments 5
iqamah al-`adl 46
Iranian Islamic banking 327
Ishak, 46
Islamic and societal values 22
Islamic Banking and Finance (IBF) 19, 32, 36, 44–50, 80; *Maqasid al-Shari'ah* in 44; Maqasid-Based Performance Evaluation Model (MPEM) 47–48; research areas 86; spirit of 44
Islamic capital market 36, 50–51
Islamic Centre Sheikh Zayed 19
Islamic civilization 9
Islamic commercial financial instruments 42–43
Islamic Conference of Ministers of Higher Education and Scientific Research (ICMHESR) 137
Islamic criminal law 78
Islamic economic philosophy 37
Islamic economics 31, 243
Islamic (macro) economics 32
Islamic economics and finance (IEF) 5, 11, 17–18, 20–22, 29–30, 67–68, 141, 257; courses 18; criticisms from economists 37; data center 39; educational and research institutions 36; innovating research methodology 39; Islamic accounting *11*; Islamic economics *11*; Islamic finance *11*; Islamic management 12; learning outcomes *23*; *muamalat 11*; programs 21–23; rapid development 36; research and research methodology 30–31; research conducted by academics 38; research topics applied in Islamic economics and finance 31–32; teaching methodology and technique *11*
Islamic economics and finance (IEF), teaching and methodology 1–2, 10; Indonesia 6, 10–12; industrial growth 2; Malaysia 6, 12–13; phase transformation *10*; standards and techniques 2; United Kingdom 13–14
Islamic Economics Departments 18–19
Islamic Economics Division in the Shari'ah Graduate Studies 19
Islamic economic sector, global investment *6*
Islamic economic system 10
Islamic economic theory 35, 37; incentives to academics 39
Islamic educational institution 7
Islamic family law 78
Islamic finance (ISFIN) 17–19, 31, 77, 103, 313–315; artificial intelligence 310; banks 32; big data analytics 310; blockchain 310; CAMELS system 307–309; case study research design 320–321; cloud adoption 310–311;

comparative of features 321–324; conceptual research design 317–318; consumer behavior 32; courses based on domains **88**; credit scoring model 306; financial assets 32; financial management 32; Islamic fin-tech model 309–310; issues and challenges in research 303–304; logistic regression 307; mixed method research design 319–320; Mudharabah investment model 305; neural network 306–307; qualitative research design 316–317; quantitative research design 318–319; quantum computing 310; research design methodologies 315–316; and research methodologies 306–307; risk management 32; takaful 304–306; Wakalah insurance model 304; Wakalah Mudharabah model 305; Waqf model 305–306
Islamic Finance Development Report 44
Islamic Finance Programs 73; and courses offered 76–81
Islamic finance research: challenges faced by 352–353; differences in 359
Islamic finance researchers 355
Islamic financial assets 29
Islamic financial contracts 46
Islamic financial industry 68
Islamic financial institutions (IFIs) 42, 52, 328
Islamic financial management 43
Islamic Financial Services Act (IFSA) 353
Islamic financial system 26, 32, 237
Islamic fin-tech model 309–310
Islamic Fiqh Academy 24
Islamic fiscal policy 68
Islamic Foundation in the United Kingdom 13
Islamic governance and morality 31
Islamic insurance (takaful) 51–52
Islamic jurisprudence 56, 60, 67, 355
Islamic knowledge model 28
Islamic law 77; of banking and takaful 78; of succession 78; of transactions 78
Islamic legal ruling. *see fiqh*
Islamic legal system 78
Islamic microfinance 148
Islamic microfinance institutions (IMFI) 328
Islamic Mu'āmalāt law 156
Islamic nonprofit microfinance 29
Islamic Organization for Medical Sciences (IOMS) 67
Islamic pedagogical paradigm 114–117
Islamic public equity funds 50
Islamic scholars and contextual understanding 353–354
Islamic social finance *(zakat and waqf)* 29, 42, 52–53, 148
Islamic social funds 52
Islamic social marketing 53
Islamic social reporting (ISR) 352
Islamic studies, teachings and methodologies 7; colonialism and post-colonialism period 9–10; early phase 7–8; medieval phase 8–9
Islamic theory, strengthening and developing 39
Islamic *Weltanschauung* 116
Islamic Worldview 73
Islamization 73; of educational curricula 17, 28n3; of knowledge 9–10, 12, 15, 113; of science 58
Istanbul University 21
istidlāl 96
istiḥkār 93
Istihsan 63
Istiḥsān 94
istinbāṭ 96
istiqrā' 95–96
Istiṣḥāb 94, 97
Istiṣlāh 94

Jadevicius, A. 324
jalb al-maslahah 46
John, B. 315
Jöreskog, K. 287
Jouti, A.T. 318
juristic councils and institutional fatwas 66–67
juristic counsel 66, **66**, 66–67
justification of slamic jurisprudence *(fiqh)* 34
juz'iyyat 63

kafala 29
Kahf, M. 45, 59
Kahf, Monzer 59
Kamaruddin, Hisham 53
Kamla, R. 351
khabar wāhid 100, 103
Khaldun, Ibn 113, 232

Khan, Fahim 87
Khan, M.A. 255
Khan, Muhammad Akram 58–59, 63–65
Khattab, Umar bin 43
King Abdulaziz University in Saudi Arabia 18, 20
Kizilkaya, Necmettin 58–59
Knowledge and Civilization 73
Koh, Y.Y. 147
Kothari, C. 30
Krippendorff, K. 260
Kulliyyah of Economics and Management Sciences (KENMS) 72–74, 76–77
Kulliyyah of Islamic Revealed Knowledge and Human Sciences (KIRKHS) 72–73, 75, 79–80, 87
kulliyyahs 72–73, 85
kulliyyat 63
Kuran, T. 37
kuttāb 197–198

lā ḍarar wa lā ḍirār, principle of 93
Laldin, M.A. 349
Lateh, N. 327
Lathifah, U. 211
learner-centered method 203
lecture *(qira'at)* 115
lecture method 9
lectures, avantages and disadvantages of **83**
Ledhem, M.A. 307
Lembaga Zakat Selangor (LZS) 53
Lemonade Stand 183
Lennox, R. 289
Libyan universities 20
Likert method 327
Likert scale 329–330
linear regression model (OLS method) 260–262
linear structural relationship (LISREL) model 287–288, 291
Linstone, A. 330
liquidity **308**
liquidity facility 50
logical positivism 243
logistic regression 306–307, *307*
logit and probit models 264–267
Lubis, D. 148

Mach, Ernst 243
machine learning 241
mafsadah 50, 63
Mahomedy, Abdulkader 58
mainstream economics and finance 60
mainstream techniques 247–248
Makdisi, G. 115
mal 349
Malaysia 6, 12–13; education providers of Islamic economics and finance **12**; e-learning and employability related to training program conducted in COVID-19 pandemic in 165–166; IEF system 12; International Islamic University 12; legal system 78; teaching methodology and technique in learning IEF *13*; *see also specific entries*
Malinvaud 249
māl mutaqawwim 93
management efficiency **308**
maqasid 65, 253; index 50; performance 50; theory for assessing human well-being *52*
Maqasid al-Shari'ah 2, 42–44, 46, 50, 80, 138, 245–247, 252, 314, 349, 351, 360; al-Ghazali's and Abu Zahrah's frameworks 48; based performance 47; in BAZNAS 52; capital market instruments 50; evaluation framework *49*; framework 45–46; index 320; Islamic banking 44–50; Islamic capital market 50–51; Islamic insurance (takaful) 51–52; Islamic social finance *(zakat and waqf)* 52–53; Islamic wealth management *51*; measurement tool 54; operational measurement concept 46, **47**; others (non-financial industry) 53–54; principle of obtaining benefit and avoiding harm 53; *Shari'ah* for 43
Maqasid al-Shari'ah-based methodology 251
Maqasid-based methodology 242–245; harmonization 250–252; issues in adopting mainstream techniques 248–250; mainstream techniques 247–248; Maqasid al-Shari'ah and its role 245–247
Maqasid-Based Performance Evaluation Model (MPEM) 47–48; dimensions, element, and measurement **48**
Maqsada 245
Marmara University 21
Masjid economic management program 148
maslahah 45, 50, 63
maslahah diniyyah 122

maslahah mursalah 63–64
Master of Comparative Laws (MCL) 78
mathematization of economics 61
maysir 42
mean importance score (MIS) 216
mean satisfaction score (MSS) 216
Mecca 7; Darul Arqam 7–8; *halaqah* 8
media and recreation 5
Medieval phase 8–9
Medina 7; Nabawi Mosque 8
Mekidiche, M. 307
memorization method 8–9
Merdeka Campus 139–140, 149
Mergaliyev, A. 44, 248
methodological challenges of teaching Islamic finance 152–155; analysis 159–161; curriculum 155–157; talent development 157–158
micro-econometric literature 276
microfinance institutions 42
micro-small enterprises (MSEs) 328
Microsoft Form 193
Microsoft Teams 182, 184
Migdad, A.M. 320
mind mapping (MM) 139
Mit Ghamr Bank 42
mixed method research design 319–320
modest fashion 5, 29
Mohammed, M.O. 46–48
Mohammed, W.S. 321
monetary policy transmission mechanism (MPTM) 340
Monica, J. 211
monodisciplinary styles 242
Monte Carlo simulation 323
moral law 234
moving average (MA) model 267
mu'āmalāt 100
Mu'āmalāt Interactive Game 156
Mudharabah investment model 305
Muhamalat 313
Muhammad, Haji 327
mujtahids 64, 95
multicriteria decision making (MCDM) research method 292
Munzarah Method (debate) 9
Murasalah Method (correspondence) 9
Musharakah Mutanaqisah Partnership (MMP) 353
Musharaqah Mutanaqisah 318
Muslim customers' behavior 341
Muslim educationalists 131
Muslim Friendly Hospitality Services Requirements 54
Muslim-friendly hotels 53
Muslim-friendly travel 29
Muslim investors 5
mutāwatir 100
muzaki (zakat payer) 53
muzaki in Jambi Province 53

nafs 349
narrower specialization 242–243
nasl 349
naṣṣ 101
Nasution, A. 148
national accounting standards in Islamic financing practicing countries 355–358
National Higher Education Accreditation Board (BAN-PT) 11
National Kazakh University of Al-Farabi 21
naturalia 93
Nave's Topical Index 240
Nawāzil in Islamic finance 105–106
neoclassical economic theory 37
neural networks 306–307, *307*
Noh, M.S.M 50
non-bank Islamic financial institutions 42
Noordin, K. 320
note writing *(ta'liqat)* 115
Nujaym, Ibn 97
null hypothesis 275
Nurzaman, M.S. 148

Omdurman University in Sudan 18
online classroom 181
online learning programs 143
opportunity: development of Islamic economics and finance educational and research institutions 36; potential human resources 36; rapid development of 36
ordinary least squares (OLS) method 309
organizational management 33
Organization of Islamic Cooperation (OIC) 9, 65, 137
organizations for Islamic financial institutions (AAOIFI) 304
others (non-financial industry) 53–54
Outlook Calendar 188
overall efficiency (OE) 342

panel data method 276–279
partial least squares SEM 288

Pavlov's experimentations 115
pedagogical methodologies in teaching Islamic economics 113–114; autodidactic or independent group work 125–127; critically reflective pedagogy 117–118; group research interactive teaching (GRIT) 118; Islamic pedagogical paradigm 114–117; pedagogical teaching illustration 119–124; reflections on pedagogical approaches 129–133; scaffolding 127–129
pedagogical teaching illustration 119–124
pension funds 42
Permata, A. 148
Pesaran, M.H. 275
pharma and cosmetics 5
PLATO (Programmed Logic for Automatic Teaching Operations) 183
poverty 29
Problem-Based Learning (PBL) 153
professional *shariah* audit training program 166–168
profit-loss-sharing (PLS) 236
programs and courses 24
project-based learning (PBL) 11–13, 139
Prophet Muhammad 8, 43, 97, 114
pseudo-*ijma'* 66

qā'idah 106
Qarāfi 97
qard 29
Qard hasan 318
Qaṭ' ī 101–105
qaṭ'ī al-thubūt 101, 103
Qawa'id al-Fiqhiyyah 77, 93–98, 103, 106–109
Qayyim approach 52
QISMUT 152
Qiyās 63, 94, 103; in Fiqh al-Mu'amalat 98–100
QS Global World Ranking University list 6, **7**
qualitative method 256–258
qualitative research design 316–317
quantitative research design 34, 318–319
quantum computing 310
question and answer 8
Qur'an 26, 34, 62–63, 68, 94, 103, 245
Quranic principles 229
Qur'anic terms 26
Quran Surah al-Baqarah 137
Quraysh 8

Rafah Center for Islamic Business 19
Rafikov, I. 245
Rahman, K. 319
Rammal, H.G. 351
al-Rashidun, Al-Khulafa' 8
Rasulullah SAW 43
reading method in front of teachers 9
real economy toward financial economy, shift from 90–91; Dhannī 101–105; emergence of financial economy 91–92; *'illah,* methods of determining 98–100; impact of 92–94; Nawāzil in Islamic finance 105–106; Qaṭ' ī 101–105; Qawaid Fiqhiyya 94–98; Qiyās in Fiqh al-Mu'amalat 98–100; 'Urf in Fiqh al-Mu'āmalāt 100–101; Usūl al-Fiqh 94–98, 106–109
reflection *(tadabbur)* 115
regression coefficient 286
religious education 9
religious teaching 229
remembrance *(tadhakkur)* 115
research and development (R&D)-based education 147
research gaps 358
research grants 37
research methodology 31
research topics applied in Islamic economics and finance 31–32
ribā 42, 92–93, 152; prohibition 45
Ricardo, David 69
Rigdon, D.D. 291
Rihlah 'Ilmiyyah Method (scientific adventure) 9
risk management 32
Rizaldi, D.R. 211
Roberts, B.E. 319
Rogoff, Kenneth 236
Russell, B. 243

Saaty, Thomas L. 292
Sabahattin Zaim University 21
Sabirzyanov, R. 51
sad al-zara'i 50
sadaqah 29, 148
Sadd al-Dharā'i 94
Sahih al-Muslim 137
Sakariyau, O.B. 355
Sakarya University 21
Salami, M.A. 319, 352

Salam Standard 54
Saleem, Muhammad Yusuf 251
Samidi, S. 148
Sarea, A. 352
Saribas, Hakan 59
scaffolding 127–129
Schumpeter, Joseph A. 113
SCL, PBL, and MM in teaching 137–138; conducting research or being a research assistant 142–143; entrepreneurial activities 146–147; evaluation 149–150; humanitarian project 145–146; independent study or project 147; internship or working experience 144–145; justified model 140–141; methods of application 141–149; practical solutions 138–140; student exchange 143–144; teaching assistant in an education unit 141–142; village or regional empowerment (VE) 147–149
scriptural Bible studies 240
secularization in education 9
Seif I. Tag el-Din 59
Sejahtera Academic Framework (SAF) 72
Sekaran's operationalization method 46
self-fulfillment 234
SEM. *see* structural equation modeling (SEM)
seminars 84–85
sensitivity to market risk **308**
sharia-based courses 36
Shari'ah: adoption of 22; audit 166; audit planning and program knowledge and skills **175**; audit training program 170; earning, purposes of 25; and economic dimensions 24; faculty member with Shari'ah background 25; financial transactions 23; governance 50; materials 25; non-compliance risk 52; objectives of 44; prohibition 50; rulings 349; student's background 27
Shari'ah advisory council (SAC) 46
Shari'ah committees (SC) of Islamic financial institutions 46
Shariah-compliant gold instruments 327
Shin, R.J. 275
Shir'ah 245
simultaneous equation model (2SLS method) 262–264
Skinner, B.F. 115
Skype 184, 194, **210**
smart techniques in Qur'anic principles 229; AI and big data 240–241; common methodology 237–240; current perception 229–231; economic taxonomy 235–237; globalized polar world 234–235; words of wisdom 231–234
Smith, Adam 69
social distancing 164
social science 62
social welfare 233
Sodaqah 318
soft modeling 288
S&P 500 Index *269*
spectrum of research *258*
spiritual value of research methodology 34
standard methodology for research in IEF 255–256, 327–329; ARMA/ARIMA model 267–269; autoregressive distributed lag (ARDL) 273–275; challenges in 327–346, 349–360; content analysis 258–260; cross section data method 260–262; data envelopment analysis 342–346; Delphi-ANP method 337–339; Delphi-Likert method 333–335; Delphi method 330–333; Delphi-SEM method 335–337; differences in Islamic finance research 359; dynamic panel data 278–279; econometrics modeling and conventional worldview interpretation 355; error correction model (ECM) 272–273; Islamic finance research, challenges faced by 352–353; Islamic finance researchers 355; Islamic scholars and contextual understanding 353–354; Likert scale 329–330; logit and probit models 264–267; modified conventional theory 339–342; national accounting standards in Islamic financing practicing countries 355–358; panel data method 276–279; qualitative method 256–258; research gaps 358; simultaneous equation model (2SLS method) 262–264; static panel data 276–277; time series multivariate method 272–275; time series

univariate method 267–271; volatility model 269–271
State of the Global Islamic Economic Report 5
static panel data 276–277
Statistical, Economic and Social Research and Training Centre for Islamic Countries (SESRIC) 137
stochastic frontier approach (SFA) 342
strength: justification from Islamic jurisprudence 34; methods applied 34–35; spiritual value 34
structural equation modeling (SEM) 53, 282, **283**, 287–290, 327; analysis of results 291; fitness test 291; model estimation 291; model identification 290–291; model re-specification 291; model specification 290; research, steps of SEM *290*; survey 291
ST strategy 33–34
student-centered approach 22
student-centered learning (SCL) 138–139
student-centered teaching 153–154, 159–162
study program (SP) 143
Sufian, F. 328
sukuk 50
sukuk ijarah structure 46, 50
Sunnah 26, 62–63, 68, 94, 103, 245
Sunnah of Allah 59
Super Decisions 292, 295–296
sustainable development goals (SDGs) 29, 53, 73
sustainable development in Islamic economics 6
SWOT analysis 32–34, 40; characteristics 32–33; components of **32**; defined 32–33; exteral factors 35–37; internal factors 34–35; SWOT matrix **33**, **38**; *see also* opportunity; strength; threat; weakness
Syatibi approach 52

ta'abbudī 100
tahdhib al-fard 46
Taḥqīq al-manāṭ 98–100
Taimiah, Ibn 232
Taimiyah approach 52
Takāful (Islamic insurance) 19, 108–109, 304–306, 317
Takhrīj Al-Manāṭ 98
Tanqīh Al-Manāṭ 98
taqlid (imitation) 116
tarbiya 115, 117
Tat, M. 32
Tawarruq 320
tawātur 103
tawhid 117, 315, 324; epistemology 320; worldview 116
Taymiyah, Ibn Salam Ibn 113
Taymiyya, Ibn 97
taysīr, principle of 93
teacher-centered method 203
teacher-centered teaching 153
teaching courses identification and balance **25**
teaching methodology and technique in learning IEF *14*
teaching theories *154*
technical efficiency (TE) 328
technology acceptance model (TAM) 328, 341, *341–342*
teleconferencing 181
textbooks and scientific books 24
TGARCH *(p,q)* model 271
Thaalibiya High School in Algiers 18
Theologies of the Digital Project 240
theory building in Islamic economics and finance *256*
theory of efficiency 343, *343*
thick frontier approach (TFA) 342
threat: criticisms from economists 37; lack of research grants 37
threshold generalized autoregressive conditional heteroscedasticity (TGARCH) model 270
time series multivariate method 272–275
time series univariate method 267–271
Tiorida, E. 212
travel and media 29
Treasury of Scripture Knowledge 240
tri-perspective holistic approach 161, *161*
t-test 217–218
Turk-Ariss, R. 360
Turoff, M. 330

Ulil Albaab 137
Umayyad period 8
ummah 43
Umm Al-Qura University in Makkah 19
understanding *(tafaqquh)* 115
United Kingdom (UK) 13; IEF education providers **14**; International

Association for Islamic Economics 13; universities providing Islamic education 14
University of Tripoli 20
'Urf 94
'Urf in Fiqh al-Mu'āmalāt 100–101
Usmani, Mufti Taqi 95
Uṣūl 92
Uṣūl al-fiqh 60, 62–64, 68, 78, 90–91, 93–98, 103, 106–109; application 50; mastery 50

vector autoregression (VAR) 282–287, **283**, *286*, 328
vector error correction model (VECM) 285–287, 328, 341
video conferencing 198
village or regional empowerment (VE) 147–149
volatility model 269–271

Waheed, K. 321
Wahhab, Abdul 94
Wakalah insurance model 304
Wakalah model 304
Wakalah Mudharabah model 305
Waqf 29, 52, 148, 230, 318
Waqf model *305*, 305–306
weakness: domination of conventional theory 35; lack of research topics 35; lack of secondary data 35
Webber, Max 62
web conferencing 198
webinars 188, 198
Web of Science (WoS) 317
Wehmiller, Barry 235
weighted factor (WF) 216
weighted score (WS) 216
Weill, L. 360
Western education system 9
WhatsApp 187
Wooldridge, J.M. 262
words of wisdom 231–234
World Bank Group 314
World Population Review 36
WT strategy 34

yamhaqu Allah al-riba 64
Yarmouk University 20
Yasin, F.M. 349
Youssef, M.A. 315
Yunus, Muhammad 255
Yusuf, Abu 113

Zaharah, Abu 46, 48
Zakariyah, L. 46
zakat 26, 29, 43, 52, 62, 148, 318; funds 65; institutions 53
zamān 248–249; principle of 93
Ẓannī 102–103
ẓannī al-dalālah 103
ẓannī al-thubūt 104
Zarkashi, M.B. 102
Zarqa 250
zero-sum games 237
Zoom application 181–182, **210**; accessories for safety and privacy 193–194; challenges 190–192; chat room platform feature 186; co-annotation and remote control 186; devices and digital awareness 192; easy and ad hoc planning for meetings 188–189; e-learning 183–184; features 184–185; free basic package for 100 participants 189; impacts, cases of selected 192–193; interactive features for easy meetings or classes 189; internet connection 191–192; merits 187–188; one-click notification or invitation link 189; participants manage features 185; polling quiz feature 186; privacy and technical issues 190; raise hand feature 185; screen and application sharing 185; simple to use 188; supervisor involvement 190; teaching and learning through 186–187; telephone option for audio 189; video recording option 189; whiteboard feature 185
Zoom application, teaching and learning IEF 196–197; classroom management 202; clear and shared outcomes 201; complex thinking, stimulation of 201; concerns and limitations 198–199; content-focused method 203; fostering a universal learning community 206–207; framework to guide 206; impact analysis 199–200; importance of learning from Islamic perspective 196–197; inclusivity 202; interactive or participative method 203–205; learner-centered method 203; learning environment 200–201; learning from historic Islamic perspective 197–198; motivation 202; philosophy 202; policy recommendations for governments and educational institutes 205–206; practice and

feedback 201; think-pair-share 202–203; varied content and methods of instruction 201
Zoom bombing 191
Zoom cloud meeting, impact analysis of teaching and learning IEF 210; CSI calculation 217, 223; customer satisfaction index 216; data and variables 212–213; demographic characteristics of respondents 218–220; determining weighted score (WS) 217; gap analysis 215–216, 222–223; importance performance analysis (IPA) 213–215, 220–222; t-test 217–218, 223–224
Zoom video communications 210
Zubairu, U.M. 355
Zulm 317
zWarDIal tool 191

Printed in the United States
by Baker & Taylor Publisher Services